The AWP Official Guide to Writing Programs

edited by
**D.W. Fenza, David Sherwin,
Katherine Perry & Philip Bacon**

Ninth Edition

**Associated Writing Programs
George Mason University
Fairfax, Virginia**

International Standard Book Number 0-916685-72-1

Copyright 1999 by the Associated Writing Programs.

Published for the Associated Writing Programs in cooperation with Dustbooks. Additional copies of this book may be purchased for $21.95 from either Dustbooks, Box 100, Paradise, CA 95967; or from the Associated Writing Programs, MSN 1E3, George Mason University, Fairfax, VA 22030. Add $6.00 postage & handling plus any applicable sales tax.

CONTENTS

Introduction: On Choosing the Writing Program Best for You

> "Great simplicity is only won by an intense moment or by years of intelligent effort, or both. It represents one of the most arduous conquests of the human spirit: the triumph of feeling and thought over the natural sins of language."
>
> —T.S. Eliot

1. Ranking the Best Programs

In 1967, the writers who taught at thirteen colleges and universities formed a nonprofit organization called the Associated Writing Programs (AWP). In those days, there were only a few programs that offered instruction in the art of writing fiction or poetry, and such programs were regarded with suspicion by the scholars of English departments, where the most esteemed authors were long-dead and safely entombed in libraries. One scholar quipped that it was no more appropriate to have a writer teach literature than it was to have an elephant teach zoology. The founders of AWP argued, of course, that living writers could certainly help their students understand and appreciate literature; and for students who wished to become writers themselves, there was no better way for them to expedite their artistic development than to study with accomplished writers. It was a convincing argument, and it gathered plenty of supporting evidence as young writers graduated from universities and began to publish books as noteworthy as those by their former teachers. At Duke, William Blackburn taught William Styron, Fred Chappell, and Reynolds Price. Price, in turn, taught Josephine Humphries and Anne Tyler. E.L. Doctrow taught Richard Ford at the University of California, Irvine. Donald Dike taught Joyce Carol Oates at Syracuse. Andrew Lytle taught Harry Crews. At Stanford, Wallace Stegner taught Robert Stone, Barry Lopez, Ken Kesey, Edward Abbey, Wendell Berry, Raymond Carver, and many others. Annie Dillard, Madison Smartt Bell, Lee Smith, and Henry Taylor studied at Hollins College. Many winners of the Pulitzer Prize for poetry are also graduates of writing programs: Rita Dove, Yusef Komunyakaa, and many others. And there are many other examples, as more universities have become more successful in helping one generation of writers to educate and encourage the next.

Much has changed since a baker's dozen of writing programs formed AWP over three decades ago. AWP has grown, and so have the opportunities for writers. This guide lists over three hundred academic programs and more than two hundred colonies, conferences, festivals, and centers for writers. These institutions and organizations provide the time, place, instruction, friendly advice, and fellow spirits to help a writer master a difficult and lonely craft.

Here at the offices of AWP, we often receive letters and phone calls from aspiring writers of all ages. "Which are the very best programs? How would you rank *such-and-such?*" they ask. Since these are questions they should answer for themselves, we can only refer them to this guide and reply with other questions: Which authors do you love to read? With which contemporary authors would you like to study? Do you need to improve your knowledge of literature's long history? Some callers become annoyed with us. Hearing questions in response to their own questions, they feel we are being evasive, cowardly, too diplomatic. But really, we have their best interests in mind. After all, no brand-name degree nor any amount of schmoozing with literary movers and shakers will necessarily make someone a better writer. Ultimately, a writer's career is forged in solitude, individual choice by individual choice, word by word, line by line, sentence by sentence. If you succeed as a writer, you will make billions of such choices; you can't let others make your artistic choices for you. The same is true for choosing a writing program. Rather than rely on any top-ten list made by others, you should rank these programs yourself. Just as a good writing teacher will help you see how many options you have in telling a story or shaping a poem, this guide will help you realize how many choices you have; but in the end, you must decide what's best for you and your work.

No artist wants to work without a full palette, but there are different ways of filling and mixing the colors on that palette. Some writers need to study 16th-century literature to learn how to make their rhetoric stretch with pleasure—to impart allusive music, grace, and a greater elasticity to their sentences. Other writers may find such study silly or oppressive—an antique corset stuffed with stays of whale bone—and prefer to keep only the company of moderns and fellow contemporaries. Others may wish to reclaim a heritage not represented in the literature of English-speaking countries. Some writers will find teaching assistantships necessary or inspiring; others will not. Some writers will thrive in the ruckus and hustle of a large urban university, while others would only be intimidated there. This guide will help you clarify your own preferences. The hallmarks of successful writing programs, which are enumerated in the appendix of this guide, will also help you list the features you may seek in a writing program.

2. More Questions & the Great Variety of Answers

So who are the contemporary writers you most admire? With whom would you like to study? In what genre do you plan to specialize, or do you plan to work in more than one genre? From which authors would you learn the most for the particular style of writing you hope to perfect? Which teachers write about the subject matter that inspires you most? Or do you need to find the time and financial support to write apart from the nine-to-five, work-a-day world? Would you benefit most from working on your own writing or from studying the work of other writers? Or both? Would you like, in addition to practicing the art of writing, to complete some scholarly research as well? Are you looking for teaching experience? Editorial experience? Can you spend a year, two years, or three or more years to educate yourself in your craft? Would your writing benefit from your living in a city? Beside an ocean? Close to mountains? Or a desert? A small town? Would you prefer a big program or a small program—having a dozen classmates or a hundred? Happily, the programs listed here are as various as the answers to these questions.

You should keep in mind that one writing program may differ greatly from the next, even if both programs offer the same degree. The basic requirements are listed in this guide so you may decide which curriculum is best for you. In some programs, students must satisfy many traditional requirements for literary scholarship: proficiency in one or more foreign languages; distribution requirements in the arts, sciences, and humanities; an overview of literature from three or more centuries; and a command of scholarly research and documentation skills. Other programs have few of these requirements, if any, as the emphasis is mainly on the progress of the student's writing. Most programs offer writing workshops in two genres only: poetry and fiction. A few programs offer workshops in only one genre, and an increasing number of programs offer workshops in a multitude of genres: creative nonfiction, playwriting, screenwriting, technical writing, translation, and writing for children. For admission, some programs require previous study in literature, a high grade-point average, and good scores on aptitude tests or graduate examinations; other programs will require only an original writing sample that demonstrates talent and promise.

In a writing program or conference, students learn their craft by studying the works of past and present writers; by writing and rewriting; and by examining, defending, satirizing, supporting, criticizing, and nurturing their own works in workshop, which is usually a small class of twelve or fewer students under the guidance of an accomplished writer. Conferences require short residencies, and most do not offer academic credit. Academic programs, of course, require longer residencies; the programs' workshops are complemented by courses in the study of literature; and this curriculum leads to a degree. For a graduate degree, each student must complete a thesis, which may be a novel, a collection of stories, a book-length collection of poems, a play, a memoir, or a collection of essays. The graduate programs listed in this guide are only those that accept an original work of literary writing for the thesis.

Most programs require coursework in literature and other fields as well; and in regard to this requirement, the programs vary the most. One graduate program may require 48 semester hours (s/hrs) of coursework, 24 of which may be workshops. Another program may require 48 s/hrs of total coursework, but only 12 of those may be workshops, as most of the credit must be acquired in literature courses. (A few schools are on the quarterly system; their requirements are listed in quarter hours—abbreviated q/hrs.) AWP classifies each program as one of three basic types: A Studio Program, a Studio/Academic Program, or a Program in Traditional Literary Study and Creative Writing. Studio Programs allow the most coursework in workshops and independent studies while Programs in Traditional Literary Study and Creative Writing require most of the coursework to be in the study of literature; the Studio/Academic Programs, the most common type of graduate program, seeks to strike a balance between the study of literature and the practice of the art of writing. If you already have a strong background in literature and you have already been writing a great deal—and perhaps you have been publishing some of your work, too—a Studio Program may work best for you; otherwise, you may benefit more from one of the other types of programs.

A variety of degrees are offered. At the undergraduate level, most programs confer a Bachelor of Arts (BA) degree in English literature, with a minor, an emphasis, or a concentration in creative writing. A few undergraduate programs, some of which confer the Bachelor of Fine Arts (BFA) degree, offer majors in creative writing. There are also Associate of Arts (AA) and Bachelor of Science (BS) programs that offer studies in creative writing. At the graduate level, the following degrees are offered: Master of Arts (MA), Master of Fine Arts (MFA), Doctor of Arts (DA), and Doctor of Philosophy (PhD). There is also a non-degree program offered by Stanford University, and the Master of Professional Writing (MPW) degree is conferred by a few institutions. Most degree-conferring programs require a residency of a year or more, but a few, such as the MFA programs at Antioch University in Los Angeles, Bennington College, Goddard College, Vermont College, and Warren Wilson College, are low-residency programs. These programs combine brief residencies (usually of ten days, twice a year) along with extended, independent studies which are directed through written correspondence with instructors.

The best writing programs are member institutions of AWP, and they are designated by this symbol ❖ in the pages that follow. These programs receive the publications and collective support of our association, which upholds professional standards in the teaching of writing, and which provides writers with services, advocacy, and information on employment and publishing opportunities.

The conferences, colonies, centers, and festivals listed in this guide also provide the time, places, and workshops in which writers may improve their work and meet other writers. The conferences and colonies require residencies of a few days to a few months. If you are live close to a literary center, you can commute to their writing workshops and literary readings. The best conferences are members of Writers' Conferences & Festivals (WC&F), and they are designated by this symbol ●. WC&F is a division of AWP, and WC&F members also uphold professional standards in the teaching of writing.

3. Be Prepared to Become Unlike Yourself

While you are mulling over the questions raised in this introduction, look over the many programs listed in this guide. After you have answered these questions to your own satisfaction, you should be able to narrow down your prospects to ten or fewer programs. Once you have done so, write to each school and request complete information on the program: brochures, listings of current faculty, catalog, information on financial aid, and requirements for admission and for completion of your degree. Although we make every effort to make sure this guide provides you with up-to-date information, the entries here are merely introductions to these programs. A few features of the programs may have changed since the time we prepared this guide; the program's faculty members especially may change. It is also a good idea to visit a few schools if you can afford to do so, or, at the very least, to talk with a few graduates of the programs that interest you. The same advice applies to conferences, colonies, and centers—if you plan to attend one of them, you should talk to a past attendee, if it's possible, to confirm that the organization really provides the experience you are seeking.

Probably you will not be familiar with all the writers at any particular writing program, but you should acquaint yourself with their work before you apply, and certainly before you make your final decision as to which program you will attend. Even though you may not ever hope to emulate the kinds of work some of those writers produce, do you still find merit in their work? The best advice here is paradoxical: be prepared to study with writers you like and with writers you don't like but in whom you still find substance, inventiveness, and intelligence. If you study only with writers you already admire, you may run the risk of becoming merely eclectic, imitative. Studying with a wide range of talents will probably serve you best, so look for variety in the faculty. You may learn, for example, to construct your own extraordinary stories of the ordinary in the unadorned style of Barbara Pym or one of your teachers only by first studying the redounding rhetoric of Henry James, the caustic satires of Dawn Powell, and the encyclopedic narratives of yet another one of your teachers (all of whom you may have previously resisted); in the end, you may find yourself—master of influences—writing simply in your own voice. Or you may improve your free verse by studying with advocates of formal poetry and by writing sonnets and sestinas. By doing things unlike themselves, writers grow, mature—and become artists.

Once you have selected the programs to which you will apply, you should prepare a sample of your own writing, which most programs will require, especially at the graduate level. This is what writing programs are all about; so put forward only you best work in its best form. Send only clear copies, free of errors. For many programs, this will be the most important part of your application.

4. A Few Warnings & Some High-Minded Encouragement

"'Nothing' is the force / that renovates the world," wrote Emily Dickinson. And every day, facing the empty page, the writer feels the burden and the exhilaration of that force. Unfortunately, it is also what writers are usually paid at first: nothing. In choosing a writing program, you may also want to consider the practical side of writing: what to do for a living, until both your avocation and vocation become one and the same. Please keep in mind that—although academe has never been more hospitable to living authors—the competition for full-time teaching jobs has never been more fierce.

According to statistics published by AWP and the Modern Language Association in 1998, most graduates with advanced degrees in literature and creative writing will not find tenure-track jobs as professors. The number of graduates exceeds the number of good, full-time academic jobs, while colleges and universities continue to create a larger percentage of temporary and part-time positions with low pay and poor benefits. There are, however, many vocations that require a writer's skills and creativity; and many graduates of creative writing programs have enjoyed successful careers in advertising, public relations, journalism, publishing, arts administration, and technical writing. Many programs provide internships, editorial opportunities, and courses in various kinds of professional writing that might improve your prospects in securing professional work in these fields; but if wealth and job security are your main goals, an MBA will serve you better than an MFA. Your main goal in attending a writing program must be artistic, or you will be disappointed. If you aspire to become a literary writer, you will benefit from attending one of the programs listed in this book.

As is the case in the study of music, dance, theater, painting, or sculpture, an advanced degree in writing will not ensure your artistic success. No enterprise is more challenging than the effort to become a successful artist; but no enterprise is more rewarding or more sublime, even if you fail—and failure is surely part of the process when it comes to making art, even if you do finally succeed. While the poet Frank O'Hara was still in college, he wrote, "Life for all its travails has far more zest than any ideal utopia ever would." O'Hara could just as well have been referring to a writer's career. If you love literature, it's worth the trouble and the risk. If you love literature, there is no better way to spend a year or more of your life than in the study of the art of making stories and poems. To be surrounded by people who love books is a thrilling experience—life-changing for many. In a mind-blurring age that keeps accelerating the production of disposable icons of celebrity and consumerism, the slow and profound pleasures of reading and writing are much needed antidotes. The communities created by these programs have enabled many of us to develop life-long friendships based on a shared devotion to literature. This support sustains many writers long after they have graduated. And for those graduates who finally choose other careers, the study of writing and literature remains an enduring personal asset.

"Character is higher than intellect," declared Emerson. Writers know this to be true because character includes intellect. Academic study alone will not make a great artist, nor will outrageous experiences alone, nor will smart ideas alone, nor will a wonderful style alone, nor will passion alone. It has been the wisdom of writing programs to include many kinds of writing, learning, thinking, and feeling. Writing programs may or may not be able to convert a mediocre scribbler into a lasting luminary, but they can certainly improve a writer's heart, intellect, or both. Writing programs can exercise and develop a stronger character—a greater range of sympathies, resourcefulness, and playfulness. Writers today have more means than ever by which they may sharpen their pencils and wits. And we as readers, too, are richer for that.

—D.W. Fenza
Executive Director
The Associated Writing Programs

Graduate
&
Undergraduate
Programs

http://www.gmu.edu/departments/awp

❖Abilene Christian University
Abilene, TX 79699
(915) 674-2262
FAX (915) 674-2408
e-mail: haleya@nicanor.acu.edu
website: http://www.acu.edu/

Degree offered: MA

Required course of study: 36-hour Thesis Program
Fiction Workshop: 3 hours
Poetry Workshop: 3 hours
Advanced Composition
Business/Professional Writing
Rhetoric as Written Discourse
Literary Theory/Technique
General Literature: 9-15 hours
Minor: 0-6 hours
Thesis: 3-6 hours (A writing project, e.g. a chapbook of poetry, a collection of short stories, a collection of essays, a biography, an autobiography, some type of business or professional writing)

Other Requirements: Written comprehensive examination; oral defense of thesis.

Application Deadlines: Apply in January for the autumn in which you seek admission to be considered for financial aid.

Personal, compassionate support is essential if one is to succeed at the difficult spiritual quest involved in the act of writing. For that reason, our writing program prizes, more than anything else, the one-on-one interaction between teacher and student. We do not leave you on a storm-tossed sea of words, battered by workshop comments, no guide in sight. By meeting individually outside of class, you will know where your work stands and receive comments on how to improve it. Students tell us that this process is amazingly encouraging and reminiscent of the heyday of literary publishing when a close relationship existed between editor and author.

Because of the faculty's faith-based outlook on the arts, we undertake a broad survey of literary techniques and also the subject matter that might be incorporated into creative expression. We believe a wide rather than narrow approach is the best way a person of faith can confront difficult questions presented by a world that often seems "unblessed" and is populated by many who cannot catch sight of the transcendent. Students are not asked to shy away from the complexities of real life in order to take refuge in prefabricated orthodoxy. In fact, while Abilene Christian University maintains close ties to the Churches of Christ, we hope that persons from other religious backgrounds and in various phases of their faith journey will thrive in our program, producing excellent literature that speaks to the deepest concerns of the human race.

Abilene, pop. 106,000, is a hospitable locale for the emerging writer. It is inexpensive, West Texas friendly, and still offers hints of its cowboy past. The city's isolation from fast-paced urban demands as well as the limitless blue skies are inducements to creativity. In addition, the presence of two other universities means a year-round array of plays, concerts, and readings. Visitors to Abilene campuses have included Yevgeny Yevtushenko, Gwendolyn Brooks, Naomi Shihab Nye, Larry Woiwode, Fred Chappell, Scott Cairns, and Ray Bradbury.

The creative writing faculty is headed by fiction writer Albert Haley (*Home Ground*, *Exotic*, stories in *The New Yorker*, *Atlantic Monthly*, *Rolling Stone*, and other literary magazines). Mr. Haley is the winner of the 1982 John Irving First Novel Prize. He is joined by poet and hypertext writer Chris Willerton and published short story writer Stephen Weathers.

For more information contact Albert Haley, Director, Creative Writing Program, Box 28252, at the above address.

Adelphi University
Garden City, NY 11530
(516) 877-4020
e-mail: baumel@adlibv.adelphi.edu

Degree offered: BA with Minor in Creative Writing

Adelphi University offers a BA in English with a minor in writing, requiring 18 credits of writing courses. Adelphi is increasing its focus on creative writing courses and the study of contemporary culture.

Adelphi's commitment to an interdisciplinary approach to the arts -- combining visual arts, dance, music, and literature, together with its proximity to New York City -- informs the reading series and cultural programming; it makes Adelphi a center of particular interest for the writing student.

Current faculty include poet Judith Baumel (*Now*, *The Weight of Numbers*), critic Thomas Heffernan (*Wood Quay*), dramatist Morgan Himelstein (*Drama Was a Weapon*), and Stephen Klass (*Adam Homo*, *Antara*). Visiting faculty in recent years have included David Plonte, Philip Lopate, Vivian Gornick, and Bruce Bawer.

For more information, contact Judith Baumel, Dept. of English.

Agnes Scott College
Decatur, GA 30030-3797
(404) 371-6000
FAX (404) 371-6177

Degree offered: BA in English Literature and Creative Writing

Required course of study: 30-45 s/hrs in literature and creative writing courses for the degree (124 hrs. total) in English literature and creative writing.

The creative writing offerings include courses in poetry, narrative, nonfiction, and playwriting on the introductory level, and workshops in all four genres on the advanced level. A student may also qualify to do an independent study in creative writing.

The Agnes Scott College Writers' Festival each spring semester highlights student writing in Georgia colleges and universities. Guest writers are invited to read and discuss their own work and to critique the student writing, the best of which is given an award and published in the college festival booklet. Guest writers have included Richard Wilbur, Rita Dove, Michael Harper, Richard Eberhart, Josephine Jacobsen, and Eudora Welty among many others.

For more information, contact the Chair (Linda L. Hubert), Dept. of English.

❖University of Akron
Akron, OH 44325-1906
(330) 972-7470
FAX (330) 972-8817

Degree: BA in English with Minor in Creative Writing (poetry, fiction, scriptwriting)

Required course of study: 128 s/hrs total
   Writing workshop: at least 9 s/hrs
   Literature courses: 38 s/hrs, at least 6 s/hrs
   of modern literature

Other Requirements: University distribution requirements; two years of a foreign language.

Application Deadlines: Mid-January for financial aid; mid-August for admissions.

The undergraduate English degree with a Minor in Creative Writing requires the student to take two introductory courses in poetry, fiction, or scriptwriting, and one advanced course in one of these genres; the program also requires extensive study in literature, with required surveys of British and American literature, a course on Shakespeare, and one on linguistics or the English language. The *Akros Review* is the campus literary magazine, which provides editorial and publishing experience for undergraduates. Each spring, the Zora M. Ledinko Endowed Memorial Scholarship is awarded to a student in poetry.

For more information, contact the Chair, Dept. of English, 302 Buchtel Hall.

❖University of Alabama, Birmingham
217 Humanities Building
900 South 13th Street
Birmingham, AL 35294-1260

For more information, contact the Director, Dept. of English.

❖University of Alabama
Tuscaloosa, AL 35487-0244
(205) 348-0766
e-mail: writeua@english.as.ua.edu
website: http://www.as.ua.edu/english/

Degrees offered: BA, MFA

Degree: BA in English with Minor in Creative Writing (poetry, fiction)

Required course of study: 15 s/hrs in creative writing

For more information, write the Director, Writing Program, Dept. of English, P.O. Box 870244.

Degree: MFA in Creative Writing (poetry, fiction)

Type of Program: Studio/Academic

Length of Residency: Three or four years

Required course of study: 48 s/hrs
   Thesis: up to 6 s/hrs
   Writing workshop: 20 s/hrs (major genre)
   Other writing courses: up to 6 s/hrs
   Directed reading: up to 6 s/hrs
   Literature courses: 18 or more s/hrs
   Electives: up to 6 s/hrs

Other Requirements: Written comprehensive examination, oral thesis defense.

Application Deadlines: Apply by February 15 for the best chance of financial aid.

All candidates for the MFA are required to take 48 s/hrs of graduate-level work in English, distributed as follows: 20 s/hrs of workshop in the major genre (600-level fiction or poetry); 4 s/hrs in the minor genre (500-level poetry or fiction); 6 s/hrs of thesis and/or research; 18 s/hrs of academic graduate-level English courses; and 6 s/hrs of electives (screenwriting; nonfiction prose; forms of fiction or poetry).

The MFA comprehensive examination is a 3-hour written exam requiring responses to 3 questions: 2 in the area of the student's major genre and 1 in the minor genre. The MFA thesis is a book-length work: a novel, a collection of short stories, or a collection of poems. The MFA thesis committee is chosen by the student in consultation with the thesis director.

Admission requirements include the submission of a portfolio of fiction or poetry. Teaching Assistantships are readily available for most qualified applicants. Assistantships carry a stipend of $7,825 and full tuition waiver. In addition, Teaching/Writing Fellowships ($3,625 per semester for teaching one section of beginning-level fiction or poetry writing), a *Black Warrior Review* editorship ($7,250 per year), and Graduate Council Fellowships (non-teaching) are available. For the latter, the stipend varies, and the candidates are nominated by the Department.

Graduate faculty includes poet Robin Behn (*Paper Bird, The Red Hour,* and *The Practice of Poetry: Writing Experiences from Poets who Teach* [co-editor]); poet Bruce Smith (*Mercy Seat, Silver and Information,* and *The Other Lover*); fiction writer Sandra Huss (*Labor For Love*); fiction writer Lex Williford (*McCauley's Thumb*); and fiction writer Michael Martone (*Safety Patrol, Alive and Dead in Indiana,* and *Seeing Eye*).

Each year the Endowed Chair in Creative Writing brings two distinguished writers to the campus for semester-long residencies. Recent chairholders include Ted Solotaroff, Greg Pape, Brendan Galvin, John Keeble, Heather McHugh, Mark Costello, Cornelius Eady, Desmond Hogan, George Starbuck, Marilynne Robinson, Gerald Stern, Margaret Atwood, Andre Dubus, Jack Gilbert, Russell Banks, Michael S. Harper, Kent Nelson, Lyn Hejinian, George Garrett, and Carolyn Kizer.

Recent visitors in the Visiting Writers Series include: Mark Doty, Toi Derricotte, Lynne Sharon Schwartz, Rodney Jones, Diane Glancy, Donald Revell, Nathaniel Mackey, Philip Graham, Philip Levine, Grace Paley, and Richard Wilbur.

About 130,000 people live in Tuscaloosa County, 19,000 of whom are students at the university. Situated on the Black Warrior River, Tuscaloosa enjoys a mild climate and very reasonable living costs. We are some fifty miles west of Birmingham and within a half-day's drive of Atlanta, New Orleans, the Smokey Mountains, and the Gulf Coast. The writing program has excellent support from the English Department and the University as a whole. There is a strong sense of community among the writers here.

For further information, write the Director, Program in Creative Writing, Dept. of English, P.O. Box 870244.

❖University of Alaska, Anchorage Anchorage, AK 99508

(907) 786-4330
FAX (907) 786-1382
e-mail: aycwla@uaa.alaska.edu

Degree: MFA in Creative Writing (fiction, poetry, creative nonfiction, drama/screenwriting)

Type of Program: Studio/Academic

Length of Residency: Two to three years

Required course of study: 45 s/hrs
    Writing workshops: 15-21 s/hrs
    Form and theory: 6-12 s/hrs
    Electives: 3-15 s/hrs
    Thesis: 9 s/hrs; book-length work of fiction,
      poetry, drama, or creative nonfiction

Other Requirements: A defense of thesis with an in-depth essay that puts the student's creative work into "critical perspective."

Application Deadline: March 1 for assistantships; April 1 for admissions.

The MFA in Creative Writing is a 45-hour professional degree which prepares students for various careers including those involving professional writing, teaching, and editing. It is generally a three-year degree, although some students may complete the requirements in a longer or shorter amount of time. In their program of study in the Department of Creative Writing and Literary Arts, students can take courses in four areas: creative nonfiction, fiction, poetry, and drama for stage and screen. The emphasis of courses in this department is balanced between the study and practice of craft, and the study of form and theory as they relate to style and content. Workshop courses under the CWLA prefix are "working" courses where students produce original works of literature and engage in productive critique of each other's writing. The MFA degree is flexible and designed to accommodate each student's needs.

MFA students have the opportunity to be involved in a number of professional editorial and writing activities, including working on the staff of *Inklings*, the campus literary magazine, and *Alaska Quarterly Review*, a nationally distributed and recognized literary journal. Additional opportunities exist for selected students to work with the editor of *We Alaskans*, the Sunday magazine of the *Anchorage Daily News*, a Pulitzer prize-winning newspaper.

The Department of Creative Writing and Literary Arts sponsors student readings each semester and sponsors readings and workshops that have included such writers and poets as: Tobias Wolff, Patricia Hampl, Jane Smiley, Rosellen Brown, William Gass, Gary Snyder, Carolyn Kizer, John Haines, Stuart Dybek, Roland Flint, William Kittridge, David Wagoner, Robert Hedin, Jim Heynen, Paula Gunn Allen, Gerald Vizenor, Joy Harjo, Mary Robison, Ron Carlson, Alice Fulton, Richard Ford, Alberto Rios, Toi Derricotte, and Valerie Miner. The Department also co-sponsors (with the *Anchorage Daily News*) a popular annual statewide Creative Writing Contest.

Students in the MFA program at the University of Alaska, Anchorage have been successful in publishing their work in books and an extensive range of journals, magazines, and anthologies including *Harper's*, *Yale Review*, *Playboy*, *New York Quarterly*, *North American Review*, *Kansas Quarterly*, the *Atlantic Monthly*, *Quarterly West*, *Amelia*, *Nimrod*, and many others. Several students have also been awarded Creative Writing Fellowship grants.

The Department of Creative Writing and Literary Arts' core faculty on the Anchorage campus includes: Poet and National Book Award Finalist Linda McCarriston (*Talking Soft Dutch* and *Eva-Mary*); creative nonfiction writer and Pushcart prize winner Gretchen Legler (*A Sportswoman's Notebook*); fiction writer and filmmaker Ronald Spatz (with short films broadcast on television, selected for film festivals), executive editor of the nationally-acclaimed *Alaska Quarterly Review*. McCarriston and Spatz have been recipients of NEA awards. An adjunct faculty of published writers and poets supplements undergraduate offerings.

UAA's Anchorage campus is surrounded by the spectacular Chugach Mountains and is only minutes away from wilderness recreation. At the same time, the campus is convenient to shopping, housing, and entertainment. The university is served by a public transportation system, and many facilities are within walking distance. The city of Anchorage, with a population of 260,000, is the chief business, cultural, and entertainment center for the State of Alaska. Summertime temperatures range between 60 and 70 degrees. Summer is filled with sunshine and long days as the sun sets only briefly. Winters are less severe in Anchorage than in many other U.S. cities. Normal lows range from 5 degrees below zero to 25 degrees above. UAA campus housing is available.

For more information, contact Ronald Spatz, Chair, Dept. of Creative Writing and Literary Arts.

❖University of Alaska, Fairbanks Fairbanks, AK 99775-5720

(907) 474-7193
e-mail: faengl@uaf.edu

Degrees offered: BA, MFA in Creative Writing

Degree: BA in English with Writing Emphasis

Required course of study: 36 s/hrs
  Thesis: no requirement
  Writing workshops: 9 or more s/hrs
  Literature courses: 27 s/hrs

Other Requirements: 58 s/hrs of university core requirements, including 6 s/hrs of English composition; 130 s/hrs minimum for graduation with BA in English.

Degree: MFA

Type of Program: Studio/Academic

Length of Residency: Three years for those with teaching assistantships.

Required course of study: 45 s/hrs
  Thesis: required 6 s/hrs
  Writing workshop: 9-15 s/hrs
  Other writing courses: 6 s/hrs
  Literature courses: 15 s/hrs

Other Requirements: Comprehensive examination; oral defense of thesis.

Application Deadlines: Full applications by March 15 for those wishing to be considered for teaching assistantships; deadline for admission without assistantship May 1.

The University of Alaska, Fairbanks has offered the MFA in Creative Writing since 1968. It is a small program with a close relationship between students and faculty. Students are expected to take workshops, craft courses (in at least 2 areas), as well as a selection of literature courses (mainly modern and contemporary). The thesis is a book-length collection of poetry, fiction, nonfiction prose, or a play. 15 teaching assistantships are available at a beginning stipend of $7,600 with tuition waiver. In addition to the MFA, the University offers an MA in English and an MA in Professional Writing.

Fairbanks is a community of 30,000 immediately adjacent to the Alaskan wilderness. It is in many senses a frontier community, and staff and students enjoy such activities as fishing, dog sledding, skiing, and wilderness treks. Despite its isolation, there is considerable activity in the arts (writing, painting, theatre), and a local symphony orchestra. *Permafrost*, a literary magazine sponsored by the University, is edited by English graduate students.

The faculty includes Renée Manfredi (fiction), author of *Where Love Leaves Us*, winner of the Iowa School of Letters Award for Short Fiction (1993). Poet John Morgan is author of *The Arctic Herd, The Inside Passage*, and *The Bone-Duster*. Peggy Shumaker is the author of three collections of poetry, *Esperanza's Hair, The Circle of Totems*, and *Wings Moist from the Other World*. Program Director Frank Soos (fiction and nonfiction) is author of short story collections *Early Yet* and *Unified Field Theory* (Flannery O'Connor Award, 1997), and essays, *Bamboo Fly Rod Suite*.

The program sponsors an active reading series including week-long residencies during which students confer with visiting writers. Recent writers-in-residence include: Hilda Raz, W.D. Wetherell, Lewis Nordan, Alice Fulton, Mary Robinson, Mary Gaitskill, Paula Gunn Allen, Toi Derricotte, and Robin Becker.

For more information, contact Frank Soos, Writing Program Co-Director, Dept. of English. fffms@uaf.edu.

University of Alberta, Edmonton Alberta, Canada T6G 2E5
(403) 492-3258
FAX (403) 492-8142

Degree offered: MA in English with Creative Thesis (poetry, fiction, creative nonfiction, children's literature)

Length of Residency: For full-time MA students the minimum period of residence is two four-month terms of full-time attendance at the University of Alberta for candidates with an Honors degree in English (or its equivalent); for candidates without an Honors BA in English, the residence requirement may be somewhat longer.

Required course of study: 3 full-year graduate courses or 18 s/hrs and a thesis of 6-12 s/hrs.

For more information, contact Chairman, Dept. of English.

Alderson-Broaddus College Philippi, WV 26416
(304) 457-6223
FAX (304) 457-6239

Degree offered: BA in Writing

Required course of study: 128 s/hrs total including Liberal Studies Core and Liberal Arts minor, courses in writing and literature or technology, plus 2 or 3 independent projects and/or practicum experiences.

For more information, contact Barbara Smith, Chair, Division of Humanities, Box 2158.

❖American University 4400 Massachusetts Avenue, NW Washington, DC 20016
(202) 885-2990
FAX (202) 885-2938

Degree offered: MFA in Creative Writing (poetry, fiction, playwriting, screenwriting)

Type of Program: Studio/Academic

Length of Residency: 2 years minimum; part-time students often take 3-4 years.

Required course of study:
  Internship/Teaching Track: 6 s/hrs
  Book-length Thesis

Application Deadlines: Fall, Feb. 1; Spring, Oct. 1.

American University offers the MFA degree in Creative Writing. Aside from regularly offered courses and workshops of a semester's duration, 4 visiting writers each year conduct 2-day workshops; other writers visit to give readings of their work. Visiting writers in recent years have included George Garrett, Charles Baxter, Colette Inez, William Matthews, Yusef Komunyakaa, A.M. Homes, Michael Cunningham, Terry McMillan, Mark Doty, Lynne Sharon Schwartz, and Grace Paley.

The Creative Writing faculty includes: novelist Charles R. Larson (*Academia Nuts, The Insect Colony, Arthur Dimmesdale*); fiction writer and film script writer Arnost Lustig (*Diamonds of the Night, A Prayer for Katerina Horovitzova, Precious Legacy,* Emmy Award, scriptwriting, 1986, *Indecent Dreams*); Richard McCann, poet, fiction writer, and anthologist (*Nights of 1990, Ghost Letters,* and *Landscape and Distance,* edited with Margaret Gibson); Kermit Moyer, fiction writer (*Tumbling and Other Stories*); Myra Sklarew, past President of Yaddo, 1987–1991 (*From the Backyard of the Diaspora, The Science of Goodbyes, Like A Field Riddled By Ants*); Henry Taylor, poet and translator (*The Horse Show at Midnight, The Flying Change,* Pulitzer Prize, 1986, *Understanding Fiction: Poems 1986–96*).

In addition to the permanent faculty, the Literature Department is sometimes joined by one or two Distinguished Writers in Residence, who teach in the MFA program. Recent holders of the Residency have included Joyce Johnson, Frank Conroy, Mary Morris, Marilyn Hacker, Jon Silkin, Jean Valentine, Alice McDermott, Pablo Medina, Carolyn Chute, Margaret Meyers, and Andrew Holleran.

Graduate writing students produce a literary magazine, *Folio,* a bi-weekly newsletter, *In Capital Letters,* and an annual alumni newsletter, *The Messenger.* They also have the opportunity to participate in the Lannan Poetry Program, as well as various readings. A limited number of fellowships and assistantships are available.

More information is available from Richard McCann, Myra Sklarew, or Henry Taylor, Co-Directors, MFA Program in Creative Writing, Dept. of Literature.

❖Antioch University, Los Angeles
13274 Fiji Way
Marina Del Rey, CA 90291
(310) 578-1090, (800) 7-ANTIOCH
FAX (310) 821-7426
e-mail: admissions@antiochla.edu
website: http://www.antiochla.edu

Degrees offered: BA, MFA

Degree: BA in Liberal Studies, Concentration in Creative Writing

Required course of study: Individualized program containing 40 quarter units of core courses, electives, internships, and prior learning. The Concentration provides focus on the genres of poetry, short fiction, and the novel. Courses in the curriculum are integrated by four areas of study: Theory and Critique (minimum 3 courses), Genre Workshops (minimum 4 courses), Special Topics in Reading Literature, and a Senior Seminar. Formats for classes include small groups, collaborative work, lecture/discussions, and whole group and on-line workshops. Internships provide avenues for students to venture into the world of writers and writing. Prior Learning activities permit

students to gain credit for college-level writing work and study completed before entering the program.

Degree: MFA in Creative Writing (Poetry, Fiction, Creative Nonfiction); and the Certificate in the Pedagogy of Creative Writing

Type of Program: Studio (Low Residency)

Required course of study: 48 semester units (five residencies of 10 days each; 4 project periods of 6 months duration between residencies); Certificate in The Pedagogy of Creative Writing requires one additional project period and residency beyond the MFA requirements.

Other Requirements: Successful completion of required residencies and project periods. Core Seminars in Arts, Culture, and Society (I and II); Seminar in Translation; writing workshops; genre seminars; Aesthetics/Poetics seminar; a field study; a critical paper; a book length manuscript; in the final residency, a public reading and a lecture or seminar; broad reading in the field and an annotated bibliography of that reading. For the Certificate in the Pedagogy of Creative Writing, the student must take 2 additional seminars -- Seminar in Teaching and Seminar in the Teaching of Creative Writing; a paper on the pedagogy of creative writing; and a supervised teaching internship. All students in the MFA in Creative Writing program must have access to a computer and modem.

The MFA in Creative Writing Program in poetry, fiction, and creative nonfiction is a two-year, 48 semester unit low-residency program, with 10-day residency periods in June and December at the Los Angeles campus. Besides developing the creative writing ability of the student, the program focuses attention on examining social and ethical issues related to the role of a writer in contemporary society and pluralistic culture. Students gain experience in community art/writing field study settings and attend seminars in potential career paths for writers. Faculty work with students via correspondence and the Internet during the alternating project periods. The intensive residencies consist of workshops, core seminars, lectures, classes, readings, professional development, and networking. During the residency, students design a learning project, the main focus of which is the student's own creative work, and an appropriate bibliography of required readings. For the next six months, the student submits creative and critical work every four weeks to the faculty mentor who responds with suggestions, revisions, and discussion. Students also participate in on-line conferences and critique groups. During one project period, a field study is required. At the end of the six months, the student returns to the campus to evaluate the completed learning project, participate in the next residency, and design the upcoming learning project. Student evaluation and faculty evaluation both become part of the student's record and narrative transcript. A successful residency period earns 6 semester units as does a successful learning project period. The Certificate in the Teaching of Creative Writing is an additional 12 semester unit requirement past the MFA.

Faculty are announced each year. Faculty for the December 1998 term are: Diana Abu-Jaber, fiction (*Arabian Jazz*); Wendy Bishop, fiction, pedagogy, poetry, creative nonfiction (*Working Words/The Process of Creative Writing*); Leonard Chang, fiction (*The Fruit 'N Food*); Bernard Cooper, creative nonfiction, fiction

(*Truth Serum*); Amy Gerstler, poetry (*Crown of Weeds*); Katharine Haake, fiction, pedagogy (*No Reason On Earth*); Eloise Klein Healy, poetry (*Artemis In Echo Park*); Michelle Huneven, fiction (*Round Rock*); Peter Levitt, poetry (*Bright Root, Dark Root*); Russell Leong, poetry (*The Country of Dreams and Dust*); Lisa Michaels, creative nonfiction, fiction (*Split: A Counterculture Childhood*); Rod Val Moore (*Igloo Among Palms*); Louise Rafkin, creative nonfiction (*Other People's Dirt*); Sharman Apt Russell, creative nonfiction (*The Humpbacked Fluteplayer*); and Tim Seibles, poetry (*Kerosene*). Visiting faculty are Dorothy Allison (fiction), Robin Becker (poetry), Aimee Bender (fiction), Lynell George (creative nonfiction), Sam Hamill (poetry, translation), Susan E. King (artist's books, letterpress printing), Bonnie Nadell (literary agent), Scott Russell Sanders (creative nonfiction), and Larry Siems (PEN Freedom to Write).

For more information, write or contact the MFA in Writing Program at above addresses.

Antioch University
Yellow Springs, OH 45387
(513) 767-6322
FAX (513) 767-6461

Degree offered: MA in Creative Writing (poetry, fiction, nonfiction, playwriting, screenwriting)

Type of Program: Studio & Studio/Academic (Low Residency)

Length of Residency: Two 4-day residencies

Required course of study: 60 q/hrs total
Thesis: 10 q/hrs
Degree plan: 5 q/hrs
Learning components: 45 q/hrs

Application Deadlines: Admission dates are October 1, January 2, and July 1.

Students interested in creative writing can design individualized curricula in fiction, poetry, drama, film script writing, or nonfiction prose. Some students in drama who want to pursue playwriting also have a strong background in directing or acting, or a combination of both.

The Antioch program differs from other programs in two fundamental ways -- it has two minimum residential sessions in Yellow Springs, after which you study in your community, where you recruit your degree committee, and the curriculum is individualized: you design your course of study with the help of your committee.

The Individualized Master of Arts (IMA) appeals to two categories of writers -- those who have had some success who want to earn a master's degree in order to improve their professional standing, and those who want to use the program to improve their writing in order to publish. The emphasis in this program is on the student as a writer. For unpublished writers, the goal is to become published.

The IMA program has an administrative and academic structure that allows each student to design and write a curriculum called a degree plan that meets the student's individual needs while meeting professional standards for a master's degree in creative writing. In writing a degree plan, students begin surveying writing programs to see what they have in common. Any academic discipline has certain features that all programs will share. It is crucial that in designing an individualized program a student includes those areas of study that all programs share. The IMA students have the freedom to include special areas of study that traditional programs do not require or make available as electives. For example, one current student is studying French literature and history while writing experimental, multi-media poetry, while another student is interested in diversions from realistic short story aesthetic norms. If you have a special interest, you can usually study it in the IMA if it is academically sound. The study of literature is inseparable from learning the craft of writing. Technique is a means to an end and not an end in itself, so students should study select writers who serve as models of good writing.

The IMA is a student-centered and initiated program which has many benefits, but also has responsibilities that place the obligation on the student to find his or her degree committee members and faculty. At first this may seem an obstacle difficult to overcome, but in fact, students find one of the real benefits of the program is picking the degree committee members and faculty with whom to study. There are faculty who have worked with different students and are available to work with new students. Students need to identify faculty in their communities. This is not as difficult as it sounds, and the Antioch faculty adviser to IMA creative writing students can play an active role in helping each student find the right committee members. Students can usually find committee members by contacting English departments at local universities, state-based arts councils, and directories such as one provided by *Poets & Writers* that has a state by state breakdown. One contact then leads to other contacts.

The degree committee plays a significant role in helping the student design a degree plan that meets the student's particular focus as a writer. Besides the degree plan, the committee evaluates the student's progress at mid-point review and candidacy status review meetings. A major role of the committee is providing guidance to the student in writing his or her thesis, which can be a novel, a collection of short stories, play, film or television script, or a collection of poems.

The minimum number of credits needed to complete the program is 60, the maximum 75. A 60-credit program consists of five credits for the degree plan, 45 credits of academic study divided into three-to-five-credit learning components consisting of independent study, tutorials, course-based study, and workshops, and ten credits for the thesis. Students recruit individual faculty members who serve as mentors for learning components. The degree committee can serve in this capacity in addition to their committee responsibilities.

Antioch's IMA in creative writing provides an academic structure that students use to design individualized curriculum to realize their goals as writers. The advantages are many. The program fits the ways writers work and learn best. Writers work by themselves and need constructive criticism of their writing -- both the form and content. Writers want individual instruction that responds to their artistic vision. The IMA provides that.

For further information, contact Office of Admissions, Antioch University, 800 Livermore, Yellow Springs, OH 45387.

❖Arizona State University
Tempe, AZ 85287-0302
(602) 965-7454

Degrees offered: BA English, MFA Creative Writing (poetry, fiction, creative nonfiction, playwriting)

Degree: MFA with Major in Creative Writing

Type of Program: Studio/Academic

Required course of study: 48 s/hrs total in poetry and prose, 60 s/hrs total in playwriting
   Thesis: 9 s/hrs
   Writing workshops: 15 s/hrs
   Literature courses: 24 s/hrs

Other Requirements: Written comprehensive exam; Practicum and Practicum Performance.

The Master of Fine Arts Degree with a Major in Creative Writing is an interdisciplinary program offered jointly by the Department of English in the College of Liberal Arts and Sciences and the Department of Theatre in the College of Fine Arts. This program offers students a unique opportunity to tailor a course of study to fit individual needs, talents, and goals. The Department of English administers the program and reviews applications for admission.

The 48/60 hour program is designed to provide students of demonstrated intelligence, motivation, and creative talent with the opportunity to work under the direction of faculty who are practicing, published writers of fiction, poetry, creative nonfiction, plays, and screenplays. The program includes equal components in literature and writing. A practicum project is required of all students: a book-length volume of poetry, short stories, novel, drama, or creative nonfiction (except literary criticism). The last requirement for the degree is that the candidate read from the practicum project before students and members of the faculty. A final comprehensive examination is required, covering 20th century literature and critical theory. For playwrights, the examination covers European and American drama and dramatic theory and criticism.

One of the unique features of this interdisciplinary program is that, because it utilizes the faculty creative/research/teaching interests of two academic units, collaborative production occurs with musicians, fine printers, and visual artists. Students have the opportunity to edit and publish a national literary magazine, *Hayden's Ferry Review*, a student publication. Candidates may direct the ASU Community Writers' Workshop or work as mentors in a high school outreach program. An annual reading, lecture, and conference series brings to ASU writers, editors, publishers, and artists who focus attention on issues in publishing creative work. Recent visiting faculty and writers have included Demetria Martínez, Anjana Appachana, Bill Loizeaux, Randall Kenan, Jean Valentine, Roland Flint, Stephen Dunn, Martin Espada, Alison Deming, Ai, and others.

Faculty members in poetry are: Norman Dubie, author of sixteen books of poetry, including *Radio Sky*, *Groom Falconer*, and *Selected and New Poems*; Alberto Rios, author of eight books, including *The Curtain of Trees* and *Pig Cookies*; Jeannine Savard, author of *Trumpeter* and *Snow Water Cove*; and Beckian Fritz Goldberg, author of *In the Badlands of Desire*, *Body Betrayer*, and *Never Be the Horse*. In fiction, faculty members are Ron Carlson, author of *The Hotel Eden*, *The News of the World*, *Truants*, and *Betrayed by F. Scott Fitzgerald*; Jay Boyer, author of *As Far Away As China*; Melissa Pritchard, author of *The Instinct for Bliss*, *Spirit Seizures*, *Phoenix*, and *Selene of the Spirits*; Jewell Parker Rhodes, author of *Voodoo Dreams: A Novel of Marie Laveau* and *Magic City*; and playwright Guillermo Reyes, author of *Chilean Holiday*, *The Hispanic Zone*, and *Men on the Verge of a His-Panic Breakdown*.

For more information, contact Karla Elling, Program Coordinator, Creative Writing Program, Dept. of English.

❖University of Arizona
Tucson, AZ 85721-0067
(520) 621-3880

Degrees offered: BA, MFA

Degree: BA with Major in Creative Writing

Required course of study: 33 s/hrs
   Writing workshop: 15 s/hrs
   Literature courses: 18 s/hrs

Other Requirements: 120 s/hrs for the BA.

Degree: MFA with Major in Creative Writing (poetry, fiction, creative nonfiction)

Type of Program: Studio/Academic

Required course of study: 36 s/hrs
   Thesis: Manuscript of poetry, fiction, or nonfiction
   Writing workshops: 12 s/hrs
   Literature courses: 12 s/hrs
   Electives: 12 s/hrs

Other Requirements: Exit interview for MFA poetry students.

The University of Arizona's Graduate Program in Creative Writing offers an opportunity for students of superior ability to develop their creative and critical skills through the practice of writing and the study of literature, leading to the MFA degree. The Program is adaptable to the interests of the individual student, with a concentration in poetry, fiction, or creative nonfiction. It is ranked among the top 5% of graduate Creative Writing Programs in the nation by *U.S. News and World Report*.

The fundamental purpose of the MFA Program is to help talented writers prepare for writing careers: at the completion of study, the student is expected to have produced a work of literary worth and size agreed upon between teacher and student. Because there can be no guarantee of professional or commercial success for any writer, a side benefit of the Program is that it can often qualify students for writing-related jobs, such as technical writing, editing and publishing, or working in the media -- and, with the degree plus publications, for the teaching of writing.

A limited number of teaching assistantships in Composition and in Creative Writing are available to MFA students. (The Creative Writing assistantships are not available to entering students.) Application for the Composition assistantships must be made on the form provided by the English department, and should be submitted with the other materials for admission. A few nonresident tuition scholarships are also offered, and several prizes and awards are available to students already enrolled in the Program.

Faculty members include: Jon Anderson (five books of poetry, including *The Milky Way -- Poems 1967-1982*; winner of The Shelley Memorial Award for Career Achievement from The Poetry Society of America); Geoffrey Becker, visiting (*Bluestown*, a novel, and *Dangerous Men*, stories, winner of the Drue Heinz Prize); Elizabeth Evans (*Locomotion*, stories; *The Blue Hour*, a novel; winner of the James Michener Award for her novel, *Man in the Moon*); Alison Hawthorne Deming (*Temporary Homelands*, essays; *Science and Other Poems*, which won the Walt Whitman Award, and *The Monarchs: A Poem Sequence*); Robert Houston (ten novels, including *Bisbee '17, The Nation Thief, The Fourth Codex*; Fulbright Professor to Peru); Jane Miller (books include *American Odalisque, Memory at These Speeds*, poetry; *Working Time*, nonfiction; winner of a Lila Wallace/Reader's Digest Fellowship); Alison Moore (*Small Spaces Between Emergencies*, stories; *Synonym for Love*, novel); Steve Orlen (four books of poetry, *Permission to Speak, A Place at the Table, The Bridge of Sighs*; winner of 3 NEA grants); Jonathan Penner (*Going Blind, The Intelligent Traveler's Guide to Chiribosco*, novels; *Private Parties*, stories, winner of the Drue Heinz Prize); C.E. Poverman (*Susan, Solomon's Daughter*, novels; *Skin*, stories; Chesterfield Award); Boyer Rickel, Asst. Program Director (*arreboles*, poetry; *Taboo*, essays, forthcoming); Richard Shelton (11 books of poetry, including *The Tattooed Desert*, winner of the International Poetry Forum's United States Award, *The Bus to Veracruz* and *Going Back to Bisbee*, winner of Western States Book Award for Nonfiction); Peter Wild (over 30 books, including *Cochise, New and Selected Poems*, and *Easy Victory*, poetry; *Pioneer Conservationists of Western America*, nonfiction).

Writers on the literature and composition faculties include Barbara Cully (*The New Intimacy, Shoreline Series*, poetry); N. Scott Momaday (fiction and poetry, including *House Made of Dawn* and *The Names*; winner of the Pulitzer Prize for Fiction); Tenney Nathanson (*The Book of Death*, poetry).

Faculty visitors have included Dagoberto Gilb, Ron Hansen, Rust Hills, Susan Howe, Kit McIlroy, Nancy Mairs, Grace Paley, Mary Elsie Robertson, and Joy Williams. The University of Arizona Poetry Center, directed by Alison Deming, has reading rooms and one of the nation's most extensive collection of poetry, including magazines and recordings. The Poetry Center sponsors readings by visiting writers and student poets. The Writers at Work series brings visiting fiction and nonfiction writers to campus, and sponsors student and faculty readings. In 1996, the first annual Publishing and Writing Conference brought former faculty member Terry McMillan back as its keynote reader.

The Program also partners with the *ArtsReach* foundation to teach creative writing in Native American schools.

Tucson is a center for writers. In addition to the many poets and writers who live here, such as Barbara Kingsolver, William Pitt Root, and Leslie Marmon Silko, Tucson is also home to several literary magazines and presses, including *Sonora Review, Arizona Quarterly, Persona, Suntracks* (magazine and press, specializing in Native American writers), Kore Press, and *Saguaro* (specializing in Hispanic-American writers).

For more information contact Robert Houston, Director of Creative Writing, Dept. of English.

❖Arizona Western College
Box 929
Yuma, AZ 85364
(520) 344-7689

Degree offered: AA with a Creative Writing Component

Application Deadlines: April 15 for financial aid; no deadline for admissions.

Arizona Western College, an equal opportunity, affirmative action institution, offers classes in creative writing for beginning and advanced writers in fiction, poetry, and creative nonfiction. Currently, a creative writing degree is not offered. The creative writing courses are part of the requirements for an AA in English. They also meet a community need.

Our courses are designed to give the students practice in creative writing, to provide each writer with an immediate critical audience, to develop the students' critical senses, to introduce them to basic form and theory of poetry, fiction, and nonfiction, to direct their reading toward appropriate contemporary models, to teach the terminology used in discussing the craft of writing, to help the students establish self-discipline and direction by assigning a quota of finished writing and by giving writing assignments, to introduce the students to contemporary and established writers as models for their own craft, and to give them guidance in preparing manuscripts.

By no means are creative writing students required to choose a genre and work in it exclusively. They may do so if they enter the class with a preference, but everyone, and especially the beginning writer, is encouraged to experiment in an attempt to discover strengths and weaknesses as a writer. All creative writing classes are run as workshops. On assigned dates during the semester, the student distributes copies of his or her work to the instructor and other students in the class. That manuscript is addressed (or critiqued) the following class period. Through extensive reading and discussion of published stories, poems, and articles early in the semester, students learn how to approach a manuscript as a writer and discuss it in terms relevant to the craft, a process distinct from doing literary analysis.

Current director of the AWC Writing School is David Coy (*Rural News*; poetry in *Intro*). Recent visiting writers/teachers include James Whitehead, Richard Shelton, Madeline DeFrees, Mark Spencer, Dick

Bakken, Eloner Kelton, David St. John, John Knoepfle, and Stephen Dunn.

For further information, contact David Coy or Cecilia Lim, English Dept.

Arkansas College
P.O. Box 2317
Batesville, AR 72503

Contact the Creative Writing Program Director, Dept. of English.

❖Arkansas Tech University
Russellville, AR 72801
(501) 968-0256
FAX (501) 964-0812

Degrees offered: BFA in Creative Writing; BFA in Creative Writing with Teaching Certification

Degree: BFA in Creative Writing

Required course of study: 124 s/hrs total
Thesis: no requirement
Writing workshop: 9 s/hrs
Other writing courses: 6-12 s/hrs
Practicum: 3-9 s/hrs
Literature courses: 15-24 s/hrs

Other Requirements: 12-16 s/hrs foreign language (French, German, Classical Greek, Japanese, Latin, or Spanish); 3 s/hrs Advanced Composition; 3 s/hrs Methods of Research; 46 s/hrs general education courses.

Degree: BFA in Creative Writing with Teaching Certification

Required course of study: 124 s/hrs total
Thesis: no requirement
Writing workshop: 9 s/hrs
Other writing courses: 6-12 s/hrs
Practicum: 3-9 s/hrs
Literature courses: 15-24 s/hrs

Other Requirements: 12-16 s/hrs foreign language (French, German, Classical Greek, Japanese, Latin, or Spanish); 3 s/hrs System of Grammar; 3 s/hrs Advanced Composition; 3 s/hrs Introduction to Linguistics; 3 s/hrs History of the English Language; 3 s/hrs Methods of Research; 40 s/hrs certification courses; 46 s/hrs general education courses.

Through the Creative Writing Program, the Department of English and Foreign Languages at Arkansas Tech University offers student writers a chance to develop writing skills as part of a broad liberal arts curriculum. In addition to their creative writing courses, students who major in creative writing complete courses in English language and literature, courses in staffing and editing a literary magazine, and a program of general studies that covers mathematics, natural science, social science, and humanities. Many creative writing majors also take advantage of the Department's microcomputers for word processing.

Students generally begin the creative writing program with honors courses in Expository Writing and Imaginative Writing. Thereafter, the recommended curriculum offers specialized classes in literature as well as developmental courses in creative writing, including Creative Writing; Form and Theory; Creative Writing Workshop, Poetry; Creative Writing Workshop, Fiction; Science Fiction and Fantasy; and a senior-level Seminar in Creative Writing. Independent study projects are always open, on a tutorial basis, to those students who wish to pursue a specific aspect of writing.

In addition to courses in writing, the Department of English and Foreign Languages also offers creative writing majors courses in magazine publishing and editing. Arkansas Tech University publishes *Nebo*, a semi-annual literary journal that includes poetry and fiction by nationally known authors as well as the work of Tech students and faculty. *Nebo* is edited by a panel of students and faculty members, and the students receive academic credit for work on the magazine.

Arkansas Tech University actively seeks out promising young writers at the high school level by sponsoring an annual Creative Writing Contest. 6 winners receive ATU scholarships that range from a first prize of $1,000 to 3 honorable mention awards of $300. The contest is held each fall, and high school seniors who are interested should send a sample of their poetry, fiction, or drama to Creative Writing Contest; Department of English and Foreign Languages; Arkansas Tech University; Russellville, AR 72801 before January 15 of their senior year in high school. The scholarship winners are notified in February. Creative writing majors who are enrolled at Tech can compete for a Francis Gwaltney Scholarship. Named in memory of the novelist who helped develop Tech's creative writing program, this full-tuition scholarship is awarded competitively on the basis of submitted poetry, fiction, or drama each semester. The student editor of *Nebo* is awarded a full-tuition scholarship.

Arkansas Tech University sponsors Creative Writing Workshops that are open to Tech students and interested high school students. In past years, the Workshops have featured writers such as Norman Mailer, Howard Nemerov, Ellen Gilchrist, James Lockwood, Jack Butler, and James Whitehead.

The senior member of the Tech creative writing faculty is B. C. Hall, a novelist and nonfiction writer whose publications include *The Burning Season, Big Muddy*, and *The South*. Professor Hall has also written screenplays, poetry, and nonfiction articles. The other primary teacher of creative writing is Paul Lake, a poet and novelist, who has published *Another Kind of Travel* (poetry), *Among the Immortals* (novel), and *Walking Backward* (poetry). Professor Lake has published short fiction, poetry, and nonfiction articles in many literary journals. Professors Hall and Lake are assisted by Dr. Michael Ritchie, advisor for *Nebo* and a published poet and translator, and Dr. Stan Lombardo, a specialist in science fiction and adventure writing.

For further information, write Dr. Carl Brucker, Head, Dept. of English or e-mail him at <egcb@atuvm.atu.edu>.

❖University of Arkansas, Fayetteville
Fayetteville, AR 72701

(501) 575-4301
FAX (501) 575-5919
e-mail: english@cavern.uark.edu

Degrees offered: MFA, Creative Writing; MFA, Translation

Degree: MFA, Creative Writing

Type of Program: Studio/Academic

Length of Residency: Three years

Required course of study: 60 s/hrs
    Thesis: 6 s/hrs
    Writing workshop: 15-18 s/hrs
    Other writing courses: 9-12 s/hrs
    Literature courses: 24-30 s/hrs
    Tutorials or directed reading: 6-9 s/hrs

Application Deadlines: March 1

The courses offered in the Program in Creative Writing are essentially of four kinds: (1) workshop sessions in which student work is read and discussed, (2) form and theory classes in poetry and fiction, (3) reading courses designed by the students in consultation with the staff, and (4) regular classes in literature offered by the Department of English. Students who take the MFA degree at Arkansas -- a 60-hour studio-academic degree -- will have both a broad general grasp of literature and a firm understanding of the history and techniques of the genre in which they do their work. The program also offers workshops in screenwriting, creative nonfiction, and translation.

We do not suggest that the program can "make a writer" and we feel, in many cases, that a writer's particular gifts might develop faster and better outside the academic scene. We do, of course, believe that the community the program offers -- the community and education -- is exactly right for many people. Some writers will take only the studio and recent literature courses, will develop their skills, and leave without a degree. Those writers who do take the MFA degree are prepared to teach a wide range of courses at the college and university level. The program is well suited to those who wish to become writers who teach. In keeping with the AWP guidelines, we believe that our MFA should be considered a terminal degree when the graduate has supported the degree with the publication of a book. Our students have become teachers, freelance writers, arts administrators, and editors, to name a few of the ways they have gone on to support themselves. Graduates of the programs, and writers who have attended workshops, have published their works in many magazines and anthologies. Many have published important books of poetry and fiction.

Each year guest writers visit the program to teach workshops, give readings, and hold conferences with the students. In a given year a student will usually have manuscript conferences with at least 3 of the regular staff members -- and the student will also have no less than 2 manuscript conferences with our distinguished guests. Guests over the last several years have included Jack Gilbert, Donald Justice, Rick Bass, Allen Gurganus, Sandra McPherson, Linda Gregg, Henry Taylor, Li-Young Lee, Rodney Jones, Martha Kaplan, Howard Nemerov, Lee K. Abbott, Kelly

Cherry, Omar Pound, C. Michael Curtis, Al Young, and Richard Ford.

The program is able to offer teaching assistantships with stipends of $8,600-$9,000 to virtually all incoming students. All tuition and fees are waived. University Fellowships, worth $3,000 per year and renewable up to three additional years, are available to exceptionally qualified incoming students. Additional $1,000 fellowships are also available on a competitive basis after the first year. Literary prizes are awarded each year. In addition, MFA students have opportunities to staff the Arkansas Writers-in-the-Schools program and receive stipends for specific work.

The permanent staff of the Arkansas program includes John DuVal, whose books of translations include *Long Blues in A Minor*, *Tales of Trilussa*, and the award-winning *The Discovery of America*; Donald Hays, author of two novels and editor of an anthology of Southern short fiction; Michael Heffernan, the author of 6 volumes of poetry, including *The Cry of Oliver Hardy*, *To the Wreakers of Havoc*, and *Love's Answer*; Joanne Meschery, author of *In a High Place*, *A Gentleman's Guide to the Frontier*, and *Home and Away*; Enid Shomer, author of three books of poetry, including *This Close to the Earth* and *Black Drum*, and a novel, *Imaginary Men*, winner of the Iowa Fiction award; James Whitehead, the author of the novel *Joiner* and 3 books of poetry, including *Domains* and *Near at Hand*; and Miller Williams, who has written or edited 28 books including, most recently, *The Ways We Touch*. In 1995 he received the Academy Award for Literature from the American Academy of Arts and Letters.

For further information, write The Program in Creative Writing, Dept. of English.

Degree: MFA, Translation

Type of Program: Studio/Academic

Length of Residency: Three years

Required course of study: 60 s/hrs
    Thesis: 6 s/hrs
    Writing workshop: 21-25 s/hrs (at least 12
        s/hrs translation workshop: 6-9 s/hrs
        poetry and fiction workshops)
    Form and Theory, fiction, poetry, translation:
        9 s/hrs
    Literature courses: 24 s/hrs
    Foreign Language

Other Requirements: Good reading knowledge of 2 foreign languages.

Application Deadlines: March 15.

Miller Williams, Founder of the Program in Translation, describes it as follows: "We treat translations as a happy contention between scholarship and creative writing, requiring the translator to know not only both languages involved, but both cultures, the criticism relating to the author, the historical context in which the piece was written, if it's not a contemporary work, and the author's own life story as it relates to the work and its time. We require a knowledge of the history of the English language as well as the Form and Theory of Poetry and the Form and Theory of Fiction, and we expect our translators to be able to write fair poems and stories of their own. We broaden the base of the

Program -- the first MFA in translation in the country, and one that requires a full 60 s/hrs of workshop and academic credit -- by bringing in at least once each semester an established translator to direct one workshop session and hold manuscript conferences with all of the translators. Visitors have included John Ciardi, Donald Justice, John Nims, Margaret Peden, Gregory Rabassa, Ranier Schulte, Lucien Stryk, Frederic Raphael, and Omar Pound.

"During the final semester in the program, a translator takes an 8-hour written comprehensive examination over the tradition and theories of translations and meets with a panel of 3, on which is at least one translator, one writer, and one scholar (all 3 may be all 3) to discuss the book-length translation or collection of translations which serves as the MFA thesis, and hopefully to have it accepted by them.

Required courses for the MFA in Translation are taught by the creative writing staff and by the foreign language faculty. John DuVal, Kay Pritchett, or Miller Williams regularly direct the translation workshop.

For more information, contact John DuVal, Translation Program Director.

University of Arkansas, Little Rock
2801 S. University Ave.
Little Rock, AR 72204
(501) 569-3161

Degree offered: BA in English with Creative Writing Emphasis

Required course of study: 33 s/hrs
Thesis: no requirement
Writing workshop: 6-12 s/hrs
Form and Theory courses: 3-6 s/hrs
Literature courses: 15-20 s/hrs

The English Department of the University of Arkansas at Little Rock offers a degree in English with Creative Writing Emphasis. Students pursuing such a degree may choose to work in fiction and/or poetry writing. They are required to complete the regular sequence of courses leading to the English major and to take at least 4 of the 8 creative writing courses regularly offered: Introduction to Creative Writing; Fiction Writing I; Fiction Writing II; Poetry Writing I; Poetry Writing II; Screenwriting; The Form and Theory of Fiction; The Form and Theory of Poetry; and Advanced Creative Writing Project.

Creative writing majors also may choose to work on the editorial staff of *Equinox*, the university's student literary magazine. Occasionally, advanced students will serve as editorial assistants for *Crazyhorse*, the national literary journal published at UALR.

The faculty includes poets Ralph Burns (author of *Any Given Day, Mozart's Starling*, and *Swamp Candles*) and fiction writer and poet David Jauss (author of *Improving Rivers, Black Maps*, and stories in the *O. Henry, Pushcart*, and *Best American Short Stories* anthologies).

For further information, contact David Jauss or Ralph Burns, Co-Directors of Creative Writing, Dept. of English.

❖University of Arkansas, Pine Bluff
Pine Bluff, AR 71601

Contact the Creative Writing Program Director, Dept. of English.

❖Armstrong Atlantic State University
11935 Abercon Street
Savannah, GA 31419-1997

Contact the Creative Writing Program Director, Dept. of English.

❖The School of the Art Institute of Chicago
Chicago, IL 60603-6110
(800) 232-7242
FAX (312) 899-1840
e-mail: admiss@artic.edu
website: www.artic.edu

Degree offered: MFA in Writing; Post-Baccalaureate Certificate in Writing

Degree: MFA in Writing

Type of Program: Studio

Required course of study: 60 s/hrs total
Tutorial Graduate Project Advising: 24 s/hrs
Writing workshops: 12 s/hrs
Writing or Interdisciplinary Seminars: 12 s/hrs

Other Requirements: 12 s/hrs in Electives or Internships.

Application Deadlines: Fall entry February 1; Spring entry November 1.

The MFA in Writing program is for writers of fiction, poetry, essays, scripts, and creative nonfiction, as well as for artists who work with both image and text and who want to focus on text. It is an integral part of the School's graduate division and thus closely associated with the MFA in Studio Art. Conceived by faculty at the School who are writers of poetry and prose and artists in performance, film, video, visual communication, printmaking, and painting, the two-year program is distinct from more conventional writing programs. It brings together a community of writers and artists at one of the nation's leading colleges of art and draws on a faculty with diverse artistic and intellectual concerns. This core group of faculty is augmented by visiting writers, artists, and scholars. It is expected that in this unique community of writers and artists hybrid works, new forms, and collaborative projects will evolve.

The program provides a flexible structure to accommodate individual needs and exploration. The majority of coursework is devoted to the development of student writing through tutorial Graduate Project advising and writing workshops. Seminar courses, many with strong generative components, are offered by both the Writing program and the graduate division of the School. In these seminar courses students -- either with other writers or with a mix of writers and artists drawn from throughout the graduate division

-- engage a variety of subjects, e.g. the work of individual writers or artists, literary or art theory and criticism, and issues in contemporary culture. Electives allow writers to develop new skills or strengthen work in any of the studio areas of the School or to select from an array of courses in art history, theory, and criticism; liberal arts; arts administration; and historic preservation. Through internships which offer art-related work experience throughout the Chicago area and in several U.S. cities, students may also satisfy elective credit.

The core writing faculty includes: fiction writer Janet Desaulniers (Director of the Writing program); fiction and nonfiction writer Carol Anshaw (*Seven Moves, Aquamarine*); poet and nonfiction writer James Armstrong; scholar Paul Ashley; writer and critic Carol Becker (*Zones of Contention: Essays on Art, Institutions, Gender, and Anxiety; The Subversive Imagination: Artists, Society and Social Responsibility*); poet, fiction writer, essayist, and playwright Rosellen Brown (*Before and After, Cora Fry's Pillow Book*); poet and nonfiction writer Calvin Forbes (*Blue Monday, From the Book of Shine*); fiction writer and filmmaker M. Evelina Galang (*Her Wild American Self*); writer-performer Matthew Goulish; poet, playwright, and essayist Dan Howell (*Lost Country*); editor, fiction and nonfiction writer Geoff Johnson; poet, fiction and nonfiction writer James McManus (*Going to the Sun, Great America*); writer, painter, and performer Michael K. Meyers; fiction writer, poet, playwright, and essayist Phyllis Moore; fiction writer Beth Nugent (*Live Girls, City of Boys*); playwright and songwriter Beau O'Reilly; artist and writer David Robbins (*The Camera Believes Everything, Foundation Papers from the Institute for Advanced Comedic Behavior*); nonfiction writer George H. Roeder, Jr. (*The Censored War: American Visual Experience During World War II, Forum of Uncertainty: Confrontation with Modern Paintings in Twentieth Century American Thought*); and poet and critic Daniel Tobin (*Where The World Is Made*).

Each semester, students may select an advisor from this core or from the school-wide Graduate Advisor roster to focus on their work in private sessions. Typically, the school-wide roster includes poets, novelists, short fiction, and nonfiction writers, as well as painters, photographers, printmakers, performance artists, filmmakers, video artists, art historians, critics, and scholars. In addition, over one hundred artists, critics, and scholars visit the School each year to lecture and critique student work. Recent visitors of interest to Writing program students include: Lee K. Abbott, Stuart Dybek, Nikki Finney, Mary Gordon, Donald Justice, Yusef Komunyakaa, Li-Young Lee, Doris Lessing, David Mamet, Molly Peacock, David Sedaris, Laurie Stone, Mark Strand, and Helen Vendler.

The School of the Art Institute of Chicago maintains an extensive financial aid program. Once an applicant has completed the needs analysis documents and been admitted, a financial aid package can be determined and mailed to the student. Financial aid is also available through Teaching Assistantships (MFA candidates only) in undergraduate programs and departments and through Graduate Assistantships (MFA and Post-Baccalaureate candidates) in offices and programs throughout the School.

Catalog requests and inquiries about admission procedures should be directed to Graduate Admissions at (800) 232-7242; inquiries about the MFA in Writing

degree program or the Post-Baccalaureate Certificate in Writing program may be directed to the Writing program office (312) 899-5094. Both Admissions and the Writing program are located at The School of the Art Institute of Chicago, 37 South Wabash Avenue, Chicago, IL 60603-6110.

Certificate: Post-Baccalaureate Certificate in Writing

Required course of study: 30 s/hrs total
Tutorial Independent Project Advising: 12 s/hrs
Writing workshops: 6 s/hrs
Writing or Interdisciplinary Seminars: 6 s/hrs

Other requirements: 6 s/hrs of Electives or Internships.

Application Deadline: May 1

The Post-Baccalaureate Certificate in Writing program is customized to help students develop a portfolio of work that will be competitive at the graduate admissions level. In the year-long program of study, students are individually advised and participate in a studio curriculum that combines the tutorial aspect of graduate school with advanced seminars and workshops in literary craft. Students admitted to the program study with the faculty of the MFA in Writing program and also have the option to elect one course per semester in any area of the School.

Applicants to the program may be recent graduates of BFA, BS, or BA degree programs who would like to increase both the depth and breadth of their instruction in writing, artists who wish to pursue a strong emphasis on text, persons who have come to writing after work in a different or unrelated field, or international students requiring a year of intensive focus on their writing before beginning an MFA program. Admission is limited to those who show clear promise for advanced study in the literary arts. An interview is required. Potential applicants are reminded that completion of the Post-Baccalaureate Writing Certificate does not guarantee admission to a Master of Fine Arts program in Writing and that credits taken while a post-baccalaureate student cannot count towards an MFA degree should the student later be accepted into such a program.

For catalog requests, Post-Baccalaureate financial aid, and program inquiries, see information listed under MFA in Writing degree program.

Ashland University
Ashland, OH 44805
(419) 289-5979

Degree offered: BA with Creative Writing major or minor

Required course of study: 128 s/hrs total

Creative Writing Major:
Form and Technique course: 3 hours
Writing workshop: 8 hours
Genre courses in short story, poetry, drama, essay, the novel: 12 hours
Literature courses: 12 hours

Creative Writing Minor:
Form and Technique: 3 hours
Writing workshop: 4 hours
Genre courses in short story, poetry, drama, essay, the novel: 6 hours
Literature courses: 6 hours

Other Requirements: University distribution requirements, 44–56 hours.

Our creative writing majors generally begin with an introductory class in the form and technique of poetry and fiction. Students spend half the semester writing metrical exercises, and exercises in such forms as the ghazal and pantoum. The other half of this introductory course involves writing exercises in perspective, dialogue, description, narration, etc. Students then take a two-credit workshop in poetry, a two-credit workshop in fiction/nonfiction, a three-credit junior year workshop ("Problems in Creative Writing"), and a one-credit finishing course, taught on a tutorial basis, in which students revise extensively work in one genre, and put together a creative writing portfolio. A strong component of the program is the study of literature, giving the students ample opportunity to grasp the ongoing tradition of the writer and do intensive study on one or more of the major writers. The literature courses are taught by a strong faculty with specializations in all the periods of English and American literature. Creative Writing majors take four upper level literature courses, and four genre-specific courses in which they write analytical essays in response to poetry, drama, short fiction, the novel, and/or the creative essay.

Special features of the program include a series of student readings sponsored by the Literature Club, an Arts and Humanities lecture/reading series by guest poets and fiction writers, and a bi-annual student-run literary journal. The Ashland Poetry Press, an adjunct of the university, has been in existence since 1969 and has published some forty titles. Interested students have an opportunity to gain editing and publishing experience when a book is in progress.

Visiting writers in recent years include, among others, Mark Jarman, Andrew Hudgins, Pattiann Rogers, Joseph Langland, Jack Matthews, Wendy Battin, Carolyne Wright, Rebecca McClanahan, and David Young.

Full-time creative writing faculty include Stephen Haven (poems, essays, translations in *American Poetry Review, Crazyhorse, Salmagundi, The Writer's Chronicle*) and Joe Mackall (former editor of *Cleveland Magazine*, stories and articles in the *Cleveland Plain Dealer Sunday Magazine, Cleveland Magazine, The Washington Post*). Robert McGovern, Emeritus Professor (poems in *The Nation, Kansas Quarterly, Hollins Critic*) continues to teach one or two creative writing courses per year, and to direct the Ashland Poetry Press.

For more information on the program contact Stephen Haven (419–289–5979) or Joe Mackall (419–289–5142), co-directors of Creative Writing.

❖Auburn University
Auburn, AL 36849-5203
(334) 844–4620

Degrees offered: BA in English with Concentration in Creative Writing; MA in English with Concentration in Creative Writing

Required course of study: 50 q/hrs total in English for BA; 40 q/hrs total in English (including three 5-hour workshops) and a 6 hour creative thesis for MA.

The Department of English at Auburn offers introductory and advanced undergraduate courses in both fiction and poetry, as well as specialty courses, such as supernatural fiction, and the option to take independent study beyond the advanced courses. Poetry and fiction workshops are offered on the graduate level, in addition to a master's section for particularly promising students. All degree candidates in writing are expected to fulfill the basic requirements for degrees in English on the undergraduate and graduate level, including the language and comprehensive examination requirements. Special students not seeking degrees, however, are not discouraged.

The current faculty includes Stephen Gresham (*Dew Claws, Midnight Boy, Moon Lake*, and others) in genre fiction; Elly Welt (*Joanna Reddinghood* and *Berlin Wild*) in fiction; R.T. Smith (*From the High Dive, Birch-Light, The Cardinal Heart*) in poetry and fiction; and Judy Troy (*Mourning Doves*) in fiction.

Visitors to campus have included John Engels, Brendan Galvin, Ann Deagon, Betty Adcock, Mary Lee Settle, and Janet Burroway.

Recent graduates have published poetry in *Shenandoah, Southern Poetry Review, Poetry Northwest, International Poetry Review, Texas Review, Poet Lore, Black Warrior Review*, and others.

Southern Humanities Review is located in the department. Auburn also operates a small writing conference each spring, offers an Academy of American Poets Prize annually, and is a member of AWP.

Graduate teaching assistantships are available at approximately $9,000 per year with a load of 1 class per quarter.

For further information, write Dr. Dennis Rygiel, Chairman, Dept. of English.

Austin Peay State University
Clarksville, TN 37044
(615) 648–7891

Degrees offered: BA or BS in English; MA in English with a Creative Thesis Option

Required course of study: 30 s/hrs total in the major; 18 s/hrs total for a writing minor; 24 s/hrs junior level introductory courses in poetry, fiction, nonfiction, and playwriting; 9 s/hrs senior level writing workshops in poetry, fiction, and nonfiction; 9 s/hrs graduate writing workshops in poetry, fiction, and nonfiction; 24 s/hrs undergraduate courses in technical and professional writing.

The Department of Languages and Literature has a Writing Program heavily supported by the university's Center of Excellence in the Creative Arts. A visiting writer is in residence for one semester each year to teach a writing workshop and a literature course. (Past writers-in-residence: Al Young, Peter Meinke,

Dave Etter, Patsy Sims.) In addition, numerous writers visit the campus for readings and workshops (In 1987–88: Howard Nemerov, Allen Ginsberg, Ishmael Reed, Gwendolyn Brooks, and others). An endowed chair in the creative arts brings a writer to the university for a lengthy residency in creative writing every several years (past recipients: Arthur Kopit, Carolyn Forché).

The Department and the Center also sponsor the nationally circulated poetry journal *Zone 3* and a student literary magazine, *The Red Mud Review*. There are also 8–10 $1,000 creative writing scholarships available.

Faculty in the program: poet Malcolm Glass (*Bone Love, In the Shadow of the Gourd*); poet David Till; fiction writer Barry Kitterman (stories in *Flyway*, etc.); nonfiction writer J.D. Lester (*Writing Research Papers* and *Interactions*); James Clemmer and Mickey Wadia, who teach technical writing.

For more information, contact Malcolm Glass, Dept. of Languages and Literature.

❖Ball State University
Muncie, IN 47306
(765) 285–8580
FAX (765) 285–3765
BITNET: D000ENG@BSUVAX1
e-mail: tkoontz@gw.bsu.edu
website: http//www.bsu.edu/english

Degrees offered: BA, BS

Degree: BA or BS in English with Emphasis in Creative Writing (poetry, fiction, essay)

Required course of study: 45 s/hrs English total
    Creative Writing: 15 or more s/hrs
    Literature: 15 or more s/hrs

Other Requirements: University distribution requirements; writing competency exam.

Application Deadlines: March 1 for admissions and for financial aid.

Courses in creative writing are designed to contribute to the student's preparation for a rich personal and professional life, by emphasizing the nature of the creative processes, the use of language for both self-expression and communication, and the specific techniques and devices that are used by artists for effective writing in the literary genres. The campus literary and fine arts magazine, *The MT Cup Revue*, is edited by undergraduates with majors in English and other arts; its Editor-in-Chief is an English major, who receives an English Department scholarship. Each year the Barry Wright Memorial Fellowship is awarded for excellence in poetry writing. Students with non-English majors may take a 9 s/hr Emphasis in Creative Writing, or a Minor in English that includes 15 s/hrs of creative writing.

For more information contact Tom Koontz, Creative Writing Coordinator, Dept. of English.

University of Baltimore
Baltimore, MD 21201
(410) 837–6038

Degrees offered: BA, MA

Degree: BA in English with Concentration in Creative Writing

Required course of study: 30 s/hrs in the major
    Thesis: up to 6 s/hrs (optional)
    Writing workshop: up to 9 s/hrs
    Other writing courses: 3–15 s/hrs
    Tutorials or directed reading: up to 6 s/hrs
    Literature courses: 9–15 s/hrs

Other Requirements: 12 s/hrs in coursework outside the major.

Degree: MA in Publications Design

Required course of study: 36 s/hrs
    Thesis: 3 s/hrs
    Writing workshop: up to 3 s/hrs
    Other writing courses: up to 15 s/hrs
    Tutorials or directed reading: up to 6 s/hrs

Other Requirements: 6 s/hrs internship; 12 s/hrs publishing and design courses.

The faculty includes Kendra Kopelke (poetry) and Stephen Matanle (fiction).

For more information, contact Kendra Kopelke, Writing Program Director, Dept. of English.

Baruch College
City University of New York
New York, NY 10010
(212) 387–1280

Degree offered: BA in English: Journalism and Creative Writing

Required course of study: 30 s/hrs for the major
    Writing courses: 12 s/hrs in journalism,
        9 in creative writing
    Literature courses: 9 s/hrs

Other Requirements: 6 s/hrs of composition; 3 s/hrs of great works survey; 3 s/hrs on the introductory "Perspectives on the News"; 6 s/hrs foreign language; 3 s/hrs art or music; 3 s/hrs philosophy; 3 s/hrs history; 8 s/hrs natural sciences; 3–5 s/hrs math or statistics; 3 s/hrs computing; 12 s/hrs social and behavioral sciences.

The BA in English with a journalism and creative writing emphasis does not require a thesis, but students are encouraged to take an internship and/or to write for *Dollars and Sense*, recent recipient of the Gold Crown Award for "superlative excellence in student publishing."

Writing faculty includes poet Grace Schulman and has featured such visitors as Pulitzer Prize winner Murray Kempton and Jack Newfield (*City for Sale*). Professional staff includes writers for the *New York Times*, the *Village Voice*, and *Fortune* magazine.

For further information, contact Prof. John Todd, Chair, Dept. of English, or Prof. Roslyn Bernstein, Asst. Chair and Director of Journalism and Creative Writing.

❖Baylor University
Waco, TX 76798-7404

(254) 710-1768

Degrees offered: BA, MA

Degree: BA in Professional Writing; MA in English with Creative Thesis

Application Deadline: December 1 for spring; May 1 for summer or fall.

Courses in writing are offered to students pursuing either a BA or MA in English. Introductory and advanced courses in Creative Writing: Poetry; and Creative Writing: Prose, along with Professional & Technical Writing and Advanced Expository Writing, are offered.

In addition to the elective courses in the BA English program, a major in professional writing is also offered. Majors in professional writing register for 9 s/hrs of literature and 15 s/hrs of writing courses. Advanced Argumentative and Persuasive Writing, Advanced Technical Writing, Writing for the Popular Market, Special Topics courses, Advanced Writing for the Popular Market, and an Internship in Professional Writing build on skills learned in introductory courses.

With a traditional MA degree program which emphasizes literary and critical study, graduate students take workshops in the writing of poetry and fiction. A creative thesis is an alternative to the standard scholarly/critical thesis. Candidates for the MA are eligible for financial assistance as graduate or research assistants. In addition, tuition scholarships are available to outstanding students.

Creative Writing faculty are: William Virgil Davis (Writer-in-Residence; Yale Series of Younger Poets Award; Calliope Press Chapbook Prize), Greg Garrett (Faulkner Prize), J.R. LeMaster (1976 Ohio Poet of the Year).

Recent visitors: Eavan Boland, Robert Olen Butler, Peter Davison, Mona Van Duyn, Carolyn Forché, George Garrett, Louise Glück, Donald Hall, Anthony Hecht, Donald Justice, W.S. Merwin, Naomi Shihab Nye, Louis Simpson, W.D. Snodgrass, Cathy Song, Larry Woiwode, Charles Wright.

The English Department sponsors a student literary magazine, *The Phoenix*, which appears annually.

For more information, contact the Dept. of English, Baylor University, P.O. Box 97404, Waco, TX 76798-7404.

Behrend College
Erie, PA 16563

(814) 898-6151

Degree offered: BA in English (poetry, fiction, creative nonfiction)

Required course of study: 124 hrs total
Writing workshops: 12 hrs
Literature: 12 hrs

Other requirements: Senior thesis (6 hrs) -- two-semester project.

The undergraduate option in Creative Writing offers coursework in the areas of poetry, fiction, and creative nonfiction. Students may also receive credit for working on the College literary magazine, *Tempus*.

For more information, contact Division of Arts and Humanistic Studies.

❖Beloit College
700 College St.
Beloit, WI 53511-5596

(608) 363-2000

Degree offered: BA in Creative Writing

Required course of study: 9 units in writing and literature plus a senior project (book-length manuscript or public presentation).
Writing workshops: 5 units
Literature courses: 4 units

Application Deadlines: Rolling applications -- no deadlines.

For nearly 50 years Beloit College has been a leader among undergraduate institutions in the study of creative writing. Our Creative Writing major requires introductory and advanced work in at least two writing genres, chosen from among fiction, poetry, playwriting, and creative nonfiction. A minor course of study in journalism is also available. Class size in all writing workshops is limited to 15 students to ensure individualized instruction. In addition, students may apprentice themselves to instructors for one-on-one Special Projects courses. Credit internships with professional publishing groups are also available for students wishing to gain practical experience in writing or editing.

Among the opportunities available is the *Beloit Fiction Journal*, a national literary magazine with an editorial board comprised of Beloit College undergraduates. Student writers may compete for a number of annual awards, including the $1,000 Lois Wilson Mackey Prize in Creative Writing and the $1,000 Nick Adams Short Fiction Contest. Occasionally, overseas writing seminars are offered in Glasgow, Scotland.

The writing faculty includes program director Clint McCown (*The Member-Guest*, novel; *Sidetracks* and *Wind over Water*, poems), twice winner of the American Fiction Prize; poet/translator John Rosenwald; poet Lisa Fishman Morren and nonfiction writer Shawn Gillen. In addition to the regular faculty, the Lois Wilson Mackey Chair in Creative Writing provides each year for the hiring of a nationally prominent writer to teach an advanced writing course. Past chairholders have included Raymond Carver, Tess Gallagher, William Stafford, Ursula K. LeGuin, Rick Bass, Carolyn Kizer, Peter Matthiessen, Edward Hoagland, and Denise Levertov. Other guest writers who have visited in recent years include Gwendolyn Brooks, Lucille Clifton, Galway Kinnell, and Carolyn Forché.

For more information, contact Clint McCown, Dept. of English.

❖Bennington College
Bennington, VT 05201
(802) 440-4452
FAX (802) 440-4453

Degree offered: MFA in Writing and Literature
(concentrations in fiction, nonfiction, or poetry)

Type of Program: Studio/Academic (Low Residency)

Required course of study: A successfully completed semester's work is granted 16 hours of graduate credit. To receive the MFA, each student will create and submit a manuscript of fiction, nonfiction, or poetry at the end of the program. To complete the program, four semesters and five residencies are required.

Application deadlines: For the January residency: September 15; for the June residency, March 15. Financial aid applications are due at the same time.

The Bennington Writing Seminars offers a low-residency Master of Fine Arts (MFA) degree in Writing and Literature. This two-year graduate program involves intense 10-day residency periods at Bennington College during January and June of each year. Between residencies, students spend the six-month semesters corresponding directly with faculty who teach as part of the program's core staff. Additional faculty participate as associate staff during the 10-day residency periods, teaching literature from a writer's point of view. The five residencies feature workshops, readings, lectures, and discussions of literature, and an ongoing investigation of what constitutes the world of letters.

In keeping with Bennington's progressive tradition, the course of study in the Seminars is structured largely by the student. Students, in concert with the core staff, form their own reading lists, and submit interpretive and original work -- fiction, nonfiction, and poetry -- for critique at regular intervals throughout the semester. The development of individual work is at the heart of the program. Students are expected to devote at least 25 hours each week to their writing and reading.

During each residency, workshops in fiction, non-fiction, and poetry will be conducted by the core staff. Associate staff will visit to conduct five-day residencies, teaching literature in three lecture/discussions sessions. Whatever the genre in which a student is working, all students are expected to attend the session of associate faculty in a least two genres. Students will design their course of study for the coming semester -- readings and writings -- in consultation with the core faculty member with whom the student will be corresponding. Workshops are small, never more than 12 people, and an intimate student/teacher ratio will be maintained throughout the program.

The first two semesters are devoted to original and interpretive work, with a minimum 10-page critical paper, based on one's reading list, to be submitted to the core staff member and the students in one's genre at the end of each semester. The third semester requires that each student complete, in addition to original work, a minimum 20-page critical work,

which will then be revised and presented to the faculty and students in a lecture during the fourth residency period.

Students are admitted to the program primarily on the strength of the original manuscript submitted with the application.

Core Faculty: Fiction: Douglas Bauer, Susan Dodd, Maria Flook, Lynn Freed, Amy Hempel, Alice Mattison, Jill McCorkle, Askold Melnyczuk, Martha Cooley, Elizabeth Cox, and Rick Moody. Nonfiction: Sven Birkerts, Susan Cheever, Bob Shacochis, Lucy Grealy, Phillip Lopate, and George Packer. Poetry: David Lehman, Liam Rector, Jason Shinder, Thomas Sayers Ellis, Jane Hirshfield, and Carol Muske.

Associate Faculty (recent): Robert Bly, Lucie Brock-Broido, Robert Creeley, Bruce Duffy, Donald Hall, Barry Hannah, Edward Hoagland, Lewis Hyde, E. Ethelbert Miller, Sue Miller, Robert Pinsky, Tree Swenson, Mark Doty, Karen Finley, George Garrett, Richard Howard, Carole Maso, Howard Norman, Mary Robison, and Tom Wicker.

For more information contact: Writing Seminars Office at Bennington College, Bennington, VT 05201.

❖Berry College
Mount Berry, GA 30149-5010
(706) 236-2279
website: http://www.berry.edu/main.html

Degree offered: BA in English with Minor in Writing

Required course of study: A major in English consists of 39 s/hrs in English; the writing minor consists of 18 s/hrs chosen from a wide range of writing courses offered in the English and Communication departments. A total of 124 hours is required for graduation.

Berry offers creative writing courses at both the 300 and 400 level in poetry, fiction, and playwriting. Students may elect to do a creative project for the senior thesis requirement. *Ramifications*, an award-winning literature and arts magazine edited by students, showcases original poetry and fiction by Berry students. The editors also organize a student and faculty poetry reading each semester.

The English Department gives a number of annual awards in creative writing, including The Academy of American Poets, Gordon Barber, Eleanor B. North, and Hammond awards. The department also sponsors the Southern Women Writers Conference, a biannual event which offers students a unique opportunity to interact with nationally recognized writers. Associated with the conference is a writer-in-residence program; this year's writer-in-residence is fiction writer Mary Hood (*How Far She Went, And Venus is Blue, Familiar Heat*). The department also sponsors a reading series which brings nationally known writers to campus for readings throughout the school year.

Founded in 1902, Berry is a small, comprehensive, coeducational college with approximately 1,800 students and is located in the scenic northwest Georgia mountains next to Rome, midway between Atlanta and Chattanooga, Tennessee. Berry's campus encompasses 28,000 acres of forests, fields, lakes, and streams. The college has been ranked as one of America's best colleges by *Peterson's Guide to Competitive Colleges, U.S. News & World Report*, and others.

For more information, contact Dr. Sandra Meek, Dr. Michael Cooley, or the Dept. of English Coordinator.

Bethel College
3900 Bethel Drive
St. Paul, MN 55112

(612) 638-6130

Degree offered: BA in English with Concentration in Creative Writing or Professional Writing

Required course of study:
Essay Writing (4 s/hrs)
Literary Theory or Ethics (4 s/hrs)
Creative or Professional Writing (15 s/hrs)
Other writing courses (17 or more s/hrs)

Other Requirements: Required senior reading.

Several Bethel faculty have published memoirs, stories, and poems, and together have edited an anthology of Christian poetry. Visiting writers in recent years have included Madeleine L'Engle, Calvin Miller, and Luci Shaw.

For more information, contact Thomas Becknell, Chair, English Dept.

❖Binghamton University
Binghamton, NY 13902

(607) 777-2168

Degrees offered: BA, MA, PhD

Degree: BA with Specialization in Creative Writing

Required course of study: 48 s/hrs in the major
Thesis: 4 s/hrs
Writing workshop: 16 s/hrs
Other writing courses: 4 s/hrs
Literature courses: 16 or more s/hrs
Tutorials or directed reading: optional

Other Requirements: 8 s/hrs foreign language or translation workshop; senior thesis is a book of poems, a collection of stories, or a novel.

Degree: MA with Specialization in Creative Writing

Type of Program: Studio/Academic

Required course of study: 36 s/hrs beyond the BA
Thesis: 4 or more s/hrs
Writing workshop: 8 or more s/hrs
Literature courses: 24 or more s/hrs
Tutorials or directed reading: optional

Degree: PhD with Creative Writing Dissertation Option

Type of Program: Traditional Literary Study and Creative Writing

Required course of study: Minimum of 24 s/hrs of literature beyond the MA, appropriate number of s/hrs of dissertation.

Other Requirements: Field exams in three distinct fields of study, and one foreign language exam.

The aim of the Creative Writing Program at Binghamton University is to foster in its students a powerful, disciplined, and skilled creativity. The program is designed to educate and guide the talented young writer of poetry and fiction. Students are introduced to all the ways of their art, its tradition, modes and masters, its pleasures and responsibilities, its materials and crafts.

Graduate assistantships ranged from $7,637 to $7,937 in 1993–94, with full tuition scholarship. The department currently has 56 such assistantships to award, of which 20 to 35 usually go to creative writing students, who may be asked to teach freshman writing or the introductory creative writing course to undergraduates. Two annual Newhouse Prizes of $1,000 are offered to the best applicants in creative writing, and a Link Fellowship -- a full tuition waiver and full stipend -- is awarded to a PhD candidate in his or her final year of study.

The staff includes: L.M. Rosenberg (*The Angel Poems, The Fire Music, Children of Paradise*); Barry Targan (*Harry Belten and the Mendelssohn Violin Concerto, Surviving Adverse Seasons, Falling Free*); Gayle Whittier; John Vernon (*Ann, Lindbergh's Son, Peter Doyle*); Milton Kessler (*Sailing Too Far, Woodlawn North, The Grand Concourse*); Ruth Stone (*Second Hand Coat, Who Is The Widow's Muse*); and Arthur Clements (*Common Blessings*).

Every spring semester, either a visiting writer joins the staff or a mini-course is offered wherein four nationally known writers are brought in to guest-teach and share with our students their preoccupations as writers.

Recent visitors have included Ron Hansen, Clarence Major, and Marilyn Hacker. In addition, the program sponsors a series of readings and workshops by visiting writers each year. Readings by graduate students and staff members occur regularly.

For more information, contact Robert Mooney, Creative Writing Program Director, Dept. of English.

❖Boise State University
1910 University Drive
Boise, ID 83725

Degree offered: MFA in Creative Writing

Type of Program: Studio/Academic

Required course of study: 48 s/hrs
Thesis: 6 s/hrs
Workshops: 12 s/hrs
Literature courses: 18 s/hrs
Electives: 12 s/hrs

Application Deadlines: Though there is no formal deadline, apply by February 15 for the best chance at being accepted into the program.

The MFA program at Boise State University offers maximum flexibility to writers seeking a place to focus on their craft in a way best suited for them. Our program is small and friendly, allowing for close counsel of your work. For writers seeking to eventually teach, we offer course work in form and theory and the teaching of creative writing, as well as invaluable teaching experience in the creative writing classroom.

The program is able to offer several teaching assistantships with stipends of $8,400. All tuition and fees are waived. TA's typically teach composition and literature classes. These assistantships are available on a competitive basis, and candidates are encouraged to apply early if interested in an assistantship.

Our MFA publication, *The Idaho Review*, offers a chance for students to work on a national literary journal, either as graduate assistants, or for credit through course work or internship. The journal has included work from Ann Beattie, Richard Bausch, Lynne Sharon Schwartz, George Garrett, Allen Wier, Kelly Cherry, Gordon Weaver, Bill Morrissey, Robert Wrigley, Michael Blumenthal and others. Our regional literary publication, *cold drill*, is entirely run by MFA students, and offers extensive experience in designing, managing, and editing a literary magazine.

Students can also gain editing experience working for Ahsahta Press, a nationally recognized publisher of poetry. Established in 1974, Ahsahta Press publishes up to three volumes each academic year. Our book arts program offers additional opportunities in design and publishing.

The creative writing faculty in fiction includes program director Robert Olmstead, who has published three novels including *America By Land*, a story collection, *River Dogs*, and a textbook, *Elements of the Writing Craft*. Mitch Wieland has published the novel *Willy Slater's Lane*. Our semester long writer-in-residence also teaches classes in creative writing. Recent writers in our writer-in-residence series have included Michael Blumenthal, Debora Greger, Ann Jones, and Dennis Covington. We anticipate our new poetry hire to start in the fall of 1999.

Visiting writers have included Gary Snyder, N. Scott Momaday, Margaret Atwood, Donald Hall, James Baldwin, Mark Strand, and Lawrence Ferlinghetti.

Those candidates interested in the program at Boise State University are encouraged to visit our website at <http://english.idbsu.edu/mfa>, or write Robert Olmstead in care of the English Dept.

❖Boston College
1 Carney Hall
Chestnut, MA 02167

For more information, contact the Director, Dept. of English.

Boston University
236 Bay State Road
Boston, MA 02215

(617) 353-2510

Degrees offered: BA, MA

Degree: BA in English

Creative writing courses at all levels -- beginning, intermediate, and advanced -- are taught by novelists and poets. Other courses in the English Department are taught with the awareness that fiction-writing, poetry-writing, and experimentation in literary styles old and new are a natural part of the learning of language and literature. For the students who pursue and develop their writing abilities, there are special opportunities for honors work, for work in student literary publications, and for advancement as undergraduates into the graduate-level writing courses. *Agni Review* is associated with our program and encourages interns. *Partisan Review* is also at Boston University.

Degree: MA in Creative Writing

Type of Program: Studio/Academic

Length of Residency: One year

Required course of study: 32 s/hrs
  Thesis: required
  Writing workshops: 16 or more s/hrs
  Literature courses: 12 or more s/hrs

Other Requirements: Demonstrate competency in a foreign language either through coursework or SATII, or past credits, or participation in translation seminar.

Eight courses are taken (usually 4 a semester), at least half in the workshops of the creative writing program, the rest either from the Graduate Department in English, the Translation Center, or related programs in literature. Not more than 12 students in poetry, 12 in fiction, and 8 in playwriting, including occasional applicants who qualify in 2 genres, are accepted each year. Admission is almost entirely dependent upon the quality of the manuscript submitted, although students must do reasonably well on the GREs.

The heart of the program is the workshop, in which no more than 12 students may be enrolled. The same students remain together in the workshop 2 semesters and take their remaining courses in literature, often from such regular faculty artists as Elie Wiesel, Saul Bellow, and Geoffrey Hill. A thesis -- 80 to 90 pages of prose, or a portfolio of poetry -- is required at the end of the year.

Boston University Fellowships are available, each worth $4,400 plus full tuition, though at times these may be split. A number of teaching assistantships, which involve full or partial tuition remission plus stipend, are also available to graduate students.

The regular faculty consists of: in fiction, Leslie Epstein (*Steinway Quintet Plus Four*, *King of the Jews*, *Pinto & Sons*), who is also program director; in poetry, Derek Walcott (*The Fortunate Traveller*, *The Star-Apple Kingdom*, *The Arkansas Testament*) and Robert Pinsky (*History of My Heart*, *An Explanation of America*, *The Situation of Poetry*); in playwriting, Derek Walcott (*The Joker of Seville*, *O Babylon!*, *OMEROS*).

Visiting faculty come full-time every year -- in recent years, only in fiction. They have included C.K. Williams, Stephen Dobyns, John Cheever, John Barth, Donald Barthelme, Charles Simic, Geoffrey Wolff,

Rosellen Brown, Stanley Elkin, Tom Lux, Penelope Mortimer, Richard Yates, Linda Gregerson, Gloria Naylor, Sue Miller, Lynne Sharon Schwartz, Jayne Anne Phillips, Amos Oz, Aharon Appelfeld, Margot Livesey, and Jose Donoso. Saul Bellow and Elie Wiesel are also at Boston University. They welcome CWP students.

For more information, contact Leslie Epstein, Creative Writing Program.

Bowie State University
Bowie, MD 20715

Contact the Creative Writing Program Director, Dept. of English.

❖Bowling Green State University
Bowling Green, OH 43403
(419) 372-8370
FAX (419) 372-6805

Degrees offered: BFA, MFA

Degree: BFA in Creative Writing

Required course of study: Major–39 s/hrs
   (Minor–20 s/hrs)
   Craft classes: 6 s/hrs
   Writing workshop: 18 or more s/hrs
   Literature courses: 15 s/hrs

Other Requirements: 14 s/hrs foreign language; 6 s/hrs science and math; 9 s/hrs social science; 15 s/hrs humanities; public reading of student's work.

Bowling Green State University's undergraduate Creative Writing Program leads to a Bachelor of Fine Arts Degree in Creative Writing. Designed to give the undergraduate writer both maximum writing time and time for independent work with the writing staff, the program offers 18–24 s/hrs (6 courses) in workshop. World literature courses, craft courses, and modern and contemporary courses offer the student craft, content, and vocabulary. In their senior year, students create a manuscript of their own writings and participate in a public reading. The Creative Writing Program has hosted readings by such nationally known writers as James Baldwin, Galway Kinnell, C.K. Williams, Stephen Dunn, Marge Piercy. See graduate listing for information on the faculty.

For more information on the undergraduate program, contact the BFA Program Director, Dept. of English.

Degree: MFA in Creative Writing

Type of Program: Studio/Academic

Required course of study: 40 s/hrs
   Thesis: minimum 6 s/hrs
   Writing workshop: 16 or more s/hrs
   Other writing courses: 18 s/hrs
   Tutorials or directed reading: 5 s/hrs

Other Requirements: Final oral examination.

The MFA Program in Creative Writing is a composite of 40 s/hrs, mostly work in writing itself, at least one course in the study of poetry or fiction technique, and the remainder in either recommended courses or electives. A creative thesis and an oral examination are required for graduation.

Graduate writers will be allowed to choose electives from a number of fields which have been as wide-ranging as philosophy, physics, history, art, novel writing, desktop publishing, and creative writing program administration, allowing valuable opportunity to increase knowledge in many relevant areas. Students choose a body of electives early in their programs and need only show a relationship between their specific goals as writers and the electives.

Four summer fellowships are awarded yearly to winners of the Devine Memorial Fellowships. All qualified students wanting teaching assistantships receive them, usually 100% of our students. Applications to the program must include a portfolio of the student's work; applications are due by February 15 for admission the following fall.

The faculty includes Sharona BenTov, poet and critic (*After the Cease-Fire*); George Looney, poet and editor of *Mid-American Review* (*Animals Housed in the Pleasure of Flesh*); Wendell Mayo, fiction writer (*Centaur of the North, In Lithuanian Wood*); Howard McCord, novelist and poet (*The Man Who Walked to the Moon, The Duke of Chemical Birds, Jennifer*); Richard Messer, poet, critic, and fiction writer (*Murder in the Family*).

For more information, contact Wendell Mayo, Director, Creative Writing, Bowling Green State University, Bowling Green, OH 43403.

❖Bradley University
Peoria, IL 61625
(309) 677-2480
FAX (309) 677-2330
e-mail: kstein@bradley.edu
website: http//www.bradley.edu/

Degrees offered: BA with Creative Writing option, MA with Writing option

Degree: BA in English with Creative Writing option

Required course of study: 124 s/hrs
   Writing Workshop: up to 18 s/hrs
   Literature Courses: 27 s/hrs
   Senior Project: 3 s/hrs

Other Requirements: Creative Project may replace the Senior Project; university general education requirements totaling 40 s/hrs; proficiency in one foreign language.

Application Deadline: March 1 for financial aid; Bradley adheres to a rolling admissions policy.

The BA with Creative Writing option encourages students to pursue their own writing while engaging the work of writers from diverse cultures and time periods. The goal is for students to refine their individual skills, informed by a broad aesthetic and cultural background. Students may choose from workshops in poetry, fiction, autobiography, and nature writing, up to 18 s/hrs. This work may culminate in a Creative

Project, a compilation of the student's own poetry, fiction, or nonfiction. Students will find that the campus literary and arts magazine, *Broadside*, is entirely edited and designed by our strong community of student writers and visual artists. That coalition of writers and artists also organizes and directs its own series of student readings and art displays. In addition, the English Department sponsors a Visiting Writers Series which brings to campus outstanding writers such as Rita Dove, Robert Coover, Yusef Komunyakaa, Philip Levine, and William Matthews. Finally, the Department offers two yearly competitions: the Academy of American Poets Prize and the Sipple Poetry Award, the latter awarding $500 to the winning student.

Degree: MA with Writing option (poetry, fiction, creative nonfiction)

Type of Program: Studio/Academic

Length of Residency: Two years

Required course of study: 30 s/hrs
Theory and Practice of Writing: 3 s/hrs
Literary, Writing, or Language Theory: 3 s/hrs
Internship in Writing: 3 s/hrs

Other Requirements: Portfolio of written work; individually designed examination evaluating each student's synthesis of workshop and classroom studies.

Application Deadline: March 1 for financial aid; Bradley adheres to a rolling admissions policy.

Students choosing our MA with Writing Option find extensive exposure to the practice and theory of creative writing. Our program offers workshop experience in poetry, fiction, autobiography, and nature writing, as well as the opportunity for related independent study. Our workshops are small, designed to maximize individual attention and to welcome varied approaches to writing. Students combine this focus on writing with broad study of literature and theory of writing. Our goal is to enable students to design a program of study that not only meets their individual creative needs but also provides means to study literature from a range of aesthetic, cultural, and theoretical perspectives. The assumption is that good writers read, and this program encourages students to do just that. Most importantly, the modest size of the program ensures that each student's work receives considerable personal attention from faculty members.

Visiting writers in recent years have included Rita Dove, William Matthews, Yusef Komunyakaa, Robert Coover, Brigit Pegeen Kelly, Michael Van Walleghen, Philip Levine, Ed Ochester, David Wojahn, Larry Heineman, and Maura Stanton. The Visiting Writers Series brings in both emerging and established writers, all of whom meet with students and workshops in addition to the usual public reading of their work.

Internships require students to work closely with creative writing faculty in designing and leading creative writing workshops. The program awards assistantships which offer students the opportunity to work as writing liaison to the Colleges of Business and Engineering, as well as to instruct in the campus writing center.

The faculty includes poet and critic Kevin Stein (*Bruised Paradise, A Circus of Want*, winner of the Devins Award for Poetry); creative nonfiction and poetry writer James Ballowe (*The Coal Miners*, winner of Illinois Arts Council Awards for poetry and creative nonfiction); fiction writer and poet George Chambers (*The Scourging of W.H.D., Wretched Hutchinson, The Last Man Standing*); fiction and creative nonfiction writer Thomas Palakeel; and poet and fiction writer Demetrice Worley (ed. *African American Literature*, ed. *Spirit and Flame* and *Reflections on a Gift of Watermelon Pickle... and Other Modern Verse*, anthology).

For more information, contact Kevin Stein, Director, Creative Writing Program, at the above address.

Brandeis University
Waltham, MA 02254-9110
(617) 736-2130
FAX (617) 736-2179

Degree offered: BA

Degree: BA in English with Creative Writing major (poetry, fiction)

Required course of study: 3 period courses, 1 genre course, 2 writing workshops, 1 studio arts or performing arts course, senior thesis (two semesters), tutorial reading list.

Other Requirements: General University distribution requirements.

Application Deadline: The Creative Writing major, also known as the Creative Writing Track, is a small, competitive program, requiring application in the second semester of the sophomore year, before the spring break. A Creative Writing Minor is also available, and is not competitive.

The program offers 4-7 workshops in poetry and fiction each year, as well as literature courses taught by writers (Carolyn Forché's Poetry of Witness, Thylias Moss's Black American Female Perspective). The faculty includes a poet-in-residence, currently Olga Broumas, a fiction-writer-in-residence, currently Jayne Anne Phillips, as well as the poets Mary Campbell and John Burt. A poet and fiction writer of national renown join the program each year as distinguished Fannie Hurst visitors -- Alice Walker, Marilyn Hacker, Louise Glück, Mark Doty, Jayne Anne Phillips, Stephen MacCauley. The "School of Night" reading series brings several outstanding poets and writers to campus each semester, and there is lively literary activity among students, including literary magazines, student-run readings at coffee-houses, and WBRS.

For more information contact Olga Broumas or the Dept. of English.

❖Brigham Young University
Provo, UT 84602
(801) 378-3053
FAX (801) 378-4720
website: http://English.byu.edu/

Degrees offered: BA, MA in English, emphasis in Creative Writing

Degree: MA in English with Creative Thesis

Type of Program: Traditional Literary Study and Creative Writing

Length of Residency: One to two years

Admission Requirements: Reading knowledge of one foreign language (French, German, or Spanish preferred); GRE Advanced Literature Exam optional; undergraduate English major or equivalent, including history of language and literary criticism.

Required course of study: 31 s/hrs; includes thesis and oral defense of thesis
   Introduction to Graduate Studies: 1 s/hr
   Rhetoric course: 3 s/hrs
   English language course: 3 s/hrs
   Theory-intensive literature course: 3 s/hrs
      (optional)
   Creative writing courses: 9–12 s/hrs
   Electives from literature, language, or
      rhetoric courses: 6 s/hrs
   Thesis: 6 s/hrs

Other Requirements: Oral examination of coursework; thesis defense.

Application Deadlines: March 15 for fall semester admission; March 1 for financial aid.

For the MA, the creative thesis can be a novel, personal essays, an autobiography, a collection of short stories or poems, or a full-length play written under the direction of the thesis chair. Students who elect the creative thesis must submit as an application a thesis prospectus and a representative sample of their creative work to the creative writing section head for approval by three members of creative writing faculty.

Creative writing faculty includes creative writing section head associate chair Sally Taylor (poetry, *A Little Light at the Edge of Day*); Linda Adams (editing and publishing); John Bennion (fiction, *Breeding Leah*); Chris Crowe (fiction, *Two Roads*); Susan Elizabeth Howe (poetry); B.W. Jorgensen (fiction, poetry, and criticism); Lance Larsen (poetry); Leslie Norris (fiction, *The Girl From Cardigan*; poetry, *Sequences*); Louise Plummer Spencer (fiction, *My Name Is Sus5an Smith, The 5 Is Silent*); Douglas Thayer (fiction, *Mr. Wahlquist in Yellowstone*); Dean Hughes (fiction, *Rumors of War*).

The university publishes *Inscape*, a literary magazine featuring student work. Creative writing contests, open to both graduate and undergraduate writing students, award about $3,500 in prizes annually. Essay contests award about $10,000 annually. Graduate students may apply for assistantships teaching in the freshman composition program and in the reading and writing laboratories.

For more information and applications, contact the English Dept. For graduate student assistantships, contact the Coordinator of Composition, English Dept.

University of British Columbia
Vancouver, B.C. Canada V6T 1Z1

(604) 822-0699 Secretary
(604) 822-2712 Info Line
FAX (604) 822-3616
e-mail: patrose@unixg.ubc.ca

Degrees offered: BFA, MFA, Diploma in Nonfiction, Joint MFA degrees: CRWR/Film and CRWR/Theatre

Degree: BFA in Creative Writing

Required course of study: 36 credits
   Thesis: no requirement

Other Requirements: 2 years of general studies, and in years 3 and 4, a Creative Writing major (5 writing workshops/tutorials plus 4 or 5 outside courses) and honors (7 writing workshops/tutorials and thesis) plus 5 outside courses. 3 genre requirement. Double Majors can be taken as BFA or BA, where there is agreement of the Departments involved. Student can then name the degree.

Application Deadline: April 30.

The Creative Writing Program of the Department of Theatre, Film, and Creative Writing offers a program of study leading to the degree of Bachelor of Fine Arts. Instruction is based on the premise that promising student-authors can benefit from judicious criticism and the chance to develop their abilities in an academic setting. Workshops, conferences, and tutorials are designed to focus attention on the student's own work. Reading assignments may be made in the department's magazine of current writing, *Prism International*, and other relevant journals and books. There are no examinations, and grades are based on the writing done and on participation in workshops throughout the year. Course offerings include workshops and tutorials in Children's Literature, Radio Plays, Nonfiction Prose, Screen and TV Plays, Stage Plays, Novel or Novella, Short Story, Poetry, and Translation.

Each course is restricted to 15 students. Applicants wishing to enter freshman/sophomore classes will be admitted if their submission of 20–25 pages of recent original fiction, imaginative nonfiction, drama, or poetry, or a combination of these, is judged acceptable by the department. Students wishing to pursue a major in Creative Writing should apply at the end of their second year of study by submitting to the department a written request accompanied by a 30-page manuscript.

Degree: MFA in Creative Writing (poetry, fiction, creative nonfiction, theater, film, radio, children's literature, translation)

Type of Program: Studio

Required course of study: 36 credits
   Thesis: 6 credits

Other Requirements: 2 years of intensive writing in workshops/tutorials within department. 3-genre requirement, except for inter-departmental programs in Creative Writing and Theatre for programs in Stage or Screenplay-writing.

Application Deadline: November 1 for fall admission.

The Department of Creative Writing offers a 2-year course of resident study leading to a Master of Fine Arts in Creative Writing.

Creative Writing, taught at UBC since 1946, became a fully independent department in 1965. In 1995 Creative Writing merged with the Dept. of Theatre & Film becoming the Creative Writing Program of the Dept. of Theatre, Film and Creative Writing. The faculty members employ different methods of instruction, but all instructors try to help each student to find and develop his or her individual voice through workshops, tutorials, and conferences. The program is not one to which a student writer may come to work only on a single project. The program is a studio program that makes certain demands of both faculty and students. Students are asked to write in 3 of the 8 genres offered by the program; to produce regular, substantial quantities of work; and to maintain continuing interaction with the staff.

Workshops, conferences, and tutorials are designed to focus attention on the student's own work in advanced studies in the writing of poetry, fiction, drama (stage, screen, television, radio), imaginative nonfiction, translation, and children's literature. MFA degrees are offered in Creative Writing (including a concentration in translation), in Creative Writing-Theatre for playwrights, and Creative Writing-Film for screenwriters. The latter must be accepted by both program faculty.

Thirty-six credits of work, including a creative thesis, are required for the MFA. Candidates must complete a program of workshops in 3 or more of the following areas: Children's Literature, Radio Plays, The Novella or Novel, Imaginative Nonfiction, Screen & Television Plays, Stage Plays, Short Fiction, Poetry, and Translation. (Students concentrating in translation need work in only one other genre.) Each workshop is a one-year course carrying 6 credits; a candidate enrolls in 3 courses each year to complete the 36 credits required for graduation.

All candidates are selected on the basis of work submitted. Please write for guidelines.

Faculty includes George McWhirter, poet, short story writer, novelist, translator, winner of Commonwealth Poetry Prize, Ethel Wilson Prize for Fiction, F.R. Scott Prize for Translation; C.J. Newman, novelist, poet, short story writer; Sue Ann Alderson, children's literature; Linda Svendsen, short story writer, screenwriter; Keith Maillard, novelist, winner of Ethel Wilson Prize for Fiction, poet, winner of Gerald Lampert Prize for first book of poetry; Bryan Wade, dramatist; Peggy Thompson, screenwriter, Gemini Award, Best Screenplay.

The Arnold and Nancy Cliff Endowment supports Writers-in-Residence, with varying terms of residence, who meet with students in tutorial during the winter term. Past guests have included Alice Munro, Carol Shields, Audrey Thomas, Thomson Highway, Joan McLeod, Evelyn Lau, and Sandra Birdsell.

Some UBC Graduate Fellowships, Graduate Assistantships, and prizes are available. Applicants to the MFA program should indicate their wish to be considered for aid and the degree of their need when they submit their materials to the department.

For more information, contact the Creative Writing Program of the Dept. of Theatre, Film, and Creative Writing, Buch. E462-1866 Main Mall, University of British Columbia, Vancouver, B.C., Canada V6T 1Z1. Please include self-addressed, stamped envelope with Canadian stamps or International Reply Coupons.

❖Brooklyn College
2900 Bedford Avenue
Brooklyn, NY 11210-2814

(718) 951-5195

Degree offered: MFA in Creative Writing

Type of Program: Studio/Academic

Length of Residency: Two years

Required course of study: 36 s/hrs
Writing workshop: 12 s/hrs
Tutorial: 12 s/hrs
Literature courses: 12 s/hrs

Other Requirements: Comprehensive examination; thesis.

Application Deadlines: November 1 for spring semester; March 1 for fall semester.

Students choose a concentration in one of the following: fiction, playwriting, or poetry. Fiction and poetry applicants must offer at least 12 credits in advanced courses in English. Thirty pages of original fiction or 20 pages of original poetry must be submitted for evaluation. Playwriting applicants must offer at least 12 credits in English or theater. One original full-length play or 2 or more one-act plays must be submitted for evaluation. Applicants who do not meet course requirements but whose manuscripts show unusual talent are considered for the program.

Students normally take a writing workshop, a writing tutorial, and a literature course each semester for four semesters.

Program directors are: (fiction) Jonathan Baumbach (*Chez Charlotte and Emily, Separate Hours, Twelve Wives*); (playwriting) Jack Gelber (*The Connection, Square in the Eye, Starters*); and (poetry) Louis Asekoff (*Dreams of a Work*).

The faculty includes: poet Julie Agoos (*Above the Land*); and fiction writer Peter Spielberg (*Twiddledum Twaddledum, Crash-Landing, Hearsay*). Visiting writers in recent years have included Maureen Howard, Ann Lauterbach, C.K. Williams, Gregory Corso, William Matthews, Irini Spanidou and others.

Brooklyn Review, an annual literary magazine, is edited and published by students in the program. Students are also encouraged to give readings from their own works. In addition, the college sponsors readings each semester by well-known writers as well as by former students of the program who have published substantial bodies of work. Other advantages of the MFA program include the limited size of workshops (10 students maximum), and the availability of teaching assistantships.

Completion of the MFA requires the submission of a substantial manuscript of publishable quality. Students concentrating in fiction are required to submit a novel or a collection of stories. Students concentrating in poetry must submit a collection of poems. Students concentrating in playwriting must submit a full-length play or a number of one-act plays, in producible form. Efforts are made to produce the student's major work in cooperation with the Theater Department.

For more information, contact Nancy Black, Deputy Chairman, Graduate Programs, Dept. of English.

Broward Community College
Fort Lauderdale, FL 33314
(305) 475-6637
FAX (305) 474-7118

Degree offered: AA in English

For more information, contact Chairman, Dept. of English, BCC, Central Campus.

❖Brown University
Box 1852
Providence, RI 02912
(401) 863-3260
FAX (401) 863-1535
http://www.brown.edu/Departments/English/

Degrees offered: MFA in Writing (poetry, fiction, playwriting), **AB in English with honors in Creative Writing** (poetry, fiction, playwriting)

Type of Program: Studio/Academic

Length of Residency: Two years

Application Deadlines: January 2 for all applications.

Students take 8 courses over the 2 years: 4 writing courses and 4 electives. This arrangement allows maximum time for writing.

Students ordinarily enroll in a workshop in their genre for each of the first 3 semesters and in their last semester complete a thesis under the direction of a particular faculty writer. The thesis must be an original manuscript: a novel or substantial part of a novel, a collection of stories or poems, a full-length play or group of one-acts, etc. Each student will, over the 2 years, have worked with at least 2 different members of the writing faculty, probably with 3.

Many, though by no means all, recipients of this degree have gone into teaching or, less often, publishing. The academic setting of the program and the possibility of actual teaching experience suggest this. But the program is not specifically oriented towards these careers. The emphasis is on the writing itself -- writing as an art. The 4 elective courses allow flexibility and individual direction. Students most often take courses in literature and languages, but many turn to studio or performing art courses.

A rather small percentage of applicants can be accepted, since the aim each year is for a class of 15 or fewer. Applicants must submit samples of writing in a particular genre -- poetry, fiction, playwriting. This sample is the most important part of the application. GRE test scores are not required. Interviews are optional with applicants.

The writing faculty includes Robert Coover, Michael Harper, Carole Maso, Aishah Rahman, Meredith Steinbach, Paula Vogel, Keith Waldrop, and C.D. Wright.

For further information, contact the Graduate Writing Program.

❖Bucknell University
Lewisburg, PA 17837
(717) 524-1853

Degree offered: BA in English with Emphasis in Creative Writing

Students majoring in English distribute their courses as follows: in five historical periods of English or American literature, in three genres, a pro-seminar, and two seminars. Creative writing courses may be taken at any time, with the permission of the instructor, as electives counting toward the required eight courses for the major in English.

In addition to the BA in English with course work in creative writing, the Department of English offers a minor in creative writing for students not majoring in English. Consisting of 5 courses, the minor requires a student to select 3 from among the following: Introduction to Creative Writing, Intermediate Workshop in Fiction Writing, Intermediate Workshop in Poetry Writing, Advanced Workshop in Fiction Writing, Advanced Workshop in Poetry Writing, Tutorial in Fiction or in Poetry Writing. In addition, at least one course above the elementary level in which drama, fiction, or poetry is studied as a genre must be taken. With the permission of the instructor, all courses in creative writing may be taken by students who do not elect the minor.

Within the Department of English, the Stadler Center for Poetry offers a number of programs in poetry writing. The annual Bucknell Seminar for Younger Poets provides undergraduates and graduating seniors in 4-year colleges and universities an opportunity to write poetry, attend workshops, participate in tutorials with the staff, and interact with other young poets over a 4-week period in June. Admission is by selection, based chiefly on a portfolio of work, by the staff. Each of the 8 poets selected is awarded a fellowship that covers all expenses except travel. The Seminar does not carry academic credit.

The Stadler Semester for Younger Poets offers 1 undergraduate who is a senior or junior in a 4-year college or university a full-credit semester of concentrated work in poetry writing each spring. A member of the writing staff serves as advisor and tutor for an independent course in poetry writing. The student also takes the advanced workshop in poetry writing, conducted by the poet-in-residence, and elects a course in reading poetry and one other related course. Admission is by selection, based largely on a portfolio of work, by the staff. The student selected is responsible for the tuition/room/board costs he/she would pay at his/her own college or university. When Bucknell's charges exceed those of the home institution and the student can demonstrate need, a scholarship is available.

The Bucknell Poet-in-Residence program brings a distinguished poet to campus each spring semester and for 2 weeks of the Younger Poets Seminar program. Past poets-in-residence have been Mary Oliver, Wendell Berry, Madeline DeFrees, Irving Feldman, Jean Valentine, Louis Simpson, Colette Inez, Molly

Peacock, Gerald Stern, Bruce Smith, William Matthews, Afaa M. Weaver, and Tess Gallagher.

During the fall semester, the Stadler Center for Poetry offers an annual Philip Roth Residence in Creative Writing. This honorific post offers a working poet or fiction writer an opportunity to devote herself or himself entirely to her or his work over a period of 4 months. Bucknell University provides a studio, a 2-bedroom apartment, and a stipend of $1,000. The Philip Roth Resident is appointed by the staff.

During the Annual Bucknell Poetry Festival, a dozen or so writers convene on campus for 2 days of poetry events. Student poetry readings are held from time to time. Two undergraduate literary magazines, *The Red Wheelbarrow* and *Giving Voice*, offer outlets for publication on campus. Both are edited by students. From time to time students may participate in and earn credit for editorial work on *West Branch*, an internationally distributed literary magazine edited by Professors Karl Patten and Robert Love Taylor.

The Stadler Internship offers a nationally competitive young writer and recent MFA or MA the opportunity to receive professional training in a thriving poetry center and at an active university press. This intern will assist at the Poetry Center for ten hours each week and at the Bucknell University Press for ten hours each week, receiving hands-on experience by helping to organize Center events, assisting at Bucknell University Press, and possibly working as an editorial assistant for *West Branch*. Bucknell University has much to offer an intern: a well-established Poetry Center; the opportunity to work with nationally renowned poets for two spring semesters; the opportunity to team-teach workshops (and thereby receive some solid mentoring and experience in teaching) during two Bucknell Younger Poets Seminars each June; and finally, professional editorial training working at the Bucknell University Press and *West Branch*.

The permanent staff includes Nicole Cooley, winner of the 1996 Walt Whitman Award; Robert Love Taylor, novelist and short story writer, whose work includes *Loving Belle Starr, Fiddle and Bow*, and *The Lost Sister*; Cynthia Hogue, director of the Stadler Center for Poetry, and Mark Svenvold, winner of the 1997 Vachel Lindsay Award.

For further information, write to John Rickard, Chair, Dept. of English, or Cynthia Hogue, Director, Stadler Center for Poetry.

California Lutheran College
Thousand Oaks, CA 91360-2787
(805) 493-3243
website: http://www.callutheran.edu

Degrees offered: BA in English; BA in Communication Arts

For more information, contact Writing Program Director, Dept. of English.

California Polytechnic State University
San Luis Obispo, CA 93407
(805) 756-2596

Degree offered: BA

For more information, contact the English Dept.

❖California State University, Chico
Chico, CA 95929-0830
(530) 898-5124
FAX (530) 898-4450

Degrees offered: BA, MA

Degree: BA in English with Creative Writing Minor (poetry, fiction, playwriting)

Type of Program: Studio/Academic

Required course of study: 124 s/hrs total
Creative Writing Minor: 26 s/hrs total
  4 s/hrs Creative Writing; 16 s/hrs selected from Poetry, Fiction, Playwriting and Advanced Poetry, Fiction, Playwriting
Literature Course Requirements: 3 s/hrs Survey of American Literature; 3 s/hrs selected from Modern Poetry, Modern Drama, Contemporary Drama, The Modern Novel, Seminar in American Literature

Application Deadlines: Nov. 1–30 for fall, Aug. 1–31 for spring admission; query about financial aid.

The undergraduate concentration requires the student to take beginning Creative Writing (poetry, fiction, playwriting) and then to focus on one or more genres. *Watershed* is the literary magazine, which uses student editors; English courses are offered in Literary Editing and Editing for Publication. The English Department offers a Creative Writing Award each fall.

Degree: MA in English with Creative Dissertation (poetry, fiction, playwriting)

Type of Program: Studio/Academic

Required course of study: 30 s/hrs
Thesis: 3–6 s/hrs
Writing Workshop: up to 6 s/hrs
Tutorials or directed reading: up to 6 s/hrs
Literature courses: Core requirement (Literature prior to 1900) plus 3 s/hrs in modern or contemporary poetry, novel or drama

Students who plan to do a creative dissertation must have permission from the Creative Writing Coordinator and must have completed the requirements for the Creative Writing pattern. The foreign-language requirement must be completed before a student can advance to candidacy. All students completing a dissertation must sit for an oral examination on that work. All students are required to present publicly portions of their theses. Members of the graduate creative writing workshop often give a joint public reading of their work. Visiting authors read in the Writer's Voice series, an ongoing literary event; twice a year a *Watershed* reading is given, to coincide with publication of the current issue. Graduate students are eligible to compete for the English Department's Creative Writing Award and to have their work submitted for AWP's *Intro* prize awards. In recent years, students have won three *Intro* awards in fiction and poetry. Teaching Assistantships and Graduate Assistantships are available; current T.A. deadlines: October 15 for spring, April 1 for fall. Inquire, since dates are subject to change.

California State University, Chico has a long tradition of commitment to Creative Writing. Among Chico's distinguished former faculty are authors Ana Castillo, Sandra Cisneros, John Gardner, Debra Greger, and George Keithley. Raymond Carver studied at Chico with John Gardner. Recent publications by creative writing graduates are Joe Kane's *Running the Amazon* and Candace Favilla's *Cups*. Undergraduate and graduate students have published in such little magazines as *New England Review, Permafrost,* and *Quarterly West.* Chico's Creative Writing graduates have continued their study at such institutions as Arizona State, Colorado State University, Cornell, Warren Wilson and the University of Iowa.

Current full-time Creative Writing faculty are: Fiction: Clark Brown, author of a novel, *The Disciple,* and short fiction in anthologies such as *Stories of the Modern West, Best Fiction from Writers' Forum,* and *California Childhood.* He has taught at Stanford and UC Berkeley, and has been an NEH Fellow at Princeton.

Play Writing: Lynn Elliott, author of six plays, two teleplays, a children's novel, and three screenplays. He has won the George Kernodle play writing award from the University of Arkansas, the San Francisco "DramaRama" award, California Polytechnic, San Luis Obispo's "New Plays" award, and Mill Mountain's annual "Theatre in the Square" award. His play *Pirandello's Wife* is in print and he has received grants and awards from the California State University system and the NEH.

Poetry: Carole Simmons Oles and Gary Thompson. Oles is the author of five books of poetry, most recently *The Deed* and *Stunts.* She has received a NEA Grant in Poetry, a Pushcart Prize, and the Virginia Prize for Poetry. She has taught at the University of Massachusetts, Hollins College, and Sweet Briar College, where she was Banister Writer-in-Residence. She has been on the faculty of Bread Loaf, Bennington, and Port Townsend Writers' Conferences. Thompson's poems have appeared in many magazines and anthologies. His book, *Hold Fast,* was published by Confluence Press in 1984. He has been awarded a NEA Grant in Poetry and the *New Letters*/William Carlos Williams Award.

Part-Time Creative Writing faculty includes Joanne Allred, organizer of the Writer's Voice series, who has received the poetry prize from Writers at Work in Park City, Utah, and has won publication of her chapbook, *Whetstone,* by Flume Press.

For more information, please contact Carole Simmons Oles, Creative Writing Coordinator, Dept. of English.

California State University, Dominguez Hills
Carson, CA 90747
(310) 516-3322

For more information on offerings in creative writing, contact the Dept. of English.

❖California State University, Fresno
Fresno, CA 93740-8001
(209) 278-3919
e-mail: charles_hanzlicek@csufresno.edu

Degrees offered: BA, MFA

Degree: BA in English with Concentration in Creative Writing

Required course of study: 36 upper division s/hrs
  Writing workshop: up to 16 s/hrs

Required for the BA in English are 36 units of upper division course work. Students interested in the creative writing option may take as many as 16 units in the writing of poetry and fiction.

Degree: MFA in Creative Writing

Type of Program: Studio/Academic

Required course of study: 54 s/hrs
  Writing workshop: 16 s/hrs
  Form courses: 8 s/hrs
  Literature courses: 12 s/hrs
  Electives: 12–14 s/hrs
  Thesis: 4–6 s/hrs

Other Requirements: Foreign language exam or translation of poetry or prose project.

Course work for the degree centers around the minimum requirements of 16 s/hrs of writing workshops, 8 s/hrs of form courses, and 12 s/hrs of literature seminars. 4–6 s/hrs are awarded for work on the thesis. 70% (38 s/hrs) of courses counted toward the degree must be from graduate level courses.

The program staff includes poets C.G. Hanzlicek (*Stars, Calling the Dead, When There Are No Secrets*), and Corrine Hales (*January Fire, Underground*), and fiction writers Steve Yarbrough (*Family Men, Mississippi History*), and Liza Wieland (*Names of the Lost, Discovering America*).

Graduate students may apply for positions as tutors in the English Department Writing Lab and as graduate teaching assistants.

Inquiries should be sent to C.G. Hanzlicek, Director, Creative Writing Program.

California State University, Hayward
Hayward, CA 94542
(510) 885-3153

Degrees offered: BA, MA

Degree: BA in English with Creative Writing Option

Required course of study: 64–76 q/hrs for major, including:
Core curriculum: 32 q/hrs
Writing workshop: 20 q/hrs
Project & portfolio: 4 q/hrs
Upper division English electives: 8 q/hrs
One year college–level foreign language (or exam)

Workshops are in fiction, creative nonfiction, and poetry. Some sections have a hypertext component and meet in a networked computer lab. Translation and drama as independent study only.

Minor in Creative Writing

Required course of study: 32 q/hrs
Writing workshop: 24 q/hrs
Upper division literature: 8 q/hrs

Degree: MA in English with Creative Thesis

Type of Program: Studio/Academic

Required course of study: 45 q/hrs
Thesis: up to 9 q/hrs
Writing workshop: up to 16 q/hrs
Literature courses: 28–45 q/hrs

Other Requirements: Reading knowledge of 1 foreign language; comprehensive exam in 1 period of British/American literature (2 periods if no thesis is submitted).

Students pursuing the MA in English may submit a creative thesis (0–9 units) and may include creative writing workshops (8–17 units) among the 45 quarter-units required for the degree. Other requirements for the degree are 28 quarter-units of courses in literary history and theory, reading knowledge of one foreign language, and one written comprehensive examination in a period of British or American literature (2 examinations if a thesis is not submitted). Reading lists are supplied for the examinations.

The faculty includes Writing Program Director Sara McAulay (fiction and nonfiction), Stephen D. Gutierrez, Donald Markos.

For further information, write Sara McAulay, Director of Creative Writing Program, Dept. of English.

❖California State University, Long Beach
**1250 Bellflower Blvd.
Long Beach, CA 90840-2403**
(562) 985-4223

Degrees offered: BA, MA, MFA

Degree: BA in English with Creative Writing Emphasis

Required course of study: 41 s/hrs for the major
Writing workshop: 9 or more s/hrs

Other Requirements: 15 s/hrs lower level composition and literature courses; 9 s/hrs in Literary Genres, Literary Criticism, and/or Recent Literature; electives to complete 41 s/hrs.

Degree: MA in English with Creative Thesis Option

Type of Program: Studio/Academic

Required course of study: 30 s/hrs for the major
Thesis: 6 s/hrs

Other Requirements: 4 s/hrs Seminar in Literary Criticism and Research; foreign language requirement; students who elect to write a thesis are not required to write the final comprehensive examination.

Graduate Study leading to the Master of Arts in English is aimed at broadening and deepening the student's understanding of the intellectual, cultural, and aesthetic traditions of British and American literature and language, and developing advanced skills in critical reading, writing, and scholarly research. In general, the degree program is designed to provide an enriched learning experience for students of varied interests and backgrounds.

A student wishing to pursue a thesis in Creative Writing must submit samples of their work to a member of the Creative Writing faculty for approval. Such samples (composed of 2 or 3 short stories, or 2 or 3 chapters of a novel, or 10 to 12 pages of poetry) shall not be included in the final thesis, if the student is approved to pursue such a thesis.

Degree: MFA in Creative Writing

Type of Program: Studio/Academic

Required course of study: 60 s/hrs for the major
Thesis: 6 s/hrs

Students applying for admission to the MFA degree program must have completed a bachelor's or master's degree in English from an accredited institution with a 3.2 GPA in upper division English courses, meet university admission requirements, and submit evidence of creative ability in fiction or poetry. Additional preparation may be required before the student can be considered for classified status in the degree program.

Admission to the MFA program in Creative Writing is based on the evaluation of a sample of the applicant's recent work, which should include one of the following: 20–30 double-spaced pages of fiction (either one or more short stories or a section of a novel) or 10–15 pages of poetry. Admission to the program will be in one genre only. Manuscripts must be typewritten or printed and will be returned only if accompanied by a self-addressed stamped envelope.

In addition to submitting manuscripts, official college or university transcripts must be provided with the application. Two letters of recommendation, though not required, may also be sent.

The faculty includes Stephen Cooper, Elliot Fried, Suzanne Greenberg, Gerald Locklin, Charles Webb, and Ray Zepeda.

For more information, contact Creative Writing Coordinator, Dept. of English.

❖**California State University,
Los Angeles
5151 State University Drive
Los Angeles, CA 90032-8629**

Contact the Creative Writing Program Director, Dept. of English.

❖**California State University,
Northridge
Northridge, CA 91330**
(818) 667-3431
FAX (818) 667-3872

Degrees offered: BA, MA

Degree: BA in English with Creative Writing Option

Required course of study: 45 s/hrs in the major
Writing workshop: 15-21 s/hrs
Theory course: 6 s/hrs
Literature courses: 27 s/hrs
Senior seminar: 3 s/hrs

The undergraduate major requires intensive study in both creative writing and literature. After an initial multi-genre, introductory creative writing course, students may choose to specialize in a single genre. Students may receive elective credit for participating in the campus literary magazine, *The Northridge Review*, which draws work from the larger Los Angeles area. Annual prizes in English include the Rachel Sherwood Poetry Prize, the Helen Marcus Fiction Prize, the Oliver W. Evans Writing Prize, and the Eva Latif Writing Prize in Children's Literature.

Degree: MA in English with Creative Thesis

Type of Program: Studio/Academic

Length of Residency: Two years, on average

Required course of study: 30 s/hrs total
Creative writing core course: 3 s/hrs
Writing workshop: 3-12 s/hrs
Critical Theory course: 3 s/hrs
Linguistics course: 3 s/hrs
Literature courses: 6 s/hrs
Elective: 3 s/hrs
Thesis: 3 s/hrs

Since 1992 our MA program has been substantially revised. The new curriculum requires that all graduate students in English take two core courses: one in critical theory and one in linguistics. In addition to its specialization in Creative Writing, the department offers a specialization in Literature and, under the new curriculum, offers a specialization in Rhetoric and Composition. Those students selecting either Creative Writing or Rhetoric and Composition will continue to be required to submit a qualifying writing sample during their first semester of graduate residency. Teaching Assistantships are available in the second year of graduate work. The new curriculum represents our commitment to a strong intra-disciplinary approach that strives to nurture the individual writer while introducing him or her to the professional concerns that affect creative writers in the world.

The Creative Writing faculty includes: Dorothy Barresi, poetry (*All of the Above*); Larry Gibson, fiction; Katharine Haake, fiction (*No Reason on Earth*, short stories); Jack Lopez, fiction and creative nonfiction (*Cholos & Surfers*); Jan Ramjerdi, fiction and poetry (in *Denver Quarterly, Mid-American Review, PRISM International*).

For more information on these programs, contact Jack Lopez, Creative Writing Program Director, Dept. of English.

**California State University,
Sacramento
Sacramento, CA 95819**
(916) 278-6586

Degree offered: MA in English with Creative Writing Concentration and Creative Thesis

Type of Program: Studio/Academic

Required course of study: 30 s/hrs in English
Thesis: 3 s/hrs (counted as writing course)
Writing courses: 12 s/hrs
Literature courses: 12 or more s/hrs of
American & British core courses, plus
English 200 (3 s/hrs), Methods and Materials
of Literary Research

The MA with a Concentration in Creative Writing requires the submission of a creative thesis: a collection of short stories, a novel, a full-length filmscript or teleplay (fiction or nonfiction), or a series of shorter filmscripts or teleplays, or a collection of poetry, for completion of the degree. The work is shaped, developed, and completed through required graduate courses. The 15 s/hrs required in writing include workshop, a tutorial, and a seminar in creative writing; the tutorial and the seminar may be repeated for credit.

Application requirements include the submission of a sample of work, which should be sent directly to the Chair at the time of application to the University.

Graduate writing faculty includes: novelist Richard Bankowsky (*A Glass Rose, On A Dark Night, The Barbarians at the Gates*); poet, novelist, and screenwriter Mary Mackey (*Skin Deep*, poems; *The Kindness of Strangers*, a novel; *McCarthy's List*, a screenplay); poet Dennis Schmitz (*Goodwill, Inc., String, Eden*).
Undergraduate writing courses are also offered by the Department; these are taught by poets Olivia Castellano (*The Blue Horse of Madness*), Kathryn Hohlwein, who also teaches nonfiction prose writing (*Touchstones: Letters Between Two Women*), and poet and critic Ronald Tanaka (*The Shino Suite*).

For more information, write the Creative Writing Committee Chair, Dept. of English.

**California State University,
San Jose
San Jose, CA 95192-0090**
(408) 924-4425
FAX (408) 924-4580

Degrees offered: BA in English; BA in Creative Arts, Creative Writing Emphasis; English Minor in Creative Writing; MA in English with Concentration in Writing (poetry, fiction, creative nonfiction)

Degree: BA in English

Required course of study:
   48 s/hrs in major, 12 of which may
      be in Creative Writing
   Foreign language: 10 s/hrs
   Total required to graduate: 124 s/hrs

Degree: BA in Creative Arts, Creative Writing Emphasis

Required course of study:
   45 s/hrs in major, 25 of which may
      be in Creative Writing
   Total required to graduate: 124 s/hrs

Degree: English Minor in Creative Writing

Required course of study:
   Introductory college-level Creative
      Writing course as prerequisite
   Creative Writing workshop: 15 s/hrs
   Reading course in appropriate literary
      genre: 3 s/hrs

Degree: MA in English, Concentration in Creative Writing

Type of Program: Studio/Academic

Required course of study:
   Core course: 3 s/hrs
   Creative Writing courses: 9 s/hrs
   Creative Writing thesis: 6 s/hrs

Other Requirements: Additional 12 s/hrs of approved courses (bringing total to 30 s/hrs); foreign language examination; MA comprehensive examination.

Application Deadlines: Write to Office of Admissions and Records.

Situated in the heart of the Silicon Valley cultural center, SJSU's Creative Writing Program balances literary study with studio work, offering workshops in poetry, fiction, creative nonfiction, children's and young adult fiction, and speech writing. Graduate classes average 12 students.

The English Department publishes *Reed* magazine, one of the oldest campus literary journals on the West Coast, with over 60 years of continuous publication. *Reed* is student-produced and offers opportunity for editing experience and active involvement in the Program, as well as a possible publishing venue. Graduate students have representation on the Creative Writing and Graduate Committees. Over $6,000 in creative writing awards are given annually by the Department. MA candidates in Creative Writing are eligible for Teaching assistantships. SJSU alumni include Lorna Dee Cervantes, James D. Houston, Steven Lopez, Sandra McPherson, Jeredith Merrin, Luis Valdez, and Amy Tan.

The English Department is in a partnership with the Center for Literary Arts, which brings many visiting faculty to conduct one-time workshops connected with a campus visit. Visitors have included Sherman Alexie, Margaret Atwood, Eavan Boland, Lucille Clifton, Carolyn Forché, Robert Hass, Carolyn Kizer, Maxine Hong Kingston, Adrienne Rich, Jane Smiley, Gary Snyder, Luis Valdez, Derek Walcott, C.K. Williams, Tobias Wolff, Toni Morrison, William Styron, and Seamus Heaney.

Connie and Robert Lurie have recently endowed a visiting professorship for distinguished writers. The first Lurie chair, award-winning author Ursula K. LeGuin, will be on campus for the entire spring semester of the 1999-2000 academic year.

Regular Faculty include:

Poetry: Virginia de Araujo (*The Minus Sign*), Samuel Maio (*The Burning of Los Angeles; Creating Another Self*), Nils Peterson (*The Heart Wants What It Wants; The Comedy of Desire*), Alan Soldofsky (*Staying Home*).

Fiction and Nonfiction: Gabriele Rico (*Writing the Natural Way; Pain and Possibility*), Robison Swigart (*Vector; Little America; The Book of Revelation*), Louis Rew (*God's Green Liniment; Editing for Writers; Introduction to Technical Writing: Process and Practice*), and Eric Miles Williamson (*East Bay Grease*), winner of *The Iowa Review*'s Tim McGinnis Award for Fiction and Book Review Editor of *Chelsea*.

For more information, contact Paul Douglass, Chair.

❖University of California, Davis
Davis, CA 95616

Degrees offered: BA, MA

Degree: BA in English, Writing Emphasis

Required course of study:
   44 q/hrs in the major (above freshman level)
   Thesis: no requirement
   Writing workshop: 12 q/hrs
   Literature courses: 24 q/hrs

Other Requirements: 4 q/hrs English Literature/Linguistics.

Application Deadline: January 15

The University of California, Davis offers the BA with a Writing Major. The undergraduate writing major includes courses in fiction, poetry, nonfiction writing, advanced composition, article writing, and magazine editing. The student in the writing major is required to take 16 distributed units of British and/or American literature in the historical periods, 8 units from major authors (Chaucer, Shakespeare, or Milton) which may not satisfy the historical requirement, 4 units of English language/linguistics, 3 creative writing courses (12 units) in fiction, nonfiction, and/or poetry, as well as 1 seminar.

The Writing Major Program particularly benefits from the English Department's graduate creative writing program, which has brought dozens of famous authors to the campus. All undergraduates in the writing major are especially encouraged to take advantage of these readings and visits.

For more information, contact the Admissions

Office or the English Undergraduate Studies Office, 118 Sproul Hall.

Degree: MA in Creative Writing

Type of Program: Studio/Academic

Length of Residency: One year minimum; normally two years.

Required course of study: 36 q/hrs
Thesis: 6 q/hrs
Writing workshops: 12 q/hrs
Theory course: 4 q/hrs
Literature courses: 14 q/hrs

Other Requirements: Oral defense of thesis; aesthetic statement.

Application Deadline: January 15

The MA in Creative Writing is a 2-year program culminating in the presentation of a thesis (a collection of poems, short fiction, or a novel). Teaching assistantships paying $12,015 per year may be available for qualified students.

Application requirements include submission of GRE scores (including the Advanced Test in English Literature), 3 letters of recommendation, and samples of creative work (poetry and/or prose) which are judged by the Creative Writing Committee of the English Department.

The MA program in Creative Writing is normally a 2-year program, although it is possible for an exceptional student to finish in one year. Required course work includes 4 q/hrs in either Fiction Theory or Poetics and 12 q/hrs in Creative Writing Workshops. The thesis (6 q/hrs) must be judged of professional quality by the candidate's thesis committee and is accepted following a successful oral interview and submission of an aesthetic statement. Elective courses (in English and American literature) make up the remaining 14 q/hrs.

Permanent faculty teaching in the graduate Creative Writing program include Max Byrd (*California Thriller, Target of Opportunity*, and *Jefferson: A Novel*); Sandra Gilbert (*The Madwoman in the Attic, No Man's Land, The Summer Kitchen*); Jack Hicks (Director, *Cutting Edges: Young American Fiction For The 70's*); Clarence Major (*My Amputations, Such Was the Season, Painted Turtle: Woman with Guitar*); Sandra McPherson (*The Year of Our Birth, Patron Happiness, Streamers*); Gary Snyder (*Turtle Island, Axe Handles, Left Out in the Rain*); Katherine Vaz (*Saudade, Mariana*); Alan Williamson (*Presence, The Muse of Distance, Introspection and Contemporary Poetry*). Recent visiting writers in residence were Tom Jenks, Sally Tisdale, Edward Hoagland, and Margaret Atwood.

For more information, write to the Graduate Advisor, Dept. of English.

❖University of California, Irvine
Irvine, CA 92697-2650
(949) 824-6712
FAX (949) 824-2916
e-mail: aaread@uci.edu

Degrees offered: BA, MFA

Degree: BA in English with Creative Writing Emphasis

Required course of study: 180 q/hrs for the BA

For further information, write the Director, The Program in Writing, Dept. of English and Comparative Literature.

Degree: MFA in Writing

Type of Program: Studio/Academic

Required course of study: 18 courses (72 q/hrs)
Thesis: required
Writing workshop: 6 courses (48 q/hrs)
Literature courses: 6 courses (24 q/hrs)

The founders and directors of the MFA Writing Program have deliberately kept it small in order to insure the high quality of the students, to restrict workshop enrollment, and to permit a good deal of teaching on a one-to-one tutorial basis. The ratio of students to faculty is low. The program is the same size today that it was when it was formed in 1965, enrolling about 12 students in poetry and 12 in fiction.

Central to the Program is the Graduate Writers' Workshop, 1 section in poetry and 1 in fiction. Student manuscripts are examined in discussion groups with a different faculty leader each quarter. A creative thesis (fiction or poetry) of publishable length and quality is required for graduation. In addition to the faculty of the Writing Program, there are poets, novelists, short story writers, and biographers on the faculty of the Department of English and Comparative Literature. Writers and editors who have taught in the Program include: Ethan Canin, E.L. Doctorow, Stuart Dybek, Amy Gerstler, Louise Glück, Judith Grossman, Rust Hills, Donald Justice, Brigit Pegeen Kelly, Thomas Kenneally, X.J. Kennedy, Galway Kinnell, Margot Livesey, Thomas Lux, Peter Matthiessen, Heather McHugh, Elizabeth Tallent, C.K. Williams, and Joy Williams.

The Writing Program faculty includes novelist and Professor Emeritus Oakley Hall (*The Downhill Racers, Warlock, Corpus of Joe Bailey*); novelist and biographer Professor Geoffrey Wolff (*Black Sun, The Duke of Deception, Providence*); novelist and Professor Michelle Latiolais (*Even Now*); poet and Professor James McMichael (*Each in a Place Apart, Four Good Things, The World at Large*, etc.); poet and Professor Michael Ryan (*God Hunger, Secret Life*, etc.).

Normally the Department of English and Comparative Literature supports its MFA Candidates with Teaching Assistantships during their course of study. Some Tuition Waivers for out-of-state applicants, and some Research Assistantships for minority students, are available.

For more information, contact the Administrator, The Program in Writing, Dept. of English and Comparative Literature.

University of California, Los Angeles
405 Hilgard Ave.
Los Angeles, CA 90095-1530
(310) 825-4174

Degree offered: BA in English with Creative Writing Track

Required course of study: 88 q/hrs in the major
  Thesis: no requirement
  Writing workshop: 12 q/hrs
  Literature course: 48 q/hrs

Other Requirements: 20 q/hrs foreign language.

Undergraduate students in the writing track of the English major are expected to take at least 3 workshop courses in one genre and 3 courses paralleling the writing specialization, as well as the remaining distribution requirements for the BA degree (total 180 q/hrs). There is no comprehensive exam for the BA.

The writing faculty includes poet and fiction writer Jascha Kessler (*Death Comes for the Behaviorist and Other Stories; Classical Illusions*); novelist Carolyn See (*The Rest is Done with Mirrors; Mothers, Daughters; Golden Days*); poet and fiction writer Paula Gunn Allen (*The Woman Who Owned the Shadows; A Cannon Between My Knees*); fiction writer David Wong Louie (*Pangs of Love*); poet Harryette Mullen (*Trimmings*); poet and critic Cal Bedient (*Candy Necklace*); and poet and critic Stephen Yenser (*The Fire in All Things*).

Recent and future visiting professors of writing, who ordinarily teach quarter-long workshops, include Louise Glück, John Barth, Carolyn Forché, Robert Pinsky, Daniel Menaker, Tina Howe, Robert Coover, Donald Justice, J.D. McClatchy, Peter Sacks, Alice Fulton, Judith Hall, Carol Muske, and David St. John. The English Department also helps to sponsor a diverse series of readings every year at the Armand Hammer Museum.

For more information, contact Stephen Yenser, Director of Creative Writing, Dept. of English.

❖University of California, Riverside
Riverside, CA 92521-0318
(909) 787-5312
FAX (909) 787-3933

Degree offered: BA in Creative Writing

Required course of study: 68 q/hrs total
  Lower division workshops and courses: 12 q/hrs
  Upper division workshops and courses: 32 q/hrs
  Senior thesis: 4 q/hrs by invitation of faculty
  Concentration in approved subject: 20 q/hrs

Other Requirements: University distribution requirements.

Application Deadlines: See University of California, Riverside catalogue for deadlines for applications each quarter.

The Creative Writing Department, the only one of its kind in the University of California system, is designed to assist undergraduates seriously interested in the writing of poetry, fiction, and drama. Many of its courses are workshop seminars limited to 18 students (20 on the introductory level). In addition, content courses, usually limited to 40, examine literature from a writer's point of view. These include such topics as fiction and film, metafiction, verse drama, poetic schools, fictional style, and fundamental and advanced concepts and writing for journalists. The Creative Writing faculty also offers directed reading and tutorial courses designed to meet individual needs.

The Department sponsors an annual Writers Week each February which includes readings by more than 20 poets, writers of fiction, and scriptwriters, and features some of the country's most significant literary figures (Maxine Hong Kingston, Joyce Carol Oates, and John Barth in recent years). In addition, it offers a Reading Series which brings to campus several guest readers each quarter (Anthony Hecht, C.K. Williams, and Thomas Lynch, among others). The Department sponsors a literary magazine, *Mosaic*, which has been in continuous publication for more than 30 years.

The Department offers fiction and poetry contests each year, including the $2,250 Chancellor's Performance Award for incoming freshmen and transfer students who demonstrate promise, the Ina Coolbrith and Poet Laureate prizes (an intra-intercampus California state competition), the Abraham Lincoln Polonsky Fiction Award, the Roy T. Thompson Poetry Award, the Birk Hinderaker Poetry Prize (commencement award), an Outstanding Fiction Award, and an Outstanding Poetry Award.

The faculty in the Creative Writing Department includes: poet and nonfiction writer Christopher Buckley (*Fall From Grace, Camino Cielo, Dark Matter*), Professor of Creative Writing and Chair; poet Maurya Simon (*The Enchanted Room, Days of Awe, Speaking in Tongues*), Professor of Creative Writing; novelist, short fiction and nonfiction writer Susan Straight (*Aquaboogie, I Been in Sorrow's Kitchen and Licked Out All The Pots*), Assoc. Professor of Creative Writing; poet and fiction writer Judy Kronenfeld (*Shadow of Wings*), lecturer; fiction writer and poet Frances McConnel (*Gathering Light, One Step Closer*), lecturer; poet and dramatist Derek McKown (*Pacific Review, Defined Providence, Salt Hill Review*), lecturer; professors emeriti -- fiction writer Stephen Minot (*Bending Time*); novelist Ben Stoltzfus (*Black Lazarus*); novelist Eliud Martinez (*Voice-Haunted Journey*).

For further information, contact Christopher Buckley, Chair, Creative Writing Dept.

University of California, San Diego
La Jolla, CA 92093-0410
(619) 534-3210
FAX (619) 534-8686
e-mail: ndhesketh@ucsd.edu

Degree offered: BA in Literature/Writing

Required course of study:
  Thesis: no requirement
  Writing workshop: 24 q/hrs
  Other literature electives: 24 q/hrs

Other Requirements: 24-40 q/hrs; second language proficiency.

The Literature/Writing Major at the University of

California, San Diego offers a BA in Writing. The core of the program is 6 workshops in at least two genres, depending on the student's interests. All students must take a lower-division literature sequence and at least 6 upper-division literature electives beyond the workshops. In addition, writing majors take a 3-course lower-division sequence in the Craft of Writing: one course each in fiction, poetry, and nonfiction prose. All students must complete the Department of Literature's foreign (secondary) language/literature requirement which demands 3 courses, at least one of which must be upper division, taught in a second (non-English) language, with texts read in the foreign language.

The structure of requirements for a BA in Writing is intended to produce writers who are also readers and readers who are literate in at least 2 national literatures. Because the Writing Section is only one of 9 sections in the UCSD Literature Department, it maintains close ties to those other sections and to their curricula. Coinciding with this comparatist focus is the program's interest in writing as a practice of multiple genres and disciplines. Students may take workshops in investigative journalism, personal narrative, screenwriting, radio playwriting, persuasion, and magazine writing, in addition to traditional poetry, experimental writing, television writing, intercultural writing, prose poem, etc., and fiction courses. Students who intend to pursue a career as teachers of writing may draw from a range of courses in composition and pedagogy: the history of writing, the writing process, forms of written discourse, stylistics, and grammar.

Students who specialize in poetry and fiction have a number of non-curricular activities to supplement their education. The UCSD New Writing Series brings poets to campus every week throughout the academic year. A number of student-run journals provide access to publication, and students regularly participate in on- and off-campus readings. In addition, the Archive for New Poetry in the central library is one of the world's largest depositories of small-press magazines, books, and manuscripts. Students regularly work in that collection, making use of its extensive print and audio tape resources.

The curriculum is taught by a combination of ladder-rank faculty members and a rotating group of visiting writers. Permanent faculty include Fanny Howe, Jerome Rothenberg, Pasquale Verdicchio, Quincy Troupe, Eleanor Antin, Linda Brodkey, Sherley Anne Williams, David Antin, Bram Dijkstra, Donald Wesling, Michael Davidson, Charles Cooper, Barbara Tomlinson, Stephanie Jed, and Wai-lim Yip.

Visitors to the program during the past few years have included Ed Dorn, Lyn Hejinian, Carey Harrison, Leslie Scalapino, Kathy Acker, Victor Hernandez Cruz, Amy Greenfield, Carla Harryman, Paul Keegan, Barrett Watten, Indira Ganesan, David Bradley, Clayton Eshleman, and Bobbie Louise Hawkins.

For further information, contact Jerome Rothenberg, Dept. of Literature, UCSD mailcode 0410.

University of California, Santa Cruz
Santa Cruz, CA 95054

(408) 459-4591

Degree offered: BA in Literature-Creative Writing

The literature major with an emphasis in creative writing is available to a limited number of students. Usually, interested students apply during the first or second quarters of their junior year by submitting a portfolio of work (poetry, short stories, or a novel in progress) to the Creative Writing Caucus. Students accepted into the program take four lower-division and five upper-division literature courses, and three upper-division writing seminars. They must also complete a creative writing thesis by the final quarter of their senior year. Work on the creative writing thesis normally involves from 5 to 10 units of individual study under the close supervision of a member of the Creative Writing Caucus.

Currently teaching in the program are Ron Hansen, Louis Owens, Page Stegner, and David Swanger. Affiliated with the program are Charles Atkinson, James D. Houston, and Carter Wilson.

For further information, contact David Swanger, Chair, Creative Writing Caucus, c/o Literature Board.

❖Cardinal Strich College
6801 North Yates Road
Milwaukee, WI 53217-3985

For more information, contact the Director, Dept. of English.

❖Carlow College
Pittsburgh, PA 15213-3109
(412) 578-6346
FAX (412) 578-6019

Degree offered: BA in English with Concentration in Writing

A writing major may be fulfilled by a concentration in either Creative Writing or Writing for Business and Industry. Major Requirements for Creative Writing require 33-35 credits.

The Writing Minor or Certificate Program is designed for undergraduate students who are pursuing degrees in other areas but who recognize that the ability to communicate well is valued in many careers. Students who have earned undergraduate degrees may also enroll in the certificate program. The minor or certificate requires 15 credits in undergraduate writing courses chosen in consultation with an advisor.

Degree: The Women's Creative Writing Program (poetry, fiction, nonfiction)

Type of Program: Studio

Length of Residency: Flexible

Required course of study: 36 C.E.U.'s (Continuing Education Units)
    Writing Workshops: 12 C.E.U.'s
    Contemporary Literature Courses: 12 C.E.U.'s
    Craft of Writing Courses: 12 C.E.U.'s
    Completion of full-length manuscript in poetry, fiction, or creative nonfiction

Application Deadlines: April 1 for admissions.

Our program is designed to meet the particular needs of women writers, especially those who may have other professional and personal commitments. Carlow has educated a diverse community of women for over 60 years and has offered non-credit workshops in creative writing since 1979. We believe that many aspiring adult women writers prefer to work in a challenging environment, but one that is also aware of the complexities of their lives. Our curriculum is designed for the student who wishes to do intensive work in writing, but who is not preparing primarily for a career in college or university teaching. The Women's Creative Writing Center emphasizes the vocation of writing. Its wide variety of courses, class times, and locations (evening and weekend classes; a safe campus; on-site day care), individually designed class schedules, a flexible residency requirement, and consultation with faculty advisors all aim at providing rigorous study of literature and intensive work in writing designed for and by each student. Literature, craft lectures, and workshops are all taught from the perspective of the working writer; our critical stance, therefore, is practical rather than theoretical.

All courses of study are focused on the writer's production of a publishable book-length manuscript of fiction, nonfiction, or poems. We expect that each writer will focus on one genre, but encourage students to participate in as many genres as desired.

We have hosted workshops and lectures by many notable women writers, including: Maggie Anderson, Jane Cooper, Tess Gallagher, Marita Golden, Maxine Kumin, Naomi Shihab Nye, Mary Oliver, Tillie Olsen, Linda Pastan, Molly Peacock, Marge Piercy, and Anneliese Wagner. Writers who have been part of our lecture series *Focus on Women* include: Margaret Atwood, Barbara Ehrenrich, Frances Fitzgerald, Nikki Giovanni, Dorothy Kearns Goodwin, Mary Gorden, Germaine Greer, Jane Howard, Fran Lebowitz, Penny Lernoux, Paule Marshall, Toni Morrison, May Sarton, and Judith Viorst.

We will offer a series of "mini-courses" each semester to be taught by visiting women writers. Prominent writers, in residencies lasting from two weeks to a month, will be available for craft lectures, workshops, and readings. The number of Continuing Education credits earned will depend on the length and type of courses offered. We expect to welcome three writers, one in each genre, each semester.

Pittsburgh has a vibrant literary life on and off its campuses, which include the University of Pittsburgh, home to the Pitt Poetry Series, Carnegie-Mellon University and its University Press, Duquesne University, Chatham College, and others. Readings are regularly scheduled at all universities and at many community locations. The International Poetry Forum and the Three Rivers Lectures Series bring prominent poets, fiction writers and nonfiction writers to Pittsburgh. Other local publishers include Cleis Press and Mill Hunk Books. There is a wide variety of new and used bookstores in and around Pittsburgh.

The core creative writing faculty includes: poet Patricia Dobler (*Forget Your Life, Talking to Strangers, UXB*); nonfiction writer Ellie Wymard (*Divorced Women, New Lives*).

Admission will be based on the manuscript sub-mission: 10 pages of poems or 20 pages of fiction or nonfiction.

For more information, contact Patricia Dobler, Director, The Women's Creative Writing Center, Carlow College, 3333 Fifth Avenue, Pittsburgh, PA 15213-3109.

❖Carnegie Mellon University Pittsburgh, PA 15213
(412) 268-2850

Degree offered: BA in Creative Writing

Required course of study: 122 s/hrs
 Forms courses: 6 s/hrs
 Writing workshop: 12–24 s/hrs
 Other writing courses: 6–18 s/hrs
 Literature courses: 18 or more s/hrs

The English department at Carnegie Mellon offers a series of courses leading to the BA in Creative Writing. At the same time, students may also double-major in professional writing, English, or technical writing.

Creative writing majors begin the program by taking at least 2 Survey of Forms courses in their sophomore year. These courses introduce majors to the different genres of fiction, poetry, nonfiction, and scriptwriting. At the heart of the program is the workshop. During the students' junior and senior years, they are required to take at least 4 workshops. The workshops emphasize constructive criticism and the incorporation of criticism in revision. Students learn to practice their craft, to experiment, and to grow. Exceptionally gifted students may also work individually with a faculty member to create a Senior Honors Thesis -- a book of poems, a collection of stories or essays, a novella, or a novel.

Students may take writing courses in journalism, magazine writing, biography, and personal essay. They may also take courses in literature and rhetoric within the English Department.

The Creative Writing Program offers a number of showcases for student writers. Most important among these are the campus publications in which students may publish their work. These include *The Oakland Review*, the student literary magazine, and *Dossier*, the literary supplement to the student newspaper. Students have also published in national magazines such as the *Carolina Quarterly, Ploughshares, Quarterly West, Antioch Review, Kansas Quarterly, The Cimarron Review*, and many others.

Both the Visiting Writers Series and the student reading series are central to our program. The Visiting Writers Series brings 8 distinguished writers to campus each school year to meet with students and to read from their work. Recent visitors include poets Stanley Kunitz, Rita Dove, Philip Levine, and Carolyn Kizer, and fiction writers Hilma Wolitzer, Russell Banks, and Alison Lurie. The student readings, which also number 8 per year, offer a showcase for the best student writing.

The highlight of the year is the presentation of the Adamson Student Writing Awards. These awards are for student excellence in poetry, fiction, screenwriting, and various forms of nonfiction. They are selected by prominent outside writers and are presented in a formal ceremony in the Adamson Wing on campus. Cash prizes currently total over $2,000 per year. Other student writing awards include the Academy of American Poets Prize, and the Carnegie Mellon University Press Prize in both poetry and fiction.

At Carnegie Mellon, students can also gain practical experience through internships and editorial positions. Internships are available with the Carnegie Mellon University Press in the production, publication, and marketing of works of fiction, poetry, and criticism. Students also take internships within the community -- in business, public relations, journalism, television, and advertising. Many graduates currently hold jobs in these fields. Others have gone on to some of the best graduate writing programs in the country, including Johns Hopkins, Brown, Bowling Green, University of California-Irvine, University of Arizona, Columbia, Ohio University, University of New Hampshire, and many others.

The writing faculty includes: poet Gerald Costanzo (*Nobody Lives on Arthur Godfrey Boulevard, In the Aviary, The Laps of the Bridesmaids*); fiction writer Hilary Masters (*Home is the Exile, Success, Last Stands*, and others); poet Jim Daniels (*Blessing the House, M-80*, and others); fiction writer Sharon Dilworth (*Women Drinking Benedictine, The Long White*); Jane Bernstein, novelist (*Departures*, nonfiction; *Loving Rachel*) and screenwriter; fiction writing Jane McCafferty (*One Heart, The Director of the World*); poet Carol Hamilton (*Fortune Cookies, Xenophilia*).

For more information, contact Jim Daniels, Creative Writing Program Director, English Dept.

❖Case Western Reserve University
Cleveland, OH 44106-7117
(216) 368-2340
FAX (216) 368-2216

Degrees offered: BA, MA

Degree: MA in English with Creative Dissertation (poetry/fiction)

Type of Program: Traditional Literary Study and Creative Writing

Required course of study: 27 s/hrs
Thesis: up to 6 s/hrs
Literature courses: up to 18 s/hrs
Tutorials or directed reading: 3-6 s/hrs

Other Requirements: Comprehensive examination; oral defense of thesis.

Application Deadlines: Graduate: applications accepted at any time; fellowship decisions April 15. Undergraduate: consult the Office of Undergraduate Admissions.

For more information, contact the Director of Graduate Studies, Dept. of English.

❖Central Connecticut State University
New Britain, CT 06050
(860) 832-2795

Degrees offered: BA, BS, MA, MS

Most undergraduate degree programs can include a minor in writing or journalism. The Minor in Writing requires 18 credit hours beyond Freshman Composition, with the option of concentrating in either expository writing, creative writing, or journalism. In expository writing, the University offers 4 courses beyond Freshman Composition, in creative writing 6 courses, in journalism 8 courses.

The creative writing courses are workshops, with at least 1 workshop in fiction and 1 in poetry offered each semester. Special opportunities for creative writing students include the yearly statewide student poetry contest, with the 5 winners traveling throughout the state giving readings, and the student literary magazine, *The Helix*.

The Minor in Journalism requires 18 credit hours beyond Freshman Composition, all in journalism. The journalism students have the opportunity to work on student publications such as the newspaper and the literary magazine. They also have available to them internships on local newspapers, such as *The Hartford Courant* and *The New Britain Herald*.

The faculty teaching the various writing courses include Sue Ellen Thompson, poet (author of 2 volumes of poems); Tom Hazuka (*The Road to the Island*, a novel; co-editor of *Flash Fiction* and *A Celestial Omnibus: Short Fiction on Faith*; short stories in many magazines); Anthony Cannella (a former editor at *The Miami Herald*, articles in various newspapers).

For more information, write Dr. Loftus Jeston, Assistant Chair, English Dept.

❖University of Central Florida
Orlando, FL 32816
(407) UCF-2212

Degrees offered: BA, MA

Degree: BA in English (creative writing track)

Required course of study: 120 s/hrs total
Creative writing: 18 s/hrs
English language and literature: 18 s/hrs

Majors take writing courses in at least two genres, chosen from fiction, poetry, nonfiction, and screenwriting. *The Cypress Dome*, a journal of student writing edited by undergraduate students, won the 1995 AWP Program Directors' Award for literary content.

Degree: MA in English (creative writing track)

Type of Program: Studio/Academic

Length of Residency: Two years

Required course of study: 36 s/hrs total
Creative writing: 12 s/hrs
Creative thesis: 6 s/hrs
Literature: 18 s/hrs

Other Requirements: A thesis and individualized reading list form the basis for the candidate's thesis defense.

Recent visiting writers have included William Styron, Joseph Heller, Toni Morrison, E.L. Doctorow, Joyce Carol Oates, John Barth, Maxine Kumin, W.S. Merwin, and Bharati Mukherjee.

The Florida Review, a nationally recognized literary journal, offers internships for both undergraduate and graduate students.

Graduate students are eligible for teaching assistantships in composition and creative writing.

The creative writing faculty includes nonfiction writer Jocelyn Bartkevicius (work in *The Best American Essays*); poet and translator Judith Hemschemeyer (*I Remember the Room Was Filled with Light, Very Close and Very Slow*, and *The Ride Home*); fiction writer Susan Hubbard (*Walking on Ice*, AWP Short Fiction Prize); fiction writer Jeanne Leiby; fiction writer Pat Rushin (*Puzzling Through the News*); poet and nonfiction writer Don Stap (*Letter at the End of Winter*, poetry; *A Parrot Without a Name*, nonfiction; recipient of NEA creative writing fellowship).

For more information about the graduate program, contact Dr. John Schell. All other information can be obtained from Dr. Dawn Trovard, Chair, Dept. of English.

❖Central Michigan University
Mt. Pleasant, MI 48859
(517) 774-3171 (English Dept.: ask for Creative Writing Coordinator)
FAX: (517) 774-1271
website: http://www.cmich.edu

Degrees offered: BS/BA, MA

Degree: BS/BA in English; Creative Writing Concentration

Required course of study: BS/BA degrees require a minimum 124 s/hrs, including competency requirements in written English, oral English, and mathematics as well as 30 hour University Program (general education). BA requires equivalent of two years of a foreign language. 39 s/hr English major: Creative Writing concentration includes 12-hr Creative Writing core in addition to required courses in literature, criticism/theory, language/linguistics.

Application Deadlines: For financial aid, apply by Feb. 15 for fall, Oct. 1 for spring. Otherwise apply at least six weeks before start of semester in which you plan to enroll.

Degree: MA in English: Creative Writing Option (poetry, fiction)

Type of Program: Studio/Academic

Required course of study: 30 s/hr degree requires 6 hours (two semesters) graduate workshop, 6 hours thesis, 6 hours literature seminars, courses in composition, criticism, language/linguistics.

Application Deadlines: for financial aid, apply by March 15; otherwise, at least six weeks before start of semester in which you plan to enroll.

We are a growing program with two new positions

(fiction, poetry) approved for 1999-2000. We offer five undergraduate courses in writing poetry and fiction, one each in playwriting and creative nonfiction (an area we're in the process of expanding). Undergraduate concentration in Creative Writing has been in place since 1996-97. MA in English with Creative Writing Option (fiction and poetry) should be in place for 1999-2000 (MA with creative thesis, graduate fiction, poetry courses already in place). Carroll Arnett Creative Writing scholarship, honoring the late Cherokee poet and long-time faculty member Gogisgi/Carroll Arnett, offered for the first time 1997-98. Significant number of teaching assistantships in composition available to graduate students. Expanded visiting writers series began 1998-99 (fall: Gary Gildner, Janet Kauffman, Barney Bush/Annette Arkekata; spring, E. Ethelbert Miller, two more TBA). Graduates have won several NEAs, published with Algonquin, Carnegie-Mellon, Missouri; MA graduates have gone on to MFA/PhD at Pitt, Michigan, Bowling Green, Vermont College, etc.

1998-99 faculty include Ann Bardens (*Stone and Water*), poetry; Robert Root (*Wordsmithery, The Fourth Genre*), creative nonfiction; Sandra Seaton (*The Bridge Party, The Will*), fiction and playwriting; and Eric Torgersen (*Good True Stories, Dear Friend*) fiction and poetry.

For more information, contact Creative Writing Coordinator (a rotating position), Dept. of English.

❖Central Missouri State University
Warrensburg, MO 64093
(660) 543-4425
FAX (660) 543-8544

Degrees offered: BA, MA

Degree: BA in English with Creative Writing Minor; BA in Creative Writing (an individualized major)

Required course of study: 124 s/hrs total
Major: 35 s/hrs
Writing workshops: 9-12 s/hrs
Writing project: 3-6 s/hrs
Directed reading: 3-6 s/hrs
Literature survey courses in student's genre: 6 s/hrs
Literature, rhetoric, and/or writing courses in English, theater or communication: remaining s/hrs

Application Deadlines: No application deadlines for admission; financial aid deadline March 1.

The undergraduate concentration requires the students to take Creative Writing (intro), Advanced Creative Writing, and Creative Writing for Publication (the latter may be taken twice and for graduate credit). Program also requires study in selected literary era or genre. Students may use the writing project hours for revision of work completed in workshop courses. Students are encouraged to complete a book-length work by graduation. Volunteer upper-level students serve as student-editors with *Pleiades*, a nation-wide literary journal.

Degree: MA with Optional Thesis, may be creative thesis

Type of Program: Academic

Length of Residency: Two years

Required course of study: 32 s/hrs, min. literature; optional thesis.

Other Requirements: Written comprehensive exam before completion of program.

Volunteer students work with *Pleiades*. Writing awards offered each year.

Director of Creative Writing: R.M. Kinder, fiction (*Sweet Angel Band*). Editor of *Pleiades* and Pleiades Press. Keven Prufer, poetry (*Strangewood*). Co-editor of *Pleiades* and Pleiades Press.

❖University of Central Oklahoma
100 University Drive
Edmond, OK 73034-0184
(405) 341-2980, ext. 5667
FAX (405) 330-3823

Degree offered: MA in English with Creative Writing Emphasis

Required course of study: 32 s/hrs
Thesis: 4 s/hrs

Founded in 1965 by now Dean of Liberal Arts, Clifton L. Warren. Over 100 books have been published by faculty & students, ranging from genre historical romances to thrillers to technical manuals. Several former students have become "bestselling" authors, including Georgina Gentry, Jeri Cook, Sara Orwig, and Deana James. The department sponsored the first state intercollegiate poetry contest in 1996. Degree requires 32 hours, of which 4 are credited for a creative thesis. Students complete 5 literary period courses, 2 translation courses, literary criticism, and writing courses. Two full-time faculty members hold doctorates, as well as the current artist-in-residence. Six adjuncts with advanced degrees complete the staff.

Graduates of this program teach at the college level, pursue PhD studies, and work in editing and publishing as well as business. Offerings of the department include courses in novel writing, poetry, romance (contemporary and historical), science-fiction, horror, creative nonfiction, writing for children, and detective fiction. Sara Orwig, who supervises mainstream novel-writing, has published over 40 novels in 10 languages. Linda McDonald, screen and playwriting teacher, has had her plays produced by Circle Repertory in New York City. Jeri Van Cook's current nonfiction work "Going Undercover" is a guide drawing on his years in law enforcement. Betty Shipley consistently produces prize-winning poets from "organic poetry" classes. Dr. Laura Apol brings expertise in writing for children and young adults. Dr. Christopher Givan is the author of two chapbooks of poetry and is a noted Shakespeare scholar. Current chair, Dr. Lynette L. Wert, has published in nonfiction, novels, and short stories.

The artist-in-residence normally serves for two years and teaches both graduate and undergraduates. Students in the MA program may elect to have the artist-in-residence direct the thesis. Some past award-winning artists-in-residence include Alec Waugh, James Dickey, Marilyn Harris, Geoffrey Bocca, John Bishop, Milan Stitt, Edward Allen, and Steward O'Nan. The present artist-in-residence, Carolyn Wheat, holds a juris doctor and specializes in mystery novels.

The *New Plains Review*, an interdisciplinary journal which publishes poems, stories, and essays of contemporary interest, is managed and edited by students and directed by its founder and Executive Editor, Professor Gwynne Hunter. *NPR* provides training in the editing and publication of a literary journal, offering valuable practicum experience for future jobs.

The MA program can be completed in 2 semesters and a summer, though many take longer. Classes are offered day and evening to accommodate those working full-time.

The program consists of many different kinds of writing courses as well as some courses in historical periods (for example: 17th, 18th, 19th-century British and classical and modern American literature). Students who have never studied some of these traditional periods at the undergraduate level will need to take them in this program. A foreign language requirement can be met either by having had 2 semesters of a language or by taking 2 courses of literature in translation at the graduate level. A course in literary criticism is also required. This mix of traditional English courses with creative writing classes has prepared graduates to work as teachers of composition, literature, and creative writing. Other career paths have been those of public relations, media consultant, editor, journalist, and communications writer for industry.

Four of 32 units in the program consist of independent work done to write a thesis which consists usually of a novel, a group of short stories, a collection of poems, a full-length play, a screenplay, or at times, a group of nonfiction essays. Classes are small and a good deal of personal instruction takes place. A sense of community seems to exist among the students, whose diverse backgrounds and ages add a mixture of viewpoints.

For further information contact the Creative Studies Department, Dr. Lynette L. Wert, Chair at (405) 341-2980, ext. 5667. We will be glad to mail the prospective student a brochure outlining the program.

Central Washington University
Ellensburg, WA 98926
(509) 963-1546

Degree offered: BA in English; minor in Creative Writing

The minor includes choices from two poetry writing classes, two fiction, one creative nonfiction, and one upper-division writing seminar. It also includes four literature classes.

Writers on the staff include Philip Garrison (*A Woman and Certain Women, Lipstick, Away Awhile, Augury*); Mark Halperin (*Backroads, A Place Made Fast, Measure of Islands*); and Joseph Powell (*Counting The Change*).

For more information, write Chair, Dept. of English.

❖Chapman University
Orange, CA 92866
(714) 997-6750
FAX (714) 997-6697

Degrees offered: BA, MA, MFA

Degree: BA in English with Emphasis in Creative Writing

Required course of study: 124 s/hrs for the BA
Writing workshop: 9 s/hrs
Other writing courses: 9 s/hrs
Literature courses: 24 s/hrs
Tutorials or directed reading: variable

Other Requirements: 3-6 s/hrs Internship or Cooperative Education recommended; 3-9 s/hrs Communications.

Degree: BA in English with Emphasis in Media Writing

Required course of study: 124 s/hrs for the BA
Writing workshop: 6 s/hrs
Other writing courses: 6 s/hrs
Literature courses: 21-27 s/hrs

Other Requirements: 3-6 s/hrs Internship or Cooperative Education recommended; 3-9 s/hrs Communications.

Degree: BA in English with Emphasis in Journalism

Required course of study: 124 s/hrs for the BA
Writing workshop: 6 s/hrs
Other writing courses: 21-24 s/hrs
Literature courses: 15-18 s/hrs
Tutorials or directed reading: variable

Other Requirements: 3-6 s/hrs Internship or Cooperative Education recommended.

Degree: BA in English with Emphasis in Professional Writing

Required course of study: 124 s/hrs for the BA
Writing workshop: 9 s/hrs
Other writing courses: 6-12 s/hrs
Literature courses: 21 s/hrs
Tutorials or directed reading: variable

Other Requirements: 6 s/hrs Internship or Cooperative Education recommended.

Degree: MA in English with Concentration in Media Writing (poetry, fiction, media writing, creative nonfiction, translation, children's literature, and playwriting)

Type of Program: Studio/Academic

Length of Residency: Two years

Required course of study: 36 s/hrs for the MA
Writing workshop: 6-9 s/hrs
Other writing courses: 6-9 s/hrs
Literature courses: 21-24 s/hrs
Tutorials or directed reading: variable

Other Requirements: Comprehensive examination during last semester of coursework.

Degree: MFA in Creative Writing

Type of Program: Studio/Academic

Length of Residency: Three years

Required course of study: 60 s/hrs for the MFA
Writing workshop: 24-30 s/hrs
Other writing courses: 3-9 s/hrs
Literature courses: 21-27 s/hrs
Tutorials or directed reading: variable

Other Requirements: Comprehensive examination during last semester of coursework; submission of creative thesis (manuscript of original poems, prose, drama, or script).

The Department of English at Chapman University offers courses in writing, language, and literature. The programs of study, derived from these courses, foster critical and creative thinking, an awareness of languages as an instrument of mastery, a mode of expression, and a form of relationship. From courses in literature and critical thinking, students encounter the evolution of human thought and develop thinking skills. Workshops in writing and courses in writing process enable students to develop their own sophisticated and unique means of expression.

Undergraduate English majors at Chapman University may elect, among other concentrations, programs emphasizing Creative Writing, Journalism, Media Writing, and Professional Writing. The Creative Writing emphasis is elected by those students who want to develop their potentials as imaginative and disciplined writers of poetry, fiction, and drama. The emphasis in Journalism prepares students for careers in the print media, while the Media Writing emphasis enables students to develop skills in writing for broadcast and film media. The Professional Writing emphasis, recommended for students with a double major in a technical field or the sciences, prepares students to write for business, government, or the professions. All majors are required to become proficient in computer word processing in anticipation of the medium's influence in writing, editing, and publishing.

Graduate students in English may select, among other concentrations, the MA in Media Writing or the MFA in Creative Writing. Students electing the Media Writing concentration refine their thinking, writing, and marketing skills to write for film and television media. The MFA in Creative Writing develops expressive, creative, and mechanical skills in talented, sensitive, prospective writers. Students in the MFA program complete a major creative work -- fiction, poetry, or drama -- and are encouraged to publish their works through professional contacts they cultivate through the program. Students in the MFA may also compete for positions in colleges and universities.

Students design their programs of study in consultation with faculty advisors. Courses in the elected programs may be drawn from a wide range of writing workshops, small seminars in theory and form, and courses in literature and allied disciplines. One of the advantages of a small private university is the effort made by faculty to assist undergraduates and graduate students in constructing individualized, but coherent and integrated, programs of study.

Undergraduates are encouraged to complete at least one internship or co-op education experience relating to their emphasis. This opportunity enables students to acquaint themselves with occasions in the community for applying their academic talents and for introducing themselves to a network of social, cultural, and business leaders. Co-op or intern placements may be described as apprenticeships in law, editing, and business offices, print production and retail firms, film, theatre, and television production companies, magazines, newspapers, libraries, schools, and brokerage offices. Students with writing emphases will be prepared and encouraged to submit their work as part of the professional dossiers for possible publication, or for placement with an agent.

The Chapman University writing programs seek to foster a creative learning environment for students to cultivate writing, thinking, and professional skills. Students in the writing programs may choose to participate in master classes, workshops, and lectures or readings conducted by major literary figures. The Distinguished Writers series has hosted writers of national and international merit including Kurt Vonnegut, Gwendolyn Brooks, Joyce Carol Oates, Diane Wakoski, John Barth, John Hollander, Joseph Heller, Tom Wolfe, and others. Weekend Writers' Workshops, offered each semester, bring students and area writers and agents together, generating opportunities for students to study and interact with representatives from the lively local creative writing community. Students may also compete in the annual departmental writing contest for cash awards, and may contribute to the student journal or campus newspaper, yearbook, or magazine. Besides workshops, publishing, and competition opportunities, the department participates in an exchange program for undergraduate students with King Alfred's College in England. Chapman University, in conjunction with the California State Poetry Society, publishes *California Quarterly*, a journal of original poetry, and sponsors monthly poetry readings.

The faculty who teach writing hold professional credentials in the fields of poetry and fiction, journalism, screenwriting, and media writing and production. They are: Mark Axelrod, Creative Writing and Media Writing (fiction and screenplays; awards from Sundance Institute, Writers Guild of America West, Writers Guild of America East); Terri Brint Joseph, Creative Writing (translations and original poems); Tom Massey, Creative Writing (original poetry and fiction); Martin Nakell, Creative Writing (poetry and fiction); Paul Frizler, Professional and Media Writing (*Getting Wasted*, screenplay, Second Prize Houston Film Festival, 1981; *Sloppy Murders*, screenplay; *Soft Explosion*, screenplay); Gordon McAlpine, Creative Writing (*Joy in Mudville, Everafter*); Richard A. Watson, Professional and Media Writing (*Snail-Headed, Ghosttracks, Models of Man's Future*); and Myron Yeager, Professional Writing and Journalism (editor of 2 books and business writing consultant).

The Department offers performance scholarships, merit scholarships, and partial tuition waivers for exceptional students. Financial aid is available through the University for qualifying undergraduates. Write to Anthony Garcia, Chair, Dept. of English.

College of Charleston
Charleston, SC 29424
(843) 792-5664

Degree offered: BA in English, Minor in Creative Writing

Required course of study: Major: 36 s/hrs at or above the 200 level of which at least 30 s/hrs must be selected from courses at or above the 300 level; Minor: at least 18 s/hrs, 9 of which must be at or above the 300 level.

Application Deadlines: None.

Founded in 1770, the College of Charleston offers a wide selection of writing courses above the freshman composition level. They include Poetry Writing I, Poetry Writing II, Fiction Writing, Advanced Fiction Writing, Writing the Novel, Writing for the Mass Media, Advanced Composition, Interdisciplinary Composition, Advanced Creative Writing, and Independent Studies on special projects in poetry or fiction writing.

The College of Charleston hosts an annual writers' conference. The emphasis is on allowing ample opportunity for emerging writers from around the country to meet more established national authors; students play an active role in helping produce the conference. 1996 Conference: Joyce Carol Oates, Eleanora Tate, Andrew Hudgins, Robert Olmstead, Martha Collins, Erin McGraw, Andrea Hollander Budy, Ralph Keyes, Gregory Pincus. 1995: Yusef Komunyakaa, Paul Hoover, Kelly Cherry, Sydney Lea, Bret Lott, Jill McCorkle. 1994: Charles Baxter, Scott Cairns, Yusef Komunyakaa, Shannon Ravenel, Chuck Verrill, Sylvia Wilkinson.

Directors: Fiction: Bret Lott (*The Man Who Owned Vermont, A Stranger's House, Jewel*). Poetry: Paul Allen (*Four Passes, American Crawl*).

For more information, contact the Directors, Creative Writing, Dept. of English.

Chicago State University
95th and King Drive
Chicago, IL 60628
(312) 995-2189
FAX (312) 995-3809

Degree offered: BA in English with Professional and Technical Writing Option

Required course of study: 51 s/hrs in the major
Writing courses: 18 s/hrs
Literature courses: 27 s/hrs
Linguistics and Speech courses: 6 s/hrs

Other Requirements: 6 s/hrs in composition; 36 s/hrs in general education; 27 s/hrs in electives selected with the department advisor's approval; passing examinations on the state and federal constitutions.

Application Deadline: March 1.

Course offerings include Writing for Publication, Feature Writing, Business News Writing, Technical and Scientific Writing, Writing for Topical Markets, Writing for Advertising, Editing, Informative Writing,

News Writing, Problems in School Journalism I, II, and III, Business Writing, Writing Research Papers, Writing the Short Story, The Writing of Poetry, Playwriting, Advanced Rhetoric, Continuity Writing for Radio and TV, Dramatic Writing for Radio and TV.

Students in the Professional and Technical Writing option may select 1 of 4 concentrations: creative writing, journalism, broadcast journalism, or technical writing. Each concentration blends a liberal arts education and English coursework while providing the student flexibility to pursue coursework relative to his or her career interests.

Faculty in the program include Chris List, Caryn Cleeland, Haki Madhubuti, Sherwood Snyder, and Donda West.

For more information, contact Jesse Green, Chairperson, Dept. of English, Speech, and Modern Languages.

❖University of Cincinnati
Cincinnati, OH 45221-0069
(513) 556-3946 Writing Program
(513) 556-3906 Graduate Program
FAX (513) 556-5960
e-mail: druryjp@ucenglish.mcm.uc.edu

Degrees offered: BA, Graduate Certificate in Professional Writing, MA, PhD

Degree: BA with Writing Certificate

The Writing Certificate is the equivalent of a minor field of concentration, allowing students to specialize in creative writing (poetry and fiction), journalism, and professional writing (business and technical). This program of courses is made available by the Department of English not only to English majors, but to students majoring in any field offered by the baccalaureate colleges of the University of Cincinnati.

Students in the Writing Program earn the certificate by completing 27 q/hrs of courses in writing, ending with the Senior Writing Seminar (9 q/hrs) in their chosen areas of specialization. Typically, a student in the Creative Writing track will take 9 q/hrs of creative writing workshops (fiction or poetry), beginning with the sophomore year and ending with the Senior Seminar. Students are encouraged to publish their work and may gain additional experience as members of the staffs of several local and student publications. In the journalism and Professional Writing tracks, students intern as writers with various University publications and a number of national and local organizations, including daily newspapers, media stations, public service institutions, and technical industries. Multiple sections of at least 20 different writing courses are offered each year, ranging in focus from playwriting to technical writing and copy editing; many of the writing classes are conducted in a state-of-the-art word processing lab. In an annual competition, the Department awards prizes to outstanding student writers in seven areas, including poetry, fiction, the essay, and journalism.

For further information, contact John Drury, Director of the Writing Program, Dept. of English, P.O. Box 210069.

Degree: Graduate Certificate in Professional Writing

Required course of study: 20 hours (5 courses) beyond the baccalaureate degree. Includes 2 required courses: either Rhetoric or Professional Writing Theory, and either Document Design or Computer Applications.

Other requirements: None.

Application Deadline: February 1 for those seeking financial aid; otherwise, applications accepted throughout the academic year.

The Graduate Certificate in Professional Writing is open to applicants with a variety of backgrounds, from English and communication to the health sciences, engineering, and business. It is intended primarily for working professionals who wish to extend their writing and publishing skills or to gain a more solid academic foundation for these skills. The GRE may be waived for students with extensive work experience.

Degree: MA in English with Creative Writing Option
(fiction, poetry)

Type of Program: Studio/Academic

Length of Residency: Two years

Required course of study: 54 credits beyond the BA (including 20 q/hrs of graduate writing workshops and 18 hours elective English courses). Courses in playwriting and creative writing pedagogy are available.

Other Requirements: Foreign language; teaching experience; creative thesis; and 3-part comprehensive examination testing knowledge of British and American literature and critical methods.

Degree: MA in English -- Professional Writing Option, Editing and Publishing Option

Type of Program: Studio/Academic

Length of Residency: Two years

Required course of study: 54 q/hrs beyond the BA (including courses in rhetoric, editing, publications management and design, article and essay writing); up to 12 q/hrs may be taken in elective courses.

Other Requirements: Language or research tool; professional internship; research thesis or portfolio/critical paper; specially designed 2-part comprehensive examination and defense of thesis or portfolio/critical paper.

Options in Editing and Publishing and in Professional Writing lead to an MA in English but are designed to prepare students for writing careers in business and industry. Students in Creative Writing may take selected courses in these areas.

Degree: PhD in English with Creative Dissertation
(fiction, poetry)

Type of Program: Emphasis on 20th-Century literature, theory, and creative writing

Required course of study: 54 graduate course credits beyond the MA, including a maximum of 16 workshop hours and one required course, Contexts of 20th-Century Literary Study. Minimum total of 135 q/hrs (MA hours and PhD hours).

Other Requirements: 2 foreign languages, 1 of which should be French, German, or Latin; teaching experience; qualifying examinations.

Application deadline: February 1.

A student in the PhD program may, with approval, write a dissertation in creative writing (a novel or a book-length collection of poems or short stories) accompanied by a critical essay. A student in this program must fulfill all the other requirements for the PhD in English.

The student who has been admitted to this program submits a specific dissertation prospectus while completing all other PhD requirements, including coursework, language examinations, and PhD qualifying examinations. The number of those approved for this option is very small; it is made available only to students who demonstrate unusual potential.

The qualifying exam consists of 2 parts. The written portion is 3 take-home exams in 3 areas: one a post-1900 literature area, one a theory area or composition pedagogy, and one any pre- or post-1900 literature area. The oral portion is a 90-minute follow-up to the written exam.

The Department's Writing Program emphasizes writing as both a practical and a creative art. Since 1951, for example, the George Elliston Poetry Foundation at the University of Cincinnati has fostered the development of promising poets and honored the achievements of established poets. Each year, through the Poet-in-Residence program, a distinguished poet is brought to campus for a full quarter to conduct poetry seminars, readings, and workshops for undergraduates, graduates, and public audiences. John Berryman, Stephen Spender, Robert Lowell, Robert Frost, Randall Jarrell, Karl Shapiro, Richard Eberhart, Denise Levertov, John Ashbery, and Mary Oliver have been Elliston Poets in years past. One of the best collections of contemporary poetry in the world -- more than 10,000 books, magazines, records, and tapes relating to contemporary poetry -- is now housed in the Elliston Poetry Room located in the University library. The Elliston Foundation also supports a lecture series that has brought recent speakers such as Nobel Laureate Czeslaw Milosz, Adrienne Rich, Seamus Heaney, and Margaret Atwood to campus. In addition, the Helen Weinberger Center for the Study of Drama and Playwriting, a joint program of the College of Arts and Sciences and the College Conservatory of Music, was launched in 1991. The Weinberger Center brings to campus each year such distinguished playwrights as Joan Schenkar, Lee Blessing, Michael Weller, and Edward Albee. The journal *American Drama* is also housed here.

The 21 full-time members of the Department of English who offer courses in the Writing Program have been recognized for their excellence in teaching in addition to their scholarly and creative work. Current faculty have received the PEN Gold Medal, Whiting Fellowship, Poets' Prize, B.F. Conners Poetry Prize, Betty Calladay Award for Poetry, and the AWP Prize for Poetry. All faculty above the rank of instructor teach both undergraduate and graduate courses.

Creative Writing faculty includes poet Don Bogen (*The Known World, After the Splendid Display*); poet James Cummins (*The Whole Truth, Portrait in a Spoon*); poet John Drury (*The Poetry Dictionary, The Stray Ghost*); poet Andrew Hudgins (*The Glass Anvil, The Never-Ending, Babylon in a Jar*); playwright Norma Jenckes (*Edward Albee: American Dreamer, Dark Horse*); fiction writer Erin McGraw (*Lies of the Saints, Bodies at Sea*); fiction writer Josip Novakovich (*Yolk, Apricots from Chernobyl, Salvation and Other Disasters*); fiction writer Martha Stephens (*Children of the World, Cast a Wistful Eye*); and poet Terry Stokes (*Sportin' Life, Natural Disasters*). In addition, the Writing Program includes courses offered by 3 full-time faculty in composition and rhetoric, 3 in journalism and publishing, and 5 in professional writing.

The university offers an array of financial aid to graduate students, and the majority of full-time students in writing are awarded Graduate Assistantships or university Graduate Scholarships. Special tuition-remission awards and several endowed scholarships -- such as the Elliston Poetry Fellowship (for doctoral students), the Lanzit Fellowships (for master's student in creative writing), Taft Fellowships, the Cincinnati-Wesleyan and the Armstrong-Hunter Awards, the Ricking Scholarship, the Lanzit Poetry Award, and the University's Minority Graduate Fellows and Scholars Program -- allow the Department to reward excellence in its programs as few other departments can. Internships at *Story* magazine are also available for graduate students.

Application can be made for any quarter, but applicants for financial aid are urged to submit files by February 1 for the following autumn.

For more information, contact Professor Kathryn Rentz, Director of Graduate Studies, Dept. of English, P.O. Box 210069.

❖City College of New York
City University of New York
New York, NY 10031
(212) 650-6694

Degree offered: MA in Creative Writing (poetry, fiction, playwriting, creative nonfiction, translation)

Type of Program: Studio/Academic

Length of Residency: Two years

Required course of study: 30 credits total; 12 workshop credits; 15 literature credits; 3 credits in thesis tutorial.

Other Requirements: Thesis of publishable work in chosen genre; foreign language proficiency exam (a translation exam).

Application Deadlines: June 1 for Fall; January 1 for Spring (Separate inquiries should be made for Financial Aid, 650-6656, 6654)

Since 1971, the City College of New York has offered a Master's degree in Creative Writing to students with a BA whose work in fiction, poetry, playwriting, creative nonfiction, and translation shows developed talent. The emphasis is on placing a few students in workshops with the best contemporary writers. The Graduate Program enrolls no more than 50 students and limits the workshops to 14.

All classes are held after 4:15, Monday to Thursday, to enable students to continue working while enrolled in the Program.

Associated with the Program is the international magazine, *Fiction*, edited by Mark Mirsky. There are fellowships for students interested in training at the magazine.

Students in the program are eligible to compete for the annual $3,000 DeJur award in Creative Writing, as well as the several other awards for fiction and nonfiction writing. A limited number of fellowships are also available.

Visiting writers in recent years have included Francine du Plessix Gray, Maureen Howard, John Guare, Alan Lelchuck, E.M. Broner, Susan Thames, Walter Mosley, Walter Bernstein, Claudia Dreifus, Charles Bernstein, Edna O'Brien, Cynthia Ozick, Grace Paley, Susan Sontag, and Elizabeth Hardwick. Twice a semester the Program hosts readings and informal discussions with such writers as Philip Levine, C.K. Williams, Stanley Plumly, Charles Wright, Donald Revell, Cynthia Mcdonald, and Heather McHugh, among others.

Current Creative Writing faculty includes: fiction writer Frederic Tuten (*Tintin in the New World, The Adventures of Mao on the Long March, Van Gogh's Bad Cafe*); fiction writer Mark Mirsky (*Thou Worm Jacob, The Red Adam*, Editor of *Fiction* magazine); fiction writer Linsey Abrams (*Double Vision, Charting by the Stars*, Editor of *Global City Review*); nonfiction writer Barbara P. Solomon (Editor, Great Marsh Press); visiting poet Judith Baumel (*The Weight of Numbers*, Walt Whitman Prize, *Now*); visiting poet Elaine Equi (*Surface Tension, Decoy*); visiting writer Stacy Doris (*Kildare* (poetry), *La vie de chester Steven Wiener écrite par sa femme* (prose)); visiting fiction writer David Bradley (*South Street, The Chaneysville Incident*, awarded the PEN/Faulkner Prize); and visiting fiction writer George Lamming (*In the Castle of My Skin, Natives of My Person*, Fulbright Fellowship).

For further information, please contact Rosana Chang, Administrator, either by mail or telephone. Telephone Monday to Thursday between 3 and 6 p.m., EST.

❖Clackamas Community College
Oregon City, OR 97045
(503) 657-6958, ext. 2285

Degree offered: AA, English Emphasis

Clackamas Community College offers introductory and advanced courses in Fiction writing, Poetry writing, and Playwriting. The classes are held in a workshop setting and are designed for people who are interested in professional writing or intend to make writing an important part of their lives. The workshops teach close critical reading, theory of writing in the respective genre for the course, and develop students' revising and editing skills. The program also offers participation through an Editing/Publishing class on the student-run literary magazine, *Synesthesia*, and student internships on the *Clackamas Literary Review*.

Visiting writers and readers in past years have included Naomi Shihab Nye, Ron Carlson, Stephen Dobyns, Alberto Rios, Sharon Olds, Phillip Red Eagle, Charlotte Watson Sherman, Edward Albee, Sherman Alexie, Li-Young Lee, Coleen McElroy, and Diana Abu Jaber.

The Creative Writing Staff includes: Craig Lesley and Tim Schell (fiction); Diane Averill, Kate Gray, and Jeff Knorr (poetry); and Sue Mach (playwriting).

For further information contact Emily Orlando, Dept. Chairperson.

Clarion University of Pennsylvania
Clarion, PA 16214
(814) 226-2480

Degrees offered: BA, BS, and MA in English

The English Department at Clarion offers 3 creative writing courses at the undergraduate level: Beginning Creative Writing, Craft of Fiction, and Craft of Poetry. Also available at the undergraduate level is a minor in writing. Available at the graduate level are courses: Independent Study in Writing, Practicum in College Composition, and Seminar in Writing Theory and Research.

For further information, contact Dr. Darlynn Fink, Director of Writing, Dept. of English.

❖Clarkson University
School of Liberal Arts
Box 5750
Potsdam, NY 13699
(315) 268-3967
e-mail: duemer@clarkson.edu

Degree offered: BS in Technical Communications

Clarkson University offers the BS degree in Technical Communications. There is also the opportunity to pursue an interdisciplinary writing minor in conjunction with this or other degree programs.

For more information, contact Joseph Duemer at the above address, phone, or e-mail.

❖Cleveland State University
RT 1814
Cleveland, OH 44115
(216) 687-4522
FAX (216) 687-6943

Degrees offered: BA, MA

Degree: BA in English with Creative Writing Concentration

Required courses of study: 128 s/hrs total
Writing workshop: 12 s/hrs
Literature: 16 s/hrs minimum

Application Deadlines: Open admissions and applications.

Financial Aid: General University Financial Aid is available to qualifying undergraduates. Application kits may be requested from the Cleveland State University Financial Aid Office each January for the upcoming academic year. In addition, twice annually substantial tuition credit is awarded to student writers through program-sponsored literary competitions.

Undergraduate creative writing majors progress from elementary, general creative writing through the study of at least two specific genres to advanced workshops in a single genre. Through the junior and senior years, they can accumulate a considerable portfolio for application to a graduate writing program.

Degree: MA in English with Creative Writing Concentration and Creative Writing Thesis

Type of Program: Studio/Academic

Length of Residency: Two years

Required course of study: 33 s/hrs total
Thesis: 5 s/hrs
Workshops: 4 s/hrs minimum
Form and Technique: 8 s/hrs minimum
Literature: 8 s/hrs minimum

Other Requirements: Candidates must pass an oral Master's Examination in which they will be expected to relate their work to that of traditional as well as contemporary practitioners in their genre.

Application Deadlines: Open applications; February 1 for financial aid.

This growing program has a strong teaching bias and very accessible faculty. Cleveland State is a large urban university in a rebounding, sometimes turbulent city. Program students are often older, often returning to the university with a wealth and surprising variety of life experience. As a consequence, workshop and course discussions are especially rich and productive. Natural student association and numerous informal working groups augment course work and teacher/student mentoring relationships to foster interchange and energy and, in fact, a remarkable degree of publishing success among our students. Cleveland winters can be bitter; nonetheless, we have a healthy and heartening climate here for ambitious writers.

Cleveland State has an extensive reading series and each year a writing residency. Recent residents and readers have included: Charles Baxter, Diane Wakoski, Richard Garcia, Joanne Greenberg, Phyllis Barber, Belle Waring, William Tremblay, John Nichols, David Foster Wallace, Cornelius Eady, Reginald McKnight, Ruth Stone, Pat Murphy, Tim Seibles, Maureen McHugh, Ron Hansen, Robert Hill Long, Theodore Deppe, Andre Dubus III, Mark Brazaitis, John Thorndike, Jacki Lyden, Joan Connors, Toi Derricotte, Leigh Allison Wilson, and James Patrick Kelly.

The Cleveland State University Poetry Center conducts a major poetry competition and publishes several book-length manuscripts annually in the CSU Poetry Series. In addition, the University publishes *Whiskey Island*, a student sponsored and edited literary magazine which draws on a national audience and is now well into its third decade of publication. Some internships or staff positions are available on these publications.

MA candidates are eligible for both program and English department assistantships, which pay full tuition plus a stipend (of $6,960 for 1990–2000). There are also full and partial tuition scholarships available. Awards are competitive and based initially on 1) portfolio submissions and 2) academic record.

The Creative Writing permanent faculty includes poet Ruth Schwartz (*Accordion Breathing and Dancing*, AWP Poetry Award winner, *The Zenith of Desire*, and *My Lover is a Woman*); poet and nonfiction writer David Evett (*Strange Loops*): poet and librettist Leonard Trawick (*Beast Forms, Severed Parts, Mary Stuart*); poet Alberta Turner, emerita (*Learning to Count, Lid and Spoon, A Belfry of Knees*); fiction writer and novelist Sheila Schwartz (*Imagine a Great White Light*, 1993 National Endowment for the Arts Fellowship, 4 Pushcart Prizes); fiction writer and critic Daniel Melnick (National Endowment for the Humanities Fellowship, Ohio Arts Council Individual Artist Fellowship); fiction writer and playwright Neal Chandler, Director (*Benediction, Appeal to a Lower Court*); fiction writer and critic John Gerlach (Ohio Arts Council Individual Artist Fellowship); and fiction writer and novelist Adrienne Gosselin (winner of the 1989 Raymond Carver Short Story Award).

For further information, write to Neal Chandler, Creative Writing Program Director, Dept. of English.

Colby College
Waterville, ME 04901
(207) 872-3295
FAX (207) 872-3555

Degree offered: BA in English with Concentration in Creative Writing; BA (any major) with minor in Creative Writing (poetry, fiction)

Required course of study: 120 s/hrs total
Literature major: 48 s/hrs beyond composition
Workshops: sequence of 3 (12 s/hrs) plus a 4th course (2 may count towards literature major)
Thesis: up to 12 s/hrs, required for Honors only

Other Requirements: College distribution requirements, language proficiency.

Application Deadlines: January 15 for admissions and financial aid.

Colby College offers a comprehensive creative writing program with two options:

1) The Concentration within the English Major includes a sequence of three workshops in a single genre, an additional workshop in another genre or an independent study in writing, plus twelve courses in literature; three entry-level, four period and genre courses, two special subjects courses, a senior seminar, and two additional upper level literature courses. The advanced writing workshop and independent study course may count toward the literature major.

2) Students in other majors may elect a Creative Writing minor that includes a sequence of three

workshops in a single genre plus a fourth workshop or independent study in writing, and three upper-class literature courses. Workshops are limited to 15-20 students, and advising is on an intensive and individual basis.

The English Department offers prizes for excellence in the writing of poetry and fiction, honors in English for a Creative Writing thesis, and a college-wide year-long Senior Scholar program. *The Pequod* is a campus arts and literary magazine offering experience in editing, layout, and publishing. The Colby College Visiting Writers Series, funded by the college, has 4-6 readings a year by such writers as Edward Albee, Martin Cruz Smith, Grace Paley, Toni Cade Bambara, Alix Kates Shulman, James Tate, Derek Walcott, Lucille Clifton, William Stafford, and Charles Baxter.

The creative writing staff includes: Program Director Susan Kenney, fiction writer (the novels *In Another Country, Sailing, Garden of Malice*); Ira Sadoff, poet and fiction writer (five collections of poetry, most recently *Emotional Traffic* and *A Northern Calendar*, the novel, *Uncoupling*); Program Director, Peter Harris, poet and editor (poems, editor of Poetry Chronicle for *Virginia Quarterly Review*); Richard Russo, fiction writer (novels *Mohawk, The Risk Pool, Nobody's Fool*, past Guggenheim Fellow); and James Finney Boylan, fiction writer (short stories *Remind Me to Murder You Later*, the novels *The Planets, The Constellations*).

For more information, contact Creative Writing Director, English Dept., or Admissions Office.

Colgate University
Hamilton, NY 13346

(315) 824-7262

Degree offered: AB in English

Students may *minor* in creative writing whether they concentrate in English or not. The minor offers courses in the writing of poetry, fiction, and nonfiction.

Required course of study: Minimum of 5 courses selected from among the workshops offered in the three genres. Students must take three such workshops and two literature courses, one of which must be a senior-level seminar.

Application Deadlines: January 15. For transfers, application must be made by November 15 for the Spring term, by March 15 for the Fall.

For more information, contact Frederick Busch, Dept. of English.

❖Colorado College
359 Eddy Hall
Fort Collins, CO 80523-6010

For more information, contact the Director, Dept. of English.

❖Colorado State University
Fort Collins, CO 80523-1773

(970) 491-6428
FAX (970) 491-5601
website: http//www.colostate.edu/Depts/English

Degrees offered: BA in English with Concentration in Creative Writing (poetry, fiction, creative nonfiction); **MFA** (poetry, fiction)

Degree: BA in English with Concentration in Creative Writing

The undergraduate concentration of 18 s/hrs requires the student to take Intro. to Creative Writing and then workshops in fiction, creative nonfiction, and/or poetry. *Greyrock Review* is the undergraduate literary annual, which gives a prize for the best story and best poem published. Each fall the Creative and Performing Arts Scholarship contest is held; awards are given based on the quality of writing rather than need.

Degree: MFA in Creative Writing

Type of Program: Studio/Academic

Length of Residency: Three years for those with TAs; the program may be completed in two years.

Required course of study: 48 s/hrs
Thesis: 12 s/hrs
Writing workshop: 12 s/hrs
Form & Technique in Modern Literature:
  3 s/hrs
Literature courses: 12 s/hrs
Electives: 9 s/hrs

Other Requirements: Written comprehensive examination and oral defense of thesis.

Application Deadline: January 15 for University Graduate Fellowship Awards; February 15 for admission and Graduate Teaching Assistantships.

Our first commitment is to help fiction writers and poets develop by offering useful commentary on their writing through workshops and thesis tutorials and by creating an active writers' community.

Visiting writers in recent years have included Lucille Clifton, Joy Harjo, Yusef Komunyakaa, C.K. Williams, Gretel Ehrlich, Carlos Fuentes, Gwendolyn Brooks, Carole Maso, Sharon Olds, Jorie Graham, James Galvin, Li-Young Lee, Charles Johnson, Charles Baxter, and Alison Lurie.

We offer a variety of for-credit internships in such areas as college teaching, literary editing, public education, and arts administration in literature. MFA candidates are offered an opportunity to teach Introduction to Creative Writing. *The Colorado Review* provides opportunities for graduate students to learn the process of editing a literary magazine.

The writing faculty includes: Leslee Becker, fiction (*The Sincere Cafe*); John Calderazzo, fiction and creative nonfiction (*Writing From Scratch: Freelancing*); Mary Crow, poetry and translation (*I Have Tasted the Apple, Going Home, Vertical Poetry: Recent Poems of Roberto Juarrez*); David Milofsky, fiction (*Eternal People*, novel; *Playing from Memory*, novel); Laura Mullen, poetry and fiction (*The Tales of Horror, After I Was Dead, The Surface* [winner, National Poetry Series]); John Clark Pratt, fiction (*The Laotian Fragments*, novel; *Vietnam Voices*, collage; *Writing from Scratch: The Essay*); Steven Schwartz, fiction (*A Good Doctor's Son*, novel; *Therapy*, novel; *Lives of the Fathers*); Bill Tremblay, poetry (*The Anarchist Heart, Second Sun: New & Selected Poems, Duhamel*).

Financial aid available: Teaching Assistantships and Fellowships.

For more information contact Director, Creative Writing Program, English Dept.

❖University of Colorado, Boulder
Box 226
Boulder, CO 80309-0226
(303) 492-7922

Degrees offered: BA, MA

Degree: BA in English with Emphasis in Creative Writing

Required course of study:
    Creative writing: 18 s/hrs
    Literature: 18 s/hrs

Degree: MA in English with Emphasis in Creative Writing

Type of Program: Studio/Academic

Length of Residency: Usually two years

Required course of study: 30 s/hrs
    Creative writing workshops: 8 s/hrs
    Literature: 6 s/hrs
    Studies in Poetry, Fiction, or Modernism
        (2 of these): 6 s/hrs
    Electives: 6 s/hrs
    Thesis: 4 s/hrs

Application Deadlines: January 2 for manuscripts; February 1 for balance of materials.

Offering workshops in fiction, poetry, playwriting, screenwriting, creative nonfiction, and publication production, Colorado has a faculty of diverse and productive practitioners whose works range from the ethnocentric and avant-garde to the traditional.

Practical editorial and production training is offered through the program's publication of the literary journal *Sniper Logic*. Teaching assistantships and manuscript awards totaling several thousands of dollars are available on a competitive basis.

Boulder is a crossroads-center of American literary activity and many of the country's most intriguing writers visit the community to take in its unique mix of Rocky Mountain habitat and cultural energy. More than a few live here, some permanently, some occasionally.

The faculty includes Lucia Berlin, Lorna Dee Cervantes, Sidney Goldfarb, Linda Hogan, Steve Katz, Bruce Kawin, Marilyn Krysl, Peter Michelson, Reg Saner, Ron Sukenick, and a visiting writer.

For additional information and application materials, contact the Creative Writing Program.

University of Colorado, Colorado Springs
Colorado Springs, CO 80933-7150
(719) 593-3477

The Dept. of English primarily offers a Creative Writing track toward the undergraduate major and BA degree. There is one fiction-writing workshop per semester and occasionally a poetry workshop. Independent study is also available to undergraduate and postgraduate students of proven ability. The Department is also committed to providing professional help to non-degree-seeking writers in the Colorado Springs community.

Among successful students who have been recommended to graduate programs elsewhere are Yusef Komunyakaa (author of numerous books of poetry) and Michael Pettit (whose *Peacekeepers at War* was written in one of the workshops).

Dr. Alexander Blackburn, critic and novelist (*A Sunrise Brighter Still, The Cold War of Kitty Pentacost*), teaches fiction writing and edits *Writers' Forum*, a nationally acclaimed literary magazine founded in 1974. Poetry workshops are taught by Dr. Janice Hays. Theatreworks, directed by Murray Ross, encourages original work through its annual Playwrights Forum.

For more information, contact the Dept. of English.

University of Colorado, Denver
Denver, CO 80204
(303) 556-8304

Degree offered: BA in General Writing

Required course of study: 120 s/hrs in the major

The Bachelor of Arts degree in General Writing combines a rich undergraduate liberal arts education with a wide range of intensive writing experiences, including such areas as fiction and poetry, as well as expository and technical writing. The General Writing major will prepare you to think critically, read carefully, solve problems creatively, and write with clarity, grace, and power. These are the qualities you'll need to succeed as a writer when faced with diverse writing challenges in a variety of settings, whether on the job or in school. You can't predict, before graduation, the writing tasks you'll face; but as a General Writing major, you'll be prepared to take on these tasks confidently -- and do them well.

You may choose electives as you wish. However, many General Writing majors use these elective credits to complement and strengthen their major program by taking a double major (30-40 credits) or a minor (15-18 credits) in another area. Minors are particularly recommended as good ways to enhance your writing degree. If you're interested in technical writing, for example, you might acquire a computer science minor; if you're interested in a career in public relations, you might consider a minor in psychology; or if you think you might want to go to graduate school in English, you might minor in English literature.

An internship provides on-the-job experiences which complement and extend your academic experiences. General Writing interns work both full and part-time in such fields as public relations, magazine writing, technical writing, advertising, radio and TV programming, government research, journalism, and documentary film. Some internships are paid positions; others aren't. But all award academic elective credits (up to 12 permitted) that apply toward your degree. Since you can work as an intern in a variety of different positions while you're in school, it's a good way to find out about various careers while enhancing your resume with work experiences. For more information, contact the CU-Denver Center for Internships and Cooperative Education.

For more information on the degree in General Writing, contact Director of Writing Programs, Dept. of English, Box 175, P.O. Box 173364, Denver, CO 80217-3364.

❖Columbia College
Fiction Writing Department
600 S. Michigan Avenue
Chicago, IL 60605-1996
(312) 663-1600, ext. 5611

Degrees offered: BA, MA, MFA

Degree: BA in Creative Writing (fiction)

Type of Program: Studio/Academic

Required course of study: 44 s/hrs for the major
Thesis: no requirement
Writing workshops: 24 s/hrs
Critical Reading and Writing courses: 12 s/hrs
Elective/Specialty writing: 8-12 s/hrs

Other requirements: Minors in Fiction Writing; interdisciplinary minors in Playwriting, Creative Nonfiction.

Application Deadlines: September for fall semester; February for spring semester.

Degree: MFA in Creative Writing (fiction, creative nonfiction, playwriting)

Type of Program: Studio/Academic

Length of Residency: Two years

Required course of study: 42 s/hrs total
Thesis: 6 s/hrs
Writing workshops: 24-27 s/hrs
Critical Reading and Writing courses: 9-12 s/hrs
electives

Degree: MA in Teaching of Writing

Type of Program: Studio/Academic

Length of Residency: Two years

Required course of study: 36 s/hrs total
Thesis: 3 s/hrs (one part fiction and one part pedagogical research)

Teaching Methods: 3 s/hrs
Writing workshops: 18 s/hrs
Practice teaching and tutoring: 9 s/hrs
Critical Reading and Writing courses: 3 s/hrs
(or electives in Language Issues in the Classroom or Sociolinguistics)

Degree: Combined Degree (MFA in Creative Writing and MA in Teaching of Writing)

Type of Program: Studio/Academic

Length of Residency: Three years

Required course of study: All requirements for the MA in the Teaching of Writing (36 s/hrs) plus:
Thesis: 6 additional s/hrs
Writing workshops: 9 additional s/hrs
Critical Reading and Writing courses: 9 s/hrs

Application Deadlines: For all graduate programs -- December 4 for spring semester. August 15 for fall semester. Early admission deadline for fall semester March 15. (Early application for fall is strongly encouraged.) Financial aid application deadlines: Dwight Follett Fellowships, mid-March; Graduate Opportunity Grants, mid-April; Getz Fellowships, February 1.

Full-tuition Dwight Follett Fellowships are available for selected MFA, MA, and combined MFA/MA applicants with outstanding credentials. In addition, the Graduate School offers competitive Graduate Opportunity Grants on a school-wide basis.

We use the Story Workshop approach, originated by John Schultz, as the core approach in the Fiction Writing area.

Over the past decade, *Hair Trigger*, our nationally acclaimed, annually published anthology of graduate and undergraduate writing, has received numerous awards. *Hair Trigger 17* won a first place Gold Crown award from the Columbia University Scholastic Press Association (CSPA). *Hair Trigger 14* won two top national awards: the Associated Writing Programs (AWP) Directors' Prize, and a CSPA first prize Gold Crown award. First-place Gold Circle awards for traditional fiction, experimental fiction, and magazine essay were given to individual writers in *Hair Trigger 19*, which also won a Silver Crown award and a Gold Medalist Certificate.

Our students, publications, faculty, and alumni are renowned for the awards and prizes they receive, including the 1987 National Book Award. Over the past 20 years, our students have won AWP *Intro* Awards. Most recently, our students swept all three places in the CSPA fiction awards, and captured the $5,000 first-place award in the *Ebony* magazine national competition for emerging writers of African-American descent, first prize in the Illinois Science Fiction in Chicago Competition, a first prize for fiction from the National Society of Arts and Letters, and *Red Rock Review*'s Mark Twain Award for Short Fiction. *Intro* Award fiction from our students has appeared in the *Indiana Review* and *Puerto del Sol*. Students are frequently singled out and recognized by editors, agents, and contest judges for writing published in *Hair Trigger* and other nationally known magazines, journals, and newspapers. Students have published nonfiction books, sold film and television scripts, had plays produced, and won recognition in many professional endeavors, including nomination for a regional Emmy award.

Graduates of the graduate and undergraduate programs in Creative Writing receive, in our Story Workshop and specialty writing classes, training in imaginative problem solving and writing that is centrally helpful in a variety of professional areas. Students have been able to use their training and their writing skills to get and advance in jobs in trade magazines and other forms of publishing, newspaper and TV/radio reporting, advertising, software writing, how-to writing, scriptwriting, and so on. They have also used their heightened ability to do important writing in fields as diverse as psychiatry, law, banking, social work, personnel, and insurance, among others, and to support entrepreneurial efforts.

In the Story Workshop approach, acceptance of the student's voice and background is crucial. The method helps the students find the all-important connections between their unique voice and the full range of fictional/factual/scientific/rhetorical modes and forms. These connections are continually developed in a series of Fiction Writing, Prose Forms, and specialty writing courses of increasing demand. The term "voice" *begins* with the meeting of physical speech and seeing in the mind, and goes on to include all the possibilities of fully developed writing expression.

Candidates for the MFA in Creative Writing, MA in the Teaching of Writing, and combined MFA/MA degree complete a book-length work of publishable fiction (novel, or combination of short stories, novellas, creative nonfiction, and/or drama) and attend Thesis Development workshops. In addition to core workshops, we offer elective courses in scriptwriting, playwriting, writing for children, creative nonfiction, science fiction, popular fiction, etc., plus tutor training, practice teaching, and methods courses in the Story Workshop approach to the teaching of writing. We also offer a variety of Critical Reading and Writing courses, developing broad, contextual, cutting-edge training in writer-oriented new historical approaches. Primary emphasis in the program rests on the production of original fiction.

The quality and kind of teacher training developed in the Teaching of Writing program is valued by other institutions, colleges, and graduate programs. Beverlye Brown of Maplewoods Community College in Kansas City said, "Story Workshop teacher training gives not simply a theory that describes the process of writing, but also sequentially developed methodology and practice that actually enable students to generate writing, from the first draft through a carefully edited finished product. The classroom experience of the Story Workshop approach stimulates real excitement with students of all levels and backgrounds."

Internships in jobs with writing-related skills are frequently available to advanced Fiction Writing students. Students have the opportunity to work as editors for *Hair Trigger* and to participate in readings and other literary events. Seed money from the Columbia College Albert Weisman Fellowships and from the Fiction Writing Department has enabled our creative writing students to found literary magazines which are having an impact in Chicago and around the country -- *Private Arts, Hyphen, Sport Literate*, and *Emergence*, and the *Solo!* and *Private Arts* reading series, important parts of the vibrant Chicago literary scene. Career Nights bring back alumni who talk about how they got their jobs and advanced in their jobs in such areas as advertising, trade journalism, newspaper journalism, scriptwriting for television, film, radio, and technical writing, and other jobs in which writing and creative problem-solving are centrally important.

Through the Writer-in-Residence Program, MFA and MA students have an opportunity for informal conversation and manuscript conferencing with such well-known writers and scholars as National Book Award winner Charles Johnson, Joyce Carol Oates, Ana Castillo, Jane Hamilton, Nawal El Saadawi, Scott Heim, John Edgar Wideman, Paule Marshall, Rosellen Brown, Scott Russell Sanders, Hubert Selby, Jr., James Alan McPherson, David Bradley, Cyrus Colter, Harry Mark Petrakis, Louise Meriwether, Douglas Unger, Hugh Holton, Joanne Leedom-Ackerman, Ted Solotaroff, Wesley Brown, C. Michael Curtis, and William Labov. Our "Noontime Conversations With the Author" and public readings are Chicago institutions.

Writing faculty includes: Randall Albers, chair of the program, writer, critic, co-writer and producer of videotapes on the teaching of writing, *The Living Voice Moves* and *Story From First Impulse to Final Draft*. John Schultz, Professor Emeritus and originator of the Story Workshop approach, author of the recently published *The Chicago Conspiracy Trial, Writing From Start to Finish*, and *The Tongues of Men*. Betty Shiflett, Professor Emeritus, writer, Illinois Arts Council Fellowship Award, author of *We Dream of Tours* (play), and *Phantom Rider* (music drama). Andrew Allegretti, writer, numerous Illinois Arts Council Artists Fellowship Awards. Shawn Shiflett, Coordinator of Faculty Development, writer, Illinois Arts Council Fellowship in 1985. Gary Johnson, writer, winner of the Edwin L. Schuman Award for Fiction, Northwestern University; writer and producer of award-winning public radio creative nonfiction documentaries *Gramma Elsie* and *Oak Park: The Integration Challenge*. Ann Hemenway, writer, editor, fiction and creative nonfiction in *Writing From Start to Finish, Private Arts, Emergence*, and other magazines; AWP *Intro* award winner; editor of specialty magazines. Eric Charles May, former news reporter and staff writer for *The Washington Post* (1987-91); fiction in *Angels In My Oven* and *Fish Stories*. Polly Mills, writer, AWP Intro Award winner for fiction. Patty Lewis, writer fiction and creative nonfiction, Columbia Scholastic Press Award winner for fiction. Don Gennaro DeGrazia, writer, journalist, author of *American Skin* and film of same name, scripted by Dan Yost (*Drugstore Cowboy*), managing editor *E Magazine*. Wade Roberts, creative nonfiction writer/editor, multimedia studies, creator and director of *Seasons of Grief: The Bereavement Project* on the World Wide Web.

For more information, contact Chair, Fiction Writing Dept.

❖**Columbia College**
Poetry & Professional Writing Program
600 Michigan Avenue
Chicago, IL 60605
(312) 344-8100
FAX (312) 344-8001

Degree offered: BA with a Minor in Creative Writing in Poetry, BA in Professional Writing

For more information, contact Garnett Kilberg Cohen, Dept. of English.

Columbia College
Columbia, SC 29202

(803) 786-3633

Degree offered: BA in English, Communication-Arts Concentration

For more information, write Chair, Dept. of English.

❖Columbia University
School of the Arts
Writing Division
2960 Broadway, Room 415
New York, NY 10027

(212) 854-4391
FAX (212) 854-7704
e-mail: writing@columbia.edu
website: http://www.columbia.edu/cu/arts

Degree offered: MFA in Creative Writing (fiction, poetry, nonfiction) Columbia University also offers undergraduate classes through Columbia College and the School of General Studies; please see next listing.

Type of Program: Studio/Academic

Length of Residency: Two years

Required course of study: 60 s/hrs
    Writing workshops: A minimum of 18 s/hrs
    Writing seminars and lectures : A minimum of 24 s/hrs
    Electives: 12–18 s/hrs

Other requirements: Thesis; foreign language at intermediate college level.

Application Deadlines: January 4 for fall admission; February 7 for financial aid.

The Writing Division of the Columbia University School of the Arts is a creative community of master teachers and gifted student writers. In the 30 years since it was founded in 1968, it has attracted many celebrated writers as teachers, students, and guests. Its graduates have become novelists, short story writers, poets, nonfiction writers, translators, editors, publishers, critics, and teachers, and many of their thesis projects have appeared as published books.

The Division believes that writing is an intensely individual conjunction of many conscious and unconscious forces, but a writer can accomplish much through consciously perfecting his or her craft in a community of fellow artists who comfort, challenge, stimulate, and support. The Division avoids cults of personality and formulas for success and does not favor any particular aesthetic, ideology, style, or genre. It is dedicated to helping each student find and develop a distinct voice and vision.

The Division draws full upon the cultural and intellectual resources of Columbia University and New York City. As the publishing and arts center of the country, New York provides writers with opportunities and experiences not available elsewhere. The Division regularly invites writers, editors, publishers, agents, and other literary professionals to participate in seminars, lectures, panels, and informal discussions. Recent guests have included Charles Baxter, Paul Berman, Frank Bidart, Sven Birkerts, Peter Carey, Ethan Canin, Nicholas Delbanco, Joan Didion, Mark Doty, John Gregory Dunne, Jonathan Franzen, Louise Glück, Rebecca Goldstein, Linda Gregg, Patricia Hampl, Kathryn Harrison, Robert Hass, Seamus Heaney, A.M. Homes, Denis Johnson, Fenton Johnson, Donald Justice, Mary Karr, Randall Kenan, Karl Kirchwey, Brad Leithauser, Janet Malcolm, Thomas Mallon, Jaime Manrique, Brad Morrow, Campbell McGrath, Caryl Phillips, Darryl Pinckney, Robert Pinsky, Marie Ponsot, Richard Powers, David Remnick, Francine Prose, Luc Sante, Le Anne Schreiber, Lore Segal, Charles Simic, Susan Sontag, Mark Strand, Helen Vendler, Derek Walcott, and C.K. Williams.

The Division's current faculty in fiction includes Magda Bogin (*Natalya, God's Messenger,* and translator of Isabel Allende's *The House of the Spirits*), Nicholas Christopher (*Veronica, A Trip to the Stars, The Soloist*), Michael Cunningham (*The Hours, Flesh and Blood, A Home at the End of the World*), Mary Gordon (*Spending, Men and Angels, Final Payments*), Jessica Hagedorn (*The Gangster of Love, Dogeaters, Charlie Chan Is Dead: An Anthology of Contemporary Asian American Fiction*), Maureen Howard (*A Lover's Almanac, Natural History, Expensive Habits*), Binnie Kirshenbaum (*On Mermaid Avenue, A Disturbance in One Place, History on a Personal Note*), Martha McPhee (*Bright Angel Time*), Sigrid Nunez (*Naked Sleeper, A Feather on the Breath of God, Mitz: The Marmoset of Bloomsbury*), David Plante (*The Ghost of Henry James, The Family, The Accident*), Helen Schulman (*The Revisionist, Not a Free Show, Out of Time*) and Dani Shapiro (*Slow Motion, Picturing the Wreck, Fugitive Blue*).

In poetry the Division's current faculty includes Lucie Brock-Broido (*The Master Letters, A Hunger*), Alfred Corn (*Present, Autobiographies, A Call in the Midst of the Crowd*), Richard Howard (*Like Most Revelations, No Traveller, Alone with America*), Rika Lesser (*Etruscan Things, All We Need of Hell*), and Alice Quinn (poetry editor of *The New Yorker*).

The Division's current nonfiction faculty includes Lis Harris (*Rules of Engagement, Holy Days: The World of a Hasidic Family*), Richard Locke (former deputy editor of *The New York Times Book Review*, founding editor of the new *Vanity Fair*, and frequent reviewer for *The Wall Street Journal* and other publications), Patricia O'Toole (*Money and Morals in America: A History, The Five of Hearts: An Intimate Portrait of Henry Adams and His Friends*), and Michael Scammell (*Solzhenitsyn, A Biography*, and translator of Nabokov's *The Defense* and *The Gift*).

Notable alumni include Jonathan Ames, Sophia Cabot Black, Lucie Brock-Broido, Henri Cole, Camilla T. Crespi, Patty Dann, Michael Drinkard, Jill Eisenstadt, Suzanne Fox, Suzanne Gardinier, Daniel Halpern, Marie Howe, Tama Janowitz, Tom Jenks, Cynthia Kadohata, Nancy Lemann, Stephen McCauley, Campbell McGrath, Musa Mayer, Susan Minot, Rick Moody, Fae Myenne Ng, Craig Nova, Sigrid Nunez, Gregory Orr, Vince Passaro, Leila Philip, Katha Pollitt, Richard Price, Anna Rabinowitz, Mark Rudman, Valerie Sayers, Helen Schulman, John Scieszka, Mona Simpson, Matthew Stadler, Sandra Tyler, Kim Wozencraft, and Cynthia Zarin.

Some of the Division's most recent alumni -- Charlotte Bacon, Mary Jo Bang, Thomas Beller, Robert Bingham, Valerie Block, Meghan Daum, Kiran Desai, Amanda Filipacchi, Emily Fragos, Philip Gourevitch, Joanna Greenfield, Scott Heim, Martha McPhee, Tom Paine, Dale Peck, Brenda Shaughnessy, Elizabeth Shepard, Michael Sledge, and Scott Smith -- have had unusually well-received publishing debuts. Current students' manuscripts regularly win national prizes and appear in magazines of all kinds from *The New Yorker*, *The Paris Review*, and *The New York Times Book Review* to zines and on-line publications, and in both hardback and paperback editions.

The Writing Division offers a 60-point course of study leading to the Master of Fine Arts (MFA) degree, a terminal degree, with concentrations in fiction, poetry, and literary nonfiction. The program consists of an interconnected system of workshops, seminars, and lectures created by writers for writers. Workshops of eight to twelve students in these concentrations, as well as in literary translation, are intense, detailed editorial discussions of current student work. The second-year thesis workshops offer instruction in the planning, development, and completion of a full-length manuscript. The Division's seminars and lectures complement the workshops and study literature from a practitioner's perspective, not that of a scholar or theorist, to learn how a wide variety of writers have confronted and resolved characteristic problems throughout literary history. Master classes are seminars composed of three four-session segments taught by visiting instructors of special expertise. Nonfiction master classes have been offered on the review, the profile, the interview, the memoir, political writing, editing techniques, and research methods. Fiction master classes have been offered on creating a character's voice, using landscape in fiction, and the comic short story. Students enroll in a workshop and two seminars or lectures in the Division each semester. The balance of their program can be filled by courses in the Film, Theatre, and Visual Arts Divisions of the School of the Arts and in other departments of the Graduate School of Arts and Sciences at Columbia University. At the end of their residency in the program, students submit a thesis project consisting of a minimum of 35 pages of poetry or 150 pages of prose.

The Division also offers its students an opportunity to edit, manage, and publish their own magazine, *Columbia: A Journal of Literature and Art*.

In addition to loans, work-study packages, and a select number of scholarships available to all School of the Arts students, Writing Division students are eligible for fellowships awarded by the Division's faculty and, in their second year, for teaching assistantships in the Columbia College Composition Program. Current students serve as interns at magazines such as *The New Yorker*, *The Paris Review*, *Grand Street*, and *Parnassus*, and at literary organizations such as PEN American Center, The Poetry Society of America, The Academy of American Poets, and Teachers and Writers Collaborative. Some twenty students a year teach creative writing to public high school students in the Liberty Partnership Project at the Bank Street College of Education. Students are also able to work as research assistants to writers who also serve as mentors, such as Paul Berman, Peter Carey, Kathryn Harrison, A.M. Homes, Phillip Lopate, Rick Moody, Francine Prose, and Anna Quindlen.

All inquiries should be directed to Writing Division,

Columbia University School of the Arts, 2960 Broadway, Room 415, Columbia University, New York, NY 10027, or by e-mail to writing@columbia.edu.

❖Columbia University Undergraduate and Nondegree Writing Creative Writing Center
2970 Broadway, Suite 612
Mail Code 4108
New York, NY 10027
(212) 854-3774
e-mail: writingprogram@columbia.edu

Degree offered: BA
Also offered is a University Statement for nondegree students completing four writing courses (12 points)
(For information on Columbia's MFA in Creative Writing, please see previous listing.)

Columbia University offers undergraduate workshops in fiction, poetry, literary nonfiction, playwriting, filmwriting, and journalism, as well as courses in literary publishing. Degree candidates in the School of General Studies may work toward a BA with a major in Literature-Writing or a minor in Writing; degree candidates at Columbia College may take a sequence of creative writing and related courses in conjunction with a major or concentration.

Nondegree students may enroll in undergraduate writing courses through the Special Students Program; although the courses carry undergraduate credit, most nondegree students already have Bachelor's degrees. Working side-by-side with Columbia degree candidates, nondegree students are part of the mainstream of Columbia's academic life.

Columbia University has a remarkable tradition in the teaching of creative writing; since 1909, tens of thousands of undergraduate and nondegree students have studied writing with Columbia's distinguished faculty. Among the notable writers who have taught here are Pearl S. Buck, Lillian Hellman, J.R. Humphreys, Stanley Kunitz, Susan Sontag, Grace Paley, Spalding Gray, A.R. Gurney, Bharati Mukherjee, Phillip Lopate, Romulus Linney, and Terry Southern.

Some former Columbia writing students who went on to noted literary careers are Paul Gallico, Carson McCullers, J.D. Salinger, Richard Yates, Evan S. Connell, Jr., and Mario Puzo. Recent students who have published include Joe Connelly, Kelvin Christopher James, Joseph Ferrandino, Patricia Volk, William Tester, Binnie Kirshenbaum, Elizabeth Tippens, Nahid Rachlin, Dick Scanlan, and Kim Wozencraft.

Various activities and publications -- including the Writers Club, Columbia Dramatists, and *Quarto* magazine -- enable students to become part of a community of writers. Recently these groups have hosted readings and full productions of student plays; readings by students, instructors, and guest writers; visits by editors and agents; and the Story Behind the Book series of panel discussions in which faculty members share their experiences of writing and publishing their works.

Instructors are drawn from New York's literary community and bring a rich store of experience to the classroom; they work with students in small classes and individual conferences. The faculty have won awards and fellowships from the National Endowment for the Arts, Guggenheim Foundation, Rockefeller Foundation, Ingram–Merrill Foundation, Whiting Foundation, the New York Foundation for the Arts, the American Academy and Institute of Arts and Letters, and the Poetry Society of America. Other awards received include an Oscar, Obie, and Bollingen Prize.

The current faculty in fiction includes Thomas Beller (*Seduction Theory*), Nicholas Christopher (*The Soloist, Veronica*), Jill Ciment (*Small Claims, The Law of Falling Bodies, Half a Life*), Michael Cunningham (*Flesh and Blood, A Home at the End of the World*), Colin Harrison (*Bodies Electric, Break and Enter, Manhattan Nocturne*), A.M. Homes (*In a Country of Mothers, The End of Alice, Jack*), Raymond Kennedy (*The Bitterest Age, Ride a Cockhorse, Lulu Incognito*), Sigrid Nunez (*A Feather on the Breath of God, Naked Sleeper, Mitz: The Marmoset of Bloomsbury*), Lucy Rosenthal (*The Ticket Out*), Dani Shapiro (*Playing With Fire, Fugitive Blue, Picturing the Wreck*), and Alan Ziegler (*The Green Grass of Flatbush, So Much To Do*).

In poetry the current faculty includes Meena Alexander (*The Storm, River and Bridge*), Nicholas Christopher (*In the Year of the Comet*), and Colette Inez (*The Woman Who Loved Worms, Alive and Taking Names, New and Selected Poems*).

Nonfiction instructors include John Bowers (*Chickamauga and Chattanooga, The Golden Bowers, In the Land of Nyx: Night and its Inhabitants*), Fenton Johnson (*Geography of the Heart; Scissors, Paper, Rock*), Bernard Lefkowitz (*Our Guys: The Glen Ridge Rape Case and the Secret Life of the Perfect Suburb, Tough Change: Growing Up on Your Own in America*), Nora Sayre (*Sixties Going on Seventies, Running Time: Films of the Cold War, Previous Convictions: A Journey Through the 1950's*), Lawrence Van Gelder (journalist with *The New York Times*), and Kal Wagenheim (editor of *Caribbean Update* and *Mexico Business Monthly* newsletters).

Playwrights and screenwriters include Loren Paul Caplin (*The Forbidden Zone, Battle in the Erogenous Zone*), Edward Pomerantz (*Caught*), Austin Flint (*Prison Light, Just War, Charity Royall*), Tony Gerber (*Side Streets*), Eduardo Machado (*Floating Islands, Once Removed, Stevie Wants to Play the Blues*), and Robert Montgomery (*Subject to Fits, Ezekiel, Genesis*).

Instructors who teach Structure & Style (the writing of poetry, fiction, and drama) include Glenda Adams (*Games of the Strong, Dancing on Coral, Longleg*), Austin Flint, Martha McPhee (*Bright Angel Time*), Donna Masini (*That Kind of Danger, About Yvonne*), Phyllis Raphael (*They Got What They Wanted*), Louise Rose (*The Launching of Barbara Fabrikant*), Matthew Sharpe (*Stories From the Tube*), Susan Thames (*As Much As I Know, I'll Be Home Late Tonight*), Sandra Tyler (*Blue Glass, After Lydia*), and Dale Worsley (*The Focus Changes of August Previco, Cold Harbor*).

Leslie Sharpe (*Editing Fact and Fiction: A Concise Guide to Book Editing*) teaches courses in editing and publishing.

The prerequisite for all classes is a college-level composition course or the equivalent. Instructors are available before or after class for individual conferences. Admission to all courses requires instructor

approval, generally after submission of a writing sample. For registration information please call (212) 854-3774.

The following courses are currently offered. *Structure & Style I* and *II*: The writing of fiction, poetry, and plays for the beginning or advanced writer. This is the suggested preparation for all other courses. *Short Prose Forms*: Short–short fiction, prose poems, and personal essays. *Narrative Forms*: An intermediate fiction workshop, with an emphasis on narrative development. *Tactics of Fiction*: An intermediate fiction workshop, with an emphasis on revision and editing. *Fiction Workshop*: An advanced workshop. *Free Verse and Poetic Forms*: An intermediate poetry workshop. *Poetry Workshop*: An advanced workshop. *News and Feature Writing*: Spot news, interviews, columns, reviews, and feature stories. *Magazine and Feature Writing*: Extended newspaper features, magazine articles, and investigative pieces. *Cultural Criticism*: Focus on the critical voice; writing about the arts, media, and/or other aspects of culture, such as politics or sports. *Creative Nonfiction Workshop*: Journalistic narrative, autobiography, and biography. *Playwriting*: An intermediate workshop. *Playwriting Workshop*: For advanced playwrights. *Filmwriting*: An intermediate workshop. *Filmwriting Workshop*: For advanced screenwriters. *The Author and the Manuscript*: The mechanics and strategies of editing one's own work and the work of others. *Literary Editing and Publishing*: The step–by–step procedures in publishing *Quarto*, a literary magazine.

For further information, contact the Creative Writing Center. (Please specify if you are interested in attending Columbia as a nondegree student or if you are interested in working toward a BA at Columbia College or the School of General Studies.)

❖Concordia College
Moorhead, MN 56562
(218) 299-3812

Degree offered: BA in English with Concentration in Literature, Writing, English Education

Required course of study: All three concentrations require 8 courses within the major (a 1-credit course at Concordia is the equivalent of a 4-s/hr course elsewhere). 31.5 total courses are required for graduation.

Other Requirements: College distribution requirements.

Application Deadlines: Ongoing. Suggested deadline for financial aid is April 1.

Concordia College is a liberal arts college of the Evangelical Lutheran Church in America. We are dedicated to the principles of a liberal arts education, particularly the development of a broad base of knowledge and experience.

The writing major within the English Department was substantially revised in 1990 and features many opportunities for students to develop substantial manuscripts at the undergraduate level. Fiction, poetry, and nonfiction each have senior-level seminar/workshops as well as junior-level introductory courses.

Concordia College provides a great many opportunities for students to gain practical experience in writing and editing. The college's newspaper, yearbook, and literary journal are each entirely student edited and staffed -- and each boasts a number of important awards won.

Recent writers and editors on campus include the editors of *The Kenyon Review*, *The New England Review*, *The Atlantic*, *Viking Books*, *Willow Springs*, etc., and writers Bret Lott, Rick Bass, William Kloefkorn, Andrea Barrett, Gillian Conoley and many others.

All members of the faculty are working writers. Recent faculty work has appeared in numerous journals.

For more information, contact the English Dept.

Concordia University
1455 de Maisonneuve Blvd. W.
Montreal, Quebec H3G 1M8
(514) 848-2342 undergraduate
(514) 848-2344 graduate
FAX (514) 848-4501
e-mail: englsgw@vaxz.concordia.ca
website: http://artsci-ccwin.concordia.ca

Degrees offered: BA, MA

Degree: BA, Major in Creative Writing, and BA, Honors in English and Creative Writing

Required course of study: 42 credits Major, 60 credits Honors

Degree: BA, Joint Specialization in Playwriting (English and Theater)

Required course of study: 60 credits in playwriting

Degree: MA in English Literature with Creative Writing Option

Type of Program: Studio/Academic

Length of Residency: Minimum of two years -- 45 credits

The English Department at Concordia University has been offering its Creative Writing Program for well over two decades. The success of the Program is largely due to the unique community of practicing writers of which the student becomes an active member. It includes a permanent faculty of poets, playwrights, and fiction writers with national and international reputations, a dedicated and highly qualified staff of part-time instructors, and a distinguished writer-in-residence as animator and resource person.

The Program has evolved over the years, adding new areas of specialization and expanding others. Thus we now offer, in addition to the traditional genres, advanced workshops in scriptwriting for all the media, and in the fields of editing, publishing, and literary translation. To playwrights, we offer a unique opportunity in our Specialization in Creative Writing and Theater.

The Program is enriched by special workshops, colloquia, and a series of Writers' Readings. Also, we have established "The Irving Layton Award for Creative Writing" at the undergraduate level and "The David McKeen Award" at the graduate level to encourage and reward excellence among our writing students.

The full-time faculty includes Robert Allen, Terence Byrnes, Mary di Michele, Gary Geddes, and Richard Sommer. The part-time faculty includes Michel Choquette, Linda Ghan, P. Scott Lawrence, S. Luxton, and R. Majzels.

For further information, contact Sharon Frank, Assistant to the Coordinator, Creative Writing Program, Dept. of English, at the address above.

❖Connecticut College
New London, CT 06320
(860) 439-2350

Degree offered: BA in English with Concentration in Creative Writing (fiction or poetry)

Concentrators must complete the ten courses required for the English major, including the introductory course and advanced seminar in either poetry or fiction writing. Students elect two additional writing courses; among the four courses, fiction writers may substitute one poetry course, and poets one fiction course. Selected students may be eligible for Honors work in creative writing.

For more information contact: Prof. Charles Hartman or Prof. Blanche McCrary Boyd, Co-Directors of Creative Writing Program, Dept. of English.

❖University of Connecticut
Storrs, CT 06269-1025
FAX (860) 486-1530

Degrees offered: BA, MA, PhD

Degree: BA in English with Concentration in Creative Writing (Poetry, Fiction, Creative Nonfiction)

The English Department offers a Certificate of Concentration in Creative Writing to those students who have taken four or more courses in creative writing and/or related courses. (See course offerings listed below.) A student fulfilling requirements for the Concentration will receive a letter of certification from the English Department following graduation. This letter of certification will help students seeking employment in editing, publishing, advertising, and other book or magazine-related fields. The Concentration in Creative Writing will also benefit students seeking a degree in creative writing at the graduate school level.

Required course of study: All students wishing to fulfill the requirements for a Concentration in Creative Writing must take English 146 and a minimum of twelve credits from among the following:

A minimum of two creative writing workshops in English 246 (Poetry) or English 247 (Prose -- fiction or creative nonfiction). English 246 and English 247 can be repeated once for credit.

A minimum of one of the following: English 211 -- Modern British and American Poetry; English 212 -- The Modern Novel; or English 216 -- The Short Story.

English 248W and English 249W are electives. English 248W, Writing Tutorial, must be taken in conjunction with either English 246 or English 247. English 248W provides students with an opportunity to read and write critical papers on literary texts in their field of creative interest. English 249W, Advanced Expository Writing, offers students an opportunity to write and analyze essays, usually on topics related to the students' individual interests and needs. (Courses required for a Concentration in Creative Writing are independent of those required for the English Major.)

Other Requirements: 4 related courses outside the major; college-wide language and area requirements.

Degree: MA in English (Poetry, Fiction, Creative Non-fiction)

Type of Program: Studio/Academic

Required course of study: Either 15 s/hrs plus MA thesis, or 24 s/hrs plus MA exam.

Other Requirements: If elected, creative thesis (poetry, fiction, creative nonfiction).

The University of Connecticut offers annual elective courses in writing that include Creative Writing I and II, Advanced Expository Writing, Writing for Prospective Teachers, and graduate courses in creative writing, rhetoric and composition, and pedagogy. Independent study in writing is available on the graduate and undergraduate levels. The English Department sponsors a publishing course that includes guest speakers; the associated Publishing Practicum teaches professional skills required in the literary marketplace. The endowed Aetna Professorship in Writing and Rhetoric makes possible a variety of innovative programs.

The Department also offers writing internships for undergraduates, which are approved assignments to publication sources, on or off campus, for supervised work. The Benton Museum, the scholarly journal *Children's Literature, The University Chronicle,* The Wadsworth Athenaeum art museum, agricultural publications, and the Greater Hartford Advertising Council are among the participating agencies. As well, the department-sponsored Connecticut Writing Program aids teachers throughout the state.

Prizes for student writing awarded by the department and sponsoring contributors include the Wallace Stevens Awards, funded by the Hartford Insurance Group and presented each spring at a ceremony honoring a visiting poet (Robert Bly in 1990, June Jordan in 1991, and W.S. Merwin in 1992) and student poets; the Hackman Prize for student fiction; and a scholarship for persons interested in careers in advertising, funded by the Greater Hartford Advertising Council.

Faculty include: Wally Lamb, Director (*I Know This Much is True, She's Come Undone*); Lynn Z. Bloom, Aetna Chair in Writing and Rhetoric (*Fact and Artifact: Writing Nonfiction*); Scott Bradfield (*The Secret Life of Houses; Sweet Ladies Good Night, Good Night; The History of Luminous Motion*); Margaret Gibson (*Long Walks in the Afternoon; The Daybooks of Tina Modoff;*

The Vigil); Joan Joffe Hall (*The Rift Zone; Romance & Capitalism at the Movies*); Samuel Pickering, Jr. (*A Continuing Education; The Right Distance; May Days*); Marilyn Nelson Waniek (*The Homeplace; For The Body; Mama's Promises*); and Feenie Ziner (*Within This Wilderness*).

Teaching assistantships, available to first-year graduate students, carry stipends of $8,295 for MA candidates and provide tuition waivers and medical and dental coverage. Lectureships carry similar stipends, without medical benefits or tuition waivers (the latter, however, may be available through the Office of Student Financial Aid). Also available are (1) Connecticut scholarships for state residents, (2) dissertation fellowships, (3) Research Foundation grants for students working on their dissertations, (4) work-study funds, (5) tuition remission. Several prizes are open to graduate students for excellence in teaching.

For more information, contact Joan Joffe Hall, Coordinator of Creative Writing, Dept. of English, U-25.

❖Converse College
580 East Main Street
Spartanburg, SC 29302
(864) 596-9186
e-mail: rick.mulkey@converse.edu
website: http://www.converse.edu

Degree offered: BA in English with Concentration in Creative Writing (poetry, fiction, nonfiction)

Required course of study: 36 s/hrs in the Major
    Writing courses: 15 s/hrs
    Literature courses: 18 s/hrs
    Senior seminar in writing: 3 s/hrs

Application Deadlines: May 1 for Creative Writing Merit Scholarship

Converse College offers a Concentration in Creative Writing within the general English major. Course work culminates in a creative writing senior thesis of 30-40 pages. The student may select from courses in poetry, fiction, nonfiction, and journalism. In addition to introductory and advanced level workshops with the permanent faculty, the student has an opportunity to work on a one-to-one basis with Matthew Self, Distinguished Writer-in-Residence, who visits the campus each Winter term and offers a one-month tutorial course in fiction or poetry. The 1999 writer-in-residence is novelist Thomas E. Kennedy.

Creative Writing Merit Scholarships up to $4,000 are available to incoming freshman. The decision to award is made by the English Department.

In addition, the English Department awards annual prizes for student work in poetry and fiction, and conducts a Poetry Slam each March. The college's literary magazine, *Concept,* and the college's newspaper, *The Conversationalist,* are edited and published by students. Student readings are held each semester.

Converse College graduates reflect the college's historic and continuing emphasis on creative endeavor. Julia Peterkin is the only South Carolinian to have won a Pulitzer Prize for literature. Ellen Bryant Voigt is winner of numerous poetry awards, as well as a finalist for the National Book Critics Circle Award. Recent graduates have won the Bucknell Fellowship for Younger Poets and received competitive scholarships to attend MFA programs at Brown University, the University of Massachusetts, and the University of South Carolina, among others.

The English Department also sponsors two reading series, The Julia Peterkin Award Series and The Elizabeth Boatwright Coker Visiting Writers Series. The visiting writers give readings of their work and also meet with students to discuss writing. Recent visiting writers have included David Baker, Carolyn Forché, Charles Wright, Doris Betts, Jean Thompson, Linda Gregg, Albert Goldbarth, Pattiann Rogers, Lucille Clifton, Joy Williams, and Mary Gordon.

The creative writing faculty includes: poet Rick Mulkey (*Before the Age of Reason*); fiction writer Rosa Shand (winner of the Katherine Anne Porter Prize, winner of the South Carolina Fiction Fellowship); and fiction writer and journalist Susan Tekulve (winner of a Breadloaf Writing Scholarship, and winner of The Walter Rumsey Marvin Fellowship).

For more information on the creative writing program, contact Rick Mulkey, Director of Creative Writing, at the above address.

❖Cornell University
250 Goldwin Smith Hall
Ithaca, NY 14853

(607) 255-6800
e-mail: english_request@cornell.edu
website: www.arts.cornell.edu/english/

Degrees offered: BA, MFA

Degree: BA in English with Creative Writing Component

Required course of study: 120 s/hrs
    Writing workshops: up to 22 s/hrs
    Literature courses: 36 or more s/hrs

Degree: MFA in Creative Writing (fiction and poetry)

Type of Program: Studio/Academic

Length of Residency: Two years

Required course of study: 40 s/hrs
    Writing workshops: 16 s/hrs
    Other courses: 24 s/hrs

Other Requirements: Completion of a book-length manuscript: a collection of poems, short stories, or a novel; oral exam concerned primarily with the thesis.

Application Deadlines: January 10. An interactive application is available through the University Graduate School's website: www.gradschool.cornell.edu. You may also request an application and information at the above address. Send the application and all supporting documents, including GRE scores, to: Admissions, The Graduate School, Caldwell Hall, Cornell University, Ithaca, NY 14853-2602.

MFA applicants must submit *samples of their fiction or poetry* before any application can be evaluated. In making selections for admission to the MFA pro-gram, the Graduate Admissions Committee puts primary emphasis on the writing sample. The writing sample should represent the applicant's best work, and should be large enough to give a sense of the work.

Students may enter the program in the fall term only. Credentials are evaluated and final decisions are made by the Graduate Admissions Committee. Those offered admission are strongly encouraged to visit the department.

Eight writers are admitted each year to the four-semester MFA program: four in poetry and four in fiction. Students participate in a graduate writing workshop each semester and take six additional one-semester courses for credit, at least four of them in English or American literature, Comparative Literature, literature in the modern or classical languages, theory, or cultural studies.

A Special Committee of two faculty members directs each MFA candidate's work. Individualized programs of study for the MFA degree are agreed upon by students and their committees.

Each year one or two students may be admitted to both the MFA program in Creative Writing and the doctoral program in English Language and Literature. These students take the MFA writing workshop courses and PhD seminars for four semesters, write an MFA thesis, and receive the MFA degree. They then proceed to complete the remaining requirements for the PhD degree. Cornell offers only the scholarly PhD, not the PhD with creative dissertation.

MFA/PhD joint-degree applicants must submit *both* a creative writing sample and a *critical writing sample*. Since admission to the two programs is decided separately, applicants might be admitted to only one of the two programs.

MFA candidates are offered a two-year support package: a first-year Assistantship working at *Epoch*, a periodical of contemporary literature published by the Creative Writing staff of the Department of English; and a second-year Teaching Assistantship; and full tuition fellowships for both years.

The Department of English, in conjunction with the Freshman Writing Program, provides excellent training for beginning teachers and varied and interesting teaching within the university-wide Freshman Seminar Writing Program.

Creative Writing faculty includes: A.R. Ammons, Lamar Herrin, Molly Hite, Phyllis Janowitz, Alison Lurie, Dan McCall, Kenneth McClane, Jim McConkey, Maureen McCoy, Robert Morgan, Edgar Rosenberg, Stephanie Vaughn, and Helena Maria Viramontes.

Further information can be obtained by writing to the Director of the Creative Writing Program, English Dept.

❖Creighton University
Omaha, NE 68178

(402) 280-2192
FAX (402) 280-2143
e-mail: spencr@creighton.edu

Degrees offered: BA, MA in English with Concentration in Creative Writing (poetry, fiction, creative nonfiction)

Required course of study: BA requires 128 s/hrs, 36 in creative writing and literature, including Intro. to Creative Writing, Narrative Forms, Poetic Forms, Seminar in Creative Writing (may be taken up to three times for credit), Senior Project, and a selection of literature courses. MA requires 33 s/hrs in a combination of workshops, seminars, and training in literature, criticism, and editing.

Type of Program: Studio/Academic

Both tracks provide extensive workshop experience and a thorough grounding in literature. Workshops are small, intensive, and individualized, with an average of 8-15 students (fewer for graduate workshops). Students enrolled in the programs enjoy not only the benefits of personalized instruction but also the opportunity to work with and become acquainted with distinguished contemporary writers. Creighton is a founding member of the Missouri Valley Reading Series, a consortium of creative writing programs on the Great Plains whose purpose is to bring well-known writers to campus. Recent visitors include Rudolfo Anaya, Charles Baxter, Eavan Boland, Tobias Wolff, Ron Hansen, Tillie Olsen, Susan Minot, William Kittredge, Patricia Foster, Robert Mezey, and Philip Lopate.

Opportunities for student writers include two student reading series, one on campus (Ray's Room) and one in the community (New Voices). Creighton is also the home of *Shadows*, gold medalist in the Columbia Scholastic Press Association's competition; *The Creighton Review*, an online literary magazine; the Creighton University Press, which provides graduate students with editing experience and training; Bluejaybards, an online poetry workshop; the Nebraska Center for Writers, a website for writers (http://mockingbird.creighton.edu/NCW/); the Creighton Young Writers' Workshop; and a chapter of Sigma Tau Delta, the International English Honor Society. Yearly cash prizes are awarded for student poetry, fiction, and nonfiction.

At present, the creative writing faculty is comprised of two full-time writers, including fiction writer Brent Spencer (*The Lost Son, Are We Not Men?*) and Irish poet/fiction writer Eamonn Wall (*Dyckman -- 200th Street* and *Iron Mountain Road*). A third full-time writer will be joining the faculty in fall 1999. Courses are also taught by part-time and visiting faculty. Several of the regular English faculty are publishing poets and fiction writers.

For more information, contact Brent Spencer, Director, Creative Writing Program, English Dept. <spencr@creighton.edu>.

Dartmouth College
Hanover, NH 03755
(603) 646-2316
FAX (603) 646-2159

Degree offered: BA in English Literature & Creative Writing

For more information, contact Writing Program Director, Dept. of English.

Delta State University
Cleveland, MS 38733

For more information, contact William S. Hays, Div. of Languages and Literature.

❖Denison University
Granville, OH 43023
(740) 587-6419
FAX (740) 587-6417
e-mail: baker@denison.edu

Degree offered: BA in English with Concentration in Writing

Required course of study: 9 courses (36 s/hrs) or more in English; 4 or more of these courses in Creative Writing.

Other Requirements: Foreign language proficiency; General Education courses in fine arts, humanities, natural sciences, and social sciences; 127 s/hrs for graduation.

Application Deadline: April 1.

Denison University has offered a Writing Concentration within its English major since 1953. This program encourages student writers to develop their skills in one or more genres while fulfilling the requirements for a major in English and for a liberal arts education.

The typical sequence for a student in the writing program begins with an introductory Creative Writing course, continues with at least one advanced course in a particular genre, and culminates with a 2-semester, senior-year project -- a collection of poems or stories, a novel, a play or film script, or some combination of these forms -- under the guidance of a member of the writing staff. Except in unusual circumstances, a student does not enroll for more than one writing course in any semester.

Because the writing program is an essential part of the English department and the English major, student writers are expected to achieve the same knowledge of literary history as do other students majoring in English. In addition, they are encouraged to take literature courses which focus on the genres being explored and developed in their own writing.

Denison's writing program was developed by Paul Bennett, author of several books and presently the college's Poet-in-Residence. The writing faculty includes David Baker, Director, author of *The Truth About Small Towns, Sweet Home Saturday Night*, and other books of poetry and criticism; Mathew Chacko, stories in *Missouri Review, Story*, and elsewhere; and Ann Townsend, winner of *The Nation/Discovery Award* and a Pushcart Prize, and author of *Dime Store Erotics* (poems).

In addition to the regular staff, 8 to 12 professional writers are brought to campus each year by the endowed Harriet Ewens Beck Lectureship in English. Such writers as Eudora Welty, Ernest Gaines, Gary Snyder, Alice Walker, William Stafford, John Barth, Edward Albee, Bharati Mukherjee, Joseph Heller, Rita Dove, Tim O'Brien, and Carolyn Forché, as well as many younger authors, have visited for readings, workshops, or periods of residence. Denison is a regular stop in the Ohio Poetry Circuit, and annually hosts the winners of the Great Lakes College Association awards in fiction and poetry.

Student writers are encouraged to seek publication in or to serve as editors for *Exile*, the college's literary magazine since 1954, and to participate in Thursday evening informal workshops with townspeople, faculty members, and each other.

In June members of the writing faculty, along with student writers and recent graduates of the writing program, conduct the Jonathan R. Reynolds Young Writers Workshops, a ten-day program for high-school students talented in and seriously committed to creative writing.

Denison University is strongly committed to enrolling good students, regardless of their financial means. Any prospective writing student with financial need should not hesitate to apply for aid by writing to the Director, Office of Financial Assistance and Student Employment.

For further information about the Writing Program, contact David Baker, Director, at the above address, or at the Dept. of English, Denison University, Granville, OH 43023.

❖University of Denver
Denver, CO 80208
(303) 871-2266
FAX (303) 871-2853

Degrees offered: BA, MA, PhD

Degree: BA in English, with Concentration in Creative Writing

Required course of study: 44 q/hrs in English
Thesis: None required except in Honors Program
Writing seminars: 12 or more q/hrs
Literature courses: 24-36 q/hrs
Foreign language: 15 q/hrs

Degree: MA in English/Creative Writing (poetry, fiction)

Length of Residency: Two years

Required course of study: 45 q/hrs
Thesis: Book-length collection of stories
or poems, or novel, with critical preface
Writing seminars: 12 or more q/hrs

Other Requirements: Reading knowledge of one foreign language.

Degree: PhD in English/Creative Writing

Length of Residency: Three years (additional)

Required course of study: 90 q/hrs
Dissertation: Book-length collection of
stories or poems, or novel, with critical
preface: 15 hours
Writing seminars: Poetry and fiction
required: 16 or more hours

Other Requirements: Comprehensive examination in 4 literary periods chosen from 6, reading knowledge of two foreign languages, or significant expertise in one.

Since 1947, when the program in writing at the University of Denver was founded by the dean of small-press publishing in America, Alan Swallow, the Department of English has offered the MA and PhD degrees in creative writing with emphasis on poetry or fiction. The program has evolved over the years to continue to serve the serious writer, and graduates such as Heather McHugh, Reg McKnight, and Mark Harris have gone on to do serious work. But the program is also designed to serve the potential teacher of writing and literature. It presupposes that writing demands an important commitment of time and effort, the development of intelligence, and the acquisition of knowledge. The program is designed to help the writer understand the nature of the creative process in oneself and others -- rather than to foster "success" in a too-easy sense of the term. Although the Writing Program accepts a small number of MA students, the large majority of students are in the PhD program.

The Writing Program is an integral part of the Department of English, and its requirements and goals are essentially the same as those of the Department as a whole. It is not, however, a mere addendum to the Department. Fully half of the students in the Department of English are in the Writing Program -- students in the MA or PhD programs take most of the same courses as students in the academic program, in addition to the workshop courses, courses in history and theory of genre, and the occasional ad hoc course designed to serve a particular need of the writers. Thus the writing students are exposed to many more of the faculty than the four full-time writers who make up the writing program.

Current writing faculty include Rikki Ducornet, author of, among other books, *The Stain*, *The Jade Cabinet*, and *Phosphor in Dreamland* (winner of the Critics Choice Award of 1995) and winner of a 1994 Lannan Foundation Literary Fellowship for Fiction; Bin Ramke, who is the author of five books of poems, including *The Erotic Light of Gardens* and *Massacre of the Innocents*, and who edits the contemporary poetry series for the University of Georgia Press; Cole Swensen, director of the writing program, poet and translator, author of *Noon, Numen*, and *New Math*, as well as a translation of Pierre Alferi's *Natural Gaits*; and Brian Kiteley, author of *Still Life with Insects* and *I Know Many Songs, but I Cannot Sing*, and a former NEA, Guggenheim, and Whiting Fellow.

The Denver Quarterly, edited by Bin Ramke, is an essential part of the writing experience at the University of Denver, and serves as a focus for many graduate activities, including an editorial assistantship. Other Teaching Assistantships are available, as are a limited number of scholarship hours.

For more information and for application forms, contact Director of the Writing Program.

DePauw University
Greencastle, IN 46135
(317) 658-4675

Degree offered: BA in English, Concentration in Writing

For more information contact Chairman, Dept. of English.

❖Dillard University
2601 Gentilly Boulevard
New Orleans, LA 70122-3097
(504) 286-4805 or 286-4689
FAX (504) 286-4799
e-mail: mlsalov@dillard.edu
website: www.dillard.edu

Degrees offered: BA in English, Minor in Creative Writing, works also with the **BA in Theatre, or Mass Communications**

Required course of study: See catalogue for BA area; 16 hours total in Creative Writing
    Form, Invention, and Technique: 6 hours
    Writing workshop: 6 hours
    Professional preparation: 4 hours

Other requirements: University distribution requirements; creative thesis; satisfactory completion of all courses.

The English area offers a minor in Creative Writing. The required course of study, in the form of a series of five classes, one per semester, is offered as (consecutively): English 307, 308, 309, 310, and 312. The course sequence is designed so a student, at whatever level and at whatever skill, may join the current class and feel comfortable. This flexibility allows students with creative ability and those wishing to develop creative skills in writing to support their creativity.

In addition to the five courses taught in sequence, the Creative Writing Program, under the leadership of the Director, administers public programming, a publication, and literary prizes. There are two levels of programming: 1) the Fat Tuesday Visiting Writer Series and mini residency -- features distinguished writers of national reputation; spring writers visiting are: Ishmael Reed, Ernest Gaines, Yusef Komunyakaa, and Kalamu ya Salaam; 1998 guest writers included Charles Johnson, Pearl Cleage; former guests include Brenda Marie Osbey, Al Young; and 2) Café Lit, a literary salon -- features writers in performance sharing works in progress or reading from published works; to generate the ambiance of a literary salon, these writers are featured after a musical guest warms the atmosphere; coffee, snacks, punch are served; in addition, Café Lit presents one or two students in a public reading each spring -- these students are encouraged into the professional arena.

Each semester, students solicit, edit, and publish student work in the literary tabloid *To Be Continued: continuing our craft, culture, and literature*. With this tabloid, the director trains interested students in publishing outside of the classroom.

Annual Literary Prizes: These contests continue each semester in the form of a literary prize, Poetry in the Fall and Fiction or Plays in the Spring; awards are in cash.

Currently in development, The Tom Dent Scholarship in Creative Writing will support a writer who exemplifies Dent's ideals in craft, cultural activism-development-community support, and publishing.

For more information contact: Mona Lisa Saloy, Director of Creative Writing.

Dowling College
Oakdale, NY 11769-1999
(516) 244-3155

Degree offered: BA in English with Certificate in Writing

For more information, contact Writing Program Director, Dept. of English.

Drake University
Des Moines, IA 50311
(515) 271-3777
FAX (515) 271-3977

Degrees offered: BA, MA

Degree: BA in English

Required course of study: 124 s/hrs total; Freshman Seminar in Reading and Writing course; Literary Study course; Literary Theory and Criticism course; 27 s/hrs other English courses.

Other Requirements: College general education requirements.

Application Deadlines: For Fall admission, March 1.

The English major requires the student to take the Seminar in Reading and Writing, the Literary Study course, the Literary Theory and Criticism course, and nine other courses in English studies: one at the lower (20-99) level, six at the mid (100-174) level, and two at the senior seminar (175-99) level. At least two courses must cover material dating from before 1900. Courses engage students in writing and reading a diverse range of types of texts: autobiography, science fiction, narratives of intercultural encounter, personal essays, song criticism, discourse theory, linguistics, detective fiction, literacy studies, film and material cultural artifacts, as well as work in the study of traditionally acknowledged genres and long-established British and American writers and texts.

The department is committed to the study of the power of language to mediate relations between people and the world around them and to a pedagogy emphasizing the interdependence of reading and writing that challenges traditional notions of "English Studies" by diversifying the writers, texts, topics, and methods of study employed, and demanding of students a critical awareness of the implications of language use, both in order to assess and develop their own ideas and to better understand the constraints which competing discourses might place upon those ideas.

For more information, contact Chair, Dept. of English.

Duquesne University
Pittsburgh, PA 15282-1703
(412) 396-5091

Degree offered: BA in English

For more information, contact Chairman, English Dept.

Dutchess Community College
Poughkeepsie, NY 12601
(914) 471-4500

Degree offered: AA, Writing Emphasis

For more information, contact Chairman, Dept. of English.

❖East Carolina University
Greenville, NC 27858-4353
(252) 328-6041
FAX (252) 328-4889

Degrees offered: BA, MA

Degree: BA in English with Writing Emphasis (Creative and/or Technical)

Required course of study:
  Writing courses: 18 s/hrs
  Literature courses: 18 s/hrs

Other Requirements: General college; foreign language; minor.

Application Deadlines: Admission -- March 15 (for Fall enrollment); Dec. 1 (Spring enrollment); April 15 for financial aid.

The program is aimed at students who want to be professional writers or writers in the professions, with courses offered in creative writing and technical writing.

Degree: MA in English with Creative Writing Emphasis (poetry, fiction, creative nonfiction, scriptwriting)

Type of Program: Creative Writing

Length of Residency: Two years

Required course of study: 30 s/hrs
  Writing courses: 9 s/hrs
  Literature courses: 9 s/hrs
  Research seminar: 3 s/hrs
  Literary criticism: electives
  Thesis: 3 s/hrs

Other Requirements: Reading knowledge of a foreign language; a comprehensive examination.

Application Deadlines: April 15 for financial aid; June 1 (Fall admission), Oct. 15 (Spring admission).

East Carolina University offers a master of arts degree in English with a concentration in creative writing designed for people who are interested in professional writing or who intend to make writing an important part of their lives. Students in the program concentrate in a particular genre -- poetry, fiction, nonfiction, or scriptwriting -- and complete a creative thesis in their chosen area.

The primary method of instruction is the advanced writing workshop. The workshops teach close critical reading and develop students' revising and editing skills. The program also offers the possibility of internships on two journals, *North Carolina Literary Review* and *Tar River Poetry*.

Visiting Writers in recent years have included Lucille Clifton, Li-Young Lee, Rita Dove, Brendan Galvin, Gwendolyn Brooks, Thylia Moss, Marilyn Waniek, Gordon Weaver, Samuel Hazo, and Amiri Baraka.

The Creative Writing Staff includes: Alex Albright (creative nonfiction), *Satori in Rocky Mount: Kerouac in North Carolina*; Patrick Bizzaro (poetry), *Fear of the Coming Drought, Responding to Student Poems: Applications of Critical Theory*; Julie Fay (poetry, translation), *Portraits of Women, The Woman Behind You*; William Hallberg (fiction), *The Rub of the Green, Perfect Lies, Van Gogh's Ear*; Peter Makuck (poetry and fiction), *The Sunken Lightship, Pilgrims* (chapbook), *Where We Live, Breaking and Entering* (short stories); Robert Siegel (scriptwriting), *Overlooking the Park, Night Into Water*; Luke Whisnant (nonfiction, fiction), *Watching TV With the Red Chinese* (novel), *Street* (poetry chapbook).

Degree: MA in English/Technical and Professional Communication

Length of Residency: Two years

Required course of study: 30 s/hrs
  Writing courses: 12 s/hrs
  Issues in Technical Communication: 3 s/hrs
  Research in Technical Communication: 3 s/hrs
  Composition Theory or Linguistics: 3 s/hrs
  Literature/Rhetoric courses: 6 s/hrs
  Thesis: 3 s/hrs

Other Requirements: Significant computer skills or a reading knowledge of a foreign language.

Application Deadlines: April 15 for financial aid; June 1 (fall admission), Oct. 15 (spring admission)

A rigorous graduate program led by nationally known scholars, East Carolina University's technical and professional communication concentration stresses a combined theoretical and practical approach for writing and research in technical, scientific, and administrative communications. Students in the MA program are encouraged to publish in the field's major journals and attend professional conferences, and they are encouraged to enroll in the graduate cooperative education program or internship program, working as technical communicators for companies in the Research Triangle Park or in companies or governmental agencies throughout the state and nation.

While some graduates go on to pursue PhDs in technical communication, others are currently working in research, software documentation, public relations, contract communications, and other areas as professional writers, editors, and documentation managers. All graduates are working as either technical communicators, managers, or teachers.

The technical communication faculty includes: Jo Allen, Sherry Southard, Bertie Fearing, Keats Sparrow, and Janice Tovey.

For further information, visit our website at

www1.ecu.edu/˜ecucw/home.html, or contact Luke Whisnant, Dept. of English (whisnant@mail.ecu.edu).

East Stroudsburg University
East Stroudsburg, PA 18301

Contact the Creative Writing Program Director, Dept. of English.

Eastern Oregon State College
La Grande, OR 97850
(541) 962-3629

Degree offered: BA in English with Writing Concentration

Required course of study: 186 cr hrs total for BA, of which
  - 60 cr hrs must be in gen ed
  - 60 cr hrs must be in upper div

Major:
  - 18 cr hrs Engl core
  - 20 cr hrs Wr core
  - 23 cr hrs Wr concentration

Other Requirements: 1. Admission to English Degree program, a. 45 minimum credit hours of college work with a GPA of 2.5 or better, b. completed 10 graded credit hours of writing or literature courses with a GPA of 3.0 or better, c. attempt Writing proficiency Exam, d. file for admission and obtain two recommendations from members of the English/Writing faculty; 2. complete all general education requirements; 3. complete both core curriculum and concentration area curriculum; 4. maintain a 3.0 GPA in major course work; 5. complete foreign language requirement; 6. Capstone Senior Project.

Application Deadlines: Priority deadline is August 1; Financial Aid no later than March 1.

The following courses lead to a BA in English with a Writing Concentration: Writing Core Curriculum: Newswriting; Writing of Poetry or Writing of Fiction; Advanced Prose Writing; Introduction to Discourse Studies. Writing Concentration Curriculum: Writing Nonfiction; Writing of Fiction or Writing Poetry; Short Story Writing; Writing Theory; Advanced Poetry Writing; Directed Writing; Practicum; Senior Project. Literature Electives: Shakespeare; Applied Literary Criticism; Major British Writers I and II; Major American Writers I and II; Literary genres; History and Structure of English; Historic Literature; Contemporary Literature; Literary Theory; Major Authors.

There is also a 2-track minor available in Literature and Writing. Each track requires 30 credit hours at 200-level and above.

Typically, writing students participate as editors and writers for *Oregon East*, the student literary magazine, and *The Beacon*, the student newspaper.

Ars Poetica, the literary reading series, has sponsored 35 years of continuous lectures and workshops by visiting writers. Recent visiting writers include: Gary Gildner, Madeline DeFrees, Craig Lesley, Ingrid Wendt, William Stafford, John Haines, Czeslaw Milosz,

Garrett Hongo, and Patricia Goedicke, among many others.

Creative Writing Faculty: David Axelrod (*Jerusalem of Grass, The Kingdom at Hand*, poetry, nonfiction), Jodi Varon (fiction and translation), George Venn (*Sunday Afternoon Grande Ronde, Off the Main Road, Marking the Magic Circle*, poetry), Donald Wolff (writing theory).

Contact David Axelrod, (541) 962-3525.

❖Eastern Washington University
705 W. First Avenue MS-1
Spokane, WA 99204
(509) 623-4221

Degrees offered: BA, MFA

Degree: BA in Creative Writing

Required course of study: 180 q/hrs
  Writing courses: 20-32 q/hrs
  Literature courses: 29-40 q/hrs

Other Requirements: 10 q/hrs college writing; 20 q/hrs natural sciences; 20 q/hrs humanities; 15 q/hrs social sciences.

Degree: MFA in Creative Writing (poetry, fiction, creative nonfiction)

Type of Program: Studio/Academic

Length of Residency: Two years

Required course of study: 72 q/hrs
  Thesis: 6-12 q/hrs
  Writing workshops: 15-20 q/hrs
  Form & Theory Courses: 10 q/hrs
  Literature courses: 15-20 q/hrs

Other options: A Secondary Emphasis of 15-20 q/hrs may be pursued in one of the following areas: (1) Literary Editing, (2) Technical and Professional Writing, (3) Teaching Composition, (4) Developmental Instruction, (5) Teaching English as a Second Language, (6) Studies in Modern Literature, or (7) Studies in another art form -- music, dance, photography, etc.

Application Deadlines: For admission, March 1, recommended. For Teaching Assistantships, March 1.

Eastern Washington University offers the BA in Creative Writing and a Master of Fine Arts in Creative Writing.

The MFA Program offers a studio/academic degree of 72 q/hrs, with at least half of the work done in workshops, form and theory courses, and on the thesis, which must be of publishable quality. Each student is required to take a written comprehensive examination in his or her major genre.

The Creative Writing staff includes: poet Nance Van Winckel, who has published *Bad Girl With Hawk* and *The Dirt*, and a short story collection, *Limited Lifetime Warranty*; John Keeble, who has published the novels *Broken Ground, Yellowfish*, and *Out of the Channel* (nonfiction); and Ursula Hegi, the author of *Unearned*

Pleasures and Other Stories, Stones from the River, and *Salt Dancers*; Christopher Howell, author of six collections of poetry, including his most recent, *Memory in Heaven*; Carolyn Kremers (director), author of *Place of the Pretend People: Gifts from a Yup'ik Eskimo Village*; Gregory Spatz (visiting), author of the novel *No One But Us*.

Carolyn Kizer, Honorary Professor of Poetry, received the Pulitzer Prize for Poetry in 1985 for *Yin* (Boa Editions, 1984). Her other books include *The Ungrateful Garden* and *Nearness of You*. Each year a Distinguished Visiting Writer serves on the MFA faculty, recently Jack Gilbert, author of *The Great Fires*.

Other visiting writers in recent years have been Rick Bass, Tess Gallagher, Robert Hass, Barry Lopez, Czeslaw Milosz, Gary Snyder, Shirley Ann Williams, Ted Solotaroff, William Stafford, Al Young, Linda Hogan, and Russell Banks.

Willow Springs, founded in 1977, has received grants and awards from the NEA and G.E. Foundation, as well as a Citation of Excellence for Editorial Vision from the CCLM. Recent issues include work by Madeline DeFrees, Sharon Doubiago, Diane Glancy, Albert Goldbarth, Robin Hemley, Lisel Mueller, Jack Myers, Donald Revell, Alberto Rios, Charlie Smith, William Stafford, and Bruce Weigl. An integral component of the MFA Program, *Willow Springs* offers students the opportunity for editing experience.

Students can also gain editing experience working on the EWU Press, a nationally recognized book publishing company. As press interns, students learn many aspects of book production from manuscript editing to cover and page design to marketing.

Many MFA students participate in EWU's Writers in the Community project, where they gain teaching experience. Students work as Creative Writing instructors in local prisons, public schools, alternative schools, and other community programs.

Our graduates have published with St. Martin's Press, Copper Canyon Press, City Lights Press, Confluence Press, Paulist Press, Blue Cloud Abbey, and Beaver Row (Ireland). They have received numerous honors including the Yale Younger Poets Award, NEA grants, American Poetry Center Russian Tour, and The O. Henry Prize Story.

Summer Writing Workshop in Ireland: Eastern annually holds a Summer Writing Workshop in Dublin, Ireland, directed by James McAuley. Participants attend workshops led by prominent Irish writers, including Eavan Boland, Michael Davitt, Benedict Kiely, Mary Lavin, John McGahern, Tom McIntyre, and Paula Meehan.

For more information, contact Director, Creative Writing Program.

Eckerd College
St. Petersburg, FL 33733
(727) 864-8281
FAX (727) 864-8354
website:
http://www.eckerd.edu/academics/cra/writing

Degree offered: BA in Creative Writing

Required course of study: 36 semester hours
   Thesis: 3–9 s/hrs
   Writing courses: 12 or more s/hrs
   Literature courses: 18–30 s/hrs

Other Requirements: Oral defense of thesis.

The basic requirements for a Creative Writing major at Eckerd College include six literature classes, four writing workshops, and a senior thesis, plus the general education requirements. Student writing projects may be undertaken in Independent Study as well as in workshops.

The program features small classes, an active schedule of visiting writers, and particular emphasis upon the writing of a substantial senior thesis.

There are workshops in fiction and poetry each semester; workshops in the one-act play, in journalism, screenwriting, journals, letters, and diaries, the personal essay, and other special topics are offered periodically.

We are a young school, but many of our graduates are already making their mark, e.g., James Nolan, James W. Hall, William Miller, and Dennis Lehane.

The Writing Workshop has its own permanent room with current periodicals, records, tapes, bulletin boards with news of literary interest, etc. It is the center of an informal but lively community. Scholarships are available to creative writers. Writing workshop students contribute to the Eckerd College student newspaper, *The Triton Tribune*, and edit *The Eckerd Review*, Eckerd's literary magazine. Additional media opportunities on campus include the student-managed radio station WECX and cable TV station, EC-TV.

The faculty includes: novelist Sterling Watson (*Deadly Sweet; The Calling; Blind Tongues*) and poet Scott Ward (*Crucial Beauty; Portraits*). Noted poet and fiction writer, Peter Meinke, a past Director of the Eckerd College Writing Workshop, is a guest lecturer in creative writing courses.

Many outside writers visit for readings, lectures and workshops. In the past these have included Howard Nemerov, Margaret Atwood, William Meredith, Richard Eberhart, Gwendolyn Brooks, Gary Gildner, Jim Daniels, and many others.

For more information, contact Sterling Watson, Director of the Writing Workshop, or visit our website.

❖El Camino College
16007 Crenshaw Blvd.
Torrance, CA 90506

For more information, contact the Director, Dept. of English.

❖Elon College
Elon College, NC 27244
(336) 538-2749

Degree offered: BA in English with a Concentration

in Creative Writing or Professional Writing. Minors in Creative Writing and Professional Writing are also available.

English majors at Elon may choose from four areas: Creative Writing, Professional Writing, Literature, or English Education. Students in the Creative Writing Concentration take four creative writing classes (including the Senior Seminar), five literature courses, and one course on the history of the English language or linguistics. Elon offers introductory and advanced classes in the writing of poetry, fiction, screenplay, drama, and creative nonfiction.

Writers who have visited Elon recently include Edward Hirsch, Francine Prose, W.D. Snodgrass, Robert Olmstead, Michael Parker, Stuart Dischell, Gregory Orr, Margaret Gibson, Gerald Stern, Alan Shapiro, and Rikki Ducornet.

For more information contact the English Dept. Chair.

❖Emerson College
Boston, MA 02116-1523

(617) 824-8600

Degrees offered: BFA in Writing, Literature, and Publishing; MA in Writing and Publishing; MFA in Creative Writing

Degree: BFA in Writing, Literature, and Publishing: Creative Writing Concentration

Required course of study: 56 s/hrs in the major
Literature surveys (Literary Foundations, American Literature, British Literature): 8 s/hrs at sophomore level
Writing workshops: 20 or more s/hrs at advanced levels
Literature courses: 12 s/hrs at advanced levels
Electives: 12 s/hrs
Senior Project: 4 s/hrs

Other Requirements: 8 s/hrs composition; 12 s/hrs communication studies; 28 s/hrs liberal arts core (literature, fine arts, philosophy, history, ethics and values, science, social science); 4 s/hrs U.S. Multiculturism; 4 s/hrs Non-western Civilizations and Cultures.

In addition to satisfying all their general education requirements, Creative Writing concentrators take Introduction to Creative Writing in their freshman or sophomore year, a course designed to help them explore their talent for writing. At this level there are 5 areas: Poetry, Prose, Drama, Children's Literature, and Comedy Writing.

As the students progress, they are offered an advanced section in each of the writing areas until they reach the courses of greatest importance: the Seminars in Creative Writing. These courses are taught by Writers in Residence or Visiting Specialists. Writers who have taught the seminars include Richard Yates, Pamela Painter, Theodore Weesner, Bill Knott, Thomas Lux, Martin Espada, and Stratis Haviaras.

As a capstone to their studies, a Senior Project is required in any area of writing. This may be, for instance, a 40-page collection of stories, a one-act play, or a chapbook of poems.

Students are encouraged through electives to explore the interdisciplinary opportunities of the college, as a leading communications school, especially in the areas of Performing Arts, Film, and American culture.

To give students actual experience in publishing, the Department offers a publication practicum, which includes editing the undergraduate literary magazines, *The Emerson Review, Gangsters in Concrete,* and *Hyena,* the comedy magazine. In addition, regular readings by guests, faculty, and students are featured, and internships are encouraged at local magazines and publishers, such as *Ploughshares,* which is published by Emerson, *The Partisan Review, Boston Review, Boston Magazine,* Houghton Mifflin Co., The Beacon Press, and David R. Godine, Publisher.

Degree: BFA in Writing, Literature, & Publishing: Writing and Publishing Concentration

Required course of study: Same as above, with the exceptions of 24 s/hrs or more in Publishing courses at advanced levels, 12 s/hrs in literature at advanced levels, and 8 s/hrs in writing, as well as 12 s/hrs in electives, and 4 s/hrs in the Senior Project.

The Writing and Publishing concentration follows a sequence analogous to that of the Creative Writing concentration, starting with Introduction to Professional Writing at the freshman or sophomore level, progressing to Advanced Professional Writing and culminating in senior seminars in the areas of Book and Magazine Publishing, Copyediting, Desktop Publishing, and Literary Editing.

Degree: MA in Writing and Publishing

Type of Program: Studio/Academic

Length of Residency: 1 1/2 years (5 years maximum)

Required course of study: 40 s/hrs, with 24 s/hrs in Writing and Publishing courses, 8 s/hrs in Literature courses, and 8 s/hrs in division electives, including internships. Students must also submit a master's project showing evidence of accomplishment in an area of publishing and/or writing.

Writing and Publishing courses include offerings such as Book Publishing, Magazine Publishing, Copyediting, Book Marketing and Promotion, Desktop Publishing, Literary Editing; and Fiction Writing, Nonfiction Writing, and Screenwriting. The program is designed to meet the needs of students who are interested in pursuing careers in publishing or as professionals in a writing-related field. It emphasizes an interactive "guided apprenticeship" in writing and publishing.

Internships and apprenticeship opportunities are available in Boston publishing and production firms and advertising agencies. Screenwriting-related internships are also available in the film industry through Emerson's Los Angeles Program. The book publishing sequence is endorsed by the Education Committee of the Association of American Publishers.

Most courses meet once weekly in the late afternoon or in the evening, to allow students to complete their education while employed full or part-time.

Degree: MFA in Creative Writing

Type of Program: Studio/Academic

Length of Residency: 2 1/2 years (5 years maximum)

Required course of study: 52 s/hrs, including 20 in writing courses, 16 in literature courses, 16 in electives including 4 given to the thesis, in Writing, Literature, or Publishing courses or in courses from related graduate programs at Emerson, such as those in video, film, or Performing Arts.

Application Deadlines: Rolling acceptances, primarily February through August.

Emerson's MFA is characterized by its range of specializations -- in poetry, fiction, nonfiction, children's writing, playwriting, and scriptwriting. The MFA is a terminal degree for those who wish to teach writing and literature on the college level from the writer's perspective. It also provides a community of practice, study, and discussion in which to produce publishable or producible work. Literature courses include Novel into Film, Contemporary World Fiction, Contemporary Short Story, Modern Poetry, Contemporary Drama, American Women Writers, Autobiography, and Literary Theory and Criticism. Writing courses include workshops in Poetry, Short Story, Nonfiction, Novel, Playwriting, and Screenwriting. A course in Learning to Teach Freshman Writing is required for students seeking teaching assistantships. A final book-length thesis of publishable quality must be presented and defended.

Full-time Department faculty includes: John Skoyles, Chair; Jonathan Aaron; Douglas Clayton, MA Coordinator; William Donoghue; Eileen Farrell; Robin Riley Fast, Undergraduate Coordinator; Flora Gonzalez; DeWitt Henry; Bill Knott; Maria Koundoura; Uppinder Mehan; Pamela Painter, MFA Coordinator; Donald Perret, Foreign Language Coordinator; and Jessica Treadway. Writers-in-Residence currently are: Lisa Jahn-Clough, Margot Livesey, Ralph Lombreglia, Gail Mazur, Michael Stephens, and Christopher Tilghman.

The Office of Financial Aid administers a college Work Study Program and other tuition remission and loan programs.

All inquiries should be addressed to Graduate Admissions, Emerson College, 100 Beacon Street, Boston, MA 02116, phone: (617) 824-8610.

Inquiries regarding undergraduate admissions should be addressed to Office of Undergraduate Admissions, the same address as above.

Emory & Henry College
Emory, VA 24327

(703) 944-3141

Degree offered: BA in English: Writing Track

For more information, contact Chairman, Dept. of English.

❖Emory University
Humanities Building 302
Atlanta, GA 30322

(404) 727-4683

Degree offered: BA in English/Creative Writing

Required course of study: Academic requirements of the creative writing major are ten courses beyond the introductory courses in English presently required by the college (English 101 or 110). Four of those ten courses are to be writing seminars and the other six are to be advanced-level English classes in literature and criticism (300- and 400-level courses). This framework provides enough flexibility so that creative writing majors can work out individual programs of study in consultation with their advisors. University distribution requirements must also be met.

Application Deadlines: April 1 for summer term; February 1 for fall term.

During the academic year, the program also sponsors the Creative Writing Reading Series, a special feature that reaches out to the entire Emory community and brings nationally prominent writers to campus for workshops and public readings. Approximately five visiting writers come to Emory each semester. Writers who have been part of the series in the last few years include Louise Glück, Yusef Komunyakaa, John Edgar Wideman, N. Scott Momaday, and Grace Paley.

The Lullwater Review is a literary journal associated with Emory, edited by undergraduate and graduate students, which appears three times yearly and features poetry, fiction, and artwork by students as well as creative writers nationwide. Theater Emory and the Creative Writing Program share an ongoing collaborative effort resulting in the teaching of cross-listed classes. The creative writing faculty includes Frank Manley, the director of the Program, a prizewinning poet and playwright, whose most recent publication is a novel called *The Cockfighter*; Lynna Williams, author of a collection of short stories, *Things Not Seen and Other Stories*; and Xuefei Jin, who writes under the name of Ha Jin. His most recent publications are two collections of short stories, *Ocean of Words: Army Stories*, which won the 1997 Ernest Hemingway Foundation/PEN Award, and *Under the Red Flag: Stories*, winner of the 1996 Flannery O'Connor Award. The program hosts various visiting faculty each semester who enrich the program in their various writings. Awards Night honors the best works in poetry, fiction, drama, and essay written by our students. Prizes are awarded in these various categories.

In addition to the Creative Writing Reading Series, the Creative Writing Program also sponsors a Summer Writers' Institute each July, available for college credit. This culminates in the Summer Writers' Festival, a collaboration of several visiting writers who join in panel discussions and give readings of their works and conduct workshops.

For further information on the Creative Writing Program, Creative Writing Reading Series, or the Summer Writers' Institute, please call or write Paula Vitaris, (404) 727-4683, coordinator of the program.

❖Emporia State University
Emporia, KS 66801-5087
(316) 341-5216
FAX (316) 341-5547

Degrees offered: BA with Creative Writing Minor; MA with Creative Thesis

Application Deadline: February 15 for financial aid.

The undergraduate creative writing minor may be obtained in conjunction with any major of the student's choosing.

Emporia State University offers graduate-level study in the writing of fiction and poetry as part of its MA program in literature, which is thorough and rigorous. Students who are accepted for the creative writing option are expected to enroll in creative writing workshops and to produce a manuscript of publishable quality.

Creative Writing students may participate in any or all of the following: *Quivira*, a student project in continuous annual publication for 38 years; The Bluestem Award, a national poetry competition involving selection of a winning manuscript which is then published by the university's Bluestem Press (a $1,000 cash award comes with publication); and The Visiting Writer's Series.

For further information, contact Chair, Dept. of English.

❖University of Evansville
1800 Lincoln Avenue
Evansville, IN 47722-0001

(812) 479-2962

Degrees offered: BA, BFA

Degree: BA in Creative Writing (poetry, fiction, screenwriting)

Required course of study: 124 s/hrs total
Survey of English language: 3 s/hrs
Creative writing courses: minimum 21 s/hrs
Literature courses: minimum 15 s/hrs

Other Requirements: University general education requirements.

Application Deadlines: March 1 for financial aid; May 1 for admissions.

The BA in Creative Writing gives the student exposure to both poetry and fiction writing but allows emphasis in either genre as well as screenwriting and creative nonfiction. It begins with Introduction to Imaginative Writing and continues with courses in poetry and fiction writing at both introductory and advanced levels; workshops, one-on-one projects, and internships are available to upper-level students. An annual university writing contest with generous cash prizes is sponsored by the Department; best contest entries are published in *On Time*, a student edited journal. *The Evansville Review*, a student association-sponsored literary magazine, also publishes student work. *The Formalist*, an international poetry journal, is edited and published by Dr. William Baer, a member of

the writing faculty. Although the journal generally publishes submissions by recognized poets such as Mona Van Duyn, Donald Justice, Richard Wilbur, and John Updike, some students do get their poems in *The Formalist* as well.

Degree: BFA in Creative Writing (poetry, fiction, and screenwriting)

Required course of study: 124 s/hrs total
Creative writing: 40 s/hrs (recommended)
Literature courses: 20 s/hrs (recommended)
Total in writing and literature: 60 s/hrs (required)

Other Requirements: University general education requirements.

Application Deadlines: March 1 for financial aid; May 1 for admissions.

The BFA in Creative Writing is very selective; it is designed with only those in mind who are likely to be accepted into the top creative writing graduate programs in the country. The selection committee will look at freshman applications but prefers to observe students in writing classes before recommending them for the program. Decisions are based on grades, test scores, portfolios of writing, and assessment of general overall promise as quality writers. Students may be admitted to the program up to the end of sophomore year.

In addition to regular creative writing and literature faculty, visiting writers-in-residence and guest writers offer supplementary workshops and individual critiques as well as readings. In recent years these have included Julia Kasdorf, Phillip Lopate, Dave Smith, Bruce Weigl, Nancy Willard, Al Young, Molly Peacock, Mary Jo Salter, and Edward Hirsch.

For more information, contact Chairman, Dept. of English.

❖Fairfield University
Fairfield, CT 06430
(203) 254-4000, ext. 2795
FAX (203) 254-4131

English majors at Fairfield take ten courses beyond the first-year sequence. Five core courses are required of all majors: one in pre-19th literature, one in 19th-century literature, and one in 20th-century literature as well as one genre course and one theory course. The remaining five courses are chosen, with the help of an advisor, to highlight the student's individual interests and needs.

Many students pursue independent study projects, working one-on-one weekly with a faculty member. Fairfield also offers internships at such places as *The New Yorker* and Walden Books.

Offerings range from workshop courses in poetry, fiction, and drama to courses in journalism, persuasive writing, and advanced composition.

Fairfield students have published in such journals as *Willow Springs, Queen's Quarterly, The Laurel Review, Quarterly West*, and *The Spoon River Poetry Review* and have been chosen for the AWP Intro Award Series and the Connecticut Student Poetry Series. In addition, the department offers numerous awards in writing as well as a creative writing scholarship. The English Department and Fine Arts Department co-sponsor a Black Box presentation of student plays and a reader's theatre presentation of creative writing students' work. Fairfield's literary magazine, *The Sound*, appears twice a year.

Visiting authors have included Julia Alvarez, Maya Angelou, Nikki Giovanni, Le Ly Hayslip, June Jordan, Galway Kinnell, Frank McCourt, Gloria Naylor, Joyce Carol Oates, Sharon Olds, Michael O'Siadhail, and Michael Waters.

The creative writing faculty is as follows: Director Kim Bridgford (poetry and fiction), Ben Halm (playwriting), and Nicholas Rinaldi (poetry and fiction).

The adjunct faculty is as follows: Janet Krauss (poetry), and Tony Sanders (poetry).

For more information, contact Dr. Kim Bridgford, English Dept.

Fairleigh Dickinson University
Florham-Madison Campus
Madison, NJ 07940
(973) 443-8710
FAX (973) 443-8713
e-mail: cross@alpha.fdu.edu

Degrees offered: BA in English with Concentration in Writing, MA

Type of Program: Studio/Academic

Length of Residency: Four years

Required course of study: 128 s/hrs
  Writing workshop: 12–21 s/hrs
  Literature courses: 15 s/hrs
  Tutorial or directed readings: up to 12 s/hrs

Other Requirements: University distribution requirements; senior independent writing project.

Application Deadlines: Rolling

Our program emphasizes the range of writing possibilities with individual attention to student interests and development. Students take an advanced writing workshop (3 hrs) and between 12 and 21 credits in writing courses in various genres (creative; scientific and technical; news; public relations; critical reviewing; drama). Up to 12 hrs of independent projects can be arranged and all students must complete a senior project. 15 credits of literature study are required. Members of the faculty edit *The Literary Review*. Students produce their own literary magazines. Writing faculty: Walter Cummins, Bill Zander, Mary Cross, Michael Goodman.

The department also offers a Master's program geared to working corporate professionals and those expecting to work in the field. This MA offers courses in managerial writing, professional writing and editing, technical communication, oral presentation, audio-visual media, and computer graphics in addition to various courses in management, communication theory, and corporate culture. Program sponsors an annual national conference with published proceed-

ings. A visiting professorship brings a notable professional to the department to offer seminars and public lectures. 2–3 fellowships are available annually; fellows assist in research and administration or work in the university's public affairs office.

For more information, contact the Chair, Dept. of English.

Fisk University
Nashville, TN 37208-8533

Contact the Creative Writing Program Director, Dept. of English.

Florida Institute of Technology
150 W. University Boulevard
Melbourne, FL 32901-6988
(407) 768-8000, ext. 8082
FAX (407) 984-8461

Florida Tech offers undergraduate and graduate degrees in business communication and technical writing.

Florida Tech's master's program aims to prepare students for careers as technical writers/editors, technical and scientific journalists, publications editors, proposal writers, corporate communication consultants, public relations specialists, copy writers, technical trainers, and media and presentation specialists.

A limited number of teaching assistantships are available to full time students in the program.

For further information, contact Dr. Judith B. Strother, Chair, Graduate Program, Technical and Professional Communication.

❖Florida International University
North Miami Campus
North Miami, FL 33181
(305) 919-5857
FAX (305) 919-5734

Degrees offered: BA, MFA

Degree: BA in English, Creative Writing Emphasis

English majors at FIU may choose from 3 areas of emphasis: Creative Writing, Literature, or Language and Linguistics. A student pursuing the creative writing track takes a minimum of 30 s/hrs of junior-senior level coursework in the Department, including 12 s/hrs of designated Literature courses and at least 12 s/hrs of Creative Writing coursework, including a senior project.

Degree: MFA in Creative Writing (fiction, poetry, creative nonfiction, screenplay)

Type of Program: Studio/Academic

Length of Residency: Two to three years

Application Deadlines: February 15.

The program is a 48 s/hr studio/academic curriculum leading to the Master of Fine Arts degree. It includes a minimum 18 s/hrs of writing workshop, 15 s/hrs of literature, 3 s/hrs of form and theory, and 6 s/hrs of thesis. There is no language requirement. Graduate workshops include short fiction, the novel, popular fiction, screenwriting, creative nonfiction, and poetry. The program places great emphasis upon the preparation and completion of a book-length creative thesis. Applicants must have 1) a baccalaureate degree, 2) a 3.0 GPA, or a 1000 combined score on the GRE, and 3) a minimum of 9 s/hrs of undergraduate work in creative writing. However, admission is based primarily on the strength of the applicant's submitted writing sample.

The 1996 *U.S. News and World Report* named Florida International University, founded in 1965, one of America's top 150 Universities. Barron's Guide lists FIU among its "most prestigious universities." FIU, with some 28,000 students, is the State University of Florida at Miami. The Creative Writing Program is housed at the North Miami Campus, directly on Biscayne Bay, where on-campus housing is available. Study at FIU is a rich multi-ethnic, multi-cultural experience. Miami/Ft. Lauderdale is a dynamic community of more than 3 million with a distinctive Latin American and Caribbean flavor in its many dance, theatre, art, and music institutions. Writers enjoy the opportunity for editorial experience on *Gulf Stream* magazine, the annual FIU Literary Awards Competition, the FIU Writers Workshop, the Miami Book Fair International, and the Writers on the Bay Series, which has included residencies by such writers as Rita Dove, Louis Simpson, John Wideman, Elmore Leonard, Derek Walcott, Luisa Valenzuela, Tony Hillerman, Robert Pinsky, and Gay Talese.

FIU's commitment to creative writing has been strong from the outset; over the years such major writers as James Jones and George Garrett have served on the faculty. Former students have published widely, with their credits including the Iowa Short Fiction Award, the Wesleyan Poetry Series, and books with Knopf, Dutton, Harcourt Brace, and the University of Texas Press. Current faculty members include novelist and nonfiction writer Dan Wakefield (*Starting Over, New York in the 50's*); novelist and poet James W. Hall (*Under Cover of Daylight, Buzz Cut, False Statements*); Edgar Award winning fiction writer Lynne Barrett (*The Secret Names of Women, The Land of Go*, stories in *Redbook* and *Mondo Barbie*); award-winning fiction and nonfiction writer John Dufresne (*The Way That Water Enters Stone, Louisiana Power and Light*); and poet Campbell McGrath (*Capitalism, American Noise, Spring Comes to Chicago*), winner of the 1997 Kingsley-Tufts Award. Director of the program is fiction and screen writer Les Standiford (*Spill, Presidential Deal*, screenplays for Pathe/MGM), an NEA fiction fellowship recipient. Visiting faculty have included Maxine Kumin, Rust Hills, and Paul Zimmer.

Edward Fiske lists FIU among its "Best Buys" in college education. Graduate tuition is approximately $110 per s/hr for Florida residents, $360 for non-residents. Fellowships, teaching assistantships, and tuition remission scholarships comparable to those of most other institutions are available on a competitive basis.

The annual FIU Writers Conference takes place each fall at Seaside, Florida. The week-long program covers all genres, including film writing and creative nonfiction. Past faculty have included Henry Taylor, Dave Smith, Joy Williams, Madelaine Blais, Richard Bausch, James Crumley, Carolyn Forché, John Katzenbach, and agent Nat Sobel.

For further information, contact the Creative Writing Program Director.

❖Florida State University
Tallahassee, FL 32306-1036
(850) 644-4230
website: www.english.fsu.edu/crw

Degrees offered: BA, MA, PhD

Degree: BA in English with Concentration in Writing

Required course of study: 33 s/hrs in the major
   Thesis: no requirement except in Honors
      Program 6 s/hrs
   Writing courses: 15-18 s/hrs (including 9
      workshop s/hrs)
   Literature courses: 15-18 s/hrs
   Tutorials or directed reading: up to 6 s/hrs

Other Requirements: Minor in another field, usually 12 s/hrs; completion of the final course of a 12 s/hr sequence in a foreign language. In the Honors Program, an oral defense of the creative thesis is required.

Degree: MA in English with Concentration in Writing

Type of Program: Studio/Academic

Required course of study: 33 s/hrs
   Thesis: 6 s/hrs
   Writing workshop: 15-18 s/hrs
   Literature courses: 15-18 s/hrs
   Tutorials or directed reading: up to 6 s/hrs

Other Requirements: Reading knowledge of one foreign language; oral defense of creative thesis.

Degree: PhD in English with Creative Dissertation

Type of Program: Traditional Literary Study and Creative Writing

Required course of study:
   27 s/hrs of course work beyond the MA
   Thesis: 24 s/hrs
   Writing workshop: 1 of 2 required seminars
      must be in writing
   Literature courses: 12 s/hrs of area requirements
   Tutorials or directed reading: up to 12 s/hrs

Other Requirements: Preliminary examination; foreign language proficiency in 1 or 2 languages; oral defense of creative dissertation; 3 hrs in language or linguistics; 3 hrs in research methods course, 3 hrs in literary theory.

The English Department of Florida State University offers the BA, MA, and PhD degrees with emphasis in writing. Students in these programs enroll in literature and linguistics courses as well as in Writing workshops.

Workshops are offered in poetry, fiction, drama, and nonfiction. Enrollment in the workshops is limited, giving students the opportunity to work closely with their instructors. In addition to techniques courses and workshops in each of the genres, courses and internships in editing are offered on both the undergraduate and graduate levels. The current writing staff includes Ralph Berry (*Plain Geometry and Other Affairs of the Heart*); Van K. Brock (*The Hard Essential Landscape*); Janet Burroway (*Raw Silk, Writing Fiction, Cutting Stone*); Hunt Hawkins (*The Domestic Life*); David Kirby (*Diving For Poems, Sarah Bernhardt's Leg, Saving the Young Men of Vienna*); Wendy Bishop (*Working Words*); Douglas Fowler (*Reading Nabokov*); Joann Gardner; William T. Lhamon, Jr. (*Deliberate Speed*); Sheila Ortiz-Taylor (*Faultline, Imaginary Parents*); and Virgil Suárez (*Iguana Dreams, Latin Jazz*). The program is directed by Mark Winegardner (*The Veracruz Blues, Elvis Presley Boulevard, We Are What We Ate*). Bob Shacochis (*Easy in the Islands, Swimming in the Volcano*) is currently our Visiting Faculty Writer.

The Writing Program regularly sponsors readings and workshops by visiting writers and, annually, a three-day Spring Festival of Writers. Visitors in recent years have included Tom Stoppard, George Plimpton, Margaret Atwood, Donald Justice, Donald Hall, Ernest Gaines, Rosellen Brown, Richard Russo, Tom Drury, Cristina Garcia, Jill McCorkle, and David Haynes.

The Tallahassee area features weekly public readings by students, faculty, and local writers. There are 2 literary magazines, *Sun Dog: The Southeast Review* and *Kudzu Review*, affiliated with the university, as well as the independent journals *International Quarterly* and *The Apalachee Quarterly*, and The Anhinga Press, which publishes a chapbook series, and other independent presses and newsletters. The department also sponsors the annual *World's Best Short Short Story Contest*, which attracts thousands of entries from around the world, and the Richard Eberhart Poetry Prize.

On the graduate level, teaching assistantships regularly provide students the opportunity to teach writing on the freshman level. A few advanced doctoral students are invited to teach introductory creative writing technique courses as well as introductory survey courses in literature.

For more information or an application, write Mark Winegardner, Director, The Writing Program. For an application via e-mail, visit our website.

❖University of Florida
Gainesville, FL 32611-2036

(352) 392-0777

Degree offered: MFA in Creative Writing

Type of Program: Studio/Academic

Length of Residency: Two years

Required course of study: 48 s/hrs
  Thesis: 12 s/hrs
  Workshops: 12 s/hrs
  Literature courses: 9 s/hrs
  Electives: 6 s/hrs
  Reading tutorials: 9 s/hrs

Application Deadlines: We accept applications for the fall. We begin reading manuscripts at the end of December, and continue into April. Though there is no formal deadline, we receive almost all applications by January 15. Applications for minority fellowships (worth $8,000) should be submitted by January 1.

The writing program at Florida was founded in 1949, and in its early years was headed by Andrew Lytle, the Southern fiction writer who later became editor of *The Sewanee Review*. We offer a degree that requires an equal interest in writing and in literature, and assume that the intelligent regard of one will invite intelligent appraisal of the other. The writers in our program come from many states and write in a variety of styles. We don't believe in any particular school of writing, and have no wish to foster or found one. Criticism should attempt to fulfill the design of a poem or story on its own terms, and not force all writing into the same set of aesthetic commonplaces.

Writers are often viewed with suspicion by critics, and it is only fair that they sometimes peer suspiciously back. Writers produce the art that critics wrangle over. Randall Jarrell once attended a conference where critics were discussing Wordsworth. What, after all, did Wordsworth know about poems? The critics knew how they were put together; poor Wordsworth just put them together: "In the same way, if a pig wandered up to you during a bacon-judging contest, you would say impatiently, 'Go away, pig!' What do you know about bacon?" Critics occasionally need to be reminded of their proper place, though the critics at Florida show the writers an intelligent concern and unusual interest. In the last decade the department has attracted one of the strongest graduate faculties in the country. They offer courses, from *Beowulf* to deconstruction, that encourage the necessary exercise of a writer's critical skill.

That skill is most finely demanded in the workshop, where the writer weekly offers his work in an atmosphere of rigor and respect, criticism and sympathy. Writers learn as much from their fellows as they will from their teachers. The writing faculty therefore accepts each year a diverse group of students who have already displayed their talent as writers, and provides them with a serious and provocative set of courses. Florida possesses a climate conducive to a writer's warm temperament, and flora and fauna shockingly unfamiliar to those from out of state. After 2 years in the program a writer will have produced a thesis of publishable work: the course of study is meant to lead to a degree of mastery, not merely a degree.

Since Gainesville has a low cost of living, we are able to offer generous financial aid. Writers almost always receive half-time teaching assistantships ($8,100), and teach 3 courses over 2 semesters. They usually have the opportunity to teach another course during the summer, if they wish. In their second year, the writers have the chance to teach creative writing to undergraduates. The teaching assistantships come with a tuition waiver that reduces the cost of graduate education to a nominal amount. There are also Alumni Fellowships (up to $2,000 added to a teaching assistantship).

The faculty in poetry consists of William Logan (winner of the National Book Critics Circle Citation for Excellence in Reviewing, and author of *Vain Empires, Difficulty,* and *Sullen Weedy Lakes*), Debora Greger

(*Desert Fathers, Uranian Daughters*, and *The 1002nd Night*), Sidney Wade (author of *Empty Sleeves* and *Green*), and Michael Hofmann (*Nights in the Iron Hotel, Acrimony*, and *Corona, Corona*). In fiction, the faculty includes Nancy Reisman (stories in *Glimmer Train* and *The Best Unpublished Short Stories by Emerging Writers*), and Padgett Powell (nominated for an American Book Award for *Edisto*, and also author of *Aliens of Affection* and *Edisto Revisited*). Each year there is also a varied list of visiting writers.

For more information, write William Logan, Director of Creative Writing, Dept. of English.

Fordham University
Bronx, NY 10458
(718) 817-4005

Degree offered: BA in Communications with Concentration in Creative Writing

For more information, contact Director, Creative Writing Program, Dept. of Communications.

Francis Marion University
Florence, SC 29505
(803) 661-1500
FAX (803) 661-1219

Degree offered: BA in English with Minor or Collateral in Creative Writing

Required course of study: 120 s/hrs total
27–36 s/hrs in English major
Minor requires 12 s/hrs in Beginning and
Advanced Poetry and Fiction plus 6 s/hrs of
advanced writing courses
Collateral requires 12 s/hrs in Beginning and
Advanced Poetry and Fiction

Application Deadlines: Varies for both admissions and financial aid. Contact Admissions Office at 803-661-1231.

Francis Marion University offers a BA in English with a minor or collateral in creative writing. English majors who concentrate in creative writing must fulfill all regular requirements of the English degree. Five creative writing courses are available, in Beginning and Advanced Poetry, Beginning and Advanced Fiction, and Playwriting. The basic courses in creative writing are offered every semester.

The English department also sponsors publication of a student-edited magazine of creative writing, the *Snow Island Review*. The Janet Wilson Award is given each year to outstanding student writers of poetry and fiction. Moreover, several working scholarships are awarded to students participating in the annual Francis Marion Writers' Conference. A reading series provides opportunities for students to hear and meet visiting writers. Recent writers at the Conference and in the reading series include Donald Hall, Henry Taylor, Kaye Gibbons, Russell Banks, and Jane Kenyon.

The faculty currently includes poet Ken Autrey, fiction writer Lynn Kostoff (*A Choice of Nightmares, The Work of Hands*), poet Robert Parham (*Dark Corners and New Light*), and playwright Jon Tuttle (*Terminal Cafe, I Wanna Be a Cowboy*).

For more information about the program, please contact Dr. Robert Parham, Chair, Dept. of English.

❖Gainesville College
P.O. Box 1358
Gainesville, GA 30503

For more information, contact the Director, Division of Humanities.

Gannon University
Erie, PA 16541
(814) 871-7504
e-mail: moore001@mail1.gannon.edu

Degrees offered: BA in English with Emphasis in Writing, MA

Required course of study: 128 s/hrs
Field of concentration: 21 s/hrs
Emphasis: 9 s/hrs

Application Deadline: Applications accepted throughout the year for admission in September and January.

Gannon University offers a BA in English with the student's choice of an emphasis in writing, literature, or applied communications. With the writing emphasis, students may take a variety of courses in literary composition, including Creative Writing, Poetry Workshop, Fiction Workshop, and Advanced Prose Style. Students may also take more practical courses such as Writing for the News Media, Feature Writing, Editing for the Print Media, Public Relations, and others. Qualified students may train as peer writing consultants for positions in the university's writing center and may apply for admission into the university's honors program. In addition, a communications curriculum offers students TV and radio opportunities as well as a Webmaster minor. Internships with local businesses and arts groups are also available for credit.

Gannon offers an MA in English; five teaching assistantships are available.

In addition, the English Department supports writing and writers through many co- and extra-curricular activities. Gannon's student-produced literary and art magazine, *Totem*, is a first place winner in the American Scholastic Press Association's 1996 and 1997 competitions. The *Knight*, also student-produced, is Gannon's weekly newspaper. Both publications are desk-top published using the latest computer technology. Writing contests in poetry, journalism, and research writing are offered each year and judged by professional writers. Visiting writers conducting seminars and giving readings have included Galway Kinnell, Gwendolyn Brooks, Donald Hall, A.R. Ammons, Lucille Clifton, William Matthews, W.D. Snodgrass, Kelly Cherry, and Lisel Mueller.

For more information, contact Berwyn Moore, association professor of English at above phone number or e-mail address.

❖Garland County Community College
Hot Springs, AR 71913
(501) 767-9371, ext. 260
FAX (501) 767-3427
e-mail: rfox@jull.gccc.cc.ar.us

Contact Communications/Arts Division Chair, at the above numbers.

❖George Mason University
Fairfax, VA 22030
(703) 993-1185

Degrees offered: BA, MA, MFA

Degree: MFA in Creative Writing (poetry, fiction; we will soon add a track in creative nonfiction. Expected initial enrollments, Fall 1999, with a small class and normal enrollments starting Fall 2000)

Type of Program: Studio/Academic

Length of Residency: Two years

Required course of study: 48 s/hrs
Thesis: 6 s/hrs
Writing workshops: 15–24 s/hrs
Other writing courses: 3–12 s/hrs
Literature courses: 15–24 s/hrs

Other Requirements: 12 s/hrs undergraduate credit in a foreign language, required for degree; students may also satisfy this requirement by passing a proficiency exam; Poetry: 4–hour written examination on the student's own list of 30 authors (chosen in consultation with the faculty); Fiction: written exam on list of authors, or completing MFA project (separate from thesis).

The Master of Fine Arts in Creative Writing (48 s/hrs) is for students with demonstrated ability who have a strong commitment to writing fiction or poetry. The MFA program involves diversified coursework and intensive work in writing: it consists of up to 6 workshops in one genre, a writing seminar on technique in that genre, up to 3 workshops in other genres, and at least 4 courses in literature. Students complete a thesis such as a publishable collection of poetry or short fiction, or a novel. In consultation with the faculty, each poetry student draws up a reading list of 30 authors which forms the basis for a written exam. Fiction students complete comparable or similar work in consultation with the faculty.

Degree: MA in English with Concentration in Professional Writing and Editing

Required course of study: 30 s/hrs
Thesis: nonfiction work or editorial project: 3 s/hrs
Research course: 3 s/hrs
Literature courses: 9–12 s/hrs
Nonfiction writing: 3–6 s/hrs
Professional development courses: 9 s/hrs

Other Requirements: 12 s/hrs undergraduate credit in a foreign language required for degree; students may also satisfy this requirement by passing a proficiency exam.

The Master of Arts with Concentration in Profes-

sional Writing and Editing (30 s/hrs) is for students who wish to combine the advanced study of literature with training in the writing of nonfiction and in editing. The program offers a balance of courses in writing and literature and includes at least one workshop in nonfiction, 3 professional courses (in editing, technical writing, desktop publishing, scientific writing, theory of composition, or internships in writing or editing), a course in literary scholarship, and at least 3 literature courses. Students write a thesis such as a monograph or series of feature articles or complete a substantial editing project.

Degree: MA in English with Concentration in Teaching of Writing and Literature

Required course of study: 30 s/hrs
Thesis: up to 3 s/hrs (optional)
Writing workshops: 6–12 s/hrs
Other writing courses: 6 s/hrs
Literature courses: 12–18 s/hrs
Tutorials or directed reading: up to 6 s/hrs

Other Requirements: 12 s/hrs of undergraduate credit in a foreign language required for degree; students may also satisfy this requirement by passing a proficiency exam.

The Master of Arts in English with Concentration in the Teaching of Writing and Literature (30 s/hrs) is for teachers who wish to develop their classroom skills while pursuing graduate study. The program offers a balance of courses and includes a minimum of 2 writing workshops, a course in linguistics, a course in literary scholarship, at least 3 courses in literature, a course in the teaching of writing, and a course in the teaching of literature. 3 elective s/hrs may be taken in writing, literature, teaching, or to complete a thesis.

Degree: BA with Major in English (Fiction or Poetry writing, or Nonfiction writing and editing)

Required course of study: 30 s/hrs in the major
Thesis: no requirement
Writing workshops: 6 s/hrs
Literature: 12 s/hrs of literature courses,
    including English 325, Dimensions of
    Literature, plus at least 6 s/hrs in
    upper–level English courses of the
    student's choice
Tutorials or directed reading: up to
    6 s/hrs (optional)

Other Requirements: 12 s/hrs humanities (composition and literature); 3 s/hrs communication; 12 s/hrs foreign language; 3 s/hrs logic or math; 3 s/hrs philosophy or religion; 3 s/hrs fine arts; 12 s/hrs social sciences; 8 s/hrs natural sciences; 6 s/hrs nonwestern culture.

George Mason University is a young, rapidly growing institution located on 600 wooded acres 16 miles from Washington, D.C., and the libraries, theatres, museums, and other resources of a major, international cultural center. The University is particularly concerned with innovative and interdisciplinary education, and has established itself as a regional and national center for the arts. By way of the Writing Program, George Mason offers the MFA, 3 writing or writing-related MA degrees, and the BA in English with an emphasis in writing. All programs combine the rigorous study of literature with intensive work in writing, and all programs work to establish a rapport with other disciplines in the arts and sciences. At the graduate level, the Writing Program offers 17 separate courses in creative writing, professional writing, editing, and the teaching of writing, as well as internships with schools, businesses, and government and arts organizations. A number of these offerings are "umbrella courses" and provide a context for workshops in such areas as playwriting and scriptwriting, short short fiction, the novella, the topical essay, reviewing, children's writing, biography, and autobiography.

Each year, from 8 to 12 poets, fiction writers, essayists, dramatists, children's authors, and editors visit George Mason to give readings and lectures, conduct workshops, and take part in short-term conferences and symposia. Well over 130 writers have visited the campus since The Graduate Writing Program was inaugurated in 1980, including Margaret Atwood, Jorge Luis Borges, Gwendolyn Brooks, Frederick Busch, Robert Hass, Seamus Heaney, Galway Kinnell, Maxine Kumin, Stanley Kunitz, Jayne Anne Phillips, Manuel Puig, Adrienne Rich, Gerald Stern, Robert Stone, William Styron, D.M. Thomas, Derek Walcott, Paul West, John Edgar Wideman, Richard Wilbur, and Adam Zagajewski. Each semester the Graduate Writing Program offers a number of one-credit-hour sections of English 699, "Visiting Writer Seminars," enabling students to enroll in intensive, short-term workshops with nationally and internationally recognized authors from outside the program.

George Mason is the home of The Mary Roberts Rinehart Fund, The Federal Theatre Project Research Center, The Northern Virginia Writing Project, *Phoebe: a journal of literary arts, So to Speak*, and the GMU Writers' Club. The Mary Roberts Rinehart Fund, established to perpetuate the memory of one of America's best known writers, each year awards 2 fellowships to promising writers outside George Mason University, and 2 fellowships for students in the MFA program in creative writing. The Federal Theatre Project Research Center contains the major collection of playscripts, radioscripts, set and costume designs, and other materials produced by the Federal Theatre of the 1930s. It includes additional scripts and memorabilia from the Robert Breen Theatre Collection and materials from the American National Theatre and Academy. The Northern Virginia Writing Project, under the direction of Donald Gallehr, works cooperatively with Northern Virginia public schools to improve the quality of writing by students at all levels and in all disciplines. The Project offers graduate courses in teaching writing and sponsors lectures and workshops by leading figures in writing research such as Janet Emig, Donald Murray, Donald Graves, Pat D'Arcy and Lee Odell. *Phoebe*, the student-edited literary quarterly, publishes poems, short fiction, essays, interviews, and photography for a national audience.

Faculty of the Writing Program include: Richard Bausch, author of numerous novels and story collections, including *Violence, Mr. Field's Daughter*, and *The Fireman's Wife and Other Stories*. Alan Cheuse is the author of the novel *The Light Possessed*, the collection of short fiction *The Tennessee Waltz*, and the nonfiction work *Fall Out of Heaven: An Autobiographical Journey*. He is a regular contributor to National Public Radio's "All Things Considered." Playwright Paul D'Andrea's plays include *The Trouble with Europe, A Full Length Portrait of America*, and *The Einstein Project* (co-authored with Jon Klein). Carolyn Forché has published three volumes of poetry, *Gathering the Tribes, The Country Between Us*, and *The Angel of*

History. Fiction and nonfiction writer Stephen Goodwin is the author of the novels *Kin* and *The Blood of Paradise*. He has also written *The Greatest Masters*, a study of golfing as a sport. Peter Klappert has published five collections of poetry, including *Lugging Vegetables to Nantucket, Circular Stairs*, and *Distress in the Mirrors*. Roger Lathbury has published the novel *Numin's Curse*, a collection of poems, *The Carbon Gang*, and *An Editing Workbook*. Poet Eric Pankey is the author of *Apocrypha, Heartwood*, and *For the New Year*. Fiction writer Susan Richards Shreve is the author of seven novels, including *A Fortunate Madness, Dreaming of Heroes*, and *A Country of Strangers*. Susan Tichy is the author of two collections of poetry: *The Hands in Exile*, selected for the National Poetry Series, and *A Smell of Burning Starts the Day*.

The Program offers financial assistance in several forms. A limited number of students work as teaching assistants, for which they are paid a stipend and given a full tuition waiver so long as the course they propose taking meets their degree requirements. In-house fellowship funds are awarded by the faculty to both incoming and returning students. Privately contributed fellowships or endowments are used to reward especially promising applicants or returning students. Sizes of fellowship awards vary.

In addition, the Fiction faculty each year selects one outstanding student as the Heritage Writer for the coming academic year. The student receives $10,000 as a stipend to allow him or her time to write. This award is usually given to a second- or third-year student.

For an application and for further information, write to William Miller, Administrator, The Writing Program, Dept. of English, MSN 3E4, George Mason University, Fairfax, VA 22030.

❖George Washington University Washington, DC 20052
(202) 994-6180

Degree: BA or BS with a Minor in Creative Writing

In addition to majors in American Literature, English Literature, and Literature in English, GW's English Department offers undergraduates a minor in creative writing. The creative writing curriculum includes a mixed-genre introductory workshop and intermediate workshops in fiction, poetry, and playwriting. Creative writing minors take the introductory workshop (3 s/hrs), satisfy a literature survey prerequisite (6 s/hrs), then take an additional 12 s/hrs of upper-level English courses, *at least 9 of which* must be intermediate or advanced creative writing workshops.

The creative writing faculty includes: essayist and fiction writer Faye Moskowitz (*A Leak in the Heart; Whoever Finds This: I Love You; And the Bridge is Love*); poet Jane Shore (*Eye Level; The Minute Hand; Music Minus One*); fiction writer and playwright Patricia Griffith (*The Future is Not What it Used to Be; Tennessee Blue; The World Around Midnight*); poet and fiction writer Maxine Clair (*Coping with Gravity; Rattlebone*); poet David McAleavey (*Holding Obsidian; Shrine, Shelter, Cove; The Forty Days*); poet Jody Bolz; poet Judith Harris; and Vikram Chandra (*Red Earth and Pouring Rain*).

Visiting writers (holding the prestigious one-year Jenny McKean Moore Writer in Washington position) enrich the program's offerings with an upper-level workshop, seminar, or lecture course each term. To date, visitors have included Rika Lesser, Lonnie Carter, Richard McCann, Bobby Jack Nelson, Pablo Medina, John Haines, Carole Maso, Linda McCarriston, Beverly Lowry, Vikram Chandra, Cornelius Eady, and Anne Caston. The Moore Fund Writer in Washington also teaches a free community workshop for area residents outside the university. A monthly reading series co-sponsored by the Moore Fund and the English Department brings to campus locally and nationally prominent writers each year.

For further information, contact David McAleavey, English Dept.

❖Georgia College & State University Milledgeville, GA 31061

(912) 445-4581
FAX (912) 445-5961
e-mail: mlammon@mail.gcsu.edu
website: http://www.gcsu.edu

Degrees offered: BA, MA

Degree: BA in English with Creative Writing Minor

Required course of study: 120 s/hrs
Creative Writing courses for minor: 18 s/hrs
English Major Requirements: 24 s/hrs

Other Requirements: University core curriculum requirements; competence in a foreign language at the level of the fourth university course.

Application Deadlines: March 15 for financial aid; July 15 for admissions.

The undergraduate minor in Creative Writing requires that students take Introduction and Advanced Creative courses; a choice of three single-genre workshops (fiction, poetry, creative nonfiction, or script writing); and a "capstone" course, Creative Writing Seminar. The English major requires studies in literature ranging from the Medieval to Modern periods. As the state's only public liberal arts university, Georgia College & State University encourages undergraduates to be active participants in the arts and sciences. *The Peacock's Feet* is the undergraduate, student-edited magazine featuring both written and graphic works. Superior senior creative writing students may also intern with *Arts & Letters Journal of Contemporary Culture*, a national journal devoted to literature, cultural commentary, and the graphic arts. Students participate in AWP's national Intro Awards competition. Students participate often in public readings of their own works. Furthermore, students meet and work with a wide range of visiting writers who come to campus via the Georgia Poetry Circuit, the annual Georgia Festival of Arts & Letters, the university's Artist-in-Residence program, and other special events.

Degree: MA in English with Creative Thesis option (poetry, fiction)

Type of Program: Traditional Literary Study and Creative Writing

Length of Residency: Two years

Required course of study: 36 s/hrs
Creative Thesis: 9 s/hrs
Required Seminars: 9 s/hrs
Major Area: 18 s/hrs (6 s/hrs in Creative Writing)

Application Deadlines: April 15 for financial aid; three weeks prior to date graduate study commences (July 15 for normal fall semester study) for admission.

Although primarily an undergraduate institution, Georgia College & State University offers unique graduate opportunities in creative writing. Working closely with full-time and visiting faculty, a student focuses on completing a collection of stories or poems. In addition, the student also completes a substantial paper that addresses one's creative work in a critical or literary context. Students develop their work in directions relevant to their own writing and career goals, in close consultation with a thesis advisor.

Writers who have visited campus the last two years are Andrea Hollander Budy, Fred Chappell, Betsy Duffey, Cornelius Eady, Clyde Edgerton (artist-in-residence), Alice Fulton, Ernest Gaines, Margaret Gibson, Terry Kay, Maxine Kumin, Donald McCaig, David Mason, W.S. Merwin, Ethelbert Miller, Barbara Ras, and Bobbie Ann Mason.

Arts & Letters Journal of Contemporary Culture is a national journal devoted to literature, cultural commentary, and the arts. Special features include the "Mentors Interview Series" and "World Poetry Translation Series." Contributors include Robert Bly, Maritza Dávila, Annie Dawid, Ernest Gaines, Caroline Langston, W.S. Merwin, Ethelbert Miller, Dinty W. Moore, Katherine Soniat, Virgil Suarez, Carolyne Wright, and Michael Waters. The journal sponsors the Georgia Festival of Arts & Letters and a national competition in poetry, short fiction, and the one-act play, *The Arts & Letters Prizes*.

The program offers one or more assistantships to students who serve as assistant editors at *Arts & Letters*. Students participate in all facets of literary editing, publishing, and business management. Other assistantships related to editing, publishing, and writing are available with *The Flannery O'Connor Bulletin*, a journal devoted to O'Connor scholarship, and with the GC&SU Writing Center.

The 1998–99 creative writing faculty includes: Martin Lammon, poet, Fuller E. Callaway endowed Flannery O'Connor Chair in Creative Writing (1997 Arkansas Poetry Award for *News from Where I Live*; Editor, *Written in Water, Written in Stone: Twenty Years of Poets on Poetry*); David Muschell, playwright (*Amelia, Once More; Mixed Emotions; Sweet Dreams*); Dale Ray Phillips, fiction writer (*My People's Waltz: Stories*; selection in *Best American Short Stories* and *Best New Stories from the South*). Additional faculty include Dr. Sarah Gordon (Editor, *The Flannery O'Connor Bulletin*).

For more information, contact Martin Lammon at Box 44, Dept. of English, at the above mailing address, e-mail address, or phone.

❖Georgia Perimeter College
2101 Womack Road
Dunwoody, GA 30338

For more information, contact the Director, Dept. of English.

❖Georgia State University
Atlanta, GA 30303-3083

(404) 651-2900

Degrees offered: BA, MA, MFA, PhD

Degree: BA in English with Emphasis in Creative Writing

Required course of study: 20 s/hrs in Creative Writing courses beyond the required 20 hours in Literature.

Degree: MA in English with Emphasis in Creative Writing

Type of Program: Traditional Literary Study and Creative Writing

Required course of study: 27 s/hrs of graduate coursework, including 12 hours in creative writing classes.

Other Requirements: Foreign language exam and the standard comprehensive MA exam; thesis completed under a director with the approval of a second and third reader.

Degree: PhD in English with Emphasis in Creative Writing (poetry, fiction, biography)

Type of Program: Traditional Literary Study and Creative Writing

Required course of study: 36 s/hrs of graduate coursework beyond the MA level, with 12 s/hrs in Creative Writing Workshops, plus 20 s/hrs of dissertation research.

Other Requirements: Reading proficiency in a second foreign language is required; comprehensive examinations; dissertation completed under a director with the approval of a second and third reader.

Degree: MFA in Creative Writing (poetry, fiction)

Type of Program: Studio/Academic

Required course of study: 42 s/hrs of graduate coursework (15-21 of which will be in Creative Writing Workshops), plus 6 hours of thesis research.

Other Requirements: Foreign language exam and a final MFA exam; thesis completed under a director with the approval of a second and third reader.

Our department is a founding member of the Georgia Poetry Consortium, which brings several established poets to the state each year for readings at member campuses. Throughout the school year, the GSU English Department sponsors readings by distinguished poets and fiction writers, as well as newer voices. Writers who have recently read or conducted workshops at Georgia State include: W.S. Merwin, Charles Wright, Toni Morrison, Ellen Bryant Voigt, Richard Bausch, Dave Smith, Jane Hirshfield, Joyce Carol Oates, Louis Simpson, and Tess Gallagher. The Atlanta area provides many additional opportunities to hear writers, to see new plays and films, and to attend concerts and exhibitions that feed and sustain a writer's life.

Five Points, a tri-quarterly edited by David Bottoms and Pam Durban, publishes poetry, fiction, and essays by many of the finest writers in America. The *GSU Review*, a student-edited literary magazine, publishes twice a year. Students will find a number of opportunities to work on these magazines.

The writing faculty includes poet and novelist David Bottoms (*Shooting Rats at the Bibb County Dump, In a U-Haul North of Damascus, Under the Vulture-Tree*); biographer Virginia Spencer Carr (*Dos Passos: A Life* and *The Lonely Hunter*, a biography of Carson McCullers); fiction writer Pam Durban (*All Set About with Fever Trees* and *The Laughing Place*); fiction writer John Holman (*Squabble* and *Luminous Mysteries*); poet Leon Stokesbury (*Often in Different Landscapes, The Drifting Away*, and *Autumn Rhythm*).

A number of assistantships are available to qualified students in several categories: tutoring in the Writing Center, assisting with faculty research, and teaching in the lower division. The fiction section also offers the Paul Bowles Fellowship in fiction writing.

For further information, contact David Bottoms, Director of Creative Writing.

❖University of Georgia
Athens, GA 30602

(706) 542-2659
FAX (706) 542-2181
e-mail: jcheckow@arches.uga.edu
website:
http://parallel.park.uga.edu/~creative/creative.html

Degrees offered: MA and PhD in English with Creative Thesis or Dissertation

Degree: MA in English with Creative Thesis (poetry, fiction, creative nonfiction)

Type of Program: Traditional Literary Study and Creative Writing

Length of Residency: Two years

Required course of study: 27 hours of coursework in English and American Literature and Related fields
    Writing workshops: 6 hours
    Creative Writing topics: 3 hours
    Thesis: 3 hours

Other Requirements: Written examination, oral defense of thesis, proof of reading knowledge of an approved foreign language.

Degree: PhD in English with Creative Dissertation (poetry, fiction, creative nonfiction)

Type of Program: Traditional Literary Study and Creative Writing

Length of Residency: Four years

Required course of study: If entering with MA, 27 hours of coursework in English and American Literature and Related Fields. If entering with BA: 45 hours of coursework in English and American Literature and Related Fields

Writing workshops: 12 hours
Creative Writing topics: 3 hours
Thesis: additional hours

Other Requirements: Written qualifying exam, comprehensive examinations, oral defense of dissertation, proof of reading knowledge of two approved foreign languages *or* proficiency in one foreign language *or* reading knowledge in one foreign language and competence in specified research skills.

Application Deadlines: January 1 for all materials. Application for both the MA and PhD program currently requires three separate but related efforts: 1) application to the UGA Graduate School, 2) application to the English Department, 3) application to the Creative Writing Faculty.

1) Application to the UGA Graduate School: Application for Admission form, official copies of transcripts from *all* institutions where you have taken college courses for credit, official report of GRE scores in both the General Test for MA and PhD candidates and the Subject Test in English for PhD candidates only. Send to: The University of Georgia, Office of Graduate Admissions, Boyd Graduate Research Center, Graduate School, Athens, GA 30602-7402.

2) Application to the Department of English: A statement of intent describing your reasons for applying to a graduate program in English (2-3 typed pages), a critical writing sample (10-15 pages), three letters of recommendation (must be sent by the referees directly). Send to: English Department Graduate Office, Park Hall 234, The University of Georgia, Athens, GA 30602.

3) Application to the Program in Creative Writing: Five copies of no more than 25-30 pages of fiction or creative nonfiction or 10 pages of poetry (one poem per page), with name, address, and phone # on the first page of the manuscript only, five *signed* copies of a statement of your personal goals and intentions in pursuing a graduate degree in Creative Writing at the University of Georgia (*note that this is different than the statement of intentions for the English program*), no more than 2 pages, and a stamped, self-addressed postcard. Send to: Prof. Julie Checkoway, Director, Graduate Program in Creative Writing, Park Hall 102, The University of Georgia, Athens, GA 30602.

Important: Students may find that they have been admitted to the MA or PhD program in English without being admitted to the Creative Writing Program. Admission to the Creative Writing Program is confirmed *only* by a written invitation from the Director. Students who are admitted to the MA or PhD program in English may matriculate in the English Department and reapply to the Creative Writing Program after their first year at UGA, but admission to the Creative Writing Program is *not* guaranteed.

The University of Georgia offers both the MA and the PhD in English and is one of the few universities that requires, along with workshopping, rigorous coursework in literature. Graduates of our program are well-prepared as both writers and scholars to greet with confidence and success both the national literary scene and the academic job market. Students offered TAships have the opportunity to teach literature or composition; all PhD students are offered teaching apprenticeships in creative writing. Paid internships are available for select students at *The Georgia Review*. Members of the creative writing faculty are excellent teachers and mentors committed to close and careful reading of student work and the cultivation of diversity in student voices.

Creative Writing faculty: Julie Checkoway, fiction and creative nonfiction (*Little Sister: Searching for the Shadow World of Chinese Women, Creating Fiction*), Judith Ortiz Cofer, poetry, fiction, and creative nonfiction (*The Latin Deli, Terms of Survival, Silent Dancing*), James Kilgo, fiction and creative nonfiction (*Deep Enough for Ivorybills, Inheritance of Horses, Daughter of My People*), Judson Mitcham, fiction and poetry (*The Sweet Everlasting*), and Kevin Young, poetry (*Most Way Home*, John Zacharis Prize, one of *Swing* magazine's 30 most powerful people under 30).

Recent visiting writers, many of whom give not only readings but master classes, include: Andrei Codrescu, Denis Covington, Donald Hall, Tony Kushner, Jill Ker Conway, Mary Hood, Czeslaw Milosz, Joyce Carol Oates, John Updike, Terry Tempest Williams, Toi Derricotte, Michael Martone, Cornelius Eady, and Philip Levine.

The University of Georgia is located in green, hilly Athens, a city of some 150,000 people. It is home not only to a rich musical culture (the B52s, REM, and Widespread Panic all had their start here), but also to many poets and novelists, including Coleman Barks (Professor Emeritus), Philip Lee Williams, and Terry Kay. Athens has a busy literary culture that includes *The Georgia Review*, The University of Georgia Press, Hill Street Press, Byhalia Books, the Athens Film Festival, and numerous reading series, including the student-run Writers Bloc. The University is also home to the student-run journals *Stillpoint, Broad River* (online), and *Mandala*.

For more information, contact Julie Checkoway, Director of Creative Writing, at (706) 542-2659, or jcheckow@arches.uga.edu. Specific questions about the English program should be directed to Professor Nelson Hilton at (706) 542-2197 or <nhilton@english.uga.edu>.

❖Goddard College
Plainfield, VT 05667-9700

(802) 454-8311

Degrees offered: BA, MA, MFA

Degree: BA with Concentration in Creative Writing in any genre (poetry, fiction, creative nonfiction, children's literature, playwriting, filmmaking, mixed genres)

Required course of study: 120 s/hrs total

Other Requirements: Level reviews at semesters three and six, senior study thesis, graduating presentation.

Application Deadlines: For financial aid, contact financial aid office; rolling deadlines for admissions.

Ungraded self-directed program with level review during the third and sixth semester and student and faculty evaluations. "Senior study" consists of an independent project and process paper. Like other BA students, those concentrating in Creative Writing may enroll in the resident or non-resident programs. Non-resident students are required to attend a ten-day residency at Goddard each semester.

The undergraduate concentration, like other Goddard concentrations, has no set requirements, but is tailored to each student's individual goals, which are outlined in the beginning of each semester in self-generated study plans. For students concentrating in creative writing, the "senior study," completed throughout the last semester in close conjunction with a faculty advisor, consists of a creative thesis and process paper.

Graduate Degrees: MFA in Creative Writing (in any genre or mixed genres: fiction, creative nonfiction, poetry, playwriting, children's and young adult literature, screen plays)

A three-semester MA degree with a concentration in literature or the teaching of writing is also offered. Students in the MA or MFA programs may also gain a high-school teaching certification.

Type of Program: Studio/Academic (Low Residency)

Length of Residency: The MFA is a four-semester, two-year non-resident program; students are required to attend a ten-day residency at Goddard each semester and to correspond with their advisors by mail throughout the semester.

Required course of study: 48 s/hrs, minimum of four semesters.

Application Deadlines: Contact financial aid office for financial aid; open rolling admissions for both fall and spring semesters.

Each semester consists of a balance of studio or creative and academic or critical work. In addition to ongoing creative work during each semester, additional requirements for each semester are as follows: one and two: short critical papers; two or three: a one-semester supervised teaching practicum and teaching essay; two or three: a long critical paper; four: creative thesis and process paper.

In the MFA program, we realize that our students are adults who have chosen a low-residency program because of their need to balance work on the MFA with other responsibilities and jobs, and we try hard to create a challenging, flexible, and non-competitive environment where this will be possible. We encourage students to set their own goals and to stretch their own boundaries as writers by experimenting with different genres and styles. We respect and value individual differences and needs, and are committed to working together to create a program which will be open and welcoming to everyone.

The MFA program at Goddard has existed, under different administrations, for the past fifteen years. Visiting writers have included: Jaime Manrique, Safiya Henderson-Holmes, Marilyn Waniek, Frank Bidart, and Kathryn Davis.

Up to two MFA students per semester may apply to live on campus and complete the teaching practicum in the resident undergraduate program.

Faculty includes: novelist and essayist Marina Budhos (*The House of Waiting*); poet, playwright, and memoirist Kenny Fries (*Body, Remember, The Healing Notebooks, Anesthesia*); poet, memoirist, and editor Michael Klein (*1990, Buried Softer, In the Company of My Solitude*); poet and playwright Joan Larkin (*Housework, A Long Sound, The AIDS Passion*); poet Nora Mitchell (*Proofreading the Histories, Your Skin is a Country*); poet and fiction writer Nicky Morris (anthologized in *Word of Mouth, 1 in 3: Women with Cancer Confront an Epidemic, Wanting Women*); poet and fiction writer Mariana Romo-Carmona (anthologized in *Cuentos: Stories by Latinas, Fight Back!, Beyond Geography and Gender*); novelist and essayist Sarah Schulman (*Rat Bohemia, My American History, Empathy*); playwright and librettist Paul Selig (*Mystery School, Pompeii Travelling Show, Terminal Bar*); poet and essayist Jane Wohl (anthologized in *Tumblewords Anthology, Sharp and Sandy Grains*).

For more information, contact Brighde Mullins and Paul Selig, Co-Directors, Admissions.

❖Goucher College
Dulaney Valley Road
Towson, MD 21204
(410) 337-6282

Degrees offered: BA, MFA

Degree: BA in English with Concentration in Creative Writing (poetry, fiction)

Required course of study: Minimum of 33 hrs of English courses at or above 200-level, including a minimum of 12 hrs of creative writing courses. There are three sequentially tracked courses for each genre, with the remaining credits for the concentration to be completed by independent study. Students may complete the course sequences in both genres if they wish. A creative thesis is optional under the College guidelines for the honors thesis.

Application Deadlines: February 1 for admissions, February 15 for financial aid.

The Goucher College English Department offers a program in Creative Writing for students of all levels of interest and ability -- from those who want to experiment to those who seriously plan careers as fiction writers or poets. For especially talented and committed students, a concentration in Creative Writing Program is available within the English Major. Well-qualified freshman and transfer students may enter the program during their first year at Goucher. Counseling about publication and graduate-level Creative Writing degrees is a specialty of this program.

The Goucher Creative Writing Concentration is a three-tiered program which offers qualified students the opportunity to specialize in poetry, fiction writing, or a combination of the two for a three-year period, or, in exceptional cases, for four years. The first tier of the program consists of the 200- and 300-level poetry workshops and the 200- and 300-level fiction workshops. These courses are typically, though not necessarily, taken consecutively in the same year, and are designed to introduce students to the second tier: the Advanced Creative Writing Seminar, a team-taught course in which poetry and fiction students are combined in a single group. Students may continue into 400-level tutorials, which provide a one-on-one editorial experience for students who may be working to complete a novel or a cycle of stories or poems, or who may be preparing a creative thesis.

Goucher College offers two $500 Reese Awards for students in both poetry and fiction, and also sponsors the Sarah Deford Academy of American Poets Prize. *Preface*, the college literary magazine, is published twice annually.

Visiting writers have included Carolyn Chute, David Bradley, Anthony Hecht, W.S. Merwin, George Garrett, Jill McCorkle, Reginald McKnight, Russell Banks, Robert Stone, A.R. Ammons, Mary Gaitskill, Louise Redd, Denise Giardina, and Frank Bidart, plus alumnae authors such as Eleanor Wilner, Sujata Bhatt, Janet Shaw, Mary Stewart Hammond, Clarinda Harris, Jonathan Jackson, Gilmore Tamney, Darcy Steinke, and Jenn Crowell.

Undergraduate creative writing faculty includes fiction writer Madison Smartt Bell (*Ten Indians, All Souls' Rising, Save Me Joe Louis*) and poet Elizabeth Spires (*Annonciade, Swan's Island, Worldling*).

For more information contact Madison Smartt Bell, Director, Creative Writing Program, English Dept.

Degree: MFA in Creative Nonfiction

The MFA in Creative Nonfiction at Goucher College offers non-traditional students nationwide a rigorous and exciting graduate level limited-residency writing program that balances original writing with critical reading. The program can be completed in two years and includes four semesters of work (36 credit hours), three two-week summer residencies, an internship experience, and submission of a 150 page manuscript of publishable quality work. The MFA program provides instruction in the following creative nonfiction sub-genre: the personal essay, memoir, literary journalism, travel/nature/science writing, biography/profiles, and narrative nonfiction. What distinguishes Goucher's program from other graduate creative writing programs, including those that take advantage of the limited or low-residency format, is its exclusive focus on a single genre.

Core faculty for the MFA program include Jane Bernstein, Julie Checkoway, Philip Gerrard, Lee Gutkind, Lisa Knopp, Jeanne Marie Laskas, Leslie Rubinkowski, and Lauren Slater. Larry Bielawski is the program director.

The tuition cost of the MFA program in the academic year 1999-2000 is $4,385 per semester, and room and board costs for the 1999 summer residency are $55 per night. Application deadline for the August 1999 residency is April 1, 1999.

For more information, contact Larry Bielawski, Director at (800) 697-4646 or visit the creative nonfiction program's website at: <www.goucher.edu/cnf>.

❖Grand Valley State University
1 Campus Drive
Allendale, MI 49401

For more information, contact the Director, Dept. of English.

❖Hamilton College
Clinton, NY 13323
(315) 859-4459
FAX (315) 859-4993

Degree offered: BA in English with Concentration in Creative Writing

Required course of study:
   11 course-credits (40 s/hrs) for the
      concentration (1 credit per course;
      4 courses per semester)
   Thesis-Senior seminar: 2 course credits
      (see Senior Program below)
   Writing workshops: 4 courses
   Literature courses: 5 courses
   Senior Honors thesis option
   Proficiency in foreign language encouraged

The concentration in Creative Writing consists of 9 courses: 5 courses in English and American literature, including Introduction to English Literature, and genre courses in fiction, poetry, and/or genre; and 4 courses in creative writing (Introduction to Creative Writing, Intermediate Fiction, Intermediate Poetry, and the Senior Seminar in Creative Writing), and a final semester independent project is available to Honors students. With the permission of the Department, students may use 1 upper-level course in a foreign literature in the original as 1 of the required literature credits.

Twenty prizes are awarded annually for essays, poetry, and fiction. The Thomas E. Meehan Prize in Creative Writing is awarded annually to 2 juniors who have distinguished themselves in creative writing; the William Rosenfeld Chapbook Series publishes a distinguished portfolio by a graduating senior. Each year a poet or prose writer is invited to spend a week as writer-in-residence, meeting with classes and individual students. Approximately 7 visiting writers come each year for readings and to meet classes. Student publications include 2 literary magazines, a humor magazine (occasionally printed as a recording), and 2 student-faculty opinion journals.

Full-time faculty includes Lucy Ferriss, fiction writer (*Against Gravity, The Gated River, Philip's Girl*); Naomi Guttman, poet (*Reasons for Winter*), and Doran Larson, fiction writer (*The Big Deal, Marginilia*).

For more information, contact Director, Dept. of English.

❖Hamline University
1536 Hewitt Avenue
Saint Paul, MN 55104-1284
(612) 523-2047
FAX (612) 523-2490
e-mail: gradprog@piper.hamline.edu
website:
  http//www.hamline.edu/depts/gradprog/gls_html

Degrees offered: MALS, MFA

Degree: MALS with an Area of Concentration in Writing (fiction, creative nonfiction, poetry)

Type of Program: Traditional literary study and creative writing

Length of Residency: Seven years maximum

Required course of study: 36 s/hrs total
  Synthesis: 4 s/hrs
  Writing concentration courses: 16 s/hrs
  Electives: 12 s/hrs
  Core Seminar: 4 s/hrs

Other Requirements: Oral defense of creative synthesis; synthesis advisors may request a scholarly introduction to the creative synthesis.

Application Deadlines: July 15 (fall), December 1 (spring), and April 15 (summer) for admission and financial aid.

The MALS program at Hamline, begun in 1980, has about 350 active students. MALS students seek to broaden their awareness of the human cultural heritage and gain insights into the complexities of contemporary life while looking toward shaping the future. Students range in age from their twenties to their seventies, in occupation from engineer to teacher to writer. Most students work full time and take courses evenings and weekends. Thirty per cent of classes are team-taught.

One of seven concentrations in MALS, the Area of Concentration in Writing provides theoretical study and practical application of creative writing techniques in a variety of genres under the direction of distinguished published authors. The faculty of the MALS and MFA programs at Hamline is identical, and over half of the courses for the MALS overlap with those in the MFA program. Class size for writing courses is limited to 18.

Degree: MFA in Writing (fiction, creative nonfiction, poetry, mixed genre)

Type of Program: Studio/Academic

Length of Residency: Seven years maximum

Required course of study: 48 s/hrs total
  Thesis: 8 s/hrs
  First-tier Writing courses: 12 s/hrs
  Interdisciplinary courses: 12 s/hrs
  Second-tier Writing courses: 12 s/hrs
  Core Seminar: 4 s/hrs

Other Requirements: Oral defense of thesis; students may pursue one independent study and/or directed readings with a faculty member in place of work with a class.

Application Deadlines: July 15 (fall), December 1 (spring), and April 15 (summer) for admission and financial aid.

Hamline's MFA in Writing, started in 1994, is unique in its connections to the interdisciplinary MALS degree (listed above). By reading widely, MFA students inform their writing as they hone their craft, working with master practitioners in fiction, creative nonfiction, poetry, or a combination of genres. Writing classes are limited to 18 students, and some second-tier project tutorials are limited to 8 students.

Hamline's location in the Twin Cities, the artistic center of the Upper Midwest, provides opportunities for significant contact with many emerging and nationally-recognized authors. Each year, Hamline co-sponsors many readings and events with The Loft, one of the nation's largest literary centers. The Loft Mentor Series has brought Samuel B. Delany, Wanda Coleman, Rick Bass, and Edwin Toreres to the Hamline campus. Since the MFA Program began, visiting writers include Tim O'Brien, Li-Young Lee, Bernard Cooper, and Sandra Benitez.

Each year, the program offers the W. Quay Grigg Award for Excellence in Literary Study. Although teaching assistantships are not yet available at Hamline, the program has become a center for information on local writing internships. Internships are encouraged at fine local presses such as Graywolf, Milkweed Editions, New Rivers Press, and Coffee House Press. *Water-Stone*, edited by a board of MALS and MFA students and professors, provides the opportunity for students to edit and produce a literary journal for degree credit.

The creative writing faculty includes creative nonfiction writer Barrie Borich (*Restoring the Color of Roses; My Lesbian Husband: Landscapes of a Marriage*); nonfiction writer Scott Edelstein (*The Indispensable Writer's Guide*); fiction and nonfiction writer Patricia Weaver Francisco (*Telling Details; Cold Feet; Village Without Mirrors*); nonfiction writer and poet Margot Fortunato Galt (*Up to the Plate: The All-American Girls Professional Baseball League; The Story in History: Writing Imaginatively into the Past; Turning the Feather Around: My Life in Art – George Morrison as told to Margot Fortunato Galt*); fiction writer David Haynes (*Heathens; Live at Five; Right By My Side*); fiction writer Judith Katz (*Running Fiercely Toward a High, Thin Sound; The Escape Artist*); poet Deborah Keenan (*Happiness; Looking for Home, Women Writing About Exile; The Only Window that Counts*); poet and children's book author Patricia Kirkpatrick (*Plowie: A Story from the Prairie; Learning to Read*); poet Roseann Lloyd (*War Baby Express; Tap Dancing for Big Mom*); poet Jim Moore (*The Long Experience of Love; Freedom of History; What the Bird Sees*); fiction writer Sheila O'Connor (*Tokens of Grace*); fiction writer Mary François Rockcastle (*Rainy Lake*); nonfiction writer Larry Sutin (*Divine Invasions: A Life of Philip K. Dick; Jack and Rochelle: A Holocaust Story of Love and Resistance*); and nonfiction writer Stephen Wilbers (*Writing for Business*). Faculty members have received prestigious awards for their writing from national organizations such as the Guggenheim Foundation, the National Endowment for the Arts, and from local organizations such as the Minnesota State Arts Board, Minnesota Voices Project, and the Jerome, Bush, and McKnight foundations.

In the past two years Hamline graduate students

have been nominated for a Pushcart Prize, have won The Loft Mentor Series in Poetry and Fiction, and fellowships from the Minnesota State Arts Board.

For more information, contact Program Assistant, Graduate Liberal Studies Programs, at the above address.

❖Hardin-Simmons University
Abilene, TX 79698
(915) 670-1214

Degree offered: MA in English with Concentration in Creative Writing (poetry, fiction)

Type of Program: Traditional Literary Study and Creative Writing

Length of Residency: Two years

Required course of study: 33 s/hrs
Thesis: 3 s/hrs
Writing workshop: 6 s/hrs
Writing tutorial: 3 s/hrs
Literature courses: 6 s/hrs must be outside
    the creative writing concentration

Other Requirements: 3 s/hr Methods of Research course is required of all English graduate students; 12 s/hrs may be taken outside the English Department. If the student chooses to minor in English, these 12 s/hrs usually will be literature courses.

Application Deadlines: Early April for graduate assistantship; Mid-August for admission to the graduate school.

When you begin looking for a writing workshop, unless you're from Abilene, Merkel, Roscoe, or maybe Rising Star, you may not think of Hardin-Simmons. Abilene is situated in the middle of what West Texans metaphorically call the Heart of the Big Country. That means Abilene is a good three hours from everywhere, so you won't come here on purpose. Of course there's always a chance that when you're on your way to Fresno, the VW bus may break down just past Clyde, and you'll have to hitchhike into Abilene. While you wait for Ed of Sonny's Wrecking to tow in the bus, you might as well have a cup of coffee and some pink thumbprint cookies at Mac's Driveateria. You might decide to stay. You might even sign up for a creative writing course at Hardin-Simmons or choose to pursue an MA in English with a Creative Writing Emphasis.

Hardin-Simmons, founded in 1891, is a small, private, liberal arts university of 2,000 students. Poet Robert Fink (*The Tongues of Men and of Angels, The Ghostly Hitchhiker, Azimuth Points*, winner of the 1981 *Texas Review* Poetry Chapbook Award), has directed HSU's creative writing workshops since 1977, and is always on the lookout for someone to throw a baseball around with or compare notes on the best flies for Colorado trout or, especially, talk poetry and fiction.

Hardin-Simmons offers two courses in creative writing. The first course, Creative Writing: English 4315/5315, is open to undergraduates, graduates, and to anyone in the region or passing through who is serious about improving his or her poetry and fiction. Other than the 9 s/hrs of core curriculum English

courses required of undergraduates pursuing a degree, the only prerequisite for this workshop is a dedication to improving writing. The advanced workshop, Advanced Creative Writing: English 4316/5316, follows in the spring semester and is a continuation of the beginning workshop. After completing 5315 and 5316, graduate students may apply to write a creative thesis (fiction or poetry).

Isolated as Abilene is, recognizable writers still manage to find their way to Hardin-Simmons to give readings and to talk about writing. Among the writers who have been on campus since 1978 are: Betty Adcock, Max Apple, David Bottoms, William V. Davis, Alison Hawthorne Deming, Lynn Emanuel, George Garrett, Reginald Gibbons, Donald Hall, Andrew Hudgins, Richard Hugo, X.J. Kennedy, Thomas Lux, Walter McDonald, Jack Myers, Linda Pastan, Louis Simpson, David Wagoner, James Welch, Allen Wier, Lynna Williams, and Miller Williams. The HSU library also subscribes to around 70 literary journals, and students have the opportunity to submit their work to the campus art/literary magazine, with the literary editor being one of the workshop members.

Next time you're heading for the coast and you need a break from I-20, stop off in Abilene. Bob Fink will introduce you to a plate of Harold's barbecue, the best you'll ever have, and ask if you brought your glove, and talk trout fishing. You don't even have to mention you write poetry or fiction; but if you do, forget about making El Paso by nightfall.

For further information, write Robert Fink, Box 15114.

❖Harvard University
Cambridge, MA 02138
(617) 495-2533

Degree offered: BA in English & American Literature with Emphasis in Writing

Application Deadlines: Contact GSAS Admissions, (617) 495-5315.

Faculty: Natalie Kusz, Chair, nonfiction; Henri Cole, poetry; Patricia Powell, fiction; and Brad Watson, fiction.

No graduate program offered. For further information, contact Writing Program Director, Dept. of English.

Haverford College
Haverford, PA 19041
(215) 896-1157

For information on offerings in creative writing, contact the Dept. of English.

❖University of Hawaii at Manoa
1733 Donaggho Road
Honolulu, HI 96822
(808) 956-7619
FAX (808) 956-3083

Degrees offered: BA, MA, PhD

Degree: BA in English with Concentration in Creative Writing

Required course of study: 33 s/hrs
Thesis: required for Honors only (3 s/hrs)
Writing workshop: 3–18 s/hrs
Other writing courses: 0–15 s/hrs
Literature courses: 18 or more s/hrs

Other Requirements: The core program consists of 18 s/hrs humanities; 9 s/hrs natural sciences; 4 s/hrs laboratory science; 12 s/hrs social sciences; 3 s/hrs logic or math; 6 s/hrs history; 12 s/hrs language.

The English Department at the University of Hawaii offers BA students the opportunity to specialize in creative writing through its electives program. The introductory course is followed by an upper-division sequence in poetry and in fiction, with form and theory courses and a writing workshop in each genre. One course in autobiography, one in creative nonfiction, and one in special topics in creative writing is offered. Of these courses, 15 credit hours may count toward fulfilling the basic 33 s/hrs of work required of the English major. Honors candidates may present a thesis comprised of a collection of work in poetry, fiction, drama, or a combination of genres.

Degree: MA in English with Creative Writing Thesis

Type of Program: Studio/Academic

Required course of study: 30 s/hrs
Thesis: 6 s/hrs
Writing workshop: up to 6 s/hrs
Literature courses: 18 s/hrs

Other Requirements: Foreign language proficiency; written final examination; oral defense of thesis.

Degree: PhD in English with Creative Writing Specialization and Dissertation

Type of Program: Traditional Literary Study and Creative Writing

Required course of study: Minimum residency of 3 full-time semesters
Dissertation: at least one semester course for dissertation research
Writing workshop: no minimum
Literature courses: 18 s/hrs of graduate course work in English

Other Requirements: 2 foreign languages; 6 s/hrs in a related field outside of English and a seminar in advanced literary research; 3 area exams (two publishable papers may be substituted in lieu of one area exam); final oral examination on dissertation.

The Graduate Program in English offers the MA and PhD degrees in English and American literature, with the option of specializing in creative writing with a thesis or dissertation in several genres, including poetry, fiction, translation, and biography. The MA requires 30 s/hrs of credits including up to 6 for thesis preparation and up to 6 for writing workshops.

For the PhD, students must satisfy a minimum residency requirement of 3 full-time semesters. But required courses beyond the MA are not the focus of the program. Only one seminar in Advanced Literary Research is specifically required by the department. Students are free to move through a program which includes workshops, writing, literature, and interdisciplinary coursework. At the same time, advising is seen as an essential part of the program, and advisory committees and doctoral committees actively aid students in preparing themselves systematically for the examinations that direct their progress.

The department has a number of graduate assistantships that are intended to give students experience in college teaching. PhD students with prior teaching experience may apply for lectureships in the department, and several scholarships and tuition waivers are available to graduate students.

The department is home to *Hawaii Review*, a student-sponsored national journal; *Biography*, a prominent professional journal that is international in scope; and *Manoa: A Pacific Journal of International Literature*. Students have the opportunity to work with these journals in various capacities.

In particular, the department is proud that the creative writing program is in no way an adjunct to English studies. Students work and study with academic faculty and fellow students in literature, criticism, and composition theory; their common purpose is a thorough understanding of the broad field of English.

The creative writing staff includes fiction writers Ian MacMillan (*Light and Power*, winner of the AWP Award Series in Short Fiction; *Proud Monster*; and *Orbit of Darkness*); Robert Onopa (*Pleasuretube*; former editor of *TriQuarterly*); Steven Goldsberry (*Maui: The Demigod*); Philip Damon (stories in journals, the O. Henry Prize collection, and *Best American Short Stories*); Rodney Morales (*The Speed of Darkness*); Robert Shapard (editor of *Sudden Fiction Series*; winner of the GE/CCLM Award for Younger Writers); and Roger Whitlock (stories in *MSS.*, *Seattle Review*, and other journals). The poetry staff includes Nell Altizer (*The Widow's Suite; The Man Who Died En Route*; winner of the Juniper Prize); Frank Stewart (*The Open Water; Flying the Red Eye, The Natural History of Native Writing*; winner of the Whiting Writers' Award); Faye Kicknosway (author of 11 volumes including *All These Voices: Selected and New*); and Rob Wilson (*Waking in Seoul; The American Sublime*). In addition, the department augments the program with a full-time distinguished visiting writer each semester. Visiting writers have included Robert Stone, Carolyn Kizer, Michael Ondaatje, Maxine Hong Kingston, and Eleanor Wilner.

The university and local organizations also sponsor an active and distinguished series of readings, workshops, and colloquia by eminent national and international writers each semester.

For more information, contact Director of Creative Writing, Dept. of English.

Hiram College
Hiram, OH 44234

(330) 569-5152

Degree offered: BA with Minor in Writing; BA in English with Creative Writing Emphasis

The minor in writing requires a firm commitment on the part of the student and approval by the Writing Board. Five courses (4 s/hrs each) must be selected from the following list: Art of Poetry, the Moral Positions of Poetry, Advanced Poetics, Advanced Expository Writing, Fiction Writing, Nonfiction Writing, Playwriting, Writing Autobiography, Travel Writing, Metafiction, Writing for Business, Technical Writing, Teaching and Supervising of Writing, Writing for Science, The English Language, Writing for Publication, Literary Theory, Rhetorical Criticism, Survey of Journalism, and Grammar for Writers.

In addition, students are required to complete the minimum of a two-hour writing internship. Also, all minors are expected to prepare a fifty-page senior portfolio (in three genres) and present it to the Writing Committee during the spring of their senior year.

Consistent with Hiram's commitment to writing across the curriculum, we are interested in offering a rich Minor that benefits all interested writers on campus, regardless of their majors. Students can tailor a program that complements and strengthens their primary discipline.

English majors with a serious interest in creative writing may opt for an English major with an emphasis in creative writing. This degree is recommended for students intending to apply for graduate programs in writing or planning to enter careers in writing immediately after graduation. In lieu of the English electives in literature required of traditional English majors, majors with an emphasis in creative writing select courses marked CW from the writing menu. Students with this specialized major are permitted to generate a senior seminar project that allows them to explore a specialized interest in writing poetry, literary nonfiction, fiction, or plays.

The writing faculty includes Hale Chatfield, poetry; David Fratus, English Language; Carol Donley, science writing; David Anderson, nonfiction; Sandra Parker, autobiography and travel writing; Ellen Summers, playwriting; Joyce Dyer, fiction and nonfiction. The faculty is widely published.

For more information, contact Joyce Dyer, Director of Writing and Associate Professor of English.

Hofstra University
Hempstead, NY 11550

(516) 463-5454

Degree offered: BA in English with Concentration in Creative Writing, Literature, and Publishing

Required course of study: 36 credits in writing and literature; 3 credits in history.

Creative writing workshops are offered in: fiction, poetry, children's books, playwriting, advanced fiction, advanced poetry, and tutorials. Courses in publishing procedures and editing are offered, as well as a concentration in publishing studies. Literature courses are offered in contemporary American literature, literary sources, and British literature.

For more information, contact Director of Creative Writing, English Dept.

❖Hollins College
Roanoke, VA 24020

(540) 362-6317
FAX (540) 362-6097

Degrees offered: BA, MA

Degree: BA in English with Concentration in Creative Writing

The program is a flexible one; students may choose among poetry and fiction workshops, form and theory courses, and independent studies. About 40 s/hrs are offered in writing courses. Though there is no thesis requirement, seniors who wish to submit an original manuscript may do so. For Honors, a thesis of approximately 60 pages is required.

Degree: MA in English: Creative Writing, Contemporary Literature, and Literary Criticism (poetry, fiction, creative nonfiction, screenwriting, playwriting)

Type of Program: Studio/Academic

Length of Residency: One year

Required course of study: 40 s/hrs
  Thesis: 8 s/hrs
  Writing workshop: up to 8 s/hrs
  Other writing courses: up to 32 s/hrs
  Literature courses: up to 32 s/hrs
  Tutorials or directed reading: up to 32 s/hrs

Other Requirements: Foreign language proficiency; 3 hour comprehensive examination on coursework.

Application Deadlines: February 2

Our primary purpose is to enable a serious writer to work in an open-minded atmosphere with other writers and a staff of professional writers, while at the same time developing his or her knowledge of modern literature.

Though students are encouraged to take courses both in writing and literature, each student pursues an individually-designed course of study. The range of possibilities permits a student wishing to do so to take nearly all of the required 40 s/hrs in writing courses; on the other hand, he or she may complete most of the 40 hours in literature courses. In addition to workshops in fiction and poetry, which are offered once a semester, there are courses in scriptwriting and playwriting and independent writing projects. The thesis may be a book-length collection of poetry, fiction, plays, or screenplays.

The faculty includes: novelist and screenwriter Pinckney Benedict (*Town Smokes, The Wrecking Yard, Dogs of God*); poet, critic, and novelist R.H.W. Dillard (*The Greeting: New & Selected Poems, The First Man on the Sun, Omniphobia*), who directs the program; poet and novelist Cathryn Hankla (*Negative History, A Blue Moon in Poorwater, Afterimages*); poet and novelist Jeanne Larsen (*James Cook in Search of Terra Incognita, Silk Road, Manchu Palaces*); film scholar Carl Plantinga; and poet, critic, and fiction writer Eric Trethewey (*Dreaming of Rivers, In the Traces, Evening Knowledge*). 12 visiting writers appear on campus each year in addition to a distinguished writer-in-residence.

For more information contact R.H.W. Dillard, Program Director, Dept. of English.

❖Hope College
Holland, MI 49423

For more information, contact Jack Ridl, Director of Creative Writing Program. English Dept.

❖University of Houston
Houston, TX 77204-3012

(713) 743-2932 for BA
(713) 743-3015 for MA, MFA, PhD
FAX (713) 743-3215

Degrees offered: BA, MA, MFA, PhD

Degree: BA in English with Concentration in Creative Writing (poetry, fiction)

Required course of study: 122 s/hrs total
Basic Skills: 18 s/hrs
Knowledge Base: 19 s/hrs
Knowledge Integration: 6 s/hrs
Other university Requirements: 14 s/hrs
Humanities & Fine Arts: 12 s/hrs
Literature (other than those taken to satisfy
   above): 24 s/hrs
Writing workshops: 15 s/hrs
Electives: 14 s/hrs

Other Requirements: Writing proficiency exam; minimum GPA of 3.0 in certain writing workshops for entry to and exit from concentration.

For more information, contact Undergraduate Advisor, Dept. of English.

Degree: MA in Literature & Creative Writing with Creative Thesis (poetry, fiction)

Type of Program: Studio/Academic

Required course of study: 30 s/hrs
Thesis: 6 s/hrs
Writing workshops: 9-12 s/hrs (includes
   cross-genre & forms)
Literature courses: 9-12 s/hrs

Other Requirements: 3 s/hrs of literary theory; foreign language proficiency.

Degree: MFA in English: Creative Writing with Creative Thesis (poetry, fiction)

Type of Program: Studio/Academic

Required course of study: 42 s/hrs
Thesis: 6 s/hrs
Writing workshops: 15-18 s/hrs (includes
   cross-genre and forms)
Literature courses: 9 s/hrs
Modern Thought: 6 s/hrs
Electives: 6 s/hrs

Other Requirements: Foreign language proficiency.

Degree: PhD in Literature & Creative Writing with Creative Dissertation (poetry, fiction)

Type of Program: Traditional Literary Study and Creative Writing

Required course of study: 57 s/hrs
Dissertation: 6 s/hrs
Writing workshops: 15-18 s/hrs (includes
   cross-genre & forms)
Literature courses: 30 s/hrs (includes
   15 s/hrs of electives)

Other Requirements: 6 s/hrs Theory (includes bibliography, rhetoric, linguistics, criticism, or theory); working knowledge of two foreign languages or intensive knowledge of one; PhD Written Examination and PhD Oral Examination.

Application Deadlines: January 15.

The English Department of the University of Houston offers flexible studies in literature and creative writing leading to the Master of Arts, Master of Fine Arts, and PhD degrees. Students have an opportunity to work closely with writers who represent a diverse range of aesthetic styles. The Creative Writing Program has become the spearhead for literary activity throughout the city. With Inprint, Inc., it sponsors the Margarett Root Brown Houston Reading Series, a distinguished showcase for contemporary writers. Such major writers as Michael Ondaatje, Ann Beattie, Ernest J. Gaines, E. Annie Proulx, Cynthia Ozick, Russell Banks, Richard Rodriguez, Adrienne Rich, and Czeslaw Milosz have been included in the Series. Each year, four of the twelve visiting Series writers conduct four-day residencies with Program students.

Students may work in editorial positions on *Gulf Coast*, the student literary magazine, and participate in the Writers in the Schools program, which places writers in grades Kindergarten through 12 to teach creative writing in schools throughout the Houston community.

Qualified students will be awarded teaching fellowships. During his or her first semester, the teaching fellow is usually assigned to work in the basic composition program. After the first year, teaching fellows generally teach 6 s/hrs of freshman or sophomore-level courses. All teaching fellows pay resident tuition and fees, approximately $1,000 per semester.

Students interested in applying for financial aid must complete a separate Financial Aid Application. Outstanding applicants may be nominated for Ehrhardt Fellowships, Mitchell Fellowships and Inprint Fellowships -- awards of up to $10,000 -- to supplement their teaching stipends. Once in the Program, students are also eligible for a number of fellowships, such as the Barthelme Memorial, Inprint, and Michener Fellowships, in amounts up to $15,000. In addition, local awards such as the Cultural Arts Council of Houston Creative Artist Program Awards are offered each year.

The permanent faculty includes Kathleen Cambor, Chitra Divakaruni, Mark Doty, Edward Hirsch, Cynthia Macdonald, Robert Phillips, Daniel Stern, and Adam Zagajewski, and in conjunction with the School of Theatre, Edward Albee. Visiting writers in recent years have included Mary Gaitskill, Alan Hollinghurst, Robert Hass, Brenda Hillman, Lucille Clifton, Grace Paley, Rick Moody, Michael S. Harper, Amy Hempel, and many others.

Applicants should request an application from the Creative Writing Program, which details all application and admission requirements. Admission is highly competitive; applicants must meet the requirements of the English Department.

Address all correspondence to Creative Writing Program, Dept. of English.

Howard University
Washington, DC 20059

Contact the Creative Writing Program Director, Dept. of English.

❖Humboldt State University
Arcata, CA 95521

(707) 826-3758
FAX (707) 826-5939
website: http//www.humboldt.edu/~english

Degrees offered: BA in English Literature, MA in Literature, MA in the Teaching of Writing (MATW)

Type of Program: Studio/Academic

A core of regular literature courses is required for the BA in literature, but students may take creative writing courses as electives. The department offers 3 different courses, which students may repeat. A creative writing option is also available for students in the teacher preparation program.

Graduate students pursuing the MA in literature may prepare a final project in creative writing. The core of the MATW curriculum is a series of graduate courses and seminars devoted to theories and methods of teaching composition. In addition, students improve their own writing skills through a writing workshop and other advanced writing courses.

Teaching in the creative writing program are Jim Dodge (*Fup, Not Fade Away, Stone Junction*), and Jerry Martien (*Shell Game* and various poetry chapbooks). The program includes a reading series with regular visits from poets and fiction writers, *Toyon* (our annual literary magazine), and the Raymond Carver Short Story Contest.

Located about three hundred miles north of San Francisco on Humboldt Bay, Arcata offers, in addition to a setting of rare natural beauty, a varied cultural climate remarkable for its size. Humboldt State University, part of the California State University system, was established in 1913 and presently enrolls approximately 7,000 students.

For further information, write Jim Dodge, Director, Creative Writing, Dept. of English.

Idaho State University
Campus Box 8056
Pocatello, ID 83209-8056

(208) 236-2478

Degrees offered: BA, MA, DA

Degree: MA in English with Creative Thesis Option

Type of Program: Traditional Literary Study

Length of Residency: The program generally requires two years of full-time study for completion

Required course of study: 30 s/hrs (33 for T.A.s)
Literature courses: 12–15 s/hrs

Other Requirements: Proficiency in one foreign language; oral defense of thesis; public reading of thesis material.

Degree: DA in English with Creative Paper Option

Type of Program: Traditional Literary Study

Length of Residency: At least two consecutive semesters. The program generally requires two to three years of full-time study for completion.

Required course of study: 48 s/hrs beyond the MA
Language and literature courses: 24 s/hrs
Interdisciplinary courses: 12 s/hrs
Pedagogy: 12 s/hrs

Other Requirements: 2 DA papers; public colloquium; proficiency in one foreign language; comprehensive written exam.

Application Deadlines: Financial Aid: Fall semester -- March 1, Spring semester -- October 1. Admissions: May 1 for summer, July 1 for fall, December 1 for spring.

For more information, contact the Director of Graduate Studies, English & Philosophy.

❖University of Idaho
Moscow, ID 83843

(208) 885-6156

Degrees offered: BA, MFA

Degree: BA in English with Creative Emphasis

Required course of study:
39 s/hrs for the major
Writing workshop: 18 s/hrs
Literature courses: 21 s/hrs

Other Requirements: 2 years college-level of 1 foreign language, or secondary school equivalent (4 years); 21 s/hrs in a supporting field.

The University of Idaho offers a BA in English with a Creative Emphasis. Presently this degree entails 21 credits in literature and 18 credits in creative writing courses and workshops (both fiction and poetry).

Degree: MFA in English (poetry, fiction, creative nonfiction)

Type of Program: Studio

Length of Residency: Two years

Required course of study: 48 s/hrs
Faculty-taught workshops: 15 s/hrs
Workshops by visiting writers: 6 s/hrs

Graduate–level courses: 15 s/hrs
Courses in other fine arts disciplines: 6 s/hrs
Thesis: 6 s/hrs

Application Deadlines: March 1.

Faculty includes Mary Clearman Blew, author of the acclaimed memoir *All But the Waltz*, two collections of short stories, and numerous essays and short fiction; Tina Foriyes, poet and founder of the creative writing effort at UI; Ron McFarland, former Idaho Writer–in–Residence, poet and editor; and Lance Olsen, author of eight books of and about postmodern fiction including *Tonguing the Zeitgeist*, finalist for the Philip K. Dick Award for best science fiction of 1994.

In addition to the above, each semester two distinguished writers visit the University of Idaho to teach intensive one- and two–week seminars, interact closely with students, and give readings. They have included such diverse poets and novelists as Derek Walcott, Ann Beattie, Gary Snyder, Carolyn Forché, Stanley Kunitz, Marilynne Robinson, William Stafford, Roberta Hill Whiteman, David Wagoner, Sandra McPherson, Ron Carlson, Gary Soto, David Foster Wallace, Li-Young Lee, David Long, Raymond Federman, Kathy Acker, and Samuel R. Delany.

The creative writing program also sponsors many readings throughout the semester by writers from around the area and country, and serves as home for the growing literary journal *Fugue*.

The University of Idaho is the state's only comprehensive educational institute, enrolling about 11,500 students. Located in Moscow, an attractive town of 18,500, the university is part of a larger college community: Pullman, WA, the home of Washington State University, is eight miles away. The closest city is Spokane, WA (population 300,000), 90 miles north; Seattle and Portland are six or seven hours away by car. The climate is mild: summers are warm and dry, and in the winter the temperature seldom drops below 20 degrees. White–water rafting, wilderness hiking and camping, skiing, sailing, and white–sand river beaches are all within a two–hour drive.

Please include 20 pages of fiction or 10 of poetry, transcripts, three letters of recommendation, and GREs. TAships are available for outstanding students.

For more information, please contact Director of Creative Writing, English Dept.

❖Idyllwild Arts Academy
P.O. Box 38
52500 Temecula Road
Idyllwild, CA 92549

For more information, contact the Director, Dept. of English.

❖Illinois State University
Normal, IL 61790-4240
(309) 438-3667
FAX (309) 438-5414

Degrees offered: BS, BA, MS, MA, PhD

Degree: BS or BA in English Studies with a Minor in Writing, Creative Writing Track

Required course of study: 120 s/hrs total
36 s/hrs beyond freshman composition
24 s/hrs for Minor in Writing, including
15 s/hrs of required courses and 9 s/hrs
elected from listed writing courses,
including 6–9 s/hrs in studio courses

Courses taken for the Writing Minor may not count for the English major. BA recipients must complete 2 years of foreign language study. The Writing Minor offers 3 areas of concentration: Creative Writing, Expository Writing, and Technical Writing (including Desktop Publishing). Many opportunities for internships in professional writing areas are available.

Degree: MS or MA in English Studies or Writing with Emphasis in Creative Writing

Type of Program: Studio/Academic

Length of Residency: Two years

Required course of study: 33 s/hrs total
Genre studies: 6 s/hrs
Studio courses: 6 s/hrs minimum
Poetics, narratology, or theory: 3 s/hrs
Literature: 12 s/hrs
Intro. to graduate study: 3 s/hrs
Thesis: 6 s/hrs

Other Requirements: Students are admitted to the creative writing option by portfolio. There is a creative thesis with a critical preface or afterword and a 3–hour integrated written examination. MA candidates must have second year college proficiency in a foreign language.

Degree: PhD in English Studies

Required course of study: The degree requires 14 courses distributed among required doctoral core seminars, 3 electives (2 in literature), 2 courses in reading, learning theory, statistics, or curriculum, 4 electives and the internship. Combination creative/theoretical/pedagogical dissertation for those interested in teaching creative writing. Exemplary recent dissertations focus on theoretical and pedagogical issues of voice.

Other Requirements: Dissertation and a comprehensive examination of 15 hours.

At all degree levels, the Creative Writing Program at Illinois State University is an integral part of the English curriculum, and at all degree levels, the curriculum is an integrative English Studies curriculum model. The English Department faculty of approximately 60 to 70 strong have designed specialized writing and teaching writing tracks which lead to degrees that are balanced in the breadth of their coursework and specialized in selected areas of depth. The Department has gathered together a community of writers/scholars who have national reputations in fiction, poetry, nonfiction, theory, translation, and writing pedagogy.

The level of graduate assistantship support is quite high at both the masters and doctoral levels, funding about 60 students a year in a program of over 100 graduate students. In addition, there are special assistantships in editing and crative writing: one in fiction, for ISU's *Fiction Collective II*, and one in poetry for *The Spoon River Quarterly*, which includes an outreach program in the schools, and several editing/desktop publishing internships in the Department's Unit for Contemporary Literature. Although the doctoral degree in English at Illinois State is not a studio degree, students frequently specialize in various aspects of teaching writing, including creative writing.

The creative writing and professional writing programs encourage participation on large joint projects among the students. For example, the students in technical writing and desktop publishing work with the student creative writing group Druid's Cave, which includes both undergraduate and graduate students, to produce a first-rate, perfect-bound magazine of student creative work. Druid's Cave works actively with Black Writers' Forum to hold manuscript workshops sessions, and jointly they sponsor an active guest reading series each year.

The ambiance at Illinois State, particularly among the graduate students, is serious, informal, and sociable. The Department encourages and facilitates student participation at conferences, as well as student research and publication. Graduates have enjoyed good success in publishing, and several have won major awards and fellowships. There is a healthy atmosphere of inquiry, effort, enthusiasm, and an excellent rapport between faculty and students. One of ISU's greatest assets is the largeness and the largesse of the English Department.

Faculty and past students have received many creative writing awards and fellowships, among them: MacArthur, Whiting, Lannan, Fulbright, NEA, Bunting (student), Stegner (student), Ruth Lilly (student), Rona Jaffe (student), I.A.C., State Author of the Year, Governor's Award for the Arts, AWP Intro, Capricorn, Ann Stanford, Pablo Neruda. There is an annual $1,000 student creative writing award at ISU.

The creative writing faculty includes: poet, translator, critic, and editor of *The Spoon River Poetry Review*, Lucia Cordell Getsi (*Intensive Care, No One Taught This Filly to Dance, Georg Trakl: Poems* [translation]); fiction writer and critic Curtis White, director of FCII/Black Ice Books (*Memories of My Father Watching TV, The Idea of Home, Metaphysics in the Midwest*); poet and critic Jim Elledge (*Into the Arms of the Universe, Earth As It Is, Various Envies,* and director of poetry press Thorngate Road); and fiction and nonfiction writer David Foster Wallace (*Infinite Jest, The Broom of the System, Girl with Curious Hair*).

Past Writers-in-Residence have included Carole Maso, Carole Oles, Ray Federman, Robert Creely, Ishmael Reed, Stacy Levine, and Ricardo Cruz.

The Unit for Contemporary Literature houses *The Spoon River Poetry Review*; two literary fiction presses, Dalkey Archive and FCII/Black Ice; the poetry chapbook press for gay/lesbian/bi-sexuals Thorngate Road; and TransGen(d)re, a poetry press for experimental genre crossings published by *The Spoon River Poetry Review. The Review of Contemporary Fiction* and *The American Book Review* are also edited and published at Illinois State. These presses and journals, and the literary advocacy that the Unit sponsors, form the largest hub of literary activity in the state outside Chicago.

Deadlines for applications for fall, October 1 and spring, Feb. 1. For more information, contact the Director of Graduate Studies or Drs. Lucia Getsi and Curtis White.

❖University of Illinois at Chicago
Chicago, IL 60607-7120
(312) 413-2229
FAX (312) 413-1005

Degrees offered: MA, PhD

Degree: MA in English with Specialization in Creative Writing

Type of Program: Studio/Academic

Length of Residency: Two years

Required course of study: 32 s/hrs
   Thesis: required
   Writing workshop: 12-16 s/hrs
   Literature courses: 16 s/hrs
   Tutorials or directed reading: 8 s/hrs

Application Deadlines: Fall, March 15; Spring, Oct. 1.

Degree: PhD in English with Specialization in Creative Writing

Type of Program: Traditional Literary Study and Creative Writing

Required course of study: 64 s/hrs beyond the MA
   Thesis: up to 32 s/hrs
   Writing workshop: 12 s/hrs
   Other writing courses: 8 s/hrs
   Literature courses: variable
   Tutorials or directed reading: 8 s/hrs

Other Requirements: Foreign language proficiency; written and oral comprehensive examinations.

Application Deadlines: Fall, Feb. 1; Spring, Oct. 1

The University of Illinois at Chicago offers an MA in English with specialization in creative writing, and a PhD in English with specialization in creative writing.

Workshop courses are offered in fiction (both short story and novel writing), poetry, translation, experimental writing, and the teaching of creative writing. Courses for graduates and undergraduates have recently been introduced in nonfiction writing. Theory is offered in literature courses specifically designed for writing students and taught by members of the writing faculty.

The MA program requires 16 s/hrs of literature without specification of area. That is to say, the work is designed not only for those interested in writing and editing, but for those who may wish to prepare for college-level teaching as well. The small and selective PhD program is designed to prepare students for combined careers in writing and university teaching. In order to provide them with university-level teaching experience in writing, every effort is made to give advanced doctoral students teaching responsibilities in the English Department's extensive offerings in undergraduate creative writing courses.

Financial assistance for UIC graduate students takes the form of tuition and fee waivers, teaching assistantships, and, occasionally, university fellowships. Students may enter the graduate programs in any semester. Financial aid, however, is normally arranged on a yearly basis, and decisions committing a significant portion of the available funds are made in Feb. for PhD's and in May for MA's.

In the 17 years of its existence, the graduate writing program at UIC has come to play an important role in the cultural life of Chicago. A number of publications and small presses have either originated on campus or been connected by close ties to the graduate writing program, among them *Milk Quarterly*, *Oink!*, *Mojo Navigator*, *Another Chicago Magazine*, The Wine Press, Another Chicago Press, The Yellow Press, all recipients of grants from the National Endowment for the Arts or the Illinois Arts Council, or both. Printing facilities in the College of Art and Architecture have been made available by individual arrangement.

Because it is a commuter campus, UIC has placed emphasis on assembling a permanent writing faculty and stressing the continuing relationship between teacher and student. The following are members of the permanent faculty: novelist and biographer James Park Sloan (*War Games, The Case History of Comrade V., The Last Cold War Cowboy*), poet-fiction writer Michael Anania (*Riversongs, The Sky at Ashland, The Red Menace*), novelist-critic Alan Friedman (*Hermaphrodeity, The Turn of the Novel*), fiction writer Cris Mazza (*Exposed, Revelation Countdown, Is it Sexual Harassment Yet?*), poet-critic Ralph J. Mills (*A Man to His Shadow, Door to the Sun, Each Branch*), and fiction writer and program chairman Eugene Wildman (*Montezuma's Ball, Nuclear Love*).

For more information, contact Eugene Wildman, Chairman, Program for Writers.

❖University of Illinois at Urbana-Champaign
Urbana, IL 61801

(217) 333-2391

Degree offered: AB in English (Major in Rhetoric)

Required course of study:
English: 15 s/hrs
Rhetoric: 15 s/hrs
Thesis: for Honors only
Writing workshop: 15 or more s/hrs
Literature courses: 15 or more s/hrs

Other Requirements: The equivalent of 4 college semesters in a given language; at least 6 s/hrs each in biological sciences, mathematics or physical sciences, and social sciences; a cognate (minor) consisting of at least 20 s/hrs in a department or departments other than English.

The University of Illinois at Urbana-Champaign offers an AB in English (Major in Rhetoric). A minimum of 15 hours in workshop courses and 15 hours in literature courses are required of the Rhetoric major. No thesis is required except of students working toward Honors.

The creative writing faculty includes: fiction writer

Mark Costello (*The Murphy Stories; Middle Murphy*); fiction writer and Program Director Paul Friedman (*And If Defeated Allege Fraud; Serious Trouble*); fiction writer Philip Graham (*The Art of the Knock; Interior Design: Stories; How to Read an Unwritten Language*); poet Brigit Kelly (*To The Place Of Trumpets; Song*); poet Laurence Lieberman (*Dark Songs: Slave House and Synagogue; Compass of the Dying; The Mural of Wakeful Sleep*); poet Michael Madonick; Richard Powers (*Three Farmers On Their Way To A Dance; Prisoner's Dilemma; Galatea 2.2*); fiction writer Jean Thompson (*The Gasoline Wars; Little Face; The Woman Driver*); and poet Michael Van Walleghen (*The Wichita Poems; More Trouble with the Obvious*).

For more information, contact Paul Friedman, Director of Creative Writing, Dept. of English.

❖Illinois Wesleyan University
Bloomington, IL 61702-2900

(309) 556-3246
FAX (309) 556-3411
e-mail: jmcgowan@titan.iwu.edu

Degree offered: BA in English with Concentration in Writing

Writing courses available at Illinois Wesleyan include workshops at beginning and advanced levels in fiction (including hypertext fiction), poetry, creative nonfiction, and journalism. Two student literary journals are published annually, and several writing clubs are also run by students and open to anyone interested in feedback and discussion.

The program director is James McGowan. Recent visiting writers include writers-in-residence Carolyn Forché and John Knoepfle. Other recent visitors have included Carlos Fuentes, Derek Walcott, Lorian Hemingway, Martha M. Vertreace, Elaine Fowler Palencia, Sandra Steingraber, and Steve Fay.

For more information, contact James McGowan, Dept. of English.

Indiana State University
Terre Haute, IN 47809

(812) 237-3164
FAX (812) 237-3156

Degrees offered: BA, MA

Degree: BA in English with Creative Writing Minor

Required course of study: 39 s/hrs (major) and 18 s/hrs (Minor); 6 s/hrs may be applied to both major and minor
Writing workshop: 12 s/hrs
Techniques: 6 s/hrs
Literature: 21 s/hrs
Linguistics: 3 s/hrs
Literary Criticism: 3 s/hrs

The creative writing minor is also available to undergraduates with a major other than English. Typical workshop or techniques class has 12-15 students. We try to accommodate the needs of a varied student body, ranging from those who see creative writing as a liberal art to those who are pre-professional. Many of our students go on to graduate school; several have been graduated from the best MFA programs.

A few scholarships are available to high school seniors; others may apply at the end of the sophomore year.

The student creative writing club offers opportunities to edit and publish in its magazine, *The Dolphin*, and the Department conducts two contests as well as several open readings each year.

Degree: MA in English with Specialization in Writing

Required course of study: 32 s/hrs
English Core: 9 s/hrs
Research Theory: 6 s/hrs
Creative Writing: 12 s/hrs (includes 6 hrs
  for creative thesis)
Electives: 6 s/hrs (outside the Department, may
  include playwriting, theatre)

Other Requirements: Foreign language proficiency through courses or proficiency exam. Note: No more than 6 s/hrs of transfer credit will be accepted.

Creative theses are collections of stories, poems, or short plays, or full-length novels or 3-act plays. Faculty includes published authors Matt Brennan (poetry), Howard McMillen (fiction and drama), and Jennifer Drake (poetry).

Three-fourths of students are supported by teaching assistantships that include a stipend and tuition waiver. Internships are available on such Department journals as *Snowy Egret, Indiana English*, and *African-American Review*. Recent visiting writers have included Donald Hall, Scott Sanders, Patricia Henley, Marianne Boruch, David Wojahn, Dexter Westrum, Maya Angelou, and A.E. Stringer.

For more information, contact Stan Evans, Chair, Creative Writing Committee.

❖Indiana University
Bloomington, IN 47405
(812) 855-8224

Degrees offered: MA, MFA

The Department of English at Indiana University has offered a degree in Creative Writing since 1948, when Peter Taylor proposed the MA in English with a concentration in Creative Writing. In 1980 the department added an MFA degree to its offerings. The Creative Writing Program is supplemented by *Indiana Review* and the Indiana University Writers' Conference. *Indiana Review*, in its 21st year, is edited and managed entirely by graduate students, with the Editor and Associate Editor both receiving graduate financial assistance. The IU Writers' Conference, second oldest in the country, is directed by a faculty member (currently Maura Stanton) and attracts writers of national reputation to its week-long workshops every June. The 2 Assistant Directors are normally students in the MFA Program and are supported by graduate financial assistance.

Degree: MFA in Creative Writing

Required course of study: 60 s/hrs
Thesis: 4–12 s/hrs
Writing workshop: 16 or more s/hrs
Literature courses: 16 or more s/hrs
Other writing courses: 4 or more s/hrs

Degree: MA in English with a Concentration in Creative Writing

Type of Program: Studio/Academic

Length of Residency: MA, 2 years; MFA, 3 years

Required course of study: 30 s/hrs
Thesis: 4 s/hrs
Writing workshop: 8 s/hrs
Literature courses: 20 s/hrs
Foreign Language Requirement

Application Deadlines: January 15.

Indiana University offers 2 graduate degrees in creative writing: an MFA in Creative Writing and an MA in English with a Concentration in Creative Writing. Both degrees are awarded in fiction or poetry only. To be admitted to the MFA, students must fulfill the usual departmental requirements and submit a sample of work (20 pages of poetry or 30 pages of fiction). At least 48 of the 60 s/hrs required for the degree must be taken in residence. Course requirements include a minimum of 16 s/hrs in graduate courses from among the department's literature and language offerings; 16 s/hrs in writing workshops, and 4 s/hrs in Teaching Creative Writing, Topics in Current Literature, or Theory and Craft of Writing. Students are expected to concentrate in a single genre, but they are encouraged to take courses in other genres as well. The final requirement, the thesis, is a book-length manuscript, ideally of publishable quality, of the best work a candidate can put forward. Theses must be approved by a thesis director and 2 readers.

Assistantships, called Associate Instructorships, are available. In 1998 they paid at least $9,500 plus a fee scholarship. Awarded by competition upon submission of manuscripts, these assistantships are available for up to 3 years and involve teaching 3 courses per year, two-thirds in Creative Writing, one-third in Composition. The Lilly and Hemingway-Wilson Fellowships provide a year with limited teaching duties for entering students. Applicants to the program are automatically considered for these awards and for the Samuel Yellen Award in poetry.

Permanent creative writing faculty includes: novelist and short story writer Tony Ardizzone (*The Evening News, In the Garden of Papa Santuzzu*), winner of the Flannery O'Connor Award; poet Catherine Bowman (*1-800-HOT-RIBS, Rock Farm*), winner of the Kate Frost Discovery Award; Afro-American specialist and novelist John McCluskey (*Look What They Done to My Song, Mr. America's Last Season Blues*); novelist and short story writer Alyce Miller (*The Nature of Longing, Stopping for Green Lights*), winner of the Flannery O'Connor Award; poet, essayist and critic Roger Mitchell (*The Word for Everything, Braid*); fiction writer and critic Cornelia Nixon (*Lawrence's Leadership Politics and the Turn Against Women, Now You See It*), first place O. Henry Award winner; novelist, essayist, and fiction writer Scott Russell Sanders (*Bad Man Ballad, The Paradise of Bombs*), winner of the AWP Award for Creative Nonfiction; poet and fiction writer Maura

Stanton (*Life Among the Trolls*, *The Country I Come From*), winner of the Yale Series of Younger Poets Award; and poet and critic David Wojahn (*Late Empire*, *The Falling Hour*), winner of the Yale Series of Younger Poets Award.

For more information, write to the Director, Creative Writing Program, Dept. of English.

❖Indiana University, Purdue
CM 145
2101 Coliseum Boulevard East
Fort Wayne, IN 46805-1499

For more information, contact George Kalamaras, Director, Dept. of English and Linguistics.

Indiana University, South Bend
South Bend, IN 46634

(219) 237-4304

Degree offered: BA in English with Concentration in Writing

For more information on the writing program, contact Chair, Dept. of English, IU-South Bend, 1700 Mishawaka Avenue, P.O. Box 7111, South Bend, IN 46634.

❖Iowa State University
203 Ross Hall
Ames, IA 50011-1201

(515) 294-2180
FAX (515) 294-6814

Degrees offered: BA, MA

Degree: BA in English

Iowa State offers a variety of creative writing courses at the undergraduate level, from introductory classes to small, intensive workshops.

Degree: MA in English with Creative Writing Emphasis (poetry, fiction, creative nonfiction, screenwriting)

Type of Program: Studio/Academic

Length of Residency: Two years

Required course of study: 30 s/hrs
  Thesis: 3 s/hrs
  Writing workshop: at least 6 s/hrs
  Literature courses: 9 s/hrs
  Linguistics: 3 s/hrs
  Electives: 9 s/hrs

Other Requirements: Master's candidates must satisfy a foreign language requirement through one of several options.

Application Deadlines: Feb. 1 for financial aid, Hogrefe fellowship, and admissions.

An emphasis in Creative Writing is one option for candidates for a master's degree within the English Department at Iowa State University. The Creative Writing Program offers the promising young writer a broad range of courses, an opportunity for fellowships and assistantships, and a collegian atmosphere suited to hard work and steady development. The 9 full-time faculty members are experienced teachers who have devoted much thought and energy to the creative writing classroom. At the same time, the creative writing faculty are active and ambitious artists, as many recent awards and publications attest.

The Creative Writing Program offers courses in writing fiction, writing poetry, and writing creative nonfiction. and in the pedagogy of creative writing, as well as occasional classes in writing drama and screenplays. While the program is most accurately described as a combination of literary study and creative writing, students may arrange to take up to 15 of the required 27 s/hrs of coursework in creative writing.

Each year the Creative Writing Program schedules writers, editors, and publishers for readings and to work with students in the classroom. Past speakers have included John Barth, Hilma Wolitzer, Gordon Lish, Denise Levertov, Robert Bly, Tracy Kidder, Ann Beattie, Joy Harjo, and Richard Bausch. The Creative Writing Program supports *Flyway*, an innovative literary journal of prose and poetry.

Creative Writing students may obtain financial aid through Pearl Hogrefe Fellowships or through assistantships in the Department of English. The Hogrefe Fellowships, granted for a 9-month academic year, provide a monthly stipend and pay tuition in full. Teaching assistants teach 3 classes per academic year, normally in Freshman English. Research assistants work 10 hours per week on individual faculty projects.

The Graduate Faculty includes: poet Neal Bowers (*Night Vision* and *Words for the Taking*); novelist and nonfiction writer Fern Kupfer (*Before and After Zachariah*, *Love Lies*, columnist for *Newsday*); fiction writer and playwright Joe Geha (*Through and Through*, plays produced in regional theatres); fiction writer Barbara Haas (*When California Was an Island*); poet and fiction writer Stephen Pett (*Pulpit of Bones and Sirens*); poet and nonfiction writer Mary Swander (*Driving the Body Back*, *Heaven and Earth House*, and *Out of This World*); poet and performance artist Debra Marquart (*Everything's a Verb* and jazz poetry CD recording, *A Regular Dervish*); and poet and nonfiction writer Sheryl St. Germain (*Making Bread at Midnight*, *How Still the Breath of God*).

For more information, contact the Graduate Studies Office, Teresa Smiley, (515) 294-2477.

❖University of Iowa
Iowa City, IA 52242

(319) 335-0416
(800) 553-IOWA

Degrees offered: BA, MFA

Degree: BA in English

Undergraduate students majoring in English may count up to nine study hours in writing courses toward a concentration in creative writing. Courses may be repeated.

Undergraduate Poetry Workshop and Undergraduate Fiction Workshop are open to any undergraduate who submits an acceptable manuscript for admission to the course. These two courses are taught by members of the staff and conducted much in the manner of the graduate workshops. Additional courses in basic techniques of writing fiction and poetry are available to students (graduate and undergraduate) who have little experience in writing. A manuscript is not required for admission to these basic writing courses: Creative Writing, Fiction Writing, and Poetry Writing.

For further information, contact Director of Undergraduate Studies, Dept. of English.

Degree: MFA in Creative Writing (poetry, fiction)

Type of Program: Studio

Length of Residency: Two years

Required course of study: 48 s/hrs total
 Writing workshops: up to 24 s/hrs

Other Requirements: 12–24 s/hrs electives.

Application Deadlines: November 1 – January 3 for Fall admission; January 3 for financial aid; April 15 for Summer (Non–degree coursework only).

The program in Creative Writing, known informally as the Iowa Writers' Workshop, offers the Master of Fine Arts in English, a terminal degree qualifying the holder to teach creative writing at the college level. As a *workshop* we provide an opportunity for the talented writer to work and learn with established poets and/or novelists and short story writers. Though we agree in part with the popular insistence that writing cannot be taught, we exist and proceed on the assumption that talent can be developed, and we see our possibilities and limitations in that light. Accordingly, the fact that the Workshop can claim as alumni nationally and internationally prominent poets, novelists, and short story writers is, we believe, more the result of what they brought here than of what they gained from us. We continue to look for promising talent in our conviction that writing cannot be taught, but that writers can be encouraged.

The course of study leading to the degree is flexible. The candidate must satisfactorily complete four semesters of graduate work, totaling at least 48 s/hrs. Up to 18 s/hrs of graduate credit may be transferred, but this does not change the residency requirement. Roughly half of the candidate's work during residence will be in actual writing courses in the program — while the rest of the work will include some coherent grouping of graduate courses (or in some cases, undergraduate courses taken for graduate credit) in a field of interest to the student and of relevance to his or her writing. The program culminates with the writing of a creative thesis and a take–home exam during the student's last semester of work.

Courses available through the program are divided into writing courses and literature courses, all of which may be repeated for credit. These consist of Graduate Poetry Workshop, Graduate Fiction Workshop, Form of Poetry, Form of Fiction, as well as seminars in fiction and poetry.

Traditionally, a number of Workshop students also take the Translation Workshop class which is offered through another department.

The writing faculty includes: fiction writer and Director Frank Conroy (*Stop–Time, Body and Soul*), fiction writer and 1978 Pulitzer Prize winner James Alan McPherson (*Elbow Room, Hue and Cry*), fiction writer Marilynne Robinson (*Housekeeping, Mother Country*), fiction writer Ethan Canin (*Emperor of the Air, Blue River, The Palace Thief*), poet Marvin Bell (*Selected and New Poems, Iris of Creation, The Book of the Dead Man*), poet James Galvin (*God's Mistress, Lethal Frequencies, The Meadow*), and poet Jorie Graham (*Dream of the Unified Field, Earth Took of Earth*). The staff of visiting professors for 1998–99 is Barry Unsworth, Stuart Dybek, Lyn Hejinian, Carl Phillips, Mark Levine, and Lan Samantha Chang.

Financial aid is available through Research Assistantships ($6,660 per school year); Graduate Teaching Assistantships in the Liberal Arts College ($9,265–$14,820 per school year); and Teaching–Writing Fellowships ($15,320 per school year). Through the generosity of James A. Michener and the Copernicus Society of America, the Writers' Workshop is able to award several annual grants of approximately $12,000 each for writers working on prose books which are near publication. Also, James A. Michener established the new Paul Engle awards of $12,000 each. Recipients will normally have completed the program and thus will be able to spend an additional year on their project.

Applications can be made for summer school only. Manuscripts must be sent between March 1st and April 15th.

All inquiries should be addressed to The Writers' Workshop, 102 Dey House, 507 N. Clinton Street, Iowa City, IA 52242–1000.

Degree: MFA in Nonfiction Writing

Type of Program: Studio/Academic

Length of Residency: Three years

Required course of study: 48 s/hrs total
 Forms and Workshop courses: 24 s/hrs or more
 Thesis work: 4–8 s/hrs

Application Deadline: January 1.

The University of Iowa's Program in Nonfiction Writing, known informally as the Nonfiction Writing Program, is home of Iowa's MFA in nonfiction, a degree program that provides accomplished and promising students the opportunity to study and write literary nonfiction. The requirements of the 48 semester-hour MFA are flexible enough to allow extensive work both inside and outside the program; the degree culminates in a thesis, a work which may present a sustained piece of literary nonfiction or a collection of shorter pieces. Graduates of the program have recently published in such magazines as *The New Yorker, Harper's, The Georgia Review*, and *Creative Nonfiction*; they have also published book–length collections of literary nonfiction.

Most program courses are either "forms" or "workshop" courses. The forms courses are centered on a kind of literary nonfiction (e.g. the travel essay) or on a special topic (e.g. unreliable narrators). The forms courses consist of both readings and writing projects. The workshop courses focus primarily on the writing of workshop participants.

The program faculty includes: Director Paul Diehl, Carol de St. Victor, Patricia Foster, David Hamilton, Brooks Landon, Sara Levine, and Susan Lohafer.

Visiting writers in recent years have included Patricia Hampl, Mary Swander, Pam Houston, Terry Tempest Williams, Gayle Pemberton, Honor Moore, Adam Hochschild, Scott Russell Sanders, and Phillip Lopate.

Financial aid is available in the form of fellowships, scholarships, teaching assistantships, and research assistantships. The term "financial aid" refers only to the kinds of fellowships, scholarships, and assistantships listed below and does not apply to other forms of financial assistance (such as loans) available through The University of Iowa and other sources. The following kinds of financial aid are available to MFA students in the Nonfiction Writing Program:

1. Iowa Arts Fellowships (IAF). IAFs are highly competitive three-year appointments awarded by the Graduate College to a small number of students recently admitted to MFA programs at The University of Iowa. IAFs are based on applicants' demonstration of exceptional promise in a particular area of the fine arts. An Iowa Arts Fellow in the Nonfiction Writing Program receives a grant the first year and a teaching assistantship the second and third years. Tuition and fees are paid all three years by the Graduate College.

2. Graduate Opportunity Fellowships (GOF). The GOFs are one-year appointments awarded by the Graduate College to a small number of highly talented applicants from underrepresented populations. A Graduate Opportunity Fellow in the Nonfiction Writing Program receives a one-year stipend and has tuition and fees covered by the Graduate College and the Department of English.

3. Tuition Scholarships: Occasionally the Nonfiction Writing Program is able to offer scholarships to cover tuition and fees. All financial aid applicants are considered for this award.

4. Teaching Assistantships: Teaching assistantships are the predominate form of financial aid in the Nonfiction Writing Program. An appointment to teach three courses for the academic year is referred to as a half-time teaching assistantship. A teaching assistant usually teaches in the Rhetoric Department. Experienced teaching assistants and applicants with appropriate teaching experience are also eligible to teach the elective nonfiction writing course in the Department of English. A quarter-time or more appointment qualifies a teaching assistant for resident tuition.

5. Research Assistantships: Research assistantships are occasionally available when the department identifies a faculty member who needs assistance with a research project or with a literary journal such as the *Iowa Review*. Such appointments are rarely more than quarter-time; a quarter-time or more research assistantship qualifies a research assistant for resident tuition.

Admission decisions are made once a year, usually by early March. Requests for admission materials should be addressed to Vicky Dingman, Secretary for Graduate Studies in English, Dept. of English, 308 English–Philosophy Building, The University of Iowa, Iowa City, IA 52242. All other inquiries should be addressed to The Director of the Nonfiction Writing Program, Dept. of English, 308 English–Philosophy Building, The University of Iowa, Iowa City, IA 52242.

Jacksonville State University
Department of English
Jacksonville, AL 36265
(205) 782-5861 or 5413

Degree offered: BA with Minors in Creative Writing and/or Business and Technical Writing

The minor in creative writing is designed for students who wish to write poetry, fiction, and/or nonfiction. The minor in business and technical writing is designed for those students who wish to acquire those professional writing skills used in business, scientific, and legal professions; this minor is also designed to aid students planning to undertake graduate study. An active writing club, a program of visiting speakers, and a program encouraging public readings compliment both minors.

For further information, write the Dept. of English.

❖James Madison University
Harrisonburg, VA 22807
(540) 568-6202

Degrees offered: BA, MA

Degree: BA

At the undergraduate level, James Madison University provides students with the opportunity to major in English with a concentration in creative writing. Such students would take 33 hours of English courses, of which 15 would be in poetry, poetics, fiction writing, narrative form, and related courses. Students may choose an emphasis in poetry or fiction but are not constrained to do so. Writers may opt to do a senior thesis or honors thesis, if eligibility requirements are met.

Degree: MA in English with Concentration in Creative Writing

A 33-hour degree, the creative writing MA includes 15 hours of conventional literature courses, six hours of creative thesis, and the remainder of course work in workshops or methods classes. Though candidates will emphasize fiction or poetry, the program allows for considerable crossover between the genres. There are also related offerings in play, script writing, and grammar and composition. Creative thesis is required. Second-year teaching assistantships are available and are competitive.

The Creative Writing faculty includes Mark Facknitz (fiction), Susan Vaclavicek Facknitz (poetry), and Laurie Kutchins (poetry). Play and scriptwriting experts at James Madison include Roger Hall and Tom

O'Connor. Among distinguished visitors in recent years have been Nikki Giovanni, Lee Smith, Charles Wright, Dave Smith, William Stafford, John Casey, Michael Ryan, and Lisa Russ Spaar.

For further information, contact Director of Graduate Studies, Dept. of English.

❖John Carroll University
University Heights, OH 44118
(216) 397-4746
e-mail: gbilgere@jcu.edu

Degrees offered: BA, MA

Degree: BA in English with Creative Writing Minor (poetry, fiction, and nonfiction)

Required course of study: 128 s/hrs total. English major is 39 s/hrs; six of these may be used toward the 18 s/hr Creative Writing Minor, which comprises introductory workshops in fiction, poetry, and the essay, advanced workshops in fiction and poetry, plus one 400-level 20th-Century literature class.

Application Deadlines: Rolling admission deadline; March 1 for financial aid.

Degree: MA in English (with creative-writing thesis)

Type of Program: Program of traditional literary study; creative thesis allowed, but most of the degree work is in the study of literature.

Length of Residency: Two years

Required course of study: 30 s/hrs total
Thesis: 6 s/hrs

Other Requirements: Written comprehensive exam.

Application Deadline: February 1 for teaching assistantships, March 1 for admission.

John Carroll University provides -- on both the graduate and undergraduate levels -- traditional, historically based degrees in English. It is a small (3,500-student) Jesuit university on the east side of Cleveland, a terrific resource for any student (the Cleveland Public Library, for example, is the second-largest open-stack library in the world). This is a good place to come if you want to ground your training as a writer in your training as a reader. The English department is friendly, rigorous, and nurturing. All workshops and all graduate classes are limited to 15 students.

Visiting writers in recent years have included Richard Bausch, Charles Baxter, Neal Bowers, T. Coraghessan Boyle, Elena Castedo, Donald Finkel, Carol Frost, Mary Gaitskill, Jane Hamilton, Mark Helprin, Ann Hood, Reginald McKnight, Antonya Nelson, Tim O'Brien, Wyatt Prunty, Liz Rosenberg, Richard Russo and Robert Stone. John Carroll University has been a national leader in Writers Harvest: Share Our Strength's National Fiction and Poetry Reading to benefit hunger relief.

Six teaching assistantships are available each year; these cover full tuition and provide a $7,500 stipend.

The creative writing faculty includes poet George

Bilgere (*The Going*; honoree in *Best American Poetry*) and novelist Maureen McHugh (*Mission Child*).

For further information, contact George Bilgere, Dept. of English.

❖Johns Hopkins University
Baltimore, MD 21218-2690
(410) 516-7562
FAX (410) 516-6828

Degrees offered: BA, MA

Degree: BA in the Writing Seminars

Required course of study: 120 s/hrs for the BA

The preliminary course for undergraduate students in The Johns Hopkins Writing Seminars is Introduction to Fiction and Poetry Writing (IFP), a prerequisite for all majors and others who want to take advanced courses in writing. Requirements for the BA include 2 semesters of philosophy, 3 semesters of history, 4 courses in English literature; a foreign language through the intermediate level; 3 advanced semesters in the humanities; and 8 advanced semesters in The Writing Seminars. Undergraduate awards and fellowships available to Writing Seminars students are 3 Louis Azrael Fellowships, the Jacob H. Hollander Prize, the Robert Arellano Award, the Mary Farrell Camerer Award, and the Three Arts Club of Homeland Award.

Degree: MA in The Writing Seminars

Type of Program: Studio/Academic

Length of Residency: One year

Required course of study: 6 semester-length courses

The Writing Seminars selects students on a competitive basis from throughout the country as candidates for the MA in Fiction, Poetry, Nonfiction Prose, or Science Writing. Each class convenes for one academic year and includes no more than 12 students, a maximum of 6 in the Science Writing program. Candidates in the Fiction and Poetry programs will take 3 courses a term, 2 of which must be within the department, and must submit an original work -- a novel, collection of stories or poems. Candidates in the Nonfiction program will take 3 courses a term, one of which must be within the department. Science Writing students will submit an original work which may be a portfolio of articles or a portion of a more extended work, about science or science policy. All candidates for the MA in the department must demonstrate an ability to read and translate a foreign language.

About 15 students will be awarded teaching assistantships consisting of a full tuition fellowship and a stipend. The Teaching Assistants will teach one section each of Introduction to Fiction and Poetry Writing. Some students in the Nonfiction and Science Writing programs will teach courses in nonfiction prose.

The faculty includes Jean McGarry, Chair (*Gallagher's Travels, Home at Last, The Very Rich Hours*); Stephen Dixon (*Gould, Interstate, The Stories of Stephen Dixon*); John T. Irwin (*Just Let Me Say This About That, Mysteries to a Solution, The Heisenberg Variations*); Allen Grossman (*The Woman on the Bridge over* the Chicago River, Of the Great House, The Ether Dome); Richard Macksey (The Structuralist Controversy, Velocities of Change); Alice McDermott (Charming Billy, At Weddings and Wakes) and Carol Burke (The Creative Process, Close Quarters).

Recent visiting faculty have included Julian Barnes, J.D. McClatchy, Francine Prose, Chaim Potok, Cynthia Zarin, Wayne Biddle, Mark Hertsgaard, Edna O'Brien, Robert Stone, Grace Paley, and Andrew Hudgins.

Financial aid is available through full Tuition Fellowships and Stipends; others are eligible for 80% Tuition Fellowships and 50% Tuition Fellowships.

For more information on the writing program, contact Regina Woloszyn, Admissions Secretary, The Writing Seminars.

❖Johns Hopkins University
Part-time Graduate Writing Program
School of Arts and Sciences
1776 Massachusetts Ave. NW, Ste. 100
Washington, DC 20036
(410) 516-6057
FAX (202) 930-9857 or (410) 516-6017
e-mail: pgp-as@jhu.edu
website: www.jhu.edu/pgp-as

Degree offered: MA in Writing (fiction, poetry, nonfiction, science/medical writing)

Type of Program: Studio

Length of Program: 2-5 years part-time, depending on workload

Required course of study: 9 semester-length courses (equivalent of 4 s/hrs per course)
  2 foundation courses
  3 workshops
  3 electives
  1 thesis

Application Deadlines: Students may apply year-round for admission and financial aid and may begin study in any semester.

The Part-time Graduate Writing Program allows students to study, write, and earn a degree at their own speed. The program strives to creative a demanding, innovative environment in which students can develop as writers. The goal is to help students move as close as possible to the creative of publishable material, whatever their writing interests. Current students include all age groups, with most students holding full-time jobs. Courses are taught three semesters a year in the evenings and on Saturday mornings. Students take one or two courses per semester but often skip summers or other semesters as needed. Most students complete the program in three years; some finish in two, and others need the maximum of five years. Most classes are held in the Dupont Circle area of Washington, D.C., with an occasional course at the Hopkins Montgomery County Center in suburban Maryland. (*Part-time courses are not offered at the main Homewood Campus in Baltimore. See the Hopkins full-time program: The Writing Seminars.*) Although early applications are suggested,

students can apply at any time for any semester. Acceptance is based primarily on a competitive examination of a statement of purpose and an extensive writing sample in the desired concentration. Because many applicants are older adults who have not been in a classroom in years, the program does not require a graduate entrance examination. The program sometimes offers noncredit preparatory courses for students who want to create writing samples for an application, although the courses do not guarantee admission. The program emphasizes a structured approach early in a student's study, with broad flexibility later. Admitted students take required foundation courses, workshops in their concentration, and electives, which are offered in literature and in specialized forms or issues such as voice, novels, essays, playwriting, reviews, structure, experimental fiction, and screenwriting. Students are encouraged to take an elective outside their concentration. The program also offers cross-boundary courses that attract students of different concentrations to the same classroom. Workshops and other writing courses have target limits of 12 students. In the final "Thesis and Publication" course, students revise a manuscript of their best writing from previous courses. The thesis class also publishes a literary journal, Mass Ave Review, and spends much of the semester learning about the business of writing and of getting published. In the past two years, students or program graduates have published or sold two novels and four nonfiction books, in addition to many articles, essays, short stories, poems, and other work.

Financial aid is available, including regular financial aid for eligible students taking two courses per term and loan programs for students taking a single course per term.

Veteran journalist David Everett, whose writing has won major awards from the National Press Club, the Society of Professional Journalists, the Overseas Press Club, and other groups, is an instructor and the full-time coordinator of the program. The rest of the faculty is adjunct, although members of a Primary Faculty teach during most semesters and advise students: Poets Greg Williamson (The Silent Partner) and Joseph Harrison; poet, editor, and fiction writer Richard Peabody (Buoyancy and Other Myths, The Morton Salt Girl, the Mondo anthologies); fiction writers Mark Farrington and E.W. Summers (This Never Happened); poet, Pushcart-winning essayist, and fiction writer Aurelie Sheehan (Jack Kerouac Is Pregnant); nonfiction writers Mary Collins (National Public Radio, Taking Control of Your Life), and Sara Taber (Dusk on the Campo); science/medical writers Ruth Levy Guyer and Mary Knudson (A Field Guide for Science Writers); and writers Christine Higgins and Elizabeth Rees. Visiting and Guest Writers who have taught courses include writer and critic Alan Cheuse (The Grandmothers' Club, The Tennessee Waltz), Pulitzer-winning journalist Steve Twomey, nonfiction author Bill Loizeaux (Anna: A Daughter's Life, The Shooting of Rabbit Wells), novelist and filmmaker Fabienne Marsh (Long Distances, The Moralist of the Alphabet Streets), nonfiction author Charlotte Allen (The Human Christ), screenwriter Marc Lapadula, and novelists Mary Kay Zuravleff (The Frequency of Souls) and John Gregory Brown (Decorations in a Ruined Cemetery, The Wrecked, Blessed Body of Shelton Lafleur). Guest lecturers and readers have included novelists Madison Smartt Bell and Patricia Browning Griffith, fiction writers Edward P. Jones and Maxine Clair, nonfiction authors Christopher Joyce and Marc Gunther, and the regular and guest faculty from The Writing Seminars in Baltimore, including poets Alan Grossman, Peter Sacks, and Mark Strand, fiction writers Stephen Dixon, Alice McDermott, Jean McGarry, Julian Barnes, and Robert Stone, critic and essayist Mark Crispin Miller, and science writers Ann Finkbeiner and Barbara Culliton.

For more information, contact David Everett, coordinator of the Part-time Graduate Writing Program, at the address above, or write: Part-time Graduate Programs, School of Arts and Sciences, The Johns Hopkins University, 102 Macaulay Hall, 3400 N. Charles Street, Baltimore, MD 21218.

Johnson State College
Johnson, VT 05656
(802) 635-2356 ext. 1340
FAX (802) 635-1294

Degree offered: BFA in Writing

Required course of study: 120 s/hrs for the BFA

Requirements for the Bachelor of Fine Arts degree in writing include the following: 12 hours in Creative Writing courses, 6 hours in Journalism courses, 6 hours in Form and Theory, 21 hours in Literature, and 3 hours in Senior Thesis. The BFA Writing Program is very active, with a strong reading series at the college and at the nearby Vermont Studio Center arts colony. Visiting writers in recent years have included Joseph Brodsky, Mark Doty, Linda Gregg, Richard Howard, Grace Paley, David Wojahn, and Al Young. The BFA Program also features two literary magazines: the national literary magazine *Green Mountains Review* and a student-edited literary journal, both of which provide opportunities for student internships.

The faculty in the Writing Program includes: poet and essayist Neil Shepard; poet, essayist, and fiction writer Tony Whedon; journalist Catherine Merrill; poet and film critic Dan Towner; poet and essayist Roberta Bienvenu; poet and literary critic Judy Yarnell; essayist Andrea Perham.

For more information on the program, contact Andrea Perham, BFA Writing Program, ext. 1341.

❖Kansas State University
Manhattan, KS 66506-0701
(785) 532-6716

Degrees offered: BA, MA

Degree: BA in English with Concentration in Creative Writing

Required course of study: 33 s/hrs in the major
Thesis: none
Writing workshop: 12 s/hrs
Literature & English language courses: 21 s/hrs

Other Requirements: For the BA, 6 s/hrs English composition; 2-3 s/hrs speech; 2 years of a modern language; 3 s/hrs mathematics; 12 s/hrs humanities; 12 s/hrs social sciences; 11 s/hrs and a lab in natural science; physical education.

The BA in English with Concentration in Creative Writing includes 6 s/hrs introductory courses in crea-

tive writing (3 hours in fiction, 3 hours in poetry). 6 hours of advanced writing workshops, in at least 2 genres, are also required. All workshops are taught by professional writers. The advanced classes are workshop-seminars in which students' writing is analyzed and discussed. Courses in literature and English language complete the student's major program of study.

Degree: MA in English with Concentration in Creative Writing

Type of Program: Studio/Academic

Length of Residency: Two years

Required course of study: 30-33 s/hrs
Writing workshop: 9 s/hrs
Literature courses: 15 s/hrs
Intro to Graduate Studies: 3 s/hrs
Tutorials or directed reading and/or
writing: up to 3 s/hrs

Other Requirements: Proficiency in one foreign language or 3 s/hrs Old English; 3 s/hrs History of the English Language; written comprehensive examination over a 30-item reading list common to all students and a 15-item individual reading list.

Application Deadlines: May 1 for teaching assistantships.

The MA Program in Creative Writing and Literature offers students a full range of writing and literature courses. The writing classes are small informal workshops taught by professional writers and supplemented by private conferences between student and instructor. The program allows some specialization but encourages a degree of diversity, since students must work in more than one genre. Graduate writing workshops are offered in the following genres: poetry, short fiction, novel/novella, and drama.

The "thesis" consists of a portfolio of original creative writing approved by the major professor.

Required course work includes 3 creative writing workshops (in at least two different genres), 12 s/hrs in literature, Introduction to Graduate Studies in English (3 s/hr), and History of the English Language (3 s/hrs) or competency in a foreign language. The MA exam is a 4-hour written examination over a 30-item reading list, plus a 15-item individualized list.

The great majority of graduate students in English hold teaching assistantships. The normal stipend consists of $6,900 or more for a 9-month appointment. Students in the creative writing track may also apply for Popkins and Graduate School Fellowships ($1,000 to $5,000).

The Department of English sponsors *Touchstone*, an annual journal (edited by graduate students) of fiction and poetry by undergraduate students from colleges and universities across the nation.

The graduate creative writing faculty includes poet Elizabeth Dodd (*Like Memory, Caverns*, poetry, and *The Veiled Mirror and the Woman Poet*, criticism); playwright Norman Fedder (founder and director of the Jewish Heritage Theater; over a dozen of his plays have been produced nationally); fiction writer Steve Heller (*The Automotive History of Lucky Kellerman*, a novel, and *The Man Who Drank a Thousand Beers*, short stories, winner of numerous writing awards); and poet Jonathan Holden (*Leverage* and *The Names of the Rapids*, poems; *The Fate of American Poetry*, criticism, winner of three national writing competitions). Also teaching in the undergraduate program are writers Susan Rodgers, Christopher Cokinos, and Craig Stroupe.

Visiting writers in recent years have included Barry Lopez, Pattiann Rogers, Mary Karr, Maxine Hong Kingston, Tobias Wolff, Kathleen Peirce, Gordon Weaver, Stephen Dunn, Michael Harper, Stanley Plumly, Susan Dodd, Marianne Boruch, Dave Smith, W.D. Wetherell, and Charles Baxter.

For more information, contact Elizabeth Dodd, Director, Creative Writing Program, Dept. of English.

❖The University of Kansas
Lawrence, KS 66045

(785) 864-4520

Degrees offered: BA, MA, PhD

Degree: BA in English with Emphasis in Creative Writing

Required course of study: 30 s/hrs in English
 Writing workshop: 6-9 s/hrs
 Other writing courses: up to 9 s/hrs
 Literature courses: 15 or more s/hrs

Other Requirements: For the BA, distribution requirements in foreign language, speech, Western civilization, and mathematics, and principal-course requirements in humanities, social sciences, and natural sciences.

The English Department at KU offers students interested in creative writing an opportunity to learn and practice their craft by writing poetry, fiction, nonfiction, and drama, while at the same time obtaining a BA, although many students take creative writing courses for other reasons: to test their abilities, to explore the creative process, to prepare for other types of writing or for teaching, or to increase their sensitivity to language.

For more information, contact Bernard Hirsch, Coordinator of Undergraduate Studies.

Degree: MA in English with Creative Writing Option (poetry, fiction, creative nonfiction, drama)

Type of Program: Studio/Academic

Required course of study: 30 s/hrs
 Thesis: 6 s/hrs
 Writing workshop: 9 s/hrs
 Other writing courses: 3 s/hrs
 Literature courses: 12 s/hrs

Other Requirements: Foreign language proficiency; defense of thesis.

Admission requirements to the MA program include the submission of a portfolio. Course requirements include 4 graduate courses in literature, English and American; 3 in creative writing; and English 803, Introduction to Graduate Study in Creative Writing, a course that includes an introduction to the teaching of creative writing, skills basic to publication, and methods of research used by creative writers.

MA candidates may present appropriate work in fiction, poetry, drama, or literary nonfiction as a thesis. Creative writing courses may be taken also by PhD students, who have the option of doing a creative writing dissertation in these genres.

The faculty includes G. Douglas Atkins, co-winner of the *Kenyon Review* award for literary excellence in nonfiction prose and author most recently of *Estranging the Familiar*; James B. Carothers, author of short stories in journals and little magazines; Victor Contoski, whose books include poetic translations (*Planting Beeches* and *Unease*) as well as collections of his own poems (*Names* and *A Kansas Sequence*, among others); Carolyn Doty, author of 3 novels (*A Day Late, Fly Away Home*, and *What She Told Him*) and Director of the Prose Section of the Squaw Valley Community of Writers; Joel J. Gold, author of *The Wayward Professor* and numerous essays in humor; James Gunn, science-fiction writer (whose many books include *The Dreamers, The Listeners*, and *Crisis!*) and Director of the Center for the Study of Science Fiction; Michael L. Johnson, Chair of the Department, author of several collections of poetry and poetic translations (*Dry Season* and *The Birds From I Know Where*, among others); Alan Lichter, whose poetry has appeared in journals and little magazines, as well as in *Cezanne's Apples*; Paul Lim, playwright, whose many works include *Conpersonas* and *Mother Tongue*, as well as a collection of short stories (*Some Arrivals, But Mostly Departures*); Tom Lorenz, author of 2 novels (*Guys Like Us* and *Serious Living*), short stories, and dramatic scripts; Chester Sullivan, novelist, short-story writer, and playwright, whose publications include *Alligator Gar* and *Sullivan's Hollow*; Luci Tapahonso, author of several collections of poetry and stories, among them *Sáanii Dahataál: The Women Are Singing* and *Navajo ABC: A Diné Alphabet Book*; and George Wedge, editor of Cottonwood Press and co-editor of *Stiletto*, whose poems have appeared in journals and little magazines. In addition to the permanent staff, Writers-in-Residence visit KU each year and work with students of writing. Recently these have included Ishmael Reed, Marge Piercy, Brian Aldiss, Albert Goldbarth, and Sandra Alcosser. Writers of national prominence frequently visit the campus, including William S. Burroughs, Seamus Heaney, Elizabeth Tallent, James Lee Burke, and Marilyn Hacker.

For more information, write Iris Smith, Coordinator of Graduate Studies.

❖Kennesaw State University
1000 Chastain Road
Kennesaw, GA 30144-5591

(770) 423-6297
FAX (770) 423-6524
e-mail: tgrooms@ksumail.kennesaw.edu or
mapw.advising@ksumail.kennesaw.edu
website: www.kennesaw.edu/English/mapw

Degree offered: MAPW

Degree: Master of Arts in Professional Writing with three concentrations: rhetoric and composition, applied writing, and creative writing (fiction, poetry, creative nonfiction, screenplay writing and playwriting)

Type of Program: Studio/Academic

Length of Residency: 2 years

Required course of study: 36 s/hrs of course work focusing in two of the three concentrations
Writing Core: 3 s/hrs
Creative Writing Concentration: 15 s/hrs
Minor Concentration (either applied or rhetoric and composition): 9 s/hrs
Elective: 3 s/hrs
Portfolio or Thesis: 6 s/hrs

Other Requirements: A student must sit for an oral defense of his or her portfolio or thesis.

Application Deadlines: Semester deadlines.

A unique approach to training writers, the Master of Arts in Professional Writing at Kennesaw State University is an interdisciplinary writing program which features three concentrations: creative writing, applied writing, and rhetoric and composition. Students major in one concentration and minor in another, and are encouraged to explore writing as a holistic and dynamic profession. Thus creative writers not only study in specific imaginative genres, but develop a variety of creative, practical, and theoretical skills.

Such courses as editing, feature writing, scriptwriting, business writing, literacy theory, literary theory, and composition pedagogy are offered in addition to creative writing workshops and independent study.

Further, students are encouraged to become involved in collaborations with other departments such as Communications and Visual Arts, and with metropolitan Atlanta's exciting literary communities. (The campus is only 25 miles from downtown.) An emphasis is placed on literary arts administration, including grant proposal writing and program development. The program affords many internships, both on and off campus.

Writing workshops are limited to 15 students. The workshops offer the students opportunities to practice writing as well as to broaden their knowledge of literature and theory. Although the ratios for concentrations differ, creative writing has maintained a 1:3 teacher to student ratio.

Every Spring, we sponsor the Contemporary Literature Writing Conference, an energetic conference which promotes contemporary literature through a variety of community programs. Recently, we have been visited by Derek Walcott, Ernest Gaines, Edwidge Danticat, Joyce Carol Oates, Ishmael Reed, Stanley Fish, Gerald Early, Gloria Naylor, Gail Godwin, Charlie Smith, and Michael S. Harper, as well as an impressive array of local writers such as Jim Grimsley, June Akers Seese, David Bottoms, John Holman, Judith Ortiz Cofer, and Ha Jin. Many of the locals drop in for classroom visits.

With a student enrollment of 13 thousand undergraduates and graduates, Kennesaw State University is a unit of the University System of Georgia, committed to excellence in teaching, research, and community service. It is fully accredited by the Southern Association of Colleges and Schools. KSU is nestled in the piedmont in Atlanta's northern suburbs, and is convenient to both city and rural living, and to mountain and lake getaways.

A center for writing in Georgia, KSU is owner of the Georgia Writers Information Listserv. Its National Writing Project site, the Kennesaw Mountain Writing Project, is a frequent partner in literary programming.

The creative writing faculty include: novelist and playwright JoAllen Bradham (*Texas Review* Prize, *Some Personal Papers, Ribbons*); fiction writer and poet Anthony Grooms (NEA Arts Administration Fellow, *Ice Poems, Trouble No More*); fiction writer and critic Greg Johnson (*Pagan Babies, Distant Friends, Invisible Writer: A Biography of Joyce Carol Oates*); and poet Don Russ (*Men*). It is notable that many of the KSU faculty are published creative writers.

For more information, contact: Director, MAPW program, English Dept., at the above addresses and numbers.

❖Kent State University
Kent, OH 44242-0001
(330) 672-2676
FAX (330) 672-3152

Degree offered: BA, Writing Minor

Required course of study: 2-24 s/hrs for the Minor
Portfolio: 2 s/hrs
Writing workshop: 9-12 s/hrs
Other writing courses: 3-6 s/hrs

Other Requirements: 3 cognate courses in English and/or other departments.

The Writing Minor gives academic recognition to students who have demonstrated their ability in either imaginative writing or expository writing. The minor helps students to establish eligibility for graduate programs in writing. It is evidence of training that may be offered to prospective employers.

Courses available for the writing minor include: Introduction to Creative Writing; Writers' Workshops (two levels in fiction and poetry); Black Writers' Workshops in fiction, poetry, and drama; and playwriting. A variety of related courses in literature (including seminars on the Beat Generation, Postmodern Fiction, chapbook preparation, and little magazines and small presses, using the resources of Kent State University's special collection of modern and contemporary poetry books and manuscripts) are also available.

The most important aspect of the writing minor with an emphasis in creative writing is the writing portfolio, a sustained collection of poetry, fiction, or playwriting which the student puts together over one or two semesters in consultation with two members of the creative writing faculty. These portfolios are often used as a part of an application to an MFA program. Recent Kent State graduates have been accepted into MFA programs at Columbia Univeristy, Western Washington University, the University of Arizona, the University of Pittsburgh, and at Stanford University as a Wallace Stegner Fellow. In addition, several students who have completed the writing minor have won the Wick Poetry Program's student chapbook competition for Ohio poets and their chapbooks have been published by the Kent State University Press. Recently, two Kent State University creative writing students were chosen to attend the Stadler Seminar for Younger Poets at Bucknell University. Some of Kent State

University's creative writing students have distinguished themselves as performance poets both regionally and nationally.

A program that is particularly supportive of the writing minor is the Wick Poetry Program under the Directorship of Maggie Anderson. Wick Program activities include an undergraduate scholarship competition, a chapbook series and a first book series through the Kent State University Press, and readings by poets, including Gwendolyn Brooks, Edwidge Danticat, Lynn Emanuel, Joy Harjo, Maxine Kumin, Heather McHugh, Gerald Stern, and others. The Wick Poetry Program also sponsors workshops with visiting writers and fellowships for graduate students. Recent visiting poets include Robin Becker, Li-Young Lee, Victoria Redel, Richard Tayson, and Rosemary Willey. In addition to the special opportunities provided by the Wick Poetry Program, a lively community of readings and performances throughout northeastern Ohio supports the academic offerings in creative writing at Kent State.

The creative writing faculty includes Maggie Anderson, poetry (*Cold Comfort* and *A Space Filled with Moving*); Zee Edgell, fiction (*Beka Lamb* and *Festival at San Joaquin*); Kat Snider Blackbird, poetry (*White Sustenance* and the CD *Recreational Virgin*); Ted Lyons, fiction (editor of *The Time of Your Life*); Maj Ragain, poetry (*Burley One Dark Sucker Fired* and *Fresh Oil, Loose Gravel*); Alice Cone, poetry and fiction (*Shattering Into Blossom*); Brooke Horvath, poetry and fiction (*Consolation at Ground Zero*, co-editor of *Review of Contemporary Fiction*); Craig Paulenich, poetry (co-editor of *Beneath a Single Moon: Buddhism in Contemporary American Poetry*); Wayne Kvam, poetry (editor and translator of *Hitchhiking: Twelve German Tales* by Gabriele Eckart); and Donald Hassler, poetry and fiction (editor of *Patterns of the Fantastic*).

For more information, contact Maggie Anderson, Wick Poetry Program Coordinator, or Margaret Shaw, Writing Program Coordinator, Dept. of English.

Keuka College
Keuka Park, NY 14478

(315) 536-5374

Degree offered: BA in English with Concentration in Writing/Communication

For more information, contact Writing Program Director, Dept. of English.

King's College
Wilkes-Barre, PA 18711-0801

(717) 208-5900 ext. 5631
FAX (717) 208-5988

Degree offered: BA in English with Concentration in Writing

Required course of study: 120 s/hrs total; 33 s/hrs in major
Advanced Writing: 3 s/hrs
Lit. Surveys & Advanced Lit.: 12 s/hrs
Writing Workshops: 9 s/hrs
Senior Practicum: 3 s/hrs
Writing Electives: 6 s/hrs (min.)

Degree: BA in English with Minor in Writing (available in combination with a Major in Literature or in another field)

Required course of study: 18 s/hrs total in minor
Advanced Writing: 3 s/hrs
Tech. Writing: 3 s/hrs
Literature: 3 s/hrs
Workshops: 6 s/hrs
Practicum: 3 s/hrs

The concentration in Writing is designed for students seeking proficiency in 3 areas: creative, technical, and rhetorical writing. Workshop and Elective possibilities include the following areas: Language/Linguistics, Business & Technical Writing, Writing for Publication, Desktop Applications in English, Seminar in the Teaching of Writing, and others. A variety of writing-intensive Internships, including opportunities with CNN and some government agencies through the Washington Center Internship Program, exist and are encouraged. Majors are also able to pursue coursework or an Internship during a semester abroad through the London Program. Independent courses or tutorials in advanced creative or other specialized writing are available through the English Department and the Honors Program. Majors may work in the Writing Center as tutorial assistants, and in conjunction with the "Teaching of Writing" course may assist professors in undergraduate teaching of core writing courses. Students are encouraged to participate in *The Scop*, the literary magazine, as well as *Regis*, our yearbook, and the award-winning college newspaper, *The Crown*. The Campion Society, the campus arts association, hosts open readings and related activities each semester.

Visiting Writers in recent years have included Howard Nemerov, Elena Castedo, Maxine Kumin, David Bradley, Joanna Scott, Sam Hazo, Tobias Wolff, and Chase Twichell. As part of a 2-day residency each fall semester, writers work with students in Creative Writing Workshop and in other related courses, in addition to offering a public reading of their work. Specialized classes, such as Writing for Publication, incorporate guest writers/editors/publishers on short-term visits.

The English and Writing Program has enabled graduates to pursue MFA degrees, and to enter a number of careers, from freelance writing and editing, to legal assistance, law, journalism, the teaching of writing, technical writing, and even the management of computerized programming.

For further information or to arrange a visit, please contact the English Dept. Chairperson at the address or phone number listed above.

❖Kirtland Community College
10775 N. St. Helen Road
Roscommon, MI 48653-9699
e-mail: lafeming@kirtland.cc.mi.us

For more information, contact Gerry LaFemina at the above address.

❖Knox College
Galesburg, IL 61401

(309) 343-0112, ext. 419

Degree offered: BA in Creative Writing

Required course of study: 36 courses overall for the BA; a minimum of 10 courses for the major
   Literature survey: 2 courses
   Other literature courses: 3 courses
     including modern and contemporary
   Writing: 4 courses in any genre; a minimum
     2 courses at workshop level; advanced
     tutorials, College Honors project as
     additional options
   Senior Colloquium: 1 course in creative,
     aesthetic, critical theory

Other Requirements: At least 2 courses in each of 3 categories -- mathematics and natural science, history and social science, arts and humanities; proficiency in mathematics and one foreign language.

Application Deadlines: Early action December 1; Admission February 15; Financial aid March 1.

Knox College has included a program in writing as part of its English Department since the 1920s and has offered a major in writing since 1952. In the setting of a highly selective liberal arts college, the writing major at Knox places equal emphasis on the exploration of personal and societal values and on the disciplined development of professional competence. The varied activities of the Program in Writing are a visible and exceptionally respected aspect of campus life. It can be truly said that a community of young writers flourishes here.

The writing courses at Knox (offered at beginning, workshop, and advanced tutorial levels) include: fiction, poetry, nonfiction, translation, playwriting, and scriptwriting. All courses are open to majors and non-majors alike. There are numerous opportunities for independent work. Candidates for College Honors in Writing submit a book-length volume of work to a faculty committee and to a non-campus reviewer prominent in the field. Upon graduation, Knox writers are routinely accepted for admission into prestigious graduate writing programs; a significant number have published their work professionally while still under-graduates.

Catch, the campus literary magazine, edited and produced by students and devoted to student work, is published 3 times each year. Twice in the past 4 years, in competition with all colleges and universities, *Catch* has been named the nation's most outstanding collegiate literary magazine by the Coordinating Council of Literary Magazines (CCLM), New York.

Additionally, the Program in Writing offers student writers valuable experience through the student newspaper and student radio station WVKC-FM (which broadcasts student readings), while the outstanding Knox theater facilities offer production opportunities for student playwrights. "The Weekly Reader" is a program that encourages students to present their own poetry and fiction to a campus audience nearly every week of the academic year.

Creative Arts Scholarships, worth a maximum of $1,500 annually, are available on a competitive basis to student writers, artists, actors, and musicians. The Davenport Literary Awards, the Wilson Prize, and the White Prize (among others) offer cash prizes each year to outstanding student writers on campus. The Nick Adams Short Story Prize of $1,000 is awarded annually to a student of the Associated Colleges of the Midwest, a consortium including Knox.

The Knox College Program in Writing, along with other campus organizations, sponsors readings by outstanding professional writers on campus every year. Writers who have appeared at Knox include: Tillie Olsen, Philip Roth, Galway Kinnell, Stanley Elkin, Denise Levertov, Grace Paley, Hilma Wolitzer, David Bradley, Larry Woiwode, Etheridge Knight, R.V. Cassill, David St. John, Joan Williams, Studs Terkel, Richard Stern, Robert Pinsky, Deborah Digges, Luisa Valenzuela, and others.

Writing classes at Knox are small, averaging about a dozen students, and frequent individual conferences are an established tradition for every course. The writing faculty members, widely published, awarded, and recognized in their primary fields, include: Michael Crowell (nonfiction), Ivan Davidson (play/scriptwriting), Robert Hellenga (fiction), Frederick Hord (poetry, Black Studies), Robin Metz (fiction, play/scriptwriting), and Lisa Ress (poetry, translation, Women's Studies).

For further information, contact Robin Metz, Director, the Program in Writing.

❖Kutztown University
English Department
Kutztown, PA 19530

(610) 683-4353
FAX (610) 683-4633
e-mail: applewhi@kutztown.edu
website:
  http://www.kutztown.edu/acad/english/bapw.htm

Degree offered: BA in English/Professional Writing

At Kutztown, creative writing courses count:

● toward the professional writing degree which provides training for students wanting to pursue writing careers

● toward the Related Arts degree for students interested in some combination of English, Music, Dance and Art courses

● as electives in other degree programs, including English General, which is primarily a literature program.

Contact the Creative Writing Program Director, Dept. of English.

La Salle University
Philadelphia, PA 19141

(215) 951-1145
FAX (215) 951-1488
e-mail: haberstr@lasalle.edu

Degree offered: BA in English with Emphasis in Professional and/or Creative Writing

Required course of study:
Writing courses: 15 or more s/hrs
Literature courses: 21 or more s/hrs
Linguistics course: 3 s/hrs
English electives: 6 or more s/hrs

Other Requirements: 45 s/hrs in major; university distribution requirements.

Application Deadlines: June 1

A distinct track within the English major, Creative and Professional Writing prepares students for a variety of professions in the writing world. In addition to seven required courses in literature, advanced expository writing, and two electives, students must take five courses in specific writing disciplines, organized within three general areas: imaginative writing (fiction, poetry, playwriting); workplace writing (journalism, magazine writing, business writing, scientific and technical writing) and editing and publishing (desktop publishing, electronic publishing, Internet publishing). Students are encouraged to pursue a professional internship, for credit, during their junior or senior years. La Salle's writing faculty includes several practicing professional authors; part-time and rotating appointments supplement the full-time faculty. Outlets for student work include a student literary magazine (*Grimoire*, published twice yearly) and regular student open-mike readings. A visiting author series brings fiction writers and poets of national reputation to campus to read and discuss their work; recent visitors have included novelists Russell Banks, Frederick Busch, Madison Smartt Bell, and Elizabeth McCracken, and poets Stephen Dunn and Eleanor Wilner. Robert L. Dean Writing Scholarships (partial tuition) are awarded annually to several students within the major; there are also awards for student poetry, fiction, and expository writing. The English program has about 230 majors, with more than half in the writing concentration.

For more information, contact Patricia B. Haberstroh, Chair, Dept. of English.

Lake Forest College
Lake Forest, IL 60045
(708) 735-5277
FAX (708) 735-6291

Degree offered: BA in English with Concentration in Writing

Required course of study: 27 s/hrs in the major
Writing workshop: 6–15 s/hrs
Literature courses: 5–18 s/hrs
Tutorials or directed reading:
    up to 6 s/hrs
Senior Project or thesis: 3–6 s/hrs

Application Deadlines: February 15, for decision in late March. For applications after February 15, as conditions permit.

Lake Forest's Writing Program has been growing steadily since its inception in 1975. The college has a new curriculum of general education courses, and also requires courses in the major. For writing majors this means there are 9 required courses: 3 writing courses, 5 literature courses, and one other elective in English. The required writing courses in the creative writing track are Fiction Writing Workshop, or Playwriting Workshop, or Poetry Writing Workshop, Advanced Writing Workshop, and Senior Writing Seminar. Nonfiction writing majors must take Nonfiction Writing, an internship or practicum of their own design, and Senior Writing Seminar.

The Senior Writing Seminar, the last required course for all writing majors, is a workshop as are all the writing courses, and one in which work is then submitted as a Senior Writing Project -- similar to a senior thesis.

The 5 required literature courses consist of 3 English literature survey classes and two electives. We offer many elective English courses, such as Shakespeare, Contemporary Literature, Folklore, Women Writers, Drama, and Literary Theory.

Lake Forest College offers several academic scholarships and work-study programs to qualified students. The Writing Program selects one senior each year to receive its deHerder Award for creative writing. Students also publish a literary magazine, *Tusitala*, in April of each year.

Every year the Writing Program brings visiting writers to campus, usually a poet in the fall and a fiction writer in the spring. During their 10-day residencies, guest writers give readings, lectures, seminars, and have individual conferences with students. Past visiting poets have included Denise Levertov, Robert Bly, Tess Gallagher, William Stafford, Adrienne Rich, Kenneth Koch, Mark Strand, and Lisel Mueller.

For more information, contact Richard Mallette, Chairperson, Dept. of English.

❖Lakeland College
Sheboygan, WI 53082-0359
(920) 565-1276
FAX (920) 565-1206
e-mail: kelder@excel.net
website: http//www.lakeland.edu/acdiv/writing.htm

Degree offered: BA in Writing

Required course of study: 36 s/hrs in the major
Writing courses: 28 s/hrs
Literature courses: 8 s/hrs
Thesis: required senior writing project

Required course of study: 24 s/hrs in the minor

Other Requirements: For the BA, general studies requirements in critical thinking, world history, humanities, natural science, religion, social science, and foreign language or math.

Application Deadlines: April 1 for financial aid; April 1 for admissions.

Lakeland College is a Christian liberal arts college with a tradition of academic excellence and a long-standing commitment to career preparation. From this identity flows the mission of the college: educating men and women in such a way as to enable them to earn a living and to lead purposeful, fulfilling lives characterized by intellectual, moral, and spiritual growth.

The Division of Creative Arts offers students a variety of courses in creative writing (poetry, fiction, autobiography, prose essays, film, and drama), journalism, and literature. The favorable ratio of students to teachers (6 to 1 in the major; 15 to 1 on campus) results in accessibility to and close attention from faculty members who are themselves writers actively engaged in their craft. Many writing students choose to join the staff of the *Mirror*, Lakeland's student newspaper, and/or *Farrago*, the campus literary magazine. Many also gain practical experience as interns for a local daily newspaper, a television station, and the public affairs offices of area hospitals and corporations. In addition, writing students often enroll in film production and film criticism classes, playwriting classes and experimental courses which have been created with the writing student in mind.

Each year several Fessler Scholarships in Creative Writing ($2,000-$3,000, renewable) are awarded and 2 writing or English majors are selected to receive Writing Fellowships (approximately $1,800 work-study stipends) for editing the student newspaper. The department also awards 2 Kohler Memorial scholarships ($500, renewable). The nationally distributed literary magazine *Seems* is published at Lakeland College, and outstanding writing students are often invited to serve as assistant editors for an issue.

The writing faculty includes Fessler Professor in Creative Writing and poet Karl Elder (*Can't Dance an' It's Too Wet to Plow; A Man in Pieces; Phobophobia*), fictionist and screenwriter Jeff Elzinga (*First Aid Songs*), and media specialist Martha Schott. The Great Lakes Writers Festival is held on campus. Featured in 1995 were William Hathaway and Michael Martone. Other visitors have included Mortimer Adler, Jonis Agee, Billy Collins, Philip Dacey, Stephen Dunn, Doug Flaherty, Robin Hemley, Judith Hemschemeyer, William Heyen, W.P. Kinsella, Dave Oliphant, Sapphire, Mark Strand, Lucien Stryk, and Henry Taylor.

For more information, contact Karl Elder, Program Coordinator.

❖Lamar University
Beaumont, TX 77710

(409) 880-8558

Degrees offered: BA, MA

Degree: BA with a Writing Emphasis

Required course of study: 127 s/hrs total
Creative Writing (fiction, poetry, essay, or screenwriting emphasis): 6 s/hrs
Writing Seminar: 3 s/hrs
Technical Report Writing, Expository Writing, Editing
Technical Communications: optional
Literature courses: 32 s/hrs
A non-teacher certification student may major in English and minor in writing

Application Deadlines: April 1 for financial aid, March 1 advised; March 1 for admission -- Fall or Summer.

The undergraduate writing emphasis in creative writing usually requires students to take one or two courses in genres (essay, fiction, screenwriting, or poetry) and an advanced workshop (usually in poetry or fiction). Students may also take other courses in writing to meet their nine-hour writing emphasis requirement. *Pulse* is the student literary magazine, which provides editorial and publishing experience for all students. Poetry, fiction, essay, and outstanding student awards are given yearly.

Degree: MA with a Creative Thesis (poetry, fiction, screenwriting, or a combination)

Type of Program: Studio/Academic

Length of Residency: Two years

Required course of study:
English courses (usually an advanced workshop included): 18 s/hrs
Minor: 6 s/hrs
Thesis: 6 s/hrs

Other Requirements: Oral defense of thesis.

Application Deadlines: Thirty days prior to registration for admission, Teaching assistantships available.

The English Department at Lamar University is committed to offering a variety of writing courses at timely intervals and to providing students with individual attention. Our expanding writing program is composed of courses in specific genres and advanced workshops that complement our literature courses.

Lamar's English Department also sponsors *Pulse*, the student literary magazine, and offers cash prizes for poetry, fiction, and outstanding work in advanced classes. Further, Lamar is currently the home for the Texas Reading Circuit and thus offers readings by prominent poets and writers (Rick Bass, Miller Williams, Lynna Williams, Dagoberto Gilb, Marion Winik, and Debra Monroe).

For students who are interested in pursuing graduate study in literature or English, Lamar's English Department offers an MA in English. Here too, a student can pursue a writing emphasis, usually a graduate level course and a creative or technical thesis. Teaching Assistantships are available.

The creative writing faculty includes: poet R.S. Gwynn (*The Drive-In*, ed. *Dictionary of Literary Biography*, and literature textbooks) and prize winning fiction writer and essayist Jim Sanderson (*Semi-Private Rooms; Pulpits, Podiums and Barstools*).

For more information write either of the listed writers at Box 10023, Lamar University, Beaumont, TX 77710.

Lancaster University
Lancaster, LA1 4YN
United Kingdom

(0524) 594169

Degrees offered: M.Phil/PhD; MA in Creative Writing; MA in Creative Writing by Distance Learning

Required course of study: M.Phil/PhD negotiated individually; 60 x 3 hrs Writing Workshops for the MA.

Application Deadline: Considered at any time.

The MA course runs each year from the start of October till the end of the following August. Classes take place throughout the ten weeks of each of the three university terms.

The aim of the course is to develop the skills of experienced writers and their awareness of what it takes to express oneself in the literary media, i.e. fiction, poetry, lyrics, and scripts. Advice is available on getting work published, i.e. on dealing with editors, publishers, and agents. Entrants for the course are expected already to be able to produce publishable work.

The backbone of the course is sixty two-to-three-hour workshops, two each week from October till June (or one each week over two academic years for part-timers). At these, students meet with the writers who make up the academic staff. Students also attend workshops run by visiting professional writers. Most of our time is spent discussing and critiquing students' work in progress. Occasionally we write pieces to specific guidelines. Individual meetings are held by arrangement to discuss problems of self-expression in the light of a student's particular needs. When necessary, discussions are held on some of the key methods, terms, and ideas that crop up during sustained writing projects.

A substantial folder of finished work, brought to its best possible state during the summer after workshops have ended, is due in by September 1. It usually consists of a novel or a collection of stories or a sequence/collection of poems or one or more playscripts or a "miscellany" including work in various of these forms. It must also include a critique of the other students' work. There are usually between eight and twelve in the group.

Applicants should normally have a first degree in any subject. They must send in a folder of creative work along with their application.

The writing faculty: Linda Anderson (*To Stay Alive, Cuckoo*); and W.N. Herbert (*Forked Tongue, Cabaret McGonagall*).

Visiting writers have included: Maggie Gee, Catherine Byron, Matt Simpson, Janni Howker, David Pownall, Paddy Kitchen, Kazuo Ishiguro, Bernard MacLaverty, Graham Swift, Hugo Williams, Edwin Morgan, Iain Crichton Smith, and Russell Hoban.

A distance-learning version of the course begins in January 1999. This is a 2-year course by computer conferencing, e-mail, and a 14-day summer school at the Poets' House, Co. Donegal, Ireland.

For more information, contact Linda Anderson, Dept. of Creative Writing, e-mail l.anderson@lancaster.ac.uk.

Lawrence University
Appleton, WI 54912
(414) 832-6647

Degree offered: BA in English

Required course of study: 9 of 36 courses required for a BA must be in English

Although there is no major in writing at Lawrence, credits toward the BA are given for courses in fiction writing, verse writing, and creative nonfiction. Students have the opportunity to continue their writing in individual tutorials, and selected students may submit honors theses in creative writing in the senior year (novels, collections of verse, etc.).

The faculty member primarily responsible for creative writing is novelist Mark Dintenfass (*Make Yourself An Earthquake; The Case against Org; Figure 8*). Writers-in-residence of recent years have included Jerald Bullis, Michael McFee, and Carolyn Kizer. There is a campus literary magazine which appears regularly, and the university offers the usual program of visiting writers who give readings and hold workshops.

For more information, write Mark Dintenfass, Dept. of English.

Lehman College
City University of New York
Bronx, NY 10468
(718) 960-8556

Degree offered: BA in English, Creative Writing Specialization

Required course of study: 40–43 s/hrs in the major
Thesis: required for honors
Writing courses: 12 or more s/hrs
Literature courses: 22 or more s/hrs
Tutorials or directed reading: 3–6 s/hrs

Other Requirements: 3 s/hrs internship or 3 additional tutorial s/hrs.

The creative writing specialization in the English Department at Lehman College offers the student a wide variety of creative writing and journalism courses, as well as the opportunity to work with the Lehman College theater production program and with the undergraduate literary magazine. The student may also explore internship possibilities with Manhattan theaters, publishers, and television studios.

The program includes major courses in fiction writing, poetry writing, play and screenplay writing, critical review writing, journalistic writing, advanced workshop in creative writing, seminar in creative writing, and, required of students preparing the creative writing honors thesis: the senior honors seminar and the senior honors tutorial.

Our program is friendly, and students may have individual access over several semesters, formal or informal, to the creative writers on the staff. Faculty members primarily responsible for creative writing courses are: George Blecher, translator and fiction writer; Billy Collins, poet, author of *The Apple That Astonished Paris*; Pamela Ansaldi, playwright and short story writer; Jack Kligerman, writer of creative nonfiction prose; and Virginia Scott, poet and prize-winning editor of the literary journal *Sunbury*.

For more information, write Mardi Valgemae, Chair, Dept. of English.

94

Lesley Adult Baccalaureate College Intense Residency Option Program
29 Everett Street
Cambridge, MA 02138-2790
(800) 999-1959, ext. 8478

Degree offered: BA in Literal Arts with concentration in Creative Writing, Literature and Writing, Nonfiction Writing

Type of Program: Studio/Academic

Length of Residency: One year and a half minimum depending on credits at time of entrance.

Required course of study: 128 hrs. total; 32 in concentration. Transfer credits acceptable even if 10 years or older. Life Experience credits accepted to maximum of 48.

This program is designed for mature adults who wish to complete their bachelor's degree in an accelerated manner.

Other Requirements: Independent study in writing and relevant literature. Ten-day residency every six months. Highly individualized program similar to non-resident MFA programs. Thesis project required for graduation, which can be a manuscript plus a contextual essay.

Application Deadlines: Rolling. 9-day residencies held Oct., Feb., April, & July.

The faculty includes: fiction writer Judith Beth Cohen, author of *Seasons*, included in *How Writers Teach Writing*; poet and playwright Erica Funkhouser, author of *Natural Affinities*, elected for a Writer's Choice Award; Laurent Daloz, author of *Effective Teaching and Mentoring*.

For more information, contact Program Director, I.R.O. Program.

❖Lewis and Clark College
Portland, OR 97219
(503) 768-7405
FAX (503) 768-7418

Degree offered: BA in English with Concentration in Creative Writing (poetry and fiction)

Required course of study: Sequence of 200, 300, 400 courses with option for Honors Thesis
Literature courses: 9 s/hrs
Electives: 6 s/hrs
Total hours for major: 36 s/hrs

Other Requirements: College distribution requirements; total number of credits for graduation: 128 s/hrs.

Application Deadlines: February 1 for regular admission (financial aid deadline is February 15); November 15 for early decision.

The undergraduate concentration requires the student to take Beginning (Foundations in Form), Intermediate, and Advanced courses. The major also requires historical grounding in English and American literature, including pre-18th-century, and successful completion of a senior seminar. Qualified students may also write an Honors Thesis. The *Lewis and Clark Literary Review* provides students with opportunities to edit, direct, and otherwise take part in the compilation of a high-quality undergraduate arts magazine. The Gender Studies journal, *Synergia*, and International Studies Magazine, *Meridian*, are other student-run publications.

Visiting writers to campus and the Gender Studies Symposium include: Russell Banks, Louise Erdrich, Adrienne Rich, Reginald McKnight, Joy Harjo, Dorothy Allison, David Sedaris, and Leslea Newman. Poets include Donald Justice, Philip Levine, Lawson Inada, Garrett Hongo, Dennis Schmitz, Patricia Goedicke, Carolyn Kizer, Lynn Emanuel, Jennifer Cornell, and Marjorie Sandor.

Faculty: Vern Rutsala, poet: *Little-Known Sports, Selected Poems, Ruined Cities,* and many others. Annie Dawid, fiction writer: *York Ferry,* stories in *American Fiction, 93; Women on Women II* and others, winner, 1998 Raymond Carver Short Story Contest.

For more information, contact Annie Dawid, Director, Creative Writing Program.

❖Lewis & Clark State College
Lewiston, ID 83501-2698
(208) 799-2050 or 799-2307
FAX (208) 799-2324

Degree offered: BA in English with Concentration in Creative Writing (poetry, fiction, nonfiction)

Required course of study: 128 s/hrs
12 s/hrs in creative writing courses (in any of three genres)
36 s/hrs in literature and technique courses

The program encourages students to work with *The Talking River Review*, a literary magazine produced by LCSC students and featuring work by both beginning and established writers. Recent contributors include David James Duncan, Pattiann Rogers, and William Kittredge. In addition, some students work as interns with Confluence Press, a small, independent literary publisher headquartered at LCSC.

The program sponsors a vigorous visiting writers series. Recent visitors have included Yusef Komunyakaa, T. Crunk, Judy Blunt, Ellen Bryant Voigt, Philip Levine, Sherman Alexie, and Richard Ford. The Division of Literature and Languages also sponsors an annual Wallace Stegner Lecture Series. Lecturers have included Robert Stone, Linda Hogan, Tillie Olsen, Larry McMurtry, and James Welch.

Creative writing faculty include: Kim Barnes (*In the Wilderness, Circle of Women*); Claire Davis; Dennis Held; James Hepworth (*Silence As a Method of Birth Control*); William Johnson (*The Wilderness Boundary*); and Robert Wrigley (*In the Bank of Beautiful Sins; What My Father Believed; Moon In a Mason Jar*).

The college and the press also sponsor an annual Visiting Writers Series. Recent visitors have included Richard Ford, William Kittredge, Ellen Bryant Voigt, Norman MacLean, Larry McMurtry, Gwen Head,

Edward Abbey, N. Scott Momaday, Terry Tempest Williams, and many others.

For more information, contact Robert Wrigley, Writing Program Director.

❖Lincoln University
P.O. Box 29
Jefferson City, MO 65102-0029
(573) 681-5234
FAX (573) 681-5209

Degree offered: BA in English with Emphasis in Creative Writing

Required course of study:
Literature: 18 s/hrs
Literary History: 2 s/hrs
Creative Writing: 15 s/hrs
Seniors submit portfolio and other written work for exit evaluation

Students are required to take Introduction to Creative Writing before specializing in poetry, fiction, or creative nonfiction. Students can enroll in Internship in Editing and Publishing, a senior course that produces LU's art and literature magazine, *Under One Sun*. Each fall the program hosts Missouri Writers Read, a reading series that features writers who have some connection to the state of Missouri. Past guests have included Carl Phillips, Trudy Lewis, David Baker, Allison Joseph, H.L. Hix, and Kevin Prufer. Each spring upperclassmen can participate in the LWS Student Reading Exchange, a visiting student writers program, compete for the Cecil Blue Creative Writing Scholarship and the Scholastic, Inc. Book Awards.

For more information, contact Dr. Ginger Jones, Coordinator of Creative Writing.

Linfield College
McMinnville, OR 97128
(503) 434-2288
FAX (503) 434-2215
e-mail: bdrake@Linfield.edu

Degree offered: BA in Creative Writing

Requirements in major: 20 s/hrs in Creative Writing including 4 credits for senior thesis, and 20 s/hrs in literature including at least one American literature course. Senior thesis may be a collection of poetry or short stories, a novel, a script, or creative nonfiction. Work on the school literary magazine is strongly advised.

For more information, contact Barbara Drake, Dept. of English.

❖Lock Haven University
Lock Haven, PA 17745
(717) 893-2174

Degrees offered: BA, BS in English with a Concentration in Creative Writing (fiction, poetry, playwriting)

The creative writing concentration allows the student to elect workshop offerings in fiction, poetry, or playwriting each semester for beginning, intermediate, and advanced credits. Workshops are studio courses. Accompanying technique and theory courses are offered in each genre and are studio-academic. The campus literary magazine, *The Crucible*, affords students experience in editing and publishing. An Isabel Winner Miller Scholarship in Creative Writing is awarded each spring. There is a yearly schedule of visiting writers and students and faculty readings.

The full-time creative writing faculty includes poet and fiction writer Marjorie Maddox (*Perpendicular As I, Nightrider to Edinburgh*, Academy of American Poets Prize), and fiction writer Joseph Nicholson (*Odds Without End, The Dam Builder*, National Endowment for the Arts Literature Fellowship, Pennsylvania Council on the Arts Award).

For more information, contact Joseph Nicholson, Dept. of English.

❖Long Beach City College
4901 East Carson Street
Long Beach, CA 90808

Degree offered: AA in English with Concentration in Creative Writing

Offers a broad range of workshops and readings open to the community.

For further information contact Writing Program Director, Dept. of English.

Loras College
Dubuque, IA 52004-0178
(319) 588-7727

Degrees offered: BA, BS

Degree: BA in English/Writing

Required course of study: 33 s/hrs
Thesis
Writing workshop: 18 s/hrs (5 elective courses)
Literature courses: 15 s/hrs
(4 electives plus Literary Criticism)

Loras, a Catholic liberal arts college, offers a balanced undergraduate Writing Program with introductory and advanced courses in fiction, poetry, and nonfiction writing. English/Writing majors are required to complete a minimum of 33 credit hours in writing and literature courses, and to produce an independent thesis project during the senior year. Students may choose from a variety of regular and special courses and are encouraged to concentrate in one or more writing areas.

The faculty of the Writing program include, in fiction and nonfiction, Don Knefel (*Writing and Life, Aims of the Essay, Essays From Time*); in poetry, William Pauly (winner of Haiku Society of America's H.G. Henderson Award, poems in *Christian Century, Notre Dame English Journal, Big Sky*); and in nonfiction,

Kevin Koch (essays in *The Des Moines Register*, *DES Journal*, *The Witness*).

The Loras English Department sponsors a literary club for student readings and field trips and publishes a student-edited magazine, *Outlet*. Loras writers are active in these organizations and in the student newspaper, the *Lorian*, and the English Department's newsletter.

Our English/Writing graduates have been successful in many fields, including business, education, theology, technology, and fine arts.

For more information, contact Don Knefel, Loras Writing Program, Dept. of English.

❖Louisiana State University
Baton Rouge, LA 70803-5001

(504) 388-2236

Degrees offered: BA, MFA

Degree: BA

Required course of study:
36 s/hrs in English
Writing workshops: 12 s/hrs
Literature courses: 18 s/hrs

The BA in English with a concentration in creative writing requires students to take at least 4 writing workshops from choices in poetry, fiction, playwriting, screenwriting, and nonfiction (in addition to six literature courses).

Degree: MFA

Type of Program: Studio/Academic

Length of Residency: Two and a half years

Required course of study: 48 s/hrs
Thesis (tutorial): 6 s/hrs
Writing workshops: 18 s/hrs
Literature courses: 12 s/hrs
Electives: 12 s/hrs

Application Deadline: February 1.

The MFA program, directed by Moira Crone and the Director of Graduate Studies, is a small, intensive program, limited to 30 students who work with a core faculty of seven (two in fiction, three in poetry, one each in playwriting and screenwriting). Requirements include 48 hours of coursework: 18 hours in workshop (no more than 12 hrs in a genre), 12 hours in literature (graduate level), 6 hours of thesis work (tutorial, with a committee, to complete a final project), and 12 hours of electives. An oral defense of the thesis takes place before graduation.

The MFA emphasizes fiction and poetry, but encourages work in playwriting, screenwriting, and literary nonfiction. A thesis can be written in any of these genres.

Financial aid at LSU is competitive. Graduate Fellowships are available to exceptional applicants, at $14,000 a year for 3 years. Any student who has 18 or more hours of graduate credit in English may apply for teaching assistantships, at $8,000 per academic year, or $8,500 for students who have an MA. Teaching Assistants who have taught satisfactorily for one year usually become Teaching Associates the next year. Teaching Associates teach an extra course in the fall for an extra $2,500. Tuition is not waived for TAs; all TAs pay in-state tuition rates. Candidates for the combined MFA-PhD are eligible for other Fellowships. There are also a few editorial internships and research assistantships available.

The LSU English Department, which offers the Creative Writing Program under the Director of Graduate Studies, has a distinguished and growing national reputation for scholarship and critical study, as well as creative writing. Our tradition goes back to Robert Penn Warren and Cleanth Brooks, founders of *The Southern Review*, which has published the early works of Eudora Welty, Jean Stafford, Robert Lowell, Katherine Anne Porter, and Peter Taylor, up through Miller Williams and Walker Percy. *The Southern Review* is now edited by James Olney and Dave Smith. Among several other publications edited as LSU is Andrei Codrescu's *Exquisite Corpse*. Students edit *The New Delta Review*, publishing writers from around the country.

Our creative writing faculty includes two fiction writers, two poets, one playwright, and one screenwriter. In fiction, James Bennett has published *My Father's Geisha* and *The Moon Stops Here*, with short stories in many publications. His work has been anthologized in *New Stories From The South*. Moira Crone's fiction includes her novel, *A Period of Confinement*, and two collections of short stories, *The Winnebago Mysteries and Other Stories* and *Dream State*, and her short stories have been anthologized in several volumes.

In poetry, Andrei Codrescu is the author of *Alien Candor: Selected Poems* and *Belligerence*. His novels include *Blood Countess*. His film, *Road Scholar*, won the Peabody award for 1996. Rodger Kamenetz's books of poetry include *The Missing Jew: New and Selected Poems* and *Nympholepsy*. His nonfiction includes *The Jew in the Lotus*, *Stalking Elijah*, and *Terra Infirma*, winner of the 1997 National Jewish Book Award. Dave Smith, author of seventeen volumes of poetry, including *Cuba Night* and *The Roundhouse Voices*, and one novel, and editor of major anthologies and poetry series at several university presses, winner of the Guggenheim, NEA, and Lyndhurst foundation fellowships, teaches workshops and mentors our students in addition to his editing work at the *Southern Review*.

Our playwright is Femi Euba, who has done radio plays produced by BBC Radio in Great Britain, including *The Wig* and *Honeybee, Tortoise, and The Devil*. His anthologized one-act plays include *Crocodiles*, which was produced by the Negro Ensemble in New York. Our screenwriter is Ricky Blackwood, whose TV script *Dead Before Dawn* was broadcast by ABC. Scripts in development with major production companies include *Deadlock* and *Pyramider*.

The application process to LSU is split; part of the application (the writing submission) is mailed directly to us, and the other part (transcripts, letters, GRE scores) is mailed to the Graduate School, which evaluates, then passes these materials on to us. The writing submissions should be 8-10 poems, 20-30 pages of fiction, or a play or screenplay. We have a yearly award ceremony with awards available in all five genres.

Graduates of LSU's Creative Writing Program have been published by Atlantic Monthly Press, *Black River Journal, South Carolina Review, Northern Review, Cimarron Review, High Plains Literary Review, Writer's Forum, Cutting Edge Quarterly, Sub Rosa, Gin Mill, Great River Review, South Central Review, The New Yorker, Lear's Magazine, Harper's, Puerto del Sol,* Houghton Mifflin, William Morrow, and Ballantine Books.

Baton Rouge -- state capital, home to crawfish boils, zydeco, swamp tours, and Huey Long -- is situated in a unique and culturally rich part of the country on the east bank of the Big Muddy. Only 70 miles from the buzz of New Orleans, Baton Rouge also enjoys its own diverse and active literary community. About half our MFA students at LSU are from the South and a few are international students. Each spring, LSU sponsors the Gathering of Poets, a two-day event begun in 1973. Visiting poets have included Ai, Gerald Stern, Derek Walcott, James Tate, Amiri Baraka, Michael Harper, Carolyn Kizer, Robert Duncan, Hayden Carruth, Etheridge Knight, Tess Gallagher, Molly Peacock, Lorna Crovier, Garrett Hongo, Peter Davison, and Ellen Bryant Voigt. Readers and Writers, sponsors readings and talks throughout the year, and the English Graduate Students Association organizes readings and an annual critical/creative conference. A local park museum and some coffee houses also have occasional readings by students and other local writers. For the last two years, many students have held full scholarships to the gala Words and Music Writers Conference held in New Orleans in September.

❖University of Louisville
Louisville, KY 40292

(502) 852-6801

Degrees offered: BA, MA

Degree: BA in English

Required course of study: 30 s/hrs in English
Thesis: no requirement
Writing workshop: 6-15 s/hrs
Other English courses: 24 s/hrs

Other Requirements: General education courses; humanities and social sciences electives; free electives; foreign language proficiency.

Six s/hrs of writing workshop may be counted toward the 30 s/hrs in English, with an additional 9 s/hrs of creative writing available as free electives. At the introductory level, all students write poetry and fiction and/or drama. Intermediate-level courses focus on a single genre. The advanced level has both multi-genre and single-genre courses. Students work with a variety of teachers. Creative writing tuition remission scholarships and cash prizes are available through annual contests. Student literary magazine, *The Thinker,* and national magazine, *The Louisville Review,* offer editorial experience and/or publication opportunities. The program sponsors various series of readings by students and visiting writers.

Degree: MA with Concentration in Creative Writing (poetry, fiction, drama)

Type of Program: Studio/Academic

Required course of study: 30 s/hrs
Thesis: 3-6 s/hrs
Writing workshop: 3-12 s/hrs
Literature and other courses: up to 15 s/hrs, some designated areas

Other requirements: Introduction to Scholarship and Research; proficiency in one foreign language; discussion of thesis with committee.

In addition to offering coursework in creative writing as part of all degree programs in English (including the MA in literature, and the PhD in Rhetoric and Composition), the University of Louisville grants the MA in English with Concentration in Creative Writing. Theses in this program are original manuscripts of fiction, poetry, or drama. Students are expected to do well in literature courses as well as in writing workshops.

The creative writing faculty includes fiction writer Sena Jeter Naslund (*Ice-Skating at the North Pole*; winner of the University's Distinguished Teaching Award); poet Jeffrey Skinner (*Late Stars;* National Poetry Series selection, *A Guide to Forgetting; The Company of Heaven*); and Paul Griner (*Follow Me,* stories, and *Collectors,* a novel).

In connection with the Twentieth Century Literature Conference and other programs, over 20 guest writers give readings each year. In recent years guests have included John Ashbery, Amy Clampitt, Robert Coover, Susan Dodd, Louise Erdrich, Carolyn Forché, Marilyn Hacker, Richard Howard, Bobbie Ann Mason, W.S. Merwin, Howard Nemerov, Marsha Norman, Greg Pape, and May Sarton.

The Anne and William Axton Reading Series in the Department of English brings well-known and up-and-coming writers of poetry and fiction to the University to give public readings and interact with students in a variety of forms.

Special advantages of the Program include an emphasis on excellence in teaching and individual attention to students; a flourishing community of writers; opportunities for editorial experience and/or publication with a nationally known literary magazine, *The Louisville Review.*

Among financial aid opportunities are creative writing scholarships, service assistantships, editorial assistantships, teaching assistantships (which generally involve teaching introductory creative writing as well as composition), and university fellowships.

For more information, contact Director of Creative Writing, Dept. of English.

❖Loyola College
Baltimore, MD 21210-2697
(410) 617-2528
FAX (410) 617-2198

Degree offered: BA in Writing

The writing and media department at Loyola College offers expository, argumentative, analytical, creative writing, and journalism courses. A writing major at Loyola will follow a program of traditional undergraduate study in a strong curriculum. The major itself is a split major, a student's upper division course load is divided with study in another discipline.

The Writing/Media department prides itself on an innovative variety of not only creative writing courses but also upper division prose courses, including Autobiography/Biography, New Writers: Newer Books, The Traveling Writer, Nature Writing, Art of the Argument, History of the Essay, Audience and the Writer's Voice, and others. Students interested in creative writing may choose from several levels of fiction and poetry workshops and more specialized courses, such as Writing for the Stage, Reviewing, and Enchanted Worlds: Writing Children's Literature.

Loyola's student literary magazines, *Garland* (poetry and fiction) and *Forum* (creative nonfiction), publish student writing from the student body as a whole and invite all interested students to work as staff members.

The Writing Department also has an annual reading series, Modern Masters. A regular stream of visiting writers spend a few days on campus reading and discussing their work, visiting classes, and talking with students. These have included Elizabeth Hardwick, Tobias Wolff, Robert Coles, David St. John, Nadine Gordimer, Tatyana Tolstoya, Alice Fulton, and many others.

For more information, contact Dr. Neil Alderstein, Writing/Media Dept. Chair.

Loyola Marymount University
Loyola Blvd. at West 80th Street
Los Angeles, CA 90045

Contact the Creative Writing Program Director, Dept. of English.

❖Lycoming College
Williamsport, PA 17701-5192
(717) 321-4336
FAX (717) 321-4389
e-mail: hawkes@lycoming.edu

Degree offered: BA in English with Creative Writing Major

Required course of study: 30 hours for major: 12 in introductory course, workshops, and form and theory (fiction or poetry); 6 in survey courses; 9 in studies courses including contemporary fiction or poetry; 3 in Shakespeare or Chaucer.

The Institution: Lycoming College is a small (1,500 students), four-year, residential liberal arts college near the Susquehanna River in north-central Pennsylvania. It offers small, intensive workshops in poetry and fiction for beginning, intermediate, and advanced students. A reading series provides opportunities for students to hear and meet visiting writers. *The Tributary*, a college literary magazine, provides a vehicle for publication and editorial experience.

Faculty: Dr. G.W. Hawkes, fiction. Books: *Spies in the Blue Smoke* (stories), *Playing Out of the Deep Woods* (stories), and *Surveyor* (novel). Dr. Sascha Feinstein, poetry. Books: *The Jazz Poetry Anthology, The Second Set* (both edited with Yusef Komunyakaa), and *Jazz Poetry from the 1920s to the Present.*

❖Macalester College
1600 Grand Avenue
St. Paul, MN 55105
(612) 696-6387
FAX (612) 696-6430
e-mail: greenberg@macalester.edu or glancy@macalester.edu

Degree offered: BA in English with Concentration in Creative Writing

Required course of study: 10 course credits (40 s/hrs)
  5 Literature courses
  5 Creative Writing courses, which must include:
  Introduction to Creative Writing (prerequisite for all further creative writing courses)
  1 Workshop capstone course taken as a senior
  3 Elective creative writing courses (which may include an Internship or Independent work)

Other Requirements: College-wide distribution requirements in humanities and fine arts, social sciences, physical sciences; oral examination for creative writing students in the Honors Program.

The Creative Writing concentration within the English major is an undergraduate program leading to the BA and offering experience with both poetry and fiction. The initial focus of the Macalester program is on craft, and all participants must take the introductory creative writing course, with its strong emphasis on technique and form, as a prerequisite to further work in the program. On the advanced level, in writing workshops and in independent writing projects, students are able to explore their own directions more fully.

In addition to regular coursework, workshops, and independent projects, Macalester writing students have opportunities to participate in internships with local arts organizations and small press publishers; editorial positions on the campus literary magazine, and an Honors program, should a student choose to develop an extensive manuscript as a culmination to his or her undergraduate career.

In addition to its own resources, Macalester's location in the Twin Cities, the most active arts area in the Midwest, offers a wide array of related opportunities for writing students. The Twin Cities are a center for theater, music, and dance throughout the year, and readings by nationally known and local writers are available on a regular basis, sponsored by area colleges and arts organizations. Macalester is also a member of the Associated Colleges of the Twin Cities, a consortium that supports residencies and readings and enables students to work with writing teachers on other campuses. As further evidence of commitment to its writing program, Macalester offers several annual cash prizes for writers, one of which, the Wendy Parrish Poetry Award, has been established in memory of a talented graduate.

The Macalester Creative Writing Program faculty

includes: Alvin Greenberg, director of the program and author of several collections of short stories (*How the Dead Live, Delta q*), as well as poetry (*Heavy Wings, Why We Live With Animals*) and novels (*Going Nowhere*); and poet and playwright Diane Glancy (*Pushing the Bear, Flutie, The West Pole*). Visiting writers in recent years have included June Jordan, Diane Wakoski, Michael Harper, Jonis Agee, Patricia Hampl, Janet Beeler Shaw, Tim O'Brien, Charles Baxter, Thomas McCarthy, Jim Heynen, and Janet Holmes.

For application forms and information on financial aid (which is offered in the form of direct grants, loans, and a work-study program), contact the Director of Admissions.

For further information, contact Alvin Greenberg, Director of Creative Writing.

❖Macon State College
100 College Station Drive
Macon, GA 32106-5144

For more information, contact the Director, Dept. of Humanities.

Maharishi University of Management
Fairfield, IA 52557-1058

(515) 472-7000 ext. 5040
FAX (515) 472-1161
e-mail: jkarpen@mum.edu
website: http://www.mum.edu

Degree offered: MA in Professional Writing

Type of Program: Studio

Length of Residency: One and a half years

Required course of study: 60 units

We offer a wide-ranging and ambitious curriculum for individuals who are looking for a career as a writer, either in traditional media or on the Internet.

The curriculum offers the aspiring professional extensive hands-on experience in genres that include journalism, magazine writing, book writing, advertising, technical writing, scriptwriting, and Web site development. In addition, students may also enjoy courses in the creative areas of fiction, poetry, and literary journalism.

Practicum and internship components provide students with a range of practical experience and materials for a substantial portfolio, which is assembled as a Final Project.

All students are required to buy a Macintosh PowerBook computer (for which financial aid is available), and students become proficient in desktop publishing and on the Internet.

In addition, all students practice the Transcendental Meditation technique, which has been shown scientifically to improve a student's creativity and intelligence. Thus, students in the Professional Writing program increase their mental potential even as they gain practical writing skills.

Faculty in the program include Dr. Jim Karpen, a professional writer, editor, and Internet consultant with experience in journalism, magazine writing, and advertising; John Kremer, a nationally recognized expert in the area of book publishing and author of 12 books; William Hathaway, author of an award-winning novel, scriptwriter, journalist, poet, and advertising professional; Paul Stokstad, a specialist in advertising, marketing, and Web site development; Diane Frank, author of four books of poetry and a professional scriptwriter; Linda Egenes, a literary journalist with additional experience in advertising; and other visiting faculty who work as professionals in the areas that they teach.

For more information, contact Dr. Jim Karpen, Director, Professional Writing Program.

❖The University of Maine at Farmington
Farmington, ME 04938-1720

(207) 778-7425

Degree offered: BFA in Creative Writing

Required course of study:
    Writing courses: 21 s/hrs
    Literature courses: 15 s/hrs

Other Requirements: 1-3 s/hrs in writing apprenticeship; 3 s/hrs in a performance or studio course other than creative writing; intermediate proficiency in a foreign language.

Application Deadlines: December 15 early admission; May 1 all other.

The BFA at the University of Maine at Farmington offers its students small classes and a good deal of individual attention. Program graduates have gone on to graduate study at institutions such as Columbia University, the University of Michigan, the University of Massachusetts/Amherst, the University of Virginia, and Cornell.

The BFA emphasizes poetry, fiction, and creative nonfiction, with electives possible in journalism, screenwriting, and writing for children. As part of their 15 s/hr requirement in literature, students must take one course in contemporary literature. Their work in the BFA must include 18 s/hrs in writing courses and 3 s/hrs in the advanced writing seminar.

The BFA offers students a variety of benefits important to their formation as writers: a literary background; professional guidance in writing and thinking about writing; an active community of writers at a similar stage of development; and time to complete a body of original writing — stories, poems, or essays. Majors who wish to publish their work or gain editorial skills are encouraged to become involved with UMF's literary magazine, *The Sandy River Review*, or with *The Mainestream*, the campus newspaper. Through the required writing apprenticeship, students obtain experience as writers in the world outside the classroom. Majors commonly apprentice at Alice James Books, affiliated with UMF since 1994, doing work ranging from the screening of manuscripts to book production.

The faculty of the writing program includes poet Wesley McNair (*The Faces of Americans In 1853, The Town of No, Talking in the Dark*); fiction writer Patricia O'Donnell (stories in *The New Yorker, Agni,* and *North American Review*); nonfiction writer John D'Agata (work in *Iowa Review, Gettysburg Review, Creative Nonfiction*); and other regular and adjunct faculty in the Department of Humanities. Adjunct professors who have been involved in the program include fiction writers Mary Peterson (*Mercy Flights*) and Elizabeth Cooke (*Complicity, Zeena*); poets Peg Peoples and Betsy Sholl (*The Red Line, Don't Explain*); and nonfiction writers Robert Kimber (*Upcountry, A Canoeist's Sketchbook*) and Don Snyder (*The Cliff Walk, A Soldier's Disgrace*).

Writers who have visited the campus during the past years include Marge Piercy, Billy Collins, Lucille Clifton, Tobias Wolfe, Grace Paley, Russell Banks, Sharon Olds, Tim O'Brien, Charles Simic, Galway Kinnell, Donald Hall, Maxine Kumin, Carolyn Chute, E. Annie Proulx, and Hayden Carruth.

For further information, contact Wesley McNair, Chair of the Dept. of Humanities.

University of Maine, Orono
304 Neville Hall
Orono, ME 04469
(207) 581-3822
FAX (207) 581-3886
e-mail: english@maine.edu
website: www.ume.edu/english

Degrees offered: BA, MA

Degree: BA in English with Writing Emphasis; Concentrations in Creative, Technical, or Expository Writing

Required course of study: 36 s/hrs
  Writing courses: 9 s/hrs
  Writing tutorial: 3–6 s/hrs
  Literature courses: 24 s/hrs

Degree: MA in English with Creative Writing Concentration (poetry, fiction)

Type of Program: Traditional Literary Study and Creative Writing

Required course of study: 30 s/hrs, including thesis
  Thesis: 6 s/hrs
  Writing workshop: 6–9 s/hrs
  Literature courses: 15 s/hrs
  Teaching College Composition: 3 s/hrs (for
    graduate assistants only)

The University of Maine offers 3 writing concentrations at the undergraduate level -- creative writing, technical writing, and expository writing. For each concentration, 12 s/hrs of writing are required, ranging from introductory courses (e.g. Introduction to Creative Writing) to Directed Writing courses for the advanced student. Directed Writing courses, in particular, provide students with the unique opportunity to work closely with practicing writers in their chosen concentration.

The MA in English with a concentration in Creative Writing allows the graduate student to focus on the writing of fiction and/or poetry and to prepare a creative thesis while still receiving graduate-level training in literature and literary criticism. Graduate creative writing courses combine workshop situations with one-to-one instruction and enable students to work closely with practicing professionals.

The faculty in the creative writing program includes poet Constance Hunting (*The Myth of Horizon*) and fiction writers Welch D. Everman (*Orion, The Harry and Sylvia Stories*) and Elaine Ford (*Ivory Bright, Monkey Bay, Life Designs*), as well as visiting writers who are invited to campus each year. Recent visitors to the writing program include Allen Ginsberg, John A. Williams, Galway Kinnell, Carolyn Forché, Gregory Corso, Cathie Pelletier, Samuel R. Delany, Tim O'Brien, Elizabeth Hardwick, E. Annie Proulx, and Jorie Graham.

Along with their coursework, undergraduate and graduate students have the opportunity to do public readings on campus and to contribute to and do editorial work for a number of campus publications, including *The Maine Review* and *Stolen Island Review*.

For more information, contact the Chair, Dept. of English.

Manhattanville College
Purchase, NY 10577

Degree offered: MA in Writing

Type of Program: Studio/Academic

Required course of study:
  Summer Writers' Week: 6 credits
  Core Writing Courses: 12 credits
  Liberal Studies Electives: 12 credits
  Final Project: 2 credits

Manhattanville's MA in Writing was developed for writers, would-be writers, teachers and communications specialists. The program is designed to meet the needs of persons who have completed their undergraduate degree and who wish to develop their skills in writing while deepening their knowledge in the humanities.

Students must complete 32 credits with a G.P.A. of 3.0 or better (scale of 4.0). The program can be completed in two years.

Students will earn 12 credits in the core writing courses and 6 credits by participating in Manhattanville's Summer Writers' Week Workshops. The writing courses are interrelated and begin where every writer must begin: with a knowledge of oneself as a human being with a unique view of the surrounding world. Though the interlocking of core courses follows the natural development of skills in written communication, the courses may be taken in any sequence. Students may enter the program in fall, spring or summer semesters.

Contact Ruth Dowd, Director, The Master of Arts in Writing Program.

❖**Marquette University**
335 Coughlin Hall
Milwaukee, WI 53233
(414) 288-7179
FAX (414) 288-5433

Degree offered: BA in Writing-Intensive English

Required course of study: 128 s/hrs total
Language and Literature courses: 24 s/hrs
Writing courses: 12 s/hrs

Other Requirements: University core curriculum.

Application Deadlines: Rolling admission; apply as early as possible for financial aid.

The Writing-Intensive English major is designed for students who wish to concentrate their efforts in composition, rhetorical theory, professional writing, and creative writing. It blends the study of literature with opportunities to become proficient in various modes of creative writing as well as professional and technical writing. Workshops are offered in creative nonfiction, playwriting, poetry, and prose fiction. Students may elect to take writing and magazine editing courses in the journalism department and have the opportunity to be trained as peer writing consultants in the campus writing center. Internships with local arts groups, schools, businesses, and nonprofit organizations are also available for credit.

Each spring the Mae E. Gales prizes are awarded in poetry or short fiction along with department prizes for essay writing. The *Marquette Journal*, the campus literary magazine, provides editorial and publishing experience for undergraduates and awards prizes in fiction and poetry. Marquette Writers Ink is the student organization responsible for student and visiting writers' readings. Recent visiting writers include Charles Baxter, Martha Bergland, Stuart Dybek, Reginald Gibbons, Czeslaw Milosz, Sheila Roberts, Richard Ryan, Ntozake Shange, Ellen Bryant Voigt, and Chuck Wachtel.

For more information, contact C.J. Hribal, Director of Creative Writing.

Mary Washington College
Fredericksburg, VA 22401-5358
(540) 654-1035
FAX (540) 654-1569
website: http://www.mwc.edu/gcampbel/els.html

Degree offered: BA with Major in English

Required course of study: 39 s/hrs (13 courses) in major, up to 15 of which can be in writing courses. 6 s/hrs must be in linguistics, and 18 in literature.

Other Requirements: 120 semester hours total, including major, electives, and General Education requirements.

English majors can include courses in journalism and creative writing, selecting up to 15 credits from a list of regularly-offered courses: Creative Writing I, Creative Writing II, Seminar in Writing, News Gathering, News Writing, Magazine Writing, Topics in Writing, Internship, and Individual Study. Playwriting is available through the Department of Dramatic Arts.

Most students supplement their writing courses by working for college publications: *The Bullet*, the student newspaper; *Aubade*, the literary magazine; and *Polemic*, a magazine of opinion and commentary. Many students take advantage of the very active internship program. They have earned college credit and gained practical experience in areas as diverse as the public information office of the National Gallery of Art, the city desk of the local newspaper, and the public relations department of the Washington Redskins.

The College Student Association sponsors a year-long program of visiting poets and fiction writers. Other writers have been brought to campus through NEH grants or the College's Distinguished Visitor in Residence Program. Recent visitors include Jerome Stern, Jesse Lee Kercheval, and Carolyn Forché.

Faculty in the writing program include short story writer Henry Lewis, short story writer and journalist Steve Watkins, and 3 members of the literature faculty who have published fiction or poetry: Daniel Dervin, Donald Glover, and Raman Singh.

For further information on the English major, write or call John Morello, Chair, Dept. of English, Linguistics, and Speech.

University of Maryland,
Baltimore County
Catonsville, MD 21228-5398
(410) 455-2384
Voice/TTY (410) 455-3233

Degree offered: BA in English with a Writing Minor or an Extended Writing Minor in Creative Writing, Journalism, Professional Writing, or Rhetoric and Communication. (Note: the Writing Minor is available to all majors.)

Required course of study: 120 s/hrs total
English Major Program: 39 s/hrs
Writing Minor: 18 s/hrs
The Extended Writing Minor: 24 s/hrs

The Writing Minor offers a variety of writing opportunities for students -- from *Apostrophe*, a student produced magazine, to *Soup*, the student/faculty literary magazine, to more career-oriented writing available through Writing Internships which also include writing for the campus newspaper, *The Retriever*. Students with an interest in creative writing may try for the Malcolm Braly Prize, named for the novelist and former instructor, now deceased. This award is given annually. The English Department frequently awards two $500 scholarships to students who show exceptional promise in creative writing. The Fine Arts Scholarships range from $100 to $1,500 and are available to admitted students who display a high level of performance in the fine arts. A portfolio is required for Writing.

For more information, contact Writing Program Director, Dept. of English.

❖University of Maryland College Park, MD 20742
(301) 405-3820

Degrees offered: BA, MFA

Degree: MFA in Creative Writing

Type of Program: Studio/Academic

Length of Residency: Two years

Required course of study: 36 s/hrs
Thesis: 6 s/hrs
Writing workshop: 12 s/hrs
Literature courses: 12 s/hrs
Electives: 6 s/hrs

Application Deadlines: January 15 of each year for the following Fall term.

The University of Maryland, College Park offers an MFA in Creative Writing as well as a BA with a Creative Writing emphasis for undergraduate English majors. Graduate students participate in a series of writing workshops, seminars in form and theory, and elect a sequence of surveys and seminars from the regular English Department offerings. Undergraduates take a sequence of beginning, intermediate, and advanced poetry or fiction writing workshops, as well as seminars in special topics related to the craft of writing.

The University of Maryland has an active reading series which in recent years has brought Russell Banks, Susan Mitchell, Claire Messud, Mark Strand, Shay Youngblood, Amitav Ghosh, Billy Collins, Madison Smartt Bell, Melanie Rae Thon, Frank Bidart, Cornelius Eady, Grace Paley, Francine Prose, and Adam Zagajewski to campus. Often visiting writers attend undergraduate and graduate workshops and are available to students for consultation. Recent visiting writers include Edward Hirsch, Tom Sleigh, Patricia Hampl, Jean Binta Breeze, Alan Shapiro, and Linda Bierds.

Special opportunities for creative writing students include the possibility of taking courses at other area colleges and universities. The University sponsors annual contests for poetry and fiction contests in conjunction with the Academy of American Poets and the Estate of Katherine Anne Porter.

The University of Maryland, College Park is strategically located 20 minutes from Washington, D.C. and 45 minutes from Baltimore, and as a result affords students a wide range of unique and exciting urban, literary, political, and cultural experiences. The University itself is the largest in the area; with its libraries, film and lecture series, and course offerings, it provides the necessary resources for a full creative and intellectual environment. The Folger Shakespeare Library, Library of Congress, Kennedy Center for the Arts, and the Smithsonian Institution, which includes the Hirschorn, Sackler, and Freer galleries, are only a few of the possibilities available to area residents.

The graduate program is limited in size in order to provide students with individual attention from instructors. Full fellowships, teaching assistantships, and scholarships are available. Students in creative writing, besides having the chance to teach composition, will be eligible to teach introductory creative writing courses.

The Creative Writing faculty includes: poet Michael Collier (*The Neighbor, The Wesleyan Tradition: Four Decades of American Poetry,* and *The Folded Heart*); fiction writer and poet Merle Collins (*Angel, Rain,* and *Darling*); fiction writer Joyce Kornblatt (*Nothing to Do with Love, Breaking Bread,* and *White Water*); poet Phillis Levin (*The Afterimage, Temples and Fields*); fiction writer Reginald McKnight (*The Kind of Light That Shines on Texas, I Get Off the Bus,* and *Moustapha's Eclipse*); fiction writer Howard Norman (*The Bird Artist, Kiss in the Hotel, The Museum Guard*); poet Stanley Plumly (*Boy on the Step, Summer Celestial,* and *Marriage in the Trees*).

For more information write Michael Collier or Stanley Plumly, Co-Directors, Creative Writing Program, Dept. of English.

❖Massachusetts Institute of Technology 77 Massachusetts Ave., 14E-303 Cambridge, MA 02139
(617) 253-7894
FAX (617) 253-6910

Degree offered: BS in Humanities, with Major in Writing or Joint Major

Required course of study: Major: 5 writing subjects, 4 related subjects, 4 additional subjects in arts, social sciences. Thesis is a manuscript of original work. Joint Major: 4 writing subjects, 3 subjects in related field, 6 subjects from single science or engineering field.

Application Deadlines: Early action: November 1; regular action: January 1; Financial aid: same dates.

The M.I.T. Program in Writing and Humanistic Studies offers instruction in 3 areas: (1) Exposition and Rhetoric, (2) Creative Writing, and (3) Science and Technical Writing. Introductory, intermediate, and advanced subjects are offered in each area. Subjects cover basic expository writing techniques, as well as forms of technical writing, fiction, poetry writing, and science journalism. Efforts are made to limit classes to about 15 students in order to allow instructors to give close attention to each student's work. In all subjects, students read as well as write, but most discussions focus on writing techniques and the student's own written work.

Students studying Exposition and Rhetoric study the essay as an evolving social and literary form. Students are encouraged to write across disciplinary lines and to explore the social implications of writing -- for example, the relation between ethics and style. The Program offers courses on the origins and uses of words, on biographical writing, and on the scientific essay.

Creative writing subjects aim to help each student to find her or his own voice and to develop versatility and control in the use of the literary imagination. Students study fundamentals of sentence and paragraph structure in the beginning courses. Intermediate and advanced subjects in creative writing concentrate on specific forms and stress workshop criticism and frequent revision.

In science and technical writing subjects, students study how to organize information, shape technical and semi-technical documents, and present complex data lucidly. Students may investigate strategies for preparing proposals, technical descriptions, and oral reports for industry and government. In addition, students practice writing about science for broad, public audiences of such publications as *Technology Review.*

For more information, contact Professor James Paradis, Head, M.I.T. Program in Writing and Humanistic Studies, 14E-303.

❖University of Massachusetts
Amherst, MA 01003-0515

(413) 545-0643
FAX (413) 545-3880
website: www.umass.edu/english/mfanews

Degree offered: MFA in English (poetry, fiction, nonfiction, drama)

Type of Program: Studio/Academic

Length of Residency: Three years

Required course of study: 60 s/hrs
  Thesis: 6 s/hrs
  Writing workshop: 24 s/hrs
  Literature courses: 24 s/hrs
  Related coursework: 6 s/hrs

Other Requirements: Foreign language proficiency; oral defense of thesis.

Application Deadline: January 15.

The MFA at the University of Massachusetts at Amherst is offered to qualified students who intend to become professional writers. The 60 s/hr degree program provides a variety of writing workshops and a solid background in modern and contemporary literature. Candidates may specialize in fiction, poetry, nonfiction, or drama. The workshops, limited to an enrollment of 10-12, provide discussion of works-in-progress and issues related to writers. MFA candidates also meet regularly with staff members in private conferences. Usually, in the third or fourth semester, a candidate will select a thesis director with whom to meet until the thesis is completed.

Twenty-four of the 60 required s/hrs for the MFA in English are taken in writing workshops; 12 in modern and contemporary literature; 6 in thesis credits; 12 in elective English; and 6 s/hrs in another related field such as comparative literature, music, or speech-drama, or in internships in literary projects, publishing, arts administration, or editorial work. The foreign language requirement can be satisfied by a grade of B or better in a Translation Workshop, translation of poetry or prose fiction with the approval of a faculty advisor, completion of any foreign language literature (graduate-level) course with a passing grade, or a passing grade on the standard Graduate Foreign Language examination, an undergraduate degree in a foreign language, or undergraduate classes with

passing grades through the intermediate level of a foreign language.

Amherst is an attractive New England town in western Massachusetts near the Berkshire hills, with easy access to New York City and Boston. The University and the four colleges in the area (Amherst, Smith, Mount Holyoke, and Hampshire) cooperate in many academic, cultural, and social activities, and are accessible through a free bus system. There are numerous excellent bookstores in the town of Amherst and the nearby towns of South Hadley and Northampton. Amherst has been the home of many writers, such as Robert Francis, Robert Frost, and Emily Dickinson; that tradition has been continued by such writers-in-residence at UMass as Chinua Achebe, Josef Brodsky, William Corbett, Russell Edson, Margaret Gibson, Michael Harper, Richard Kim, Maxine Kumin, and Harvey Swados.

The Harvey Swados Prize in Fiction ($200) is awarded annually for the best piece of short fiction written by an MFA candidate. The Joseph Langland Prize in Poetry ($100), sponsored by the Academy of American Poets and the University of Massachusetts, Amherst, is awarded annually for the best poetry submission. Each year several MFA students are selected as teaching assistants assigned to teach introductory creative writing classes. Throughout the year, the University of Massachusetts Visiting Writing Series sponsors readings by poets and fiction writers, recently featuring Simon Armitage, John Ashbery, Hayden Carruth, Gillian Conoley, Gordon Lish, Gary Lutz, Jane Miller, Carl Phillips, James Salter, Christine Schutt, Mark Strand, Charles Wright, and Dean Young. Live Literature, a reading series coordinated by MFA students, provides a place for students in the program to read from new work. Other reading series at area colleges, writing centers, and bookstores provide a lively, visible arts community with a continuous program of literary events. The MFA Program publishes a yearly newsletter listing readings, publications, and achievements of faculty, students, and graduates.

Financial aid is available. A limited number of MFA Fellowships of $5,000 are available for first-year students; all applicants are automatically considered for these fellowships. The Delaney Fellowship in Fiction Writing encourages women who, after the age of thirty-five, seek to develop their talent in the writing of fiction. Inquiries into the Delaney Fellowship should be made to the office of the Director. The Deborah Slosberg Scholarship Fund awards yearly prizes of $200 to deserving students. A limited number of Graduate School Fellowships of $6,000-$10,000 are awarded competitively through the Graduate School. Minority Recruitment Fellowships in amounts up to $10,000 are available to first-year, incoming applicants who have identified themselves as minority candidates. For most of the graduate students, the primary sources of support are Teaching Assistantships, which are awarded by the Director of the Writing Program, and a variety of additional departments on campus. Availability is limited, however. To apply for a Teaching Assistantship (which carries a stipend of $10,600 and a full tuition waiver), write to Professor Peter Elbow, Director of the Writing Program, 305 Bartlett Hall, University of Massachusetts, Amherst, MA 01003 or call (413) 545-0610 for an application.

Students who file a Financial Aid form (FAFSA) with the College Scholarship Service, are encouraged to apply for work-study aid making them eligible for a broader selection of teaching jobs (including tutoring, teaching ESL, etc.) as soon as they are admitted for the Fall semester. HELP Loans are also available. For up-to-date information and to ascertain your eligibility contact the Financial Aid Office in Whitmore Administration Building, University of Massachusetts, Amherst, MA 01003. Phone: (413) 545-0801.

The Massachusetts Graduate Grant Program is open to Massachusetts residents who are full-time graduate students. To apply for the Grant, based on financial need, submit a Financial Aid Form to the College Scholarship Service, CN6300, Princeton, NJ 08541 by March 1 for the fall semester.

Applicants should complete all graduate school admission requirements before submitting a manuscript of a body of original poetry, fiction, or drama to the MFA program. All admissions are based primarily on the submitted manuscript.

The faculty includes: Agha Shahid Ali, poetry. His volumes of verse include *A Nostalgist's Map of America*, *The Beloved Witness: Selected Poems*, and *The Country Without a Post Office*. Noy Holland, fiction. Her short story collection is *The Spectacle of the Body*. Sam Michel, fiction. Michel is the author of the story collection *Under the Light*, and recently completed work on the novel *Lincoln Dahl Turns Five*. Jay Neugeboren, fiction, nonfiction, screenwriting. Neugeboren is the author of six novels. His screenplay, *The Hollow Boy*, which premiered on American Playhouse, won a Blue Ribbon at the American Film and Video Festival. His most recent publications include a memoir, *Imagining Robert*, and a collection of stories titled *Don't Worry About the Kids*. James Tate, poetry. He was the winner of the Pulitzer Prize for Poetry for his *Selected Poems*. He is the author of over a dozen books, including *The Oblivion Ha-Ha*, *Hints to Pilgrims*, and *Constant Defender*. John Wideman, fiction, nonfiction. Two of Wideman's books, *Sent for You Yesterday* and *Philadelphia Fire*, were awarded the PEN/Faulkner Award. In 1993 he was awarded a MacArthur Fellowship from the John D. and Catherine T. MacArthur Foundation. His most recent book is *Two Cities*. Dara Wier, poetry. Wier has published six collections of poems, including *Blood, Hook & Eye*, *The Book of Knowledge*, and *Our Master Plan*. Her work has been awarded fellowships from the Guggenheim Foundation and National Endowment for the Arts; in 1993 she held the Richard Hugo Chair at the University of Montana.

For more information, write to the Director, MFA Program in English, 452 Bartlett Hall.

University of Massachusetts, Boston
Boston, MA 02125-3393
(617) 287-6719

Degree offered: Certificate in Creative Writing (for undergraduates, graduates, and non-degree students)

Required course of study: 21 s/hrs
  Writing courses: 12 s/hrs
  Literature courses: 9 s/hrs

Other Requirements: Final review and approval of portfolio of creative writing.

Application Deadlines: June 1 for fall semester

(return by April 1 is recommended); November 1 for spring semester.

The U.Mass.-Boston Creative Writing Program is open to undergraduate students, regardless of major; to graduate students, most of whom are also enrolled in the English MA program; and to non-degree students, regardless of their previous academic experience. Creative Writing students are taught by practicing poets, fiction writers, and playwrights from the English and Theatre Arts departments.

Students in our program are culturally diverse; the average age of U.Mass.-Boston students is 27, and many creative writing students are considerably older. Advanced classes are generally limited to 15 students.

Visiting writers have included Denise Levertov, Gish Jen, Carole Oles, Jonathan Strong, and Paule Marshall.

U.Mass.-Boston has a literary magazine, *The Watermark*.

The Mary Doyle Curran Scholarship is offered annually to undergraduate students already in the Program. Graduate students in the English MA may apply for assistantships, which often involve assisting the teaching of undergraduate creative writing courses.

The creative writing faculty includes: poet Martha Collins (*A History of Small Life on a Windy Planet*, *The Arrangement of Space*, *The Catastrophe of Rainbows*); Poet Lloyd Schwartz (*These People; Goodnight, Gracie*); fiction writer K.C. Frederick (winner of NEA fellowship, anthologized in *Flash Fiction* and *Graywolf VII*); fiction writer Lee Grove (*Last Dance, Drowning*); fiction writer Patricia Powell (*Me Dying, Trail, A Small Gathering of Bones*); playwright Ron Nash.

For more information, contact Director of the Creative Writing Program, Dept. of English.

❖University of Massachusetts, Dartmouth
North Dartmouth, MA 02747
(508) 999-8274
FAX (508) 999-9235

Degrees offered: BA, MA

Degree: BA in English with Writing/Communications Option

Required course of study: 120 credits; 42 must be in English, of which 21 must be writing.

Application Deadlines: Rolling admissions all year; financial aid as soon after Feb. 1 as possible.

Honors program available. Numerous university publications and campus newspaper, area newspapers, radio and TV opportunities. 30 undergraduate writing courses in a variety of fields: journalism, technical, business, critical, creative, scriptwriting. Faculty widely published.

Degree: MA in Professional Writing

Type of Program: Studio/Academic

Required course of study: 30 credits total with 9-credit core curriculum. Thirty graduate-level courses offered, (concentrations in journalism, technical writing, editing/document design, scriptwriting, creative fiction, business writing, public relations, teaching writing).

Application Deadlines: Rolling admissions, for September and January admission.

Strong emphasis on diversity, versatility, and finding ways to make a living as a writer. Priority on publishing, building a portfolio. TA positions in teaching and publications. Strong computer/desktop publishing emphasis. Required thesis may be writing project in concentration.

The Department of English offers a specialized graduate program in professional writing designed to fit each student's individual needs. Students may choose a concentration in business and technical writing, journalism, creative writing, or teaching writing. Students take 9 credits from a core of 5 courses: Rhetorical Theory or Communication Theory; Language and Its Use or Stylistics; and Principles of Investigation, Research, and Validation. The program also offers a broad range of elective courses, including Editing, Layout, and Document Design; Report and Proposal Writing; Scientific and Technical Journalism; Advanced Principles in Journalism; Language and the Teaching of Writing; Public Relations Techniques; Writing Computer-User Documents; Visual Display, Formatting, and Desktop Publishing; Teaching Technical and Professional Writing; Law and Ethics in Professional Writing; and Workshops in Screenwriting, Fiction, Poetry, Literary Nonfiction, and Interactive Communications.

The teaching staff includes John M. Lannon, writing consultant and author of *Technical Writing* and *The Writing Process*; Raymond A. Dumont, author of *Business Communications Workbook* and co-author (with John Lannon) of *Business Communications*; Peter Owens, professional writer, journalist, editor, and award-winning software writer (*Superscoop, Superscoop II*, and *The Research Paper Writer*); Everett Hoagland, poet (*Black Velvet, Scrimshaw*); Tish Dace, journalist and theatre critic; Alan Rosen, screenwriter and creative consultant (script consultant, *The Wizard of Loneliness*); Catherine Houser, fiction writer and journalist; Luke Wallin, fiction writer, author of award-winning novels for young adults (*The Redneck Poacher's Son, Ceremony of the Panther, Beastiary Mountain* trilogy), and regional planning consultant; Robert P. Waxler, author and business and organizational planning consultant; Linus Travers, grant writer and fundraiser; Sue Hum, communication and composition theory.

Admission decisions are based on the quality of writing represented in the applicant's portfolio, the undergraduate record, work experience, letters of recommendation, and scores on the Miller Analogies Test.

Teaching assistantships and graduate assistantships in writing positions are available.

For further information, contact Director of English Dept. Graduate Programs.

McMurry University
Abilene, TX 79697
(915) 691-6245

Degree offered: BA in English and Writing

For further information, contact the Chairman, Dept. of English.

❖McNeese State University
Lake Charles, LA 70609
(318) 475-5326

Degree offered: MFA in Creative Writing (poetry, fiction)

Type of Program: Studio/Academic

Required course of study: We do not believe that workshops and writing courses train or prepare a person to write unless coupled with extensive reading in the history of literature and a sound knowledge of the tradition. Therefore, only fifteen to eighteen hours are spent in Workshop; six in the Form and Theory of the student's major genre, and three in the other genre; three hours in Contemporary Poetry or Fiction; the other courses are electives, with six hours being given for the thesis, a novel, collection of stories, or book of poems. One can earn the MA while pursuing the MFA.

Workshops are small and the student-teacher relationship is close. There are usually six to eight visiting writers, agents, and editors each year who come to give workshops, individual conferences, and a reading. Recent guests have included Richard Wilbur, W.D. Snodgrass, Ann Beattie, X.J. Kennedy, William Trowbridge, Dana Gioia, Dave Smith, Paul Zimmer, Susan Ludvigson, and many others. Our students have had stories in *Scribner's Best of the Fiction Workshops*, won *Poetry* magazine's $15,000 Ruth Lilly Fellowship, and been published in a wide variety of magazines.

The faculty includes Robert Olen Butler and John Wood. Butler won the 1993 Pulitzer Prize for *A Good Scent from a Strange Mountain*, and his stories have been included in *Best American Short Stories* several years in a row. He has also written six screenplays for major Hollywood studios in the last four years and he teaches a course in screen writing. Wood's books *In Primary Light* and *The Gates of the Elect Kingdom* both won the Iowa Poetry Prize, and his *Selected Poems 1968-1998* will be published in 1999. He is also an art and photographic historian whose books have won several national awards including being named one of the Best Books of 1995 by the *New York Times Book Review*.

McNeese has 8,500 students and is in a city of some 100,000. Lake Charles is between New Orleans and Houston down in the bayous of Cajun country. Assistantships pay $6,000 and include a waiver of most tuition.

For additional information write: Dr. John Wood, Director, Program in Creative Writing.

❖The University of Memphis
Memphis, TN 38152
(901) 678-2651

Degrees offered: BA, MA, MFA

Degree: BA in English with Concentration in Creative Writing

Required course of study: 24 s/hrs for the major
Thesis: 3 s/hrs
Writing workshop: 9-12 s/hrs
Literature courses: 6-15 s/hrs
Tutorials or directed reading: up to 6 s/hrs

Degree: BA in English with Concentration in Professional Writing

Required course of study: 24 s/hrs for the major
Thesis: 3-6 s/hrs
Writing workshop: 6-18 s/hrs
Other writing courses: 15-18 s/hrs
Literature courses: 6-15 s/hrs
Tutorials or directed reading: 3 or more s/hrs

Degree: MA in English with Creative Writing Thesis

Type of Program: Studio/Academic

Required course of study: 33 s/hrs (30 plus thesis)
Thesis: up to 6 s/hrs
Writing workshop: 9-12 s/hrs
Other writing courses: up to 12 s/hrs
Tutorials or directed reading: up to 6 s/hrs

Other Requirements: Reading knowledge of one foreign language; oral examination based on thesis.

Degree: MA in English with Professional Writing Concentration

Required course of study: 30 s/hrs (including thesis)
Thesis: 3 s/hrs
Writing workshop: up to 6 s/hrs
Other writing courses: up to 12 s/hrs
Tutorials or directed reading: up to 6 s/hrs
Literature: 6 s/hrs

Other Requirements: Reading knowledge of one foreign language; oral examination based on thesis.

Degree: MFA in Creative Writing

Type of Program: Studio/Academic

Required course of study: 48 s/hrs
Thesis: up to 6 s/hrs
Writing workshop: up to 18 s/hrs

The Mississippi River Delta begins in Memphis, a diverse city of a million individuals. Memphis has a rich past and is historically one of the most influential centers of literature and music in the country. Anyone familiar with the work of William Faulkner, Richard Wright, Eudora Welty, Peter Taylor, Shelby Foote, or Robert Penn Warren is aware of the hold Memphis has on the literary imagination. Memphis is also the hometown of rock 'n' roll and big-city rhythm and blues.

The Creative Writing Program at The University of Memphis offers MA and MFA degrees, as well as an undergraduate major in English with a concentration in Creative Writing. All degrees combine a studio/academic curriculum, and those on the graduate level require a book-length publishable thesis in poetry, fiction, or nonfiction.

Graduate financial assistance is available, including both Research and Teaching Assistantships. Two assistantships a year are awarded to students who work on the Program's national literary and cultural magazine, *River City*. Another assistantship is awarded to the graduate student who works for the River City Writers Series. Applications for all assistantships must be made by March 15 or October 15, respectively, for the following academic semester. Letters requesting assistantships must be addressed to the Associate Director of Graduate Studies, Dept. of English.

The Writing Program brings six internationally known writers to campus each year for readings and workshops through the River City Writers Series. In addition, a writer-in-residence position provides well-known writers with longer residencies each year. Recent visitors have included Tobias Wolff, James Tate, W.S. Merwin, Stuart Dybek, Ellen Gilchrist, Luisa Valenzuela, John Updike, Larry McMurtry, Seamus Heaney, Eavan Boland, and Czeslaw Milosz.

The current faculty includes visiting professor Randall Kenan, whose books of fiction are *Let the Dead Bury Their Dead* and *A Visitation of Spirits*. His nonfiction includes *Walking On Water: In Search of Black America*. He has been awarded a Guggenheim Fellowship and the Whiting Writers Award. John Bensko, whose books of poems are *Green Soldier* and *The Waterman's Children*; his awards include a Yale Younger Poets Prize and the John Ciardi Fellowship at the Bread Loaf Writers' Conference.

Gordon Osing's collections of poems include *From the Boundary Waters* and *Town Down-River*. He has co-translated several books of Chinese poetry.

Tom Russell has published stories and poems in numerous magazines, and has been the recipient of NEA and Carnegie Mellon Fellowships. Russell is the winner of the 1995 *Quarterly West* novella competition, and has also been awarded the Pushcart and PEN Syndicated prizes. He is editor of *River City*.

Other faculty has included Brett Singer, Greg Spatz, Jay Meek, Sharon Bryan, Justin Cronin, Mary Bush, C.J. Hribal, Shelby Foote, Peter Taylor, William Page, Barry Hannah, Margaret Skinner, Lucille Clifton, and M.L. Rosenthal.

The literary magazine *River City* publishes fiction, poetry, and nonfiction. Recent issues have focused upon the Blues and Imaginary Homelands. The journal comes out in the spring and fall and is distributed nationally. *River City* publishes the winning stories from the annual fiction competition. The contest offers First Prize of $2,000, a Second Prize of $500, and a Third Prize of $300. For contest submission guidelines, contact *River City*, Dept. of English, The University of Memphis, Memphis, TN 38152.

Mercyhurst College
Erie, PA 16546
(814) 824-2354

Degree offered: BA in English with Creative Writing Minor

Required course of study: 48 q/hrs in English
  Writing workshop: 6 q/hrs

The Creative Writing Program at Mercyhurst College offers a BA with a Creative Writing minor. An introductory course in either poetry or fiction is followed by a Form and Theory course and an advanced workshop in one of these 2 genres. Senior English majors taking a Creative Writing minor may present as their Senior Project a collection of work in fiction or poetry.

The faculty includes novelist Ken Schiff (author of *Passing Go*, a novel, winner of the Library Journal Award, Director of Mercyhurst Summer Writers Institute); and poet James W. Hood.

Visiting writers include poet Gary Myers; novelist Randall Silvis; novelist W.S. Kuniczak; novelist J. Madison Davis; Don Robertson (columnist, critic, and author of over 15 novels); novelist Terry Bisson; Chuck Rosenthal; short-story writer Steve Coyne (winner of the *Playboy* short-story contest and author of work published in *Prairie Schooner*); novelist Dan Vilmure (author of *Life in the Land of the Living*, a novel); and novelist Chris Dubbs.

For more information, contact Ken Schiff, Writing Program Director, Dept. of English.

Metropolitan State College of Denver
Denver, CO 80204
(303) 556-3211
FAX (303) 556-6165

Degree offered: BA in English with Concentration in Creative Writing

For further information, contact the Chair of the English Dept.

❖Miami University
Oxford, OH 45056
(513) 529-5221
FAX (513) 529-1392

Degrees offered: BA, MA

Degree: BA in English with Concentration in Creative Writing (poetry, fiction)

Required course of study: 128 s/hrs
  Writing courses & workshop: at least 12 s/hrs
  Literature courses: 21 s/hrs
  Theory and practice: 9 s/hrs

Other Requirements: University distribution requirements; liberal education requirements (includes foreign language requirement); 56 s/hrs at or above the 200 level.

Application Deadlines: January 31 for admission and financial aid.

The undergraduate major consists of fourteen required courses in three areas -- writing, theory and practice, and literature. All majors take Introduction to Creative Writing (poetry and fiction) before progressing to the intermediate and advanced levels, where study is in a single genre. In addition, students take five literature courses, as well as two courses in foreign language literature in translation. The theory and practice section consists of a genre course, a course in contemporary American writing, and a topics course (Issues in Creative Writing). While most students concentrate in either fiction or poetry, it is possible to balance courses so as to work in both. *Inklings* is the undergraduate literary magazine. Each spring the department awards fiction and poetry prizes on the sophomore, junior, and senior levels, judged by a nationally known writer.

Degree: MA in Creative Writing (fiction, poetry)

Type of Program: Studio/Academic

Length of Residency: Two years

Required course of study: 38 s/hrs
  Writing workshop: 16 s/hrs
  Literature: 12 s/hrs
  Issues in Creative Writing: 4 s/hrs
  Thesis: 6 s/hrs

Other Requirements: Oral examination on two reading lists (contemporary literature in the genre of the thesis; student-generated reading list on the genre, subject matter, or concerns in which the thesis is embedded); oral defense of thesis; competency in foreign language.

Application Deadlines: January 15 for financial aid; February 1 for admission.

Miami's graduate program in creative writing was begun over twenty-five years ago, and is well-established. It is small, composed of about twenty-five students. The faculty ratio is 1:4. Characterized by workshops of 8-15 people, the program is able to provide both a tutorial atmosphere and a community of ambitious peers. The faculty works closely with a diverse group of students, some of whom are non-traditional, and encourages a demanding, non-competitive environment.

The master's program consists of eight courses -- four writing workshops in which students are also expected to write detailed critiques of one another's work and to present a revised portfolio of work at the semester's end, in order to achieve skills as editors as well as writers; Issues in Creative Writing; and three literature seminars of their choice which introduce students to current theoretical and critical practices and allow them a better understanding of the tradition out of which they write.

Each student's work is directed toward the thesis -- a novel, novella, or collection of short fiction or poetry.

Recent students have been successful in careers in university teaching, publishing and editing, and public service. Their work has received Intro Awards, Honorable Mentions in the *Atlantic Monthly* Young Writer's Competition, the George Bennett Fellowship, and has been published widely in literary journals. In the spring of 1999, Alfred A. Knopf will publish *The Life I Lead*, a first novel by Keith Banner, who graduated in 1993.

Visiting writers in recent years have included: Jonathan Ames, Jimmy Santiago Baca, Rita Dove, Ron Hansen, Seamus Heaney, Susan Mitchell, Tim O'Brien, Sharon Olds, Linda Pastan, Robert Pinsky, Richard Russo, Francine Prose, Elizabeth Arthur, and C.K. Williams. Each spring semester a visiting fiction writer offers an intensive week-long one-credit course; during the last few years, the course has been taught by Bob Shacochis, Margot Livesey, Michael Martone, Nancy Willard, and Ron Carlson. Week-long poetry courses have recently been taught by Molly Peacock, Marilyn Nelson, Debra Bruce, and Stephanie Strickland.

In *Oxford Magazine*, Miami has one of the country's few student-run national literary magazines; it was recently named one of the top 50 fiction markets in the country. Work on the magazine provides the program's graduate students with direct experience in editing and publishing. Recent issues include work by X.J. Kennedy, David Citino, James Purdy, William Stafford, Philip Dacey, Baron Wormser, Eve Shelnutt, and Andre Dubus. A story by Joseph Geha won a Pushcart Prize.

As well, the Miami University Press Poetry Series publishes two books of poetry a year by poets in mid-career. The series' editor is James Reiss. Ralph Angel's *Neither World* won the 1995 James Laughlin Award of the Academy of American Poets.

The program awards teaching assistantships in its nationally recognized first-year writing program to the most qualified students. For 1998-99, the assistantship pays approximately $8,400, an additional summer stipend of $1,600, and remission of tuition and most fees. Other assistantships are available across campus, with the library, Learning Assistance, and Residence Life. Interested students should contact those places directly. In addition, we offer the Sinclair Award of $1,000 to each class's most promising applicant.

The creative writing faculty includes: fiction writer and poet Steven Bauer (*Satyrday, Daylight Savings*, winner of the Peregrine Smith Poetry Prize); poet and critic Annie Finch (*Eve, The Ghost of Meter*, and editor of *A Formal Feeling Comes*); screenwriter and novelist Eric Goodman (*In Days of Awe, The First Time I Saw Jenny Hall, High on the Energy Bridge*); fiction writer Constance Pierce (*Hope Mills*, which won the Editor's Prize from the Pushcart Press, *When Things Get Back To Normal*); poet and editor James Reiss (*The Breathers, Express, The Parable of Fire*); poet David Schloss (*Legends, The Beloved*); novelist and cultural critic Kay Sloan (*Worry Beads, Looking Far North: The Harriman Expedition to Alaska, The Loud Silents: Origins of the Social Problem Film*); and avant-garde critic and poet Keith Tuma.

For more information, contact Eric Goodman, Director of Creative Writing, External Programs.

❖University of Miami
Coral Gables, FL 33124-4632
(305) 284-2182
FAX (305) 284-5396

Degrees offered: BA, MFA

Degree: BA in English with Concentration in Creative Writing

Thirty credits in creative writing and literature, in addition to the requirements of the College of Arts and Sciences. Opportunity to write a senior-year or honors thesis. Faculty: Robert Antoni (fiction), John Balaban (poetry and fiction), Fred D'Aguiar (poetry and fiction), Lester Goran (fiction), Evelyn Wilde Mayerson (fiction), and Peter Schmitt (poetry).

Degree: MFA (in fiction or poetry)

Type of Program: Studio/Academic

Length of Residency: Two years

Required course of study: 36 s/hrs total
Thesis: 6 s/hrs
Workshops: 12 s/hrs
Literature courses: 12 s/hrs
Elective: 3-6 s/hrs
Rhetoric: 3 s/hrs (TA's only)

Other Requirements: A final exam based on a list of books in the candidate's genre of interest.

Application Deadline: February 1 for those seeking teaching assistantships.

The program provides an opportunity for students of superior ability in imaginative writing to develop their skills and critical judgment through the practice of writing and the study of literature. The aim of the program is to prepare talented students for careers in writing. Degree candidates are expected to produce a book-length work of literary value and publishable quality.

Begun through a gift from James A. Michener, our new MFA is housed on the tropical, 260-acre main campus of the University of Miami in Coral Gables. The area has great cultural vitality with strong literary and film traditions (some MFA students may wish to use their elective in scriptwriting). The Department of English, with a faculty of thirty-five, currently serves about 80 students in its MA and PhD programs.

While it is recommended that applicants have an undergraduate major in English, the program does not discourage applicants from other undergraduate disciplines. Regardless of their undergraduate major, applicants should have a 3.2 grade-point average on a 4.00 scale. Students must submit scores from the general aptitude section of the Graduate Record Examination (GRE), three letters of recommendation, transcripts of all undergraduate work, and, most importantly, writing samples. For fiction, approximately thirty pages are required; for poetry, at least twelve poems. Manuscripts should be accompanied by a stamped, self-addressed envelope if the material is to be returned. Applicants should retain copies of all work submitted.

Financial aid is available, primarily in the form of teaching assistantships in freshman composition. Teaching assistantships include full tuition and a stipend ($11,000 for the 1998-99 academic year). Teaching assistants normally teach one course per semester or serve as tutors for 12 hours per week. All assistants take a graduate seminar in Teaching College Composition and receive regular guidance in classroom or tutorial instruction. In addition to the above, the program tries to offer qualified students the opportunity to teach introductory courses in their genre of interest.

In addition to the James A. Michener Teaching Assistantships, the department provides prizes for poetry and fiction, including competitions on the national level such as the Academy of American Poets Prize.

Visitors have included John Barth, Carolyn Kizer, Bette Pesetsky, Isaac B. Singer, Derek Walcott, Richard Wilbur, Shelby Hearon, Maxine Kumin, and Nelida Pinon.

The regular faculty includes fiction writer Robert Antoni (*Divina Trace*, *Blessed Be the Fruit*, Commonwealth Writers Prize), poet, fiction writer, and translator, John Balaban (*Locusts at the Edge of Summer*, *Remembering Heaven's Face*, Lamont Prize), poet and fiction writer Fred D'Aguiar (*The Longest Memory*, *Mama Dot*, The Whitbread Prize), and fiction writers Lester Goran (*Tales from the Irish Club*, *Bing Crosby's Last Song*, *The Paratrooper of Mechanic Avenue*) and Evelyn Wilde Mayerson (*Sanjo*, *Well and Truly*, The Sidney Taylor Library Award). Together the graduate writing faculty has authored some thirty books, which have won numerous prizes and critical attention.

All queries should be sent to: Fred D'Aguiar, MFA Director, Dept. of English, University of Miami, P.O. Box 248145, Coral Gables, FL 33124.

❖Michigan State University
East Lansing, MI 48824-1036
(517) 355-7570

Degree offered: MA in Creative Writing (fiction, drama, poetry)

Type of Program: Studio/Academic

Length of Residency: Two years

Required course of study:
Degree: min. 30 credits
English (800 level or 400 lev with permission):
9–12 credits
Creative writing workshops: 9–12 credits (with
emphasis in one genre; expected to take
one workshop in a second genre)
Thesis: 4 credits

Other Requirements: Proficiency in one foreign language.

Application Deadlines: December 31 for financial aid; January 1 for fall semester admission; November 1 for spring semester admission.

The MA in Creative Writing is a terminal degree which also prepares students for further academic work, if desired. The thesis is a publishable book of stories, poems, or a full length play.

Teaching assistantships and fellowships are available.

Professors include: Diane Wakoski (poetry); Anita Skeen (poetry); Gordon Henry (fiction); W.S. Penn (fiction); Arthur Athanason (drama); and Marcia Aldrich (creative nonfiction).

Further information may be obtained from the graduate secretary of the English Dept.

❖University of Michigan
Ann Arbor, MI 48109-1003
(734) 763-4139
e-mail: graduate_English_Admission@om.cc.umich.edu

Degrees offered: BA, MFA

Degree: MFA in Creative Writing (poetry, fiction)

Type of Program: Studio

Length of Residency: Two years

Required course of study: 36 s/hrs
Writing workshops: 24 s/hrs
Literature & cognate courses: 12 s/hrs

Other Requirements: Basic proficiency in one foreign language (equivalent to 4 semesters of undergraduate work); MFA project (collection of poems or short stories, or part of a novel).

At the heart of the MFA program are the writing workshops in either poetry or fiction, where students, under the direction of professional writers, form a community who read and comment on each other's work. Students elect a total of 18 workshop s/hrs (6 each of 3 semesters) and 6 hours of thesis tutorial in the final semester. The thesis may be a collection of poems or short stories, or part of a novel.

In addition to the workshops, students must complete at least 9 s/hrs in literature or literary criticism at the graduate level, and 3 s/hrs in a cognate field. Students will also be asked to demonstrate basic reading competence (approximately equivalent to 4 semesters of undergraduate course work) in one foreign language.

Successful applicants will be admitted as writers of either poetry or fiction. Applicants must have a baccalaureate degree by the time of expected enrollment. Although the degree need not involve concentration in English, the applicant should demonstrate sufficient skill in undergraduate language and literature courses to indicate readiness for enrollment in graduate literature courses.

In addition to the complete Rackham Application Form, the applicant must submit 3 letters of recommendation, 2 of which should be from writers or teachers of writing, and which should refer to both writing skill and critical ability in discussing literature. Most important among the criteria for admission are the applicant's writing samples, which should consist of 10 or 12 poems, 3 or 4 short stories, or part of a novel. Applicants who have published work should submit a bibliography. Submission of Graduate Record Examination scores is optional, though urged.

MFA applicants are encouraged to apply for all fellowship assistance for which they may be eligible, whether funded by the University of Michigan or other sources. The Department of English offers several financial aid packages which include a range of stipend support and tuition remission. In addition, successful applicants will be considered for University and departmental awards for which they are eligible;

these include the Rackham Merit Fellowships for Historically Underrepresented Groups, Graduate Student Teaching Assistantships, non-traditional fellowships, and other awards. All students accepted into the program receive some form of financial assistance, including full tuition remission and teaching stipends in their second year.

The University of Michigan offers a series of creative writing courses on all levels -- from sophomore level to advanced graduate study. The introductory courses are multi-genre, but specialized courses are also offered in poetry, fiction, and drama.

Among the distinctive resources of the University of Michigan's program in creative writing is the Avery Hopwood endowment, which funds an extensive series of annual student writing awards. In addition to the Major and Minor Hopwood Contests, the University of Michigan also has a summer Hopwood Contest for those enrolled in writing classes in the summer, and an Underclassman Contest during the fall term for freshmen and sophomores enrolled in writing classes. Prizes such as the Cowden, the Jeffrey Weisberg Memorial Prize, the Arthur Miller Award, Dennis McIntyre Prize in Playwriting, and the Kasdan Scholarship in Creative Writing are also offered routinely.

Major Hopwood Awards are open to regularly enrolled graduate students and seniors; Minor Awards are open to all undergraduates, including seniors. In both the Major and Minor contests, awards are offered in four fields -- drama/screenplay, fiction, poetry, and essay. Though the number and amount of the awards is not fixed, the Major and Minor Hopwood awards generally range from $400 to $3,000 apiece, and other contests for undergraduate and graduate students offer awards of $100 to $2,000. Over a million dollars in prize money has been disbursed by the Hopwood Program since its inception. Judges of national reputation read manuscripts and provide recommendations to the Hopwood Committee, which makes final decisions on the awards. Judges and Hopwood lecturers have included such writers as W.H. Auden, Theodore Roethke, Lillian Hellman, W.D. Snodgrass, Pauline Kael, Walker Percy, Joyce Carol Oates, Donald Justice, and William Kennedy.

The Hopwood Room houses an extensive collection of current periodicals and books and a file of prize-winning manuscripts. A coffee hour for students and faculty is held once a week during the fall and winter terms.

The MFA writing faculty includes fiction writers Jonis Agee, Charles Baxter, and Nicholas Delbanco, and poets Alice Fulton, Linda Gregerson, Thylias Moss, and Richard Tillinghast. The program is directed by poet and critic Linda Gregerson. The English Department hosts approximately 24 visiting writers each year; recent visitors include Russell Banks, Eavan Boland, Ethan Canin, Mark Doty, Richard Ford, Louise Glück, Jorie Graham, Donald Hall, Robert Hass, Charles Johnson, Maxine Kumin, Li-Young Lee, Jay McInerney, Bharati Mukherjee, Joyce Carol Oates, Michael Ondaatje, Tim O'Brien, Robert Pinsky, Wole Soyinka, Mark Strand, Scott Turow, Derek Walcott, and Richard Wilbur.

For full information and application materials, please write MFA Admissions, Dept. of English, 3187 Angell Hall.

Middlebury College
Middlebury, VT 05753
(802) 388-3711 ext. 5276
FAX (802) 388-8637

Degree offered: BA in English with a "Field" in Writing (fiction, nonfiction, poetry)

Required course of study:
10 to 16 courses (out of 36) in
the English major
Senior Program course in literature

Application Deadlines: January 15 for regular admissions; March 1 for transfers; November 15 for early decision. Same dates for financial aid.

At Middlebury the writing and literature courses are closely integrated: an aspiring writer is expected to become an extensive reader of the tradition to which he or she aspires. Writing workshop courses are offered in poetry, fiction, and nonfiction at 2 levels: introductory, and intermediate-advanced. There are also playwriting and screen/video writing courses. A student in the major who has completed 3 workshops may elect independent writing projects (frequently undertaken as part of senior work).

There are opportunities for outstanding students to attend summer sessions in writing at Bread Loaf (both School of English and Writers' Conference). Most of the Department faculty teach writing courses; published writers include Robert Pack, Jay Parini, Julia Alvarez, Gary Margolis, Don Mitchell, David Bain, and Ron Powers. Middlebury College publishes the *New England Review*.

For more information, contact Chair, Dept. of English.

❖Midland College
Main Campus
3600 N. Garfield
Midland, TX 79705-6397

For more information, contact the Director, Dept. of English.

Millikin University
1184 W. Main
Decatur, IL 62522
(217) 424-6250
FAX (217) 424-3993
e-mail: mboaz@mail.millikin.edu

Degree offered: BA

Required course of study: 120 s/hrs
Computer Aided Publishing: 3 s/hrs
Applying Writing Theory: 3 s/hrs
Senior Writing Portfolio: 3 s/hrs
Advanced Writing Studies: 9-18 s/hrs
(Writing internship strongly recommended)
Composition & Communications: 9 s/hrs
Literature & Language: 18 s/hrs

The writing major offers a broad range of writing

experiences and editing opportunities in creative writing, journalism, and pre-professional writing. The students follow a planned curriculum which develops practical writing skills and theoretical understanding of writing and publishing as a profession.

With a required sophomore course in computer aided publishing, writing majors learn to master both the current technologies and long standing traditions of publishing. The course in applying writing theory allows students to examine their own writing processes and consider the strategies and techniques of various theories of writing. The senior writing portfolio is an independent writing project which also gathers their writing accomplishments into a professional collection for future job or graduate school applications.

Writing majors may design their own specialty by choosing to participate in various advanced writing studies, editing opportunities, and writing internships available. In addition to our student literary journal, *Collage*, most writing majors gain journalism experience writing for the student newspaper, *The Decaturian*, and other campus newsletters or impromptu anthologies.

Recent advanced writing studies include: Creative Writing, Advanced Creative Writing, Contemporary Essay, Editing & Publishing, Public Relations Writing, Feature Writing, and Electronic Publishing. Enrollment is limited to 15 writers per section of advanced writing.

Recent writers who have visited for readings and workshops include: Mark Costello, Lucien Stryk, John Knoepfle, Dave Etter, Maya Angelou, Maura Stanton, Larry Lieberman, and Gwendolyn Brooks.

For more information, write to Dr. Mildred Boaz, Chair, Dept. of English.

❖Mills College
5000 MacArthur Boulevard
Oakland, CA 94613
(510) 430-2217
FAX (510) 430-3314

Degrees offered: BA, MFA

Degree: BA in English with Emphasis in Creative Writing

Required course of study:
English and Creative Writing: 12 courses
Literature courses: 8 courses
Creative Writing: 3 courses
Thesis: Independent Project in Creative Writing

Degree: MFA in Creative Writing

Type of Program: Studio/Academic

Length of Residency: Two years

Required course of study:
English and Creative Writing: 10 courses
Creative Writing: 4 courses
Literature: 4 courses
Electives: 2 courses
Thesis: required

Application Deadlines: Feb. 1 for Fall; contact: Graduate Studies at (510) 430-3309.

The Creative Writing program at Mills is an intimate workshop setting that provides a focus in Poetry, Fiction or Creative Nonfiction. We offer workshops in creative writing as well as study of literature. Both the undergraduate writers and the writers in the MFA program benefit from the accessibility of the professors, all recognized authors themselves.

Mills also provides a professional atmosphere where readings are held and a fine literary magazine is produced. The Contemporary Writers Series has brought writers such as Dorothy Allison, Tillie Olson, Adrienne Rich, Tess Gallagher, Louise Glück, Gwendolyn Brooks, Mei-Mei Bersenbrugge, Rosemarie Waldrop, and Gail Tsukiyama to campus for readings and interactions with the students.

Our Distinguished Writer-in-Residence brings one distinguished poet and one distinguished prose writer to campus for one year, expanding our course offerings, particularly on the graduate level.

The English Department also houses The Place for Writers, a resource for creative writers who wish to publish, write grants, apply to colonies, contests, etc. In addition, the Bay Area offers many opportunities to attend readings and be involved in other writing activities.

The Walrus is the undergraduate literary magazine that provides experience in small press publishing. The volunteer staff is involved in many activities, particularly producing readings such as Writer's Harvest.

The English Department sponsors a number of awards in creative writing a year. Graduate students are eligible for scholarships their first year and for teaching assistantships their second year. Most graduate students get some in-class or tutoring experience during their study at the College.

The permanent creative writing staff includes poet and translator Chana Bloch, Director of Creative Writing, poet Stephen Ratcliffe, and prose writer Elmaz Abinader.

For more information, contact the Director, Creative Writing Program, Dept. of English.

❖Minnesota State University, Mankato
MSU Box 53
P.O. Box 8400
Mankato, MN 56002-8400
(507) 389-2117
FAX (507) 389-5362
e-mail: mfa@mankato.msus.edu
website: http://www.mankato.msus.edu/dept/english

Degrees offered: BA, BS, MFA

Degree: BA, BS in English with Concentration in Creative Writing (poetry, fiction, creative nonfiction, scriptwriting, writing for children)

Required course of study: 128 s/hrs total
For the CW major, 32 (BA) or 34 (BS) s/hours beyond

general education, distributed as follows:
    Writing workshops: 12 s/hrs
    Form and technique course (poetry or prose):
        4 s/hrs
    Contemporary literature course: 4 s/hrs
    Literature and English-language courses:
        12-14 s/hrs

Other Requirements: BA track requires one year of foreign language as part of general education.

Application Deadlines: August 15 for admission; July 1 for financial aid.

The undergraduate concentration prepares students for professions related to writing, such as publishing, editing, public relations, or freelancing. The requirements for the program encourage students to develop a strong core understanding of literature and language while gaining experience in at least two creative genres. Activities surrounding the program include three literary magazines, several reading series, and a number of student-operated writing groups and organizations.

Degree: MFA in Creative Writing (poetry, fiction, creative nonfiction, screenwriting, writing for children)

Type of Program: Studio/Academic

Length of Residency: 2-3 years

Required course of study: 48 s/hrs
    Writing workshops: 12 s/hrs (minimum)
    Form and technique courses: 6 s/hrs
    Contemporary genre courses: 6 s/hrs
    Career-related courses: 8 s/hrs
    Literature/Other courses: 12 s/hrs (maximum)
    Thesis: 4 s/hrs

Other Requirements: A comprehensive exam, a book-length creative thesis, and a public reading.

Application Deadlines: March 1 for admission the following fall term. March 1 for financial aid and/or graduate assistantship.

The MFA program in creative writing meets the needs of students who would like to strike a balance in their graduate study between the development of individual creative talent and a close study of literature and language. Candidates in the program will find it appropriate training for careers in freelancing, college-level teaching, editing and publishing, arts administration, and several other areas. New students will discover the faculty eager to work with them and a community atmosphere extremely supportive of writing.

The Good Thunder Reading Series brings emerging and established writers to Mankato State for one-day residencies, usually six per year. These visits include manuscript conferences, classroom visits, craft lectures, and public readings. Past guests have included William Stafford, Olga Broumas, Tim O'Brien, Louise Erdrich, Donald Hall, Carolyn Forché, Rick DeMarinis, Jane Smiley, and over 100 others. During spring term, the Eddice B. Barber Visiting Writer Program sponsors an extended, week-long residency by an additional poet or prose writer.

Twice each semester graduate students in creative writing sponsor the Writers Bloc series of open readings, which gives campus and community writers the opportunity to read their work in a public forum. At various times during the year, graduate students who are nearing completion of their programs will give thesis readings before audiences of faculty, fellow students, and members of the general public.

The MSU English Department houses *Mankato Poetry Review*. Both *MPR* and the MSU-sponsored *Minnesota River Review* offer opportunities for graduate students interested in learning more about editing and publishing.

The Department of English employs approximately 30 teaching assistants at stipends of $5,400 for the academic year. Teaching assistants pay in-state tuition, and receive a remission of half their graduate tuition when registered for 6 or more graduate hours per quarter. Assistants are provided office space and have faculty library privileges. Other graduate assistantships are available from Student Affairs, the Memorial Library, the Residential Life Office, and other offices of the University. Affirmative Action graduate assistantships are available for American graduate students of color.

The full-time creative writing faculty includes novelist and screenwriter Terry Davis (*Vision Quest, Mysterious Ways, If Rock and Roll Were a Machine*); fiction writer Cathy Day (*Walking on Water*); poet Richard Robbins (*The Invisible Wedding*; NEA Fellow); fiction writer Roger Sheffer (*Borrowed Voices, Lost River*); and nonfiction writer Richard Terrill (*Saturday Night in Baoding*, NEA Fellow). Additional faculty in the program include nonfiction writer Suzanne Bunkers (*In Search of Susanna*) and children's writing specialist Louisa Smith.

For more information, contact Richard Robbins, Director of Creative Writing, at the above address.

❖**University of Minnesota**
Minneapolis, MN 55455
(612) 625-6366
FAX (612) 624-8228
e-mail: creawrit@tc.umn.edu

Degree offered: MFA in Creative Writing (with concentrations in poetry, fiction, literary nonfiction)

Type of Program: Studio/Academic

Required course of study: 54 s/hrs
    Introductory multi-genre course: 4 s/hrs
    Writing workshops: 16 s/hrs
    Literature courses: 12 s/hrs
    Related field courses: 6 s/hrs
    Writing Project: 16 s/hrs

Other Requirements: MFA essay exam; public reading of written work; completion of book-length manuscript.

Program Design: The English Department at the University of Minnesota offers a specialized Master of Fine Arts Degree in Creative Writing designed to develop students' analytic and creative skills under the direction of faculty who are distinguished practicing writers. The three-year program integrates advanced study of English and American language and literature with writing workshops. Students are encouraged to read contemporary literature in a global context and to explore writing that reflects a sense of values and social responsibility.

Coursework: The Program in Creative Writing regularly offers advanced workshops, comprised of 12 to 15 students each, taught by core and adjunct faculty in poetry, fiction, memoir, and literary nonfiction. Based on the assumption that good writers must be good readers, a unique course series entitled Reading as Writers focuses on poetry, short story, memoir, contemporary novel, and contemporary dramatic fiction. Specialized workshops are offered in areas such as preparation of the book-length manuscript, playwriting, screenwriting, and professional editing. Internships with local presses, and arts and literary organizations are also available. In the summer, the University's Split Rock Arts Program offers week-long workshops in writing and other arts in the Lake Superior port city of Duluth. In their third program year, students concentrate on their creative project, a book-length manuscript suitable for publication.

Visiting Writers: The Edelstein-Keller Endowment for Creative Writing has led to remarkable growth in the University of Minnesota's Creative Writing Program. The funds have enabled the program to offer a diverse selection of courses in all genres and to sponsor a writer-in-residence series, which has brought such internationally acclaimed writers as Samuel Delany, Nikki Giovanni, Carolyn Forché, Nuruddin Farah, Grace Paley, Joy Harjo, Mei-Mei Berssenbrugge, Garrett Hongo, Isaac Bashevis Singer, Josip Novakovich, and C.K. Williams to Minnesota.

Faculty members are the poet and librettist Michael Dennis Browne (*Selected Poems 1965-1995, You Won't Remember This, Smoke from the Fires*); fiction writer M.J. Fitzgerald (*Rope-Dancer, Concertina, The Placing of Kings*); poet and essayist Ray Gonzalez (*Cabato Sentora, The Heat of Arrivals, Memory Fever: A Journey Beyond El Paso del Norte*); memoirist, poet, and fiction writer Patricia Hampl (*Virgin Time, A Romantic Education, I Could Tell You Stories: Essays on Memory and Imagination*); fiction writer and essayist Valerie Miner (*Range of Light, A Walking Fire, Rumors from the Cauldron: Selected Essays, Reviews and Reportage*); fiction writer Julie Schumacher (*An Explanation for Chaos, The Body Is Water*); and poet and memoirist Madelon Sprengnether (*The Normal Heart; Rivers, Stories, Houses, Dreams;* co-editor of and contributor to *The House on Via Gombito*).

Financial Support: The English Department at the University of Minnesota is committed to providing financial support to MFA students for three full years. Support is given in the form of graderships, teaching assistantships, research and administrative fellowships, and teaching appointments. In addition, grants and fellowships from outside the department may be available by nomination to incoming students. All forms of support provide salary or stipend and include a full tuition waiver plus health benefits. Classroom appointments carry the added benefit of teacher training.

Awards and Residencies: The program provides opportunities for annual awards in fiction, poetry, and literary nonfiction, as well as student writer residencies each summer.

Application materials may be obtained from the Director of Graduate Studies, Dept. of English, 207 Lind Hall, 207 Church Street S.E., University of Minnesota, Minneapolis, MN 55455. Application materials are due in the Graduate School and the English Dept. by December 20. No separate application fee for financial support is necessary.

❖Mississippi State University
Mississippi State, MS 39762
(601) 325-3644
FAX (601) 325-7283
e-mail: rjl@ra.msstate.edu
website: www.msstate.edu/dept/english

Degree offered: MA in English with Creative Writing Emphasis (fiction, poetry)

Type of Program: Studio/Academic

In addition to Creative Writing courses and Professional Writing classes in several fields available to undergraduates, Mississippi State University offers an MA in English with an emphasis in Creative Writing. This program requires 24 hours of English courses, plus an original work of fiction or poetry (with an introduction) in lieu of the usual academic thesis. Courses available include writing workshops, the Craft of Poetry and the Craft of Fiction. Reading courses, the Form and Theory of Poetry, and Form and Theory of Fiction, are also offered.

Fiction Faculty: Price Caldwell, Kathlene Postma. Visiting Fiction Faculty: James Wilcox and Vickie Hunt. Poetry Faculty: Gary Myers and Richard Lyons.

Teaching Assistantships are available for entering graduate students. Those interested in Creative Writing may also apply for the $2,500 (renewable) Eugene Butler Scholarship. The department further encourages students by sponsoring readings and writing contests. We participate annually in the Southern Literary Festival. Creative Writing students also edit and produce a literary journal called *The Jabberwock*.

For more information, contact Richard Lyons, Box E, Dept. of English.

Missouri Southern State College
Joplin, MO 64801-1595
(573) 625-9377

Degrees offered: BA, BSE

For further information, contact Writing Program Director, Dept. of English.

❖University of Missouri, Columbia
107 Tate Hall
Columbia, MO 65211
(314) 882-6066

Degrees offered: BA, MA, PhD

Degree: BA in English with Concentration in Creative Writing (poetry, fiction)

Required course of study: 33 s/hrs total
  Writing workshops: up to 9 s/hrs
  Literature courses: 24 s/hrs

Other Requirements: In addition to the normal requirements for the major in English, students pursuing a creative writing emphasis take one required lower division course in poetry or fiction writing, and two upper-level seminars in creative writing.

Application Deadlines: February 1 for financial aid and admissions.

The undergraduate concentration requires the student to take an Introductory Creative Writing class in poetry or fiction, and then take two more classes specializing in that genre; the program also requires extensive study in the literature of at least three centuries. The writing program as a whole offers a number of private and university sponsored creative writing awards, some of which are limited to our undergraduates.

Degree: MA in English with a Concentration in Creative Writing (poetry, fiction)

Type of Program: Studio/Academic

Length of Residency: Two years

Required course of study: 30 s/hrs total
  Writing workshops: 12 s/hrs (6 s/hrs
    seminar-level)
  Literature courses: 12 s/hrs in English
  Electives: 6 s/hrs

Other Requirements: Written comprehensive examination or Master's thesis (50–75 pages of scholarly work), portfolio of creative work (approximately 70 pages of fiction or 30 pages of poetry).

Application Deadlines: January 15.

Financial Aid: MA: $5,340 for first year (includes 10 hrs. per week of apprenticeship in teaching writing); $10,140 for second year (includes teaching two sections per semester).

The MA with a Creative Writing emphasis offers the students the opportunity to participate in a series of intensive writing workshops, work closely with resident faculty writers, and pursue a wide range of studies in Literature, Language, Critical Theory, and Creative Writing. In the creative writing workshops we are committed to keeping the class size small enough (the limit is set at 15) to give each student the individual attention necessary to encourage the growth of his or her work.

In addition to -- and hand-in-hand with -- their creative work, our students are engaged in a wide-ranging study of literature and theory covering at least five of the following fields: 1. Medieval Literature; 2. Renaissance Literature; 3. 17th-century Literature; 4. 18th-century Literature; 5. 19th-century Literature; 6. American Literature; 7. 20th-century Literature; 8. Other Approaches to Literature.

Degree: The Creative Writing PhD in English (poetry and fiction)

Type of Program: Studio/Academic

Required course of study: 30 s/hrs total
  Writing workshops: 9 s/hrs minimum;
    12 s/hrs maximum
  History or theory of literary criticism: 3 s/hrs
  Theory and practice of composition: 3 s/hrs
  History or structure of the English Language:
    3 s/hrs
  Writing for Publication: 3 s/hrs

Other Requirements: 1) a residency requirement; 2) a working knowledge of two foreign languages or an advanced knowledge of one; 3) a written Comprehensive Examination; 4) a Creative Dissertation (the PhD candidate may choose to write a novel or a book-length collection of poems or stories. Professional standards for approval of the dissertation in Creative Writing will be as rigorous as in other areas).

Application Deadlines: January 15.

Financial Aid: Creative Writing Fellowships: one PhD fellowship in poetry and one in fiction, $11,720 per year (to teach two sections per year) for four years. PhD Fellowships: four fellowships of $11,720 per year (to teach three sections per year) for three years. PhD Assistantships: six assistantships of $11,720 per year (to teach four sections per year) for five years.

The Creative Writing PhD in English is designed to offer the students a chance to pursue a course of study that emphasizes both their creative and academic interests. It is our belief that the study of literature will nurture and deepen a student's creative work; conversely, we find that our students bring with them a firsthand knowledge of writing that nurtures and deepens their academic studies. We've set up our course requirements to provide the students with the opportunity to participate in a series of intensive writing workshops, to work closely with resident faculty writers, and at the same time to pursue a wide range of studies in Literature, Language, and Critical Theory. Graduates of our program are qualified to teach in a wide range of areas, in both academic and creative writing courses.

In addition to our intensive courses, we are also committed to providing a program of outside readers of national and international reputation. In recent years that program has included Sandra Gilbert, Derek Walcott, Marilynne Robinson, Donald Justice, Francine Prose, Helen Vendler, Yusef Komunyakaa, Paule Marshall, and Anthony Hecht.

Current faculty: poet Sherod Santos, Director of the Program in Creative Writing (books include *The Pilot Star, Elegies, The City of Women*; his awards include the Delmore Schwartz Memorial Award, the Oscar Blumenthal Prize from *Poetry*, and grants from the Guggenheim and NEA Foundations); poet Lynne McMahon (books include *All Quail to the Wallowing, Devolution of the Nude, Faith*; awards include the Guggenheim and Ingram-Merrill Foundation grants); poet Sw. Anand Prahlad Folly (books include *Hear My Story and Other Poems* and *African-American Proverbs in Context*); Speer Morgan, fiction writer (books include *Frog Gig and Other Stories, Belle Starr, Brother Enemy*; awards include an NEA grant); Trudy Lewis (author of *Private Correspondences*, for which she was awarded the William Goyen Prize for Fiction).

All students admitted to the graduate program receive a fellowship or teaching assistantship. Each year the Creative Writing Program offers two named fellowships, one in each genre. Second- and third-year writing students often have the opportunity to teach Introductory Creative Writing classes. Additionally, the Creative Writing Program is pleased to offer a number of yearly writing prizes totaling almost $3,000. Students also have the chance to work on 3 campus publications; *Midlands*, the student literary magazine, and *The Missouri Review* and *The Minnesota Review* (which moved to UMC this year), both national literary journals.

For more information, write: Sherod Santos, Director of the Program in Creative Writing.

❖University of Missouri, Kansas City
Kansas City, MO 64110
(816) 235-1168
FAX (816) 235-2611

Degree offered: MA in English with Professional Writing Emphasis (poetry, fiction, journalism, playwriting, screenwriting)

Type of Program: Studio/Academic

Length of Residency: Two years

Required course of study:
  33 s/hrs in English and Professional Writing
    (areas: Poetry/Fiction; Print/Electronic
    Journalism; Stage/Screenwriting)
  Portfolio of work in chosen area
  Writing workshops: 2 offered (6 hrs)
  Other writing courses: 12–15 s/hrs
  Literature courses: 9–12 s/hrs

Other Requirements: Writing sample; GRE (60% on verbal); foreign language proficiency; 2 letters of recommendation; 6–12 s/hrs allowed in other departments.

Application Deadlines: Applications accepted year-round.

Candidates in the Professional Writing Program must choose one of three Areas of Concentration: Poetry & Fiction; Print & Electronic Journalism; or Stage & Screenwriting. Candidates are expected to do a majority of their writing in their chosen Area, although they may take some course work in other Areas. The normal 33-hour program of study consists of 18 hours of writing, 12 hours of literature, and a 3-hour tutorial course devoted to preparation of the Portfolio of work in the chosen Area (a requirement for graduation). Six hours of writing courses from other departments (e.g. Communications Studies and Theater) are allowed every candidate. An additional six hours may be allowed upon petition to the Graduate Committee of the Department of English. Candidates who show a lack of literary preparation may be asked to take an additional six hours of literature courses from the Department of English. The Portfolio requirements and all other details are available upon request, but the overall requirement of the Portfolio is that it is of professional quality.

The core faculty includes: Michelle Boisseau (*No Private Life, Understory*, poems; *Writing Poems*, with Robert Wallace, text); G.S. Sharat Chandra (*Family of Mirrors*, poems; *Logic to Their Fate, Sari Of The Gods*, short stories); Angela Elam (National Public Radio producer, host of *New Letters on the Air*); James McKinley (*Acts of Love*, short stories; *The Fickleman Suite and Other Stories, Assassination in America*, biography of Robert Graves, nonfiction; editor, *New Letters*; Director, Professional Writing Program); Robert Unger (*The Union Station Massacre*, nonfiction; National Press Club Edwin M. Hood Award for Diplomatic Correspondence; Pulitzer Prize; print journalism); Robert Stewart (*Plumbers, Letter from the Living*, poems; *Voices from the Interior*, editor); Ralph Berets (screenwriting); Gregory D. Black (*Hollywood Censored: Sex, Politics, Codes and Catholics; 1930–1940, Hollywood Goes to War: How Politics, Profits and Propaganda Shaped WWII Movies* (co-author), *The Catholic Crusade Against Hollywood: 1940–1975*, nonfiction); Charles Hammer (*Me, the Beef and the Bum, Wrong Way Ragsdale*, novels); Felicia Londré (*Frederico Garcia Lorca, Tom Stoppard, Tennessee Williams, The History of World Theater: From English Restoration to the Present*, critical biographies/theater history). In addition to the full time faculty, the program features visiting writers of national and international prominence, poetry and fiction readings, and summer creative writing workshops. Recent visiting writers include Mary Catherine Bateson, Gwendolyn Brooks, Janet Burroway, Gerald Early, Paul Fussell, Tess Gallagher, Molly Ivins, William Henry Lewis, Barry Lopez, David McCullough, Walter McDonald, Terrence McNally, Grace Paley, Richard Rhodes, William Jay Smith, Miller Williams, and Al Young.

Graduate students are encouraged to work and contribute to *Number One*, the student edited creative writing journal. *New Letters*, the nationally known magazine, also invites assistance in reading manuscripts, provides internships, and will consider contributions from students. BkMk Press, also at UMKC, has published collections of poems by former students in the program.

Graduate teaching assistantships in freshman composition and literature are available as are Work Study funds. Several scholarships are available for creative writing students of talent and promise.

For more information, contact James McKinley, Director of Professional Writing Program, or Ralph Berets, Chairman, Dept. of English, University of Missouri-Kansas City.

University of Missouri, St. Louis
8001 Natural Bridge Road
St. Louis, MO 63121
(314) 516-6845
FAX (314) 516-5781
e-mail: marytroy@umsl.edu
website:
www.umsl.edu/divisions/artscience/english/mfa.htm

Degree offered: MFA in Creative Writing (poetry, fiction)

Type of Program: Studio/Academic

Length of Residency: Final two-thirds of course work

Required course of study: 39 s/hrs total
  Writing workshop: 15 s/hrs
  Literature/Composition Theory/Journal Editing/
    Linguistics: 15 s/hrs
  Elective: 3 s/hrs

Final Writing Project: 6 s/hrs

Application Deadline: March 1.

We are committed to helping writers develop their talents by providing commentary on their writing through workshops, conferences, and final writing tutorials, and by creating a lively community of writers inside a larger lively community of writers -- the St. Louis area. The size of our program -- 30 students total -- ensures close contact between students and faculty and fosters a strong sense of each writer's identity. We offer a flexible plan of study culminating in a final writing project aimed at a book-length manuscript of fiction or poetry.

Visiting writers in recent years have included Opal Palmer Adisa, Sandra Benitez, Richard Burgin, T.M. McNally, Speer Morgan, Tim O'Brien, Ann Patchett, Jewell Parker Rhodes, Marilynne Robinson, Steve Yarbrough, Sharon Dubiago, Allison Funk, Albert Goldbarth, Pamela White-Hadas, Bob Hicok, Maurice Kenny, David Meltzer, and Eric Pankey.

In addition to the regular faculty, we feature a distinguished visiting writer, who ordinarily serves on the faculty for one semester each year, teaching workshops in either fiction or poetry and conferring with students. The visiting writer for 1998-1999 is Donald Finkel.

We publish a new, nationally distributed literary magazine, *Natural Bridge*, containing fiction, poetry, and essays. Every fall and winter term, MFA students taking the graduate course Literary Journal Editing are the first readers of all work submitted to the magazine, and they are actively involved in its editing and production.

The creative writing faculty includes: novelist, short story writer, and nonfiction writer David Carkeet (*Double Negative, The Greatest Slump of All Time, I Been There Before*); poet Steven Schreiner (*Too Soon To Leave*); poet and fiction writer Howard Schwartz (*Vessels, Gathering The Sparks, Sleepwalking Beneath the Stars*); fiction writer Mary Troy (*Joe Baker Is Dead*); and fiction and nonfiction writer Charles Wartts (works published in *River Styx, Conjunctions, Drum Voices Review*, and more).

For more information, contact Mary Troy, Director, MFA Program, at above address.

❖University of Montana
Missoula, MT 59812-1013
(406) 243-5231 or 243-2029
e-mail: kgadbow@selway.umt.edu
website: http://www.umt.edu/

Degrees offered: BA, MFA

Degree: BA in English with Creative Writing Emphasis

For the BA, students need a total of 120 semester credits. To fulfill General Education requirements, all students must successfully complete courses in 6 perspectives: Expressive Arts, Literary and Artistic Studies, Historical and Cultural, Social Sciences, Ethical and Human Values, and Natural Sciences.

The BA in English requires 42-60 credits, including Contemporary Imagination, 2 British or American survey courses, and 2 upper division courses. In addition to fulfilling these requirements for the BA in English, a creative writing student must complete one lower division poetry course, Shakespeare, one course in literary theory, two years of upper-division creative writing courses, and two years of a foreign language.

Degree: MFA in Creative Writing

Type of Program: Studio/Academic

Length of Residency: Two years

Required course of study: 45 semester credits
Thesis: up to 12 credits
Writing workshop: 12 credits, one per semester
Technique courses: 3 credits
Literature courses: 12 credits, 3 of which
  must be a literature seminar; may also
  include independent study, special topics
  courses, or Techniques of Modern Fiction

Application Deadline: February 1.

"A creative writing class may be one of the last places where you can go where your life still matters," said Richard Hugo, UM poet from 1965-82, one of many powerful influences in a writing program whose long history, including Walter Van Tilburg Clark and Leslie Fiedler, began formally in 1966 with the establishment of the MFA degree. The Writing Program is committed to the integration of academic literature and creative writing courses. As such, it is particularly suited to preparing writers who can teach a variety of courses at the college level. Former students have published widely and successfully; many teach or work in publishing across the country.

Providing students a milieu in which to develop and practice their skills as serious writers, the program offers courses in the writing of poetry, fiction, and drama. A creative nonfiction emphasis was expanded in 1992-93. Students in the program edit and publish *Cutbank*, a noted periodical featuring poetry and fiction by students and nationally known writers.

To complete their degrees, candidates in the MFA program at the University of Montana are required to complete a professional paper (thesis) acceptable to their MFA committee and to the Graduate School: at least 40 pages of poems, 80 pages of fiction or drama, or some approved combination of these. A public presentation of selected portions of the professional paper must be made.

Writing Program faculty includes: fiction writer Kevin Canty (*A Stranger in This World, Into the Great Wide Open, Nine Below Zero*--forthcoming); fiction and nonfiction writer Deirdre McNamer (*Rima in the Weeds, One Sweet Quarrel, My Russian*--forthcoming); fiction writer Debra Earling (stories in *The Last Best Place* and *Talking Leaves: Contemporary Native American Short Stories*); poet Patricia Goedicke (*The Tongues We Speak, The Wind of Our Going, Invisible Horses*); poet Greg Pape (*Sunflower Facing the Sun, Black Branches, Little America*).

Each spring quarter the Writing Program brings in a Richard Hugo Writer-in-Residence. These have included Joy Harjo, Albert Goldbarth, Pattiann Rogers, Cyra McFadden, Kent Nelson, Robert Wrigley, James

Galvin, Beverly Lowry, Dara Weir, Patricia Traxler, Jack Gilbert, and Annah Sobelman.

On occasion, professional writers from Missoula and nearby towns teach a variety of writing courses, varying from genre fiction to professional essay. To date, these have included James Crumley, Leonard Robinson, David Long, Neil McMahon, Steve Krauzer, Ralph Beer, Marnie Prange, Lowell Jaeger, Fred Haefele, Bill Vaughn, and Robert Simms Reid.

The regular student-run feature of the program is the Second Wind Reading Series which features both students and writers from the local area.

The Creative Writing Program frequently sponsors readings, workshops, and residencies by visiting writers, agents and editors. Visitors in recent years include Jorie Graham, James Tate, Robert Hass, Derek Walcott, Richard Ford, James Welch, Rick DeMarinis, Elaine Markson, Yusef Komunyakaa, Denis Johnson, Marie Howe, Ian Frazer, Kate Braverman, Lucy Grealy, Chris Offutt, Heather McHugh, and Mark Levine.

Hellgate Writers, a non-profit regional center for literary arts and artists, is an incorporated organization based in Missoula which cooperates with the department's writing program to sponsor literary programs for the community.

The Department offers several teaching assistantships for MFA students. At present, these pay about $7,900 a year with a tuition waiver and may be renewed for a second year, if the student's teaching and academic performance are satisfactory. (The degree can usually be completed in 2 years.) Teaching assistants usually have the equivalent of an undergraduate degree in English, a 3.0 GPA or above. Applicants interested in a TA should submit an expository writing sample along with their other material.

Outstanding students in fiction may be nominated at the end of their first year by faculty for Fiction and Poetry Fellowships. These fellows teach one section of Introduction to Fiction or Introduction to Poetry Writing.

For more information, contact Kate Gadbow, Director of Creative Writing, Dept. of English.

❖Moorhead State University
Moorhead, MN 56563
(218) 236-2235
FAX (218) 236-2236
e-mail: enger@mhd1.moorhead.msus.edu

Degree offered: MFA in Creative Writing

Type of Program: Studio/Academic

Length of Residency: Two and one-half years

Required course of study: 42 s/hrs

Application Deadline: April 1 for fall semester and November 1 for spring semester.

The Master of Fine Arts in Creative Writing is a degree for students who wish to improve their creative writing abilities on the graduate level. The program is designed to be completed on either a full-time or part-time basis, in two and a half to seven years. The MFA is a terminal degree, consisting of a minimum of 42 semester credits; most of a student's work will be in writing workshops, in tutorials, and in thesis preparation.

Admission Requirements:

1. University-wide admission requirements: Baccalaureate degree from an accredited institution and GPA of 2.75 on a 4.0 scale, or at least 3.25 for the last 30 credits of graded course work.

2. Submission of a representative manuscript sample of creative work: 20-25 pages of original writing in fiction, 10-20 pages of poetry, or a similar amount of material in the student's preferred genre.

3. Submission of three letters of reference from those who can speak to the student's potential and/or experience as a creative writer.

The MFA Program Coordinator, in consultation with members of the MFA staff, will evaluate the applicant's transcript, prescribing additional undergraduate credits for those who have inadequate background in English and American literature and creative writing. Exceptions may be made for outstanding students who have majored in related fields. Gifted writers may study in the program as special students with no specific degree intentions. Applicants who earned their undergraduate degrees more than 10 years before the time of application must be interviewed by the MFA Program Coordinator or his/her designee before admission. The Graduate Record Examination is not required for admission.

All application materials should be clearly labeled for the MFA in Creative Writing and submitted directly to the Graduate Admissions Office, Moorhead State University. Students will be forwarded a copy of the MSU Graduate Bulletin and a checklist for admission. Applications will also require a $15 application fee, as well as official transcripts from all institutions previously attended.

Degree Requirements:

1. A minimum of 42 semester credits.

2. At least half of the total 42 semester credits required for the degree must be taken at Moorhead State University. Transferred credit must have received a grade of either A or B, and must have been completed within seven years previous to admission.

3. 3.0 grade point average.

4. Thesis.

5. Oral discourse presented to the student's thesis committee following completion of the thesis and based on the thesis and on the student's program, and a public reading by the student from his or her thesis work.

Degree Program

Students are expected to emphasize a single genre (fiction, poetry, film, playwriting, or creative nonfiction) but they are required to take at least one workshop in a second genre. In addition to workshops offered by full-time faculty, students will also be eligible for intensive workshops occasionally taught by visiting writers. The final requirement is a thesis-length manuscript of work (usually in one genre) that has been approved by the thesis director and a thesis committee.

Course Requirements

1. *Required Courses:*

A. A minimum of three credits per year in MFA 688, graduate-level workshop, to a minimum of 15 semester credits and a maximum of 18 semester credits total.
B. A minimum of five credits in MFA 677: Tutorial: The consideration of various problems in literature or language agreed upon by the instructor and the student.
C. Four credits of MFA 699: Thesis.

2. *Elective Courses:* All candidates must successfully complete a minimum fifteen credits of electives from selected English courses taken for graduate credit, Master of Liberal Arts (MLA) courses (to be chosen in consultation with the candidate's advisor), or other graduate courses taken with permission of the MFA Program Coordinator and the candidate's advisor. Elective courses may be taken to strengthen areas of weakness; to pursue historical, theoretical, or technical studies that the candidates find useful; or to enrich their degree programs appropriately within an area of specialization. Courses taken for graduate credit in comparative literature, literature in translation, foreign language, or an applied course in another art or discipline may be taken with permission. For candidates who wish to strengthen a professional expertise, internship credit (MFA 669: Internship -- Writing, 1-6 credits) may be substituted for part of the above elective credits, if approved by the Program Coordinator and the student's advisor.

Thesis

The candidate will submit a body of original work of publishable quality. The finished manuscript must be of a length as appropriate to published books in its genre and is to be written under the direction of members of the program staff. Candidates must preface their thesis with a critical introduction which discusses influences, process, and/or issues related to the structure and content of the thesis, as well as a comprehensive bibliography completed in consultation with the thesis director and committee. Thesis credits will normally be taken at the end of a candidate's program.

For more information, contact: Lin Enger, MFA Program Coordinator, Dept. of English.

❖Morehead State University
Morehead, KY 40351-1689
(606) 783-2185
e-mail: l.taetzsch@morehead-st.edu

Degrees offered: BA, MA

Degree: BA with Minor in Creative Writing (poetry, fiction, creative nonfiction)

Required course of study: 128 s/hrs total
Writing workshops: 12 s/hrs

Literature courses: 3 s/hrs
Literature, linguistics, or foreign language electives: 6 s/hrs

Application Deadlines: Priority deadline for financial aid, February 1; for admission, August 1.

Degree: MA in English with Creative Writing Emphasis (poetry, fiction, creative nonfiction)

Type of Program: Studio/Academic

Length of Residency: Two years

Required course of study: 33 s/hrs (at least 27 s/hrs in English)
Thesis option: may substitute for 6 s/hrs
Bibliography: 3 s/hrs

Other Requirements: MA in English exam; reading knowledge of a foreign language.

Application Deadlines: Priority deadline for financial aid, February 1; for graduate assistantships, April 15; for admission, August 1.

Within the graduate program in English at Morehead State University, students have the option of taking advanced creative writing classes as electives and substituting a creative thesis for graduate electives. The program averages 3-4 graduates with this option per year.

Inscape, Morehead State University's literary and arts journal, provides opportunities for graduate students to learn the process of editing and producing a magazine.

The creative writing faculty sponsors ongoing activities to foster a supportive community, including open-mike readings, invitational readings, public radio forums on writing, a visiting writers program, and advanced writing groups. Since 1990 visiting writers have included Chris Holbrook, Jeff Worley, Patricia Foster, Yusef Komunyakaa, Richard Tillinghast, Arthur Smith, Kim Edwards, and Mary Ann Taylor-Hall.

Graduate creative writing faculty includes Christ Offutt (*The Same River Twice, Kentucky Straight, The Good Brother*), George Eklund (*The Sorrow of the King,* Al Smith Poetry Fellowship), and Lynne Taetzsch (Editor, *Hot Flashes: Women Writers on the Change of Life*).

For more information, contact George Eklund, Lynne Taetzsch, or Chris Offutt at the above address.

Morningside College
Sioux City, IA 51106-1751
(712) 274-5126

Degree offered: BA or BS in English (Writing and Language)

Required course of study: 124 s/hrs total
Writing workshops: at least 6 s/hrs
English Department offerings: 30 or more s/hrs

Other Requirements: General studies requirement for 44 hours, a minor for at least 20 hours, electives.

Application Deadlines: March 1 for first priority consideration for need–based financial aid.

Students solicit, select, and edit works for *The Kiosk*, the campus literary magazine. Occasional readings are sponsored by Sigma Tau Delta, the English honorary society.

For further information, contact the Chair of the English Dept.

❖Murray State University
1 Murray Street
Murray, KY 42071-3311
(502) 762-2401
FAX (502) 762-4545

Degrees offered: BA, MA

Degree: BA in English with Emphasis in Creative Writing

Required course of study: 33 s/hrs in the major
Thesis: no requirement
Writing workshop: 12 s/hrs
Other writing courses: 3 s/hrs
Literature courses: 15 s/hrs
Tutorials or directed reading: 3 s/hrs

Degree: MA in English with Emphasis in Creative Writing (poetry, fiction)

Type of Program: Studio/Academic

Length of Residency: Two years

Required course of study: 30 s/hrs in the major
Thesis: required
Writing workshop: 12–15 s/hrs
Literature courses: 15 s/hrs

The Creative Writing Program at Murray State University, under the auspices of the English Department, offers a Bachelor of Arts in English with Emphasis in Creative Writing as well as a Master of Arts in English with Emphasis in Creative Writing. Undergraduates may elect Creative Writing as a minor. They may also fulfill both major and minor requirements by electing an area in Creative Writing. Workshops are conducted in poetry and fiction. All workshops are open to non–degree–seeking students.

Graduate and undergraduate students form a single community of writers. Undergraduates are required to enroll in ENG 340: An Introduction to Creative Writing. Upper–level workshops include both graduate and undergraduate students. All students have the opportunity to work together on *Notations*, M.S.U.'s literary magazine, which publishes poetry, short fiction and essays. All students are also invited to help coordinate M.S.U.'s reading series and the annual Jesse Stuart Writing Symposium through the English Students' Organization (E.S.O.). Recent visiting writers have included Mark Levine, Anne Patchett, George Cuomo, Andrew Hudgins, Kae Cheatham, Larry Brown, X.J. Kennedy, Bobbie Ann Mason, Jean Craighead George, Chris Gilbert, Scott Russell Sanders, Yusef Komunyakaa, Catherine Sasanov, A. Manette Ansay, James Tate, Sena Naslund, and James Still.

Each year the Department of English administers several undergraduate literary prizes, including the Margaret Trevathan Creative Writing and Arts Education Scholarship and the Deb and Edith Wylder Creative Writing Award. Graduate students in writing are eligible to apply for a major fellowship named after Kentucky writer Jesse Stuart, whose papers are displayed on campus in the Pogue Library. Graduate students may also be eligible for teaching assistantships in composition.

Writing faculty are Squire Babcock (fiction) and Ann Neelon (poetry).

For more information, contact Squire Babcock, Director, c/o Dept. of English.

Napa Valley College
2277 Napa – Vallejo Highway
Napa, CA 94558

Contact the Creative Writing Program Director, Dept. of English.

The Naropa Institute
Boulder, CO 80302
(303) 444-0202
FAX (303) 444-0410

Degrees offered: BA, MFA

Degree: MFA

Type of Program: Studio/Academic

Required course of study: 48 hours
Thesis: 6 hours
Writing workshop: 17 hours
Other writing courses: 6 hours
Literature courses and seminars: 17 hours
Electives: 6 hours

The Master of Fine Arts in Writing and Poetics is a 48 credit terminal degree program for serious students of creative writing who wish to pursue their own practice, prepare a manuscript of professional quality, and develop skills for teaching writing and poetics to others.

The program begins with Ezra Pound's premise that one should not take criticism from anyone who has not himself or herself written a notable work of literature. The Writing Programs at The Naropa Institute, since their inception, have attracted poets and writers of the highest caliber, interested in working with younger writers through scholarship, discipline, and one-to-one critical feedback on creative work. The emphasis is on frankness and intelligent exploration between students and faculty.

Founded originally as The Jack Kerouac School of Disembodied Poetics by Allen Ginsberg and Anne Waldman in 1974, the writing and poetics program's inspiration has been to investigate the creative process involved when words and language directly and accurately express original perception. The willingness to drop preconception and write from an open state, in combination with a formal appreciation for nuance, sound, and meaning as expressed in classical and modern texts, provides the basis of the graduate student's literary training at the Institute. The program also places an emphasis on clear and attentive oral presentation of works, since it is as speech that words proclaim themselves most fully. Therefore, performance -- whether it be reading one's work, or working with dance, music, and theatre -- is a vital aspect of the program.

During the annual summer writing Programs, the academic semesters, and the guest residencies, students will study with some of the foremost contemporary poets and writers of our time. Students culminate their studies with a completed manuscript. Periodic special tracks will be introduced in the fields of translation, creative nonfiction, hermeutics, mythopoetics, and ethnopoetics, depending upon the scholarship of available faculty.

Adjunct and Visiting Faculty include Jack Collom, Diane DiPrima, Lucia Berlin, Rikki DuCornet, Ed Sanders, Robert Creeley, Amiri Baraka, Joanne Kyger, Michael Ondaatje, Hubert Selby, Jr., Eileen Myles, Jerome Rothenberg, Julie Patton, Gloria Frym, Lyn Hejinian, Clayton Eshleman, and others.

The Core Faculty includes Anne Waldman (Founder-Director), author of 20 books of poetry including *Iovis* and *Helping the Dreamer: New and Selected Poems 1966-1988*. She has edited several anthologies, and is an internationally renowned performing artist. Andrew Schelling (recent books include *Old Growth: Selected Poems & Notebooks, 1986-1994*) poet, essayist, and translator. His 1992 book *Dropping the Bow: Poems of Ancient India* won the Academy of American Poets translation prize. Bobbie Louise Hawkins, whose fiction includes *One Small Saga, Almost Everything*, and most recently, *My Own Alphabet*. Jack Collom, who was awarded an NEA Fellowship in 1980, and whose work is published in magazines and anthologies here and abroad. Anselm Hollo, whose works include *Corvus, Heavy Jars*, and *Pick up the House: New and Selected Poems*. Keith Abbott, whose fiction includes *First Thing Coming, Harum Scarum*, and *Downstream from Trout Fishing in America: A Memoir of Richard Brautigan*.

For further information, contact Admissions Director, The Naropa Institute.

❖Nassau Community College
Bradley Hall
One Education Drive
Garden City, NY 11530-6793

For more information, contact David Rosner, Director, English Dept.

❖National University
4025 Camino Del Rio South
San Diego, CA 92108-4194

Contact the Creative Writing Program Director, Dept. of English.

❖University of Nebraska at Kearney
Thomas Hall, Room 202
Kearney, NE 68849-1320

For more information, contact the Director, Dept. of English.

❖University of Nebraska, Lincoln
202 Andrews Hall
Lincoln, NE 68588-0333
(402) 472-3191
FAX (402) 472-9771

Degrees offered: BA, MA, PhD in English

Degree: MA in English with Concentration in Creative Writing (poetry, fiction)

Type of Program: Studio/Academic

Length of Residency: One year plus summer

Required course of study: 30 s/hrs total
  Thesis: 6 s/hrs
  Literature & creative writing courses: 24 s/hrs

Other Requirements: Written comprehensive examinations in two areas; distribution requirements in British and American literature.

Application Deadlines: January 15 for financial aid and admission; October 15 for admission.

Degree: PhD in English with Concentration in Creative Writing (poetry, fiction)

Type of Program: Studio/Academic

Length of Residency: Four to five years

Required course of study: 90 s/hrs beyond bachelor's degree
  Dissertation: 24-30 s/hrs
  Creative writing courses: 9-12 s/hrs
  Literature courses: 15-18 hours beyond
    master's degree

Other Requirements: Examination portfolio; written comprehensive examination in two areas; distribution and concentration requirements; residency requirement; language requirement.

Application Deadlines: January 15 for financial aid and admission.

MA candidates in literature may take an area of concentration in creative writing, and may submit a portfolio of fiction or poetry for the thesis. Candidates for the PhD in English with a concentration in creative writing must complete a dissertation in the form of a collection of poems, a novel, or a group of short stories. The examination portfolio consists of creative work normally unrelated to the dissertation which is evaluated as comprehensive examinations are graded. Graduate course offerings include seminars in the technique of poetry and fiction, as well as workshops in both genres.

The Department of English offers a number of teaching assistantships to PhD applicants. The stipend for beginning teaching assistants is at least $9,100, plus 10 hours of tuition remission each semester and summer. Senior assistants in creative writing usually have opportunities to teach introductory courses in creative writing. Recipients of teaching assistantships normally hold teaching appointments as instructors after 3 or 4 years as teaching assistants. MA applicants may apply for reading assistantships. The current stipend is $5,950 for 9 months plus 12 hours of tuition remission each semester and summer.

The English Department houses the editorial offices of *Prairie Schooner*, a nationally known literary magazine which has been in existence for over 60 years. One or two reading assistantships associated with the *Prairie Schooner* are available each year.

The Visiting Speakers Program sponsors readings and lectures each semester by nationally known creative writers. Recent visitors have included Lee Gutkind, Richard Russo, Hayden Carruth, Chrystos, Jacqueline Osherow, Joy Harjo, June Jordan, N. Scott Momaday, Tillie Olson, Reynolds Price, Stanley Plumly, and Eleanor Wilner.

Faculty: Poets: Greg Kuzma, author of *Good News, Of China and Of Greece*, and *Village Journal*; Hilda Raz, editor of *Prairie Schooner* and author of *The Bone Dish*, *What Is Good*, and *Divine Honors*; and Grace Bauer, author of *The House Where I've Never Lived, Where You've Seen Her*, and *Women at the Well*. Fiction writers: Gerald Shapiro, author of *From Hunger* (stories) and a forthcoming new collection from Zoland Press; Judith Slater, author of *The Ouija Board Murders*, *Single Lives*, and *The Baby Can Sing*; and Marly Swick, author of *A Hole in the Language* (winner of the Iowa Short Fiction Contest), *The Summer Before the Summer of Love* (stories), and *Evening News* (novel).

For additional information on the MA and PhD requirements, contact Chair, Graduate Studies, Dept. of English.

❖University of Nebraska at Omaha
Omaha, NE 68182-0324
(402) 554-4801
FAX (402) 554-3436

Degree offered: BFA in Creative Writing

Required course of study:
    71 s/hrs in major coursework
    Thesis option: 6 s/hrs
    Writing workshops: 26-38 s/hrs
    Other writing courses: up to 24 s/hrs
    Literature and theory courses: 45 s/hrs

Other Requirements: 1 year of foreign language at a post-secondary level; 15 s/hrs social science and humanities; 12 s/hrs fine arts, 11 s/hrs natural sciences and math.

The Writer's Workshop is both an academic program in the University's College of Fine Arts and a community of writers dedicated to improving their craft. In its dual role, the Workshop offers intense coursework in fiction and poetry; frequent readings by visiting writers, resident faculty, and students; and a first rate literary journal of poetry and fiction contributed by writers throughout the country.

The academic program is a 130 s/hr plan of undergraduate study leading to a Bachelor of Fine Arts degree in creative writing. At the heart of the curriculum are the studio courses in fiction and poetry, where student work is critiqued by peers under the direction of the faculty. Visiting writers regularly conduct these studio sessions as well. In addition to four semesters of studio courses in each genre, writing majors take 45 s/hrs of literature and theory courses to ground themselves in the history and development of their craft.

As a department of the UNO College of Fine Arts, the Writer's Workshop is part of a larger and active artistic community which includes the visual arts, theater, music, and the fine-art press. Writing students often participate in arts activities and courses which support their interest in literature and expand their knowledge and appreciation for other art forms. Playwriting, screenwriting, fine book design, and press work are a few of the related pursuits available to the apprentice writer.

Inquiries may be directed to Art Homer (poetry) or Richard Duggin (fiction) through the Writer's Workshop, FA 315. Information on admission to the university, financial aid, and the university catalog may be obtained from the Office of Admissions, Eppley Administration Building 101.

❖University of Nevada, Reno
Dept. of English/098
College of Arts and Sciences
Reno, NV 89557-0031
(702) 784-6755
FAX (702) 784-6266
e-mail: palwick@unr.edu
website: http://www.unr.edu/unr/colleges/arts-n-science/engl/

Degrees offered: BA, MA

Degree: BA in English, Writing Option (poetry, fiction, nonfiction)

Required course of study: 128 s/hrs total
    Literature courses: 12 or more s/hrs
    Writing workshops: up to 24 s/hrs

Other requirements: University and college distribution requirements.

Application Deadlines: February 1 for financial aid; March 1 for admissions.

The undergraduate concentration requires the student to take Introduction to Creative Writing and then to pursue advanced study of at least two genres; writing majors must also take introductory courses in literary theory and interpretation. The Department holds writing contests each spring and sponsors a literary magazine, *The Sagebrush*.

Degree: MA in English with a Writing Emphasis (poetry, fiction, nonfiction)

Type of Program: Studio/Academic

Length of Residency: One year

Required course of study: Thesis option (Plan A) 30 s/hrs; non-thesis option (Plan B) 32 s/hrs, of which 6 are thesis hours. A minimum of 18 s/hrs (Plan A) or 15 s/hrs (Plan B), must be taken in graduate composition and language seminars.

Other requirements: Portfolio, written and oral comprehensive examination, and either a thesis (Plan A) or a final oral examination (Plan B).

Application Deadlines: February 1 for financial aid; March 1 for admissions.

The MA Writing emphasis is designed for students who wish to strengthen their skills as writers while deepening their understanding of literature and language. It is intended for people who are preparing for careers in writing and editing or planning to teach writing in schools or colleges. The program is centered on the craft of writing, as experienced by professionals and by the students themselves, and offers elective courses in both imaginative and expository writing. All students in the program are active in professional activities; publishing, participating in conferences, and serving as writing interns in businesses, community agencies, or educational institutions. As the home of the Center for the Environmental Arts and Humanities, we offer particularly strong nonfiction options in environmental writing.

The writing faculty includes fiction writers Susan Palwick (*Flying in Place*), Richard Brown (*Fishing for Ghosts, Chester's Last Stand*) and Stephen Tchudi (*The Valedictorian, The Burg-O-Rama Man*); poets Gailmarie Pahmeier (*The House on Breakaheart Road*) and William Wilborn (*Rooms, Briefs*); and nonfiction writers Scott Slovic (*Seeking Awareness in American Nature Writing*, editor of *Literature and the Environment* and *Being in the World*) and Ann Ronald (*Earth Tones: A Nevada Album*).

For more information, contact Susan Palwick at the above address.

University of New Brunswick
P.O. Box 4400
Fredericton, New Brunswick
Canada E3B 5A3
(506) 453-4676
FAX (506) 453-5069

Degree offered: MA in English with a Concentration in Creative Writing (poetry, drama, fiction, nonfiction)

Type of Program: Traditional Literary Study and Creative Writing

Length of Residency: Funded students are supported for up to twenty months

Required course of study:
18 credit hours over two terms
Writing workshops: 6 credit hours
Literature courses: 12 credit hours

Other Requirements: A creative thesis in lieu of the MA thesis.

Application Deadlines: February 1 for financial aid; otherwise no deadline. A sample of creative work (20 pages maximum) must accompany the application.

The University of New Brunswick offers a graduate Creative Writing Program within the regular MA program in English. Students who qualify for this program take two one-term courses in poetry, fiction, or drama, and present a substantial manuscript in lieu of the MA thesis.

The University of New Brunswick has a long tradition of Creative Writing, dating back to the times of Bliss Carman and Sir Charles G.D. Roberts. *The Fiddlehead*, Canada's oldest functioning literary magazine, is published on the campus. Classes are run on the workshop model. Faculty include fiction writer and poet William Bauer (*A Family Album, Unsnarling String, The Terrible Word*); fiction writer Kent Thompson (*Playing in the Dark, Married Love, Leaping Up/Sliding Away*); fiction writer Peter Thomas (*The Welsher*); poet Ted Colson; and poet Don McKay (*Birding, or Desire, Sanding Down This Rocking Chair on a Windy Night, Night Field*). Professors Emeriti include Fred Cogswell, the influential editor, publisher, critic, and poet, and Robert Gibbs, the noted editor, poet, and writer of fiction.

Students who qualify for the MA in English with Creative Writing are eligible for financial assistance. Students who do not wish to pursue the degree may be admitted to Creative Writing courses at the discretion of the instructor.

For further information, contact Don McKay, Director of Creative Writing, Dept. of English.

❖New College of California
766 Valencia Street
San Francisco, CA 94110
(415) 437-3401
FAX (415) 437-3417
website: www.newcollege.edu/poetics/

Degrees offered: BA, MA, MFA

Degree: BA in Humanities with an Emphasis in Poetics

Required course of study: 120 s/hrs total
Humanities Core Courses (depending on transfer units): 3-21 s/hrs
Humanities Breadth Requirements: 24 s/hrs
Other Undergraduate Coursework: 27-63 s/hrs
Literature Breadth Requirement (fiction or drama): 6 s/hrs
Poetics courses: 24-36 s/hrs
Senior Project: 3 s/hrs

Application Deadlines: June 1 for Fall semester; November 15 for Spring semester. (Note: Priority financial aid deadline March 1 for entire year.)

Undergraduates are admitted to Poetics courses (see description of MA program below) by permission of instructor: normal prerequisite is 9 s/hrs upper-division literature credit. Students may offer a poetry manuscript or other poetic work as a Senior Project. Undergraduates admitted to MA or MFA programs may apply 12 s/hrs Poetics credit toward these degrees.

Degree: MA in Poetics

Required course of study: 36 s/hrs total
  Core courses: 15 s/hrs
  Additional Reading Courses: 6-15 s/hrs
  Writing or Interdisciplinary Study: 0-9 s/hrs
  Internship/Practicum: 0-6 s/hrs
  Thesis Project: 6 s/hrs

Type of Program: (Non) Traditional Literary Study with electives in creative writing, publishing, and cross-disciplinary work

Application Deadlines: June 15 for Fall semester; December 1 for Spring semester. (Note: Priority financial aid deadline March 1 for entire year.)

Degree: MFA in Poetics & Writing

Required course of study: 54 s/hrs total
  Core courses: 18 s/hrs
  Additional Reading Courses: 6 s/hrs
  Writing (workshops, technique courses): 12-21 s/hrs
  Internship/Practicum: 3-6 s/hrs
  Interdisciplinary Study: 0-9 s/hrs
  Thesis Project: 6 s/hrs

Type of Program: Studio/Academic; (Non) traditional creative writing/ performance/publishing combined with literary study and interdisciplinary work.

Application Deadlines: June 1 for Fall semester; December 1 for Spring semester. (Note: Priority financial aid deadline March 1 for entire year.)

Neither a traditional English Literature graduate program nor a Creative Writing MFA program, the New College Poetics Program combines aspects of both with features all its own. The program is dedicated to the critical study and creative practice of poetry (including poetic prose), taught by practicing poets. For all three degree tracks, the core curriculum provides a common frame of reference by treating four vital periods in poetry: the Elizabethan-early Stuart period, the Romantic epoch, the American mid-19th-century, and the era of high modernism between 1900 and 1950. Electives and independent study open up other avenues of investigation.

From close reading in historical context, critical essays, mimetic exercises in the strategies and forms of great poetry, and work with student writing, the program aims to push outward against established limits and definitions. One way boundaries are crossed is in the program's approach to curriculum: writing and technique courses involve analytical and theoretical reading, while reading courses often allow for imaginative as well as critical response. Another direction of outward thrust is beyond reading and writing themselves. The program offers instruction in reading/performance, printing, and desktop publishing. In addition, qualified graduate students may enroll in courses in Performance, Video, and Visual Arts offered by the Interdisciplinary Arts MA Program. Students are encouraged to develop practica that bring poetry to the wider world: teaching in the undergraduate program or in schools or community settings, working for literary organizations.

Besides a general education in poetry and poetics, the program aims to provide student poets with the means to develop not only their own "voice" (or voices) but *their own aesthetics and politics in poetry*. In keeping with this emphasis, the MA Thesis Project is an extensive critical paper, in some cases combined with a poetry manuscript; and the MFA Thesis Project, normally a book-length collection of poetry, must include an essay on the student's own poetics.

Since its founding in 1981, the program has become a fluid yet intimate community of writers and thinkers, which continually generates new ventures -- magazines, chapbooks, informal workshops, readings, and discussion groups. In addition, students can investigate more widely in the San Francisco area, a national center for poetry.

Core Faculty: Tom Clark (*Sleepwalker's Fate*, poetry collection; *The Poetry Beat*, collected essays). Adam Cornford, Chair ("The Snarling Gift," in *Terminal Velocities*, long poem; *Animations*, poetry collection). Gloria Frym (*How I Learned*, short story collection, *By Ear*, poetry collection). Lyn Hejinian (*The Cell* and *Oxota*, sequences of poems). David Meltzer (*Reading Jazz* critical anthology; *Arrows: Selected Poems 1982-92*).

For more information, contact Adam Cornford, Poetics Dept.

❖New Hampshire Institute of Art
148 Concord Street
Manchester, NH 03104-4826

For more information, contact Linda Butler at the above address, or by phone at (603) 623-0313.

❖University of New Hampshire
Durham, NH 03824

(603) 862-1313

Degree offered: MA in English with Option in Writing (poetry, fiction, nonfiction)

Type of Program: Studio/Academic

The University of New Hampshire Department of English offers a Master of Arts in Writing program for talented students who write fiction, nonfiction, or poetry.

The program is staffed by 7 distinguished writers. The staff is large, but because each member emphasizes conference teaching, only 25 to 35 graduate students can by accommodated. That number, spread among the 3 genres, provides the sort of student-to-teacher ratio the staff wishes to maintain. In addition to having individual conferences with the writing instructors, each student will take at least 2 workshop courses in his or her own genre. Such workshops provide a forum for close and detailed criticism of the manuscripts by faculty and graduate student colleagues. Students may take an additional workshop in another genre. Form-and-theory courses and literature courses complete the program.

When all course requirements have been satisfied, the student submits a portfolio of writing. The portfolio might consist of short stories, a novel, nonfiction articles, a nonfiction book, or a collection of poetry. The degree is awarded upon the approval of the portfolio by 3 writers on the staff.

The faculty includes: Fiction: John Yount, whose novels include *Hardcastle, The Trapper's Last Shot,* and *Thief of Dreams.* Mark Smith's novels include *Doctor Blues, The Delphinium Girl,* and *The Death of the Detective.* Margaret Love Denman's work includes *A Scrambling After Circumstance.* Nonfiction: Andrew Merton is the author of *Enemies of Choice: The Right-to-Life Movement and Its Threat to Abortion.* Jane Harrigan was managing editor of the *Concord (NH) Monitor.* She is the author of *Read All about It,* a day in the life of the *Boston Globe.* Sue Hertz was a reporter with *The Hartford Courant.* Poetry: Charles Simic's books include *Unending Blues, Return to a Place Lit by a Glass of Milk,* and *Classic Ballroom Dances.* He won a MacArthur award in 1984. Mekeel McBride's collections of poetry include: *Wind of the White Dresses, Red Letter Days,* and *The Going Under of the Evening Land.*

For more information, contact Director, Creative Writing Program, Dept. of English.

❖New Mexico State University
Dept. of English Box 30001, Dept. 3E
Las Cruces, NM 88003-0001
(505) 646-3931

Degrees offered: BA, MA

Degree: BA in English with Minor in Writing

Degree: MA in English with Emphasis in Creative Writing

Type of Program: Studio/Academic

Length of Residency: Two years

Required course of study: 36 s/hrs total
Thesis: 6 s/hrs
Writing workshop: 12–15 s/hrs
Literature and electives: 15–18 s/hrs

Other Requirements: Foreign language; comprehensive examination; public reading from thesis.

Application Deadlines: Open (for assistantship consideration, deadline Feb. 1).

Each student in the writing program is required to give a public reading of his/her work. He/she must compile a 40–50 page (minimum) creative thesis with a written preface.

NMSU houses creative writing journals of interest to students: *Puerto del Sol* is a national literary magazine, consistently cited for its high-quality work. Graduate students comprise the fiction and poetry assistant editorship. *La Sociedad Para Las Artes* sponsors a reading series on campus. Recent guests include: Marie Howe, Dean Young, Marcia Southwick, Ron Carlson, Mary Gaitskill, Abraham Verghese, Andrea Barrett, Charles Baxter, Ana Castillo, and Quincy Troupe.

The department awards teaching assistantships to qualified candidates.

Creative Writing faculty: fiction writer and playwright Robert Boswell (*American Owned Love, Mystery Ride*); fiction writer and playwright Denise Chávez (*Face of an Angel, The Last of the Menu Girls*); poet Tony Hoagland (*Donkey Gospel, Sweet Ruin*); fiction writer Kevin McIlvoy (*Hyssop, Little Peg*); fiction writer Antonya Nelson (*Nobody's Girl, Talking in Bed*); and poet Kathleene West (*Landbound, Four Satirical Songs, The Summer of the Sub-Comandante*).

For more information, contact the Staff, Creative Writing Program, Dept. of English.

❖University of New Mexico
Albuquerque, NM 87131
(505) 277-6347
FAX (505) 277-5573
e-mail: english@unm.edu
website: www.unm.edu/~english

Degrees offered: BA, MA

Degree: BA in English, Concentration in Creative Writing (poetry, fiction)

Required course of study: 33 hrs minimum
27 hrs in English and 6 hrs in other creative areas such as film, music, painting, dance, or journalism. Requirements include Analysis of Literature; a literature survey course; 12 hrs of workshop classes on the 200, 300, and 400 level (students must take one course at each level); 6 hrs of literature courses numbered 300 or above; and a creative writing thesis.

The English Department sponsors contests and awards for undergraduate students in creative writing, and the University supports an undergraduate literary magazine, *Conceptions Southwest.*

Degree: BA in English, Concentration in Professional Writing

Required course of study: 34 hrs minimum
Lower-division requirements include Analysis of Literature, Traditional Grammar, Intro to Professional Writing, and expository or technical writing courses. Upper-division requirements include 12 hrs in Advanced Expository Writing, Topics in Professional Writing, and/or a Senior Project, and an Internship.

The Melada Award offers financial aid to an outstanding senior Professional Writing student. Interns work at paid and volunteer positions on and off campus.

For more information, write or call the Academic Advisor, English Dept.

Degree: MA in Writing: Creative and Professional

Type of Program: Studio/Academic

Length of Residency: Two years

Required course of study: 33 hrs minimum
Required core courses include Introduction to the Profession for Writers and Genre Studies (Theory of Fiction, Poetics, Stylistic Analysis of Nonfiction). All MA Writing students should take at least 12 hrs of writing workshops. In addition they must also take 10 hrs in coursework, which includes a 4 hr seminar from at least three of groups A through E: (A: British Literature to 1660; B: British Literature 1660–1900; C: American Literature to 1900; D: Literatures in English

since 1900; E: Literary Criticism and Theory, Language and Rhetoric, Composition Theory). Finally, all MA students in Writing must enroll for 6 hrs of thesis.

Other Requirements: Foreign language proficiency demonstrated by coursework or successful GSFLT score; oral defense of the thesis.

Application Deadlines: Feb. 1 for Fall admission; Nov. 1 for Spring admission. (Applications for Teaching Assistantships are accepted only for the Fall semester and are due Feb. 1.)

The Master's Program in Writing offers students the opportunity to concentrate in professional or creative writing while taking courses from either program. Capitalizing on our department's strengths in both areas, this approach allows students to work closely with faculty members to master various genres, from technical writing to hypertext and from poetry to the novel. Our professional writing courses teach students proficiency in composition, design, and editing of projects, while creative writing workshops provide a supportive environment for developing and revising poems, short stories, works of creative nonfiction and novels. Because our writing faculty overlaps in many areas, our Master's Program in writing allows students to explore their creative and professional sides at the same time.

Creative Writing

Creative Writing students complete a substantial work of fiction, poetry, or creative nonfiction under the guidance of a faculty mentor. The program -- which consists of workshop, literature, and publishing courses -- grounds students in the rich tradition of writing.

Each spring a visiting writer teaches courses for the semester; recent visitors have included Laurie Kutchins, Chris Offutt, Mary Swander, and Pam Houston. The department also sponsors an on-going reading series featuring members of the faculty, graduate students, and local writers, as well as authors such as Michael Ondaatje, Thom Gunn, John Nichols, Ruth Stone, Diane Wakoski, N. Scott Momaday, Michael McClure, Diane Johnson, and Luci Tapahonso.

Our creative writing students also have the opportunity to apply their writing skills within professional settings. Each year a graduate student serves as Editorial Fellow for the *Blue Mesa Review*, a collection of poetry, fiction, and creative nonfiction published by the Creative Writing Program with funding from the College of Arts and Sciences. Beginning in 1999, we will host the D.H. Lawrence Summer Writers' Conference, in association with the D.H. Lawrence Ranch in Taos, New Mexico. Graduate students will be able to attend this annual conference and to apply for a Departmental fellowship to assist with its planning and execution.

Professional Writing

The Professional Writing program focuses on writing used in the workplace, such as grants, proposals, broadcasting, and documentation. Courses cover such topics as scientific communication, visual design, documentaries, publishing, and editing. The program is often thought of as an "MBA for writers," because it prepares people from various fields to become profes-

sionals in publishing-oriented workplaces.

Our graduates have been hired as editors, technical writers, development directors, public relations specialists, communications consultants, website developers, trainers, and multimedia authors. Many of our students are working professional writers who want to diversify or strengthen their writing capabilities.

For students who need to build their writing portfolios, campus-based and off-campus internships are available with major organizations. We regularly have interns working at Los Alamos National Laboratory, Sandia National Laboratories, Honeywell, Intel, and other organizations. Periodicals such as the *Albuquerque Journal* and the *Albuquerque Tribune* have also supported our interns. In some cases, these internships lead to regular employment.

The writing faculty includes Lee Bartlett, Jim Colbert, David Dunaway, David Johnson, Richard Johnson-Sheehan, E.A. Mares, Louis Owens, Charles Paine, Scott P. Sanders, Julie Shigekuni, Marcia Southwick, Patricia C. Smith, and Sharon Oard Warner.

For more information, contact the Academic Advisor, English Dept.

❖**University of New Orleans**
New Orleans, LA 70118
(504) 280-7454
FAX (504) 280-6468

Degrees offered: BA, MA, MFA

Degree: BA in English with Emphasis in Creative Writing or Professional Writing

Required course of study:
36-42 s/hrs in the major
Thesis: none
Writing workshop: 9-12 s/hrs in writing fiction and/or poetry
Other writing courses: 12 s/hrs in Professional Writing
Tutorials or directed reading: 3-6 s/hrs available
Literature courses: 27-30 s/hrs

Other Requirements: Foreign language (equivalent of 15 s/hrs), Science (8 s/hrs), mathematics (6 s/hrs), social sciences (12 s/hrs).

Degree: MA in English with Creative Thesis Option

Type of Program: Traditional Literary Study and Creative Writing

Length of Residency: Two semesters

Required course of study: 30 s/hrs
Thesis: 3 s/hrs
Writing workshop: 6 s/hrs minimum
Literature courses: 15 s/hrs

Degree: MFA (fiction, playwriting, poetry, and screenwriting)

Type of Program: Studio/Academic

Length of Residency: Five semesters

Required course of study: 45 s/hrs
Theory: 3 s/hrs
Nonfiction Writing: 3 s/hrs
Workshop: 15 s/hrs minimum
Literature: 9-18 s/hrs
Thesis: 6 s/hrs

Other Requirements: Written comprehensive examination.

Application Deadlines: February 1.

The undergraduate English Major at the University of New Orleans offers 5 areas of concentration: Literature, Creative Writing, Professional Writing, Linguistics, and Pre-Law. The Creative Writing track includes a series of Workshops in writing fiction or poetry at the beginning and advanced levels. Courses in Playwriting and Screenwriting are available as electives in the Department of Drama and Communications. The Professional Writing track includes course offerings in Advanced Composition, Professional Writing, Professional Editing, Technical Writing, and Advanced Technical Writing; it is designed to prepare the student for a career in technical writing, editing, or feature writing.

UNO is the only university in New Orleans to offer graduate-level training in creative writing. The English Department regularly offers Workshops in Poetry Writing and Fiction Writing for students pursuing both the MA and the MFA. The Department of Drama and Communications regularly offers Workshops in Playwriting and Screenwriting for its MA and MFA students. Together the two departments have formed The Creative Writing Workshop, a graduate curriculum for creative writers leading to the MFA. Graduate work in creative writing at UNO provides students easy access to such national events as the New Orleans Writers' Conference and the Tennessee Williams Literary Festival. In addition, every year contemporary writers are brought to campus to give readings and meet with students; recent visitors have included John Ashbery, Robert Olen Butler, Richard Ford, Edward Hirsch, Josephine Humphreys, Susan Kenney, Denise Levertov, Ismael Reed, Adrienne Rich, William Matthews, Bobbie Ann Mason, and others. Both English and Drama and Communications offer a limited number of Teaching Assistantships to qualified applicants seeking the MA or MFA degrees.

The faculty of the Creative Writing Workshop at UNO includes fiction writer Fredrick Barton (*The El Cholo Feeling Passes, Courting Pandemonium, With Extreme Prejudice*); poet John Gery (*Charlemagne: A Song of Gestures, The Burning of New Orleans, The Enemies of Leisure*); designer Kevin Graves; screenwriter and filmmaker Steve Hank (*The Limner, The Holdup, One to One*); director David Hoover; playwright and director Phillip Karnell (*Every Mother's Son*); poet Richard Katrovas (*Green Dragons, Snug Harbor, The Book of Complaints*); fiction writer James Knudsen (*Playing Favorites, Just Friends*); fiction writer and screenwriter Joanna Leake (*A Few Days at Weasel Creek*); and nonfiction writer Carol Gelderman (*Henry Ford, the Wayward Capitalist; Mary McCarthy, A Life; Louis Auchincloss, A Writer's Life*). Other creative writers at UNO include poets James Hietter, Kay Murphy, and Elizabeth Thomas; and fiction writer Jeanne Cunningham.

For further information, contact Joanna Leake, Director, The Creative Writing Workshop, University of New Orleans, Lakefront, New Orleans, LA 70148.

The New School
66 West 12th Street
New York, NY 10011
(212) 229-5630
FAX (212) 989-3887
website: www.newschool.edu

Degree offered: MFA in Creative Writing with Concentration in Fiction, Nonfiction, Poetry and Writing for Children

Type of Program: Studio/Academic

Length of Residency: Two years

Required course of study: 36 credits
Writing workshops: 12 credits
Literature seminars: 12 credits
Writers life colloquia: 4 credits
Masters Thesis: 4 credits
Literature Project: 4 credits

Application Deadline: January 15 for fall admission, no spring admission.

Tuition for 1998-99 is $6,354 per semester. There is a $100 university services fee charged at registration.

Federal and state grants and loans are available. In addition, The New School Writing Program awards departmental scholarships based on merit and need. A FAFSA (Free Application for Federal Student Aid) Form available from the Admissions Office must be filed to be considered for financial aid.

Faculty includes: Director Robert Polito, Associate Director Jackson Taylor, Hilton Als, Jill Ciment, Jonathan Dee, Cornelius Eady, David Gates, Lucy Grealy, Amy Hempel, A.M. Homes, David Lehman, Pablo Medina, Rick Moody, Geoffrey O'Brien, Francine Prose, Luc Sante, Dani Shapiro, Jason Shinder, Darcey Steinke, Abigail Thomas, David Trinidad, Susan Wheeler, and Stephen Wright.

Visiting Faculty: Ai, Martin Asher, Frank Bidart, Peter Carey, James Ellroy, Margaret Gabel, Glen Hartley, Pearl London, Thomas Mallon, Kate McMullan, Carol Muske, Geoffrey O'Brien, Robert Pinsky, Jon Scieszka, and Ira Silverberg.

Situated in New York's Greenwich Village, The New School has been a vital center for writing and the instruction of writing since 1931 when Gorham Munson, a Manhattan editor and influential partisan of the Alfred Stieglitz circle, introduced his now legendary workshop in creative writing.

Over more than six decades of steady innovation, The New School's writing and literature faculty has included many of this century's most acclaimed poets, novelists, literary critics, and editors.

The MFA degree marks the latest transformation in The New School's commitment to creative writing. All writing workshop and literature seminar instructors in this Graduate Program are themselves published writers and experienced teachers. Both in the classroom and through a program of distinguished visitors, including New York City magazine and book editors, publishers, literary agents, and prominent teachers of writing, The New School Graduate Writing Program aims to animate, expand, and intensify the writer's life.

The MFA Program is a full-time course of study balancing writing workshops with seminars in the reading of literature. The program is designed to be completed in four semesters. During each of their first three terms, students enroll in one writing workshop (4 credits) in their area of concentration and one literature seminar (4 credits) and must participate in the Writer's Life Colloquium (1 credit). During their final term of residence, students continue to participate in the Writer's Life Colloquium, but no longer enroll in writing workshops or literature seminars. Instead, they work closely with one or more New School writer-teacher advisors in independent study learning to the creation of a Writing Thesis (4 credits) and a Literature Project (4 credits) both within their area of concentration.

The program is enriched by over 30 readings each semester, recent authors include: Dorothy Allison, John Ashbery, Amiri Baraka, Mark Doty, Mary Gaitskill, Allan Gurganus, Eddie Harris, Richard Howard, Zia Jaffrey, Denis Johnson, August Kleinzahler, Carole Maso, Ed McBain, Claire Mesud, Dale Peck, Richard Powers, Adrienne Rich, Art Spiegelman, and Jeanette Winterson.

For more information, contact the Director, Dept. of English.

❖New York University
Graduate Program in Creative Writing
19 University Place, Room 200
New York, NY 10003
(212) 998-8816
FAX (212) 995-4864
e-mail: creative.writing@nyu.edu
website: http://www.nyu/edu/gsas/dept/english

Degrees offered: MFA, MA

Degree: MFA in Creative Writing (fiction, poetry)

Type of Program: Studio/Academic

Length of Residency: Two years

Required course of study: 32 credits total
Writing workshop: 16 s/hrs
Craft of Fiction/Craft of Poetry: 4–16 s/hrs
Electives: 12 s/hrs

Other requirements: Four courses from any school or department of the University with the permission of the advisor and the department selected. MFA students may also take the Craft of Poetry or the Craft of Fiction more than once if taught by a different instructor each time. In their last semester, students must submit a creative thesis.

Application Deadline: January 4 for admission and financial aid.

The MFA is designed to offer students an opportunity to concentrate more intensively on their writing. It is designed to offer a wider selection of courses from which students may choose those they feel will help them as writers.

Degree: MA in English with a Concentration in Creative Writing (fiction, poetry)

Type of Program: Studio/Academic

Length of Residency: Two years

Required course of study: 32 credits total
Writing workshop: 16 s/hrs
Literature courses: 12–16 s/hrs
Craft course: 4 s/hrs

Other requirements: Students must also demonstrate proficiency in reading a foreign language by passing a foreign language written exam. In their last semester, students submit a writing project bringing together the fiction or poetry they have written during their time in the Program. This program is designed to offer students an opportunity to perfect their own writing and at the same time develop their knowledge of English and American Literature. Four of the 16 credits drawn from the graduate offerings in the English Department may include one Craft of Fiction or Craft of Poetry seminar taught by a member of the CWP faculty and open only to students enrolled in the program. This program is recommended for students who may want to consider applying to a PhD program in English Literature or teaching literature as well as writing at the secondary school level.

Application Deadline: January 4 for admission and financial aid.

The Graduate Creative Writing Program at New York University has distinguished itself for almost twenty years as a leading national center for the study of literature and writing. The program enables students to develop their craft while working closely with some of the finest poets and novelists writing today. Students also have an opportunity to enjoy America's most literary terrain, benefiting from the extensive cultural resources of the University and New York City.

Each year the faculty selects a talented group of writers and offers them rigorous and supportive teaching. Most candidates take one workshop and one other course each semester and complete the program in two years; only one writing workshop may be taken per semester. The maximum time allowed to complete the degree requirements is five years. In the final semester, students present a creative thesis consisting of a substantial body of finished work in poetry or fiction.

The NYU Creative Writing program provides an environment which enables students to work seriously at their craft and, through outreach programs, the literary journal *Washington Square*, and public readings, bring the art of writing to the larger community of New York City. This is a serious community of writers engaged in an exceptional program of study.

Each year the permanent faculty is joined by a rotating group of illustrious writers. In the past fifteen years, these have included: Yehuda Amichai, Margaret Atwood, Robert Bly, Joseph Brodsky, Wesley Brown,

Peter Carey, Edwidge Danticat, Toi Derricotte, Cornelius Eady, Allen Ginsberg, Jessica Hagedorn, Marie Howe, Thomas Keneally, Philip Levine, William Matthews, Mary Morris, Edna O'Brien, Michael Ondaatje, Jayne Anne Phillips, Marie Ponsot, Robert Stone, and Jean Valentine.

Washington Square is the literary review of New York University's Graduate Creative Writing Program. A biannual literary magazine, it is staffed and edited by CWP students. It includes work by established writers as well as current students. It sponsors a student reading series open to the public, offers opportunities for NYU's CWP students to present their work, and enables students to experience working on a literary magazine in all phases of its production.

NYU's Creative Writing Program offers a prestigious literary reading series, free and open to the public. (Support is provided by NY Community Trust.) Guest writers are invited to meet informally with students during their visit. Recent guests have included A.R. Ammons, Robert Creeley, Charles Simic, Annie Dillard, Miroslav Holub, William Kennedy, Yusef Komunyakaa, Toni Morrison, Edna O'Brien, Amos Oz, Grace Paley, Adrienne Rich, Robert Stone, C.K. Williams, and Adam Zagajewski.

Several innovative CWP projects have enabled eligible students to apply for fellowships that involve teaching in literary outreach programs. These programs have become national models for excellence in literary outreach:

The New York Times Foundation Creative Writing Fellowships – Each year, five students admitted to the Program are named New York Times Company Creative Writing Fellows. Spending two days a week in selected New York City high schools, New York Times Fellows conduct creative writing workshops for students under the guidance of an experienced high school teacher. The NY Times Fellowship provides a stipend of $10,000 and New York University matches the grant with full tuition.

Goldwater Writing Project Fellowship – Students may apply for six semester-long fellowships which are awarded each year for teaching at Goldwater Hospital, a public facility for the severely physically challenged located on Roosevelt Island. Goldwater Fellows conduct weekly Creative Writing workshops for patients, meet with them in individual conferences, and help transcribe their work.

The Starlight Foundation Teaching Project – The Starlight Foundation offers two to four fellowships each semester. All students are eligible to apply. Starlight Fellows teach creative writing one day a week to seriously ill children at local hospitals and to the learning disabled at a local high school.

English Department Teaching Assistantships – Approximately 20 (the number varies according to undergraduate enrollment and demand) undergraduate English Department teaching positions are offered to Creative Writing Program graduate students during their second year in the Program. Recipients of these Assistantships design and teach a semester-long introductory workshop in creative writing for undergraduates. Participating students take a year-long teaching practicum in the Creative Writing department.

The distinguished permanent faculty members of the NYU Graduate Program in Creative Writing are: E.L. Doctorow (fiction), who has garnered the National Book Critics Circle award twice, the National Book Award, the PEN/Faulkner Award, the Edith Wharton Citation for Fiction, and the William Dean Howells medal of the American Academy of Arts and Letters. His many novels include *The Book of Daniel, Billy Bathgate*, and *The Waterworks*. Paule Marshall (fiction), is the author of several novels including *Brown Girl, Brownstones; The Chosen Place, The Timeless People*; and *Daughters*. She is a MacArthur Fellow, a winner of the Dos Passos Prize for Literature, and was designated a Literary Lion by the New York Public Library. Sharon Olds (poetry), was recently named the New York State Poet. Her books of poetry include *Satan Says, The Dead and the Living*, and *The Wellspring*. She has received the San Francisco Poetry Center Award, the Lamont Poetry Award, and the National Book Critics Circle Award. Galway Kinnell (poetry), a former MacArthur Fellow, won the Pulitzer Prize and the American Book Award for his *Selected Poems*. His many other volumes of poetry include *The Book of Nightmares*, and most recently, *Imperfect Thirst*.

For further information please contact Melissa Hammerle, Director, Graduate Program in Creative Writing, at the above address.

❖New York University Liberal Arts Program Paul McGhee Division, SCPS Shimkin Hall 50 West 4th Street New York, NY 10012-1165

(212) 998-7090
FAX (212) 995-4132
website: http://www.edu.nyu/sce/

Degree offered: BA in Liberal Arts with concentration in Creative Writing (poetry, fiction, playwriting, screenwriting, nonfiction prose, performance)

Required course of study: 128 credits total
Liberal Arts Core: 64 s/hrs
Concentration: 28 s/hrs
B.A. electives: 24–28 s/hrs
Culminating Experience: 4–8 s/hrs

Prerequisites and recommended courses: Students entering the Creative Writing concentration should already have completed Writing Workshops I and II, with a combined average of B; Introduction to Literature; and Foundations of Creative Process.

Concentration Courses: Students select eight credits from each of the following three categories: Studio, Workshops, and Literature. The four additional credits may be from any courses within the concentration including practicum (e.g. editing) courses.

Application Deadline: Year-round admission. Semesters begin in September, January, and May. Financial aid available.

The Creative Writing Program is aimed at serving the needs of adult students seeking an undergraduate degree in writing. We provide a program for beginning and experienced writers who wish to develop their craft while working towards a bachelor's degree. We also provide courses for individuals who want to write in professional or personal contexts, as well as courses for individuals preparing for professions in which an understanding of language and of creative processes would be a significant asset.

A basic course -- "Foundations of the Creative Process" -- is required of all students planning to enter this concentration and is also open to all interested students.

Studio courses in poetry, prose (fiction and nonfiction), and writing in performance (including stage, screen, and emerging performance art forms) are beginning craft courses in which students concentrate on generating text and on learning the practice of particular forms. The Workshops are more advanced and focus on preparing work for publication. A final interdisciplinary seminar prepares students for Senior Projects. In Creative Writing these projects consist of a collection of original work written under the supervision of a mentor.

Editorial conferences make it possible for students to individualize their programs. *Icarus* is the student-run literary magazine. Those students working on the editorial board may earn academic credits for their efforts. The magazine sponsors an annual student literary reading. Readings that bring together faculty writers with writers from outside of the institution are held several times each year.

Guest writers in 1997-1998 included: Ann Beattie, Jennifer Egan, Toi Derricotte, Jean Valentine, Tomaz Salamun, Harry Mathews.

Faculty includes: Poetry: Paul Violi (*Likewise, Splurge*); Andrew Levy (*Curve*); Michael Heller (*In the Builded Place*); Karen Volkman (*Crash's Law*); Ruth Danon (*Triangulation from a Known Point*). Fiction: Peter Bricklebank. Screenwriting: Michael Zam, Michael Golder. Prose nonfiction: Joline Blais, M. Mark. Drama: Steven Smith.

For more information, contact Ruth Danon, Master Teacher of Creative and Expository Writing, at the above address.

Norfolk State University
Norfolk, VA 23504

Contact the Creative Writing Program Director, Dept. of English.

❖University of North Alabama
Florence, AL 35632-0001

Contact the Creative Writing Program Director, Dept. of English.

❖North Carolina State University
Raleigh, NC 27695-8105

(919) 515-3870

Degrees offered: BA, MA

Degree: BA in English with Emphasis in Creative Writing

At the undergraduate level, 12 s/hrs of creative writing courses are offered, plus the opportunity for independent study (writing a novel, for instance).

Degree: MA in English with Creative Thesis Option

Type of Program: Studio/Academic

Required course of study: 31 s/hrs
Thesis: 3 s/hrs
Writing workshop: 9 s/hrs
Literature courses: 18 s/hrs
Bibliography/Methodology: 1 s/hr

Application Deadlines: Nov. 1 for Spring, April 1 for Fall, Feb. 1 for Teaching Assistantship.

The MA Program offers coursework in English and American literature, rhetoric and composition, linguistics, and creative writing. A minimum of 31 s/hrs is required of all MA students, in the following general areas: 12 hours of distribution requirements, 3 hours of thesis, 12 hours of electives. At least 15 hours of coursework must be in English or American literature.

Teaching Assistants will have a 34-hour program, since they take ENG 696 (Problems in College Composition) to prepare for teaching freshman English. This requirement is professional training that is added to the 31 hours of coursework for the degree.

Students choose their courses and take Fiction Writing Workshop or Poetry Writing Workshop for elective credit. An additional special topics workshop is offered every other semester. The thesis project may consist of a single creative work or a series of shorter works, as agreed with the thesis director.

Special advantages of graduate work in creative writing at NCSU include the limited size of the program and resulting individual attention from instructors; the chance to take courses in technical writing, composition, or journalism; the richness of cultural opportunity afforded by the Raleigh/Durham/Chapel Hill area; and the availability of graduate teaching assistantships. Thesis possibilities include a novel, a collection of short stories, or poems.

Visiting writers in the past few years have included Galway Kinnell, Russell Banks, Elizabeth Spencer, Jill McCorkle, Annie Dillard, Miller Williams, Reynolds Price, Harry Crews, Clyde Edgerton, Amy Tan, and John Grisham.

The faculty in the Creative Writing Program includes: fiction writer Lee Smith (*Saving Grace, The Devil's Dream, Fair and Tender Ladies*); fiction writer John Kessel (*Good News from Outer Space, Meeting in Infinity, Freedom Beach*; winner of Nebula Award, SF Writers of America 1982); fiction writer Angela Davis-Gardner (*Felice, Forms of Shelter*); fiction writer Tim McLaurin (*Cured by Fire, Keeper of the Moon, Woodrow's Trumpet*); fiction writer William McCranor Henderson (*I Killed Hemingway, Stark Raving Elvis*); poet Gerald Barrax (*Leaning Against the Sun, Another Kind of Rain, An Audience of One*; editor of *Obsidian II Magazine*); poet Thomas Lisk (*A Short History of Pens Since the French Revolution*); poet Steven B. Katz, and others.

For more information, contact Tom Lisk, Dept. Head, Creative Writing Program.

❖University of North Carolina at Asheville
One University Heights
Asheville, NC 28804-8509
(828) 251-6600, 251-6411
FAX (828) 251-6603
e-mail: rchess@unca.edu

Degree offered: BA in Literature and Language with Concentration in Creative Writing (poetry, fiction, playwriting, screenwriting, nonfiction prose)

Required course of study: 120 s/hrs total
Literature courses: 24 s/hrs
Writing workshops: 9 s/hrs
Senior Project: 3 s/hrs

Other Requirements: Comprehensive exam; university general education requirements; a creative thesis.

Application Deadlines: March 1.

UNCA is a small, public, liberal arts university with the declared mission of developing in all its students "a breadth of perspective, a capacity to think both critically and creatively, and an understanding of the role of values in thought and action." To these ends, the Department of Literature and Language offers a course of study that encourages students to approach literature from cultural and historical perspectives and challenges them to expand their intellectual capabilities through various forms of critical and creative writing.

The program in Creative Writing enables students to combine a liberal arts study of world literature with a strong program of creative writing. It features a sequence of workshops in which students share their work with students and faculty and receive assistance in realizing their vision and developing their craft as writers of fiction, poetry, plays, and nonfiction prose. Students in the Creative Writing program take most of the same courses required for all majors -- period surveys, genre studies, special courses chosen from a wide selection -- as foundation for their own writing.

The program in Creative Writing offers a number of opportunities for practical development outside the classroom. *Headwaters*, UNCA's literature and arts magazine, is edited and published by students in literature, and the Pisgah Players, the production arm of the Playwriting Workshop, encourages student participation in every aspect of creation and performance. Furthermore, on- and off-campus, thanks to Asheville's literary atmosphere, students will be able to hear and meet the many established writers who visit this area.

The Literature Club welcomes all students interested in the study of literature and language. It sponsors writing contests, holds meetings where students may exchange ideas with each other and with engaging visitors, publishes *Footnotes* (the department of Literature and Language newsletter) and arranges frequent student-faculty parties to advance the camaraderie of the Department.

The department awards four writing prizes each year: the Thomas Wolfe Fiction Prize, the Carl Sandburg Poetry Prize, the Francis P. Hulme Drama Prize and the Wilma Dykeman Award for University Writing. The department also offers the Gullickson Award for outstanding rising senior and the Bryan Award for best senior paper, as well as prizes for the best freshman essays each year.

The creative writing faculty includes Richard Chess (*Tekiah*), Jan Harrow (fiction and nonfiction prose), David Hopes (*A Childhood in the Milky Way; A Sense of the Morning; The Glacier's Daughters*), Peggy B. Parris (*Waltzing in the Attic*; winner of PEN Syndicated Fiction Award), and Jeff Rackham (short fiction; *Creativity and the Writing Process; The Rhinehart Reader; Windows on Human Values*).

For more information, contact Richard Chess at the Dept. of Literature and Language.

❖University of North Carolina at Chapel Hill
Chapel Hill, NC 27599-3520
(919) 962-4000

Degree offered: BA in English with Minor in Creative Writing

The Creative Writing Program at Chapel Hill offers one of the most outstanding and respected programs for undergraduates in the country. Our students proceed through a sequence of courses which can lead to a Minor in the discipline or graduation with Honors in Creative Writing. Currently we number 10 full or part-time faculty and teach around 250 students each semester. Many alumni have gone on to distinguish themselves as successful novelists, poets, editors, filmmakers, and teachers. They include Randall Kenan, Jill McCorkle, Tim McLaurin, Lawrence Naumoff, Michael Parker, Russell Banks, Jim Grimsley, Leon Rooke, Will Blythe, Alane Mason -- although this is by no means a comprehensive list.

Teachers in the past 30 years have included Pulitzer prize-winning poet Carolyn Kizer, Louis D. Rubin (founder of Algonquin Books), Max Steele, Lee Smith, Elizabeth Cox, and Elizabeth Spencer. Today's staff attempts to mentor students rather than mold them, and although many faculty have national profiles, dedication to teaching remains their primary focus. In 1998-1999 our staff included Daphne Athas, Doris Betts, Marianne Gingher, Robert Kirkpatrick, Michael McFee, Ruth Moose, James Seay, Alan Shapiro, Bland Simpson, Max Steele, and Tim Mizelle. Visiting lecturers were novelist Sarah Dessen and poet Michael Chitwood.

Each year our writing students compete for five major literary prizes and are presented cash awards. Extracurricular activities for young writers include a "Second Sunday" reading series that features many of North Carolina's brightest talents such as Reynolds Price, Kaye Gibbons, and Fred Chappell. The Blanche Armfield Poetry series brings a prominent American poet to campus each spring. The Morgan Writer-in-Residence Program invites an outstanding writer or group of writers to campus each year for panel discussions, lectures, and informal meetings with students. Recent guests have included Annie Dillard, Beth

Henley, Shelby Foote, Richard Ford, Robert Pinksy, Rita Dove, and Richard Wilbur. In addition, the "Youth Angst Society" sponsors regular student readings at the Bull's Head Book Store on campus.

In the spring of 1998, the University sponsored the first North Carolina Literary Festival, a mega-celebration of writers and readers. Writers in attendance included Alice Adams, Derek Walcott, Allan Gurganus, Ariel Dorfman, and John Grisham.

Two well-established literary magazines, the *Carolina Quarterly* and *Cellar Door*, are housed on campus and welcome student participation as staff members.

Ours is an energetic program at a lively and supportive university. For more information, contact our secretary Frances Coombs at (919) 962-4000 or Marianne Gingher, Director of Creative Writing, at (919) 962-0468, or write for our brochure.

University of North Carolina at Charlotte
Charlotte, NC 28223
(704) 547-2296

Degrees offered: BA, MA

At present, we are building our graduate and undergraduate offerings in creative writing. We have a sequence of courses on the graduate and undergraduate levels, but no formal degrees in creative writing yet. Our faculty includes, in fiction: Robin Hemley (*All You Can Eat; The Last Studebaker*) and Nanci Kincaid (*Crossing Blood*), and in poetry: Christopher Davis (*The Tyrant of The Past and the Slave of the Future*) and Robert Grey (*Saving The Dead*).

We offer a MA degree in English with a Creative Thesis in poetry, fiction, or creative nonfiction.

For more information, contact the Chair, Dept. of English.

❖University of North Carolina at Greensboro
P.O. Box 26170
Greensboro, NC 27402-6170
(336) 334-5459
FAX (336) 334-3281

Degrees offered: BA, MFA

Degree: BA in English with Concentration in Creative Writing

The University of North Carolina at Greensboro allows a writing concentration for undergraduate English majors. Courses in journalism, expository, technical, and creative writing, and publishing are available for a maximum of 15 s/hrs, with 21 s/hrs to be taken in literature courses. The student may plan a course of study suited to individual needs, whether those be practical or artistic. All resources of the graduate writing program (permanent faculty, visiting writers, campus publications) are open to undergraduates electing this concentration. A limited number of scholarships are available to undergraduates in creative writing.

Degree: MFA in Creative Writing (poetry, fiction)

Type of Program: Studio/Academic

Length of Residency: Two years

Required course of study: 36 s/hrs
Thesis: 6 s/hrs
Writing workshop: 6-12 s/hrs
Tutorials: 6-12 s/hrs
Literature (and other academic) courses: 12-18 s/hrs

Other Requirements: Written comprehensive examination focusing on the student's own writing.

While recognizing that the study of literature is vital to writers, our program emphasizes writing rather than an academic curriculum designed to produce teachers. While many of our graduates have made very successful careers in teaching, we feel strongly that students who do not plan to teach should not be forced to prepare for a career in which they have no interest. In addition to workshops, students spend a great deal of their time writing in tutorials with individual contact with one or more members of the writing staff.

The English Department's core of editing courses allow students to develop skills in contemporary publishing. Students may take internships for in-classroom teaching experience, and strong course offerings in rhetoric and composition afford further training in the teaching of writing.

Campus literary publications include *The Greensboro Review*, a national literary journal sponsored by the program, staffed by faculty and selected students; and *Coraddi*, a magazine of the arts independent of the English Department. Both magazines regularly publish student work. The English Department is also home for *English Literature in Transition, 1880-1920*. Each year several writers visit the campus for readings, workshops, and tutorials with students. The program sponsors the St. Mary's House Poetry/Fiction series, featuring readings by students and regional writers.

The Randall Jarrell Fellowship is offered annually to one or more outstanding writing students. Students holding an MA degree in English may seek a teaching assistantship ($9,000 minimum stipend for 9 months). Research assistantships ($8,000 for 9-month assignment) are also available. Out-of-state tuition waivers may accompany assistantships to out-of-state students. Applicants seeking an assistantship are advised to have all application materials in by February 1. All applications for the fall semester must be received by March 15.

Current faculty includes poet and novelist Fred Chappell (winner of the Bollingen and T.S. Elliot Prizes; 7 novels, 13 books of poetry, 2 volumes of critical essays, and 2 collections of short stories); fiction and nonfiction writer Jim Clark (stories and nonfiction in a variety of magazines, editor of *The Greensboro Review*); poet H.T. Kirby-Smith (poetry in many journals and two books, *The Origins of Free Verse* and *A Philosophical Novelist: George Santayana and "The Last Puritan"*); poet Stuart Dischell, (*Good Hope Road* and

Evenings & Avenues); fiction writer Lee Zacharias (*Helping Muriel Make It Through the Night*, stories, and *Lessons*, a novel); and fiction writer Michael Parker (*Hello Down There*, a novel, and *The Geographical Cure*, novellas and stories).

For more information, contact Jim Clark, Writing Program Director, Dept. of English.

❖University of North Carolina at Wilmington
Wilmington, NC 28403-3297

(910) 962-7401 (voice)
(910) 962-3320
FAX (910) 962-7186
e-mail: mfa@uncwil.edu
website: www2/uncwil/eng

Degrees offered: BA, MFA

Degree: BA in English with a Concentration in Creative Writing (fiction, poetry, literary nonfiction)

Required course of study: 124 s/hrs total; 21 s/hrs core literature and language; 21 s/hrs writing concentration including senior seminar with senior ms.

Other Requirements: 45 s/hrs basic studies; optional minor.

Application Deadlines: February 1 for fall.

In the UNCW Professional and Creative Writing Program, we value and promote cross-genre versatility. The undergraduate concentration requires a student to take a beginning creative writing course in the chosen genre and then specialize in one or more genres, including a combination of creative writing and professional writing (journalism, technical writing), culminating in a mixed-genre senior seminar, a manuscript project, and a reading. Courses are also offered in screenwriting and playwriting. In addition, the degree requires courses in British and American Literature, linguistics or language history, and essay writing. *Atlantis* is the undergraduate literary magazine, fully staffed by student editors. Each year, based on a judging of undergraduate manuscripts, the program awards the Sam Ragan Prizes in Poetry (3) and the Jessie Rehder Short Story Awards (3). Students have the chance to meet visiting Writers-in-Residence and speakers in our Writers & Readers Series.

Degree: MFA in Creative Writing

Type of Program: Studio/Academic

The Department of English offers a program of study leading to the Master of Fine Arts in Creative Writing, an appropriate terminal degree for the writer teaching in the university and for the writer wishing to pursue various other career paths in writing and editing. The MFA program is an intensive studio-academic apprenticeship in the writing of fiction, poetry, and creative nonfiction. Courses include workshops in the three genres, special topics workshops, and a range of courses in literature, criticism, theory, and language. Students are urged to pursue the MFA primarily as a way of mastering their art by rigorous study and practice among a community of other dedicated writers, and only secondarily for the teaching credential, since

the MFA without supporting publications does not guarantee employment. Each student will be expected to demonstrate mastery of one genre and proficiency in at least one other.

Admission Requirements: Applicants seeking admission to the Master of Fine Arts Program in Creative Writing are required to submit the following six items to the Graduate School before the application can be processed:

1) A double-spaced, typed manuscript in the applicant's primary genre: 15 pages of poetry, 30 pages of fiction, or 30 pages of creative nonfiction. The manuscript should demonstrate mastery of basic craft and unmistakable literary promise. Applicants are advised not to apply with a mixed-genre manuscript.

2) An application for graduate admission.

3) Official transcripts of all college work (graduate and undergraduate).

4) Official scores on the Graduate Record Examination (GRE), no more than five years old.

5) At least three recommendations from individuals in professionally relevant fields addressing the applicant's achievement and promise as a writer and ability to successfully complete graduate study.

6) Essay on the applicant's goals in pursuing the MFA (300–500 words).

An applicant must have successfully completed a BA in English, a BFA in Writing, or another appropriate undergraduate degree with at least a "B" average in the major field of study. But acceptable fulfillment of all the above constitutes the minimum requirements for, and does not guarantee, admission to the MFA program.

In general, we are seeking candidates who show artistic commitment and literary promise in their writing and whose academic background indicates they are likely to succeed not only in graduate study but as publishing professional writers. Therefore, in evaluating candidates, the admissions committee places great emphasis on the quality of the manuscript.

The deadline for receiving applications is March 1 for the fall semester and November 1 for the spring semester. All interested applicants will be considered for graduate assistantships, which will be awarded on a competitive basis as they become available. Applicants seeking graduate assistantships are urged to complete their applications well before the deadline.

Degree Requirements:

1) An MFA candidate must successfully complete a minimum of 48 semester hours of graduate study: 21 hours in writing; 6 hours of thesis; and 21 hours in other graduate English courses, with an option of substituting for up to six of those hours study in a related discipline, as determined by the student's advisor and the MFA coordinator.

2) A maximum of six semester hours of graduate course credit may be transferred from another accredited institution in partial fulfillment of the MFA. UNCW regulations will be applied in determining the transferability of course credits, and requests for transfer must be approved by the MFA coordinator and the Dean of the Graduate School.

3) An MFA candidate is required to complete at least six hours of writing workshops in a primary genre, and at least three hours of workshop in a second genre.

4) A minimum GPA of 3.0 (on a 4.0) scale must be

maintained in all graduate coursework; a "B" average is required for graduation.

5) An MFA candidate must complete a book-length manuscript of literary merit and publishable quality acceptable to the thesis committee: this ordinarily will be a novel; a collection of short stories, poems, or essays; a single long poem; a long nonfiction narrative; or some combination of the foregoing. Nonbinding guidelines: 75 pages of poetry, 200 pages of prose.

6) An MFA candidate must pass the Master of Fine Arts Examination.

7) An MFA candidate must maintain residency during all course work except thesis and transfer hours.

8) All requirements must be completed within five calendar years.

Writing faculty: Wendy Brenner, fiction. Author of *Large Animals in Everyday Life.* Winner of the Flannery O'Connor Award in 1996. Stanley Colbert, distinguished visiting professor, creative nonfiction, formerly CEO of Harper-Collins, Canada. Clyde Edgerton, fiction. Author of seven novels, most recently *Where Trouble Sleeps.* Awards include a Guggenheim Fellowship. Philip Gerard, fiction and creative nonfiction. Author of three novels, most recently *Desert Kill.* Rebecca Lee, fiction and creative nonfiction. Her short stories have appeared in *The Atlantic Monthly.* Dennis Sampson, poetry. Author of two books of poetry. Michael White, author of two collections of poetry, winner of the 1998 Colorado Poetry Prize. Paul Wilkes, author of two collections of poetry.

Please direct all inquiries to Darcy White, Graduate Administrative Assistant, Dept. of English, University of North Carolina-Wilmington, 601 S. College Road, Wilmington, NC 28403.

❖University of North Dakota
Box 7209
Grand Forks, ND 58202
(701) 777-3321
FAX (701) 777-2373

Degrees offered: BA, MA, PhD

Degree: BA in English with Concentration in Creative Writing

Required course of study: 36 s/hrs in major
Thesis: no requirement except in Honors program
Writing courses: up to 16 s/hrs plus
independent study

Other Requirements: Foreign language proficiency; general graduation requirement of 8 s/hrs science; 8 s/hrs social science; 5 s/hrs English composition; 125 total s/hrs required for degree.

Degrees: MA and PhD in English with Creative Thesis/Dissertation Options (poetry, fiction)

Type of Program: Traditional Literary Study and Creative Writing

Required course of study: 30 s/hrs for MA; 90 s/hrs for PhD.

The graduate and undergraduate writing programs at UND are designed to encourage independence and self-motivation within a supportive and stimulating environment. Students design their own program of study in consultation with their advisor and usually take a combination of courses in imaginative writing, literary studies, language, and related fields such as philosophy, history, and art.

The undergraduate courses in imaginative writing are English 305, Creative Writing, an introductory course covering fiction, poetry, and drama; and English 411 and 412, The Art of Writing, the advanced courses. Normally, English 305 is open to sophomores and juniors, and English 411 and 412 are open to juniors and seniors. Each course can be repeated once. Independent Study is also available.

On the graduate level, the option of a creative thesis or dissertation is available for MA and PhD programs that combine traditional literary study with the writing of fiction and poetry. Normally, students will enroll in the graduate writing workshop, English 515, before beginning independent study, Research in Creative Writing, which can be repeated. Eventually, each student will work with an advisor in putting together a book-length work of publishable quality. Teaching assistantships are available to students in both the MA and PhD programs.

Internships are available with *North Dakota Quarterly* as well as opportunities to edit the student publication, *North Country.*

The writing faculty includes fiction writer James Robison (*The Rumor and Other Stories, The Illustrator*), poet Jay Meek (*Headlands: New and Selected Poems, Windows, Stations*), and poet Martha Meek (*Rude Noises*).

The annual Writers Conference, held each spring, brings together nationally-known writers to give readings, engage in panel discussions, and meet with students. Recent writers have included Rosellen Brown, Martin Espada, Diane Glancy, Tim O'Brien, Czeslaw Milosz, Michael Ondaatje, Carol Shields, and Luisa Valenzuela.

For further information, contact Jay Meek, Director of the Writing Program, English Dept.

❖North Lake College
5001 N. MacArthur Blvd.
Irving, TX 75038-3899

For more information, contact the Director, Dept. of English.

❖University of North Texas
English/UNT Box 311307
Denton, TX 76203-1307
(940) 565-2117

Degrees offered: BA, MA, PhD

Degree: BA in English (with concentration in writing)

Required course of study: 128 s/hrs total; English: 36 s/hrs, 12 of which are basic comp rhet and world lit. At the advanced level, the option in writing requires 24 s/hrs including tech writing, comp rhet, creative writing, and 6 hrs upper div. lit.

Degree: MA in English (with a concentration in creative writing)

Type of Program: Studio/Academic

Required course of study: 36 s/hrs total
    Literary Criticism: 3 s/hrs
    Literature: 9–15 s/hrs
    Writing workshops: 6–12 s/hrs
    Practicum (Form and Theory): 3 s/hrs

Other Requirements: Foreign language requirement, comprehensive exam, thesis defense.

Application Deadline: January 15.

Degree: PhD in English (concentration in contemporary literature with a creative dissertation)

Type of Program: Traditional Literary Study and Creative Writing

Required course of study: 90 s/hrs beyond BA, as follows:

Note: UNT offers a five-year, direct-track doctoral program, admitting 15 students (holding undergraduate degrees) each year. Students who, upon admission to the PhD program, have already earned an MA or MFA may receive transfer credit for classes which correspond to those required by the five-year plan.

First year, fall semester: Old English, Methods of Teaching Composition (or alternate assigned by senior tutor), Bibliography and Methods of Research.

First year, spring semester: Studies in Medieval Lit., Studies in British Renaissance, Scholarly and Critical Writing.

Second year, fall semester: Studies in British Lit. of Romantic Period, 18th-century British Lit., Studies in Literary Criticism.

Second year, spring semester: Studies in American Lit., 1800–1865, Seminar in British Lit., 1780–present, a contemporary American or British literature course.

Third year, fall semester: three courses assigned by senior tutor.

Third year, spring semester: three courses assigned by senior tutor.

Fourth year, fall semester: three courses in the major assigned by senior tutor. The student will undergo the fourth year oral examination at the end of this semester.

Fourth year, spring semester: 9 s/hrs dissertation research.

Fifth year, fall semester: 3 s/hrs Special Problems, 6 s/hrs Dissertation.

Fifth year, spring semester: 3 s/hrs Special Problems, 6 s/hrs Dissertation.

Other Requirements: Foreign language requirement, oral exam, dissertation defense.

Application Deadlines: January 15.

Our graduate programs are essentially English literature programs which supplement literary study with creative writing workshops and which culminate in the production of a creative thesis or dissertation. Our approach assumes a necessary relationship between literary study and literary production, and encourages students to actively engage their traditions for the purpose of responding both critically and creatively. Our faculty and students are encouraged to participate in regional, national, and international conferences as both scholars and writers.

Visiting writers have included Donald Barthelme, Rick Bass, Charles Baxter, Ron Carlson, Richard Howard, Andrew Hudgins, Phillis Levin, Cynthia Mcdonald, Walter MacDonald, Sandra McPherson, Larry McMurtry, W.S. Merwin, Naomi Shihab Nye, Adrienne Rich, Pattiann Rogers, David St. John, W.D. Snodgrass, and Richard Wilbur.

Departmental publishing projects include *American Literary Review, Studies in the Novel, North Texas Review*, and a book award series, The Vassar Miller Prize in Poetry.

The permanent creative writing faculty includes: poet Bruce Bond (*Radiography, The Anteroom of Paradise, Independence Days*); screenwriter Ken Harrison (*Hannah and the Dog Ghost, Last of the Caddoes, Mr. Horse*); poet Austin Hummell (*The Fugitive Kind, Audible Ransom*); fiction writer Lee Martin (*The Least You Need to Know, Traps*); and fiction writer Barbara Rodman (*Flying Saucer*).

For more information, contact Lynn Eubank, Director of Graduate Studies in English.

❖Northeastern University
406 Holmes Hall
360 Huntington Avenue
Boston, MA 02115
(617) 373-2512
FAX (617) 373-2509

Degrees offered: BA, MA

Degree: BS/BA in English with concentration in creative writing (poetry, fiction, playwriting)

Required course of study: 176 q/hrs total
    Intro to Creative Writing: 4 q/hrs
    Creative Writing: 4 q/hrs
    Workshop in one genre: 4 q/hrs
    Publication Arts: 4 q/hrs
    Literature courses: 56 or more q/hrs

Other Requirements: Arts and sciences core curriculum requirements; electives in Directed Study: 4 q/hrs and Creative Thesis: 8 q/hrs are available for those wishing to do substantial creative projects under close, direct supervision.

Application Deadline: February 1 for financial aid; March 1 for admission.

The undergraduate program requires the student to take an introductory class, then a mixed-genre workshop, then a workshop in at least one particular genre. Through the course in publication arts and the cooperative education program, students gain experience in the editing, publishing, and marketing of publications. The undergraduate creative writing club mounts an informal program of workshops and readings; a number of those involved in the club also work on *Spectrum*, the campus literary magazine.

Degree: MA in English with concentration in writing, focus in creative writing and composition (poetry, fiction, prose nonfiction, playwriting, composition studies)

Type of Program: Traditional literary study/creative writing; this is a two-year MA program requiring 42 q/hrs (14 courses) and a comprehensive examination, with a creative thesis option.

Application Deadlines: February 15 for a teaching assistantship; rolling admissions process for admission without award.

For more information, contact Stuart Peterfreund, Director, Creative Writing Program.

❖Northern Arizona University
Flagstaff, AZ 86011
(520) 523-4911
FAX (520) 523-7074

Degrees offered: BA, MA

Degree: BA in English

The BA in English is a uniquely flexible major which permits interested students to do coursework in both poetry and fiction writing at all levels. Small special topic seminars are available to seniors.

Degree: MA in English with an Emphasis in Creative Writing

Type of Program: Studio/Academic

Length of Residency: Two years

Required course of study: 36 s/hrs
  Writing workshop: 12 s/hrs
  Creative thesis: 4–6 s/hrs
  Other English courses: 3 s/hrs
  Literature Courses: 12 s/hrs

Application Deadlines: Sept. 1 to April 15. Graduate Assistantships due by Feb. 15.

The MA in English with an Emphasis in Creative Writing allows the student to balance academic coursework in English with the serious study of creative writing. To be admitted to the program, applicants must submit an acceptable 10- to 20-page manuscript of original poetry or fiction to the Creative Writing Director, and must meet those academic requirements for admission to graduate English studies outlined in the Graduate Catalogue. Students accepted for graduate study are eligible for Graduate Assistantships.

NAU is situated in the Coconino National Forest, at the base of the 12,600 foot-high San Francisco Peaks, near the Grand Canyon and 6 other national parks and monuments. The 4-season climate affords ample opportunities for year-round recreation.

NAU's creative writing faculty includes Ann Cummins (fiction), Barbara Anderson (poetry; *Junk City* and *1–800–911*), Jim Simmerman (poetry; *Moon Go Away, I Don't Love You No More*, and *Kingdom Come*), Allen Woodman (fiction; *The Cows Are Going To Paris* and *Saved by Mr. F. Scott Fitzgerald*), and Jane Armstrong (creative nonfiction and fiction).

For more information, contact Creative Writing Coordinator, Dept. of English, Box 6032.

University of Northern Iowa
Cedar Falls, IA 50614-0502
(319) 273-2821
FAX (319) 273-5807
e-mail: vince.gotera@uni.edu
website: http://www.uni.edu/english/webfiles/cw

Degrees offered: BA, MA

Degree: BA in English, or in English Teaching (secondary certification), **with writing minor, Creative Writing Emphasis** (poetry, fiction)

Required course of study: 18 hours total in the minor. Required core courses: Introduction to Literature or Critical Writing About Literature; Beginning Poetry Writing and/or Beginning Fiction Writing; Craft of Poetry and/or Craft of Fiction; Poetry Workshop and/or Fiction Workshop. Electives, if necessary, in a studio or performance course in art, music, or theatre; electives may also be taken in creative writing and/or literature, including literature in a language other than English.

Application Deadlines: August 15.

Degree: MA in English (Creative Thesis Option)

Type of Program: Studio/Academic

Length of Residency: Two years

Required course of study: 30 hrs total. 24 hours of courses in creative writing and literature; 6 hours of creative thesis. Note: We are currently creating a true graduate emphasis in Creative Writing.

Other Requirements: Written comprehensive examination, competency in one foreign language, one semester of Introduction to Graduate Study.

Application Deadlines: March 1 for graduate assistantships; for admission, at least one month prior to commencement of study.

The University of Northern Iowa provides a stimulating and challenging environment for both undergraduate and graduate students in creative writing. The renowned journal *North American Review* is housed at our campus. We also host *Literary Magazine Review*. *Inner Weather*, the student-run campus literary magazine, appears once a year and offers experience in editing as well as a place to publish.

Outside class, students can share their work in an informal student creative writing group that meets online in a computerized e-mail discussion list. The English Club sponsors readings, workshops, and other literary activities. Writers also visit campus each year through the Northern Iowa Reading Series. Every year, we sponsor the Roberta S. Tamres Science Fiction Award for fiction, poetry, or essays. Students are also within easy reach of events sponsored by the Iowa Writers' Workshop in Iowa City.

The creative writing faculty includes fiction writer and poet Robley Wilson (*A Pleasure Tree, Dancing for Men, Kingdoms of the Ordinary*), editor of the *North American Review*; poet Vince Gotera (*Dragonfly, Radical Visions*), winner of an NEA creative writing fellowship; Susan Rochette-Crawley; and Grant Tracey, editor of *Literary Magazine Review*.

For more information, contact Vince Gotera, Coordinator, Creative Writing.

❖Northern Michigan University
Marquette, MI 49855
(906) 227-2711
FAX (906) 227-1096

Degree offered: MA in English with Emphasis in Writing (poetry, fiction, creative nonfiction, technical and professional writing, screenwriting)

Type of Program: Studio/Academic

Required course of study: 32 s/hrs minimum
  Thesis: 4 s/hrs
  Writing workshops and thesis: 12 s/hrs
  Electives: 12-17 s/hrs
  Required: EN 504, Principles of Critical
    Investigation and one additional 500-level
    literature course

Application Deadlines: February 1 for graduate assistant applications.

The MA in English with an Emphasis in Writing is intended for writers of fiction, nonfiction, poetry, and technical and professional works. The degree is also intended for prospective teachers of writing. The core courses in the program are the writing workshops in fiction, nonfiction, poetry, and technical and professional writing. Each student plans an individual course of study with the Director of Graduate Studies to include writing workshops in at least 2 of the 4 workshop areas. Since the department regards as axiomatic that there is an intimate link between good reading and good writing, literature courses are a necessary and vital part of the degree.

Graduate assistantships ($6,760 per year minimum) are offered on a competitive basis and include a tuition scholarship for up to 16 credits a year. Assistants usually teach one 4-credit section of the freshman English course. Teaching Assistants are required to take a four-credit-hour Teaching of Composition course.

Primary writing faculty include Ronald L. Johnson, fiction and creative nonfiction (*Women's Work: A Memoir*, Editor's Prize, *Missouri Review*, 1997); Paul Lehmberg, nonfiction (*In the Strong Woods*); Beverly Matherne, poetry, French-English translations (*Revue de Louisiane, Kansas Quarterly*, New Rivers Press); Anne Youngs, poetry (*The Third Coast Anthology, 13th Moon*, and *Thirty Octaves Above Middle C*, winner of the Quentin R. Howard Poetry Prize 1997, offered by

Wind Magazine); John Smolens, nonfiction and fiction (*Winter By Degrees, Angel's Head*); and visiting fiction writer Katie Hanson (*Prairie Schooner, Shenandoah, North American Review*). Recent visiting writers include: Kurt Vonnegut, Melanie Rae Thon, Kitsi Watterson, Edie Clark, Gordon Henry, Ray Young Bear, Sharon Dilworth, Jim Daniels, and Jack Gantos.

Faculty members encourage students to submit their outstanding writing for publication, and our students and recent graduates have published their work in *American Poetry Review, Country Journal, Michigan Natural Resources, Mid-American Review, The Third Coast, Midwest Quarterly*. The English Department publishes the literary quarterly *Passages North*, which in 1998 was listed in "Fifty Best Fiction Markets" by the *Writers' Digest*. The MA in English program presently has between 50 and 60 active candidates. In 1999 the English Department hopes to expand the graduate writing program by offering an MFA in poetry, fiction, and creative nonfiction, currently under development.

Marquette, in Michigan's Upper Peninsula, is a city of 23,000 on the scenic south shore of Lake Superior. The area is noted for its forests and lakes and its clean, natural environment.

For additional information and application materials, write to Dr. Peter Goodrich, Interim Director of Graduate Studies, Dept. of English.

❖Northwestern University
Evanston, IL 60208
(847) 491-7294
FAX (847) 467-1545

Degree offered: BA, English Major in Writing

Requirements of the Writing Major:
  Prerequisites: 2 B-level courses
  Fundamentals of Prose for Writers (C95)
  One "Theory and Practice" sequence
  The Situation of Writing (C92)
  6 literature courses

Other Requirements: At least two quarters of one of the following sequences in History or European Thought and Culture: History of the United States; History of England; American Intellectual History; The Intellectual History of Europe; Patterns of Western Thought and Culture.

Application Deadlines: Students may apply for admission to the Writing Major through the English Office, University Hall 215, in the early spring of each year.

The English Major in Writing is an undergraduate concentration within the English Department at Northwestern University that emphasizes the writing of poetry and fiction. While the Major in Writing is clearly designed for the instruction and encouragement of promising writers, that is not its only end: it is also designed to produce better *readers* of literary texts. By asking that students acquaint themselves with poems and prose works from the perspective of the writer, and by encouraging students to apprentice themselves, as energetically as possible, to the best literary models, the Writing Faculty hopes to create a more discerning readership for the writers of the future.

On the B-level, no prior knowledge of the genre is required; all students interested in the Writing Major are required to take two introductory writing courses, one in poetry and one in fiction, before applying to the program. The C-level advanced course sequences, which extend across one entire year, are enrolled on a competitive basis. No writing course may be taken pass/fail or audited. The reading of literary texts is an integral part of the courses, as are essay-writing and explication on the one hand, imitation and original work on the other. These three-semester sequences, also called "The Theory and Practice of Poetry and Fiction," begin in the fall semester with specialized courses in the fundamental technical and rhetorical bases of each genre. Poetry students study the theory of prosody, including both the major form of poetry in English (accentual-syllabic verse) and the minor forms (accentual, syllabic, and free verse). Fiction students consider the tenets of naturalism and its substitutes, and practice different uses of plot, narrative technique, and point of view. The second term of the "Theory and Practice" writing sequences is devoted to intensive writing practice in a wide array of shorter then longer works in each genre. Each of the "Theory and Practice" sequences thus begins with technical work, principles and fundamentals of the genre, and imitation; proceeds in the winter to intensive writing practice in the more circumscribed forms within that genre; and leads in the spring to the production of a longer original work: a poem of at least 120 lines; a novella or part of a novel. Students may not enroll in these courses out of sequence.

But the work of poetry and fiction students is not restricted to "creative writing" alone. A required course in prose style and argument (C95, Fundamentals of Prose for Writers) helps students focus on logical method, authorial tone, and the techniques of presenting discourse and description.

The writing curriculum also strongly emphasizes literature and the study of the theory and principles of writing. (See list of requirements below.) In addition, students are asked to take a second course designed especially for Majors, "The Situation of Writing" (C92), generally offered once in the spring of the year, which asks about the writer's relation to the culture, both currently and historically. The course addresses such questions as the relation of criticism to imaginative literature, the rise and fall of specific literary genres, the effect of the university on the production and consumption of literary works, and the writer's changing sense of audience.

A third unique feature of the Major is the Honors Tutorial (C99), in which, after qualifying, the student works individually with a faculty member on a final writing project. Scheduled during one of the quarters of the senior year, the Final Project is usually a combination of older work, which the student revises, and new work; the tutorial term also involves an analytic component, so that the student gains further expertise in the close reading of writers who will be of immediate pertinence to the particular original projects that are to make up the final manuscript of work. The Final Project is reviewed by a committee of Writing Faculty, and the grade suggested by the C99 instructor is subject to the approval of that committee.

More than half the members of the staff of the Writing Major are or have been editors of literary quarterlies, small presses, or established publishing houses. Thus, instruction in the theory and practice of fiction, poetry, and the essay is augmented by the faculty's considerable knowledge of publishing, editing, and book preparation. Furthermore, all of the Writing Major faculty members are currently publishing their own work in journals and in book form. (See list of faculty.) Contributing to the lively atmosphere for undergraduate writers at Northwestern are several publishing and academic initiatives: *TriQuarterly* magazine, an international journal of writing, art, and cultural inquiry, is published at Northwestern three times a year. A new writing initiative, the University-wide Center for the Writing Arts, will also host visitors, colloquia, a publishing series, and new courses for writers. Writing by students at Northwestern is recognized by the award-winning student literary magazine, *Helicon*, and by the annual spring competition for English Department Prizes (last year, over $4,000 was awarded for essays, poetry, fiction, and drama).

Another attractive feature of the English Major in Writing is the Writers-in-Residence Program. Each year we bring to campus at least one writer in each genre for one week of writing classes and advanced seminars, a public reading, and individual conferences with advanced writing students. Writers-in-Residence from past years include Frank Conroy, Robert Coover, J.V. Cunningham, Stuart Dybek, Jonathan Penner, Julia Randall, Gjertrud Schnackenberg, Vikram Seth, Louis Simpson, Josef Skvorecky, W.D. Snodgrass, Timothy Steele, Arturo Vivante, C.K. Williams, Eleanor Wilner, Robley Wilson, Anne Winters, Larry Woiwode, and Tobias Wolff. Fiction writer Lee Smith came to campus in 1995, as did Irish poet Eavan Boland. In the spring of 1996, poet Mark Strand and fiction writer Lynne Sharon Schwartz were in residence.

Teaching Staff of the English Major in Writing: Joanna Anos, poet. Gian Balsamo, fabulist, translator, fiction writer, theorist, and author of *Sentimental Rousseau*. Paul Breslin, author of a critical study, *The Psycho-Political Muse*). Tony Eprile, author of many nonfiction articles about South Africa and a collection of stories, *Temporary Sojourner*. Joseph Epstein, editor of *The American Scholar*; author of *Partial Payments, A Line Out for a Walk*, and *The Goldin Boys* (stories). Reginald Gibbons, editor of *TriQuarterly*; author of poetry collections, *The Ruined Motel, Maybe It Was So*, and a novel, *Sweetbitter*. Mary Kinzie, author of poetry collections, including *Summers of Vietnam, Autumn Eros*, and *Ghost Ship*. Johnny Payne, author of fiction, translations, and criticism, including *Triumph of the New Word*. Poet and critic Charles Wasserburg teaches poetry and fiction.

For more information, contact Mary Kinzie, Director, English Major in Writing, Dept. of English.

❖University of Notre Dame
Notre Dame, IN 46556-0368
(219) 631-7526
e-mail: english.righter.1@nd.edu
website: http//www.nd.edu

Degree offered: MFA

Type of Program: Studio/Academic

Length of Residency: Two years

Required course of study: 36 s/hrs
 Thesis: required
 Writing workshops: 12 s/hrs
 Literature courses: 12 s/hrs
 Tutorials: 12 s/hrs

Application Deadline: February 1.

The program in creative writing at the University of Notre Dame is relatively new, but it is built on a long-standing tradition within an English Department with a distinguished history in creative writing, its teachers over the years preparing young writers-to-be from Edwin O'Connor (class of '36) to Barry Lopez (class of '66) to Michael Collins (class of '87), the recipient of the 1988 Young Writer of the Year Award in the Republic of Ireland. *The Space Between*, an anthology of Notre Dame poetry edited by James Walton, includes work by 19 well-known poets associated with the university from 1950 to the present, including Ernest Sandeen, John Frederick Nims, Henry Rago, Anthony Kerrigan, John Logan, Paul Carroll, Samuel Hazo, John Engels, and Michael Ryan.

Notre Dame's program aims to be small and selective, with the expectation that students will work closely with the creative writing faculty on a thesis project that consists of a volume of the student's work, usually a novel, a collection of short stories, a volume of poetry, or a work of literary nonfiction. *The Notre Dame Review*, our new national literary magazine, has positions for graduate students as Editorial Assistants, as well as Managing Editor. The program also sponsors, along with the University of Notre Dame Press, the Sandeen/Sullivan prizes, a second book (or later) rotating short story and poetry volume competition.

The full-time writing faculty includes poet and novelist Sonia Gernes (*The Mutes of Sleepy Eye, Brief Lives, The Way to St. Ives*), poet and translator John Matthias (*Bucyrus, The Battle of Kosovo*, and *Contemporary Swedish Poetry*), novelist William O'Rourke (*The Meekness of Isaac, Idle Hands*, and *Criminal Tendencies*), novelist Valerie Sayers (*Due East, How I Got Him Back*, and *The Distance Between Us*), and novelist James Walton (*Margaret's Book*). Visiting writers have been coming to Notre Dame since 1968 in the context of The Sophomore Literary Festival, a week of readings, workshops, and related events. These authors include Norman Mailer, Joseph Heller, Ralph Ellison, John Barth, Robert Duncan, Gwendolyn Brooks, Tennessee Williams, Edward Albee, Denise Levertov, Margaret Atwood, Czeslaw Milosz, John Irving, Mary Gordon, Seamus Heaney, Marge Piercy, Susan Sontag, and Derek Walcott.

The Creative Writing Program offers full tuition scholarships and a limited number of fellowships. For application or further information, write or call: The Director of Creative Writing, Dept. of English.

❖Nottingham Trent University
Clifton Lane
Nottingham
England NG11 8NS

44-115-948-6335
FAX 44-115-948-6632
e-mail: mahendra.solanki@ntu.ac.uk
website: http://human.ntu.ac.uk/foh/pg/mawrit.html

Degree offered: MA in Writing (autobiography, biography, features, fiction, hypertext, internet, poetry, technology, travel)

Type of Program: Studio

Length of Residency: 15 months full-time, 24 months part-time.

Required course of study: Students can expect to attend for a total of 140 contact hours throughout the course, plus extra independent writing time. Most of these contact hours are spent in workshops and tutorials. (Please note that these are English *contact* hours and do not correspond to the American system of semester hours.)

Other Requirements: Students take 2 from a choice of 4 options: Feature Writing, Fiction, Lifewriting, Poetry.

Application Deadlines: Admissions: July 31 (NB: the UK teaching term usually begins around the last week of September/first week of October.) Financial Aid: We regret there is no financial aid available at this time.

The MA in Writing invites students to develop their writing strengths by providing a framework of workshops supported by occasional seminars or lectures. It encourages them to discuss their own and each other's work and promotes rigorous editorial criticism. It is of use to all practicing writers interested in exploring the ways in which writing is made, from inspiration and research right through the final draft, and is keen to encompass the growing links between writing, virtuality, and the Internet. To this end, there is an opportunity to collaborate in *trAce*, a new WWW-based writing project. As well as providing an intellectual and creative challenge, the course also offers the opportunity to work with a variety of professional authors and fosters a stimulating environment for practical and imaginative development. Classes generally comprise around ten students.

Visiting Writers: In recent years we have hosted three Writers-in-Residence, and we are especially pleased to welcome Michele Roberts and Miranda Seymour as Visiting Writing Fellows. Other guests have included Meena Alexander, Simon Armitage, Jackie Brown, Carolyn Caughey, Mary Chauhan, Gillian Clarke, Michael Donaghy, Kevin Fegan, Alison Fell, David Gale, Martin Glyn, Paul Hyland, Mark Illis, Kathleen Jamie, Gwyneth Jones, Graham Joyce, Janice Kulyk Keefer, Sarah Lefanu, Jeremy Lewis, Glyn Maxwell, James Melville, Peter Mortimer, Andrew Motion, Kathy Page, Kate Pullinger, Carole Satyamurti, and Martin Stannard.

Nottinghamshire has a history of producing challenging writers, perhaps the best known being D.H. Lawrence, Lord Byron, and Miranda Seymour, and the area features a range of creative influences from the post-Victorian multiculturalism of the city to the rural farmlands and forestry of the surrounding countryside.

The MA in Writing makes its own contribution to this culture with regular public events where authors are invited to read and discuss their work. For example, the major event for 1996 was held in conjunction with a local restaurant: *Recipes for Pleasure: Food as inspiration? Food as seduction? Food as fashion? Food as addiction?* These public events are supported by smaller and more personal visits where the MA students meet with authors, agents, and editors.

The permanent creative writing team includes poet and lifewriter Catherine Byron (*Out of Step: Pursuing Seamus Heaney to Purgatory, The Fat-Hen Field Hospital: Poems 1985–92, Settlements & Samhain*); biographer Katherine Frank (*Lucie Duff Gordon: A Passage to Egypt, Emily Brontë, A Voyager Out: The Life of Mary Kingsley*); novelist and journalist David Gale (*A Diet of Holes, Slips, The Art of Tripping*); novelist and Internet writer Sue Thomas (*Correspondence, Water, Wild Women*); poet and critic Gregory Woods (*Articulate Flesh: Male Homo-Eroticism in Modern Poetry, We Have the Melon, This is No Book*).

For more information, contact Mahendra Solanki, Course Leader, at the above address.

Oberlin College
Oberlin, OH 44074
(440) 775-6567
FAX (440) 775-8124
e-mail: martha.collins@oberlin.edu or
pamela.alexander@oberlin.edu

Degree offered: BA in Creative Writing

Required course of study: 37 s/hrs
Creative Writing: 25 s/hrs
Literature: 12 s/hrs

Application Deadlines: Contact Admissions Office.

The Creative Writing Program is a rigorous course of study which provides training in poetry, fiction, playwriting, creative nonfiction, and translation. Two large first-year courses introduce students to some of the techniques of poetry and fiction; subsequent courses are limited to 12 students. The introduction poetry/prose workshop, Creative Writing 201, acquaints students with workshop protocol and critiquing methods, and is a pre-requisite for most advanced courses. Students must also complete workshops in three of the five genres mentioned above, and intermediate and advanced projects in at least one of those genres; the projects involve weekly one-on-one meetings with an advisor. By the end of their final year, graduating majors are expected to turn in a substantial portfolio of completed work and to give a senior reading. The curriculum is based on the view that reading is essential to a writer's training, and most courses include extensive reading assignments. An English major with a concentration in creative writing (15 semester hours of creative writing) is also available.

Several student publications, run by various groups on campus, provide creative writing majors the opportunity to see their work in print. The Oberlin College Press is run by professors who are creative writers, and includes among its publications *Field*, an internationally recognized journal of poetry and ongoing series in poetry and translation. A few students have worked for the Press throughout the year, and many have had internships with literary magazines and publishing houses throughout the country during winter term. Winter term also offers students a chance to work independently with individual instructors, or collectively under the sponsorship of advanced students.

The Creative Writing faculty includes: poet Pamela Alexander (*Navigable Waterways; Commonwealth of Wings; Inland*); poet and translator Martha Collins (*The Catastrophe of Rainbows; The Arrangement of Space; A History of Small Life on a Windy Planet*); fiction and nonfiction writer Sylvia Watanabe (*Talking to the Dead*; editor, *Into the Fire, Asian American Prose* and *Home to Stay: Asian American Women's Fiction*); and poet, translator, and nonfiction writer David Young (eight books of poems, including *Henry Vaughan and Night Thoughts; The Planet on the Desk; Earthshine*; numerous books of translations of Holub, Rilke, and others). A visiting writer (currently fiction writer Dan Chaon) is hired every year, and faculty from other departments who teach for the program include poet Jessica Grim, nonfiction, fiction, and poetry writer Calvin Hernton, director and theatre specialist Caroline Jackson-Smith, poet Carol Tufts, nonfiction writer Thomas Van Nortwick, and poet and translator David Walker.

On-campus readings and meetings with students have featured such writers as Toni Morrison, Margaret Atwood, Charles Simic, Charles Wright, Rita Dove, Miroslav Holub, Grace Paley, Maxine Hong Kingston, and Adrienne Rich.

For more information, contact Director, Creative Writing Program, at above address.

❖Ohio State University
164 West 17th Avenue
Columbus, OH 43210-1370
(614) 292-2242
FAX (614) 292-7816
e-mail: griffin.6@osu.edu

Degrees offered: BA, MFA

Degree: BA in English with a Concentration in Creative Writing

Application Deadline: January 15 for financial aid and admission.

The undergraduate concentration in creative writing requires up to 20 hrs of creative writing workshops in addition to 40 hrs of other English courses and a creative thesis. Honors students may design an undergraduate English major in creative writing, and write a creative thesis.

Degree: MFA in Creative Writing (poetry, fiction, nonfiction)

Type of Program: Studio/Academic

Length of Residency: 2–3 years

Students in the MFA program must complete 65 hrs of course work including: 25 hrs of graduate creative writing workshops; 20 hrs of English other than creative writing workshops, 5 of which could be Individual Studies; a minimum of 10 hrs of 700 or 800-level literature classes in an historical period; any other 5-hr graduate-level course offered by the Department of English; 5 hrs of a course in literary form; 5 hrs of electives in related areas outside the Department or any other relevant course approved by the student's faculty advisor; 10 hrs of creative thesis tutorial; and an approved creative thesis, followed by an oral defense.

Other Requirements: One course in the teaching of freshman composition (this does count toward the 65 hrs of course work).

Application Deadline: Postmarked no later than December 31.

The aim of the Creative Writing Program is to help undergraduate and graduate students develop to the fullest their talents and abilities as writers of poetry, fiction, and creative nonfiction, with the expectation of eventual publication. A further goal is to create and sustain an active community of writers, faculty, and students -- a critical mass of artists serving as a resource for each of its members. It is the belief of the faculty that writers learn by writing and reading. Creative writing classes are conducted as workshops or tutorials, with emphasis given to student manuscripts. Literature courses, with some exceptions, are those of the English program of graduate study. It is the intention of the Creative Writing faculty to maintain a fairly small (ca. 40 students total), highly selective MFA program. Students compete for University Fellowships and Teaching, Research, and Administrative Associateships. Every admitted student receives full funding for not less than two years.

Students work with resident faculty and distinguished visiting writers, usually two a year in residency. These writers of national and international stature offer short courses for academic credit and deliver a public reading. Recent distinguished visiting writers have included John Barth, Brenda Hillman, Edward Hirsch, Maxine Kumin, Alison Lurie, Alice McDermott, Tillie Olsen, Robert Pinsky, Mary Robison, Geoffrey Wolff, Josef Skvorecky, Tim O'Brien, Robert Olmstead, Frederick Busch, Alice Fulton, Ron Carlson, Carol Muske, Phillip Lopate, and Billy Collins.

Once each year the Writer-in-Residence at the Thurber House offers a 5-credit quarter-long course in the Program (in the recent past, the Thurber House Writers have included Pinckney Benedict, Enid Shomer, Leila Phillip, Alfred Corn, John Daniel, Patricia Traxler, and Meg Files).

Established in 1973, *The Journal: The Literary Magazine of The Ohio State University* has offered the university's best writing students an opportunity to work as student editors of a publication with a growing national reputation. Students work on the staff of *The Journal* through the university's Work/Study Program, and compete on the graduate level for the Managing and Associate Editorships. Each year, through the Ohio State University Press/*The Journal* Award in Poetry, a full length manuscript of poems is selected in an open competition. The author of the winning manuscript receives $1,000, and the book is published by OSU Press.

The OSU Creative Writing MFA Program also co-sponsors with the University Press The Sandstone Prize in Short Fiction. An independent judge selects one manuscript for this annual award. The winning author receives a cash prize of $1,500, publication under a standard book contract, and an invitation to direct a creative writing program workshop and to perform a public reading. Winner is announced in May each year.

The resident faculty in Creative Writing at Ohio State: Lee K. Abbott, Director of the Creative Writing Program (*Wet Places at Noon, The Heart Never Fits Its Wanting,* and *Dreams of Distant Lives*). Among his awards are two NEA Fellowships, and two nominations for the Pulitzer Prize in fiction. David Citino, poet (*The Book of Appassionata: Collected Poems, Broken Symmetry, The Weight of the Heart*). Among his awards are the Distinguished Teaching Award from Ohio State, the Exemplary Faculty Award from the OSU College of Humanities, The Nancy Dasher Award from the College English Association of Ohio, and a Fellowship in Poetry from the National Endowment for the Arts. Kathy Fagan, poet (*The Raft*, National Poetry Series selection, and the forthcoming *Revisionary Instruments*, winner of the 1998 Vassar Miller Prize for Poetry). She is the recipient of Fellowships in Poetry from the National Endowment for the Arts, the Ingram Merrill Foundation, and the Ohio Arts Council. Michelle Herman, fiction (*A New and Glorious Life* and *Missing*, which was awarded the Harold Ribalow Prize for best Jewish fiction). Among her awards are NEA Creative Writing Fellowship, a James Michener Fellowship, and an Individual Artist's Fellowship from the Ohio Arts Council. Jeredith Merrin, poet, is the author of a book of criticism, *Marianne Moore, Elizabeth Bishop, and the Uses of Tradition*, and of *Shift*, a book of lyric poetry. Bill Roorbach, nonfiction (*Summers with Juliet, Writing Life Stories*). Melanie Rae Thon, fiction (*Iona Moon, Meteors in August, Girls in the Grass*). She has received grants from the Massachusetts Artists Foundation, the New York Foundation for the Arts, and the National Endowment for the Arts. In 1997 she received a Whiting Writer's Award and in 1996, *Granta* named her one of the "Best Young American Novelists."

For further information, contact Lee K. Abbott, Director, Creative Writing Program.

❖Ohio University
Athens, OH 45701-2979
(740) 593-2838

Degrees offered: BA, MA, PhD

Degree: BA in English with Concentration in Creative Writing

Required course of study: 56 q/hrs in major (beyond freshman level coursework)
  Thesis: no requirement
  Writing workshop: 20 q/hrs

Other Requirements: English composition; foreign language proficiency; 18 q/hrs humanities; 19 q/hrs social sciences; 19 q/hrs natural sciences.

At the undergraduate level, Ohio University offers creative writing workshops in fiction, poetry, nonfiction; courses in form and theory of these three genres; and independent projects in each genre.

Degree: MA in English with Creative Thesis (poetry, fiction, creative nonfiction)

Type of Program: Literature as well as Creative Writing

Required course of study: 70 q/hrs (60 q/hrs for pre-doctoral candidates)

Thesis: 5-15 q/hrs
Writing workshop: 15-20 q/hrs
Literature courses: 35-40 q/hrs

Other Requirements: Bibliography and methods course or history-of-English course; form and theory course; oral defense of thesis.

Application Deadline: March 1.

Degree: PhD in English with Creative Dissertation (poetry, fiction, creative nonfiction)

Type of Program: Literature as well as Creative Writing

Required course of study: 45-60 q/hrs beyond the MA (total 105-120 q/hrs)

Other Requirements: Comprehensive written exam; reading knowledge of one foreign language; oral defense of creative dissertation.

Application Deadline: March 1.

Since its establishment in 1964, the Creative Writing Program at Ohio University has remained an integral part of the English curriculum. The interaction and cooperation between the Creative Writing Program and the Literature Program are extensive and mutually enriching. The Creative Writing Program is relatively small but plays a vigorous and visible role in Department and University life. Collegial relations among faculty and MA candidates and PhD candidates are continuous and energetic.

Graduates of the Creative Writing Program have won numerous national awards. Distinguished alumni include William Heyen, Bin Ramke, Stanley Plumly, Dave Smith, Patricia Goedicke, Robert Taylor, Wendell Mayo, and Ed Allen.

Both the MA and the PhD programs culminate in a book-length manuscript deemed by the Creative Writing faculty to be of publishable quality. The dissertation is expected to be of greater length and complexity than the MA thesis, and to include a significant critical/scholarly component.

Teaching assistantships are available at both MA and PhD levels.

The Creative Writing faculty includes: Joan Connor, fiction (*Here on Old Route 7*); David Lazar, nonfiction (*Conversations With M.F.K. Fisher, Michael Powell: Interviews*); Jack Matthews, fiction (*Crazy Women, Dirty Tricks, Storyhood As We Know It*); Darrell Spencer, fiction (*Our Secret's Out, Blood Work*); Mark Halliday, poet, director of Creative Writing (*Little Star, Tasker Street, Selfwolf*); Mary Ruefle, visiting poet 1998-1999 (*Cold Pluto, Post Meridian*).

Each year the Program brings visiting writers to campus, often for three-day residencies. The annual Spring Literary Festival, a nationally noted event, brings five distinguished writers to Ohio University for three days of public events. Recent Festival writers include John Ashbery, Russell Banks, Anne Carson, Richard Ford, Jorie Graham, Kenneth Koch, Philip Levine, and Grace Paley.

For more information, write to Creative Writing Program, Dept. of English.

Ohio Wesleyan University
Delaware, OH 43015
(800) 922-8953
(740) 368-3592
e-mail: RJFlanag@cc.owu.edu

Degree offered: BA in English with Concentration in Creative Writing

Required course of study: At least 10 English courses and a senior portfolio (about 40 s/hrs), including 5 writing workshops, 4 literature courses, and 1 elective.

Application Deadline: March 1 for admission and financial aid.

The writing program is an integral and dynamic part of Ohio Wesleyan's English Department; nearly half of the department's current majors are in Creative Writing or nonfiction writing.

The Creative Writing concentration offers workshops in Writing Fiction, Playwriting, Writing Poetry, and Screenwriting as well as Advanced Creative Writing. Students also may take Independent Studies in writing and/or work as editing apprentices in Literary Magazine Editing, the course which produces *The Owl*, a student literary magazine published each semester.

The writing environment at Ohio Wesleyan includes a Visiting Writers program which brings 4 to 6 writers to campus each year for readings or periods of residence -- in the past few years, guests have included novelists Joyce Carol Oates and Kurt Vonnegut, poets Brenda Hillman and Robert Pinsky, and essayists Scott Russell Sanders and Richard Selzer; student/faculty readings each semester hosted by the literary magazine; the OMNI-Versal Readings, a student poetry reading series; Theatre's Lunchbox Showcase at which student plays are read or performed; an annual campus-wide literary competition and a dozen writing awards in a variety of genres, with cash prizes.

Writing faculty includes: program director Robert Flanagan, a fiction writer, poet, and screenwriter (*Loving Power; Maggot: Naked to Naked Goes*); novelist and literary editor Lynette Carpenter (*Six Feet Under; Fade to Black; Haunting the House of Fiction*); poet and specialist in modern poetics Jeffrey Peterson (*Unpaged*); and playwright and theater director Bonnie Milne Gardner (*Daddy's Home; Day Old Bread; Forever Fraternal*).

A number of writing majors have gone on to graduate school in creative writing at Columbia University, Cornell University, Johns Hopkins University, New York University, University of Colorado, and University of Iowa. Others have worked as editors at Harper & Row, Random House, Little, Brown & Co., *Paris Review*, the *New York Review of Books*, and *The Village Voice*.

For further information, contact Robert Flanagan, Director of Creative Writing, Dept. of English.

Okanagan University College
7000 College Way
Vernon, B.C. Canada V1B 2N5

Degree offered: BA

Okanagan University College is a four-year university college with main campuses at Salmon Arm, Vernon, Kelowna, and Penticton, B.C. OUC's creative writing program, offered through the English Department, is designed to provide beginning writers an opportunity to improve their skills in writing and reading contemporary fiction, poetry, scripts and creative nonfiction.

At present (1993-94), a total of six sections of creative writing are offered at OUC's Vernon and Kelowna campuses. These sections enroll about 100 students at the introductory, intermediate, and advanced levels.

Introductory creative writing classes are open to any registered OUC student. No portfolio is required. Successful completion of introductory courses, however, is a prerequisite for the next highest level of instruction. To enroll for advanced study, intermediate courses must be successfully completed, and third-year student status obtained.

The introductory workshop in creative writing (English 116/126) is a two-term, multigenre course, intended to expose students to various techniques and strategies in contemporary literature. Two-term intermediate courses currently are offered in short fiction (English 217/227) and poetry (English 216/226). In these classes students further refine their writing skills and broaden their knowledge of modern and contemporary practitioners of their chosen genre. Advanced courses (Creative Writing 409 [Short Fiction] and Creative Writing 410 [Poetry]) offer further exposure to, and practice in, the student writer's area of specialty. OUC's advanced courses at present are classified as on-site offerings of the University of B.C.'s Creative Writing Department.

All three levels of OUC's creative writing program are credit courses, fully transferable to other post-secondary institutions. Our creative writing faculty members in 1993-94 were: Chris Castanier, Nancy Holmes, John Lent, and Tom Wayman. All are working writers, fully engaged with the Canadian literary world. A creative writing student club publishes a campus literary magazine, *Chiaroscuro*. Public readings by students are held, both as part of the curriculum and outside it.

For more information on OUC's creative writing program, contact John Lent at the Vernon campus at (604) 545-7291 or Nancy Holmes at the Penticton campus at (604) 492-4305. Or write either John Lent or Nancy Holmes c/o Dept. of English, OUC, 3333 College Way, Kelowna, B.C. 1V1 1V7.

❖Oklahoma State University
Stillwater, OK 74078-4069
(405) 744-9474
FAX (405) 744-6326
e-mail: dalmcl@okway.okstate.edu
website: http://www.writing.okstate.edu/english

Degrees offered: BA, MA, PhD

Degree: BA in English with Concentration in Creative Writing (poetry, fiction, dramatic script)

Required course of study: 53 hours total (in Major)
Writing workshops: 15 hours
Literature courses: 21 hours
Non-English electives: 17 hours

Other requirements: Cross-genre study is required, as is literary study in both British and American areas. A Senior Seminar serves as a capstone course and a creative thesis is submitted to the faculty.

The undergraduate writing community is served by The English Club, and by the Creative Writers' Association, both of which sponsor readings and social events, often in conjunction with our thriving graduate program. *Papyrus* is the campus literary magazine which provides editorial and publishing experience for undergraduates. Undergraduate writers are eligible for all program awards competitions.

Degree: MA in English with Concentration in Creative Writing (poetry, fiction, dramatic script)

Type of Program: Studio/Academic

Length of Residency: Two years

Required course of study: 30 s/hrs total
Thesis: 6 hours
Writing workshops: 6-9 s/hrs
Literature courses: 15-18 s/hrs

Other Requirements: Written comprehensive examination; oral defense of thesis; reading knowledge of one foreign language; required course in rhetoric/composition teaching methods for teaching assistantships.

Application Deadlines: April 1 for both financial aid (teaching assistantships) and admission to graduate college.

Degree: PhD in English with Concentration in Creative Writing

Type of Program: Traditional Literary Study and Creative Writing

Length of Residency: Three to five years

Required course of study: 60 s/hrs total
Dissertation: 15-20 s/hrs
Writing workshop: 9-15 s/hrs
Literature courses: 25-36 s/hrs

Other Requirements: Written comprehensive examination; oral defense of dissertation; mastery of one foreign language or reading knowledge of two; required course in rhetoric/composition teaching methods for teaching assistantships.

Application Deadlines: April 1 for both financial aid (teaching assistantships) and admission to graduate college.

Since 1975, our creative writing program has been an integral part of a Department committed to diversity in its offerings and to helping students make the correct educational choices for a career in teaching. OSU's English graduate program in creative writing focuses on the vital relationship between the literary arts of fictional, poetic, and dramatic composition and the larger literary tradition of our language. In both the MA and PhD programs, students select course work to balance their writing courses and literary study. Creative writing students meet the examination requirements for all engaged in the study of literature, augmenting those studies with writing workshops, and submit original creative works in place of the traditional scholarly thesis or dissertation. Doctoral students also have the option of testing in the Practical Poetics and Fictional Rhetoric comprehensive examination area. We are proud of our excellent placement record.

The creative writing faculty welcome students from various backgrounds and we function well with an eclectic range of student writing. We all find personal contact with student writers to be rewarding, we encourage cross–genre study, and we limit enrollment in workshops to 10 students, allowing for rigorous, yet supportive, educational settings. Our PhD program attracts a diverse population of writers holding both MA and MFA degrees. Typically, the program consists of 25–30 writers in any given semester.

We host, on average, five visiting writers per year. Visiting writers during the past five years include: Lynn Emanuel, Jack Myers, Pattiann Rogers, Ralph Angel, Edward Allen, Jonathan Holden, Albert Goldbarth, Walter Wetherell, T.R. Hummer, Gladys Swan, Debra Monroe, Richard Price, Kent Nelson, Richard Jackson, Ben Marcus, Luci Tapahonso, François Camoin, Louise Glück, Stanley Plumly, Janet Peery, Bret Lott, Mark Doty, C.D. Wright, John Yau, Ralph Burns, and Gordon Lish.

Cimarron Review, a quarterly literary journal published since 1967, is edited and produced by the program; staff members include program students. The department also publishes *Common*, a literary annual devoted to criticism and theory, also staffed by program students. Program students present frequent readings in cooperation with the Creative Writers' Association and the English Graduate Student Association, and support is available to assist program students to travel to regional conferences and workshops.

The Department awards teaching assistantships to qualified program students, and also offers annual literary prizes for students (OSU Short Fiction and Poetry Awards, Academy of American Poets Prize).

The creative writing program faculty includes poet Mark Cox (*Smoulder*, *Thirty-seven Years from the Stone*, recipient of a Whiting Writers' Award, a Pushcart Prize, and a Kansas Arts Commission Fellowship); fiction writer Brian Evenson (*Altmann's Tongue*, *Father of Lies*, recipient of NEA and Helm fellowships); poet Lisa Lewis (*The Unbeliever*, *Silent Treatment*, recipient of the Brittingham Prize, National Poetry Series, a Pushcart Prize); film historian Leonard J. Leff (*Hitchcock and Selznick*, *The Dame in the Kimono: Hollywood, Censorship, and the Production Code from the 1920's to the 1960's*, *Hemingway and His Conspirators*).

For more information, contact: Mark Cox, Director.

❖University of Oklahoma
760 Van Vleet Oval
Norman, OK 73019-0240
(405) 325-4661

Degrees offered: BA, MA

Degree: BA in English in Track 2 -- Writing

Required course of study: 33 hrs of coursework beyond freshman composition, of which a minimum of 12 hrs must be in writing courses, at least 9 hrs of which must be upper division.

Degree: MA in English with Creative Thesis Option

Type of Program: Studio/Academic

Length of Residency: 75% of course work

Required course of study: 30 hrs of course work, 9 of which are required in literature and criticism; of the 15 elective hrs, at least 6 must be in writing courses; up to 6 hours are allowed for the thesis.

Other Requirements: A reading knowledge of a foreign language.

Application Deadline: April 1.

The University of Oklahoma's Department of English offers an undergraduate major, as well as a minor, with a concentration in writing. The Department also offers the MA with the Creative Thesis Option to any qualified student enrolled in its graduate program: application for admission to the option must be made to the Creative Writing Committee at least 2 semesters prior to receipt of the degree. This admission will be based on manuscripts submitted by the student. The thesis will consist of a significant collection of short stories, poems, plays, or other creative prose introduced by a critical/theoretical essay in which the writer defines and places her/his work within its generic and traditional contexts. A thesis defense is required.

The department regularly offers a variety of courses and workshops on both the undergraduate and graduate levels taught by the publishing creative writers in the department: George Economou, Robert Murray Lewis, Michael Flanigan, Geary Hobson, Janet McAdams, Susan Kates, and Vinay Dharwadker, along with adjunct and visiting faculty such as George Bilgere, Frank Chin, Maurice Kenny, Georgina Kleege, David Matlin, Rochelle Owens, Elizabeth Robinson, and Jerome Rothenberg. The program sponsors a series of readings by local writers. In addition, many writers come to campus to give readings and lectures; recent visitors have been Clayton Eshleman and Luci Tapahonso. The literary atmosphere of the OU campus is also charged by the presence of the international journal *World Literature Today*, which awards the Neustadt Prize in Literature and sponsors the Puterbaugh Conference on Writers of the French–Speaking and Hispanic World.

For more information, contact Robert Murray Davis, Creative Writing Committee Coordinator, Dept. of English.

❖Old Dominion University
Norfolk, VA 23529-0078
(757) 683-3991

Degrees offered: BA, MFA

Degree: BA in English with Creative Writing Concentration

Required course of study:
43 s/hrs in English (in addition to other graduation requirements)
Creative Writing courses: 15 s/hrs
Literature courses: 21 s/hrs
Linguistics courses: 3 s/hrs
Intro to English Studies: 1 s/hr
Capstone course: 3 s/hrs

Application Deadlines: Fall: May 1 (freshmen), July 1 (transfers), Spring: December 1, Summer: April 15.

Degree: MFA in Creative Writing

Type of Program: Studio/Academic

Length of Residency: Three years

Required course of study: 54 s/hrs
Workshops: 12-18 s/hrs
Form and Theory courses: 6 s/hrs
Literature courses: 12 s/hrs
Other approved electives: 12 s/hrs
Thesis: 6-12 s/hrs

Other Requirements: Minimum 3.0 overall GPA; mid-program review, competency in one foreign language, successful completion of written comprehensive exams and a book-length manuscript in a single genre.

Application Deadline: Feb. 15 for financial aid consideration; March 1 for all others.

Our MFA is designed to prepare students for careers as published writers of fiction, poetry, and literary nonfiction; college-level teachers; script or speech writers; translators, editors, or publishers.

Regular faculty include: Scott Cairns, poetry (*Recovered Body, Figures for the Ghost, The Translation of Babel*), Maria Luisa Carino, poetry and nonfiction (*In the Garden of the Three Islands, Blood Sacrifice, Encanto*), Michael Pearson, nonfiction (*Imagined Places: Journeys into Literary America, John McPhee, and Dreaming of Columbus: A Boyhood in the Bronx*), Janet Peery, fiction (*The River Beyond the World, Alligator Dance*), Sheri Reynolds, fiction (*A Gracious Plenty, The Rapture of Canaan, Bitterroot Landing*), and Tim Seibles, poetry (*Kerosene, Hurdy-Gurdy, Body Moves*).

For more information, contact: Michael Pearson, Graduate Program Director, Dept. of English, (757) 683-4770, or mpearson@odu.edu.

❖Oregon State University
238 Moreland Hall
Corvallis, OR 97331
(541) 737-3244
e-mail: tdaugherty@orst.edu or msandor@orst.edu

Degrees offered: BA, MA

Required course of study: 48 hrs total
Writing workshops: up to 15 hrs
Forms courses: 15 or more hrs

Other requirements: University distribution requirements; thesis defense.

Application Deadline: February 1.

The creative writing faculty includes: Jennifer Cornell (*Departures*); Tracy Daugherty (*Desire Provoked, What Falls Away, The Woman in the Oil Field*); Ehud Havazelet (*What Is It Then Between Us, Like Never Before*); and Marjorie Sandor (*A Night of Music, The Night Gardener*).

Contact the Creative Writing Program Director, Dept. of English.

❖University of Oregon
Eugene, OR 97403-5243
(541) 346-3944
FAX (541) 346-0537
e-mail: catelay@oregon.uoregon.edu

Degrees offered: BA, MA, MFA

Degree: MFA

Required course of study: 72 q/hrs
Thesis: up to 18 q/hrs
Writing workshop: 36 q/hrs
Literature/craft courses: 20 q/hrs
Tutorials or directed reading: up to 10 q/hrs

Other Requirements: No language requirement.

Application Deadlines: February 1.

Kid Tutorial: This is a $1.14 million endowment which funds a special program of prizes and tutorials in creative writing for undergraduates.

The creative writing faculty includes: poet Garrett Hongo (*Yellow Light* and *The River of Heaven*); poet Dorianne Laux (*Awake* and *What We Carry*); poet Pimone Triplett (*Ruining the Picture*); and fiction writer Peter Ho Davies (*Ugliest House in the World*).

For further information, contact Dorianne Laux, Director, Program in Creative Writing, 114 Columbia Hall.

❖Otterbein College
Westerville, OH 43081
(614) 823-1218
FAX (614) 823-1315

Degree offered: BA in English with Writing Concentration

Required course of study:
45 q/hrs beyond core courses in composition and literature
Thesis: 5 q/hrs
Writing workshop: 15 q/hrs
Other writing courses: 5 q/hrs
Literature: 20 q/hrs

For more information, contact Norman Chaney, Chair, Dept. of English.

Pace University
New York, NY 10038

(212) 346-1402

Degrees offered: BA, MS

Degree: BA in English, Writing & Literature Concentration

Required course of study: 36 credits
Professional Writing & Editing
Professional Writer's Forum
Critical Writing & Analysis

In addition, (3) of the following courses may be selected and should precede ENG 225 and 226.
Report Writing
Advanced Writing
Creative Writing -- may be taken more than
once; includes Poetry, Short Fiction, & Drama
Journalism

This concentration is designed for students who look to careers as professional writers or who realize that writing well is a marketable skill that will bring them substantial rewards, whatever career path they might follow. The program offers a wide variety of writing courses, such as Report Writing, Journalism, TV News Writing, Feature Writing, Creative Writing, and many more. Upon completion of this concentration, many students find employment on newspapers and magazines, at TV and radio stations, in public relations, or in editing corporate in-house newsletters and magazines.

Degree: MS in Publishing

Required course of study: 36 credits
Principles of Publishing
Book Production & Design or
Marketing Production & Design
Financial Aspects of Publishing
General Interest Books: Acquisitions,
Subsidiary Rights, Promotion & Distribution,
the Publishing Contract
Information Systems in Publishing
Editorial Principles & Practices

This program educates its students in all aspects of the publishing business: finance, production, sales and marketing, the legal intricacies of acquisitions and subsidiary rights, editing.

For information on offerings in Creative Writing, contact the Dept. of English.

Pasadena City College
Pasadena, CA 91106

(818) 585-7371

Degree offered: AA

Required course of study: 60 s/hrs total
Humanities Division courses: 18 s/hrs
General Education requirement: 33 s/hrs
PE and Health Ed: 2 s/hrs each

Application Deadlines: Friday before first day of semester.

The Creative Writing program at this two-year college consists of an introductory course, Short Story Writing, Poetry Writing, Play Writing, and publication of the campus literary magazine, *Inscape*. In addition to earning the AA degree, students may satisfy the lower division requirements for transfer in advanced standing at four-year colleges and universities; these requirements may include specific courses in literature as well as those in creative writing, and vary according to the school.

For further information, contact Writing Program Director, Dept. of English.

❖Pennsylvania State University
117 Burrowes Building
University Park, PA 16802

(814) 865-6381

Degrees offered: BA, MFA

Degree: BA in English, emphasis in creative writing

Required course of study: 36 s/hrs (major)
Thesis: 3 s/hrs (Honors only)
Writing workshops: 15 s/hrs
Literature courses: 15-21 or more s/hrs

Other Requirements: None, except honors thesis for students enrolled in Honors Program.

Classes in both the undergraduate and graduate writing programs at Penn State are small, and students' manuscripts receive the close attention of a writing faculty that consists of poets, short story writers, novelists, radio and television script writers, and nonfiction writers.

Undergraduate requirements are designed to meet the needs of a wide range of students, from the student who wishes to explore a variety of writing forms to the one who wishes to concentrate primarily on one form. Beyond the core requirement, students may take courses from a broad "pool," which takes advantage of the resources of a large university. This pool includes, in addition to the basic sequences in fiction, poetry, and nonfiction, courses in journalism, film writing, theatre writing, television writing, radio drama, biography, science writing, technical writing, and editing.

Several internships with established public publications or television stations are available on a regular basis for qualified undergraduates, each involving some combination of editing, research, nonfiction writing, and even publicity writing. The program allows majors to gain practical experience in publishing and to develop a portfolio of published work as a source of on-the-job references.

The Department sponsors 2 undergraduate writing competitions annually: The Nichols Award for the best stories submitted in the introductory fiction writing courses in a given year, and the Katey Lehman Creative Writing Awards in fiction, poetry, nonfiction writing, and journalism -- a university-wide competition with annual prize money of approximately $1,000 in each category.

Degree: MFA in Creative Writing (poetry, fiction, literary nonfiction)

Type of Program: Studio/Academic

Required course of study: 48 s/hrs
Thesis: 6-12 s/hrs
Writing workshop: 15 s/hrs
Elective courses: 6-12 s/hrs
Literature courses: 15 s/hrs

The Department of English of Pennsylvania State University offers a flexible 2 to 3-year program in poetry writing, fiction writing, and creative nonfiction writing leading to the Master of Fine Arts degree. The program provides an opportunity for students of superior ability in imaginative writing to develop their skills and critical judgment through the practice of writing and the study of literature. The course of study is highly adaptable to individual interests. The aim of the program is to help talented students prepare for a career in writing. Degree candidates are expected to produce a book-length work of literary value and publishable quality.

While it is recommended that applicants have an undergraduate major in either English or creative writing, the program does not discourage applicants from other undergraduate disciplines. Regardless of the undergraduate major, applicants should have a 3.20 grade-point average on a 4.00 scale. Students must submit a score for the general aptitude section of the Graduate Record Examination, 3 letters of recommendation, transcripts of all undergraduate work, and, most important, writing samples. For fiction and creative nonfiction, at least 30 pages are required; for poetry, at least 12 poems. These samples are expected to show enough writing skill and experience to suggest that by the end of the program, students will be able to meet the writing project requirement. Manuscripts will not be returned. Applicants should retain copies of the work submitted. Since decisions about admissions are usually made for the fall semester in March, applications, including GRE scores, must be received by the director of graduate studies by January 15. Application forms and an information packet may be obtained by calling (814) 863-0369 or by writing to Graduate Admissions, Dept. of English, Penn State University, University Park, PA 16802. Applicants for assistantships must file an assistantship application, as well as a third letter of recommendation, preferably one indicating teaching potential.

Candidates for the MFA degree must complete a total of 48 credits, 27 of which are taken in the area of writing specialization. These include workshop courses (15 credits) and the final writing project (12 credits). The remaining 21 credits are taken in literature (15 credits) and electives (6 credits). The final writing project must be a book-length manuscript in the area of specialization. In fiction and creative nonfiction, a minimum length of 200 pages is expected; in poetry, at least 50 pages.

In the final semester, candidates will be administered a take-home examination on topics set by the MFA committee. In addressing the topics, students will be asked to demonstrate knowledge of both contemporary and modern literature.

Financial aid is provided in several varieties. The Katey Lehman Fellowship (of $13,000 stipend and tuition) is awarded annually to an incoming student.

Teaching assistantships are available on a competitive basis. Teaching assistants generally teach freshman composition in their first year, introduction to creative writing in their second year, and, when available, an introductory course in their area of specialization in their third year. Applications for such positions must be made on the form provided by the director of graduate studies. There are no special forms for the Lehman Fellowship. All of these positions carry full remission of tuition and related fees.

Seven writers comprise the MFA faculty. Poet Robin Becker, whose books include *All-American Girl*, *Giacometti's Dog*, and *Backtalk*, has been a Bunting Fellow and won fellowships from the NEA and the Massachusetts Artists' Foundation. Cecil Giscome is a poet and essayist whose published books of poetry include *Giscome Road*, *Here*, and *At Large*. His work is widely anthologized and he has received numerous awards, including an Illinois Arts Council grant and a NEA fellowship. Novelist, essayist, and short story writer William J. Cobb's *The Fire Eaters* won the Associated Writing Programs' Award for the Novel in 1992. His awards include a NEA Fellowship. Fiction writer Charlotte Holmes' stories are collected in *Gifts and Other Stories*. She has received grants from the Pennsylvania Arts Council, the Writers' Exchange Award from Poets & Writers, Inc., and Penn State's Atherton Award for excellence in teaching. Fiction writer Peter Schneeman's collection of short stories, *Through the Finger Goggles*, was a winner of the University of Missouri Breakthrough Series. He has received grants from the Pennsylvania Arts Council and Penn State's Liberal Arts Outstanding Teaching Award. Nonfiction writer Vivian Gornick's books include *The End of the Novel of Love*, nominated for a National Book Circle Critics Award, *Aproaching Eye Level*, and *Fierce Attachments*. Nonfictionist Toby Thompson is the author of *Positively Main Street: A Biography of Bob Dylan*, *Saloon*, and *The '60s Report*, and is a frequent contributor to *Vanity Fair* and many other magazines. Recent visiting writers include Deborah Eisenberg, Stanley Plumly, Bill Collins, Heather Sellers, Adrian Oktenberg, Margot Livesay, Mark Doty, Mary Karr, Hettie Jones, Reetika Vazirani, Tim Seibles, Sarah Schulman, Tess Gallagher, Liliana Ursu, Marilyn Nelson, and William Matthews.

For more information, contact Director, MFA Program, 117 Burrowes Building, Dept. of English.

❖University of Pennsylvania
Philadelphia, PA 19104-6273
(215) 898-7347

Degree offered: BA in English with Creative Writing Concentration

Required course of study: 33 credit units including 13 in English of which 6 comprise the Creative Writing concentration (3 writing courses plus 3 in related literature).

Visiting writers are brought to the campus to read their work and often take part in workshops. Recent visitors: Donald Hall, Ron Silliman, Lyn Hejinian, Susan Howe, Allen Ginsberg, Robert Creeley, Norman Mailer, and Eavan Boland.

Writing students may edit and publish at 9 literary magazines including *Philomel*, sponsored by the oldest collegiate literary society in the U.S., the Philomathean. In addition to readings by visiting writers, student readings are arranged by the Philomathean Society and the Graduate English Club.

The Writing Program staff includes: novelist and memoirist Lorene Cary (*Black Ice, The Price of a Child*); novelist Diana Cavallo (*A Bridge of Leaves*); poet Gregory Djanikian (*Falling Deeply into America, About Distance*); novelist Albert DiBartoloemeo (*The Vespers Tapes, Blood Confessions*); poet Bob Perelman (*The Captive Audience, Virtual Reality*); playwright and script writer Marc Lapadula (*Distant Influences, Night Bloom*); nonfiction writers Paul Hendrickson (*The Living and the Dead*) and Ben Yasoda (*Will Rogers: A Biography*); novelist Karen Rile (*Winter Music*); and poet Susan Stewart (*The Forest, The Hive*).

For more information, write Gregory Djanikian, The Writing Program, Dept. of English.

❖Phoenix College
1202 W. Thomas Road
Phoenix, AZ 85013
(602) 285-7348
FAX (602) 285-7700
e-mail: lmiller@pc2.pc.maricopa.edu

Degree offered: Certificate of Completion in Creative Writing (poetry, fiction, screenwriting)

Required course of study: 20-23 s/hrs
Introductory genre classes: 9 s/hrs
Workshop: 8-10 s/hrs
Literature: 3-4 s/hrs

Other Requirements: Students applying to the certificate program must submit a 20-page portfolio of original creative work.

Application Deadlines: Continuous admission.

The Phoenix College Creative Writing program provides a writing community that inspires and encourages, while allowing each individual to follow his or her own path in creative work. The program is especially suited to non-traditional students, including adults with established careers in other fields, minority writers, and seniors. Introductory courses in fiction, creative nonfiction, poetry, and screenwriting prepare students for workshops in a variety of topics, including: children's literature, the novel, the short short story, poetic forms, musical elements of poetry, dialogue, magical realism, dream writing, journaling, memoirs, revision, and publishing. Courses are offered weekdays, evenings, and weekends in 4, 8, 10, 12, and 16-week units. Many workshops are multi-genre, allowing students to concentrate on a chosen genre or experiment with several.

Most classes have no prerequisites and are open to any students at Phoenix College. The highest level workshops are reserved for certificate students only and include such diverse topics as exploring obsession, revisionist myth, and the writer as witness.

Certificate students may choose a mentor from the residential and adjunct faculty or from a pool of participating authors. Via mail, computer, or in person, the mentor comments on and directs the student's writing and progress in the program. Current and past participating mentors include: Alison Deming, Jim Cervantes, Ellen Palestrant, Juanita Havill, Mark Hollis, Lusia Slomkowska, and Gus Edwards.

Writing students may also participate in internships with the public schools; local magazines such as *Arizona Highways*; and adult daycare centers. Other individualized, for-credit projects can be designed. The program sponsors several writing contests, and certificate students are invited to give a public reading each semester.

Residential faculty: Marty Etchart (screenwriting), David Pineda (fiction and poetry). Regular adjunct faculty: Jed Allen (poetry), Barbara Nelson (fiction), Tracy Trefethen (poetry), Paul Morris (poetry, nonfiction), Jaunita Havill (children's), Laraine Herring (playwriting).

The Program offers many readings, lectures, and non-credit workshops. Visiting writers in recent years have included: Ron Carlson, Alison Deming, Gus Edwards, Carolyn Forché, Ken Kesey, Nikki Giovanni, Bob Powers, Luis Rodriguez, Roger Weingarten, Beckian Fritz-Goldberg, Rick Noguchi, M.C. Helldorfer, Sneed B. Collard, Pat Mora, Natalie Lemberg, Jewell Parker Rhodes, and David Guterson.

For more information, contact Lisa Miller, Director.

Pittsburg State University
Pittsburg, KS 66762
(316) 235-4689
FAX (316) 232-2430

Degree offered: BA in English with Emphasis in Creative Writing (poetry, fiction)

Required course of study: 124 s/hrs total
Core courses in literature, grammar, linguistics, and composition: 15 s/hrs
Intro to Creative Writing: 3 s/hrs
Form and Theory: 3 s/hrs
Fiction Writing: 3 s/hrs
Poetry Writing: 3 s/hrs
Workshop: 3 s/hrs
Literature: 9 s/hrs or more

Other Requirements: University general education requirements, 43 s/hrs. Minor, 20 or more s/hrs.

Application Deadlines: April 1 for financial aid. June 1 for admission of out-of-state students; August 1 for admission of in-state students.

The undergraduate student takes introductory and intermediate courses in poetry writing and fiction writing before specializing in one genre. *The Cow Creek Review*, the campus student literary magazine, provides editorial and publishing experience. Each spring Sigma Tau Delta, English honorary society, sponsors a literary contest offering cash prizes for poetry and fiction. The Visiting Distinguished Writers Series brings four prominent writers to campus each year for public readings and class sessions with students and faculty. Recent writers in the series include Joy Harjo, Donald Hall, Rachel Hadas, Henry Taylor, Yusef Komunyakaa, Gordon Lish, Kathleen Peirce, Jeanne Murray Walker, Gerald Stern, and others.

For more information, contact: Dr. Stephen Meats, Chairperson, English Dept.

❖University of Pittsburgh–Bradford
300 Campus Drive
Bradford, PA 16701
(814) 362-7590
FAX (814) 362-5094

Degree offered: BA in Writing (poetry, fiction, creative nonfiction, journalism, professional)

Application Deadlines: March 1 for financial aid; rolling admissions.

The degree in writing allows students to combine courses in creative writing (poetry, fiction, creative nonfiction) with courses in professional writing (newswriting, feature writing, writing for management, technical writing). The program also requires a two-course sequence in a foreign language and a handful of literature courses, as well as a minor in a chosen field. Students can earn credit working on the newspaper (*The Source*) and the literary magazine (*Baily's Beads*). Student achievement is recognized each year by prizes associated with the literary magazine and by the annual Robert C. Laing award, given to a writing student of promise.

The Writing Program Readers Series brings four writers of national reputation to campus each year to read and visit writing classes. Recent guests have included Lynn Emanuel, Li-Young Lee, C.D. Wright, Scott Russell Sanders, Patricia Hampl, Barry Paris, Jewell Parker Rhodes, Donald Hall, William Matthews and Larry Heinemann. The creative writing faculty includes David McKain, author of the AWP award-winning *Spellbound: Growing Up in God's Country*; Dr. Paula Closson Buck, Writing Program Director; Hellen Ruggieri, Assistant Professor of Writing; and Dr. Don Ulin, Assistant Professor of English and Writing.

For more information, contact Paula Closson Buck, Writing Program Director, at the above address.

❖University of Pittsburgh–Greensburg
1150 Mt. Pleasant Road
Greensburg, PA 15601
(724) 836-9894
FAX (724) 836-7133

Degree offered: BA in English Writing with Concentrations in Creative Writing (poetry, fiction) **and Journalism**

Required course of study: A total of 36 credits are required for the major, including 24 credits (8 courses) in writing and 12 credits (4 courses) in literature.

Other Requirements: University distribution requirements; university core course requirements in communication skills, critical reasoning, and mathematics.

Application Deadlines: Rolling deadline for admissions; May 1 for financial aid.

The Writing Major requires the student to take at least 2 of 3 introductory courses in Poetry, Fiction, or Journalism, and then to specialize in one of the genres, with a variety of electives. *Pendulum* is the campus literary magazine which provides editorial, computer-generated production, and publishing experience for undergraduates. *Perspectives* is the student news magazine, which offers similar experience in publishing, as well as involvement in campus speaker/visitor programming. Each spring the Writing Program offers the Gerald Stern Poetry Prize to a writing major whose poetry shows promise. Each year, senior journalism majors are placed in community-based writing internships at area newspapers, magazines, or public relations, advertising, and social service agencies.

For more information, contact the Dept. of English.

❖University of Pittsburgh–Johnstown
Johnstown, PA 15904
(814) 269-7140
FAX (814) 269-7196

Degree offered: BA in Creative Writing

Required course of study: 33–51 s/hrs
    Writing courses: 15–21 s/hrs
    Literature courses: 18–30 s/hrs

Other Requirements: 4 terms in a foreign language or 3 courses of literature in translation; internships.

The writing program at the University of Pittsburgh, Johnstown, offers students a BA in Creative Writing with a flexible program of requirements. Students in the program publish a literary magazine, *Backroads*.

Related degrees at the University include a BA in Journalism, which requires 30–36 s/hrs, and a BA in Composite Writing, which requires 24–30 s/hrs. For both these degrees, a secondary area of specialization is strongly recommended.

The faculty includes: Gladys Clifton, David Ward, Ronald Reinbold, Catharine Kloss, Michael Cox, Richard Strojan, Charles Clifton, Frederick Fornoff, and Lee Wood.

For more information, contact Dr. Carroll Grimes, Chair, Division of Humanities.

❖University of Pittsburgh
Pittsburgh, PA 15260
(412) 624-6506
FAX (412) 624-6639
website:
  http://www.pitt.edu/doc/95/52/54269/English.html

Degrees offered: BA, MFA

Degree: BA in English with Concentrations in Fiction, Poetry, Journalism

Required course of study: 30 s/hrs in the major
    Thesis: no requirement
    Writing workshops: 18 s/hrs
    Literature courses: 12 s/hrs

Other Requirements: Senior seminar in writing.

The University of Pittsburgh's undergraduate writing program is the oldest and one of the largest in the United States. Undergraduates may concentrate in fiction, poetry, or journalism (newspaper or magazine). The maximum size of writing classes is 20, and a large variety of writing courses is available. The program emphasizes individualized attention for all of its students, and maintains a relaxed and informal workshop atmosphere. All writing courses for the major are taught by professional writers, the large majority of whom are tenure-stream faculty; part-time faculty in journalism and general nonfiction include senior editors and reporters from *The Pittsburgh Post-Gazette* and officers of major Pittsburgh corporations. Internships at local newspapers, magazines, television and radio stations, and in other writing-related jobs are regularly available as part of the undergraduate program. In recent years Pitt undergraduates have achieved an unusual degree of professional success, publishing in a wide variety of journals –– *The New Yorker, American Poetry Review, Ms.*, and many others –– and publishing many books. Our undergraduates regularly find employment with newspapers, and in public relations, publishing, and other writing-related jobs; many continue their education in graduate and professional schools, particularly in writing, journalism, and law.

In addition to writing internships, special opportunities at Pitt include the Academy of American Poets Prize, The Montgomery Culver Fiction Prize, the Frances Wright Weber Memorial Award for Journalism, the University Honors Program, and undergraduate teaching assistantships. Many students choose to work with one or more of our numerous student publications. Each year dozens of well-known professional writers come to Pittsburgh to read and discuss their work.

For more information, write for the College of Arts and Sciences Bulletin (Office of Admissions, Bruce Hall). Additional inquiries about undergraduate writing offerings should be addressed to Office of Undergraduate Advisors, Dept. of English.

Degree: MFA in English (fiction, poetry, and creative nonfiction)

Type of Program: Studio/Academic

Length of Residency: Three years, with teaching assistantship

Required course of study: 36 s/hrs
　　Writing workshops: 12 s/hrs
　　Literature courses: 12 s/hrs
　　Elective: 12 s/hrs

Application Deadlines: February 1 for financial aid; April 1 for admission.

The MFA offers concentrations in fiction, poetry, and creative nonfiction, emphasizing small seminars and individual instruction. A total of 36 credits is required; 12 must be earned in graduate writing courses, 12 in English and American literature courses, and an additional 12 in elective courses (these may be graduate writing seminars). Each student must also complete an acceptable book-length final manuscript. Scheduling is arranged so that the MFA is attainable by students enrolled on a part-time basis.

The great strength of the MFA program is the individual attention given students. Workshops are small (average size: 10) and the large majority of faculty are writers in the tenure-stream faculty of the University. We think visiting writers are an important part of any program –– visitors who have taught at Pitt include Gerald Stern, Angus Wilson, Galway Kinnell, Louis Simpson, Maggie Anderson, Christopher Gilbert, Belle Waring, Siv Cedering –– but major emphasis here is placed on permanent faculty who can establish longer-term teaching relationships with students.

The Program currently has a total of 24 teaching assistantships available for MFA students. In the first year, all TA's teach composition courses (one each term for two terms); in subsequent terms TA's may teach in Writing, Composition, Literature, or Film. Every effort is made to honor requests for assignment to Writing Program classes.

The Writing Program regularly brings to campus well-known writers and editors for readings and lectures. These have included Ray Carver, Grace Paley, David Halberstam, Scott Turow, Larry Levis, Dave Smith, Cornelius Eady, Tobias Wolff, Carolyn Forché, Richard Ford, Alan Cheuse, Ernesto Cardenal, Minnie Bruce Pratt, David Wojahn, Toni Morrison, and many others. The program also sponsors weekly readings at Hemingway's Cafe, adjacent to the campus. Participants include Pitt students and faculty, local writers, and visitors. The program is run by Pitt students, and the crowds are large and gregarious.

The University of Pittsburgh Press publishes the Pitt Poetry Series. The press offers the Agnes Starrett Prize for a first book of poetry ($2,500 and publication) and the Drue Heinz Literature Prize ($10,000 and publication) for a book-length collection of short fiction. In recent years MFA students have worked as assistants at the Press, and several have gone on to full-time jobs in publishing. Other activities include the annual Academy of American Poets Prize for student writing, the Scott Turow Fiction Prize, and the Frances Wright Weber Memorial Award for Journalism. Pittsburgh is home for a number of other lively magazines and presses, including *5 AM*, Carnegie Mellon University Press, Cleis Press, and Slow Loris Press.

The graduate/undergraduate writing faculty includes Dennis Brutus, poetry (*Letters to Martha, A Simple Lust, Stubborn Hope*); Fiona Cheong, fiction (*The Scent of the Gods*); Toi Derricotte, poetry (*Captivity, The Empress of the Death House, Natural Birth*); Bruce Dobler, nonfiction (*The Last Rush North, Icepick, I Made It Myself*); Lynn Emanuel, poetry (*Hotel Fiesta, The Dig, Oblique Light*); Catherine Gammon, fiction (*Isabel Out of the Rain*); Lee Gutkind, nonfiction (*Many Sleepless Nights, Bike Fever, The Best Seat in Baseball But You Have to Stand*); Chuck Kinder, fiction (*Snakehunter, Silver Ghost*); Lewis Nordan, fiction (*Welcome to the Arrow-Catcher Fair, The All-Girl Football Team, The Music of the Swamp*); Ed Ochester, poetry (*Changing the Name to Ochester, Miracle Mile, Dancing on the Edges of Knives*); Anthony Petrosky, poetry (*Jurgis Petraskas*); and Patsy Sims, nonfiction (*Can Someone Shout Amen, Cleveland Benjamin's Dead, The Klan*).

For more information, contact Sue Borello, Graduate Secretary.

150

Pomona College
Claremont, CA 91711
(909) 607-2212
FAX (909) 621-8296

Degree offered: BA in English with Concentration in Writing; BA in Writing, Special Major

Degree: BA in English with Concentration in Writing

Required course of study: 128 s/hrs
Thesis: no requirement
Writing workshop: 12-20 s/hrs
Literature courses: 35-52 s/hrs

Degree: BA in Writing, Special Major

Required course of study: 128 s/hrs
Thesis: varies (each graduating senior pre-
prepares an edition of his or her own
writing to that point)
Writing workshop: 12-32 s/hrs
Other writing courses: varies
Literature courses: varies
Tutorials or directed reading: varies

Other requirements for both degrees: 1 foreign language; 12 s/hrs each in humanities, social studies/history, physical science/math; distribution of courses within the major to cover 4 of 6 historical periods in English & American literature; senior seminar.

Application Deadlines: January 15; for early decision, November 15.

The writing program at Pomona is in keeping with Pomona's character as a small, independent liberal arts college. The only degree offered is the BA, for which students must satisfy distribution requirements in the humanities, natural and social sciences.

Two writing majors are offered. The ordinary one, elected by most of our majors, is like the literature major and would prepare a student to go on to graduate school in English. A special major is offered to talented students with well-defined career interests that probably wouldn't include an advanced degree in literature. An oral exam, based on a reading list negotiated by the student, is required of the ordinary writing major. For special majors, the coursework, senior exercise, and comprehensive examination are directed by a 3-member committee chosen by the student, under the scrutiny of the curriculum committee. Requirements are usually more rigorous than those for the ordinary major, but the program resembles closely what the student would like to do. Often such a major combines disciplines: theatre/writing, poetry/dance, art/writing, etc.

The course offerings look deceptively simple. There is an introductory course open to all students and designed partly as a studio introduction literature course. At present there is only one advanced course, required of all majors; the program may add a poetry workshop and fiction workshop as elective advanced courses. The advanced course may be repeated for credit, or a student may take independent study with a professor. There is also a course in playwriting offered by the Theatre Department, and depending on where the faculty strength is, students are encouraged to take writing courses at the other Claremont Colleges. We believe it all adds up to an extremely simple, flexible, and effective program, and one unusually responsive to the individual needs or abilities of the student.

On the extracurricular side, the program is equally strong. Poetry and fiction readings are frequent and free; we often have brief residencies by such writers as Donald Justice, Gary Snyder, Maxine Kumin, Robert Bly, Allen Ginsberg, and Denise Levertov. Pomona, Pitzer, and Scripps students all publish separate literary magazines; as often as not there is a counter-establishment *salon-des-refusés* literary magazine at Pomona, surreptitiously aided by the English Department, which does not interfere with or support the established student magazine. A recent innovation has been visits by successful alumni -- a screenwriter, a writer of thrillers, a professor, a printer and publisher of fine editions, a novelist, a poet who creates software for computer word processing -- to talk about what they do in the world.

The faculty includes poet and Program Director Richard Barnes (*Lyrical Ballads; Hungry Again the Next Day; The Real Time Jazz Band Storybook*); poet Robert Mezey (*A Door Standing Open; Small Song; Selected Translations*); Steven Young (*1:1,000,000*, with Mowry Baden; *Picture Talk*, with Jan Raithel); fiction writer Brian Stonehill (produced *Children of Paradise, Laserdisk*); and Paul Mann, poet and translator (*Rimbaud in Africa, Dog of Hearts*).

Tuition is high, but we have a "need-blind" admissions policy, and about half the students receive financial aid. Requests for information should be made to Patricia A. Coye, Director of Financial Aid, Le Bus Court.

For more information, contact Richard Barnes, Director of Writing Program, Dept. of English.

Prairie View A & M University
Prairie View, TX 77446-2779

Contact the Creative Writing Program Director, Dept. of English.

Princeton University
Princeton, NJ 08544
(609) 258-4712

Degree: AB in English with Concentration in Creative Writing

The early faculty of Princeton's Creative Writing Program, founded in 1939, included R.P. Blackmur, Randall Jarrell, John Berryman, and Elizabeth Bowen. Currently the Program offers a dozen or more small (limited to 10 students) workshops in poetry, fiction, and translation each semester. Each year approximately 15 students in various majors write a creative senior thesis -- a novel or a collection of poems, short stories, or translations -- under the direction of Program faculty.

The faculty of the Creative Writing Program includes novelists Paul Auster (*In the Country of Last Things, Moon Palace*), Russell Banks (*Continental Drift, Hamilton Stark*), Maureen Howard (*Expensive Habits*,

151

Grace Abounding), Edmund Keeley (*A Wilderness Called Peace, The Salonika Bay Murder*), Toni Morrison (*Beloved, Song of Solomon*), Joyce Carol Oates (*You Must Remember This, Them*), Joanna Scott (*The Closest Possible Union, Fading, My Parmacheene Belle*), and Michael Stephens (*Season at Coole, Heaven, Earth, Human*), and poets Julie Aggos (*Above the Land*), Charles Bernstein (*Four Poems, The Sophist*), Andrew Hudgins (*Saints and Strangers, After the Lost War*), Ann Lauterbach (*Before Recollection, Greeks*), J.D. McClatchy (*Scenes from Another life, Stars Principal*), Paul Muldoon (*Meeting the British, Selected Poems*), James Richardson (*Reservations, Second Guesses*), and Chase Twichell (*Northern Spy, The Odds*).

The Program sponsors numerous readings by workshop and senior thesis students, faculty, and visiting writers, and operates its own library of contemporary poetry and fiction. It shares a newly renovated building with *The Quarterly Review of Literature* (edited by Theodore and Renee Weiss) and Princeton's programs in Theater and Dance (which teaches playwriting) and Visual Arts (which offers courses in film and video). Workshops in journalism and nonfiction are available through the Council of the Humanities.

For further information, write to James Richardson, Director, Creative Writing Program, 185 Nassau Street, Princeton, NJ 08544.

❖Providence College
Providence, RI 02918-0001

For more information, contact Jane Lunin Perel, Director, English Dept.

University of Puget Sound
Tacoma, WA 98416
(206) 756-3235
(206) 756-3211

Degree offered: BA in English with Emphasis in Creative Writing

Required course of study:
3 literature survey courses
2 introductory workshops
2 advanced workshops
1 upper-level literature course

Other Requirements: University core-curriculum requirements; 2 ancillary courses in philosophy, religion, and/or world literature.

Application Deadlines: March 1 for fall admission.

The University of Puget Sound offers an undergraduate English major with an emphasis in creative writing. Students may take courses in fiction, poetry, and playwriting. The literary magazine *Crosscurrents* appears twice a year and is student-run. The creative writing emphasis also includes course work in literature surveys and seminars in rhetoric and composition.

Recent readings and guest workshops have featured Rita Dove, Gillian Conoley, Lex Runciman, Irene Fornes, David Wagoner, and Madeline DeFrees. Enrollment at Puget Sound is 2,800.

For further information, contact English Dept. or Admission Office.

❖Purdue University
West Lafayette, IN 47907
(765) 494-3740
FAX (765) 494-3780
website: www.sla.Purdue.edu/academic/engl

Degrees offered: BA, MFA

Degree: BA in Creative Writing

Required course of study: 33 s/hrs for major
Writing workshop: 12 or more s/hrs
Literature courses: 18 or more s/hrs

In addition, the Department of English offers a BA in Professional Writing, which is a 33 s/hr program. 12 s/hrs in literature and linguistics, 18 s/hrs in writing courses, 3-6 s/hrs in an internship in professional writing. Both degrees require immediate proficiency in a foreign language.

Degree: MFA in English (poetry, fiction)

Type of Program: Studio/Academic

Required course of study: 42 s/hrs
Thesis: 12 s/hrs
Writing seminars: 12 s/hrs
The Craft and Theory course (poetry or fiction): 3 s/hrs
Five other graduate departmental/university electives (one of which may be taken in another art form): 15 s/hrs

Length of Residency: Three years

Other Requirements: Foreign language proficiency (satisfied in various ways); oral defense of the thesis; a public thesis reading in the final semester.

Application Deadlines: Although we have no specific deadline -- the process is ongoing -- we urge those interested to apply by late February, the earlier, the better. This is particularly true of those who wish to apply for a teaching assistantship.

Established in 1987, the English Department's graduate program in creative writing gives poets and fiction writers the opportunity to develop their work in a serious, non-competitive atmosphere which values originality and a vital literary tradition. The three year program is small and flexible to ensure personal attention, allowing writers to design study plans to their specific needs. Workshops and classes are completed in the first two years; the third year is dedicated to intensive work on the thesis -- a novel or a book-length collection of poetry or fiction -- through individual tutorials with a writer chosen from the MFA faculty.

Teaching assistantships, which begin in the student's first semester, can include composition and creative writing, and, in 1998-99, provided a stipend of $10,000, plus the remission of tuition and fees (a figure adjusted yearly). Fellowships for ethnic minority students are available and carry dependence and research allowances. Program members staff *Sycamore Review*, an award-winning national journal, and participate in readings throughout the year. Accomplishments of program graduates include book and journal publication, *The Nation* Discovery Prize, numerous AWP "Intro" Awards, the Loft/McKnight Prize in poetry, Breadloaf fellowships, and a range of state arts awards.

The writing faculty includes poet Tom Andrews (*The Hemophiliac's Motorcycle, The Brother's Country*, poetry, and *Codeine Diary*, memoir); fiction writer Patricia Henley (*Friday Night at Silver Star, The Secret of Cartwheels*, fiction, and *Back Roads*, poetry); another full-time faculty fiction writer to be hired in a national search, and to begin teaching in fall 1999; and poet and program director Marianne Boruch (*Descendant, Moss Burning*, poetry, and *Poetry's Old Air*, essays). Past visiting writers (for a semester or more) have included Li-Young Lee, Brigit Pegeen Kelly, Richard Cecil, Sharon Solwitz, Elizabeth Inness-Brown, John Woods, May Swenson, Mark Harris, and Susan Neville. There is also an active reading series which sponsors a number of visits by writers every year, recently among them Eavan Boland, Mark Halliday, Charles Baxter, Jane Hamilton, Wesley Brown, Joan Silber, Denise Levertov, Adrienne Rich, Kathleen Peirce, Margaret Drabble, Russell Banks, John Barth, Grace Paley, and Derek Walcott.

For further information, write to Marianne Boruch, Director, MFA Program in Creative Writing, Dept. of English, Heavilon Hall.

Queens College
City University of New York
Flushing, NY 11367-0904
(718) 997-4600

Degrees offered: BA, MA

Queens offers an undergraduate English major with a concentration in creative writing. Students take 12 one-semester courses (36 credits), including 4 or 5 writing workshops, and the rest in literature. Advanced workshops are offered in poetry, fiction, prose nonfiction, and plays.

Queens also offers an MA in Creative Writing. 15 credits in writing and 15 credits in literature are required. The writing credits consist of 4 writing workshops in 1 or 2 genres and an advanced writing project (for example, a novel, or a collection of poems or short stories). The MA program is designed to prepare students for joint careers as professional writers and as teachers of writing in literature in colleges or secondary schools.

Degree: MA

Type of Program: Traditional Literary Study and Creative Writing

Length of Residency: Two years

Application Deadline: February 1.

The writing faculty includes Derek Mahon, Charles Molesworth, Joseph McElroy, Fred Buell, Richard Schotter, Evan Zimroth-Wollman, Kimiko Hahn, and John Weir.

Undergraduates are eligible to enter an annual writing contest, which features prizes in various categories. The top prize is the $1,000 John Golden Award.

Each year the Queens College Evening Reading Series brings distinguished writers to the campus. The list of recent visitors includes William Styron, Peter Matthiessen, Molly Peacock, Paule Marshall, and Czeslaw Milosz.

For further information, contact Professor Charles Molesworth, Chairperson, Dept. of English.

Radford University
Radford, VA 24142
(703) 831-5614

Degree offered: BA or BS in English with Concentration in Writing

For more information, contact Chairman, Dept. of English.

❖Randolph-Macon Woman's College
Lynchburg, VA 24503
(804) 947-8511
FAX (804) 947-8138

Degree offered: AB in English with Concentration in Creative Writing

Required course of study: 30 s/hrs
  Senior Seminar and Thesis: 6 s/hrs
  Writing courses: 12 s/hrs
  Literature courses: 12 s/hrs

The student may select from courses in journalism, poetry, fiction, creative nonfiction, and playwriting. In years when a visiting writer offers a class, it may be counted toward the concentration. Independent study is also available.

Special opportunities for writing students include a literary magazine, annual contests in poetry writing and explication, and an annual visiting writer program. Past visitors have included Eudora Welty, Peter Taylor, Maxine Kumin, Richard Wilbur, Nikki Giovanni, John Casey, Cathryn Hankla, Daniel Mark Epstein, Paule Marshall, May Sarton, Denise Levertov, Margaret Walder, Sherley Anne Williams, Margaret Atwood, and Maxine Hong Kingston.

For more information, contact Jim Peterson, Dept. of English, Creative Writing Program, Randolph-Macon Woman's College, 2500 Rivermont Avenue, Lynchburg, VA 24503.

❖University of Redlands
1200 E. Colton Avenue
Redlands, CA 92373-0999
(909) 793-2121, ext. 4260
FAX (909) 793-2029

Degree offered: BA in English/Creative Writing

Required course of study: 132 s/hrs total
44 units in the major
Thesis: Senior Portfolio in the area
of specialization
Writing workshop: 28–32 units
Literature courses: 8–12 units
Tutorials or directed reading: recommended

Application Deadlines: February 1 if applying for the Talent Scholarship; March 1 for financial aid; all other deadlines are revolving.

The Creative Writing Program is one of a very few in the country to offer an aspiring writer the opportunity to pursue a Bachelor of Arts degree in Creative Writing with an emphasis in poetry, fiction, or nonfiction. The intimate nature of the college, along with the accomplished poets, novelists, and nonfiction writers on the faculty, offers the student a unique experience, providing both an in-depth study of literature and at the same time a vigorous pursuit of creative expression and professional craft. Many Program graduates go on to leading graduate schools in creative writing, see their creative work published or produced, and pursue careers in fields of communications.

The Creative Writing Program offers 4-year talent scholarships to promising writers, a Visiting Writers Reading Series, which brings to campus writers of national and international reputation, and an Academy of American Poets Prize and an annual fiction prize. Students take introductory, intermediate, and advanced workshops in the writing of poetry, fiction, and nonfiction, and in the senior year have an opportunity to work with resident faculty on major projects in their areas of interest. Writing students also take advantage of a nationally recognized internship program, expert career advising, and extensive alumni-networking.

The writing faculty includes: Ralph Angel, poet (*Neither World*, 1995 James Laughlin Award, *Anxious Latitudes*); Greg Bills, novelist (*Fearful Symmetry, Consider This Home*); Leslie Brody, essayist and playwright (*Red Star Sister: Between Madness and Utopia*, NEA and McKnight Fellowships); Patricia Geary (*Strange Toys, Living in Ether*, Bunting Fellowship); Joy Manesiotis, poet (poems in *The American Poetry Review, The Antioch Review, Threepenny Review*, etc., Graves Award).

Recent visiting writers have included: Poets: Louise Glück, Tomaz Salamun, Ellen Bryant Voigt, and Charles Wright. Novelists and short story writers: Valerie Martin, Ishmael Reed, Tom Robbins, and Lawrence Thornton. Journalists and essayists: Frances Fitzgerald, Jack Tobin, and Simon Winchester.

For more information, contact the Creative Writing Program Director, English Dept.

❖Rhode Island College
600 Mt. Pleasant Avenue
Providence, RI 02908
(401) 456-8115, 456-8027
FAX (401) 456-8379
e-mail: tcobb@ric.edu

Degrees offered: BA, MA

Degree: BA in English with focus in Creative Writing (poetry, fiction)

Required course of study: 120 hrs total
Writing workshops: 9 hrs minimum
Literature courses: 27 hrs minimum

Other Requirements: General education, writing requirement, mathematics requirement.

Application Deadlines: March 1 for financial aid, May 1 for applications.

The undergraduate degree is a degree in English with a focus in creative writing. It requires 36 hours in literature classes and a minimum of nine semester hours in upper division workshops (poetry, fiction, nonfiction prose), as well as Introduction to Creative Writing. Concentration on a genre is not required. Undergraduate students are invited to work on the magazine *Shoreline*, and elective credit may be earned. The Jean Garrigue Award and the English Faculty Writing Award are open to undergraduates in creative writing.

Degree: MA in English/Creative Writing (poetry, fiction)

Type of Program: Studio/Academic

Length of Residency: Two years

Required course of study: 30 s/hrs total
Writing workshops: 9 s/hrs minimum
Literature: 12 s/hrs
Thesis: 6 hrs

Application Deadline: April 1 for financial aid.

The Master of Arts in English/Creative Writing fosters skills, discipline and support for writers at an early stage of their career. Small workshop classes and individual study provide plenty of student/teacher contact and personal guidance through the program. Other benefits include flexible schedules, day and evening classes, and low tuition. Financial aid and a limited number of assistantships are available.

Visiting writers in recent years have included Robert Pinsky, Ann Harleman, Thomas Lux, James Tate, Rosellen Brown, Wally Lamb, Ann Hood, Daniel Asa Rose, Andrew Hoffman, Charles Simic, and Richard Price.

The creative writing faculty includes poet Cathleen Calbert (*Lessons in Space* and *Bad Judgment*), poet Mark Anderson (*The Broken Boat* and *Serious Joy*), and fiction writer Thomas Cobb (*Crazy Heart*).

For more information, contact Thomas Cobb, Director of Creative Writing, at the above address.

❖Rhodes College
Memphis, TN 38112
(901) 843-3794

Degree offered: BA in English with Concentration in Writing

Required course of study: 44 s/hrs beyond composition

Literature: 27 s/hrs (includes senior seminar in critical theory and form and theory course in selected genre)
Writing courses: 15 s/hrs
Senior project: 2 s/hrs, production of a thesis of creative work

The writing program at Rhodes College offers a balance in the study of literature and writing. Students complete a senior writing project in either poetry or fiction. Students may also bridge the writing major in English with other majors in other departments such as foreign languages, international studies, or art.

For more information, contact Dr. Tina Barr, Writing Program Director, Dept. of English.

Rice University
Houston, TX 77251

(713) 527-4840

Degree offered: BA in English

For further information, contact Writing Program Director, Dept. of English.

University of Richmond
Richmond, VA 23173

(804) 289-8292

Degree offered: BA in English

Required course of study: 30 s/hrs in English
Thesis: no requirement
Creative writing workshop: up to 15 s/hrs
Literature courses: 30 or more s/hrs

The University of Richmond offers several creative writing courses for undergraduates, including an introductory workshop in fiction and poetry and advanced workshops in the short story, the poem, and the one-act play. Most courses are taught by Dr. Steven Barza, fiction writer and poet. Students may join the college literary magazine, *The Messenger*, and avail themselves of Richmond's cultural activities. The University's Tucker-Boatwright Literary Festival regularly brings nationally important writers to campus. (Recent festival guests have included John Updike, Larry McMurtry, Annie Dillard, E.L. Doctorow, Gary Snyder, Galway Kinnell, Jay McInerney, Isabel Allende, and Ray Bradbury.)

For more information, contact Steven Barza, Director of Creative Writing, Dept. of English.

❖Roanoke College
221 College Lane
Salem, VA 24153-3794

For more information, contact the Director, Dept. of English.

University of Rochester
Rochester, NY 14627

(716) 275-4091
FAX (716) 442-5769

Degree offered: BA in English, with a Minor in Creative Writing (also Minors in Journalism and Composition)

Required course of study: The creative writing minor may be taken by English majors and by non-majors. Minimum of six courses: two introductory workshops in poetry and fiction (one each), an advanced workshop in one or the other, a course in rhetoric and style, and selected literature courses. Special tutorials in creative writing are also available.

Application Deadlines: January 31 for admissions; February 3 for financial aid.

The Program in Creative Writing is closely integrated with the curriculum of the English Department, and draws on its strengths and diversities. For example, advanced creative writing courses may be counted toward a regular concentration in English; students in the English Honors program may elect to do creative writing Honors theses; student-writers may take courses in the Film Studies Program as part of their study of writing and literature; those interested in editing, publishing, and arts management may take "hands-on" internships at Rochester's celebrated downtown literary center, Writers and Books Inc. The creative writing program offers workshops (generally twelve students or fewer) in poetry and fiction on three levels: introductory (for undergraduates who, having made their beginnings, are far enough along to profit from criticism), advanced (for undergraduates who have done introductory work or are otherwise ready for advanced study, and for graduate students interested in writing), and graduate (for advanced graduate writers and exceptional undergraduates). No graduate degree in creative writing is planned at present: the idea is to offer graduate-level work in writing to students in our regular MA and PhD programs in literature.

In addition to regular coursework, writing students on all levels can participate in the UR student literary magazine, *LOGOS*, in "Writers at Large," a student/faculty writing support group, and they can take part in the Plutzik Memorial Poetry Series, which brings a diverse slate of poets and writers to campus each semester to read and meet with students. Recent Plutzik Series visitors include Yusef Komunyakaa, Maureen Howard, Alice Fulton, Dana Gioia, Orson Scott Card, Alison Lurie, and William Matthews.

The creative writing faculty includes novelists Thomas Gavin (*Kingkill; The Last Film of Emile Vico*), Sarah Higley (*Star Trek* scripts), and Joanna Scott (*My Parmacheene Belle; The Closest Possible Union; Arrogance*), and poets Jarold Ramsey (*Love in an Earthquake; Dermographia; Hand Shadows*), Barbara Jordan (*Channel*), and James Longenbach (*Nation* "Discovery" Award, 1995).

For more information, contact Chair, English Dept.

Roger Williams University
Bristol, RI 02809

(401) 254-3149 or (401) 254-3217

Degree offered: BFA in Creative Writing

Required course of study: 120 s/hrs total
51 s/hrs in the major
Thesis: 6 s/hrs
Writing workshop: 9 s/hrs
Other writing courses: 30 s/hrs
Literature courses: electives available
Tutorials or directed reading: arranged

Other Requirements: University gen/ed requirements; thesis examination by faculty.

Roger Williams University offers a BFA in Creative Writing. Students majoring in Creative Writing must satisfy the College's total requirement of 40 courses for the baccalaureate. 17 courses (51 s/hrs) are required for the major: Beginning Creative Writing; Intermediate Creative Writing; Advanced Creative Writing; Introduction to Poetry; Introduction to Fiction; Autobiography; Contemporary American Poetry; Contemporary American Fiction; one modern literature course; 2 literature electives; one problems course in fiction and poetry; 2 Fine Arts courses (Art, Dance, Music, Theatre); Thesis I; and Thesis II. Upon completion of Thesis II the student submits a thesis -- a book-length collection of poems or stories, a combination of poetry and fiction, or a novel -- which is examined and approved by a faculty director.

The writing and literature courses are complemented by directed readings in selected authors. Students are also offered a substantial selection of minors in related fields such as career writing-communications.

The Matthew Wolfe Memorial Scholarship is available each spring, based on quality of writing, academic record, and need.

The Creative Writing Program's staff includes Robert McRoberts (*Lip Service*); Geoffrey Clark (*What the Moon Said*); and Martha Christina (*Staying Found*).

For the past 20 years the Program has carried on a reading series and writer-in-residence schedule that has brought to campus Paul Zimmer, Mary Oliver, Peter Matthiessen, Nancy Willard, Richard Yates, Mark Doty, Tim Seibles, Terri MacMillan, Lucien Stryk, and many others to read from their work and examine and discuss student writing. 4 to 6 writers visit the program each year.

Creative Writing courses approach literature from the writer's point of view: a poem, short story, or novel is studied as something in process, from the moment a writer first senses a pattern in a set of human experiences, through its first commitment to paper to the final draft. We believe, as Richard Hugo has said, that "the creative writing class is a refuge for the nameless quality that makes us human and what we learn about ourselves, our loves, and our losses, we can best learn in the creative act itself. Unless we learn about ourselves, we are not educated."

For more information, write Robert McRoberts or Martha Christina, Creative Writing Program.

Rollins College
Winter Park, FL 32789-4499

(407) 646-2216

For information on offerings in Creative Writing, contact the Dept. of English.

Rosary College
7900 W. Division
River Forest, IL 60305

(708) 524-6840

Degree offered: BA in English with Concentration in Creative Writing (poetry, fiction, playwriting)

Required course of study: 124 s/hrs total
30-48 s/hrs in the major
Thesis: 50-page portfolio required
Writing courses: 12 or more s/hrs
Literature: 15 or more s/hrs

Other Requirements: Senior comprehensive examination; college distribution requirements.

Application Deadlines: "Rolling" for both admissions and financial aid.

The program requires students to take Introduction to Creative Writing and two available advanced writing courses; the senior seminar and comprehensive exam require students to study and report on a wide variety of literary periods and genres. *The Eagle*, Rosary's literary magazine, provides students experience in editing and publishing their work.

For more information, contact Mary Scott Simpson, Director of Creative Writing.

❖Rowan University
201 Mullica Hill
College of Communication
Glassboro, NJ 08028-1701

For more information, contact Richard Ambacher at the above address.

Rutgers University, Camden
Camden, NJ 08102
(609) 225-6121
website:
http://Camden-www.rutgers.edu/dept-pages/english

Degrees offered: BA, MA

Degree: BA in English with a Minor in Creative Writing

Required course of study: 42 s/hrs in English, 18 credits in writing courses; for the Minor, requirements include 18 s/hrs: Short Fiction Writing, Poetry Writing, Advanced Creative Writing, Review Article Writing, and Freelance Article Writing.

Degree: MA in English with Concentration in Writing

Type of Program: Studio/Academic

Required course of study: 30 s/hrs
Writing workshop: 12 s/hrs
Rhetoric or linguistics: 3 s/hrs
Literature courses: 15 s/hrs
Thesis: 3 s/hrs; substantial body of creative
work may be submitted in partial fulfillment
of the MA comprehensive examination

For further information, contact Tim Martin, Chairman, Dept. of English, or Geoffrey Sill, Graduate Program Director.

❖Saddleback College
Mission Viejo, CA 92692

Contact the Creative Writing Program Director, Dept. of English.

St. Ambrose University
Davenport, IA 52803

Contact the Creative Writing Program Director, Dept. of English.

St. Andrew's Presbyterian College
Laurinburg, NC 28352
(919) 277-5000
FAX (919) 277-5020

Degree offered: BFA in Creative Writing (poetry, fiction, playwriting). Thesis may be in one of the above or mixed genres.

Required course of study: 120 hours total. 3 hours of creative writing (general), 6 to 12 hrs in genre writing, 4 hrs thesis and presentation credit, in addition to an additional 31-40 hrs on approved contract. Writing workshops, internships, practica, and guided independent projects available. Electives encouraged in psychology, philosophy, and cinema as well as literature.

Application Deadlines: April 15 for financial aid; rolling admissions deadline.

St. Andrews College Press originates on campus, as does the student literary magazine, *Cairn*. The flagship magazine, *Sandhills/St. Andrews Review* (founded 1970) issues from the Sandhills campus. Contributors to each have included James Laughlin, Romulus Linney, Barry Gifford, Grace Freeman, all frequent campus visitors; weekly Fortner Writers' Forums for students and professionals reading together have included the above, Tom Wolfe, Carolyn Kizer, Donald Keene, Judith Johnson, Robert Orr, and many others. Annual junior-senior chapbook competition (blind judging by professionals). Scholarships available, including Knight Awards of up to $2,500 per year. Loans and work-study available.

For more information, contact Director of Admission, St. Andrews Presbyterian College.

The College of St. Catherine
St. Paul, MN 55105
(612) 690-6557 or 6548

Degree offered: BA in English: Writing Concentration

Required course of study:
10 courses in major
Writing courses: 4
Literature: 4
Language course: 1
Senior seminar: 1
Further courses as student determines for program

Other Requirements: 13 courses in Liberal Arts Core: foreign language, mathematics, or science, philosophy and theology, fine arts, history, social science.

A liberal arts college for women, The College of St. Catherine offers a writing concentration in the English Department. Most students choose the creative writing track with supplemental courses in the expository writing area as she determines. Introduction to Creative Writing is designed to help students understand the fundamentals of fiction and poetry writing, and is the required course for the other levels. The 2 intermediate courses offered in Poetry or Fiction may both be taken by the student. The Advanced Workshop and Independent Studies are available to students wishing to prepare portfolios for Honors and/or Graduate school or publication.

Since our creative writing program is affiliated with those of 4 other private liberal arts colleges in the Twin Cities, our students have the additional opportunity of taking courses with writers on the other campuses. This exchange provides a diversity of experience in the workshops and permits greater development of creative abilities. The Association of Creative Writing Programs sponsors a 5-week residency by a fiction writer or poet each year. During this residency, the writer spends a week on each campus working closely with students in conferences and classes.

In addition, the program at CSC maintains an active role in the rich variety the Twin Cities writing community offers.

Visiting writers to the campus in recent years include Alice Walker, Maya Angelou, Laura Jensen, Mona Simpson, Eamon Grennan, Carol Bly, Diane Wakoski, Leslie Adrienne Miller, and James McKean.

Through this program students develop confidence in and facility with imaginative language. They are urged to pursue their own style, voice, and sensibility, and to work with an eye to specific goals they individually determine for themselves as writers: personal satisfaction, freelance careers, publication, or graduate programs in writing. Our best students publish before graduation and continue their writing in graduate programs across the country.

The Director of Creative Writing, Robert Grunst, has published poems and essays in several magazines. He teaches creative writing and literature courses. Fiction writer Susan Welch's prize winning stories have appeared in *The Pushcart Prize* and *Love Stories for the Time Being*.

For more information, contact Robert Grunst, Director of Creative Writing.

St. Cloud State University
St. Cloud, MN 56301-4498
(612) 255-3061 or 3062

Degrees offered: BA, MA

Degree: BA in English with Creative Writing Emphasis

Required course of study: 48 q/hrs
Core: 21-22 q/hrs
Writing workshops: 10-11 q/hrs
Electives in English: 15-17 q/hrs

Degree: BA in English with Writing Emphasis

Required course of study: 48 q/hrs
Core: 18-19 q/hrs
Rhetoric and business writing: 10 q/hrs
Electives in English: 18-19 q/hrs

Both BA degrees have a required core including advanced expository writing, linguistics, English literature survey, and American literature. The emphasis allows a concentration in either creative writing or expository and business/technical writing. Electives for either emphasis may include additional creative writing workshops or professional writing courses as well as literature courses.

Degree: Creative Writing Minor in a BA or BS degree

Required course of study: 32 q/hrs for minor
Writing workshop: 18 q/hrs
Literature courses: 7-8 q/hrs
Electives in English: 6-7 q/hrs

St. Cloud State University offers a 32-credit creative writing minor which can be elected as part of a BA or BS degree with any major or with the English major.

The creative writing minor gives students an opportunity to develop their talents and individual expression through the writing of poetry, fiction, and plays, both on the introductory and the advanced levels. The courses, taught by published writers, provide students with individualized attention as they focus on an awareness of writing technique, imaginative expression, and critical self-appraisal. Elective courses in literature add a well-rounded perspective.

The creative writing program has sponsored an annual Writer-in-Residence program which includes readings and writing workshops by prominent authors. Other campus readings by nationally recognized and regional authors are given each year. A campus literary magazine is published annually.

The Mississippi River Creative Writing Workshop in Poetry and Fiction is an annual 2-week summer workshop featuring four visiting poets and fiction writers. It may be taken for either undergraduate or graduate credit.

For more information, contact Robert Inkster,

Creative Writing Program Director, or Richard Dillman, English Dept. Chair.

Degree: MA in English with Creative Thesis Option

Type of Program: Studio/Academic

Required course of study: 48-50 q/hrs
Thesis: 6 q/hrs (offered on a limited basis)
Literature seminar: 8 q/hrs
Writing workshops: 3-19 q/hrs
Electives in English: flexible

The MA in English offers a Creative Work Option (Non-Thesis Option) in which the student is required to write two starred papers, one of which will be a creative work.

The MA program is a combination of traditional literary study and writing workshop courses with opportunity for writing pedagogy and academic and professional writing courses as well. Students have the flexibility to design an individualized graduate program with an adviser. There is no foreign language requirement.

Students applying for approval to select the Creative Starred Paper or Creative Thesis option in poetry, fiction, or playwriting must successfully complete advanced creative writing courses at St. Cloud State University or show acceptable advanced courses in creative writing at another institution and must have the recommendation of 2 graduate creative writing faculty members verifying that the student's writing is of thesis-level quality. The Creative Thesis must include a 5-page Statement of Artistic Intent and receive approval in an oral examination by the committee.

Creative writing faculty include William Meissner, Program Director, poetry and fiction (*Learning to Breathe Underwater*, *The Sleepwalker's Son*, and *Hitting into the Wind*); Steve Klepetar and Steve Crow, poetry; Caesarea Abartis, fiction; and Sidney Parham, playwriting. Specialists in rhetoric and business/professional writing are Sharon Cogdill, Donna Gorrell, Robert Inkster, Philip Keith, Judy Kilborn, and David Sebberson.

Graduate assistantships for teaching composition and tutoring in the writing center are available each year. For information on these positions or the graduate program, contact Donna Gorrell, Director of English Graduate Studies, or Robert Inkster, Dept. of English Chair.

❖St. Edward's University
Austin, TX 78704-6489
(512) 448-8560
FAX (512) 448-8492
e-mail: laurted@admin.stedwards.edu

Degree offered: BA in English Writing and Rhetoric

Required course of study: 42 s/hrs for the major
Writing courses: 66 s/hrs
Literature courses: 6 or more s/hrs
Internship: 3-9 s/hrs

Other Requirements: University degree requirements; 120 s/hrs for the BA.

Application Deadlines: March 1 for priority financial aid; August 1 for admission.

The writing major provides a wide range of course work for students wishing to enter careers involving writing, editorial, and communication skills. Students gain experience writing in a variety of forms, to a variety of audiences, for a variety of purposes.

Students take 10 core courses and 4 courses in specialized writing areas. They are encouraged to double major or minor in other disciplines -- such as behavioral or social science, computer science, business, education, literature, photocommunications, or science -- in order to prepare for careers in these fields. Core requirements include American Grammar or Intro. to Linguistics, Research and Argumentation, Revising and Editing, Text and Discourse Analysis, Technical and Report Writing, Theories of Rhetoric, Literary Criticism, Writing for Publication, Advanced Writing Seminar, and Internship.

Specialized courses include Principals of Style, Journalism I and II, Writing with Computers, Desktop Publishing, Advanced Editing, Personal Essay, Creative Nonfiction, Legal Writing, Fiction, Poetry, Advanced Creative Writing Workshops, Screenplay and Drama, Special Topics in Creative Writing, and Media Writing.

There are a variety of opportunities for paid internships on campus including Teaching, Communication Lab, and Reading Lab, as well as off-campus internships with The Austin Writers League and other local businesses.

SEU has two student-run campus magazines: *Aesthetic Voice*, the creative writing journal; and *Areté*, the award-winning academic journal. The campus newspaper, *Hilltop Views*, offers a variety of positions and publishing opportunities.

Our Visiting Poets and Writers Program hosts a writer once a semester for a reading and to work with students. Recent visitors include Philip Levine, David Bradley, Jorie Graham, Dinty W. Moore, and Gary Soto. The program also sponsors four Open Mike Night readings a year and an annual Creative Writing Contest.

Writing faculty members are Alan Altimont, Brion Champie, Anne Crane, Virginia Dailey, Laurie Drummond, Barbara Filippidis, Marcia Kinsey, Bro. George Klawitter, Cecil Lawson, Michele Moragne Silva, Brother John A. Perron, CSC, Catherine Rainwater, and Anna Skinner.

For more information, contact Anna Skinner, Director of Writing Programs, School of Humanities.

❖St. Lawrence University
Canton, NY 13617
(315) 229-5125
FAX (315) 229-5628
e-mail: aglo@music.stlawu.edu

Degree offered: BA in English with Creative Writing Emphasis

Required course of study:
40-48 s/hrs in English

Writing workshop: 8 or more s/hrs
Other writing courses: 8 or more s/hrs
Tutorials: no requirement (up to 8 s/hrs optional)
Literature courses: 20 s/hrs

The English Department at St. Lawrence University offers a 2-step series of writing courses in each of 5 genre concentrations: fiction, poetry, creative nonfiction, journalism, and screenwriting. The series includes an introductory techniques course and advanced workshop in each genre. Courses are also offered in intermediate and advanced expository prose as well as in playwriting. Independent work is optional.

Excellence in writing is also fostered by 3 literary magazines, a writer's club, a weekly newspaper, and numerous prizes and awards for original writing. Every effort is made to bring major writers to campus for readings and workshops as part of the ongoing cultural life of the community. Recent visitors include: A.R. Ammons, Tim O'Brien, Susan Griffin, Gloria Naylor, Amiri Baraka, Robert Creeley, Michael Ondaatje, John Irving, Lorrie Moore (a graduate of the program), Anne Waldman, Richard Tillinghast, and Rosellen Brown.

Writing major faculty are: Peter J. Bailey, critic, fiction writer (*Reading Stanley Elkin*); Joe David Bellamy, fiction writer, poet, critic (*Suzi Sinzinnati, The Frozen Sea, Olympic Gold Medalist*); Robert Couser, creative nonfiction writer; Albert Glover, poet, editor (*Next, A Curriculum of the Soul, The Dinner Guest and Other Poems*); Natalia Rachel Singer, fiction and creative nonfiction writer; and journalists Kerry Grant and Susan Ward. Year-long visiting faculty have included Michael Burkard, Tess Gallagher, Elizabeth Inness-Brown, Patricia Donegan, and David Shields.

For further information, contact Natalia Singer, WPD, Dept. of English.

❖Saint Leo College
Dept. of English
P.O. Box 6665, MC 2127
Saint Leo, FL 33574
(352) 588-8294

Degree offered: BA in English with Concentration in Writing

Required course of study: 124 s/hrs total
Foundation courses: 12 s/hrs
History and Structure of English Language: 3 s/hrs
Senior Seminar: 3 s/hrs
Writing workshop & classes: at least 12 s/hrs
Upper-Level English courses: 9 s/hrs
Credits for major: 27 s/hrs

Application Deadlines: April 1 (preferred deadline) for financial aid; June 1 for admission.

In addition to the composition and literature courses offered to all English majors, those on the writing track choose from among 8 writing courses designed to prepare them academically and professionally.

The college publishes 2 magazines yearly and sponsors various readings and artistic events. Students concentrating in writing also have the opportunity to work/study in the college's Writing Center or intern at newspapers, magazines, or television stations.

For more information, contact Kurt Van Wilt, (352) 588-8839, e-mail kwilt@saintleo.edu.

St. Mary College
Leavenworth, KS 66048-5082
(913) 758-6147

For information on offerings in Creative Writing, contact the Dept. of English.

St. Mary's College
Notre Dame, IN 46556
(219) 284-4474

For more information on offerings in Creative Writing, contact the Dept. of English.

❖Saint Mary's College of California
P.O. Box 4686
Moraga, CA 94575-4686
(925) 631-4088
FAX (925) 631-0938
e-mail: writers@galileo.stmarys-ca.edu

Degree offered: MFA in Creative Writing (poetry, fiction, and playwriting)

Type of Program: Studio/Academic

Length of Residency: Two years

Required course of study: 42 s/hrs, plus thesis
  Thesis
  Writing Workshop: 24 s/hrs
  Seminar in Contemporary Thought: 3 s/hrs
  Craft Course in genre: 3 s/hrs
  Contemporary Literature in genre: 3 s/hrs
  Literature & related courses: 9 s/hrs

Application Deadlines: February 1.

The Saint Mary's MFA Program takes as its central mission the education and formal training of serious writers. It is distinguished by its commitment to the writer as an intellectual functioning within a cultural context. We believe that writing is one of the primary ways of knowing and that contemporary writers participate in an ongoing conversation with the great works of the present and the past.

The core of our program is the Writing Workshop, which provides an opportunity for talented student writers to work with established poets, prose writers, and playwrights on developing their own voice, material, and style. Workshop leaders are dedicated to fostering an atmosphere of mutual respect and professionalism; we strive to create a community within which students are challenged and supported as they hone their craft and explore their visions. Maximum size of the workshop is 15 MFA students. Students are also required to take courses in literature and in the craft of writing, and they are encouraged to pursue elective courses in other areas (e.g. history, education, theatre) related to their individual plan of study. A unique feature of our program is the Seminar on Contemporary Thought required of all first-year students; this discussion-oriented course is designed to give writers greater critical awareness of the cultural context in which they themselves are working.

MFA courses are typically scheduled during fall and spring semesters, but students may choose to take electives during the Saint Mary's January Term. For this term, students take one course for four weeks of intensive study, meeting several hours a day, four days a week. Spread over the broadest spectrum imaginable, courses during January Term have included Primo Levi: Understanding the Holocaust; Writing From the Land; Creativity in Late Life; An Introduction to T'ang Poetry; Shamanic Knowledge in Native America; Contemporary Arab Women Writers; The Stalinist Experience through Memoirs and Novels; Screenwriting; The Roots of Country Music; and specialized courses on such writers as Cervantes, Dostoevsky, Woolf, Freud, and Baldwin. Students not taking January Term courses have from mid-December to mid-February free to write.

In addition to our permanent faculty, outstanding visiting writers in residence are a regular part of our MFA program. Each year we will feature one Writer-in-Residence in each genre who will conduct a semester-long workshop. We will also feature at least one Visiting Writer in each genre, who will be on campus for a short visit to lecture, read, and conduct intensive workshops. In its first two years, the program has hosted as guest faculty: Alice Adams, Frank Bidart, Ethan Canin, Lynn Freed, Robert Hass, Pam Houston, Michael Palmer, and Christopher Tilghman.

Saint Mary's College also sponsors an annual Creative Writing Reading Series, which has included such writers as Robert Alexander, Andrea Barrett, Charles Baxter, Michael Chabon, Lucille Clifton, Joshua Clover, Bernard Cooper, Carolyn Forché, Louise Glück, Philip Kan Gotanda, Jorie Graham, Ron Hansen, Garrett Hongo, Maxine Hong Kingston, Galway Kinnell, Yusef Komunyakaa, Tony Kushner, Denise Levertov, Li-Young Lee, Czeslaw Milosz, Charlie Moraga, Bharati Mukherjee, Sharon Olds, Michael Ondaatje, Oyamo, Luis Rodriguez, Mona Simpson, Gary Snyder, Susan Straight, and Charles Wright.

The program offers a teaching internship in which the student serves as co-instructor with a Mentor Teacher, teaching an undergraduate course in writing or literature. These positions are open to second-year students.

The creative writing faculty includes Director, Diem Jones; poets Brenda Hillman (*Bright Existence*, recipient of the Delmore Schwartz Memorial Award and a Guggenheim Fellowship) and Phyllis Stowell (*Who is Alice? Assent to Solitude*); fiction writers Louis Berney (*The Road to Bobby Joe and Other Stories*) and John Fleming (*The Legend of the Barefoot Mountain*); and playwright Carol Lashof (*Medusa's Tale, Fraulein Dora*, recipient of a Joseph Kesselring Playwriting Award from the National Arts Club of New York for *The Story*).

Located in the rolling east bay hills of the Moraga Valley, Saint Mary's College is a half-hour's drive from San Francisco, one of the country's most vibrant literary centers.

160

For more information contact Director, MFA Program in Creative Writing, at the above address.

❖Saint Olaf College
1520 Saint Olaf Avenue
Northfield, MN 55057-1001

For more information, contact the Director, Dept. of English.

St. Thomas Aquinas College
Sparkill, NY 10960
(914) 398-4134

Degree offered: BA in English (A Writing Concentration is being developed)

Writing courses available at St. Thomas Aquinas include Creative Writing -- Poetry, Fiction, Expository Prose, and Magazine Writing. The student literary journal, *Voyager*, is published semi-annually.

The program director is Gerald McCarthy (*War Story*). Recent visiting writers include David Ignatow, David Kelly, Gloria Emerson, W.D. Ehrhart, Raymond Patterson, etc.

For more information, contact Gerald McCarthy, Humanities Division.

❖University of St. Thomas
2115 Summit Avenue #30F
Saint Paul, MN 55105-1096
(800) 328-6819, ext. 5600
e-mail: jebukowski@stthomas.edu
website: http://www.stthomas.edu

Degrees offered: BA, MA

Degree: BA in English with Writing Emphasis (poetry, fiction, nonfiction)

Required course of study: 132 s/hrs total
Freshman courses: Critical Reading and
   Writing: 8 s/hrs
Four writing courses (ENGL 252 or above):
   16 s/hrs
One additional course (ENGL 300 or above):
   4 s/hrs
Senior Seminar: 4 s/hrs

Other requirements: University core curriculum requirements.

Application Deadlines: Rolling admissions; April 1 priority deadline for financial aid.

The undergraduate Writing Emphasis major (or minor) is designed to provide choices that will enable you to specialize in an area of interest (poetry, fiction or nonfiction). Or you can choose a series of courses that will enable you to gain experience with a range of genres. The *Summit Avenue Review* is the campus literary magazine, and won the AWP prize for content in 1996. A Literary Magazine Practicum course is offered which provides editorial and publishing experi-

ence. Several scholarships are awarded specifically to English majors of high academic standing; internships are held at local publishing houses; and many interdisciplinary and study abroad opportunities are available. Two academic journals are published out of the University of St. Thomas and edited by English faculty: *New Hibernia Review* (a quarterly record of Irish Studies), and *Logos: A Journal of Catholic Thought and Culture*. There is an active Literary Club and a chapter of the English Honor Society, Sigma Tau Delta.

Degree: MA in English (general degree, writing courses can be taken as electives)

Type of Program: Literary Study and Creative Writing

Length of Residency: 2-7 years (full or part-time study allowed); all classes meet in the evening

Required course of study: 30 s/hrs
Issues in Literary Criticism: 3 s/hrs
Pre-1900 American Literature: 3 s/hrs
Pre-1800 British Literature: 3 s/hrs
Multicultural Literature: 3 s/hrs
Five elective courses: 15 s/hrs
Master's Essay: 3 s/hrs

Application Deadlines: November 1 for spring admission; April 1 for fall and summer admission.

Fellowships: Three fellowships are awarded each year on a competitive basis to full-time students of exceptional promise. These fellowships carry a waiver of tuition and a stipend of $4,000 per semester.

The MA in English program affords students the opportunity to develop their analytical, writing, and editing skills; to deepen their knowledge of English and American literature, to broaden their perspective through multicultural courses and to enhance their understanding of the essential role language has in thought, values, and self-development. The program aims to provide students with the opportunity to expand their personal and professional qualifications, to improve the effectiveness of teachers, and to prepare students considering further study for the PhD. Our class size averages 10-15 students, with an average total of 50 students enrolled per semester.

Minneapolis and St. Paul are the home of several nationally distributed small presses: Coffee House, Milkweed, New Rivers, Hungry Mind, and Graywolf. Writers find support for their work at The Loft for Writers, one of the largest literary centers in the country. Visiting writers in recent years include Allen Ginsberg, Bharati Mukherjee, Toni Morrison, James Kelman, Gary Snyder, Robert Bly, Eugene McCarthy, Tim O'Brien, Jim Heynen, Sally Fitzgerald, Barry Lopez, Jane Smiley, Carlos Fuentes, Eavan Boland, Edward Hirsch, and Gordon Henry.

The creative writing faculty includes Leslie Adrienne Miller (*Yesterday Had a Man In It, Ungodliness, Staying up for Love*), whose recent awards include the Loft McKnight Award of Distinction and the *Nebraska Review* Poetry Award; Mary Rose O'Reilley (*The Peaceable Classroom, Radical Presence*), whose recent awards include a Bush Foundation Fellowship; Lon Otto (*A Nest of Hooks*), and Heid Erdrich (*Fishing for Myth*), recent winner of the Minnesota Voices Project through New Rivers Press.

For information call: Jeanne Van Slyke Bukowski,

AWP <u>Official</u> <u>Guide</u> <u>to</u> <u>Writing</u> <u>Programs</u>

Program Coordinator, (800) 328-6819 ext. 5628, or e-mail jebukowski@stthomas.edu, and visit our website at www.stthomas.edu/www/gpeng_http/frame1.htm.

❖Salisbury State University
Salisbury, MD 21801-6837
(410) 543-6445
FAX (410) 543-6068
e-mail: mgwaters@ssu.edu

Degrees offered: BA in English with Concentration in Writing; MA in English with Creative Thesis

For further information, contact Dr. Michael Waters, Dept. of English.

❖Sam Houston State University
English Department
Huntsville, TX 77341
(409) 294-1403 or 1992
FAX (409) 294-1408

Degrees offered: BA, MA

Degree: BA in English with Concentration in Creative Writing (poetry, fiction, familiar essay, scriptwriting)

Required course of study (English Writing Option): 36 s/hrs in major
Freshman composition: 6 hrs
200-level literature course: 3 hrs
Introductory Creative Writing: 3 hrs
Journalism writing course: 3 hrs
Radio/Television/Film writing course: 3 hrs
Advanced Composition: 3 hrs
300-level literature course: 3 hrs
Advanced Creative Writing: 3 hrs
Writing Seminar: 3 hrs
400-level literature courses: 6 hrs

Degree: MA with Creative Writing Emphasis

Required course of study: 36 s/hrs total
Literature courses: 18 hrs
Writing Seminar: 6 hrs
Graduate Writing Workshop: 6 hrs
Thesis (in preferred discipline): 6 hrs

Other Requirements: Comprehensive examination, oral defense of thesis.

The Creative Writing Program at Sam Houston State University produces two publications -- *The Sam Houston State Review* and *The Texas Review* -- and operates *Texas Review* Press, which publishes several books a year, including the winning manuscripts in the annual Southern and Southwestern Writers Breakthrough competition in poetry and fiction.

At the graduate level teaching assistantships are available; in some instances teaching assistants will be assigned duties on the staff of *The Texas Review* or *Texas Review* Press in lieu of teaching positions, giving them invaluable experience in editing and publishing. All graduate students in the Creative Writing Program are given the opportunity to serve in some capacity on the journal and/or press staffs.

The creative writing faculty includes Phillip Parotti (*The Greek Generals Talk, The Trojan Generals Talk, Fires in the Sky*) and Paul Ruffin (*Lighting the Furnace Pilot, Our Women, The Storm Cellar*).

For more information, contact Eugene Young, Chair, Dept. of English, or Paul Ruffin, Director, Creative Writing Program.

❖San Diego State University
San Diego, CA 92182-8140
(619) 594-5443

Degrees offered: BA, MFA

The writing program at San Diego State University offers a balance between studio and academic, traditional and experimental, commercial and aesthetic approaches. Undergraduate writing courses progress from fundamentals courses through techniques classcs and senior-level workshops. The graduate program has two stages -- graduate workshops followed by intensive study with one or more professors in tutorials and thesis preparation.

Degree: BA in English, with Emphasis in Creative Writing

Required course of study: 27 s/hrs in the Major
Thesis: no requirement
Writing workshop: 9-15 s/hrs
Other writing courses: 3-9 s/hrs
Literature courses: 12-18 s/hrs

Application Deadlines: Applications received during the month of November; write to Admissions and Records, SDSU, for more information.

Degree: MFA in Creative Writing

Type of Program: Studio

Required course of study: 54 s/hrs
Thesis: 6 s/hrs
Writing workshop: 24 s/hrs
Literature courses: 18 s/hrs

Other Requirements: 6 s/hrs electives.

Application Deadlines: March 1; application available from the Director of Creative Writing.

The MFA Program offers a concentration in either poetry or fiction. In addition to Distinguished Visiting Writers, the faculty includes Jerry Bumpus, who teaches fiction workshops (2 novels and 4 books of short stories including *The Civilized Tribes* and *Things in Place*); Sandra Alcosser, who teaches poetry, fiction, and feminist poetics (AWP Award Winner for *A Fish to Feed All Hunger*); Marilyn Chin, who teaches workshops in poetry, theory, and form (*Dwarf Bamboo*); Glover Davis, Director, who teaches workshops in poetry, theory, and form (4 books of poems including *Legend*); David Matlin, who teaches fiction writing, creative nonfiction, and American literature (*How the Night is Divided*, a creative writing nonfiction book on the American prisons, and several books of poems); and Dr. Harold Jaffe, who teaches workshops in fiction and contemporary theory (*Beasts, Mourning Crazy Horse, Dos Indios*).

162

Each year, The Living Writers Series brings approximately 20 writers and editors to the campus for readings and residencies. Recent guests have included Maxine Hong Kingston, Robert Hass, William Stafford, Maxine Kumin, and John Williams. Professors Jaffe and Larry McCaffery edit the award-winning journal *Fiction International* at SDSU. *Pacific Review*, the SDSU literary journal, is edited by students.

Graduate Teaching Assistantships are available on a competitive basis; for applications, write to the Program Director. We arrange internships for our advanced students in arts administration, academic and professional services, editing, and publishing, for which we award research assistantships and/or unit credit. Information on scholarships and other financial aid is available from The Financial Aid Office.

For more information on the program, contact MFA Program Director, Dept. of English and Comparative Literature.

❖San Francisco State University
1600 Holloway Ave.
San Francisco, CA 94132-4162
(415) 338-1891
e-mail: cwriting@ceres.sfsu.edu
website: http://www.sfsu.edu/~cwriting

Degrees offered: BA, MA, MFA

The Creative Writing Department offers approximately 50 courses per semester in fiction, poetry, and playwriting. Besides workshops, our curriculum includes Modernist Women Writers, Teaching Creative Writing, Writers on Writing, specifically focused process seminars on topics relating to the art, and many other courses.

An important dimension of the program is the Poetry Center, now in its 45th year. The Center sponsors 30 readings a year by poets and prose writers. The Poetry Center Archive of videotapes is the largest holding in the country.

The permanent faculty includes: In fiction, Michelle Carter, Molly Giles, Maxine Chernoff, and Robert Gluck. In poetry, Myung Mi Kim, Daniel J. Langton, Toni Mirosevich, and Frances Mayes. In playwriting, Brighde Mullins and Roy Conboy.

Current part-time faculty members are: Jewelle Gomez, Nona Casperts, Aaron Shurin, Phyllis Burke, and Paul Bailiff. Several rotating part time positions are filled by writers in the San Francisco Bay Area. Recent faculty includes: Ethan Canin, Cyra McFadden, Lissa McLaughlin, Cecil Pineda, Josephine Carson, Gillian Conoley, Mary Gaitskill, Jane Miller, Gail Tsukiyama, Camille Rog, Michael Palmer, Justin Chin, and Sherril Jaffe.

Degree: BA in English with Concentration in Creative Writing

Required course of study: 39 s/hrs for concentration
Thesis: portfolio requirement
Writing workshop: 12 s/hrs
Other writing courses: 12 s/hrs
Literature courses: 12 s/hrs
Elective courses: 3 s/hrs

Application Deadlines: August for admission in the spring; November for admission in the fall; apply to the Admissions Office.

The Creative Writing Program emphasizes the primary importance of the study and practice of writing fiction, drama, and poetry. The writing and creative process courses offered by the Department provide this training. The undergraduate major in Creative Writing has been designed primarily to take cognizance of a certain difference between the educational objectives of the student concentrating in creative writing and one concentrating in a traditional English program.

Graduates are prepared to continue graduate studies in English, and are prepared as well to continue as MA or MFA candidates in a creative writing program.

Degree: MA in English with Concentration in Creative Writing

Type of Program: Studio/Academic

Required course of study: 30 s/hrs
Thesis: 3 s/hrs
Writing workshop: 9 s/hrs
Other writing courses: 9 s/hrs
Literature courses: 9 s/hrs

Application Deadlines: January 15 for admission in the fall.

The MA program in English with Concentration in Creative Writing serves a double purpose: to extend and broaden the student's familiarity with literature and the art of writing, and to provide the help of a faculty of professional writers and critics in developing the student's own potential as a professional writer.

Courses offered include advanced fiction writing, poetry writing, playwriting, novel writing, special study and projects courses, Seminar in the Creative Process, and Directed Reading in Selected Major Authors. A creative thesis (poetry, fiction, or a play) is required for graduation.

Admission requirements include the submission of a portfolio of work (short stories totaling 15 pages of prose, 15 pages of a novel, a complete play for theatre only, or 15 to 20 poems) and two letters of recommendation, along with a Creative Writing Department application form, sent to the Creative Writing Department.

Degree: MFA in Creative Writing (poetry, fiction, playwriting)

Type of Program: Studio/Academic

Required course of study: 54 s/hrs
Thesis: 6 s/hrs
Writing workshop: 18 s/hrs
Other writing courses: 6 s/hrs
Literature courses: 12 s/hrs
Correlative courses: 12 s/hrs

Application Deadlines: January 15 for the fall.

The MFA is a smaller program than the MA, and emphasizes small classes and individual directed writing projects. It also develops the student's understanding of the history and theory of literature. The "correlative courses" requirement enables students to minor in a field related to particular interests.

Courses offered include MFA level workshops in fiction, poetry, or playwriting, with enrollment limited to ten students; MFA Craft and Process tutorials in fiction, poetry, or playwriting; Teaching Creative Writing; Individual Projects in Directed Writing; and Community Projects in Literature, in which students are placed in work positions in community literary organizations. A Creative Thesis (poetry, fiction, or a play) is required. Admission requirements include the submission of a portfolio of work (short stories totaling 15 pages of prose, 15 pages of a novel, 15 to 20 poems, or a complete play for theatre only) and two letters of recommendation, along with a Creative Writing Department Application form, sent to the Creative Writing Dept.

For both the MA and MFA, formal application (transcripts, etc.), must also be made to the Graduate Division Office by the above deadline dates. Contact the Graduate Division office at (415) 338-2234 for their application forms. For information on student loans and university scholarships, write the Financial Aid Office.

The Creative Writing Department offers several awards in short fiction, the novel, playwriting, and poetry. Students publish two literary magazines, *Transfer* and *Fourteen Hills: The SFSU Review*. Each year six to twelve current graduate students are given part-time teaching positions.

For more information and MA/MFA application forms, contact the Creative Writing Dept., or see our webpage.

University of San Francisco
Lone Mountain 212
2130 Fulton Street
San Francisco, CA 94117-1080
(415) 666-6208
FAX (415) 666-2346
e-mail: Barrows@usfca.edu

Degree offered: MA in Writing (poetry, fiction, non-fiction, drama)

Type of Program: Workshop/Academic

Length of Residency: Two years

Required course of study: 33 units total
Major project (thesis): 6 units (2 independent studies)
Writing Workshops: 12 units (4 workshops)
Methods and Literature Courses: 15 units (5 courses)

Application Deadline: February 1 of the year in which the course begins (program begins in August).

The Master of Arts in Writing is designed to encourage students to develop their talents in imaginative and professional writing and editing, drawing upon the rich cultural and aesthetic resources of San Francisco. Students in the MAW program are practicing writers who work as teachers, managers, editors,

administrators, secretaries, actors, and in many other capacities. The program is structured so that students may attend while continuing their careers. Classes meet once a week in four-hour sessions for approximately 24 months, with some time out for semester breaks and holidays. Students can expect to spend about 20 hours per week on course assignments. Students develop their writing abilities through the study of contemporary and classical literature, while bringing a problem-solving approach to the activities of reading and writing. In the process, students learn to read with a writer's eye, and to write with a reader's sensibility. At the heart of the program is the students own writing -- in academic courses, in the writing workshops, and in the Major Project. Twenty-five to thirty new students are accepted into the program each year. Last year, the program received over a hundred applications. Class sizes vary. Workshops have between 5 and 10 students; courses between 5 and 15.

Creative Writing Faculty includes: Poetry: Kim Addonizio (*The Philosopher's Club*, poems); Jeanne Foster; Jane Hirshfield (*Of Gravity and Angels*); August Kleinzahler (*Red Sauce, Whiskey and Snow*); Aaron Shurin (*Into Distances*). Fiction: Catherine Brady (*Dailey's Girls*); Toni Graham (*The Daiquiri Girls*); Judith Greber (*As Good as It Gets*); Lynn Klamkin (*Hello, Good-bye*); Ruthanne Lum McCunn (*One Thousand Pieces of Gold*, made into a movie); Floyd Salas (*Buffalo Nickel*); Steven Simmons (*Body Blows*). Nonfiction: Peter Carroll (*Abraham Lincoln Brigade*); Lowell Cohn (*The Bill Walsh Story*); Martin Lasden; Michael Robertson; David Rompf. Drama/Screen: Andrea Onstad, Mira Kopell. Academic Courses: Alan Heineman, Deborah Lichtman, Barbara Ohrstrom, Darrell Schramm, Edward Stackpoole.

For more information, contact: Dr. Anne Barrows, Director, Master of Arts in Writing.

Sangamon State University
Springfield, IL 62794-9243
(217) 786-6778

For information on offerings in Creative Writing, contact the Dept. of English.

❖Santa Clara University
Santa Clara, CA 95053
(408) 554-4308
FAX (408) 554-4837

Degree offered: BA in English with an Emphasis in Writing (poetry, fiction, nonfiction)

Required course of study: 65 q/hrs in major
Writing workshop: 15 or more q/hrs
Thesis: no requirement except in Honors Program

Other Requirements: Foreign language proficiency; 65 q/hrs in University Curriculum and College of Arts and Science Curriculum; 175 q/hrs required for degree.

Santa Clara University offers a BA in English with an Emphasis in Writing, including fiction, poetry, nonfiction, and playwriting. Courses include Fundamentals of Creative Writing, Poetry Writing, Fiction

Writing, Magazine Writing, Craft of Fiction, Craft of Poetry, Advanced Poetry Writing, Advanced Fiction Writing, Play Writing, and Literary Journalism. Students choose an upper-division core of courses in the writing of poetry, fiction, or nonfiction.

Students who take writing courses have the opportunity to work on the *Santa Clara Review*, the University's literary magazine, published three times a year, with 150 pages an issue, a 3,000-copy run, and which includes fiction, essays, poetry, book reviews, art, and photography from the Santa Clara University Community and the Bay Area. In the Literary Magazine Practicum, a one-unit course offered every quarter, students select and discuss poetry and prose submissions. Students also have the possibility of working on copy editing and promotion for the magazine, and on production through a state-of-the-art desktop publishing system. Stipends for Editors range from 3/4 tuition to quarterly salaries. Positions include Editor, Associate Editor, Poetry Editor, Fiction Editor, Nonfiction Editor, Production Editor, and Assistant Editors.

A Practicum in Writing, offered every quarter and repeatable for credit, gives students the opportunity to become interns at companies in Silicon Valley (Hewlett-Packard, Amdahl, Intel), throughout the Bay Area (Harper San Francisco, KQED, KGO, KRON), and, during the summer, at newspapers around the country.

A number of nationally known writers are brought to campus to read and conduct workshops, along with many award winning San Francisco Bay Area writers. In addition, numerous writers read at The San Jose Center for Poetry and Literature, at nearby Stanford University, San Francisco State University's Poetry Center, and the University of California at Santa Cruz and Berkeley. Recent visiting writers include: Adrienne Rich, John L'Heureux, Isabel Allende, Gwendolyn Brooks, Ethan Canin, Ron Hansen, Gary Soto, Alice Walker, William Stafford, Juan Rulfo, John Knowles, James Galvin, Donald Revell, and Sandra Gilbert.

Each year the Department of English administers two literary prizes for undergraduates. The Shipsey Prize is given annually for the best poem written by an undergraduate, and the McCann Prize for the best short story. The winning compositions receive cash awards and are published in the *Santa Clara Review*.

Writers on the staff include: Terry Beers, nonfiction (*Quarry West* and *Robinson Jeffers Newsletter*); James Degnan, nonfiction and fiction; Ron Hansen, fiction and screenwriting (*Atticus, Mariette in Ecstasy, Nebraska*); Claudia McIssac, poetry; Cory Wade, poetry and fiction (*July in Georgia*); Edward Kleinschmidt, AWP Poetry Prize 1998, poetry and fiction (*Magnetism, First Language, To Remain*); Mark Clevenger, fiction; Toni Graham (*The Daiquiri Girls*, AWP Short Fiction Award 1997); Cheryl Dumesnil, poetry; and Nick Barrett, poetry.

For more information, contact Richard Osberg, Chair, Dept. of English.

❖College of Santa Fe
1600 St. Michaels Drive
Santa Fe, NM 87505
(505) 473-6200
FAX (505) 473-6510

Degree offered: BA

Required course of study: 128 hours total
Form and Theory: 6 hours
Writing workshop: 15 hours
Literature and other: 23 hours

Other Requirements: University core curriculum, senior reading.

Application Deadlines: June 30 for financial aid; March 30 for admission.

The Bachelor of Arts degree in Creative Writing prepares new students with a Candidate Forum involving writing exercises and literary discussion. In the sophomore year, majors will take two form and theory courses in emphases of their choice, and enroll in an Introduction to Creative Writing Workshop. In the junior year, majors enter two intermediate workshops in emphases of their choice. Throughout the course of study, majors will enroll in literature courses as required.

The college literary magazine, *Glyph*, offers publication opportunities and cash awards for winning entries. The college's national literary magazine, *Countermeasures*, offers publications practicums for credit. The program features many nationally-known visiting writers and strong ties to the Santa Fe literary community through the Creative Writing Advisory Council.

Jack Butler and Greg Glazner are Co-Directors of the Creative Writing Program.

Contact the Creative Writing Program Directors through the Dept. of Humanities.

Santa Fe Community College
6401 Richards Avenue
Santa Fe, NM 87505
(505) 471-8200
e-mail: jwilson@santa-fe.cc.nm.us
website: http://www.santa-fe.cc.nm.us

Degree offered: AA in General Studies

Required course of study: 65 s/hrs total
Creative writing: 6 s/hrs
English: 9 s/hrs

Other requirements: Core requirements in communications, science, math, computer science, behavioral/social sciences, health, humanities, and other electives.

Application Deadlines: Up to the dates of registration at the beginning of each semester.

We offer two courses in creative writing at the sophomore level, one in poetry and one in fiction. We also offer an advanced nonfiction essay course. Several members of our faculty are writers who are actively publishing. Writing is encouraged by contests with awards and publication in a student literary magazine. Of course, at the community college level our program serves general education purposes, but we also hope to begin developing those who wish to explore creative writing at higher levels.

For more information, contact the English Dept.

❖Sarah Lawrence College
Bronxville, NY 10708

(914) 337-0700

Degrees offered: BA, MFA

Degree: BA

Required course of study: 120 credits

Sarah Lawrence is a small, coeducational, liberal arts college with an unusually strong and varied writing faculty. Students may take fiction or poetry writing for 3 or even 4 years, and the presence of at least a dozen writers on campus makes this a unique undergraduate concentration. Normally, each student takes only 3 courses per year, each 10 credits, so it's possible for writing to constitute up to one-third of an undergraduate's total work towards the BA. At present, about 23% of the student body is enrolled in writing courses.

But this is not a program in any way limited to students who want to become writers. Taking a writing course can be a way of understanding how a story or poem or novel is made and so increases the joy of reading. Or it can be a way of exploring resources of language and becoming more aware of the life around us. For students who want to take writing for more than one year, the only stipulation is that they study with different teachers, because to find out how much the teachers differ, is, as Grace Paley says, to learn something of the "luck and loneliness of the true writer."

During the year funds from the college, matched by Poets and Writers, Inc., and from the Henfield Foundation, make possible a series of readings. Whether introducing writers of first books, or nationally- or internationally-known poets and fiction writers, these readings are open to the entire college community. Also, faculty-student readings are held every other week, as well as a variety of faculty readings and panels. The award-winning *Sarah Lawrence Literary Review* comes out once a year, and other once-a-year events are the Academy of American Poets poetry prize contest, the Nancy Lynn Schwartz Fiction Award contest, and participation, along with a number of other colleges and universities, in the Henfield Foundation's *Transatlantic Review* Awards competition for fiction.

For further information and application forms, write to the Admissions Office. Various financial aid packages are available for undergraduates, but those seeking financial aid should be sure to apply before February 1. A creative sample may be included with completed application materials, but is by no means necessary.

Degree: MFA in Writing

Type of Program: Studio/Academic

Required course of study: 36 credits, plus thesis

What distinguishes the Sarah Lawrence Master of Fine Arts Program in writing is the close attention given by workshop teachers, who meet bi-weekly with each student in individual conferences as a part of every semester-long course. The thesis -- a manuscript of stories, poems, or a novel -- naturally becomes the focus of the ongoing work in writing. On the one hand, the student is urged to study with different teachers so as to be exposed to different approaches to subject matter and craft, and on the other, there is a consistent overview dialogue with a thesis advisor in the final year. In this way, the graduate program is a clear outgrowth of the philosophy of the college, which stresses a high degree of individual development that is essentially non-competitive in nature, while encouraging growth in both subject matter and technical skill.

There are always at least a dozen professional writers on campus, offering courses in fiction and poetry to undergraduates and graduate students alike. On permanent contracts are fiction writers Linsey Abrams (*Our History in New York*) and Myra Goldberg (*Rosalind: A Family Romance*), and poets Marie Howe (*The Good Thief*), Kate Knapp Johnson (*This Perfect Life: Poems*), Thomas Lux (*Split Horizon*), and Jean Valentine (*Pilgrims*). On extended contracts are fiction writers Susan Daitch (*Storytown*), Mary LaChapelle (*House of Heroes and Other Stories*), William Melvin Kelly (*A Drop of Patience*), Mary Morris (*House Arrest*), and Lucy Rosenthal (*The Ticket Out*). Melvin Bukiet (*While the Messiah Tarries: Stories*), Kathleen Hill (short stories in various publications), John Silber (*In the City*), Brook Stevens (*The Circus of the Earth and the Air*), and Susan Thames (*As Much As I Know*) are on guest contracts in fiction. On extended contracts in poetry are Suzanne Gardinier (*The New World*), and Kevin Pilkington (*Reading Stone*), and on guest contracts are Michael Klein (*Buried Softer: A Racetrack Reminiscence*), Loan Larkin (*A Long Sound*), Victoria Redel (*Already the World*), and David Rivard (*Wise Poison*). Associate faculty members include fiction writers Allan Gurganus (*Oldest Living Confederate Widow Tells All*) and Grace Paley (*Later the Same Day*). Jane Cooper (*Green Notebook, Winter Road*) is poet emeritus.

In addition, other writers visit the campus frequently during the year to read from their work and meet with students. In a real sense, Sarah Lawrence can be looked on as a community of writers, sharing ideals of honesty, exploration, and open-mindedness.

In order to qualify for the MFA degree, all students are asked to take 36 credits of coursework in addition to completing the thesis. For most students, the full-time program takes 2 years. The first year consists of an elective course plus two semester-long graduate workshops and two graduate reading courses, either in poetry or fiction, focusing on matters of craft and how they affect subject matter. The second year consists of two graduate workshops and the thesis only, so that the focus is exclusively on writing. On a part-time basis the degree takes three years to complete. Normally, the elective courses are done in the undergraduate college, with regularly scheduled conferences in order to pursue more advanced or focused interests; occasionally, others develop conference courses to work individually with a faculty member. It's advisable, but not mandatory, to consider a course outside the field of writing.

Applicants to the program are asked to send a group of poems, three stories, or chapters from a novel-in-progress for consideration by the writing faculty. The single most important factor for admission is the quality of the work submitted. It is hoped that the community of graduate students will always represent a wide variety of literary and personal viewpoints. Financial aid is available on a need basis, and applicants are encouraged to request and submit the appropriate forms on time, since aid is limited.

Sarah Lawrence is located in a wooded suburban area only about 30 minutes from midtown Manhattan by car or train (just a 5-minute walk from the campus). One of the attractive things about this program is its access to the rich literary and cultural life of New York City.

For graduate application forms, write to Susan Guma, Administrative Director, Graduate Studies, or call (914) 395-2373.

❖University of Scranton
Scranton, PA 18510
(717) 941-7619
FAX (714) 941-6369

Degree offered: BA in English (Writing); **Minor in Writing**

Required course of study: 39 s/hrs in English
  Thesis: no requirement, except for Honors Students
  Writing workshops: 15 or more s/hrs
  Literature courses: 24 or more s/hrs

The University of Scranton offers a BA in English with a Track in Writing. In addition to satisfying a 24 s/hr (7 course) literature core, the Writing Track student takes a minimum of 15 s/hrs (5 courses) devoted exclusively to the production and criticism of student work. Offerings include introductory and advanced classes in Fiction, Playwriting, and Poetry as well as specialized courses in Nonfiction, Writing for Television, Technical and Business Writing, Writing for the Law, etc.

Students may also earn a Minor in Writing by taking a minimum of 18 s/hrs (6 courses) designated with the WRTG prefix.

Students edit *Esprit*, a semi-annual literary journal, and compete for the Berrier Memorial Prize in poetry and fiction. Students also take part in hosting the University Reading Series that brings several nationally-known writers to campus each year.

For more information, contact Prof. John Meredith Hill, Dept. of English.

❖Sewanee --
The University of the South
Sewanee, TN 37383-1000
(931) 598-1000, ext. 1530
FAX (931) 598-1145

Degree offered: BA in English with electives in creative writing (poetry, fiction, playwriting)

Required course of study: Only 16 s/hrs are strictly required, but majors usually take the full complement of 44 s/hrs from a wide offering of period or theme-based courses.

Other Requirements: University distribution requirements; comprehensive exam; additionally, for departmental honors, satisfactory preparation and oral defense of tutorial paper.

Application Deadlines: November 15 for early decision admissions; February 1 for regular admissions; March 1 for financial aid.

The College of Arts and Sciences incorporates a writing-across-the-curriculum program, in which many courses are designated "writing intensive." Student writing tutors are available to undergraduates in all departments. In addition to a full slate of courses in American and English literature, the English Department offers one or two writing workshops each semester in fiction, poetry, or playwriting. These workshops are open to a maximum of 15 students. Advanced students may undertake supervised independent writing projects and have opportunities to attend the Sewanee Writers' Conference. Workshop faculty has included Roberta Allen, Daniel Anderson, Manette Ansay, Elizabeth Dewberry, Tony Earley, Ron Fitzgerald, Jessica Goldberg, Ann Patchett, Wyatt Prunty, and Lisa Shea. Visiting writers have included Richard Wilbur, Mona Van Duyn, Maxine Kumin, Tim O'Brien, Tina Howe, Ellen Douglas, Richard Ford, and others.

English is the largest department in Sewanee's College of Arts and Sciences, both in number of faculty members and of majors. Together with the Student Forum and the Haines Endowment, it sponsors an active reading series in which nationally prominent poets and fiction writers visit the campus, meet with students formally and informally, and give public readings. *The Mountain Journal* is the campus literary magazine; it provides editorial and publishing experience for undergraduates. The *Journal* also sponsors an annual literary competition. The duPont Library has excellent holdings in the humanities. Sewanee is the home of the *Sewanee Review*, the oldest literary quarterly in continuous publication in the United States.

Because the University of the South annually hosts the Sewanee Writers' Conference, student writers often have opportunities to attend as scholars or staff members with full conference privileges, including workshop membership and individual conferences with members of the Conference faculty. The following writers have served as faculty members: Russell Banks, Pinckney Benedict, James Gordon Bennett, Robert Olen Butler, John Casey, Elizabeth Dewberry, Ellen Douglas, Ernest Gaines, Marianne Gingher, Amy Hempel, Ann Hood, Diane Johnson, Margot Livesey, Alice McDermott, Susan Minot, Mary Morris, Kent Nelson, Tim O'Brien, Joe Ashby Porter, Francine Prose, Mark Richard, Brent Spencer, Robert Stone, and Stephen Wright; poets Carol Frost, Emily Grosholz, Rachel Hadas, Anthony Hecht, John Hollander, Andrew Hudgins, Mark Jarman, Donald Justice, Maxine Kumin, Charles Martin, Howard Nemerov, Mary Jo Salter, Mark Strand, Chase Twichell, Mona Van Duyn, and Derek Walcott; and playwrights Kent Brown, Laura Maria Censabella, Dave DeChristopher, Horton Foote, Wendy Hammond, Tina Howe, and Romulus Linney.

For further information, contact Wyatt Prunty, Director, Sewanee Writers' Conference.

❖Skagit Valley College
Mount Vernon Campus
2405 E. College Way
Oak Harbor, WA 98277
e-mail: luckmann@skagit.ctc.edu

For more information, contact Chuck Luckmann at the above address or e-mail.

Skidmore College
Saratoga Springs, NY 12866
(518) 584-5000, ext. 2321
FAX (518) 584-3023

Degree offered: BA in English with Concentration in Creative Writing

Application Deadlines: General application to Skidmore College, February 1.

The student enters the program in the freshman or sophomore year by enrolling in the Introduction to Creative Writing, which is concerned with either fiction or poetry. Following this, the student can enroll in workshops in poetry, fiction, or playwriting, each of which can be taken twice for academic credit. In the senior year students can enroll in Advanced Projects in Creative Writing and Independent Study. An additional course called Senior Projects allows the creative writing student 2 semesters to engage in work comparable to a thesis. This senior project is required for departmental honors; terms are set individually by the student and faculty sponsor.

Once the student enters the program, there are writing course opportunities throughout the academic career every term. All of the classes are small and feature close individual attention to each student's work.

A regular stream of writers visit for campus readings and often conduct workshops and work with students. These have included Jamaica Kincaid, Seamus Heaney, Ellen Bryant Voigt, Richard Howard, Grace Paley, Donald Justice, J.M. Coetzee, Carolyn Forché, Robert Pinsky, and many others.

The writing faculty during the academic year include poets R. Parthasarathy (*Rough Passage*), Barry Goldensohn (*The Marrano*), and novelists Stephen Millhauser (*Edwin Mullhouse*), Tatyana Tolstaya (*Sleepwalker in Fog*), and Kathryn Davis (*Labrador*).

For more information, write to Barry Goldensohn, Director, Writing Program, Dept. of English.

❖Sonoma State University
Rohnert Park, CA 94928
(707) 664-2140
FAX (707) 664-4400
e-mail: william.babula@sonoma.edu
website: http://www.sonoma.edu/

Degrees offered: BA, MA

Degree: BA in English with Concentration in Creative Writing

The BA degree is a 42-unit program, Literary/Creative. Sequences of courses are available in fiction writing, poetry writing, and script writing.

Degree: MA in English with Concentration in Creative Writing (poetry, fiction, creative nonfiction, screenwriting, playwriting)

Type of Program: Studio/Academic

Length of Residency: Two years

Required course of study: 30 s/hrs

Application Deadlines: January 31 for Fall admission, October 31 for Spring.

Faculty on the staff include playwright/novelist William Babula (*St. Johns' Baptism, According to St. John, St. John and the Seven Veils*), poet Gillian Conoley (*Some Gangster Pain, Women Speaking Inside Film Noir, Tall Stranger*), poet and fiction writer Elizabeth Herron (*Desire Being Full of Distances, While the Distance Widens*). Emeritus faculty who participate as visitors to the program include poet David Bromige (*Desire* and numerous other books of poetry), fiction writer Gerald Haslam (*Okies, Hawk Flights, The Great Central Valley*), and Gerald Rosen (*Blues For a Dying Nation, The Carmen Miranda Memorial Flagpole, Growing Up Bronx*).

Recent visitors to the campus and the program have included Paul Erdman, Edward Albee, Tom Wolfe, Kurt Vonnegut, Jr., Irving Stone, Stephen Spender, Maya Angelou, Lewis Lapham, Meridel Le Sueur, and Ishmael Reed.

The literary magazine *Zaum* is published through the English Publications Workshop, an activity of the Small Press Editing course. In addition, SSU is now the home of *Volt*, a Magazine of the Arts.

We have a 30 s/hr program for the Master's degree in English that requires 24 units of formal course work plus 6 units of 500 level courses in Directed Writing. There are few course requirements, but students must pass an examination in English and American literature (either the GRE Advanced Literature in English at the 65th percentile or the Department essay examination in literature) and satisfy the foreign language requirement.

For more information, contact Chair, Dept. of English, at the above address.

University of South Alabama
Mobile, AL 36688-0002
(334) 460-6146

Degrees offered: BA, MA

Degree: MA in English with Concentration in Creative Writing (fiction, poetry, nonfiction, screenwriting)

Type of Program: Studio/Academic

Length of Residency: Two years

Required course of study: 36 s/hrs total
    Creative Thesis: 6 s/hrs
    Writing Workshop: 12 s/hrs

Literature Courses: 18 s/hrs

Other Requirements: GRE for admission; oral defense of thesis; reading competency in one foreign language.

Application Deadlines: Continuous admission; April 1 for financial aid; May 1 for graduate assistantship.

The graduate writing program is small and cares about its majors. Workshops are limited in enrollment; tutorial instruction is integral to the program. Several graduate assistantships are available each year. Current students come from around the country, including UC–Berkeley, Syracuse, Maryland, and Creighton. Most students specialize in fiction writing.

The program features writer consultants who review exceptional student work and contact the student directly. They include poet Edwin Honig, Paul Gilette (*Play Misty for Me*), producer Martin Jurow (*Breakfast at Tiffany's*), John Hermann (Editorial Director, Ticknor & Fields), and Christina Ward (head, Christina Ward Literary Agency).

Negative Capability Press publishes *Negative Capability*, a quarterly review edited by Sue B. Walker. Student internships are available. James White is publisher of Texas Center for Writers Press, which publishes fiction and anthologies. Creative Writing also sponsors student readings every quarter. As a member of the Gulf Coast Association of Creative Writing Teachers, the program also has an exchange with other schools in the region.

The faculty includes novelist James White, Director (*Birdsong, The Ninth Car*, and *California Exit*; Guggenheim Fellowship); poet Sue Walker (*Life on the Line, Shortings*); and nonfiction writer Robert Bahr (*The Virility Factor, The Hibernation Response*, and *Least of All Saints*).

For more information, please contact Sam Wilson, Writing Program Assistant, at the English Department.

❖University of South Carolina
171 University Parkway
Aiken, SC 29801

Contact the Creative Writing Program Director, Dept. of English.

❖University of South Carolina
English Department
Columbia, SC 29208

(803) 777-5063
FAX (803) 777-9064
e-mail: bpace@garnet.cla.sc.edu
website: http://www.cla.sc.edu/ENGL/index.html

Degree offered: MFA in Creative Writing (poetry, fiction, playwriting, writing for media)

Type of Program: Studio/Academic

Length of Residency: Three years

Required course of study: 45 s/hrs total
  Thesis: 6 s/hrs

Writing workshops: 15 s/hrs
Literary theory: 6 s/hrs
Literature courses: 9 s/hrs
Electives: 9 s/hrs

Other Requirements: Written comprehensive examination in genre; oral defense of thesis; competency in a foreign language.

Application Deadlines: February 15 for financial aid; May 15 for admission.

We seek talented students from diverse backgrounds and interests. Our primary goal is to nurture and develop each student's talent in whatever direction it may take. Some of our recent graduates seek academic positions, some do not; but all have written and defended a thesis which competes with work issued by university and commercial presses or with dramatic works being publicly presented. Each student's work is guided by a committee which suggests a detailed course of study combining elements of history, craft, and experimentation.

During the three years of residency, our writing students typically enter and contribute to an active intellectual and artistic community. Sometimes their participation evolves from workshops and formal academic tasks, but much of it is unstructured and discretionary, such as reading experimental work in ad hoc groups or serving on the editorial board of our nationally distributed literary journal *Yemassee*.

Our program takes advantage of being housed in a large English Department whose faculty are nationally prominent in many areas, especially 20th-century American literature. In addition to offering creative writing workshops and individual tutorials, all creative writing faculty teach literature to both undergraduate and graduate students.

There are a limited number of fellowships available, as well as internships and research assistantships, which carry both a stipend and an out-of-state tuition waiver. Students successfully completing the first year of study are eligible to apply for teaching assistantships in the second and third years of study.

Recent speakers and visiting faculty include Charles Frazier (who received his doctorate from this department in 1986), W.S. Merwin, Terrence McNally, Barbara Ehrenreich, Marilyn Nelson, Reynolds Price, Elaine Scarry, Laurence Lieberman, and John Updike. Currently, our Distinguished Writer-in-Residence is Robert Coover.

Creative writing permanent faculty includes: poet Kwame Dawes, whose seven books include *Progeny of Air*, winner of the British Forward Poetry Prize; Ed Madden, whose poetry has appeared in numerous anthologies and national journals; Amittai Aviram, author of *Telling Rhythm*, an examination of poetic theory; novelist and short story author William Price Fox, whose 12 books include *Southern Fried Plus Six*, and *Dixiana Moon*; novelist Ben Greer (*Slammer* and *Time Loves a Hero*); and playwright John MacNicholas, winner of The Roger Stevens Playwriting Award given by the Kennedy Center (*Crossings, Dumas, Deja Vu*).

For more information, contact the Director of Graduate Studies at (803) 777-5063.

❖University of South Dakota
212 Dakota Hall
414 E. Clark Street
Vermillion, SD 57069-2390

(605) 677-5486

Degrees offered: MA, PhD in English

Type of Program: Traditional Literary Study and Creative Writing

Degree: MA

Required course of study:
   Minimum of 30 s/hrs: 18 or more s/hrs of
      literature and related courses
   Thesis: up to 6 s/hrs credit for creative
      thesis, usually in fiction, nonfiction, or poetry
   Writing workshop: 6 s/hrs

Degree: PhD

Required course of study:
   Minimum of 54 s/hrs: 18 s/hrs in Creative Writing,
      12 s/hrs in electives (literature and critical
      theory), 9 s/hrs core requirements in Linguistics,
      Multicultural Literature, and Bibliography and
      Research
   Dissertation: 15 s/hrs credit for creative
      dissertation in fiction, nonfiction, and poetry

The creative writing program at the University of South Dakota is designed to give developing writers as much flexibility as possible, while providing a good grounding in literature, language, and criticism. The small size of our department makes it possible for writers in both the MA and PhD programs to work closely with individual faculty members.

Graduate classes are small. The limited enrollment in the writing workshops makes it easier to examine closely and intensively the work that has been brought to class.

The quarterly *South Dakota Review* is published in association with the English department. Many writing students work with the Vermillion Literary Project, which produces a literary magazine and sponsors coffee shop readings and other events.

The creative writing faculty includes program director and fiction writer Brian Bedard (*Hour of the Beast and Other Stories*), novelist Ed Allen (*Straight Through the Night* and *Mustang Sally*), and poet Aliki Barnstone (*Madly in Love* and *The Real Tin Flower*).

For more information, contact Brian Bedard, Creative Writing Program Director.

❖Southampton College of
Long Island University
Southampton, NY 11968

(516) 283-4000, ext. 200
FAX (516) 283-4081
e-mail: info@southampton.liunet.edu
website: http://www.southampton.liunet.edu

Degrees offered: BA, MFA

Degree: BA in Writing and Literature

Required course of study: 39 s/hrs in the major, with a minimum of 18 s/hrs in writing courses, 21 in literature. Writing classes include both "creative" workshops and those in more practical areas like journalism, critical writing, and scriptwriting.

Application Deadline: None.

The ability to write well is one of the most versatile, valuable, and marketable skills in today's society. The Writing and Literature major balances a practical knowledge of writing with a time-honored creative, humanistic, and literary background.

The arts of various kinds of writing are developed through a carefully planned curriculum, presented under the encouraging but critical direction of the humanities faculty, several of whom are published writers. All teachers work closely with their students, helping them to develop their talents in a disciplined and original style, encouraging them to explore diverse forms of writing. In addition to courses offered for that purpose, a variety of independent-study, internship, and Cooperative Education options are available to accommodate the individual needs and interests of writing majors. Furthermore, several campus outlets exist for student writing: the college newspaper, the literary magazine, and the yearbook.

One reason the Writing and Literature major is one of LIU/Southampton's best known programs is because a number of distinguished writers (some of them living in the Hamptons) have taught as adjuncts, or have participated in the Southampton College Summer Writer's Conference (open to students for writing credits), or have visited the campus as part of the John Steinbeck Lecture Series, or have given a reading under the sponsorship of Writers & Readers, the campus literary society. Recent visitors have included Galway Kinnell, David Ignatow, Robert Long, Peter Matthiessen, Joyce Carol Oates, Budd Schulberg, Louis Simpson, and Lanford Wilson.

Students intending to major in the Writing and Literature program may compete for a Campus Writing Scholarship. The competition categories are poetry, drama, fiction, and nonfiction. Scholarship awards may range from $750 to $10,000 and are renewable annually.

For more information about the Writing Scholarship Program, contact the Director of Admissions.

Degree: MFA in English/Writing

Required course of study: 36 credits.

The College offers graduate courses in English and Writing in its two regular 15-week fall and spring semesters. It also offers a full range of graduate courses during its two 6-week summer sessions. Summer session courses satisfy the same requirements and require the same number of credit hours of teaching as do regular semester courses. During the fall and spring semesters students may take up to 15 credits. Students taking courses during summer sessions may take no more than 9 credits per session.

Admission to the program is based on the evaluation of a portfolio of the applicant's writing, made in conjunction with a review of the candidate's entire academic record. The portfolio may include works in any genre, including fiction, nonfiction, poetry, or scriptwriting.

Full-time faculty in the program include nationally distinguished authors such as essayist and television commentator Roger Rosenblatt, poet and critic William Hathaway, and novelist Indira Ganesan. All full-time faculty are widely published as writers and scholars.

In addition, through its Distinguished Southampton Authors and Lecturers offerings, the program draws on the large number of noted writers living on Long Island and in the New York metropolitan region. Distinguished Southampton Authors and Lecturers for 1997–99 include novelist and screenwriter Richard Price, author Peter Matthiessen, television producer and writer Norman Lear, critic Molly Haskell, nonfiction author Shana Alexander, novelist Bruce Jay Friedman, commentator Michael Arlen, science writer Dava Sobel, and scriptwriter Jules Feiffer.

Every summer the English and Writing department sponsors the Southampton Writers Conference, an intensive program of one-credit courses in contemporary writing that includes lectures, readings, workshops, and panels featuring nationally distinguished authors who join the department's summer faculty. Past conference participants have included Edward Albee, William Burroughs, Susan Isaacs, Joyce Carol Oates, Kurt Vonnegut, Stewart O'Nan, Richard Russo, Tom Wolfe, Barbara Ehrenreich, Shana Alexander, and Bruce Jay Friedman.

Graduate students in the Writing Program are eligible for several forms of financial aid: Merit Fellowships and Teaching Assistantships.

For more information, contact the English Dept.

University of Southern California
Los Angeles, CA 90089-0354
(213) 740-2808

Degree offered: BA

The Department of English at USC offers a BA degree with an Emphasis in Creative Writing. (The Master of Professional Writing Program is a separate department and program; please see next listing.) Department requirements for the BA creative writing track include a contemporary literature class, a minimum of 4 writing workshops, 3 basic survey courses, and 2 upper division English electives.

The creative writing faculty includes T. Coraghesan Boyle (*World's End*, fiction); Michelle Latiolais (*Even Now*, fiction); Carol Muske (*Applause, Saving St. Germ*, poetry and fiction); and David St. John (*Study for the World's Body*, poetry).

For more information, contact the Dept. of English.

❖University of Southern California
WPH 404
Los Angeles, CA 90089-4034
(213) 740-3252

Degree offered: Master of Professional Writing (MPW) (Fiction Writing, Poetry Writing, Playwriting, Cinema-Television Writing, Creative Nonfiction Writing)

Type of Program: Studio

Length of Residency: Two years

Required course of study: 30 s/hrs

Other Requirements: 3 s/hrs of Survey of Professional Writing; 15 s/hrs of courses in major concentrations; 12 s/hrs of electives.

Application Deadlines: January 1 for financial aid; August 1 for admission.

One of the oldest and most distinguished graduate programs in the nation, the USC Master of Professional Writing Program is designed for individuals pursuing writing as a profession. The multi-disciplinary orientation of the Program results in well-rounded writers who are disciplined in craft and in the vocation of writing as a lifetime pursuit. *Craft, quality*, and *discipline* are key words. The MPW Program keeps its graduate seminars intimate. Only 8 to 10 students are permitted to register for any writing course, thereby ensuring that a student will receive individualized attention from an instructor. Program faculty, drawn from writers of national and international reputations, have included playwright William Inge, novelists Richard Yates and William Goyen, Academy Award winner Harry Brown, best-selling journalist/author Thomas Thompson, poet Ann Stanford, and the distinguished Soviet poet Yevgeny Yevtushenko. Mark Andrus, 1998 Academy Award nominee for Screenwriting (*As Good As It Gets*) is an MPW graduate. As a student, filmmaker George Lucas was a part of the MPW tradition. Fields of instruction are fiction writing, poetry writing, playwriting, cinema-television writing, creative nonfiction writing, and journalism. The curriculum also offers seminars and workshops focusing on the development of students' work and on completing a manuscript of publishable or production-level quality. The degree is specifically intended for writers interested in working in more than one genre.

Faculty includes: Program Director Dr. James Ragan, poet (*The Hunger Wall, Lusions*) and playwright (*Saints, Commedia*); author Betty Friedan (*The Feminine Mystique, The Fountain of Age*); Gay Talese, founder of the New Journalism (*The Kingdom and the Power, Honor Thy Father*); Shana Alexander, former CBS-TV "60 Minutes" commentator and author (*Nutcracker, Very Much a Lady*); novelist Hubert Selby, Jr. (*Last Exit to Brooklyn, The Willow Tree*); John Rechy, novelist (*City of Night, Marilyn's Daughter*) and dramatist (*Tiger's Wild*); Jerome Lawrence, Broadway award-winning playwright (*Inherit the Wind, Mame, The Night Thoreau Spent in Jail*); Pulitzer Prize winner Paul Zindel (*Effects of Gamma Rays on Man-in-the-Moon Marigolds*); Pulitzer and Tony nominated playwright Lee Blessing (*A Walk in the Woods, Oldtimers Game*); Frank Tarloff, Academy Award-winning screenwriter (*Father Goose, School for Scoundrels*) and Broadway playwright (*The Heroine*); S.L. Stebel, Australian Academy Award-winning screenwriter (*Picnic at Hanging Rock, Storm Boy*) and novelist (*Spring Thaw, The Collaborator*); Sy Gomberg, Academy Award-nominated screenwriter (*When Willie Comes Marching Home, Summer Stock*); Academy Award-nominated

171

screenwriter, Ehrich Van Lowe (*Cadillac Dreams*, Exec. Producer, "The Cosby Show"); Academy Award-nominated producer Dale Pollock (*Mrs. Winterbourne, Blaze*) and author (*Skywalking*); novelist Aram Saroyan (*The Romantic, Last Rites*); Dr. Richard Lid, author/critic (*Ford Madox Ford: The Essence of His Art*); Dr. Noel Riley Fitch (*Sylvia Beach and the Lost Generation, Anaïs: The Erotic Life of Anaïs Nin*); David Scott Milton, author/playwright (*Kabbalah, Duet*); Dr. Shirley Thomas, author (*Men of Space*) and commentator for NBC, CBS and ABC television networks; nonfiction author Tristine Rainer (*Your Life As Story*); Ben Masselink, novelist (*Green, The Danger Islands*); Donald Freed, author/playwright (*Executive Action, Secret Honor*); humorist Shelley Berman (*Up in the Air*); Shelly Lowenkopf, author and editor (*ABC-Clio Books*); poet Holly Prado (*The Garden, Specific Mysteries*); and Visiting Poet Marvin Bell (*The Book of the Dead Man*).

The USC Master of Professional Writing curriculum includes the following classes: Survey of Professional Writing, Poetry Workshop I & II, Master Class in Poetry, Fiction Writing Workshops I & II, Narrative Structure, Literature & Approaches to Writing the Novel, Film & Approaches to Writing the Novel, Principles of Dramatic Structure, Literary Marketplace, Writing Humor: Literary & Dramatic, Basic Dramatic Screenwriting, Practicum in Screenwriting, Screenplay, Story Conference, Playwright's Workshop I & II, Master Class in Playwriting, The Art of Literary Criticism, Writing the Nonfiction Book I & II, Advanced Creative Nonfiction Writing, Writing & Editing Magazine Nonfiction, Biography, and Technical Writing. In addition, Directed Research, a one-on-one study arrangement with a faculty member, is offered to second-year students.

In addition, the Professional Readers Series and Conference have showcased internationally acclaimed dramatists Friedrich Durrenmatt, Eugene Ionesco, Athol Fugard, and Edward Albee; noted poets Galway Kinnell, W.S. Merwin, Robert Bly, Allen Ginsberg, Michael S. Harper, Andrei Voznesensky, Robert Creeley, Charles Simic, Yevgeny Yevtushenko, Louis Simpson, Henry Taylor, William Matthews, and Carolyn Kizer; as well as Kurt Vonnegut, William Gaddis, Alice Walker, Carlos Fuentes, Gail Sheehy, William Gass, Christopher Isherwood, Manuel Puig, T.C. Boyle, Judith Guest, Jessica Mitford, Academy Award-winning screenwriter/author Budd Schulberg, and the Watts Writers Workshop.

Students' works are produced and presented in a variety of activities including the Festival of Writers; Jerome Lawrence's Octet student play productions; Master Class in Poetry Reading; The USC Playwrights Guild One-Act Play Festival with past judges including Paul Zindel, Mark Rydel, Piper Laurie, Tony Franciosa, Fay Kanin, Irwin Kirshner, and Arthur Hiller; and the Writers Table Lecture Series, which recently featured such guests as Emmy Award-winning producer Steven Bochco (*L.A. Law*), agent Georges Borchardt, Paramount Pictures President Ned Tanen, and Academy Award-winning screenwriters Julius Epstein (*Casablanca*), Edward Anhalt (*Beckett*), and Edmund North (*Patton*). Students also have opportunities to be involved in informal student readings, the publication of the Program's newsletter, *ManUSCript*, and the internationally recognized literary journal, *The Southern California Anthology*, edited by graduate students of the Professional Writing Program, and which also offers the annual Ann Stanford Poetry Prize.

Graduates have published poetry, novels, and nonfiction books, sold screenplays, and had successful stage productions. A large number have enjoyed a high degree of success in the film, theater, and publishing industries as well as in the college and university teaching professions. USC's Los Angeles location offers a superb climate and strong ties to the nation's top publishing houses, literary agents, theaters, film studios, and print media, including Time Inc., *Newsweek, Los Angeles Times*, and the *New York Times*.

Professional associations include film writing internships with Columbia Pictures, Walt Disney, Twentieth Century Fox, Paramount Pictures, Universal, DreamWorks, Oliver Stone's Ixtan Productions, Sony Pictures, Polygram, Miramax, Tri-Star (Tony Bill), Cathy Lee Crosby Productions, Martin Sheen Productions, AFI, and Warner Brothers; publishing liaisons with Faber & Faber, Viking, Knopf, Grove/Atlantic, Farrar-Straus, Carol Publishing, Doubleday, Avon, Houghton Mifflin, Scott Foresman, Norton, Dutton, Bantam, Harper & Row, Pinnacle, Crown, Vanguard, Warner Books, Dell, Chatto & Windus (London), and Playboy Enterprises; studio liaisons with Walt Disney, Warner Brothers, New World Pictures, PBS, NBC, CBS, HBO, and ABC television networks; theatrical liaisons with Houston's Alley Theatre, Actor's Theater of Louisville, L.A.'s Ahmanson Theater, Mark Taper Forum, The Odyssey, Beverly Hills Playhouse, CAST Theatre, Main Floor Theatre, Galaxy Theatre, and the Actor's Playhouse; as well as access to top theatrical and literary agents such as Georges Borchardt, Peter Matson, Charlotte Sheedy, Sterling Lord Literistic, Robert Lantz, and the William Morris, Creative Artists, ICM, and UTA agencies.

In addition to critical reviews of praise for our writers, the Program can claim, as alumni, nominees for the Academy Award, Emmy Award, ACE Cable Award, The Mystery Writers of America's Edgar Allen Poe Award, the Pulitzer Prize, Yale Younger Poets Series, Pushcart Poetry Prize, and winners of the NAACP Image Award, Barbra Streisand Playwriting Award, WGA-West Screenwriting Award, the CBS/Dramatists Guild New Plays Program, the N.Y. Shakespeare Play Festival, the American College Theatre Festival's Lorraine Hansberry Award, the New Dramatists/McDonald's Award, the PEN Nelson Algren Fiction Award, the American Independent Film Competition at Los Angeles' FILMEX, the Academy of American Poets Prize, AWP/Intro Award Prize, the NEA, Guggenheim, Samuel French Morse Poetry Prize, the AMPAS Student Academy Award, the Phi Kappa Phi Award, the Disney Fellowship Screenwriting Award, Nicholl Screenplay Fellowship, the Donald Davis Screenwriting Award, the Jack Nicholson Screenwriting Award, the Sundance Screenwriting Award, and the Los Angeles Arts Council's Prizes in Fiction, Poetry, and Playwriting.

A limited number of merit scholarships and teaching assistantships are available to qualified students on a competitive basis. A 3.0 undergraduate grade-point average, adequate scores on the aptitude portion of the Graduate Record Examination, a minimum 10-page writing sample, and 3 letters of recommendation are required for admission to the Program.

For more information, please write to Dr. James Ragan, Master of Professional Writing Program.

❖Southern Connecticut State University
501 Crescent Street
New Haven, CT 06515
(203) 392-6745

Degrees offered: BA in English with Concentration in Creative Writing; MA and MS in English with Concentration in Creative Writing (fiction, poetry)

Required course of study: 30 s/hrs English (BA), including 12 s/hrs of workshops, 18 s/hrs of literature. 33 s/hrs (MA), including 9 s/hrs of workshop, 12 s/hrs of literature and elective courses (with option of further workshops), 6 s/hrs of Research Methods and Critical Theory, 6 s/hrs for creative thesis. 33 s/hrs (MS), same as MA except 12-18 s/hrs in English studies and 9 s/hrs in cognate electives.

SCSU offers a BA, an MA, and an MS in English with Concentrations in Creative Writing. The MA program is small and provides close contact with the faculty and other graduate students. The current sequence of creative writing courses includes workshops in fiction, poetry, creative nonfiction, and the writing of the novel; additional seminars are offered in narrative theory, poetics, literary publishing, and other special topics.

SCSU's Creative Writing Program focuses primarily on helping each student to explore and develop his or her own interests. Our students are an unusually diverse group, many of whom have returned to school to study writing after establishing careers in other fields. New Haven boasts a strong writing community, with many opportunities for involvement in a variety of other activities. SCSU's tuition is markedly lower than that of comparable private universities; a few graduate teaching assistantships are awarded to students already enrolled in the program; adjunct teaching positions are also awarded to select graduate students with appropriate credentials.

SCSU is home to the *Connecticut Review* (edited by Vivian Shipley), winner of the 1997 Phoenix Award for Distinguished Editorial Achievement from the Council of Editors for Learned Journals. Poems from *CR* have been selected for both *Best American Poetry 1998* and *The Pushcart Prize XXIII*. Furthermore, students at both the undergraduate and graduate level contribute to and staff the campus literary magazine, *Folio*, and are able to work closely with Jeff Mock, assistant editor of the *Gettysburg Review*.

Our program provides numerous opportunities for participation in student readings, and all writing students are encouraged to attend the program's series of readings by writers from outside the school. In the past three years the readers' series has brought to campus John Edgar Wideman, Marilyn Nelson, Kevin Canty, Rita Ciresi, Joan Connor, Sydney Lea, Brad Watson, Nanci Kincaid, Buck Downs, Tony Earley, Leo Connellan, and numerous others.

The faculty in the Creative Writing Program includes Vivian Shipley, poetry (*Devil's Lane, Poems Out of Harlan County,* and *Jack Tales*); Megan Macomber, fiction; Jeff Mock, poetry (*Evening Travelers, You Can Write Poetry*); and Tim Parrish, fiction.

For further information, contact Tim Parrish, Director, Creative Writing Program, Dept. of English.

❖Southern Illinois University at Carbondale
Carbondale, IL 62901
(618) 453-5321

Degrees offered: BA, MFA

Degree: BA in English, with Creative Writing Emphasis

Required course of study: 36 s/hrs
Thesis: no requirement
Writing workshop: 15 or more s/hrs
Literature courses: 18 or more s/hrs
Other writing courses: 3 s/hrs

Southern Illinois University offers beginning, intermediate, and advanced workshops in poetry, fiction, and literary nonfiction. Students in the Creative Writing Emphasis also take either Forms of Fiction or Forms of Poetry, literature courses taught by and for writers, as well as literature courses taught by the literature faculty. All creative writing faculty (listed below) teach all levels of writing courses. *Grassroots*, a student-edited journal of student work, is produced through the English Dept., and a limited number of undergraduate interns work on the national literary magazine, *The Crab Orchard Review*. Recent creative writing majors have been accepted to graduate programs at such institutions as the University of Pittsburgh, George Mason University, Emerson College, Washington University, Iowa Writers Workshop, Western Michigan University, the University of Maryland, and Cornell University.

Degree: MFA in Creative Writing (fiction, poetry, nonfiction)

Type of Program: Studio/Academic

Length of Residency: Three years

Required course of study: 48 s/hrs total
Thesis: 6 s/hrs
Writing workshop: 20 s/hrs
Forms course: 4 s/hrs
Literature, electives, & independent study:
  18 s/hrs

Other requirements: Students with teaching assistantships are required to take a course in the teaching of composition. All students must pass an oral examination entailing both course work and a defense of the creative thesis.

Application Deadlines: January 15.

The MFA in Creative Writing is a three-year studio/academic program for students who show talent writing fiction, poetry, or literary nonfiction. The program accepts a maximum of 10 students each year, so workshops are small and faculty members work closely with students, providing both formal and informal mentoring.

SIUC is located two hours from St. Louis, near the Mississippi River, on the edge of the Shawnee National

Forest. The university offers excellent support services for students with disabilities and for nontraditional students, and the campus is exceptionally wheelchair-accessible.

Our Visiting Writers Series brings numerous writers to campus for readings and meetings with students. Recent guests have included Yusef Komunyakaa, Larry Brown, Eavan Boland, Albert Goldbarth, Mark Doty, Alan Dugan, Stuart Dybek, Nancy Willard, Paul Muldoon, Hope Edelman, C.K. Williams, Paul Levine, Bob Shacochis, Laura Hendrie, and William Kennedy.

The English Department is home to a national literary journal, *The Crab Orchard Review*. A limited number of internships with the journal, and with the SIU Press, are available.

Most students admitted to the MFA program are offered three years of financial aid as teaching assistants in composition. A limited number of second- and third-year creative writing students are offered teaching assistantships in creative writing and literature. All assistantships include tuition remission. Also, some university fellowships are available to qualified students. Applicants should request an application from the Graduate Program in English and return it with samples of their work (10–15 pages of poetry, 15–30 pages of fiction or nonfiction), transcripts, and letters of recommendation.

The writing faculty includes novelist Ricardo Cortez Cruz (*Straight Outta Compton*, winner of the Nilon Award for Minority Fiction; *Five Days of Bleeding*); novelist Kent Haruf (*The Tie That Binds*, winner of the Whiting Award; *Where You Once Belonged*); poet Rodney Jones (*The Unborn; Transparent Gestures*, winner of the National Book Critics Circle Award; *Apocalyptic Narrative and Other Poems: Things That Happen Once*, a Publisher's Weekly Best Books of 1996 selection); poet Allison Joseph (*What Keeps Us Here*, winner of the John C. Zacharis First Book Award and Women Poets Series Competition; *Soul Train; In Every Seam*); essayist Lisa Knopp (*Field of Vision*); novelist Beth Lordan (*August Heat; And Two Shall Row*); poet Lucia Perillo (*Dangerous Life*, winner of the Norma Farber First Book Award; *The Body Mutinies*, winner of the Kate Tufts Discovery Award).

For more information, contact Director of Graduate Studies, Dept. of English.

Southern Illinois University at Edwardsville
Edwardsville, IL 62026-1431
(618) 692-2060

Degree offered: BA in English with Minor in Creative Writing

For more information, contact Writing Program Director, Dept. of English.

❖Southern Methodist University
Dallas, TX 75275-1234
(214) 768-2945
FAX (214) 768-4129
e-mail: cwsmith@mail.smu.edu
website: http://www.smu.edu

Degrees offered: BA, MA

Degree: BA in English with Specialization in Creative Writing

Required course of study: 33 s/hrs for the major
Thesis: no requirement
Writing workshop: 6–9 s/hrs
Other writing courses: 3–6 s/hrs
Literature courses: 15–18 s/hrs
Tutorials or directed reading: up to 6 s/hrs

Other Requirements: 42 required s/hrs are specified outside the English/writing courses; they include studies in science, social sciences, arts, mathematics, language, and physical education. A total of 120 s/hrs is required for the degree.

The BA in English with a Creative Writing Specialization is composed of the traditional range of English courses but includes a minimum of 12 s/hrs and a maximum of 15 s/hrs in creative writing courses in fiction and/or poetry writing. The 2 fiction and poetry tracks are made up of workshops on the introductory and advanced levels and technical craft courses on the intermediate level. Directed Studies courses can also be used toward a degree.

The undergraduate literary magazine *Espejo* is published twice a year and has received a number of national awards for excellence.

The purpose of the Creative Writing Specialization is to foster awareness of and excellence in writing contemporary poetry and fiction.

Degree: MA in English with Creative Writing Emphasis

Type of Program: Studio/Academic

Required course of study: 30 s/hrs
Thesis: 3–6 s/hrs
Writing workshop: 3–6 s/hrs
Literature courses: 12–18 s/hrs
Tutorials or directed reading: 3–6 s/hrs

The Master's Degree in English with Creative Dissertation requires successful completion of 30 s/hrs of graduate study including thesis. The creative writing thesis consists of a book-length volume of high quality poetry (30–50 pages) or high quality fiction of novel length. Each candidate must pass an oral examination based on traditional and modern works of literature. It is expected that the graduate student in writing will work closely in advanced courses and conferences with his thesis advisor, one of the writers on the faculty.

Each year SMU sponsors a Literary Festival in November which features major and promising poets and writers who read from their work, attend classes, and offer panel discussions. In addition, visiting writers often teach for a term, and writers give readings through the year. There are also a number of poetry and fiction readings performed at other close-by universities and places outside the universities.

The Creative Writing faculty includes: novelist and short story writer Marshall Terry (*Old Liberty, Tom Northway,* and *My Father's Hands*), poet Jack Myers (*As Long As You're Happy, I'm Amazed That You're Still Singing,* and *Blindsided*), novelist and nonfiction writer C.W. Smith (*Thin Men of Haddam, Country Music,* and *Buffalo Nickel*), novelist Patricia Anthony (*Brother Termite, Conscience of the Beagle,* and *Cold Allies*), novelist David Haynes (*Somebody Else's Mama, Live at Five,* and *Heathens*), and poet Leslie Richardson (poems in *The Paris Review, The Hampden-Sydney Review,* and *The Cimarron Review*.

For more information, contact C.W. Smith, Director of Creative Writing, Dept. of English.

❖University of Southern Mississippi
Box 5144
Hattiesburg, MS 39406-5144
(601) 266-4321

Degrees offered: BA, MA, PhD

Degree: BA in English

Required course of study: 36 s/hrs in the major
Thesis: no requirement
Writing workshop: up to 15 s/hrs
Other writing courses: up to 6 s/hrs
Literature courses: 15 or more s/hrs upper
  division courses

At the undergraduate level, a maximum of 15 s/hrs in writing workshops and 6 s/hrs in other writing courses are allowed toward the BA degree in English.

Degree: MA in English with Creative Writing Emphasis

Required course of study: 30 s/hrs
Thesis: 6 s/hrs
Writing workshop: 6 s/hrs
Theory/Criticism: 9 s/hrs
Literature courses: 9 s/hrs

Other Requirements: Foreign language proficiency; oral defense of thesis.

Degree: PhD in English with Creative Writing Emphasis

Type of Program: Traditional Literary Study and Creative Writing

Required course of study: 54 s/hrs beyond MA
Dissertation: 12 s/hrs
Writing workshop: 12 s/hrs
Literature/Theory: 30 s/hrs in accordance
  with standard PhD requirements

Other Requirements: Proficiency in 2 foreign languages or 9 graduate hrs in related field and 1 foreign language; oral defense of dissertation; written comprehensive examination.

Application Deadlines: February 1 for financial aid.

The Center for Writers at the University of South-

ern Mississippi offers undergraduate emphasis in creative writing within the English major, as well as 2 graduate programs that allow the student to combine writing and academic studies: the MA, a 1 or 2-year program with a creative thesis, and the PhD, a 3-year program with a creative dissertation and comprehensive exams. The thesis or dissertation may be poetry or fiction and must be book-length and of publishable quality.

A number of teaching assistantships are available on a competitive basis with stipends of $7,100 for PhD and $6,800 for MA and full tuition waivers. 2 supplementary awards of $500 are available annually to graduate students from the Joan Johnson foundation. TA's may teach freshman composition, tutor in the writing lab, or work on one of the department's 6 publications, which include *Mississippi Review,* an award-winning triquarterly journal of fiction and poetry, and *Product,* a publication of student literary work. Students from the Center have published widely, in such magazines as *Poetry, Chicago Review, Intro, Grand Street, Poet & Critic,* and *The New Yorker.*

The Center's Visiting Writers Series has brought over 100 writers and editors to campus -- Molly Peacock, Ann Beattie, Charles Wright, David Leavitt, Tobias Wolff, John Barth, Tom Drury, Alice Adams, Larry McMurtry, W.S. Merwin, Richard Howard, Edna O'Brien, Charles Simic, Yevgeny Yevtushenko, Amy Hempel, Derek Walcott, and Antonya Nelson.

The Center faculty: In fiction, Frederick Barthelme (novels and collections include *Tracer, Natural Selection,* and *The Brothers*); Mary Robison (*Days, Oh!, Believe Them, Subtraction*); and Steven Barthelme (*And He Tells the Little Horse the Whole Story*). In poetry, David Berry (*Divorce Boxing*) and Angela Ball (*Quartet and Possession*). In criticism and literary theory, Kim Herzinger (*D.H. Lawrence: In His Time, Flying to America: The Unpublished & Uncollected Stories of Donald Barthelme*).

For more information, contact Rie Fortenberry.

Southern University at New Orleans
New Orleans, LA 70126

Contact the Creative Writing Program Director, Dept. of English.

❖Southwest Missouri State University
Springfield, MO 65804
(417) 836-4484

Degrees offered: BA, MA

Degree: BA in English with an emphasis in Creative Writing (poetry, fiction, drama)

Required course of study: 124 s/hrs total
Writing workshop: 12 s/hrs
Senior portfolio: 3 s/hrs
Literature courses: 18 s/hrs

Other Requirements: 12 s/hrs one foreign language; 18 s/hrs minor of student's choice; university general education and fine arts requirements.

Application Deadlines: March 31 for financial aid; beginning of academic year (mid–August) for admission.

Southwest Missouri State University offers students a studio/academic undergraduate degree in creative writing. Courses in British, American, and world literature provide a knowledge of the tradition, and workshops at introductory, intermediate, and advanced levels develop creative writing skills. The campus literary magazine offers students editorial and publishing experience.

Degree: MA in English, Creative Writing Track (poetry, fiction, drama)

Type of Program: Literary study combined with creative writing workshops/thesis

Length of Residency: One and one/half years, two years with a teaching assistantship

Required course of study: 33 s/hrs total
Core (literature, linguistics, theory): 18 s/hrs
Creative writing course work (workshops, thesis): 15 s/hrs

Other Requirements: Foreign language proficiency, written comprehensive examination.

Through the reading series, visiting lecturers, and creative publications, the faculty and students at SMSU have formed an active, distinguished community of creative writers. Program faculty members include Michael Burns, Jane Hoogestraat, W.D. Blackmon, Roland Sodowsky, and Martin Jones.

Louise Glück, Carolyn Kizer, Miller Williams, Quincy Troupe, Naomi Shihab Nye, and Demetria Martinez are writers who have recently visited our campus.

Graduate teaching assistantships are available competitively. Assistantships include full tuition waiver and a minimum stipend of $6,000.

For more information, contact the Dept. of English at (417) 836–5107.

❖Southwest State University
Marshall, MN 56258

For more information, contact Eileen Thomas, Writing Center, English Dept.

❖Southwest Texas State University
San Marcos, TX 78666
(512) 245–7681
FAX (512) 245–8546
e-mail: tg02@swt.edu
website: www.English.swt.edu/MFA.html

Degree offered: MFA in Creative Writing (fiction, poetry)

Type of Program: Studio/Academic

Length of Residency: Three years

Required course of study: 48 s/hrs total
Thesis: 6 s/hrs
Writing workshop: 12 s/hrs
Literature courses: 15 s/hrs
Form and Theory course: 3 s/hrs
Literary techniques: 3 s/hrs
Minor: 9 s/hrs

Other Requirements: Written and oral comprehensive examination. Minors available include Southwest studies cognate, fine arts cognate, and traditional academic disciplines including English.

Application Deadlines: January 15 for fall admission; November 1 for spring admission.

We offer talented writers the opportunity to develop their skills in a program that balances workshops with literature seminars. The workshops offer rigorous critiques in the context of a supportive community of writers. We encourage diversity in critical and artistic perspectives. A special feature of the program offers students the chance to work with distinguished writers who serve as adjunct faculty for thesis direction. In its eighth year, the program currently enrolls sixty writers. Southwest Texas State University is located on the San Marcos River in the Texas Hill County thirty miles from Austin and fifty miles from San Antonio. The university enrolls 22,000 students, 3,000 of whom are graduate students.

Resources of special interest to MFA students include the Therese Kayser Lindsey Endowment, visiting writer residencies, teaching opportunities in a summer creative writing camp, the Center for the Study of the Southwest, the Southwestern Writers Collection, and several journals: *The Prose Poem, Southwestern American Literature, Texas Books in Review, Excerpt,* and *The Children's Literature Association Quarterly.*

A visiting writers program has brought to campus a number of writers, including Ann Beattie, Robert Boswell, Joseph Brodsky, Sandra Cisneros, Rita Dove, Allen Ginsberg, Nikki Giovanni, Albert Goldbarth, Jorie Graham, Joy Harjo, Charles Johnson, Galway Kinnell, Maxine Kumin, Denise Levertov, W.S. Merwin, Antonya Nelson, Sharon Olds, W.D. Snodgrass, Gary Snyder, Alice Walker, James Welch, Richard Wilbur, and Charles Wright.

Teaching assistantships are available. Teaching assistants receive health benefits and remission of non–resident tuition. 1998 stipends are $6,516 for Instructional Assistants and $8,275 for Teaching Assistants. 1998 tuition and fees for nine hours are $890 resident, $2,816 non–resident.

Each year, an award–winning writer of international distinction will teach in the MFA program and deliver lectures on literature. Fall 1999–Spring 2000: National Book Award Winner Tim O'Brien.

Permanent faculty include poet Cyrus Cassells (*Beautiful Signor, Soul Make a Path Through Shouting, The Mud Actor*); fiction writer Dagoberto Gilb (*The Last Known Residenc of Mickey Acuna, The Magic of Blood*); fiction writer Tom Grimes (*A History/Anthology of the Iowa Writers Workshop, City of God, Season's End*); poet Roger Jones (*Strata*); fiction writer Debra Monroe (*The Source of Trouble, A Wild, Cold State, New–Fangled*); poet Kathleen Peirce (*The Oval Hour, Mercy, Divided Touch, Divided Color*); poet Steve Wilson

(*Singapore Express or Faith in the Knowing Hand of the Scientist, Allegory Dance*, and *The Anatomy of Water: A Sampling of Contemporary American Prose Poetry*, ed.).

Adjunct faculty include Lee K. Abbott, Rick Bass, Ron Carlson, Gillian Conoley, Charles D'Ambrosio, Andre Dubus, Shelby Hearon, Li-Young Lee, Philip Levine, Beverly Lowry, Jane Mead, W.S. Merwin, Kent Nelson, Naomi Shihab Nye, Chris Offut, Alberto Rios, Pattiann Rogers, Reg Saner, Gerald Stern, Terry Tempest Williams, and Eleanor Wilner.

For more information, contact Director, MFA Program, Dept. of English.

❖Southwestern Community College
900 Otay Lakes Road
Chula Vista, CA 91910

For more information, contact Dr. Renee M. Kilmer, Dean of Language Arts.

❖University of Southwestern Louisiana
Drawer 44691
Lafayette, LA 70504-4691
(318) 482-6908
FAX (318) 482-5071 (must include cover sheet and address to Director, Creative Writing)
e-mail: jwf4516@ucs.usl.edu

Degrees offered: BA, MA, PhD

Degree: BA in English

A total of 24 s/hrs in creative writing courses (electives), plus individual studies, are offered to students at the undergraduate level. Students in the University Honors Program may elect to write a creative Honors thesis. Second semester juniors may elect to compete for the Judge Felix Voorhies Creative Writing Award, which carries a stipend as well as its considerable honor.

Degree: MA in English with Creative Writing Option
(poetry, fiction, screenwriting)

Type of Program: Traditional Literary Study and Creative Writing

Length of Residency: Completion of minimum of 24 hours of degree program credit on this campus

Required course of study: 33 s/hrs
Thesis: 6 s/hrs
Writing workshop: 6 s/hrs
Literature courses: 15–18 s/hrs
Tutorials or directed reading: up to 6 s/hrs

Other Requirements: Bibliography course; professional colloquium; foreign language proficiency; written comprehensive examination based on coursework, oral defense of thesis.

The MA in English with the Creative Writing Option combines literary coursework with a flexible program of publication experience, culminating in a creative thesis (poetry, fiction, drama, scriptwriting) with

theoretical introduction. The program annually hosts the Deep South Writers' Conference and presents visiting writers as well as occasional resident artists.

Degree: PhD in English with Creative Writing Emphasis

Type of Program: Traditional Literary Study and Creative Writing

Length of Residency: Two semesters of full-time consecutive graduate study, not including summer sessions.

Required course of study: 72 hrs of graduate work above the baccalaureate
Writing workshop: 6 or more s/hrs
Literature courses: 24 s/hrs
Dissertation: variable s/hrs

Other Requirements: Distribution of literature courses among major period divisions; one additional foreign language beyond MA; written comprehensive examination; oral defense of dissertation.

Application Deadlines: March 1 for fall semester; November 1 for spring semester.

The faculty includes playwrights John Fiero and Joe Andriano; fiction writer and poet Burton Raffel; poets Herb Fackler, Jerry McGuire, and Darrell Bourque; and writer in residence Ernest J. Gaines, author of *A Lesson Before Dying, The Autobiography of Miss Jane Pittman*, and *A Gathering of Old Men*, for which he won the National Book Award in 1994.

A limited number of fellowships are available (MA -- $7,500; PhD -- $12,000). MA assistantships pay $4,500 plus waiver of fees and tuition, for 10 months; PhD assistantships pay $7,500 plus waiver fees and tuition, for 10 months.

For more information, contact Jerry L. McGuire, Director of Creative Writing.

❖Spelman College
Atlanta, GA 30314-4399

Contact the Creative Writing Program Director, Dept. of English.

❖Stanford University
Stanford, CA 94305
(650) 723-2637

Degrees offered: None

Degrees required for entrance: None

Required course of study: Attendance at weekly workshop.

The Stanford Writing Program is unique among programs: it confers no degree, it requires no degree for admission, and it offers a living stipend of $15,000 a year plus required workshop tuition of about $5,000 a year for a total of $40,000 in fellowship support over a 2-year residency. This program is intended for accomplished but not yet established writers who, whatever their degree of competence, can still learn from participation in a workshop.

Stanford Writing Fellows are regarded as working artists rather than as degree candidates, and though degrees are always welcome, they do not enter our consideration of a writer's suitability for our program. Rather, we presume that education, particularly a literary education, is a lifelong pursuit for any writer.

At Stanford, we have no commitment to any particular school of writing -- not realism, naturalism, modernism, experimentalism. Our commitment is to good writing, the best writing, in all its manifestations. We try, quite simply, to help writers become the best poets, novelists, and short story writers they can possibly be.

Creative Writing Fellows register for and participate in the writing workshop, that is to say, they read and criticize writing by other workshop members, put up their own writing for criticism and, having done so, they listen to it. Writers who feel they cannot profit from workshop should not apply to this program.

Every year the Stanford Writing Program supports at least 20 Fellows in Creative Writing -- 10 in fiction, 10 in poetry. There are no fellowships for work in drama or in nonfiction.

We offer all first year writers a Wallace E. Stegner Fellowship, named for the founder of the Stanford Writing Program. Other endowed Fellowships, for work during the second year, are named for Elsie P. Ettinger, Jean Lane, Joan Lane, Edith R. Mirrielees, Richard P. Scowcroft, Dorrit Sibley, Sheila and Walter Weisman, and Truman Capote.

Applicants do not apply for individual Fellowships; the Admissions Committee makes that designation. All Fellowships, named and unnamed, provide the same financial support.

The Creative Writing faculty includes: Director and poet and essayist Eavan Boland (*Object Lessons: The Life of the Woman and Poet in Our Time, In a Time of Violence, Collected Poems*), fiction writer Elizabeth Tallent (*Museum Pieces, In Constant Flight, Time with Children*); fiction writer John L'Heureux (*Woman Run Mad, The Shrine at Altimira, The Handmaid of Desire*); novelist and poet Gilbert Sorrentino (*Mulligan Stew, Crystal Vision, Aberration of Starlight*); poet, essayist and translator W.S. Di Piero (*The Restorers, Memory and Enthusiasm, Out of Eden*); poet Kenneth Fields (*The Other Walker, Sunbelly, Smoke*); and Tobias Wolff (*The Night in Question, This Boy's Life, In Pharaoh's Army*).

We have published a collection of fiction and poetry by 98 writers from the Stanford Writing Program: *The Uncommon Touch*, ed. by John L'Heureux. *The Uncommon Touch* contains work by Edward Abbey, Wendell Berry, Raymond Carver, Evan S. Connell, Harriet Doerr, Ernest Gaines, Thom Gunn, Allan Gurganus, Donald Hall, Ron Hansen, Robert Hass, Alice Hoffman, Donald Justice, Ken Kesey, Tom McGuane, Larry McMurtry, Tillie Olsen, Robert Pinsky, Alan Shapiro, Robert Stone, Scott Turow, Stephanie Vaughn, and Tobias Wolff, among others. It may be purchased from the Stanford Alumni Association.

Our selection of Fellows is made on the basis of the writing portfolio: 40 pages for fiction, about 12 poems for poetry. The closing date for the receipt of applications and manuscripts is postmarked by December 1. All applicants are notified by mid-March.

Application materials can be obtained by writing Gay Pierce, Program Coordinator, Creative Writing Program.

❖State University of New York, Albany
HU-335
Albany, NY 12222
(518) 442-4055
FAX (518) 442-4599

Degrees offered: BA, MA, PhD

Degree: BA in English

The undergraduate English program at SUNY-Albany initiated a writing sequence through the English major entitled "Writing: Rhetoric and Poetics" in Fall 1994. Regular offerings also include creative writing, advanced poetry and fiction writing, expository and advanced expository writing, critical writing, tutoring and writing (a course which trains undergraduates to work in the Department's Writing Center), and a range of literature classes designated Writing Intensive. Seniors well advanced in their work may take graduate workshops. In addition, the Department supports a very strong Journalism minor, taught mainly by active professional journalists, and featuring internships at area newspapers, public relations firms, and so on.

Each year prizes are given for the best undergraduate poem and story. Campus outlets for undergraduate work include the student newspaper, *ASP (Albany Student Press)*, and 2 literary journals: *Tangent* and *The Albany Review*. All students at Albany benefit from an exceptionally strong program of visiting writers, made possible in part by the presence on campus of the New York State Writers Institute, a non-academic organization created specifically to promote writing in New York State.

Degree: MA in English -- Writing Sequence

Type of Program: Studio/Academic

Required course of study: 30 s/hrs
Thesis: not required
Writing Theory & Practice: 12 s/hrs
Literature Seminar: 4 or more s/hrs

Other Requirements: 4 s/hrs Language Theory and Practice; foreign language proficiency; written comprehensive examination.

Degree: PhD in English (writing, teaching, criticism)

Type of Program: Studio/Academic

Length of Residency: One year minimum

Required course of study: 72 hours of graduate-level coursework, of which a maximum of 24 may be transferred from other institutions and a maximum of 12 taken outside of the Department of English.
Thesis: required
Possible genres: fiction, poetry, drama, creative nonfiction, mixed genres

Writing Workshop: 4-24 s/hrs
Required courses: "The History of English Studies,"
"Teaching Writing and Literature," "Practicum in
English Studies"

Other Requirements: Two from among 6 other 4 s/hr core courses; foreign language proficiency; one written and two oral comprehensive exams, the latter based on papers prepared by the student; one-semester internship.

The University at Albany offers a curriculum in English Studies leading to the PhD or MA degrees. The program puts writing at the center of inquiry and foregrounds issues of teaching theory and practice. It emphasizes the pervasiveness of ideological positions in the making and sharing of knowledge, and stresses disciplinary self-consciousness. The program reconfigures English Studies by integrating the activities of writing, teaching, and criticism, and by locating these practices within concrete social and historical settings. Courses foster a dialectic between theory and practice, and introduce issues of gender, race, ethnicity, and class as essential themes in the narrative of English Studies.

The program is designed to serve persons with a variety of interests -- creative writing, composition studies, literary history, theory -- and to explore the interrelationships among such interests. To that end, courses are clustered in seven interdependent areas of study, without concentrations or tracks: Writing in History; Writing Theory and Practice; Teaching Theory and Practice; Language and Language Theory; and Literary History. Students take courses in all these areas, and seek an integration evolving out of their own interests. The goal of the program is to promote coherence, not (some imagined) coverage. Creative dissertations in such forms as poetry, fiction, and drama are supported and encouraged, but candidates also have considerable latitude to mix genres, including the creative and the critical.

The program's faculty includes Judith Barlow, critic (*Final Acts: The Creation of Three Late O'Neill Plays*) and editor (*Plays by American Women, 1900-1930*), whose major interest is in American drama; Don Byrd, a poet (*The Great Dimestore Centennial*) and critic (*The Poetics of Common Knowledge*); Sarah Cohen, critic (*From Levity to Liturgy: The Fiction of Cynthia Ozick*) and playwright; Helen Elam, a literary theorist (*The Limits of Imagination*), with interests in 19th- and 20th-century poetry; Judith Fetterley, critic (*The Resisting Reader, Provision: A Reader From 19th-Century Women*), whose major focus is on 19th-century American literature and feminist criticism; Rosemary Hennessy, critical theorist who works especially in post-modern culture studies (*Materialist Feminism and the Politics of Discourse*); Judith Johnson, a poet (*Ice Lizard, Cities of Mathematics and Desire*), short fiction writer (*The Life of Riot*), and intermedia performance artist; Pierre Joris, a poet, translator, and editor (*Turbulence, Poems for the Millennium*); Laura Marello, a fiction writer (*Tenants of the Hotel Biron, Claiming Kin*); Stephen North, author of *The Making of Knowledge in Composition*, and editor of the NCTE book series "Refiguring English Studies"; Martha Rozett, a Shakespeare scholar (*The Doctrine of Election and the Emergence of Elizabethan Tragedy*) with a special interest in pedagogy (*Talking Back to Shakespeare*), and Carolyn Yalkut, Director of Journalism (undergraduate) and playwright (*Big Boy*).

The program sponsors numerous readings and lectures -- most notably, perhaps, the longstanding student-run Jawbone Series for area artists. It also houses two literary journals: *The Little Magazine* and *13th Moon*. In addition, the program benefits from its affiliation with an extraordinary range of Albany-based organizations: the New York State Writers Institute, housed on the Albany campus and directed by founder William Kennedy (whose *Ironweed* won the National Book Critics Circle Award and the Pulitzer Prize), is a non-academic organization charged with promoting writers and writing in New York State; the energetic Hudson Valley Writers Guild, a regional writers group which sponsors its own workshops, reading, and publications; and ALPS (Alternative Literary Programs), which, with funding from the New York State Council on the Arts, NEA, and the New York State Writers Institute, sponsors reading and poetry workshops throughout the state.

Teaching assistantships are available for doctoral students who have a master's degree, paying a stipend of $9,000 plus a 10-credit tuition waiver. Teaching fellows ordinarily teach one course per semester or work in the Department's Writing Center. Minority Fellowships pay a $10,000 stipend and a full tuition waiver. A few University-wide Presidential Fellowships, carrying a $15,000 stipend plus a tuition waiver, are available on a competitive basis following nomination by the Department. A very limited amount of assistance may be available for students entering the master's program. Some 25 graduate students are supported each year.

For more information, contact the Director of Graduate Studies, Dept. of English.

State University of New York at Brockport
Brockport, NY 14420
(716) 395-2503

Degrees offered: BA, BS, MA

Degree: BA or BS in English (essential difference: BA requires minimum of 2 years of a foreign language; BS does not)

Required course of study: 36 s/hrs beyond composition, General Education requirements
Writing workshop and related: 9 s/hrs minimum
Literature courses: 27 s/hrs minimum
(includes 6 s/hrs of critical theory)

For more information, contact Paul Curran, Chairman, Dept. of English.

Degree: MA with Creative Writing Emphasis

Type of Program: Studio/Academic

Required course of study:
30 s/hrs with comprehensive examination;
36 s/hrs without comprehensive examination
Thesis: up to 6 s/hrs
Writing workshop: up to 12 s/hrs
Literature courses: 15 s/hrs minimum

Both of the programs listed above are options offered by the Department. We also have tracks in literature.

For more information, contact David G. Hale, Graduate Coordinator, Dept. of English.

State University of New York, Buffalo
Buffalo, NY 14260-2575
(716) 636-2575

The English Department at SUNY–Buffalo does not offer a creative writing degree (undergraduate or graduate); it does, however, provide the opportunity for students to enroll in undergraduate courses or graduate seminars in the writing of poetry, fiction, or literary journalism (and, occasionally, playwriting). In the internationally known Poetics Program in the Department students may investigate new forms of prose and poetry and the linkages between writing poetry and writing critical scholarship. MA and PhD dissertations are, however, works of critical analysis and theory. Core faculty include Charles Bernstein, Robert Creeley, Ray Federman, Susan Howe, and Dennis Tedlock. For a description of the program as it looks to outsiders, see the *Chronicle of Higher Education*, July 28, 1995.

Opportunities for writers to read their work and to hear the work of established writers, in both academic and non-academic settings, abound in Buffalo. The *Wednesdays at 4 Plus* (under the direction of Robert Creeley and Charles Bernstein) is an established part of the academic calendar at Buffalo, and has featured such poets and writers as Lyn Hejinian, Kathy Acker, Ann Waldman, David Wagoner, Gustav Sobin, and Larry McCaffery.

Graduate seminars in poetry are offered by Irving Feldman, Susan Howe, Carl Dennis, and Ray Federman; seminars associated with the *Wednesdays at 4 Plus* are offered under the direction of Charles Bernstein (e.g. on the investigation and practice of the everyday in poetry, art, and music); seminars in modern and postmodern fiction and poetry are regularly offered by Joseph Conte, Stacy Hubbard, Neil Schmitz, and Mark Shechner.

Undergraduate classes in writing poetry or prose are offered by Irving Feldman and Carl Dennis; in playwriting by Anna K. France (on occasion), in fiction-writing by Irving Feldman and Ray Federman, and in literary journalism by Ann Haskell and Howard Wolf. Robert Creeley regularly teaches undergraduate courses in poetry. Visiting professors in recent years have included John Coetzee, Grace Paley, and Judith Betsko.

For admissions and general information, contact Stacy Hubbard, Director of Graduate Admissions, Dept. of English, 306 Clemens Hall.

❖State University of New York at
Geneseo
One College Circle
Geneseo, NY 14454

The English Department offers an undergraduate list of 18 credit hours in creative writing within the English Department curriculum. The College also offers writing courses in journalism and theater. It also offers three hours in the graduate English/education program (MS, education).

Faculty includes: Rachael Hall, fiction and creative nonfiction; and David Kelly, poetry and fiction.

For more information, contact David Kelly, Creative Writing Program, English Dept.

State University of New York at
Oswego
Oswego, NY 13126
(315) 341-2150

Degree offered: BA in English Writing Arts; BA, Minor in Creative Writing

Required course of study: 36 s/hrs
  Basic writing courses (in genres): 12 s/hrs
  Writing workshops (in genres): 6 s/hrs
  Advanced conference courses or internships
    (in genres): 6 s/hrs
  Criticism courses: 3 s/hrs
  Literature courses: 9 s/hrs

Other Requirements: 122 s/hrs for the BA, of which 42 must be in the upper division; no more than 48 s/hrs in one department; specified General Education courses required; independent studies may be taken for Writing Arts credit.

Application Deadlines: March 15 for fall semester; November 15 for spring semester.

The Program in Writing Arts of the State University of New York College at Oswego dates from 1968; it is one of the largest and best-staffed undergraduate writing programs in the United States. Eight career writers offer courses in fiction, drama, poetry, nonfiction, professional writing, juveniles, scriptwriting, and journalism to well over 100 English Writing Arts majors and many other students including double majors and Creative Writing minors.

Each semester a Writing Arts Festival is presented, featuring visiting writers in the fall and campus/area writers in the spring. Four annual awards are given: the Buckley Award to a graduating Writing Arts Senior; an Academy of American Poets Prize for the best poem or group of poems written by an undergraduate; the Mathom Fiction Award for the best story written by an undergraduate; and the Yelpin Award for the best drama written by an undergraduate. The Writers' Guild is the undergraduate writers' club. Publications on campus include *The Great Lakes Review* undergraduate literary periodical, which has in the past won a CCLM prize; *The Oswegonian* student newspaper, *The Pendulum* social issues periodical, and *The Ontarian* annual yearbook. A community periodical is *Lake Effect* magazine, a nationally distributed literary tabloid.

The facilities of the Program include the English Department Library where many of the writing classes are held. The room contains periodicals and other materials of use to students and faculty. Students have the use of the College's Experimental Theater and other auditoriums and stages, computer, television, and radio facilities through cooperative arrangements with other departments.

The faculty includes Lewis Turco, founding director, fiction and poetry; James Brett, journalism; John Knapp, III, juveniles and professional writing; Shelley Ekhtiar, nonfiction; Brad Korbesmeyer, drama and journalism; Robert O'Connor, fiction and professional writing; Stephen M. Smith, poetry, and Leigh Alison Wilson, fiction.

Scholarships and financial aid are available through the Regents and other programs for New York State residents; there is also a work-study program for students provided by the College. Inquiries should go to the Director of Admissions.

For further information, contact Lewis Turco, Director, Program in Writing Arts, Dept. of English.

State University of New York at Rockland
145 College Road
Suffern, NY 10901
(914) 574-4338
FAX (914) 574-4425

Degree offered: AA

Rockland Community College, SUNY, offers a variety of poetry and fiction courses to the student seeking an AA (a 2-year degree) in liberal arts.

Separate workshops in poetry and fiction are available every semester. Students may enroll, for credit, in one or both genre workshops during each of their semesters on campus. Other courses available to the writer include: Freshman English I and II for the Creative Writer; Introduction to Modern Poetry; Modern Fiction; Studies in the Short Story; Studies in the Novel; Science Fiction; and other related literature courses.

In addition to traditional classroom instruction, the writer may also choose to become involved in contract learning, individualized study, and self-directed media study.

Primary staff writers include: John Allman (*Walking Four Ways in the Wind; Clio's Children*; and *Curve Away From Stillness*); Dan Masterson (*On Earth as It Is, Those Who Trespass*); and Barbara Unger (*Inside the Wind, Dying for Uncle Ray*, and *Chiffon Wings*). Other writers involved in the writing program include: Suzanne Cleary, Con Lehane, Lee Slonimsky, Maria Goldberg, and David Means.

RCC/SUNY has an active visiting writers series, a campus literary magazine, and the Henry V. Larom Annual Writing Award in Poetry and Fiction. Student writers are encouraged to attend the many readings scheduled at New York City's 92nd Street Poetry Center, The Guggenheim Museum, The Donnell Library Center, and other locations, all within an hour's drive from campus.

For more information, contact the English Dept.

❖Stephens College
Columbia, MO 65201
(573) 442-2211, ext. 4668
FAX (573) 876-7248
website: http//www.stephens.edu

Degrees offered: BA, BFA

Degree: BA in English with Concentration in Creative Writing (poetry, fiction, playwriting, autobiography, creative nonfiction)

Required course of study: 120 s/hrs total
American Literatures I: 3 s/hrs
Early English Literatures I: 3 s/hrs
Women Writers: 3 s/hrs
Senior Project: 3 s/hrs
Writing Workshops, languages, and literature courses selected with an English advisor: 24-33 s/hrs

Other Requirements: 33 s/hrs College general education requirements. English BA majors must include 3 s/hrs of a foreign language as one of these college requirements.

Application Deadlines: Stephens College reviews applications on a rolling basis after September 1. Students should submit their applications early in the fall of their senior year of high school to receive preferential consideration for merit scholarships, and by March 15 for priority consideration in awarding other financial assistance.

The opportunities offered students earning the BA in English do not differ from those offered to students earning the BFA in Creative Writing. See below. The distinction between the BA and the BFA is that students have more freedom to design their program for the BA than they have in the BFA.

Degree: BA in Liberal Studies With a Concentration in Creative Writing or in Playwriting and Dramatic Literature

Required course of study: 120 s/hrs total; 18 s/hrs of courses prescribed by the English program, up to 27 s/hrs of courses prescribed by another program, also allowing students to include their disciplines in a Liberal Studies major.

Other Requirements: 33 s/hrs College general education requirements.

Application Deadlines: See above.

Stephens College has a professional theater offering a BFA in Theater. Students choosing the Liberal Studies major have the opportunity to combine creative playwriting with work in a producing theater, or with studies in Communication, Education, Foreign Languages, or Business, for example.

Degree: BFA in Creative Writing

Required course of study: 120 s/hrs total. The BFA student may include up to a total of 78 s/hrs in her major. However, these must include specified courses in general education, including 3 s/hrs of a foreign language and 3 s/hrs of Language Use and Abuse; 18 s/hrs of writing courses; 12 s/hrs of literature courses, and 12 s/hrs of Women's Studies courses.

Application Deadlines: See above.

The Stephens College BFA in Creative Writing is designed for women. (This is a Women's College.) The instructors create their workshops from feminist backgrounds and have the ability to make "safe" classrooms for serious writers.

Visiting Writers are not chosen for being feminist in orientation, but for willingness to interact with our students and to talk about their work: Among these, we can list Walter Bargen, Paule Marshall, Shirley Jordan, Catherine Parke, Pamela McClure, William Sutherland, Carol Lee Sanchez, Leslie Adrienne Miller, Demetria Martinez, and Claribel Alegria as recent visitors. Students may apply for editorial internships to produce the literary annual *Harbinger* and may apply for funding to publish a chapbook in their senior year. Two Department assistantships are available each year to students on financial aid; various internships are available to all degree students.

For more information, contact Judith Clark, Chair, Languages and Literature, at the above address.

❖Stetson University
Campus Box 8304
Deland, FL 32720

For more information, contact Dr. Michael W. Raymond, English Dept.

Stockton State College
Pomona, NJ 08240

(609) 652-4505 or 652-4354

Degree offered: BA in Literature with Concentration in Creative Writing (poetry, fiction)

Required course of study: 128 hrs total
    64 hrs in General Studies
    64 hrs in major (40 hrs Core Literature
    Courses & Cognates, e.g. Philosophy,
    History, etc.)
    24 hours in Creative Writing:
    Workshops: 12 hrs
    Intro to Genre (poetry or fiction): 4 hrs
    Major author (poet or fiction writer): 4 hrs
    Senior Project: 4 hrs

Application Deadlines: February 1.

The undergraduate concentration involves two workshops (beginning and advanced) in a genre of the student's choosing, and one workshop in the other genre. Student must take either Intro to Fiction or Intro to Poetry, one major author in student's genre, and a senior project, which will be fashioned around the student's area of specialization.

Stockpot is the campus literary magazine, which provides editorial and publishing experience for undergraduates. The Miriam Paolella Award in Fiction and the Jeannette Gottlieb Award in Poetry are awarded to outstanding writers each spring.

The Creative Writing Faculty is at this time a one-person operation. Poet Stephen Dunn, author of eight collections of poetry (most recently *Landscape at the End of the Century*) and many essays, teaches both Poetry and Fiction Writing.

Visiting writers in recent years have included C.K. Williams, William Matthews, Rita Dove, Russell Banks, Carolyn Forché, Galway Kinnell, Charles Baxter, Lucille Clifton, Sharon Olds, Robert Hass, Lawrence Raab, Jonathan Holden, and many others.

For more information, contact Stephen Dunn, Director of the Creative Writing Program.

❖Sweet Briar College
Sweet Briar, VA 24595

(804) 381-6434
e-mail: brown@sbc.edu
website: http://www.sbc.edu/

Degree offered: BA with a Major or Minor in English & Creative Writing

Required course of study: 33 s/hrs in the Major
    Thesis: senior portfolio required
    Writing workshop: 15 s/hrs
    Literature courses: 18 s/hrs

Application Deadlines: Early admissions, November 15; Admissions with academic awards, January 15; Regular admissions, March 1.

The major in English and Creative Writing at Sweet Briar College requires 5 courses in creative writing and 6 in English and American literature. Each major completes both a senior literature project and a senior writing portfolio. The aim of the major is to produce graduates who have read widely and have completed extensive projects in creative writing. We believe that students should have experience in more than one genre; however, a student may concentrate on either fiction or poetry in the workshops and in her senior portfolio. College-wide distribution requirements must also be satisfied in order to graduate.

The College awards an annual Academy of American Poets Prize and an annual Jean Besselievre Boley Prize for the best student short story. The college's literary magazine, *Red Clay*, is edited and published by students. Student readings are held in the college bookstore's Boxwood Cafe.

The Creative Writing Program is directed by John Gregory Brown, who holds the Julia Jackson Nichols Chair in English and Creative Writing. He is the author of the novels *Decorations in a Ruined Cemetery* (1994) and *The Wrecked, Blessed Body of Shelton Lafleur* (1996). He received a Lyndhurst Prize in 1993 and the Lillian Smith Award in 1994.

The creative writing faculty includes Carrie Brown, author of the novels *Rose's Garden* and *Lamb in Love*, and poet Reetika Vazirani, author of *White Elephants*, which received the Barnard New Woman Poets Prize.

The College sponsors a reading series by writers who also meet with students individually and in the workshops to discuss the students' work. Recent visitors have included Robert Olen Butler, Philip Levine, Ursula Hegi, Donald Justice, Lee Smith, Richard Bausch, Jill McCorkle, Carolyn Kizer, and Deborah Eisenberg.

The Virginia Center for the Creative Arts, an artists' colony, is located near the Sweet Briar campus. VCCA Fellows, many of whom are published writers, are invited to attend readings on campus, and other opportunities exist for formal or informal association between the two institutions.

Financial aid is available to students who can demonstrate need; those interested should write directly to the Director of Financial Aid, Sweet Briar College.

For more information, contact John Gregory Brown, Director of Creative Writing.

❖Syracuse University
Syracuse, NY 13244-1170
(315) 443-2173

Degree offered: MFA in Creative Writing (poetry, fiction)

Type of Program: Studio/Academic

Length of Residency: Three years

Required course of study: 48 s/hrs
  Thesis: 6 s/hrs
  Writing workshop: 9 s/hrs
  Literature courses: 12-15 s/hrs
  Form courses: 9 s/hrs
  Elective work: 6-9 s/hrs

Other Requirements: Third-year 5,000-word degree essay.

Application Deadline: January 1.

The Syracuse program in creative writing has long been regarded as one of the strongest in the country. Each year about 12 students are admitted in poetry and fiction, and they work closely in small workshops with an accomplished group of writers. In addition, there is a strong emphasis on the study of literature and theory -- something that has distinguished our creative writing program from other universities.

Applicant must fill out the "Basic Information Sheet" and submit a sample of poetry or fiction no later than January 1, in addition to completing the regular application for graduate study. Admission is based primarily on this sample, but also upon the academic record. Thus, letters of recommendation should address not only the students' creative work, but their general preparedness for graduate study. In their personal statements on the application for graduate study, students should state their background as writers. The writing sample (consisting of either a set of 10-12 poems for poetry, or several short stories, or two chapters of a novel for fiction) should be sent directly to Director of Creative Writing, 401 Hall of Languages, Dept. of English, Syracuse University, New York, 13244-1170.

Candidates will be expected to complete 48 hours of credit over a three-year period, including nine hours of creative writing workshops and nine hours of forms courses taught by creative writing faculty.

The remainder of the candidates' coursework will be split between 12-15 hours in other English Department courses and 6-9 hours of elective work at the graduate level to be taken outside the Department. We consider it necessary for young writers to have as wide a university experience as possible. This elective work can be taken in another artistic medium; in language, history, philosophy, religion; or in whatever area a student believes would best benefit his or her writing.

A third-year degree essay addressing some aspect of the work of a major writer (to be written as part of an Essay seminar) will also be required; this degree essay will take the place of the present MA Dossier as the culminating intellectual experience. These essays will address some aspect of the work of a single major writer. The emphasis will be on one writer's understanding in depth of another writer: What was the nature of the writer's craft and how did it develop? The seminar will see each paper through several drafts, with the final essay being about 5,000 words.

The MFA thesis (6 hours credit) will be a book length manuscript of poetry or fiction, and students will work closely with one or two creative writing faculty while preparing the manuscript.

Three kinds of financial aid are offered: Teaching Assistantships, Creative Writing Fellowships, and University Fellowships. All provide tuition remission plus a stipend. Nearly all those accepted into the program are, if they wish, eligible for teaching assistantships, which currently offer a stipend from $8,415 to $8,966 for the academic year. The program competes for University Fellowships, awarded annually to outstanding applicants in the form of multi-year packages, in which fellowships and teaching assistantships are held in alternate years. These fellowships carry a stipend of $9,398. The department also offers awards four one-year creative writing fellowships, stipends ranging from $6,684 to $10,800.

Applicants desiring financial aid should apply as early as possible, preferably during the first semester, but no later that January 10. Some aid offers will be made early in the second semester.

Each year, "The Raymond Carver Reading Series" invites at least 10 visiting writers to read from their work and to visit an undergraduate class for a question and answer session in which graduate students may participate.

Current faculty includes: poet Safiya Henderson-Holmes (*Madness and a Bit of Hope*); poet Mary Karr (*Abacus* and *The Devil's Tour*); poet Brooks Haxton (*Dominion*); fiction writer Junot Díaz; fiction writer George Sanders; fiction writer Mary Caponegro; and fiction writer Arthur Flowers.

For more information, contact Brooks Haxton, Director, Creative Writing Program, Dept. of English.

❖University of Tampa
Tampa, FL 33606
(813) 253-3333, ext. 6229

Degree offered: BA in Writing; BA in English with Writing Minor

Required course of study: 48 s/hrs
  Writing courses: 32 s/hrs

Literature courses: 16 s/hrs

Other Requirements: 47 s/hrs in General Curriculum including Academic Skills, Natural Science, Humanities/Fine Arts electives, Social Sciences, Interdisciplinary Studies.

Application Deadlines: Prefer applications by January 15 for financial aid, but aid applications are accepted and considered through July; prefer admissions applications by February 15, but UT has a rolling admissions policy, so applications are continuously accepted.

The Writing Major at the University of Tampa is unique in its combination of strong liberal arts ideals with practical, real-world applications. Students in the program are encouraged to explore 3 dimensions of writing -- the grammar and techniques of professional writing, the creative and intellectual traditions of great literature, and the inner resources, emotional depth, and creative talents unique to each individual student writer.

The Writing faculty at the University of Tampa emphasize the process of discovery and the process of learning at the heart of the writing major. Students in the program can concentrate on creative writing -- fiction, poetry, and other imaginative forms -- or professional writing -- journalism, public relations, advertising, technical writing, business communications, and writing for other media and applications.

Students enjoy a regular program each year called "Writers at the University," which brings outstanding contemporary authors to campus to meet with and share their work with students. Recent visitors have included Peter Matthiessen, W.S. Merwin, Peter Taylor, Stephen Dunn, Lee Abbott, Jane Smiley, Carol Shields, and Jane Hamilton.

Internship opportunities for the writing majors include work on major daily newspapers, experience with several magazines and small publishing companies in the Tampa Bay Area, and positions with television stations, advertising and public relations firms, and various corporations in Tampa.

Students in the program also work on the staffs of the student newspaper, *The Minaret* and the student literary magazine, *Quilt*. Faculty-edited publications on campus -- including *Tampa Review*, *The Pinter Review*, and books from the University of Tampa Press -- also expand student opportunities for learning about editing and publishing.

Each member of the writing faculty is an active professional and each has many publications. The faculty's background also includes professional experience outside the university writing and editing for newspapers, magazines, films, television, and public relations. Richard Mathews is a poet, editor, and scholar of science fiction; author of *Numbery*, a book of poems, and *Fantasy: The Liberation of Imagination*, a study of fantasy as a literary genre. Andy Solomon is a book reviewer for major media including *The New York Times* and National Public Radio. Kathryn Van Spanckeren has lectured widely abroad, has published poetry in chapbooks and magazines, and written books and articles of literary criticism, including *Outline History of American Literature*. Lisa Birnbaum writes nonfiction and fiction; her work has appeared in a number of literary journals. Don Morrill is a poet

and nonfiction writer, and has published a book in each genre, *At the Bottom of the Sky* and *A Stranger's Neighborhood*. Kathleen Ochshorn has published short fiction, book reviews, commentary, literary criticism, and a book on the work of Bernard Malamud, *The Heart's Essential Landscape*.

For more information on the writing program, contact Chair, Dept. of English, Writing, and Composition.

❖Taylor University
Upland, IN 46989
(765) 998-4971
e-mail: rchill@taylor.edu

Degree offered: BA in English with Concentration in Writing (poetry, fiction, creative nonfiction, technical, mixed genre)

Required course of study: 128 s/hrs total
39 minimum s/hrs in Major
19 in writing workshop courses
12 in lit surveys and electives
8 in writing or lit electives

Other Requirements: University gen-ed requirements, senior seminar, senior project (creative thesis with critical introduction or afterword). Taylor is an Evangelical Christian university; students are expected to attend chapel and abide by a Life Together Covenant.

Application Deadlines: Rolling admissions. Feb. 15 notification deadline.

The concentration in creative writing allows for specialization in a single genre or for a general study of writing in various courses, workshops, independent studies, and internships. Department courses offered regularly include Imaginative Writing (intro to poetry, fiction, playwriting, and creative nonfiction), Fiction Writing, Poetry Writing, Business and Technical Writing, Freelance Writing, and Advanced Writing Workshop (mixed genre). Students may also take Newswriting, Writing for Advertising, and/or Feature Writing from the communications department to fulfill Writing concentration requirements. Summer independent studies have included Writing the Novel, Children's Literature, Playwriting, Creative Nonfiction, Travel Writing, Screenwriting, and other projects in mixed genres. Student-initiated summer internships have included staff positions with magazines, advertising agencies, and publishing houses. Literature surveys and courses in area(s) of interest augment the work in writing, and students write a critical introduction or afterword to the creative thesis. *Parnassus*, Taylor's literary magazine, is student-edited and managed; 1–2 s/hrs credit per semester is offered for staff work on the magazine. Each spring, *Parnassus* awards cash prizes in poetry, fiction, and creative nonfiction.

For more information, contact Rick Hill, Writing Concentration Coordinator, at the above address, phone, or e-mail.

❖Temple University
Anderson Hall 022-29
Philadelphia, PA 19122
(215) 204-1796
FAX (215) 204-9620

Degree offered: MA in English, Creative Writing (poetry, fiction)

Type of Program: Studio/Academic

Length of Residency: Two years

Required course of study: 30 s/hrs total
Writing workshops: 12 s/hrs
Literature courses: 9 s/hrs
Master's Manuscript Tutorials: 6 s/hrs
Electives (workshops, literature courses, or
    courses from other graduate programs): 3 s/hrs

Other Requirements: Written comprehensive examination; creative thesis.

Application Deadlines: February 1 for financial aid and admission. Applications received after February 1 must be completed by March 15 to be considered for late admission.

Temple University offers a 30 credit Master of Arts Degree in English: Creative Writing. With a combination of small, intensive workshops (limited to 12 students) in poetry, fiction, translation, and nonfiction, one-to-one tutorials, university-wide electives, and a wide selection of graduate literature courses, Temple provides creative writers with an opportunity to concentrate in the genre of their choice and at the same time prepare themselves for further graduate study or entrance into the working world.

Visiting Writers have included: Susan Sontag, Robert Creeley, Ngugi wa Thiong'o, Tomas Tranströmer, William Gaddis, Ryszard Kapuscinski, Sharon Olds, Clarence Major, Charles Bernstein, Robert Coover, Harry Mathews, Paul Auster, Joseph McElroy, Kathy Acker, and Susan Howe.

Financial aid, in the form of Teaching Assistantships, Research Assistantships, Tuition Scholarships, and University Fellowships, is available on a competitive basis.

Temple's full-time creative writing faculty includes nationally recognized writers in poetry, fiction, translation, and nonfiction (literary theory and criticism, reviewing, biography).

The writing faculty includes poet Rachel Blau DuPlessis (*Wells; Tabula Rosa; The Pink Guitar: Writing as Feminist Practice*); nonfiction writer and novelist Joan Mellen (*Natural Tendencies; Bob Knight: His Own Man; The Wave at Genji's Door: Japan Through Its Cinema*); poet and novelist Toby Olson (*We Are the Fire; Utah; Seaview*; winner of the PEN/Faulkner Award); poet Sonia Sanchez (*Homegirls and Handgrenades; I've Been a Woman*; American Book Award); novelist Alan Singer (*The Ox-Breadth; The Charnal Imp; A Metaphorics of Fiction*); fiction writer William F. Van Wert (*Tales For Expectant Fathers; Missing in Action*, winner of the Nelson Algren Award); translator Lawrence Venuti (*Restless Nights: Selected Stories of Dino Buzzati; I.U. Tarchetti: Fantastic Tales*; winner of the PEN Renato Poggioli Award).

For information, please write Director of Creative Writing, Dept. of English.

Tennessee State University
Nashville, TN 37209-1561

Contact the Creative Writing Program Director, Dept. of English.

University of Tennessee at Chattanooga
Chattanooga, TN 37403
(423) 755-4238

Degrees offered: BA, MA

Application Deadlines: Applications accepted throughout the year for both programs; for various Financial Aid deadlines which are in early Spring, contact Financial Aid Office; undergraduate candidates should also apply to the University Honors Program, an extensive program of seminars in general education courses, with full scholarships.

Degree: BA in English with Concentration in Writing (creative, professional, expository)

Required course of study: 128 s/hrs total
Literature courses: 27 s/hrs minimum
Writing courses: 15 s/hrs maximum
(Creative Writing courses are studio courses)

Other Requirements: University distribution requirements; optional honors thesis of 4 hours can be in writing and added to 42 s/hrs in department listed above; total hours can be extended if 128 s/hrs for graduation is also extended; 2 years of foreign language. A Minor in writing with a major in any field consists of 21 hours, 15 s/hrs of which must be in writing, 6 s/hrs in writing or literature.

Degree: BA in Humanities with Area Concentration in Creative Writing

Required course of study: 128 s/hrs total
Writing courses: 18 s/hrs maximum to count
    in major
Humanities courses: 27 s/hrs (Literature,
    Philosophy, History, Art, etc.)
(Creative Writing courses are studio courses)

Other Requirements: As above, planned with individualized committee. Contact John Trimpey, English Dept.

Degree: MA in English with Concentration in Writing (professional, expository, creative)

Type of Program: Studio/Academic

Required course of study: 33 s/hrs total
Literature: 21 s/hrs
Writing: 12 s/hrs

Other Requirements: Students must complete a 3 s/hrs project or a 6 s/hrs thesis as part of the 33 s/hrs total, either of which can be in writing; there is a Comprehensive written exam in 5 fields and an oral thesis defense if the student chooses the thesis option.

The creative writing program is committed to giving intensive and individualized help to developing writers; it prides itself on being a supportive community of writers who respect each other's work enough to trust honest criticism. The classes are all workshops except in occasional special-topics courses that may focus on form, uses of autobiography, etc. The Meacham Fund is the anchor for an extensive program of visiting creative writers (nearly 30 last year alone) who visit the campus for a 3-day conference/workshop every semester and for individual visits. The visiting writers work closely with students. Students can also work on *The Poetry Miscellany*, a national journal, and *The Sequoya Review*. The university also offers support for an innovative program where up to 15 students, mostly undergraduates, travel to Europe (Slovenia, Italy, Yugoslavia, Hungary, Switzerland, Austria, Czechoslovakia) to attend conferences, give readings, conduct interviews, and have their work translated and published. In the past several years 100% of undergraduate students who applied won graduate fellowships; seven have published chapbooks, and dozens have published in journals such as *Iowa Review*, *Indiana Review*, and *Tar River Poetry*.

Visiting writers have included Tomaz Salamun, Jean Valentine, William Matthews, Tim O'Brien, Phil Levine, Susan Mitchell, Marvin Bell, Gladys Swan, Dara Wier, Charles Simic, Richard Wilbur, William Stafford, Robert Houston, William Matthews, and Larry Brown.

Every other spring (odd years) the Southern Literature Conference brings together readers and writers from across the country. The Fellowship of Southern Writers (about 40 famous writers) holds its meeting in the Lupton Library on the UTC campus.

The expository writing sector (professional writing, composition, and composition theory) is aimed at educating teachers, preparing students for careers in technical and business writing, and providing solid grounding in rhetorical theory. There is a successful work-study program for professional and business writing with several area companies. A number of visiting writers have conducted seminars and workshops, presented papers and met with students and faculty. The program has encouraged a writing across the disciplines approach on campus.

The creative writing faculty includes: poet Earl Braggs, author of *Hat Dancer Blue*, which won the 1992 Anhinga Poetry Prize, and who also teaches Black literature; poet Richard Jackson (*Alive All Day*, *Obljubje Svetlobe/The Promise of Light*, *Selected Poems in Romanian*) who is also the author of two books of criticism (*Dismantling Time*); fiction writer Ken Smith (*Decoys and Other Stories* and *Angels and Others*).

The expository writing faculty includes: Craig Barrow (*Montage in James Joyce's Ulysses*) and Reed Sanderlin (*Cross Country Flight at Night*) who have co-edited a casebook in the humanities; Eileen Meagher, author of essays and presentations; Marcia Noe, author of numerous journal articles; Sally Young, Director of Composition.

For information on the writing program, contact Head, English Dept., Arlie Herron, (423) 755-4238, e-mail: aherron@utcvm.utc.edu.

❖University of Tennessee, Knoxville
Knoxville, TN 37996-0430
(423) 974-5401, Undergraduate
(423) 974-6933, Graduate Studies
FAX (423) 974-6926

Degrees offered: BA, MA

Degree: BA with Concentration in Writing

Required course of study:
36 s/hrs in English, 30 of which must be upper level courses
Thesis: not required

Other Requirements: 2 years of a foreign language.

The Concentration in Writing calls for 9 English courses at the 300-400 level, including: (1) a 2 course sequence in expository, technical, or creative writing; (2) 3 other courses in writing; and (3) 4 other courses, at least 3 of which must be literature courses selected in consultation with the advisor.

At the undergraduate level, Creative Writing typically offers courses in Poetry Writing and Advanced Poetry Writing; Fiction and Advanced Fiction Writing; Writing the Screenplay and TV Play; Writing the Detective and Mystery Story; Writing Science Fiction and Fantasy; Writing for Children; Dream Works: Poetry Writing; and other Special Topics.

Degree: MA with Concentration in Writing

Type of Program: Studio/Academic

Required course of study: 24 s/hrs beyond the BA
Literature courses: 9 s/hrs
Writing courses: 9 s/hrs
Other English courses: 6 s/hrs
Thesis: creative thesis (collection of poems, novel, play, creative nonfiction; or technical writing/rhetorical theory thesis)

Other Requirements: Evidence of proficiency in a foreign language, the equivalent of two years of college study; 90-minute oral exam covering a reading list in British and American literature. A reading list of primary works designed to help MA students pursuing this Concentration is available in the graduate office.

Graduate Writing Workshops typically include intensive writing classes, seminar courses in practice and theory of poetics or fiction, and thesis hours.

Creative Writing faculty includes: Program Director Marilyn Kallet, poet, translator, critic, and editor (*How to get Heat Without Fire*; co-editor, *Worlds in Our Words: Contemporary American Women Writers*); Arthur Smith, poet (*Orders of Affection*; Agnes Lynch Starrett Poetry Prize for *Elegy on Independence Day*); Allen Wier, fiction writer (*A Place for Outlaws*; *Departing as Air*); Robert Drake, author of more than 8 books of fiction, short stories and criticism (*The Home Place: A Memory and Celebration*; *Survivors and Others*); Richard Kelly, literary historian and poet (*Graham Greene: A Study of The Short Fiction*); Jon Manchip White, Professor Emeritus, author of over 30 volumes, including novels, short stories, mystery, travel, etc. (*The Journeying Boy*); Wilma Dykeman, author of more than 16 books, State Historian, novelist, journalist, essayist; Connie Jordan Green, poetry, fiction, young adult (*Emmy; The War at Home*).

The program has a strong multicultural series in visiting writers, some of whom have included in recent years: Joy Harjo, Linda Hogan, Gloria Naylor, Li-Young Lee, Al Young, George Garrett, C.K. Williams, Robert Hass, Galway Kinnell, Sharon Olds, and many others. The Creative Writing Program offers opportunities for outreach to the public schools.

Financial aid is available: Graduate assistantships for new MA students carry a stipend of $6,000 and a tuition waiver. Second-year Teaching Associateships carry a stipend of $8,500 plus tuition waiver. Hilton Smith and Alumni Fellowships support full-time course work and pay approximately $5,000 per year. The John C. Hodges Better English Fund supports dissertation and travel fellowships, and several W.E.B. Du Bois Fellowships for black U.S. citizens.

For further information, write to Marilyn Kallet, Director, Creative Writing Program, Dept. of English.

❖Texas A & M University
College Station, TX 77843-4227
(409) 845-3452
FAX (409) 862-2292

Degrees offered: BA, MA

Degree: BA with an Emphasis in Creative Writing

Required course of study: 12 hrs worth of courses in workshops and theory in drama, fiction, and poetry.

Student's senior seminar project consists of a thirty page collection of original work with a ten page critical introduction.

Degree: MA with an Emphasis in Creative Writing (poetry, fiction, creative nonfiction, playwriting)

Type of Program: Studio/Academic

Required course of study: 12 hours worth of courses in workshops and theory in drama, fiction, and poetry.

Specialization in creative writing at the graduate level includes: Writing, Teaching Creative Writing, or Editing Journals and Reviews. The creative writing thesis option carries all the obligations of the regular MA thesis option. Candidates apply for this option by submitting creative work and having an interview. Creative writing courses are taken along with traditional literature courses.

Candidates must pass the departmental MA non-thesis written examination and an oral examination designed and conducted by the candidate's advisory committee. This exam will focus on the thesis.

The faculty includes: Ewing Campbell in fiction (recipient of an NEA grant; author of *The Rincon Triptych, Piranesi's Dream: Stories*); Paul Christensen in poetry and nonfiction (recipient of an NEA grant; author of *Signs of the Whelming, Charles Olson: Call Him Ishmael*); James Hannah in fiction (recipient of an NEA grant; author of *Desperate Measures*); Terence Hoagwood in poetry (author of *Secret Affinities*); Janet McCann in poetry (recipient of an NEA grant; author of

How We Got Here, Creative and Critical Thinking, Dialogue with the Dogcatcher); and Patricia Phillippy in poetry (recipient of the Thomas McAfee Prize).

For more information, contact Director, Creative Writing Program.

Texas Southern University
Houston, TX 77004

Contact the Creative Writing Program Director, Dept. of English.

❖Texas Tech University
Lubbock, TX 79409-3091
(806) 742-2501
FAX (806) 742-0989
e-mail: walt@ttu.edu
website: http://english.ttu.edu

Degrees offered: BA, MA, PhD

Degree: BA in English with Creative Writing Specialization (fiction, poetry)

Required course of study: 125 s/hrs total
    Writing workshop: 9 s/hrs
    Independent studies in creative writing
        (optional): up to 6 s/hrs
    Elective English courses: enough to complete
        36 s/hrs total for the major

Application Deadlines: Varies.

Undergraduate English majors, with permission of the staff, may specialize in creative writing and choose a wide range of courses in literature. Each workshop is limited to 15 to 17 students. The program sponsors each year the Robert S. Newton Creative Writing Awards.

Degree: MA in English with Creative Writing Emphasis (fiction, poetry)

Type of Program: Traditional Literary Study and Creative Writing

Length of Residency: Two years, normally

Required course of study: 30 s/hrs total, including thesis
    Thesis: 6 s/hrs
    Writing workshop: 6 s/hrs
    Literature courses: 12 s/hrs
    Courses in research, teaching or critical
        methods: 6 s/hrs

Other Requirements: Written comprehensive examination; competency in one foreign language.

Application Deadlines: Varies.

Degree: PhD in English with Creative Writing Specialization & Dissertation (poetry, fiction)

Type of Program: Traditional Literary Study and Creative Writing

Length of Residency: Varies.

Required course of study: 60 s/hrs of courses beyond the bachelor's degree, plus dissertation
   Dissertation: 12 s/hrs
   Writing workshop: 6 or more s/hrs
   Foundation courses in research, teaching and critical methods: 9 s/hrs
   British literature courses: 12 s/hrs
   American literature courses: 6 s/hrs
   A specialization of 18 s/hrs in creative writing, plus 15 s/hrs in a minor

Other Requirements: Preliminary examination; competency in two foreign languages or a high level of competence in one foreign language; college teaching experience; written qualifying examination; oral defense of the dissertation; at least one year in full-time residence at the University.

Application Deadlines: Varies.

The graduate program in creative writing is a modest but lively part of the Department of English. With permission of the creative writing staff, graduate students with exceptional ability and potential may emphasize creative writing and write creative MA theses and PhD dissertations. Such projects are the culmination of conventional, rigorous courses of academic study in literature. We strive to give students supportive and practical reading of their work, individually and in discussion workshops. Each graduate workshop is limited to 12 to 15 students. The program is an institutional member of AWP and sponsors each year the Robert S. Newton Creative Writing Awards. Poems and stories by former Texas Tech students have appeared in *Carolina Quarterly, CutBank, Intro, The Literary Review, Michigan Quarterly Review, Mississippi Review, Missouri Review, New York Quarterly, Poetry,* and *TriQuarterly.* An active creative writing club meets frequently and sponsors readings and craft discussions; many members help edit undergraduate and graduate publications.

Recent visiting writers include Edward Albee, Carolyn Forché, Ernest J. Gaines, Shirley Ann Grau, Joseph Heller, Donald Justice, Galway Kinnell, Philip Levine, Linda Pastan, Maura Stanton, Henry Taylor, Ellen Bryant Voigt, Marilyn Waniek, Bruce Weigl, James Welch, and Eudora Welty.

The Texas Tech University Press publishes books of poetry eligible under its current policy. Walt McDonald served as Poetry Editor of the Press for 20 years.

The creative writing faculty includes: fiction writer Doug Crowell (winner of the short-story award from the Texas Institute of Letters and an NEA Creative Writing Fellowship Grant); fiction writer Jill Patterson (former member of the Board of Directors of the Texas Association of Creative Writing Teachers; sponsor of the Creative Writing Club); poet William Wenthe (*Birds of Hoboken*; specialist in modern British and American poetry); Paul Whitfield Horn, Professor and Poet in Residence; Walt McDonald (*Blessings the Body Gave, Counting Survivors,* and *After the Noise of Saigon*).

For more information, contact Walt McDonald, Director of Creative Writing.

❖The University of Texas at Austin Department of English Austin, TX 78712-1164

(512) 471-4991

James A. Michener Center for Writers J. Frank Dobie House 702 East Dean Keeton St. Austin, TX 78705

(512) 471-1601
FAX (512) 471-9997

Degrees offered: BA, MA (Department of English); **MFA** (Michener Center for Writers)

Degree: BA in English

Required course of study:
   120 s/hrs; 33 s/hrs in the major

Within the English major a student may take a sequence of creative writing course work including 325 (Introduction to Fiction or Poetry), 341 (Short Story or Poetry Workshop), and an advanced course in fiction or poetry, 355K. There is a conference course in Creative Writing, 367K.

Annual undergraduate James A. Michener Scholarships are awarded to eligible students on the basis of outstanding work.

For information contact Undergraduate English Advising, Parlin Hall 114, University of Texas, Austin TX 78712-1164. (512) 471-5736; or e-mail <dcr@mail.utexas.edu>.

Degree: MA in English with Creative Writing Concentration (fiction, poetry)

Type of Program: Traditional Literary Study and Creative Writing

Length of Residency: 2 years

Required course of study: 33 s/hrs, including 9 hrs in writing courses, 6 hrs in a minor outside the department, and a 3-hr creative Master's Report.

Other requirements: 2 years' credit in a foreign language is required for all MA-level candidates in English. If waived for admission, this requirement must be fulfilled through coursework or proficiency exams before completion of the MA.

Application Deadline: January 15 for admission and financial aid.

The MA program in English with a concentration in creative writing offers work with experienced writers in both workshops and in individual conference courses. The program stresses training in literature as well as in creative writing. Readers regularly visit the campus, and in the Austin community and on campus there is considerable literary activity (small magazines, writers groups, etc.).

The creative writing faculty includes: fiction writer Laura Furman (*The Glass House, Watch Time Fly, Tuxedo Park,* founding editor *American Short Fiction*); fiction writer Zulfikar Ghose (*The Incredible Brazilian,*

Figures of Enchantment, A New History of Torments); fiction writer Elizabeth Harris (*The Ant Generator and Other Stories*); poet Kurt Heinzelman; fiction writer Rolando Hinojosa Smith (*Klail City, Dear Rafe, The Useless Servants*); poet Judith Kroll (*In the Temperate Zone, Our Elephant and That Child*); fiction writer Peter LaSalle (*Hockey Sur Glace, Strange Sunlight, The Graves of Famous Writers*); novelist James Magnuson (*Windfall, Money Mountain, Ghost Dancing*); poet David Wevill (*Child Eating Snow, Figure of Eight, Other Names for the Heart*); and poet Thomas Whitbread (*Four Infinitives, Whomp and Moonshiver*).

Visiting faculty members in creative writing in recent years have included Rick Bass, Pattiann Rogers, Li-Young Lee, Lynn Freed, Anthony Smith, Anthony Giardina, Carey Harrison, Ben Marcus, Anne Finger, Nuruddin Farah, Virgil Suarez, and James Kelman.

Graduate students in creative writing may apply for teaching assistantships with their initial application. Also, in conjunction with the Michener Center for Writers, a number of James A. Michener fellowships and scholarships are awarded each year. Financial grants from individuals and organizations allow the Department of English to conduct writing contests each fall and spring, with cash prizes.

For more information, contact Graduate Program in English, Calhoun Hall 210, University of Texas, Austin, TX 78712-1164. (512) 471-5132. Fax (512) 471-2898; e-mail <rfcooper@mail.utexas.edu>.

Degree: MFA in Writing, Michener Center for Writers (fiction, poetry, screenwriting, playwriting)

Type of Program: Studio/Academic

Length of Residency: Three years

Required course of study: 54 s/hrs, including 18 hrs of writing workshops or conferences; 15 hrs in academic studies courses; a 3-hr first-year MFA seminar; 6 hrs in a minor subject; and a 6-hr creative thesis course.

Application Deadline: January 15 for admission and fellowship support.

The unique feature of the Michener Center for Writers' MFA program is its interdisciplinary approach: our students work in at least two genres, chosen from fiction, screenwriting, poetry, and playwriting. By combining the resources of the English, Theatre, and Film graduate programs at UT Austin, we offer the student a chance to explore new voices and forms while completing a major project in a primary field. A diverse resident faculty of poets, playwrights, novelists, and screenwriters, and an eclectic and distinguished series of visiting professors and guest writers enrich the interdisciplinary experience.

The center is funded by an endowment from the late James A. Michener and Mari Sabusawa Michener, whose generosity makes it possible for us to offer $12,000 per year fellowships, plus remission of all required tuition and fees, to each candidate admitted for study. That, and the small number of students we admit every year (10), creates a tight-knit and nurturing community.

The MFA is a three-year degree; students enroll full-time, typically for three classes each in the fall and spring semesters. The requirements are flexible, so students can shape their own degree plans and take supporting courses that feed into their writing projects -- say, a literature course on the 20th-century American novel, a spoken word performance class in poetry, a cinema history survey, acting or directing. Our teaching staff includes both regular faculty of the departments of English, Theatre, and Film, and visiting professors we bring in each semester to teach in the different genres. About five or six guest writers also come each semester and hold informal seminars with the students and give evening readings.

Our permanent resident faculty in fiction include Laura Furman, Zulfikar Ghose, Elizabeth Harris, Rolando Hinojosa-Smith, Peter LaSalle, and James Magnuson. The current head of the Theatre's MFA in Playwriting program and the Michener Center's playwriting emphasis is Suzan Zeder. Screenwriting faculty are Robert Foshko, Lindy Laub, Charles Ramirez-Berg, and Horace Newcomb. Poets on faculty are David Wevill, Judith Kroll, and Thomas Whitbread.

Recent visiting faculty have included J.M. Coetzee, Denis Johnson, James Kelman, August Kleinzahler, Sherry Kramer, Naomi Shihab Nye, James Still, and Tino Villanuevo. Past guest writers have been John Ashbery, Andrea Barrett, Peter Carey, Louise Glück, David Hare, Tina Howe, Lawrence Kasdan, Kenneth Koch, Maxine Kumin, Tony Kushner, Li-Young Lee, W.S. Merwin, Lorrie Moore, Tim O'Brien, Michael Ondaatje, Richard Price, Jane Smiley, Steven Soderbergh, Robert Stone, Tom Stoppard, James Tate, Paula Vogel, and Edmund White.

For more information, contact Bruce Snider, Graduate Coordinator, Michener Center for Writers, J. Frank Dobie House, 702 E. Dean Keeton Street, Austin, TX 78705, (512) 471-1601; fax (512) 471-9997; e-mail <bsnider@mail.utexas.edu>.

University of Texas at Dallas
Box 830688 JO3.1
Richardson, TX 75083-0688
(214) 883-2756

Degrees offered: BA, MA, PhD

Degree: PhD in Humanities, Concentration in Writing & Translation (poetry, fiction, playwriting)

Type of Program: Studio/Academic

Length of Residency: One year

Required course of study: 42 s/hrs beyond the MA
    Thesis: up to 18 s/hrs
    Writing workshop: 6-12 s/hrs
    Other writing courses: 9-12 s/hrs
    Tutorials or directed reading: 3-9 s/hrs
    Literature courses: 6-12 s/hrs
    History or Aesthetics courses: 6-12 s/hrs

Other Requirements: One doctoral seminar in foreign language; one advanced workshop in foreign language or in translation workshop; four 3-hour written examinations and one 2-hour oral examination.

Application Deadlines: February 15.

The School of Arts and Humanities at the University of Texas at Dallas is dedicated to interdisciplinary studies. Students are encouraged not to settle into narrow, specific fields but rather to cross standard academic boundaries and to explore the humanities not only from literary, historical, philosophical, and dramatic perspectives but also from creative and practical directions. Courses include not only seminars stressing the interpretation and criticism of specific works and issues but also ensemble laboratories and studio workshops in which creation, performance, and application become integral components of the learning process.

For administrative purposes, the School of Arts and Humanities is loosely divided into three divisions: Aesthetic Studies, History of Ideas, and Studies in Literature. BA, MA, and PhD students, in consultation with faculty, divide their course work among these divisions, building a personal area or focus of concentration. Theory and practice play important roles in all three areas. For example, in many classes (e.g., The Literature of Fantasy and The History of the Novel), students are given the option of producing scholarly and critical work or a combination of creative and academic projects.

Students in the School of Arts and Humanities are actively encouraged to become involved in three journals produced at the University of Texas at Dallas. Students work directly with the editors not only as research assistants but also in classroom settings. They assist both research for and the editing of the journals.

Translation Review is the official publication of the American Literary Translators Association. It is devoted to the critical evaluation of literary translations from all languages into English. It specifically addresses critical and theoretical aspects of transplanting a literary text from one culture into another, and its pages provide a forum for translators to discuss the creative process involved in the transplantation of literary texts from foreign languages into English, for translators and scholars to investigate the subtle nature of linguistic, semantic, cultural, historical, and anthropological considerations underlying translation activities, for critics to establish a meaningful vocabulary to evaluate the quality of literary works appearing in translation, and for the general reader to be continuously informed about translations of literary works published in book, journal, and anthology format.

Common Knowledge is the interdisciplinary and international journal of Oxford University Press. It publishes work in the arts, social sciences, cultural studies, and intellectual history that redefines divisive terms and figures of the past and present in ways that make expanded sympathies credible. *Common Knowledge* represents a commitment to go beyond established disciplines and, more importantly, beyond the factions at war in the literary and scholarly world. In the articles, fiction, and poetry that it publishes it seeks to refine a new skepticism -- a postwar doubt of claims to knowledge and authority -- that presents no obstacle to solidarity. Among the members of the editorial board are the well-known writers Charles Johnson, Hugh Kenner, Leszek Kolakowski, Gyorgy Konrad, Greil Marcus, Czeslaw Milosz, Susan Sontag, and Tatyana Tolstaya.

Sojourn is an interdisciplinary arts journal that is published once a semester by the students of the University of Texas at Dallas. The journal contains poetry, prose, fiction, nonfiction, and graphic arts. *Sojourn* sponsors a yearly, juried competition for fiction, nonfiction, and poetry, and it also sponsors regular readings by the contributors to the journal. It looks for work that is experimental, especially in the realms of sensibility, and it is dedicated to fostering student writing and publishing at UTD.

The School of Arts and Humanities has a varying number of scholarships and teaching assistantships (not only for students in Literary Studies but also Historical Studies and Aesthetic Studies).

The creative writing faculty at UTD includes poet and critic Frederick Turner; poet and translator Rainer Schulte; and fiction writer and editor Robert Nelsen.

For further information, please write or e-mail: Robert Nelsen, Creative Writing, The School of Arts and Humanities; <nelsen@utdallas.edu>.

❖University of Texas, El Paso
El Paso, TX 79968-0526
(915) 747-5731

Degrees offered: BA, MFA with bilingual option

Degree: BA in English, Creative Writing Option

Required course of study: 123 s/hrs for the BA
  Writing workshop: 18-30 s/hrs
  Literature courses: 18-24 s/hrs

Other Requirements: Foreign language proficiency; distribution of arts and sciences requirements.

The BA in English with Creative Writing option requires 30 s/hrs of advanced-level courses in English, including 18 s/hrs of selected creative writing courses and 12 s/hrs of selected literature courses, in addition to a wide distribution of coursework in the arts and sciences and a sophomore-level language proficiency.

The Creative Writing Option is directed toward students interested in careers in writing or editing, in teaching creative writing and literature on the high school level, and in further study in creative writing and literature.

A wide range of scholarships and work-study assistance is available. For information on financial aid, write the Office of Financial Aid and Scholarship.

Degree: MFA with Bilingual Option (English/Spanish, poetry, fiction, creative nonfiction)

Type of Program: Studio/Academic

Required course of study: 48 s/hrs
  Thesis: 6 s/hrs
  Writing workshop; 18 s/hrs
  Electives: 6 s/hrs
  Literature courses: 18 s/hrs

Application Deadlines: February 1.

The MFA in Creative Writing at UTEP is the only one of its kind in that it offers English, Spanish, and bilingual components. English-speaking students can fulfill all requirements in English but the *program* as a whole reflects the bi-cultural atmosphere that flourishes on the U.S./Mexico border as well as in other parts of the country. Bilingual students have the option of taking some or all of their coursework in Spanish in the Department of Languages and Linguistics, and/or of exploring the interweaving of the two languages in their creative work. The program is designed to bring student writers together in order to examine the many literary traditions of the Americas.

We offer creative writing courses in genre fiction, screenwriting, and the literary essay in addition to the regular workshops in literary fiction and poetry. Workshop classes are limited to 15. We offer a broad choice of literature courses from which students are required to take a large portion of their semester hours. We offer structured assistance to TA's by having them work under the supervision of a faculty mentor, which gives them excellent preparation for a career in teaching. Our aim is to provide graduate creative writing students with a background that familiarizes them with their literary heritage and also fits them for career options in teaching and genre or feature writing, in addition to their ongoing creative work.

The faculty includes: poet Leslie Ullman, author of *Natural Histories*, which won the Yale Series of Younger Poets Award in 1978, *Dreams by No One's Daughter*, and *Slow Work Through Sand*, winner of the 1998 Iowa Poetry Prize. Fiction writer Rick DeMarinis, author of the novels *The Burning Women of Far Cry*, *The Year of the Zinc Penny*, and *The Mortician's Apprentice*. His collections of short stories include *Under the Wheat*, which won the Drue Heinz Literature Prize in 1986. Ben Saenz, bilingual poet, fiction, and nonfiction writer, and author of a children's book titled *A Gift from Papa Diego*, and two novels, *Carry Me Like Water* and *The House of Forgetting*. Mexican fiction writer Luis Arturo Ramos, author of novels *Intramuros*, *Violeta-Peru*, *Esta era un gato*, and *La casa del ahorcado*, plus three short story collections and five children's books. He is also former head of a major university press in Mexico, La Universidad Veracruzana. Peruvian poet and critic Miguel-Angel Zapata, author of seven books of poetry, most recently *Lumbre de la letra* and *My Hermit Crow*, and five books of criticism on contemporary Latin American poetry. He also has published several articles on contemporary American poetry.

Visiting writers have included Sandra Cisneros, Simon Ortiz, Jimmy Santiago Baca, Jim Crumley, Naomi Shihab Nye, Howard McCord, Denise Chavez, Maxine Kumin, and John Rechy.

Amid its Rocky Mountain backdrop, its desert landscape, and its endless sunshine, El Paso has developed a substantial community of writers and artists. Together with its sister city Ciudad Juarez on the South bank of the Rio Grande, El Paso offers a writer the privileges of immersion in the largest bilingual, bicultural complex on the U.S. borders.

The Rio Grande Review/Rio Brava, formerly *The Rio Grande Review*, has published student writers and nationally known writers for several years, along with photography and original artwork. It has now been expanded to publish works in both English and Spanish, from both sides of the border, and each issue will be co-edited by an English and a Spanish-speaking MFA student, with help from all interested students and also from Creative Writing faculty advisors.

Teaching Assistantships paying $7,000 plus benefits are available on a competitive basis. Awards include the remission of out-of-state tuition; and teaching load includes two composition courses per semester, with the possibility of teaching a creative writing course in the third year.

For further information, write Leslie Ullman, Writing Program Director, Dept. of English, or Director, Creacion Literaria, Depto. de Languages y Linguisticas.

University of Texas, San Antonio
6900 North Loop 1604 West
San Antonio, TX 78249

For more information, contact Wendy Barker, Dept. of English.

❖University of Toledo
Toledo, OH 43606-3390
(419) 530-2318
FAX (410) 530-4440

Degree offered: BA in English--General Writing Concentration, BA in English--Creative Writing Concentration (An MA in Creative Writing is being developed)

Required course of study: The General Writing Concentration requires a total of 34 s/hrs; 22 literature and linguistics hours, and 12 hours of Department writing courses, at least half of which must be at the 3000-4000 level. The Creative Writing Concentration requires 34 s/hrs; 12 hours of departmental literature and linguistics hours at the 3000-4000 level, and 22 hours of Department creative writing courses, which include workshops in poetry writing, fiction writing and playwriting, and at least 1 credit of independent study and a 3 credit capstone course, Senior Seminar in Writing. The minor in English (writing emphasis) consists of 22 hours of advanced English courses. Students may concentrate on Business and Technical Writing or Creative Writing.

Other requirements: Students must fulfill the general education core and distributive requirements in the College of Arts and Sciences.

Methods of instruction include lecture/discussion, peer workshop, and independent study. An Honors Program is available to meet the needs of qualified students. University College offers program options for non-traditional students.

The various writing tracks provide options for undergraduates with specific degree objectives. Unique to the University of Toledo's Programs is a working relationship with the Toledo Museum of Art and the Center for Visual Arts, making available an extensive archive of print materials and artist's books, allowing for a sequence of courses in visual language, artist's books, electronic publishing, letterpress printing, and the art and process of the book.

Students also have access to working with Aureole Press, a literary fine-press publishing work by both established and up-and-coming poets and writers. Aureole Press is also home to *Whirligig: A Journal of*

Language Arts, a literary periodical of contemporary poetry and art.

Funding from the Arts Commission of Greater Toledo and the Ohio Arts Council make possible ongoing programs of guest residencies, visiting writers, and community workshops. The Toledo Poets Center sponsors an annual visiting writers series and publishes chapbooks under the imprints of Toledo Poets Center Press and Radio Room Press.

The faculty includes Carl Sandburg Award-winning poet and playwright Rane Arroyo (*Pale Ramón* and *The Singing Shark*); NEA award-winning fiction writer and playwright Jane Bradley (short-story collection *Power-Lines* and the novel *Living Doll*); poet and printer Timother Geiger (*Blue Light Factory*, proprietor of the Aureole Press); and poet and visual artist Joel Lipman (*Mercury Vapor Lamp, Machete Chemistry/Panades Physics*, and *The Real Ideal*). The writing faculty is supplemented by other members of the Department of English.

For more information contact the English Dept. at the above address.

❖Towson University
Towson, MD 21252-0001
(410) 830-2871
FAX (410) 830-3999
website: http://www.townson.edu/english/

Degree offered: MS in Professional Writing

Required course of study: 36 s/hrs in the major
Thesis: optional

Application Deadlines: March 1 and October 1.

The English Department at Towson University offers an MS in Professional Writing with an emphasis on practical writing. The core of the program is 6 required courses providing advanced study in the theory of writing, in the functions of written communication within the professional/occupational setting, in writing techniques and style, and in the principles and techniques of editing.

The program features 2 concentrations. Writing for Public and Private Sectors provides experience in writing grant proposals, reviews, freelance articles, as well as technical and scientific material for a wide range of occupations. Writing in the Professions provides a foundation in the principles of written communication and concentrates on an area of specialization: mass media, health professions, science, creative writing, or teaching. Elective course work within these concentrations make up the remaining 6 courses (4 for the thesis option).

The graduate faculty includes active writers of poetry, prose, and pedagogical theory such as Clarinda Lott (*The Night Parrot*), Harvey Lillywhite (*Ephemeral Blues*, NEA Creative Writing Fellowship in Poetry), George Friedman (*Three Years*), and Carolyn Hill (*Writing from the Margins*), as well as faculty involved in managing and editing professional journals, consulting for corporate and government agencies and organizations, and freelance writing for newspapers and popular magazines.

Towson University and the Baltimore area provide students with an active writing community, a number of publishing opportunities in journals and by small presses such as *The Maryland Poetry Review, Baltimore Magazine*, and The New Poet Series for writers of poetry, fiction, and nonfiction.

For more information, contact Coordinator, Masters in Professional Writing Program, Dept. of English.

❖Trinity College
Hartford, CT 06106
(860) 297-2455
FAX (860) 297-5258

Degree offered: BA in English with Major in Creative Writing

Trinity College offers a special undergraduate Major in Creative Writing to a select number of students who demonstrate exceptional ability in the writing of fiction, poetry, and drama. A combination of small classes, frequent conferences with writers in residence, and a supplemental course of study in literature and related fields affords the student an unusual opportunity to prepare for a career in writing, teaching, editing, or publishing. The distinguishing feature of the Trinity program in creative writing is that it offers a BA in English with a concentration in creative writing. The Creative Writing major takes 12 courses in the major, including 6 courses in literature and 3 prerequisite workshops in creative writing. The remaining 3 electives may be taken in creative writing, literature, or critical theory.

Students in the program also have the opportunity for experience in editing and publishing through work on 3 campus publications: *The Trinity Review*, a magazine of student work, *The Trinity Tripod*, and *The Observer*, the college newspapers.

Workshops, tutorials, and conferences are handled by a permanent staff of established writers and by distinguished visitors. The staff includes: Arthur Feinsod, Dramaturg at the Hartford Stage Theatre in playwriting; in poetry, Elizabeth Libbey (*All That Heat in a Cold Sky, The Crowd Inside*, and *Songs of a Returning Soul*) and Hugh Ogden (*Gift, Looking for History*, and *Two Roads and a Spring*); in fiction, William Henry Lewis (*In the Arms of Our Elders*, other short fiction), Fred Pfeil (*What They Tell You to Forget, Shine On*, and *Goodman 2020*), and Shona Ramaya (*Beloved Mother, Queen of the Night*, and *Flute*).

Presently, our distinguished visiting writer teaching regular courses here is Michelle Cliff; other such appointments in the past have been held by Margaret Randall and Robert Abel. Other writers visiting for readings and residencies of various lengths of time include Amy Bloom, Gwendolyn Brooks, Lucille Clifton, Sam Hamill, Peter Matthiessen, Sharon Olds, Gary Snyder, John Edgar Wideman, and many others.

Scholarships are available. For more information on the creative writing program, contact Fred Pfeil, Director, Creative Writing Program, Dept. of English.

❖**Trinity University**
San Antonio, TX 78212
(210) 736-7517

Degree offered: BA in English

Required course of study: 36 s/hrs in the major
Thesis: no requirement for regular major
   Required for Honors Program
Writing workshop: up to 12 s/hrs
Other writing courses: up to 6 s/hrs
Tutorials or directed reading: up to 6 s/hrs
Literature courses: 12 s/hrs

The writing program at Trinity University includes expository, argumentative, analytical, and fiction writing courses. A student at Trinity will follow a program of traditional undergraduate study in English with an emphasis in writing. The choice of a formal Writing Concentration within the English major can emphasize fiction writing and poetry, or linguistics, or rhetoric-composition.

The English major at Trinity University includes a strong emphasis in expository and persuasive writing. On the English faculty are 2 rhetoricians, Drs. Victoria Aarons and Willis Salomon (PhD's in Rhetoric from the University of California, Berkeley). Students seeking a writing concentration are encouraged to enroll in both "Advanced Writing" and "Rhetorical Analysis." In addition, "Supervised Writing Practicum and Laboratory" are offered for those students who wish to familiarize themselves with writing pedagogy. Students enrolled in these courses serve concurrently as "Peer Tutors" in the campus Writing Center, where they assist students from disciplines throughout the curriculum. Further tutorial options are available to those students who elect the expository writing concentration, such as participation in Trinity University's "First Year Seminar Program," in which advanced students assist teaching faculty both in and out of the classroom. The English Department also includes a widely-praised Honors Program that features a variety of stimulating written and oral requirements and opportunities during a student's junior and senior year.

The writing faculty includes writer Robert Flynn (*In The House of The Lord: The Sounds of Rescue, The Signs of Hope*); poet Frank L. Kersnowski (*The Outsiders To Adam: A Bibliography of Modern Irish and Anglo-Irish Literature*). 10 to 12 visiting writers appear on campus each year.

For more information, contact Peter Balbert, Chairman, Dept. of English.

Tufts University
Medford, MA 02155
(617) 627-3459

Degree offered: BA in English

For further information, contact Director of Writing, Dept. of English.

❖**Tulane University**
New Orleans, LA 70118-5698
(504) 865-5160

Degree offered: BA in English

Required course of study: 40 s/hrs

The new 9-course English major allows a student to take up to 4 courses in creative writing for credit toward a degree. An introductory course as well as advanced courses which may be taken 4 times are available as well as a course in autobiographical writing and in writing for performance. A senior thesis in fiction or poetry or occasionally drama is possible for honors students.

Tulane belongs to the Southern Literary Festival, the Academy of American Poets, and AWP.

The faculty includes Rebecca Mark, Dale Edmonds, and Peter Cooley, poet (*The Room Where Summer Ends, The Van Gogh Notebook, The Astonished Hours*), as well as different visiting writers from the city or region each semester.

All creative writing classes are limited to 15 students.

Four named scholarships in creative writing are available, including 2 John Kennedy Toole scholarships for undergraduates. The Zale Foundation program brings a woman writer to campus each year for 1 week. Visitors have included Allison Lurie, Carolyn Forché, Nancy Willard, Gloria Naylor, Ellen Douglas, and Sonia Sanchez. Other writers to visit the campus recently have been Octavia Butler, Gloria Naylor, Rodney Jones, Stephen Dobyns, Louise Glück, and Ellen Bryant Voigt.

Please note: we have no graduate program in creative writing, only an academic English PhD.

For more information, contact Peter Cooley, Dept. of English.

❖**University of Utah**
Salt Lake City, UT 84112-0494
(801) 581-6168
website: http://www.utah.edu

Degrees offered: BA, MFA, PhD

Degree: BA with Creative Writing Emphasis

Required course of study: Maximum of 36 credit hours, of which 12 must be in creative writing workshops.

Degree: MFA

MFA candidates must spend 2 semesters in residence. The degree requires completion of 4 creative writing workshops and 5 literature and criticism courses, including a form and theory course in the genre of the student's thesis. The MFA thesis is a book-length piece of publishable writing: a novel, collection of stories, or a collection of poems.

MFA students may focus their course work in any

area of English or American literature. They are required, at the end of their second year, to pass a written examination on selected texts in their chosen genre.

Degree: PhD

Type of Program: Literary Study and Creative Writing

The PhD in Creative Writing is neither a fine arts degree nor simply a traditional literature PhD with a creative dissertation. The program is designed to help students become not only better writers, but also writers who know the history of their chosen genre and the critical theory relevant to it.

PhD requirements include 4 semesters, 2 of them continuous, in residence at the University; 10 courses beyond the MA or MFA, including 4 creative writing workshops, 4 literature courses, 2 theory courses; and a reading knowledge of 2 foreign languages or an advanced reading knowledge of one.

PhD candidates must also complete course work at the graduate level in the literature of 4 major literary periods. After finishing these courses, students take an oral examination covering the history of the chosen genre, critical theory relevant to that genre, and major modern and contemporary works in the genre. This is followed by a written examination. The dissertation is a book-length work of publishable quality.

Admission to the doctoral program carries with it the award of a teaching fellowship. Fellows teach three sections of English composition spread over two semesters. During the second and third years, they generally have the opportunity to teach one section of English 2500, Introduction to Creative Writing.

MFA candidates may apply for teaching assistantships, which are normally renewable for 2 years. Those with strong academic records may apply competitively for an assistantship in the third year as well. Assistants teach 3 composition courses over a 2 semester period.

The faculty includes: François Camoin (*The Revenge Convention in Webster, Middleton and Tourneur, Why Men Are Afraid of Women*); Jacqueline Osherow (*Looking for Angels in New York, Conversations with Survivors, With a Moon In Transit*); David Kranes (*Margins, Hunters in the Snow, The Hunting Years*); Katharine Coles (*A History of the Garden, The Measurable World*); Franklin Fisher (*Bones*); Donald Revell (*There are Three, Alcools, Beautiful Shirt*); Karen Brennan (*Wild Desire, Here on Earth*); and Richard Schramm (*Rooted in Silence*).

The Creative Writing Program brings in several nationally known writers each year to give readings, work with student manuscripts, and have conferences with student writers. Recent visitors have included Eleanor Wilner, Robert Creeley, and Alice Fulton.

For further information, contact the Director of Creative Writing, Dept. of English.

❖**Valdosta State University
1500 Patterson Street
Valdosta, GA 31698**
*(912) 333-5946
e-mail: jmckinne@valdosta.edu*

Degrees offered: BA, MA with Creative Thesis Option

We do not offer a degree in creative writing; both BA and MA are English degrees. English majors may opt for a Creative Writing Track, which can be completed by taking 60 hours of senior college curriculum. In addition to taking literature courses, students in the CRWR Track can pursue a course sequence in either poetry or fiction writing.

For more information call Dr. Joshua McKinney, Creative Writing Coordinator, Dept. of English

Vanderbilt University
Nashville, TN 37235

Degrees offered: BA

Required course of study: 33 hours

We have a vital undergraduate program in creative writing, which is part of the English major. Our faculty includes fiction writers Tony Earley (*Here We Are in Paradise*) and Walter Sullivan (*A Time To Dance*) and poets Kate Daniels (*Four Testimonies*) and Mark Jarman (*Questions for Ecclesiastes*). The Vanderbilt English Department sponsors a visiting writers program and a spring literary symposium, both of which brings writers to campus to read and meet with students. Every other spring a writer comes to teach for a semester. These visitors have included Philip Levine, James McConkey, and Marilyn Nelson.

For more information, contact Director, Creative Writing Program, Dept. of English.

❖**Vermont College
of Norwich University
Montpelier, VT 05602**
*Poetry, Fiction, Creative Nonfiction & Post Graduate
  Studies
(802) 828-8840
FAX (802) 828-8649
e-mail: crowley@norwich.edu
website: http://www.norwich.edu/acad/mfa_wrl.htm*

*Writing For Children
(802) 828-8637
FAX (802) 828-8649
e-mail: vikkiw@norwich.edu*

Degree offered: MFA in Writing

Type of Program: Studio

Length of Residency: Two years

Required course of study: 64 s/hrs

The Master of Fine Arts in Writing is a low-residency, two-year program, offering concentrations in poetry, fiction, creative nonfiction, and writing for children. Intensive 11-day residency periods are followed by six-month non-resident study projects. Immersed in a stimulating environment, students develop working relationships with more experienced poets, fiction, creative nonfiction writers, and writers of childrens' literature. The emphasis throughout all aspects of the program is on student writing and the study of contemporary letters. Post-Graduate Semester and One-Year Intensive Post-Graduate Studies options offer graduates of writing programs an opportunity to broaden their studies in specific areas of interest.

Residencies take place in January and June/July on the Vermont College campus. During the residency, each student participates in small, faculty-guided workshops in which student work is carefully examined. Daily seminars, lectures, and discussions as well as readings by faculty and visiting writers from all over the country afford students ongoing formal and informal exchange. Also during the residency, students, in concert with faculty, design a semester-long study project. As a summation of the work of residencies and semester projects, graduating students, under the guidance of faculty, give lectures and public readings of their work during the final residency. The low student/faculty ratio (5 to 1) ensures close attention to the developing skills and talents of each writer.

The non-resident six-month semester project focuses on the student's own writing. Reading and critical study components appropriate to individual backgrounds, interests, and needs expand writing skills and critical judgement. Each faculty member supervises five students through correspondence during the semester. Students submit packets of work-in-progress, revisions, and brief essays. A dialogue concerning issues of craft, criticism, and aesthetics becomes the working medium for study and growth. Students and faculty submit written evaluations of the work, which become a part of the student's record and narrative transcript. At the beginning of the next semester, the student returns to the campus to attend residency lectures and readings, and to design a new project. Through the four semester projects, students take an active role in shaping their own curricula, while participating in a sustained dialogue with experienced writers of national reputation.

Criteria for the granting of the degree include general creative writing ability, understanding literature, familiarity with contemporary letters, and experience in applied criticism. The student's record must include evidence of the following: full participation in five residencies; successful completion of four semester projects, a course taught during the final residency; an original book-length manuscript of high quality; a substantial analytical thesis; work with at least two faculty members during the student's tenure in the Program; and broad reading in literature and contemporary letters.

The Program is dedicated to alternative, hands-on education. The study of writing should resemble the work patterns of professional writers, since fruitful learning occurs both on and off campus. Residencies and faculty-guided semester projects encourage student writers to develop independent work habits and are designed to serve writers who have jobs, families, and other responsibilities, as well as conventional students.

Limited financial aid is available. Details are provided in a financial aid brochure and application form from the Vermont College financial aid office.

For more information and application materials, please write or call: MFA in Writing Program, Vermont College, Montpelier, VT 05602, (802) 828-8840.

1998-99 Poetry Faculty: Ralph Angel, Robin Behn, Mark Cox, Nancy Elmers, Jody Gladding, Richard Jackson, Sydney Lea, Jack Myers, William Olsen, Victoria Redel, David Rivard, Clare Rossini, Mary Ruefle, Natasha Saje, Betsy Sholl, Leslie Ullman, Roger Weingarten, David Wojahn.

1998-99 Fiction/Creative Nonfiction Faculty: Carol Anshaw, Phyllis Barber, François Camoin, Abby Frucht, Douglas Glover, Mary Grimm, Sydney Lea, Diane Lefer, Ellen Lesser, Bret Lott, Sena Jeter Naslund, Christopher Noel, Pamela Painter, Victoria Redel, Sharon Sheehe Stark.

1998-99 Writing for Children Faculty: Marion Dane Bauer, Brock Cole, Carolyn Coman, Sharon Darrow, Louise Hawes, Ellen Howard, Ron Koertge, Eric Kimmel, Norma Fox Mazur, Randy Powell, Phyllis Root, Graham Salisbury, Jane Resh Thomas.

Contact Louise H. Crowley, Administrative Director, for more information.

❖University of Victoria
P.O. Box 1700
Victoria, British Columbia
Canada V8W 2Y2
(604) 721-7306
e-mail: writing@kafka.uvic.ca
website: http://kafka.uvic.ca/writing

Degrees offered: BA, BFA in Writing (drama, fiction, nonfiction, poetry)

Required course of study: 60 units
   Writing workshop: 15 or more units
   Other writing courses: up to 42 units
   Literature courses: 6-26 units
   Tutorials or directed reading: up to 6 units

Other Requirements: As long as the requirements of the Department are met with regard to Writing and English courses, the student is free to choose a wide selection of courses.

The Department of Writing at the University of Victoria offers a Major Program and a Professional Writing Minor with Co-op option.

Major Only: 3 units at 1st year, 6 units at 2nd year, 15 units at 3rd and 4th year of which 4.5 units must be in a single genre workshop (drama, fiction, nonfiction, poetry).

Sophomore-level courses include the Theory and Practice of Literary Criticism; workshops in fiction, nonfiction, poetry, and drama; Introduction to Journalism; and Multimedia and Film. Third-year course offerings include: poetry, nonfiction, and drama workshops; basic and advanced Forms and Techniques in Poetry; basic and advanced Forms and Techniques in Narrative; structure courses in stage Drama and in

Cinema and Television Drama; a seminar and an Advanced Workshop in Journalism; The Medium of Print, and Directed Studies in Writing. Fourth-year courses include advanced workshops in fiction, nonfiction, poetry, and drama; and a special studies seminar.

Entrance to the introductory class does not require a portfolio, but admittance to writing classes at all levels requires permission of the Department: by March 31, journalism students must submit a resume, portfolio and current transcript for consideration. Decisions on admittance are made before June 1.

The Writing Department faculty includes Bill Gaston, Lynne Van Luven, Lorna Crozier, William D. Valgardson, Margaret Hollingsworth, Jack Hodgins, and Derk Wynand. Part-time faculty includes Tom Gore, Patrick Lane, Marilyn Bowering, Cameron Young, Brian Hendricks, Stephen Hume, and Stephen Osborne.

For more information, contact by e-mail at <writing@finearts.uvic.ca>.

❖Virginia Commonwealth University Department of English
P.O. Box 842005
Richmond, VA 23284-2005
(804) 828-1329
e-mail: eng_grad@vcu.edu
website: http://www.has.vcu.edu/eng/grad/

Degrees offered: BA, MFA in Creative Writing

Degree: BA in English, Minor in Writing

Required course of study for BA: 124 s/hrs total
30 s/hrs of upper-level English

Required course of study for Writing Minor:
Writing courses: 18 s/hrs
Writing workshops: 6-12 s/hrs available
Advanced composition: 3 s/hrs
Other writing courses

Undergraduate Application Deadlines: Feb. 1 for fall; Dec. 1 for spring (freshman applicants).

Virginia Commonwealth University offers undergraduate creative writing courses in fiction, poetry, and drama at both the introductory and advanced levels. Limited enrollment allows for individualized attention by instructors. Students frequently cite these courses as one of their most important undergraduate experiences. Of the ten upper-level courses required for the English major, undergraduates can take up to four in creative writing coursework. In addition, while no major in "creative writing" is currently offered, a minor in writing is available to all undergraduates, including English majors. The minor in writing is flexible, and students adapt it individually. It consists of 18 hours chosen from a list of selected writing courses, including creative writing, professional writing, and rhetoric courses. One of the courses in advanced nonfiction writing is required as a keystone course in the minor.

Undergraduate and graduate students have an opportunity to publish their work in two on-campus magazines: *Millenium*, VCU's literary magazine produced in affiliation with the English Department, and *Richmond Arts Magazine*, featuring both literary and visual arts work. Annual competitions in writing are also offered for students.

Degree: MFA in Creative Writing (poetry, fiction, possibly in combination with other genres)

Type of Program: Studio/Academic

Length of Residency: Usually three years for teaching assistants without previous graduate degree. Varies for part-time students.

Required course of study: 48 s/hrs total
Thesis: 6-12 s/hrs
Writing workshops: 12 s/hrs
Literature courses: 12 s/hrs
Electives: 12-18 s/hrs

Graduate Application Deadline: February 1 for admission and financial aid, including application for Graduate Teaching Assistantship.

VCU is a state institution with a total enrollment of more than 21,000 students on its two campuses in Richmond, the capital of Virginia. The Medical College of Virginia Campus is near the financial, governmental, and shopping areas of a newly-renovated downtown. The Academic Campus is in Richmond's historic Fan District, which dates back to the 19th-century. VCU is Virginia's largest urban university and features one of the nation's most comprehensive evening colleges, a nontraditional student body (nearly half of VCU's students are more than 25 years old), and a well-established, highly respected School of the Arts with programs in painting, sculpture, crafts, theatre, dance, and music. The Jazz Orchestra has many times been judged the best in the country. The city of Richmond is itself an attraction to many students. Founded in 1727, it is now one of the South's fastest-growing and most cosmopolitan cities. Rich in historic significance, Richmond was an important site in the lives of Patrick Henry, Edgar Allan Poe, and Thomas Jefferson, to name only a few. The city offers enjoyable and affordable cultural activities, including a professional symphony orchestra and ballet, several theaters, and a number of important museums devoted to art, history, and science.

Designed to attract students from varied undergraduate backgrounds who are writers of promise, the MFA in Creative Writing program is especially suited for those interested primarily in the writing of fiction or poetry. In addition, to expand students' writing experience and versatility, advanced workshops are also available in nonfiction, screenwriting, the novel, and playwriting. Students may also undertake editorial internships with *New Virginia Review*, an outstanding journal of national circulation produced by a Richmond-based nonprofit literary arts organization with close ties to our program.

Students in the program are encouraged to develop a strong personal sense of aesthetic and ethics, and to pursue excellence in writing, scholarship, and teaching. Through the workshop experience, as well as personal conferences with the writing faculty, the program aims to help students to significantly advance the quality of their writing, and to enable them to become sensitive, knowledgeable readers who are expert critics of their own and others' work. Students broaden their literary sophistication in a wide range of available courses which examine the literature of varied historical periods and geographic areas, introduce a spectrum of critical theories and perspectives, and explore the techniques and possibilities of the various literary genres. Innovative graduate seminars in topics of special interest and focus are offered each semester. Degree requirements, while rigorous, are flexible so that they can be individually tailored to fit the student's needs and goals. The program's limited enrollment allows for personal attention to the student's writing by a nationally prominent faculty (graduate workshops are limited to 12 or fewer students), as well as for establishing friendships with other developing writers in a diverse and challenging, yet mutually supportive, community of artists.

The basic course of study toward the MFA requires a minimum of 12 hours of graduate writing workshops, 12 hours of graduate literature courses, and 6 hours of thesis work. Beyond that the student is free to work out a total program of 48 semester hours (with the advice of the program's faculty and the student's thesis advisor) which is well-balanced and appropriate to that student's aims and interests. Thesis courses enables students to reserve space in their academic schedules to produce a substantial creative writing thesis. Many of our students have written award-winning manuscripts in this way, and have subsequently been able to place their work with publishers. Course work is available in other departments of the university as well, including art history, theater, history, philosophy, and mass communications.

The majority of full-time students complete the program within three years, while a few, particularly those who have previously taken graduate course work in English, are able to graduate in two years. Part-time study is also possible because a large number of courses are taught in the evening to accommodate such students. Generally, students take workshops and submit a thesis in the genre in which they have been admitted, though they may seek admission to any creative writing workshop by submitting a sample of writing in the appropriate genre to the MFA program director.

Admission to the MFA program is based primarily on the quality and vitality of the candidate's submitted creative writing portfolio. In addition, we also consider the applicant's letters of recommendation, undergraduate background, and scores on the general portion of the GRE.

A sizable number of graduate assistantships are available each year, all of which offer a full waiver of tuition plus a substantial stipend. For example, the stipend for 1998-99 was approximately $8,900. Graduate assistants receive excellent training in teaching skills and perform a variety of duties including classroom teaching and tutoring in the Department's writing center and the computer center. An MFA fellowship is also available, awarded by competition, usually in the student's final year. The program is home as well to a Truman Capote Literary Trust scholarship, awarded annually to a third-year fiction student.

Each year the Department invites a number of writers to campus for readings, discussion sessions, and workshops, often in the form of mini-residencies. Over the past several years, visitors to VCU have included Yusef Komunyakaa, Toni Morrison, Philip Levine, Henry Taylor, Deborah Digges, Jamaica Kincaid, Fred Chappell, Paul Muldoon, Carolyn Forché, Gerald Stern, David Bradley, Ellen Bryant Voigt, Lee Smith, Russell Banks, Toni Cade Bambara, Peter Taylor, William Styron, Scott Cairns, Pagan Kennedy, Jennifer Egan, Rita Dove, and many others. Along with readings given by MFA students themselves, several other readings series in the region combine to create a lively annual round of literary events.

The creative writing faculty includes playwright and literary critic Laura Browder (*Spitting Into the Wind, Modernism for the Masses: Radical Culture in Depression America*); novelist and freelance writer Tom De Haven (*Freaks' Amour, Sunburn Lake, Derby Dugan's Depression Funnies*); poet Gregory Donovan (*Calling His Children Home*, winner of the Devins Award); novelist and nonfiction writer Marita Golden (*Migrations of the Heart, Long Distance Life, Saving Our Sons: Raising Black Children in a Turbulent World*), who has established at VCU the Zora Neale Hurston/Richard Wright Foundation award for young African-American fiction writers; poet T.R. Hummer (*The Passion of the Right-Angled Man, Lower-Class Heresy, Walt Whitman in Hell*); poet Gary Sange (*Sudden Around the Bend*); and novelist and short story writer William Tester (*Darling*).

VCU is an equal opportunity/affirmative action institution and does not discriminate on the basis of race, gender, age, religion, ethnic origin, or disability. For more information on VCU's programs in English and creative writing, please call, e-mail, or write the English Graduate Programs Coordinator at the above address.

Virginia Intermont College
Bristol, VA 24201-4298

(703) 669-6101 ext. 266

Degree offered: BA in English with a Concentration in Creative Writing

Required course of study: 33 s/hrs in the major
Writing courses: 9-12 s/hrs
Literature courses: 18-21 s/hrs

Other Requirements: 48 s/hrs core curriculum; 6 s/hrs foreign language; 37 s/hrs minor and/or electives.

Virginia Intermont College offers a BA degree in English with a concentration in Creative Writing. Because the writing courses are very small (less than 10), it is possible for the instructor to respond to the writing interests and needs of each student.

The purpose of the program is to serve those students who plan to pursue the MFA degree and those who are planning to pursue careers that demand a high level of writing skill.

The courses are taught by professional writers who are currently very active in their fields. In addition, well-known poets and fiction writers visit the campus each year to conduct workshops and give readings. The college literary magazine provides yet another way for students to become involved in literary activities.

For more information, write Allen Pridgen, Dept. of English.

197

❖Virginia Polytechnic Institute and State University
Blacksburg, VA 24061-0112
(540) 231-6501
FAX (540) 231-5692
e-mail: ed.falco@vt.edu

Degree offered: BA in English

Required course of study: A maximum of 50 s/hrs in English
    Thesis: no requirement
    Writing workshop: 3–12 s/hrs

Application Deadlines: November 1 for notification by December 15; February 1 for notification by April 15.

Virginia Polytechnic Institute and State University offers a BA in English with a concentration of courses in a writing option. Most of the courses under the option are in creative writing. English majors who concentrate in creative writing must fulfill all regular requirements of the English degree. Five creative writing courses (3 s/hrs each) are available in fiction, poetry, drama, advanced poetry, and advanced fiction. In addition, a student may elect from a variety of upper division courses in contemporary fiction and/or contemporary poetry. The workshops may be repeated for credit, and independent study is available in the various areas of creative writing. The basic courses in creative writing are offered every semester and in the summer session.

As an adjunct to course offerings, *Silhouette* provides a publication outlet for outstanding creative work produced in the workshops. The Visiting Writers Series brings widely published writers to campus. Authors who have read recently in the series include Lynne Tillman, Reginald McKnight, Henry Taylor, Alice Fulton, Derek Walcott, Bobbie Ann Mason, Lee Smith, and George Garrett. Writers who have appeared in this program in the past include John Barth, Raymond Carver, Eudora Welty, and John Updike. The Virginia Tech Prize in Fiction and Poetry is awarded annually for the best story and poem produced in a creative writing workshop.

The purpose of the writing workshops is to advance the talent, individuality, critical perception, and self-confidence of student writers within the limits of their talent and dedication. Less than ¼ of the students enrolled in the workshops are English majors. Many are from such fields as engineering or science. A good percentage of our student writers have begun publishing in literary magazines, won prizes at contests and writing festivals, and have gone on to graduate work at leading creative writing programs, including the Iowa Writers' Workshop and the University of Montana's Creative Writing Program.

The writing program full-time faculty includes Edward Falco (*A Dream with Demons, Plato at Scratch Daniel's, Winter in Florida*); Nikki Giovanni (*The Sun is So Quiet, Selected Poems, Shimmy Shimmy Shimmy*); Lucinda Roy (*Lady Moses, The Humming Birds, Wailing the Dead to Sleep*); Katherine Soniat (*A Shared Life, Cracking Eggs, Winter Toys*). Many writing courses are also taught by widely published writers such as Carl Bean, Jeff Mann, Lisa Norris, and Simone Poirier-Bures.

For more information, write Edward Falco, Creative Writing Program, Dept. of English.

❖University of Virginia
219 Bryan Hall
Charlottesville, VA 22903
(804) 924-6675
(804) 924-7105
e-mail: lrs9e@virginia.edu

Degrees offered: BA, MFA

Degree: BA in English

The University of Virginia offers the following undergraduate courses in creative prose writing and poetry writing: Intermediate and Advanced Composition; Introductory, Intermediate, and Advanced Poetry Writing; Introductory and Intermediate Newswriting; Magazine Writing; Newsmagazine Writing; Introductory, Intermediate, and Advanced Fiction Writing.

Degree: MFA in Creative Writing (fiction or poetry)

Type of Program: Studio/Academic

Length of Residency: Two years

Required course of study: 36 s/hrs
    Thesis: 12 s/hrs, 6 of which may be electives
    Writing workshop: 12 s/hrs
    Literature courses: 12 s/hrs

Other Requirements: Only one writing course may be taken per semester; degree must be completed within 5 years; no language requirement; 1-hour oral defense of thesis.

Application Deadlines: January 1; February 1 for financial aid. March 31 for work-study. There is no mid-year entry into the program. No transfer credits will be accepted by the program.

We are a small program, admitting about a dozen students each year. Graduate courses in creative writing offer students an apprenticeship with an established writer. These courses are not intended to teach a student how to teach creative writing. For admission to such courses, MFA candidates have first priority, then English graduate students, then all others. MFA candidates have priority only for entrance into courses within their field (i.e., poetry or fiction). Manuscript submissions are required for all levels of graduate creative writing courses. No student, including the MFA candidates, is guaranteed entry into any one workshop. All manuscript submissions for entry into graduate workshops should be of recent work and should be submitted to the instructor at least one week prior to the first meeting of the workshop. No student may receive "double credit" for any creative writing course. Workshops may not be taken pass/fail.

The Creative Writing Program offers several Henry Hoyns Fellowships (the number and value of the fellowships may change from year to year). Hoyns application forms are available from the Creative Writing Program, Dept. of English, 219 Bryan Hall. Graduate School applications are available from the Graduate School of Arts and Sciences, Cabell Hall. Many other forms of financial aid are available. For information, contact the graduate advisor or the director, Office of Financial Aid to Students, Miller Hall.

The Creative Writing faculty includes: Fiction: George Garrett, Henry Hoyns Professor (*The Sorrows of Fat City; Whistling In the Dark; My Silk Purse and Yours*); John Casey (*Half-Life of Happiness; Spartina*); Douglas Day (*The Prison Notebooks of Ricardo Flores Magon; Journey of the Wolf; Malcolm Lowry: A Biography*). Poetry: Charles Wright (*Zone Journals; Half-Life; The World of the Ten Thousand Things: Poems 1980-1990*); Gregory Orr, Director (*New and Selected Poems; We Must Make a Kingdom of It; City of Salt*); Deborah Eisenberg (*Under the 82nd Airborne, Transactions in a Foreign Currency, Pastorale*); and Rita Dove (*Fifth Sunday; Grace Notes; Mother Love*).

MFA students have the opportunity to earn graduate credit and gain valuable experience in editing and publishing by working on *Meridian*, a semi-annual literary journal founded, managed, and edited by MFA students at the University of Virginia. The journal features poetry, fiction, and creative nonfiction, as well as interviews and a "Lost Classics Series" devoted to overlooked or unpublished work by significant writers.

Visiting writers include: Ellen Bryant Voigt, Stanley Kunitz, Carolyn Chute, Madison Smartt Bell, Jill McCorkle, Richard Bausch, Donald Justice, Ellen Douglas, Carolyn Kizer, Henry Taylor, Josephine Humphreys, James Salter, Lorrie Moore, Mark Strand, W.S. Merwin, Edward P. Jones, Marilyn Waniek, Tess Gallagher, Mary Oliver, Marianne Wiggins.

For more information, contact the Creative Writing Program, English Dept. (804) 924-6675.

❖Wabash College
301 West Wabash Avenue
P.O. Box 352
Crawfordsville, IN 47933-0352

For more information, contact the Director, Dept. of English.

❖University of Wales
College of Cardiff
P.O. Box 94
Cardiff CF1 3XB
Wales
01222-874241
FAX 01222-874242

Degrees offered: MA, PhD

Degree: MA

Type of Program: Studio/Academic

Application Deadline: March 31.

Cardiff is offering a Master's degree in the Teaching and Practice of Creative Writing. A one-year, full-time course, it is planned for writers with an interest in teaching creative writing as well as for teachers at all levels of education who are interested in creative writing practice and formal study of writing skills.

Weekly throughout the autumn and spring terms students will attend creative writing practice seminars, for which they will be encouraged to write regularly. In seminars, students will examine writing they are doing independently and also discuss set writing exercises designed to stimulate and sharpen writing skills. In the autumn term students will also attend weekly seminars in Writing and the Creative Process. This course will involve a wide range of critical and theoretical activities. Materials for discussion will be drawn from writers' drafts, notebooks, letters, and autobiographical writings. In the spring term, students will attend weekly seminars in Teaching Creative Writing. This will be a reflexive course, on one level offering further opportunities to practice and discuss students' writing, but at another level, and simultaneously, it will constitute practice in planning, leading, and teaching creative writing groups.

Students will be assessed on their portfolio of creative writing, and also on four essays or projects (two for each course) for Writing and the Creative Process and Teaching of Creative Writing. There will be no formal examination.

Degree: PhD

Type of Program: Traditional Literary Study and Creative Writing

Application Deadline: March 31.

Cardiff is offering part-time and full-time study toward the PhD in Creative Writing. Candidates will receive individual supervision from a member of the Creative Writing staff and will be encouraged to consult with other members of the staff if they so wish. On completion of their studies, they will submit a substantial folder of original writing in lieu of a dissertation. This creative work will be supplemented by a critical introduction and/or commentary.

Professional writers are increasingly expected to work with creative writing groups in the schools and the community. For many of them, it is a more important source of income than writing itself. Teachers in primary, secondary, and tertiary education are turning more and more to creative writing as an essential part of English studies. For both these groups, the MA in the Teaching and Practice of Creative Writing would provide invaluable experience.

The MA course is staffed by a group of writer-teachers who between them have experience teaching creative writing at all educational levels and in a wide variety of contexts. All of them teach on the popular BA Creative Writing course at Cardiff. Faculty members are: Anne Cluysenaar, Dr. Roger Ellis, Dr. Colin Evans, Dr. John Freeman, Dr. Peter Hunt, Norman Schwenk, and James Tucker.

Enquiries to the Secretary, MA in Creative Writing, School of English Studies.

❖Warren Wilson College
P.O. Box 9000
Asheville, NC 28815-9000
(828) 298-3325 ext. 380
FAX (828) 298-1405

Degree offered: MFA in Creative Writing (poetry, fiction)

Type of Program: Studio (Low Residency)

Length of Residency: 10 days

Required course of study: 60 s/hrs

Other Requirements: Each student is required to complete at least 4 semesters in the Program; each student is required to participate in at least 5 full residencies.

The low-residency program model was initiated at Goddard College in 1976 by Ellen Bryant Voigt and has been offered at Warren Wilson since 1981. It is designed for adults who either cannot or do not wish to join residential programs, and it offers a mode of study that closely resembles and thus prepares the student for the life of a writer.

During the residencies, students gather from all over the country to exchange their fiction and poetry, to receive criticism and advice, to find motivation and stimulation for further work, and to form lasting supportive connections among colleagues. During the 6-month semester, they return to their ongoing lives and to the hard, solitary work of writing, but they do so within the structure of the project plan and the regular detailed responses, in writing, of an experienced faculty member.

The residency is an intensive 10-day period of both instruction and lively exchange with other writers. Each day's agenda includes workshops in which the students' creative work is critiqued and discussed under the direction of 2 faculty members. Classes in literature and craft provide a broad curriculum and a strong background for the semester study projects, and each evening, there is a poetry or fiction reading presented by faculty, guest faculty, or graduating students.

During these 10 days in the Blue Ridge Mountains, the low student–faculty ratio of 4–1 enables students to have easy access to the faculty for individual instruction, counseling, and guidance for the upcoming semester project. Thus, students who had previously found themselves isolated in their commitment to writing are given regular opportunities for stimulation, exposure to new ideas and different aesthetics, contact with more experienced writers and with their own peers, and direct response to their work within a supportive writing community.

The residencies are also designed to help students choose a faculty supervisor and work closely with that supervisor to plan a semester project. Although each project includes creative work, substantial reading, and some analytical writing, the goals of the study derive from the student's own interests and are directed toward his or her development as a writer. During the 6-month term, the student submits work to the supervisor every 3 weeks (new poems or fiction, revised pieces, reports on the reading), and the faculty supervisor responds with specific suggestions as well as general advice, criticism, and support. At the end of the semester, students complete evaluations of their finished projects and return to the campus to design new study plans. Thorough evaluations of both the residency and the project become a part of the student's permanent record in the program; a successfully completed semester is granted 15 s/hrs of graduate credit.

Throughout the 6 months away from campus, a student is expected to devote at least 25 s/hrs each week to the study project; thus, students are able to maintain commitments to family or job while pursuing their studies, combining the solitude and life patterns that are necessary for creative work with a flexible structure of response, criticism, and guidance from an experienced writer and teacher.

The Warren Wilson Master of Fine Arts degree requires successful completion of 4 semesters' study and represents mastery in creative writing, contemporary letters, applied criticism, and the tradition of literature. In the final month of each semester, evaluations of the project by both the student and the supervisor, along with samples of creative and analytical writing, are submitted to the Academic Board for review. This process affords an opportunity for regular, direct counseling as the student progresses toward the degree through a series of individually tailored projects. In order to receive the degree, each student will complete an analytical paper on some topic of literature, contemporary letters, or craft; read 50–80 books; teach a class to fellow students; give a public reading of his or her work; and prepare a manuscript of fiction or poetry. Within these guidelines, however, each student devises a course of study which directly addresses the strengths and weaknesses, the aesthetic issues, and overall intention of his or her own creative work.

Admissions decisions are based primarily on the application manuscript. Application materials should evidence not only an acceptable quality of creative work, but also a level of commitment and sophistication which indicates the candidate is prepared to do independent graduate study. The Program does accept a small number of students without BA degrees or undergraduate concentrations in literature and writing; however, the application manuscripts in these cases must be exceptionally strong.

Financial aid is available for qualified students; applications for aid are handled through the College Financial Aid Office and do not affect admissions decisions.

Warren Wilson College is accredited by the Southern Association of Colleges and Schools. The College is dedicated to equality of opportunity and welcomes students without regard to race, religion, color, national origin, sex, or handicap.

Current faculty include, in poetry: Joan Aleshire, Anne Carson, Linda Gregerson, Heather McHugh, Stuart Dischell, Mary Leader, Michael Ryan, Steve Orlen, Ellen Bryant Voigt, Alan Williamson, and Robert Wrigley. Faculty in fiction are: Wilton Barnhardt, Andrea Barrett, Robert Boswell, Judith Grossman, David Haynes, Marcie Hershman, Michael Martone, Claire Messud, Kevin McIlvoy, Jim Shepard, Debra Spark, and Peter Turchi.

For more information, please contact Peter Turchi, Director, Program for Writers.

Washburn University
1700 College Avenue
Topeka, KS 66621

(785) 231-1010, ext. 1441
FAX (785) 231-1089
e-mail: zzdpen@washburn.edu or
zzaver@washburn.edu or
zzfleury@washburn.edu

Degree offered: BA in English with Writing Emphasis

Required course of study: 124 s/hrs total
 Core and writing courses: 30 s/hrs
 Capstone experience: 3 s/hrs
 Writing in other departments: 3 s/hrs
 English: no more than 40 s/hrs

Majors in English may choose 3 emphases: Literature, English Education, or Writing. All students take a common core of courses in literary history, critical theory, and language, but students who choose the writing emphasis also take courses in creative and professional writing in our department and others. For their capstone experience, students may do a writing internship with one of the many public or private institutions in Topeka, may participate in a publishing lab, may undertake a special independent writing project, or may take a course in Revising and Editing. The degree also requires completion of a second course in a foreign language.

The university supports the Woodley Press, a small press that publishes book-length collections of poetry, drama, and short stories. Excellent editing and marketing opportunities exist. The university also publishes *Inscape*, a literary magazine designed and edited by students under the direction of a creative writing professor.

Our faculty consists of 13 full-time professors. The coordinator for the writing program is Tom Averill, who has an active interest in midwestern literary history and is a widely published writer of short stories and literary essays, including *Passes at the Moon* and *Seeing Mona Naked*. Amy Fleury, poet, teaches creative writing and directs the publishing lab. An active reading series has brought to campus poets and fiction writers like Albert Goldbarth, Ted Kooser, Marly Swick, Gerald Stern, Sharon Warner, and Mary Swander.

Topeka is located on the Kansas River, 60 miles from Kansas City, 30 miles from the University of Kansas, and 50 miles from Kansas State University. The city's libraries, museums, concert series, fine arts series, live theater, and art galleries (including Washburn's Mulvane Art Museum) also offer a rich local cultural environment. Topeka is an important medical and mental health center with a cluster of hospitals and psychiatric training institutions, including Menninger. Topeka's many parks, its zoo, its golf courses, lakes, and other outdoor facilities afford varied recreational activities.

For more information, contact Robert D. Stein, Chairperson, Dept. of English.

Washington College
Chestertown, MD 21620

(410) 778-2800

Degree offered: BA in English with Minor in Creative Writing

Required course of study:
 English: 8 courses
 Writing workshops: up to 3 courses
  (including Freshman Creative Writing Workshop)
 Other writing courses: up to 2, with workshops,
  to complete Minor

Other Requirements: Creative writing thesis, scholarly thesis, or comprehensive examinations.

Application Deadlines: February 15; December 1 for early decision.

Students interested in creative writing or the study of literature will find Washington College an especially hospitable and vigorous college in which to pursue their education. Through the unusually handsome Sophie Kerr Endowment, Washington College is able to bring to campus each year a number of distinguished writers, editors, and literary scholars. There are generous scholarships for entering students.

The Writers' Union of Washington College is a student association of creative writers and students of English, American, and foreign literatures. Among the programs it sponsors are the Freshman and Senior Readings, The Writers' Theatre (for student plays), the Broadside Poetry Series, the Letterpress Workshop (where students learn the craft of letterpress printing), the Monday Series (informal talks on "matters curious and worthy"), as well as student readings and social activities.

The O'Neill Literary House -- a large Victorian house located on the edge of the Washington College campus -- is the focal point of creative writing and literary activity at the college. The facilities of the Literary House include The Readers' Room (a literary reference room), the offices of the teachers of creative writing, a student study lounge, a kitchen for student use, the Letterpress Room, the Paperback Lending Library, a performance deck for the Writers' Theatre, word processing rooms, and Literary House Fellowship Rooms for individual student use. Each year a number of individual study rooms in the Literary House are awarded to deserving students engaged in significant writing projects, such as the completion of a novel, a literary thesis, or a volume of poetry. Some of the rooms carry a modest fellowship stipend. The Literary House also sponsors small art exhibitions, the Foreign Language Poetry Reading, journalism workshops, translation workshops, and various literary celebrations.

The Sophie Kerr Lecture Series brings to campus a number of America's finest writers, editors, and literary scholars to lecture and to teach. Edward Albee, John Barth, Joseph Brodsky, Carolyn Forché, Jorie Graham, James Tate, W.S. Merwin, Toni Morrison, Alain Robbe-Grillet, Grace Paley, Max Apple, Derek Walcott, Gwendolyn Brooks, Charles Simic, Sharon Olds, Ron Hansen, and Bobbie Ann Mason have been recent visitors to Washington College.

Students interested in the craft of letterpress printing may enroll in a noncredit workshop at the O'Neill Literary House Letterpress Room. Using Chandler and Price presses, students learn the history of letterpress printing as well as how to set type, lock up forms, and run the letterpress. Advancing from "printer's devils" through "apprentices" and "journeymen" to "pressmen," students become accomplished enough to print literary posters, broadsides, literary magazines, and chapbooks.

The Sophie Kerr Prize, awarded to a graduating senior "...having the best ability and promise for a future fulfillment in the field of literary endeavor...," is the largest undergraduate literary prize awarded in the United States. Sophie Kerr Prize recipients have gone on to achieve distinction in writing and editing.

For more information contact Robert Mooney, Director, or Kathy Wagner, Associate Director, Dept. of English.

❖Washington State University
Dept. of English
P.O. Box 645020
Pullman, WA 99164-5020
(509) 335-2163
FAX (509) 335-2582

For more information, contact the Director, Dept. of English.

❖University of Washington
A101 Padelford Hall, Box 354330
Seattle, WA 98195
(206) 543-2690
(206) 543-9865
FAX (206) 685-2673

Degrees offered: BA, MFA

Degree: BA in English

At the undergraduate level, the University of Washington offers a BA in English with extensive offerings in creative writing. Between 250 and 300 undergraduates are enrolled in creative writing classes each quarter.

Degree: MFA in English with Concentration in Creative Writing

Type of Program: Studio/Academic (fiction, poetry)

Length of Residency: Approx. two years

Required course of study: 55 q/hrs
Thesis: 15 q/hrs
Writing workshop: 20 or more q/hrs
Literature courses: 15 or more q/hrs
Electives: 5 q/hrs

Other Requirements: Foreign language proficiency; one-hour oral examination on the thesis, course work, and reading list/MFA essay.

Application Deadlines: January 15 for the following autumn.

The Creative Writing Program and the English Department sponsor or support various literary activities, some that restrict themselves to the campus' literary community, some that have national scope. The Castalia reading series offers students a chance to read on campus to fellow students and faculty. Readings by prominent writers are presented throughout the year, including the annual Roethke Memorial Reading and the Watermark Reading Series.

The Seattle Review, a semi-annual literary magazine that publishes short fiction and poetry, is staffed by Creative Writing Program faculty and students.

The Seattle area has a very active literary community. There are excellent bookstores here, a few of them specializing in small press books and little magazines. City and county governments have grant programs for writers. Several magazines and small presses are located in or near Seattle. The Creative Writing Program is pleased to be a part of the community.

The faculty includes: Linda Bierds, poetry. Her books are *Flight of the Harvest-Mare, Heart and Perimeter*, and *The Profile Makers*. She received a PEN/West award and a MacArthur Fellowship in 1998. David Bosworth, fiction. His first book, *The Death of Descartes*, won the Drue Heinz Literature Prize in 1981. His most recent novel is *From My Father, Singing*. His work has appeared in many publications. Charles Johnson, fiction. He is the author of *Middle Passage, The Sorcerer's Apprentice*, and *Dreamer*. He has been scriptwriter for several PBS films, and he received a MacArthur Fellowship in 1998. Richard Kenney, poetry. His books are *The Evolution of the Flightless Bird*, which won the Yale Series of Younger Poets Competition in 1984, *Orrery*, and *The Invention of the Zero*. He won the Rome Prize in Literature and a MacArthur Fellowship. Colleen McElroy, poetry and fiction. Her books of poems include *Music From Home: Selected Poems, Queen of the Ebony Isles*, and *Bone Flames*. Her collections of short fiction are *Jesus and Fat Tuesday* and *Driving Under the Cardboard Pines*. Heather McHugh, poetry. Her books of poems are *To the Quick, Shades*, and *Hinge and Sign*. She has 2 translations: *D'Apres Tout: Poems by Jean Follain*, and *Because the Sea is Black: Poems by Blaga Dimitrova*. David Shields, fiction. His books are *Remote, Dead Languages*, and *A Handbook for Drowning*. Maya Sonenberg, fiction. Her collection of stories, *Cartographies*, received the Drue Heinz Literature Prize in 1989. David Wagoner, poetry, fiction, playwriting. His 14 books of poetry include *Collected Poems 1956-1976, Who Shall Be the Sun?*, and *First Light*. He has had 10 novels published. His most recent book is *The Hanging Garden*. Shawn Wong, fiction. His novels include *Homebase* and *American Knees*. He has co-edited several anthologies of Asian-American literature, including *Aiiieeeee!*

The writing program regularly has visiting writers teaching workshops. Recent visiting professors have included Peter S. Beagle, Tess Gallagher, Laura Kalpakian, Maxine Kumin, Denise Levertov, Charles D'Ambrosio, Jim Welch, and Al Young.

Various forms of financial aid are offered by the university. 2 letters of recommendation (3 for TA), and 3 copies of a creative work are required for admission to the graduate writing program.

Grants and Prizes: During the academic year, more than 7 awards are granted to distinguished student writers. These include the Loren D. Milliman Scholarship of $7,000 and the Edith K. Draham Scholarship of $3,000.

For more information, contact the Writing Program Director, Dept. of English.

❖Washington University
Campus Box 1122
St. Louis, MO 63130

(314) 935-5190

Degree offered: MFA in Writing

Type of Program: Studio/Academic

Length of Residency: Two years

Required course of studies: 39 s/hrs
Thesis: required
Writing workshops and directed writing:
18–21 s/hrs
Other graduate course work: 18–21 s/hrs

The Writing Program at Washington University leads to the Master of Fine Arts in Writing. It is a two-year program, requiring satisfactory completion of 39 s/hrs, a thesis (a volume of poems or short stories or a novel), and an oral examination dealing principally with the thesis.

The Writing Program has evolved into a unique community of writers, scholars, and critics. While the program is designed by writers for writers, it is an integral part of the English Department, and closely associated with other graduate programs within the university. A writer's education will obviously differ from a conventional academic program. We will recommend courses originating in the English Department as well as courses from other departments. Our primary concern is not to make critics, or for that matter creative writing teachers, out of writers, but to challenge students' cultural perspective. Individual programs will be set in consultation with advisors.

The program is rigorous and challenging, requiring a full commitment from the students. The program is, as well, selective and small. We admit only those students we think are definitely qualified and can benefit from the program. Because of our selectivity and size, we are able to offer generous financial aid. Almost all our new students receive tuition scholarships, and many receive University Fellowships. In the second year, students have the opportunity for teaching assistantships.

Faculty writers at Washington University include fiction writer and essayist Wayne Fields (*What the River Knows, The Past Has a Life of its Own*); essayist Gerald Early (*Tuxedo Junction: Essays on American Culture* and *The Culture of Bruising*); fiction writer and essayist William H. Gass (*In the Heart of the Heart of the Country, The World Within the Word*, and *Habitations of the Word*); fiction writer and essayist Charles Newman (*White Jazz, There Must Be More to Love than Death*, and *The Post-Modern Aura*); and poet Carl Phillips (*In the Blood, Cortege, From the Devotions*). The program of writers visiting Washington University is rich and varied with an emphasis on residencies from three weeks to a full semester. Visiting writers in recent years have included Mona Van Duyn, Maxine Kumin, Linda Gregg, Derek Walcott, Donald Justice, Hilma Wolitzer, Grace Paley, W.S. Merwin, Frank Kermode, Lore Segal, and Helen Vendler.

For more information, contact Dept. of English.

Wayne State University
51 West Warren Avenue
Detroit, MI 48201

(313) 577-2450

Degrees offered: BA English Major; MA in Writing with a Creative Concentration

Degree: MA

Required course of study: 33 s/hrs
Thesis: 8 s/hrs
Writing workshop: 6–12 s/hrs
Literature courses: at least 8 s/hrs
Electives: 10–16 s/hrs

The English Department of Wayne State University offers an MA with a particular emphasis in creative writing, as well as a concentration in creative writing for undergraduate majors. The Department regularly schedules workshops at both the graduate and undergraduate level in poetry, fiction, and writing for the theater. Through the Miles Modern Poetry Series, and also in association with The Writer's Voice/Detroit and The Detroit Festival of the Arts, the Department sponsors readings by internationally recognized writers. In recent years, these have included Kathy Acker, Russell Banks, Andrea Barrett, Samuel Delany, Mark Doty, Edward Hirsch, Adrienne Rich, Sapphire, and Edmund White. The department also offers two week "master classes" to advanced students, taught by distinguished visitors (1999––Charles Baxter).

There is considerable opportunity for student writers on campus. The English Department sponsors a student-run magazine, *The Wayne Literary Review*, and during the winter term conducts weekly colloquia in which students present their work in programs shared by faculty members and other local writers. There are several literary contests open to both graduate and undergraduates (the Thompkins Prize; the Bruenton Prize). Further, in the Loughead-Eldredge and the Stephen Tudor Memorial Scholarships, the department has considerable financial resources specifically available for the support of creative writing students, including a renewable grant for a student working on an extended piece of fiction.

Writers on staff include playwright William Harris (*Robert Johnson: Trick the Devil; Riffs*); novelist Christopher T. Leland (*Letting Loose; The Art of Compelling Fiction*), as well as poet and experimental prosewriter and dramatist Carla Harryman (*There Never Was a Rose Without a Thorn; Memory Play*), poet and performance artist M.L. Liebler (*Breaking the Voodoo; Stripping the Adult Century Bare*), Spanish language poet and novelist Osvaldo Sabino (*Atlántida; La historia de las panteras y de algunos de los animales conversos*); poet and experimental fictionalist Chris Tysh (*Carmen; Porné*), poet and novelist Anca Vlasopolos (*Through the Straits: At Large; Missing Members*), and poets and critics Bernard Levine (*The Dissolving Image: A Study of the Spiritual-Esthetic Development of W.B. Yeats*), John R. Reed (*Great Lakes; Life Sentences*), and Barrett Watten (*Bad History; Frame: Collected Poems 1970-1990*).

Some recent graduates have chosen to continue

their studies for a terminal degree (MFA or PhD) at such universities as those of Iowa, Chicago, and Southern Mississippi. Others have published extensively in nationally recognized journals and anthologies. Among its better known alumni are poets Sharon Dilworth and Barbara Henning, and novelist Michael Zadoorian.

As a large, urban university dedicated to diversity, Wayne State encourages application by all interested students. For further information: please contact Dr. Christopher Leland, Head, Creative Writing Section, or Dr. Henry Golemba, Director, Graduate Studies.

University of West Alabama
LU Station 22
Livingston, AL 35470
(205) 652-9661, ext. 249
FAX (205) 652-4065

Degrees offered: BA, BS in English, with concentration in writing

Required course of study: 192 q/hrs total
Basic curriculum courses: 75–80 q/hrs
Major area: 50–60 q/hr
Minor: 30–35 q/yrs
Electives: 17–37 q/hrs

Application Deadlines: Four weeks before the beginning of the quarter in which a student wishes to enroll for admission and financial aid.

University of West Alabama offers a wide range of literature, language, criticism, and writing courses, including one graduate course and three undergraduate courses in creative writing. Students in the writing program also have the opportunity to work for the Livingston Press.

For more information, contact Dr. Joe Taylor.

West Chester University
West Chester, PA 19383
(215) 436-2822

Degrees offered: BA in English with Creative Writing Minor; MA with Concentration in Creative Writing (poetry, fiction)

West Chester University offers 6 s/hrs of Introduction to Creative Writing; 3–6 s/hrs of Creative Writing; 3 s/hrs of Poetry and 3 s/hrs of Short Story Workshops; 3 s/hrs of Editing and Publishing; 3 s/hrs of either drama or Creative Nonfiction/Essay.

The creative writing faculty consists of poet Christopher Buckley (*Blue Autumn, Dark Matter, Camino Cielo*; NEA 1984, Fulbright 1989, *Pushcart Prizes X, XV, XVI, XVIII*). Fiction writer Luanne Smith (screenplay *Just For The Taking* on PBS PA).

For further information, write Christopher Buckley, Director, Creative Writing, Dept. of English.

University of West Florida
11000 University Parkway
Pensacola, FL 32514
(904) 474-2923

The University of West Florida's Creative and Professional Writing Program offers undergraduate students the opportunity to pursue their writing interests through a range of creative writing workshops and professional writing courses. Emphasis is on both writing and literature. Internships are available on local publications and on *The Panhandler*, UWF's literary magazine.

For more information, contact Dr. Laurie O'Brien, Director.

West Georgia College
Carrollton, GA 30118
(404) 836-6512

Degrees offered: BA, MA

Degree: MA in English, Literature Concentration

Type of Program: Traditional Literary Study and Creative Writing

Length of Residency: Four semesters

Required course of study: 30 hours thesis program, 36 hours nonthesis program
Thesis: 3 hours
Writing courses: up to 6 hours
Literature courses: 24 hours, thesis;
30–36 hours, nonthesis

Application Deadlines: Two weeks prior to the opening of each term.

For more information, contact Chair, Dept. of English.

❖West Virginia University
Department of English
P.O. Box 6296
Morgantown, WV 26506-6296
(304) 293-3107
FAX (304) 293-5380
e-mail: jharms@wvu.edu

Degrees offered: BA, MA

Degree: BA in English with Concentration in Creative Writing (poetry, fiction, nonfiction)

Required course of study: 128 s/hrs required for graduation

Creative Writing Concentration (15 hours) allows students to select from introductory and advanced courses in fiction, poetry, and nonfiction. The 9 hours of advanced work in the same genre culminates in a senior seminar.

Degree: MA with a creative writing thesis option

Required course of study: When applying to the graduate program, students must submit a portfolio of creative work, either fiction, creative nonfiction, or poetry, to be approved by the creative writing faculty. If approved, the student can be admitted to a specially designed graduate program which mixes literary and creative writing courses and culminates in a creative writing thesis.

The Department of English also offers a fall and spring writers series, a one-week Sturm Writer-in-Residence Workshop, and undergraduate and graduate writing contests. Students annually publish a literary journal, *Calliope*, which won the 1993 AWP Honorable Mention in both content and design. Visiting writers have included Denise Giardina, Pinckney Benedict, Lynn Emanuel, Elizabeth Cook-Lynn, Craig Lesley, Patricia Hampl, David St. John, Reginald McKnight, Maggie Anderson, Ralph Angel, Peter Cameron, Irene McKinney, Gurney Norman, Sharon Sheehe Stark, Lisa Kroger, Richard Currey, Wayne Dodd, and Valerie Colander.

Visiting faculty who offer special topics courses are hired on a semester basis. Past visiting faculty include Pinckney Benedict (Literature of the Apocalypse); Irene McKinney (Nature Writing); and Valerie Nieman (Science Fiction and Fantasy).

The Department is a cosponsor of the GoldenRod Writers Conference, an annual, regional conference affiliated with West Virginia Writers, Inc.

The following faculty teach creative writing and/or direct creative theses: fiction writer Gail Galloway Adams (*The Purchase of Order*, 1987 Flannery O'Connor Award recipient); poet John Flynn; poet Winston Fuller (co-edited *Trellis*); poet James Harms (*Modern Ocean, The Joy Addict*); fiction writer Ellesa Clay High (*Past Titan Rock: Journeys into an Appalachian Valley*, Appalachian Award winner); creative nonfiction writer Kevin Oderman; fiction writer Ethel Morgan Smith (work in *Southern Living Magazine, The Atlanta Chronicle, Grand Mothers* -- an anthology, edited by Nikki Giovanni).

For more information, contact the Chair, Dept. of English.

❖West Virginia Wesleyan College
Buckhannon, WV 26201-2995

(304) 473-8000, ext. 8329

Degree: BA in English with Concentration in Creative Writing (fiction, poetry, nonfiction)

Requirements for Major: 38 s/hrs above composition, including core and concentration requirements.

Requirements for Writing Concentration: 20 s/hrs
Writing electives: 9 s/hrs
Literature Electives: 12 s/hrs

Requirements for Writing Minor: 15 s/hrs above composition
Writing electives: 12 s/hrs

Other Requirements: Creative thesis.

Application Deadlines: March 1 for financial aid; March 31 for admissions.

The writing concentration requires a sequence of courses; 1) Intro to Creative Writing; 2) either Fiction Workshop, Poetry Workshop, or Writing for the Print Media; 3) Senior Seminar or Independent Study in the chosen genre; and 4) Senior Thesis. Students may work as editors and staff on the literary magazine *The Rickshaw*, which publishes work by students, faculty, and nationally known writers. The magazine awards prizes annually in poetry and prose. Three other awards are given annually by the college to English students, including Writing Concentration students. The Program sponsors 2-4 visiting writers annually, and hosts a Writer's Conference. Visitors in the past include Jayne Anne Phillips, Pinckney Benedict, Maggie Anderson, Patricia Dobler, Richard Currey, Susan Richards Shreve, Jonathan Holden, James Harms, and Denise Giardina.

The creative writing faculty includes poet Irene McKinney (*Quick Fire and Slow Fire, Six O'Clock Mine Report*; State Poet Laureate); poet Mark Defoe (*Bringing Home Breakfast, Palmate*); and nonfiction writer Arminta Baldwin.

For more information, contact Irene McKinney, Director of Creative Writing, at the above address.

Western Carolina University
English Dept.
Coulter Building
Cullowhee, NC 28723

(828) 227-7264
FAX (828) 227-7266
e-mail: madams@wcu.edu
website:
http://www.wcu.edu/as/english/brian/prowrite.htm

Degree offered: BA in English with Concentration in Professional Writing (poetry, fiction, nonfiction, technical writing, screenwriting, and editing); **MA in English** (Professional Writing Focus)

Degree: BA in English with Concentration in Professional Writing

Required course of study: 39 hours in the major
15 hours literature (6 must be at the junior or senior level
21 hours writing courses
3 hours off-campus coop, directed writing, or campus internship
Other university requirements including general education and minor

Other Requirements: 6 hours in Modern Foreign Language, 3 hours in approved Computing course.

Application Deadline: Rolling admission.

Western Carolina University is located in the scenic Appalachian mountain ranges at Cullowhee, North Carolina. The university consists of the main campus in Cullowhee and resident credit centers in Asheville and Cherokee. The central campus consists of about 265 acres, including beautifully wooded areas and modern academic, student residence, recreation, and athletic facilities. The Blue Ridge Parkway, Great Smoky Mountains National Park, Cherokee Indian Reservation, Fontana Lake, and many resort areas offer golf, skiing, fishing, hunting, hiking, climbing, and water sports.

Western's Writing Program combines the best of creative and professional writing courses with real-world experiences (classes in journalism, magazine publishing, and computing; cooperative assignments with businesses, magazines, and publishers; technical writing assignments for area companies; and practice in professional speaking situations). The low student-faculty ratio in our courses allows students to get one-on-one guidance in poetry, creative nonfiction, and fiction writing from such well-known authors as Kathryn Stripling Byer and Rick Boyer, and to gain new perspectives from visiting writers and writers-in-residence. In recent years, Western or area bookstores have hosted workshops and readings by such writers as James Welch, Yusef Komunyakaa, Rosellen Brown, Lucille Clifton, Clifton Taulbert, Vikram Chandra, Eavan Boland, Doris Betts, Li-Young Lee, Doris Davenport, Judith Ortiz Cofer, Fred Chappell, and Wilma Dykeman.

Students also gain experience in professional magazine production on the student magazine *Nomad*, write for the school's newspaper, *The Western Carolinian*, and host readings, open-mikes, and poetry slams at Western and in nearby Sylva and Asheville. Each year the English Department, the English club, and the local chapter of honor society Sigma Tau Delta award the Ashby Wade prize for best freshman essay, the Crum Scholarship for highest achievement in the major, and other prizes.

Degree: MA in English with Professional Writing focus

Required course of study: 30 s/hrs total
    3 hours in English 618 (Literary Research and
      Bibliography)
    6 hours in Writing Concentration
    15 hours in Literature or Theory
    6 hours Creative or Professional Writing Thesis

Other Requirements: Written comprehensive exams; reading exam in a foreign language (usually Spanish, German, or French); final oral examination.

Application Deadline: Rolling admission; application must be received six weeks before beginning of term.

The goal of the WCU graduate program in English with Writing Concentration is to foster excellent creative and professional writing skills, to increase the breadth and depth of each student's reading in English and American literature, and to carefully guide each student in developing critical skills. We offer both variety and specialization, with course work available in literature, rhetoric and composition, linguistics, teaching theory and practice, and creative writing. The graduate degree in English helps prepare students for entry into a PhD Program, a teaching position, or a variety of jobs and careers in writing.

In our program, students receive individualized attention and have ample opportunity to interact and work with our 23-member graduate faculty. Our program is small enough to be personal, and our excellent facilities support a professionally active faculty and graduate student population. The holdings in literature at Hunter Library are quite good, and, additionally, students and faculty have quick access to holdings at neary UNC institutions as well as national interlibrary loan service. Western houses a state-of-the-art Media Center with over 50 Mac and PC networked computers, offers many courses online in the school's many computer classrooms, and provides students with ample computer time in its eight different computer labs.

Financial aid is available. Teaching, research, and service assistantships ranging from $1,000 to $6,500 are awarded to well-qualified graduate students. The out-of-state portion of tuition may be waived for some but not all assistantships. Acceptance of an award requires a student to work for a specified number of hours per week. A limited number of Chancellor's Fellowships are available. The awards are based on merit and are intended to help superior students pursuing graduate studies. Fellowships are valued at $6,000 and carry no work requirement.

Faculty: Mary Adams (poetry, nonfiction); Rick Boyer (fiction, nonfiction; author of *The Giant Rat of Sumatra* and the *Doc Adams* novel series; winner of the 1982 Edgar Allen Poe award for best mystery novel); Kathryn Stripling Byer (poetry; author of *The Girl in the Midst of the Harvest*, *Wildwood Flower*); Newton Smith (technical writing, poetry); and Brian Railsback (fiction, screenwriting).

For more information, contact the Director, Dept. of English.

Western Illinois University
Macomb, IL 61455

(309) 298-1103

Degrees offered: BA, MA

Degree: BA in English, Creative Writing Minor

Required course of study: 17–18 s/hrs in creative writing (6 s/hrs, genre; 12 hours, workshop)

Degree: MA in English, Writing Option

Type of Program: Traditional Literary Study and Creative Writing

Required course of study: 31–34 s/hrs
    Thesis: required; 6 s/hrs
    Writing workshop: 3–6 s/hrs
    Literature: 18 s/hrs

For more information, contact Director of Graduate Studies, Dept. of English.

Western Kentucky University
Bowling Green, KY 42101

(502) 745-3043
e-mail: joe.survant@wku.edu
website: http://www.wku.edu or
* www2.wku.edu/~survant*

Degree offered: BA in English with a Creative Writing Emphasis

Required course of study: A minimum of 36 hours leads to the BA. This option includes five writing courses and six literature courses.

The department's literary magazine, *Zephyrus*, offers editorial and publishing experience as well as scholarships and prizes based on the quality of the writing and G.P.A.

An active visiting writers program has brought in major writers including William Stafford, Robert Bly, Bobbie Ann Mason, Wendell Berry, Jane Smiley, Ted Kooser, Carolyn Forché, James Baldwin, Truman Capote, William Matthews, Jonathan Holden, John Haines, and Lamar Herrin.

The full-time writing faculty includes fiction writer Nancy Roberts (*Women and Other Bodies of Water*); and poet Joe Survant (*We Will All Be Changed, Anne & Alpheus, 1842-1882*, winner of the 1995 Arkansas Poetry Award).

For further information, contact Joe Survant, Dept. of English.

Western Maryland College
Westminster, MD 21157

(410) 857-2420

Degree offered: BA in English with Concentration in Writing

For more information, contact Chairman, Dept. of English.

❖Western Michigan University
Kalamazoo, MI 49008-5092

(616) 387-2572
e-mail: arnie.johnston@wmich.edu
 (Arnie Johnston, Dept. Chair)
joslin@wmich.edu (Katherine Joslin, Director of
 Graduate Studies)
website: http://www.wmich.edu/english

Degrees offered: BA, MFA, PhD with Creative Dissertation

Degree: BA English Major/Minor with Creative Writing Emphasis (poetry, fiction, playwriting)

Required course of study: 35 s/hrs of English (plus English 110: Literary Interpretation 4 s/hrs, required for entry into program)
 Writing workshop: 14 s/hrs
 Other writing courses: 4 or more s/hrs
 Literature courses: 13-14 s/hrs
 Tutorials or directed reading: up to 4 s/hrs

Other Requirements: 3 s/hrs English language course.

The English Major with Creative Writing Emphasis aims at giving students intensive practice in writing and criticism in various genres in a workshop format, for general writing careers, or for prospective candidates for the MFA in Creative Writing.

A minimum of 35 s/hrs of English courses are required (plus one 4 s/hr course for entry into the program, ENGL 110: Literary Interpretation), including 14 s/hrs of course work in creative writing from among the following: Writing Fiction & Poetry (prerequisite for all creative writing courses); Advanced Fiction Writing; Advanced Poetry Writing; Playwriting; and Creative Writing Workshop (poetry, fiction, drama, or nonfiction). Literature and language requirements include: British Literature I or II and American Literature I or II; Studies in Poetry, Studies in the Novel, or Studies in Drama; and an English language course.

Degree: MFA in Creative Writing (poetry, fiction, playwriting, nonfiction)

Length of Residency: Two years

Type of Program: Studio/Academic

Required course of study: 48 s/hrs of English
 Thesis: 6 s/hrs
 Writing workshop: 12-18 s/hrs
 Literature courses: 6 s/hrs (modern)
 Tutorials or directed reading: up to 4 s/hrs

Other Requirements: Balance of program in courses in language and literature; cognate courses permitted, but not required; thesis is a book-length creative work, including public reading or performance.

Application Deadlines: February 1 for the once-a-year review of applications which will take place in March. For graduate assistant applicants, same deadline. GRE general and subject are required for all applicants.

The MFA in Creative Writing is a program for students who wish to become professional writers of poetry, fiction, drama, or nonfiction and qualifies them to teach the craft of writing on the college or university level.

The program requires 42 s/hrs of courses in writing workshops, literature, and literary theory, and a 6-semester-hour MFA Project. Workshops (12-18 s/hrs) provide for much independent work, instruction, and practical experience in criticism and rewriting, and the challenge and inspiration of working with and for one's peers. The successful MFA candidate should develop research and critical skills and a sound background in literature as well. Therefore, candidates take The Nature of Poetry, Studies in the Novel, or Studies in Drama; 6-8 s/hrs in modern literature; courses in language and literature before 1900; and courses in various cognate fields. Capping the program is the MFA Project, an original book-length work of fiction, poetry, drama, or nonfiction, including a public reading or performance, to be approved by the candidate's advisory committee.

Degree: PhD with Creative Writing Dissertation (poetry, fiction)

Type of Program: Traditional Literary Study and Creative Writing

Length of Residency: 4 or 5 years beyond the MA

Required course of study: 90 s/hrs of English
 Dissertation: 15 s/hrs
 Writing Workshop: 12 s/hrs
 Literature courses: 18 or more s/hrs
 Tutorials or directed readings: 3 or more s/hrs

Other Requirements: Prerequisites and distribution requirements; non-traditional literature requirement; teaching component (including practicum); doctoral readings and oral examination; foreign language competency requirement. Written candidacy examinations.

Application Deadlines: Same as for MFA.

WMU's new PhD program is designed to meet the needs of future scholars and writers, particularly those who intend to teach at undergraduate institutions. The program requires all candidates to have broad knowledge of English and American literature, acquaintance with non-traditional literature, practical and/or theoretical background in the teaching of English (including the teaching of creative writing), and a specialization in a single area which can be creative writing. Candidates entering with an MA are credited with 30 to 36 s/hrs depending on their degree; those entering with an MFA may be credited with as many as 45 hours in some circumstances.

In order to enrich their creative process, writers are encouraged to work in more than one genre, and the content of MFA Projects and creative dissertations frequently reflects this approach. Whatever their specialization, all candidates will receive essential experience in research, teaching, and writing in the profession, and will develop the breadth required of teachers in relatively small English Departments.

WMU hosts the Third Coast Western Michigan Creative Writing Conference in the spring with participating writers from all over the Midwest, and nationally-known writers serve as workshop faculty, panelists, and featured readers. Under the general guidance of the writing faculty, graduate students serve as the editorial and production staff of *Third Coast*, WMU's national literary journal; undergraduates, too, may gain valuable experience by working with this publication. Graduate students may have the opportunity to provide editorial and other assistance in the production of books in Western's award-winning New Issues Press Poetry Series, under the general editorship of writing faculty member and series founder Herbert Scott. Students may compete, in separate categories for graduates and undergraduates, for annual departmental awards in fiction, poetry, playwriting, and creative nonfiction; they are also eligible for other departmental awards that recognize general achievement in academics and/or creative writing.

The program awards numerous Teaching Assistantships and Doctoral Associateships, as well as assistantships for work such as helping coordinate the Third Coast Writer's Conference, editing *Third Coast* magazine, assisting the coordinator of the writing program, and assisting the Director of Freshman Composition and Basic English.

Visiting writers in recent years have included Sharon Bryan, Lisa Dillman, Alice Fulton, Jorie Graham, Mark Halliday, Amy Hempel, Denis Johnson, Donald Justice, Tracy Kidder, Maxine Kumin, Philip Levine, Barry Lopez, Peter Mathiessen, Czeslaw Milosz, Elizabeth McCracken, W.S. Merwin, Howard Norman, Deborah Ann Percy, Pattiann Rogers, Gerald Stern, David Wojahn, and Dean Young.

The writing faculty includes Stuart Dybek (fiction, nonfiction, poetry), Whiting Awardee, NEA Fellow, *Brass Knuckles, Childhood and Other Neighborhoods*, and *The Coast of Chicago*; J.D. Dolan (nonfiction, fiction), *Phoenix*; Nancy Eimers (poetry), NEA Fellow, *Destroying Angel* and *No Moon*; Jaimy Gordon (fiction), NEA and Bunting Fellow, *Circumspections from an Equestrian Statue* and *She Drove Without Stopping*; Arnold Johnston (playwriting, fiction, poetry), *The Witching Voice, Of Earth and Darkness*, and *The Zamboni Situation*; William Olsen (poetry), NEA Fellow, *The Hand of God and a Few Bright Flowers* and *Vision of a Storm Cloud*; and Herbert Scott (poetry), NEA Fellow, *Disguises, Groceries*, and *Durations*.

For further information, contact Katherine Joslin, Director of Graduate Studies, Dept. of English, at the address above.

❖Western Washington University
Bellingham, WA 98225-9055
(360) 676-3209

Degrees offered: BA, MA

Two programs lead to the Bachelor of Arts in English. One focuses on the study of British and American literature in an historical context and then, through a large number of elective credits, allows students to select English courses of their choice. The other program is a writing concentration. Here, courses in literature supplement a focus on writing courses, either creative writing (fiction, drama, poetry) or nonfiction prose, exposition, and argumentation.

Degree: BA in English with a Concentration in Writing--60 credits

Classes in poetry writing, fiction writing, and nonfiction are offered each quarter. The creative writing classes are typically taught as workshop critique sessions. Students are expected to read contemporary and traditional literature, but the focus of classroom discussion is on the students' own work. Emphasis is placed on rewriting as well as on writing.

A limited number of work/study appointments are available to qualified students. For further information, write Dr. John Purdy, Director of Undergraduate Studies.

Degree: MA in English with a Concentration in Writing--45 credits

Required course of study: Eng 501, Theories of Literature; 20 credits in writing courses to be taken from the following: Eng 500 Directed Independent Study; Eng 502 Seminar in the Writing of Fiction (repeatable); Eng 504 Seminar in the Writing of Poetry (repeatable); Eng 505 Seminar in the Writing of Nonfiction Prose (repeatable); Eng 690, Thesis Writing; 15 credits in literature, criticism, or rhetoric.

Note: A student may, with permission, take up to 10 credits in 400-level. Also, playwriting courses taught by the Theatre Arts staff are applicable toward the BA or MA in English.

Other Requirements: Reading knowledge of a foreign language or an additional 5 credits of graduate work in literature, criticism, or rhetoric, and an examination designed by a faculty committee over selected works appropriate to a student's emphasis.

Applicants interested in the writing option should send a representative selection of their writing at the same time that they apply for admission to WWU. Send 10-15 pages of poetry or 20-30 pages of prose.

The graduate and undergraduate faculty includes poet Bruce Beasley (*Summer Mystagogia, The Creation*, and other works), fiction writer Carol Guess (*Seeing Dell* and *Switch*), poet Kathleen Halme (*Every Substance Clothed* and *Equipoise*), fiction and nonfiction writer Robin Hemley (*Nola, The Big Ear*, and other works), fiction writer Rosina Lippi-Green (*Homestead* and *Into the Wilderness*), and poet and fiction writer Suzanne Paola (*Bardo, Glass*, and other works).

The English Department has its own program of visiting writers who give readings and talk to students. Some additional features are the Playwright's Theater, which provides opportunities for student playwrights to have original work produced on campus, and *Jeopardy*, a CCLM-award-winning student publication which offers the chance of editorial experiences as well as publication, and the chance to work on *The Bellingham Review*, a nationally acclaimed literary journal. The Leslie Hunt Memorial Poetry Award of $100 is given annually to a WWU student in open competition. Students may earn degree credits working as writing or editing interns for agencies or departments on campus or for businesses off campus.

Teaching assistantships and work/study appointments are available to graduate students on a competitive basis. For information concerning financial aid and admission to the graduate program, write to Graduate Director, Dept. of English.

❖Westminster College
Fulton, MO 65251

(573) 592-5287

Degree offered: BA in English with Concentration in Writing

Required course of study: 33 s/hrs in the major
   Thesis: 3 s/hrs
   Writing workshop: 3-6 s/hrs
   Other writing courses: 6 s/hrs
   Literature courses: 12 s/hrs
   Tutorials or directed reading: 3-6 s/hrs

Other Requirements: 8 s/hrs foreign language plus 6 s/hrs related studies.

Westminster College combines theory studies with writing workshops; work on the thesis is preceded by a semester of directed reading. A minimum of 24 s/hrs is expected in outside requirements. At the end of two semesters of work toward the finished paper, the creative-writing-track major has worked through at least one tutorial semester with his advisor to complete an original work in prose, poetry, or drama, which is of equal scope and rigor to the critical paper of his academic-track counterpart. This would mean a work of 30-90 pages.

The writing program faculty includes Program Director Wayne Zade (poetry) and Chuck Lewis (fiction). Visiting writers appear on campus each year.

For more information, contact Wayne Zade, Writing Program Director, Dept. of English.

Westminster College
New Wilmington, PA 16172

(412) 946-7342

Degree offered: BA in English with Concentration in Writing

Required course of study: 31-40 s/hrs in the major
   Thesis: 6 s/hrs
   Writing workshop: 3-9 s/hrs
   Other writing courses: 3 s/hrs
   Literature courses: 18 s/hrs
   Tutorials or directed reading: 3-9 s/hrs

Other Requirements: 21 s/hrs from 3 educational divisions outside the major; 12 s/hrs foreign language; 12 s/hrs physical education; 3 s/hrs religion.

Application Deadlines: March 15 for financial aid; July 15 for application.

Through its writing concentration, the Westminster College English Department offers students the opportunity to develop a basic understanding of literature and criticism as well as the opportunity to strengthen creative writing skills.

Minimum requirements for the concentration include nine courses in English, of which two must be in writing, including Independent Studies. Writing courses include: Introduction to Creative Writing; Advanced Writing: Poetry; Advanced Writing: Fiction; Advanced Writing: Drama; Advanced Exposition; and Continuity Writing.

Students may further develop communication skills through campus publications, the campus radio station, or the field experience internship program. There are generally four readings a year, two of student works and two by guest writers.

Westminster College publishes a student magazine, *Scrawl*, as well as a national literary review, *Westminster Review*.

The writing faculty includes poet and editor David Swendlow (*The Last Hill and the Wild Trees*); novelist William McTaggart (*What Happens in Fort Lauderdale*); and poet and fiction writer James A. Perkins (*The Amish: 2 Perceptions; Billy-the-Kid, Chicken Gizzards and Other Tales; Snakes, Butterbeams, and the Discovery of Electricity*).

For more information, contact James A. Perkins, Director, Writing Program, Dept. of English.

❖Westminster College of Salt Lake City
2840 S. 1300 E
Salt Lake City, UT 84105

For more information, contact the Director, Dept. of English.

❖Wichita State University
1845 N. Fairmount
Wichita, KS 67260-0014
(316) 978-3130
FAX (316) 978-3548

Degrees offered: BA, MA, MFA

Degree: BA in English Creative Writing Major

Required course of study: 33 s/hrs in major
Thesis: no requirement
Workshops: 9-15 s/hrs
Tutorials/Directed Readings: up to 6 s/hrs
Literature: 15-18 s/hrs

Application Deadlines: August 1 for fall; January 1 for spring.

The creative writing major in English provides intensive training in poetry and fiction with optional course work in nonfiction writing and playwriting. Literature requirements seek to provide a broad foundation in literary tradition and genres.

Students begin their professional training with workshops in fiction and/or poetry. Later, they may opt to take workshops in creative nonfiction and/or playwriting. Students who have at least one upper level workshop in fiction or poetry have the opportunity to work on a tutorial basis with a distinguished visiting writer. See the MFA description for a list of recent visitors.

The English Department at Wichita State is richly endowed with scholarships at the undergraduate level. At a school where the in-state tuition is less than $2,500/year, several provide over $2,000 in aid. In addition there are many smaller awards, including the Grafton Scholarship, which is specifically targeted toward creative writing majors.

Mikrokosmos, the student literary magazine, is edited and produced by graduate and undergraduate majors in the program.

Degree: MA in English with Creative Thesis

Required course of study: 30 s/hrs including thesis
Thesis: 3 s/hrs
Workshops: 9 s/hrs
Tutorials/Directed Readings: up to 6 s/hrs
Literature: 18 s/hrs

Other Requirements: 3 s/hrs Introduction to Graduate Study; written comprehensive examination; oral thesis exam.

Applicants must submit a portfolio of fiction (approximately 20 pages) or poetry (8-10 poems).

Degree: MFA in Creative Writing

Type of Program: Studio/Academic

Required course of study: 48 s/hrs
Thesis: 6 s/hrs
Workshops: 12 s/hrs
Tutorials/Direct Reading: up to 9 s/hrs
Literature courses: 15-24 s/hrs
Other Academic courses: 3-6 s/hrs

Other Requirements: 3 s/hrs Introduction to Graduate Study; 3 s/hrs in a discipline outside English; written comprehensive exam; oral thesis exam. All TA's must take 3 s/hrs Advanced Theory and Practice in Composition.

Applicants for the MFA in Creative Writing must submit a portfolio of fiction (approximately 20 pages) and/or poetry (8-10 poems) for evaluation. Students who enter the program with no significant course work in English may be required to take two or three undergraduate literature courses as background. Students with graduate work at other institutions may transfer up to 24 s/hrs of equivalent credit toward the MFA degree.

The program at WSU has earned widespread respect over the years for graduating writers who have both good professional prospects and strong teaching skills. The program emphasizes close one-to-one contact between students and teachers in their writing courses. Literature offerings attempt to broaden the student's knowledge of the literary traditions and controversies of which their work will become a part, a background which should allow them to teach or to seek other professional goals in addition to their writing.

Each semester graduate students may enroll in a one-month tutorial with a distinguished visiting poet or fiction writer. Up to three of these tutorials may count toward the degree. Recent visiting writers include Henry Taylor, Debora Greger, Michael Blumenthal, Carol Frost, Antonya Nelson, James Wilcox, Bette Pesetsky, and Robert Olmstead.

MFA candidates in their final year must take a comprehensive examination based on a reading list selected jointly by the students and their advisors. Degree work culminates with the submission of a book-length thesis of publishable quality.

The great majority of students in the graduate writing program hold teaching assistantships for all or part of their residence. All assistantships include a full waiver of tuition and fees. Two or three MFA fellowships are also available each year. Call for current information on stipends and fellowship amounts. Deadline for assistantship applications is March 1 for the fall and Nov. 1 for the spring. Applications received after those dates will still be considered for admission.

The permanent writing faculty includes poets Fred Dings and Albert Goldbarth, poet and novelist Jeanine Hathaway, and fiction writers Steve Hathaway and Phil Schneider. Richard Spilman directs the program.

For further information contact Director of Creative Writing, Dept. of English.

Wilkes University
P.O. Box 111
Wilkes-Barre, PA 18766
(717) 831-4520

Degree offered: BA in English with Concentration in Writing

Required course of study: 120 s/hrs total; 39 s/hrs in English, with a minimum of 12 s/hrs in writing, including a required course in advanced composition and presentation of a senior portfolio. Twelve s/hrs in advanced literature courses are also required.

Application Deadlines: May 1 for financial aid; rolling admissions.

The writing concentration at Wilkes includes courses in creative writing, technical writing, and rhetorical theory. Advanced workshops are offered in poetry, fiction, playwriting, and nonfiction prose. Advanced students work individually with faculty on specifically designed projects in writing and internships.

Students concentrating in writing are encouraged to work as tutors in the Writing Center, to participate in writing internships at the University and in the community, and to join the editorial staffs of the student newspaper, yearbook, and literary magazine.

The Manuscript Society, which publishes the annual literary magazine of student writing, offers scholarships to students in key editorial positions. In addition to publishing the *Manuscript*, the Society sponsors coffeehouses and readings.

The Department awards the Taft Achilles Rosenberg Naparsteck Scholarship each year to a student who shows promise in writing.

Each year, Wilkes University and the English Department sponsor a series of readings, workshops, lectures, and writers–in–residence programs. Visiting writers in recent years have included Amiri Baraka, Norman Mailer, John Barth, John Vernon, Denise Levertov, Richard Wilbur, Ruth Stone, Rashidah Ismaili, Liz Rosenberg, Loften Mitchell, and Daniel Hoffman. Writers–in–residence have included Dennis Finnell, Laura Furman, Mark Halliday, Beatrice Hawley, and Toby Olson.

For more information, contact Patricia B. Heaman, Chair, English Dept.

College of William & Mary
Williamsburg, VA 23185
(804) 221-3905

The College of William and Mary has no creative writing program per se. However, the following courses are offered: Advanced (Expository) Writing; Creative Writing -- Poetry; Creative Writing -- Fiction; Seminar in Creative Writing I and II; Seminar in Nonfiction Writing; Advanced Creative Writing I and II.

Faculty members who currently teach these courses include Thomas Heacox, David Essex, Hermine Pinson, Henry Hart, Sheri Reynolds, and Nancy Schoenberger (poetry).

For further information, contact Terry Meyers, Chair, Dept. of English.

William Paterson College
Wayne, NJ 07470
(201) 595-2254

Degrees offered: BA, MA

Degree: BA in English with Concentration in Writing

Required course of study: 128 s/hrs total
General Education courses: 59-60 s/hrs
Writing Concentration courses: 33 s/hrs
Electives: 36 s/hrs

Application Deadlines: February 1 for financial aid; March 1 for admissions.

The undergraduate concentration requires the student to take 4 core courses: Methods of Literary Analysis; Critical Writing I; Creative Writing, and Linguistics and Grammar; Development of the English Language; or Grammar and Style. The student takes three advanced writing courses in one of two writing groups: Book and Magazine Editing, Technical Writing, Advanced Creative Writing, Modern Techniques of Composition, and Writing for the Magazine Market; or Playwriting, Screenwriting, Writing for Radio and TV, Freelance Writing, and Journalism. The program also requires the student to take two of eight literature survey courses and two additional upper-level literature courses. *Essence* is the campus literary magazine, which provides editorial and publishing experience for undergraduates. Each spring the English Alumni Creative Writing Competition is held, and awards are given to students based on the quality of their writing.

Degree: MA in English with Concentration in Writing (poetry, fiction, drama, nonfiction, screenwriting)

Type of Program: Studio/Academic

Length of Residency: Two years

Required course of study: 30 s/hrs total
Required courses: 9 s/hrs
These include
Qualifying Manuscript: 3 s/hrs
Applied English Linguistics, Advanced Critical Writing, or Creative Writing: 6 s/hrs
Elective courses: 21 s/hrs
These include
Literature courses: 9 s/hrs
Print & Media writing courses: 12 s/hrs

Application Deadlines: For admission, June 1 for fall semester, November 1 for spring semester; May 1 for financial aid; April 1 for graduate assistantships.

We are committed to helping writers develop their talents by offering useful commentary on their writing as well as peer critiquing within the setting of a lively community of writers. The writing concentration offers aspiring writers, preprofessionals, teachers who wish to update their skills, or individuals who are interested in writing as process enough structure to supply a firm foundation and enough flexibility to permit individual writing goals.

Visiting writers in recent years have included novelist Bette Pesetsky (*Midnight Sweets, Stories Up to a Point*), poet and scholar Wendolyn Tetlow (*Hemingway's In Our Time: Lyrical Dimensions*), poet and Director of Academic Support Center Priscilla Orr (The Nation/DISCOVERY Award Semifinalist, National Writer's Union Finalist).

The program also awards two Graduate Assistantships in the Department (which are also open to Literature Concentration students); internships are also available.

The Writing Concentration Creative Writing faculty includes fiction and poetry writer Philip Cioffari; fiction, poetry writer, and biographer Brad Gooch (*Scary Kisses, City Poet: the Life and Times of Frank O'Hara*); and poet and nonfiction writer Charlotte Nekola (*House of Cards*).

For more information, contact Anthony J. Mazzella, Chair, English Dept.

Williams College
Williamstown, MA 01267

(413) 597-2114

Degree offered: BA in English

For further information on the writing courses offered, contact Chairman, Dept. of English.

❖University of Windsor
Windsor, Ontario
Canada N9B 3P4

(519) 253-4232, ext. 2288
FAX (519) 971-3676

Degrees offered: BA (Honours English Literature and Creative Writing); **MA** (English Literature and Creative Writing)

Length of Residency: One to 4 years, undergraduate; one to 2 years, post-graduate.

Application Deadlines: July 1, for submissions for Graduate Programme.

The Department of English offers a full spectrum of courses and programs in Creative Writing. All of the courses emphasize workshop participation and individual writing conferences. The program provides for continuous involvement from first year through the fourth year, leading to an Honours BA in English Literature and Creative Writing. The granting of a degree in this program is not guaranteed.

Students may enter the program at any point consistent with the development of their talent and experience, or they may elect any of the Creative Writing courses independently. Admission at all levels requires departmental approval based on the submission of a sample of the student's creative work. Creative Writing courses are open to English majors and non-majors alike and to part-time students. They are not available on an audit basis. A major project in any genre is required of all candidates for the degree of Master of Arts in English Literature and Creative Writing.

Members of the Creative Writing staff include Alistair MacLeod (*The Lost Salt Gift of Blood, As Birds Bring Forth the Sun*), Eugene McNamara (*Spectral Evidence, The Moving Light*), Peter Stevens (*Out of the Willow Trees*), Richard Hornsey (*Where Roads and Rivers Lead*), John Ditsky (*Friend and Lover, Scar Tissue*), Wanda Campbell (*Sky Fishing*), and Di Brandt (*Jerusalem, beloved, questions i asked my mother*).

Writers-in-Residence in the past have included: Morley Callaghan, Tom Wayman, W.O. Mitchell, Adele Wiseman, Judith Fitzgerald (1993-94), and Daniel David Moses (1995-96).

Magazines: *University of Windsor Review, Generation* (Student), and *Wayzgoose Chapbook* (Canadian/American).

For further information, contact Dr. Katherine M. Quinsey, Chair, Dept. of English.

University of Wisconsin, Eau Claire
Eau Claire, WI 54704

For more information, contact Max Garland, Dept. of English.

University of Wisconsin, Green Bay
2420 Nicolet Drive
Green Bay, WI 54311-7001

(414) 465-2727
e-mail: sweetd@uwgb.edu

Degree offered: BA in Literature and Language: English, with an Emphasis on Creative Writing (poetry, fiction)

Required course of study: 124 s/hrs total
Introductory writing work: 9 s/hrs
Fiction and/or Poetry Writing Workshops:
6-12 s/hrs
Courses in English/American literature:
15-21 s/hrs

Application Deadlines: April 15 for financial aid; August 10 for Fall admission (earlier if enrollments limits are reached).

The undergraduate concentration in Creative Writing requires students to take introductory level courses in expository, fiction, and poetry writing, an intermediate mixed genre creative writing course, and then allows students to choose to specialize in fiction and/or poetry, within the context of an English literature program.

For information on the writing program, contact Denise Sweet, Advisor, Creative Writing Program.

❖University of Wisconsin, Madison
600 North Park Street
Department of English
Madison, WI 53706

(608) 263-3374
(608) 263-3705

Degree offered: BA in English with a Creative Writing Emphasis

Required course of study: 27 s/hrs
Thesis: 3 s/hrs
Writing workshop: 9 s/hrs

Literature courses: 15 s/hrs

Other Requirements: 9 s/hrs of literature or writing are possible beyond the 27 s/hrs; 12 s/hrs science; 12 s/hrs social studies; 12 s/hrs humanities; 12 s/hrs in one language, or 9 s/hrs in one language and 6 in another (or high school equivalent; retroactive credits available); creative thesis.

Application Deadlines: February 1 for admission; March 1 for financial aid.

The Department of English offers a BA in English with a Creative Writing Emphasis. The required course of study is 27 s/hrs in the major, including 15 s/hrs of literature courses and 12 s/hrs of upper-level creative writing courses. Of the 12 s/hrs of writing, 9 s/hrs are devoted to workshops, and 3 s/hrs are devoted to a Directed Creative Writing Thesis. Majors, non-majors, graduate students, and special students are eligible to apply for workshops.

The creative writing workshops, composed of 15 students, are designed to give students professional training in the writing of fiction, nonfiction, and poetry. Some time is spent on theory and technique, some time is spent reading the work of established writers as models, and some short writing exercises are assigned. But the major focus of the courses is the analysis of student writing, in the classroom and in frequent individual conferences.

Approximately 15 workshops are offered each semester -- half at the introductory level and half at the intermediate and advanced level. Although most of the workshops focus on fiction or poetry, special topics workshops also focus on creative nonfiction, the novel, experimental writing, the short-short, genre writing, etc. Admission to the workshops and the major is competitive based on writing samples and personal interviews.

There are 6 permanent members of the creative writing staff: Kelly Cherry is the author of *Death and Transfiguration, Writing the World,* and *The Exiled Heart.* Jesse Lee Kercheval is the author of *The Dogeater, The Museum of Happiness,* and *Space.* Ron Kuka. Lorrie Moore is the author of *Self Help, Who Will Run the Frog Hospital?,* and *Birds of America.* Ronald Wallace is the author of *Tunes for Bears to Dance To, The Makings of Happiness,* and *The Uses of Adversity.* Roberta Hill is the author of *Star Quilt* and *Philadelphia Flowers.*

In addition to the regular staff, visiting writers periodically teach in the program. In past years, Lisa Ruffolo, Steve Stern, Dean Young, Debra Spark, Ann Packer, and Max Garland have been in residence.

Students in the creative writing program edit and publish *The Madison Review,* a magazine that features both student and professional writers. In past issues, the magazine has published work by such writers as John Allman, Norbert Blei, Philip Dacey, Stephen Dunn, Dave Etter, Richard Grayson, Conrad Hilberry, Ted Kooser, Lisel Mueller, Felix Pollak, James Reiss, May Sarton, Peter Wild, C.K. Williams, and John Woods. In addition to providing a market for student writing, the magazine provides valuable editorial experience for its staff members. The magazine sponsors two prizes: The Phyllis Young Prize in Poetry ($500) and The Chris O'Malley Prize in Fiction ($500).

As adjuncts to the program, distinguished writers are invited to campus each semester to read from their work and to talk to students. Over the years the following writers have appeared: Alice Adams, Margaret Atwood, Philip Dacey, Carl Dennis, Stuart Dybek, Stanley Elkin, Sharon Olds, Marge Piercy, Robert Pinsky, Adrienne Rich, Tom Robbins, William Stafford, Gerald Stern, Angus Wilson, Paul Zimmer, Donald Justice, Jorie Graham, Gary Soto, David Clewell, Alicia Ostriker, and Charles Baxter.

The creative writing program sponsors the annual George B. Hill and Therese Muller Memorial Awards Creative Writing Contest. $2,000 in prize money is awarded for the best short stories and poetry submitted by currently enrolled students.

In addition to the campus-wide competition, 3 prizes are awarded annually to creative writing majors -- the Felix Pollak Poetry Thesis Prize ($500), the Eudora Welty Fiction Thesis Prize ($500), and the Cy Howard Memorial Scholarships ($1,000). The August Derleth Prize ($300) is awarded annually to a graduate student writer.

The creative writing program also sponsors 3 national competitions. The Brittingham Prize in Poetry and The Felix Pollak Prize in Poetry, each consisting of a $1,000 prize and publication by the University of Wisconsin Press, are awarded annually to the two best book-length manuscripts of poetry submitted in an open competition. Donald Finkel, Donald Justice, Lisel Mueller, Henry Taylor, Carolyn Kizer, Philip Levine, Rita Dove, and Donald Hall have selected books by Jim Daniels, Patricia Dobler, Lisa Lewis, David Clewell, Lynn Powell, Bob Hicok, Dennis Trudell, Juanita Brunk, Olena Kalytiak Davis, Betsy Sholl, Suzanne Paola, and Chana Bloch. Manuscript submissions are invited in September ($20 reading fee).

The Wisconsin Institute for Creative Writing awards five $22,000 fellowships annually to writers who have completed an MFA or equivalent graduate degree in Creative Writing and who are working on a first book. Fellows teach one workshop per semester as artists in residence. Applications are invited in February.

For further information, write to Ronald Wallace, Director of Creative Writing, Dept. of English.

❖University of Wisconsin, Milwaukee
Milwaukee, WI 53201
(414) 229-4511

Degrees offered: MA, PhD

Degree: MA in English (Plan C, Creative Writing, poetry, fiction, some creative nonfiction)

Type of Program: Studio/Academic

Required course of study: 24 s/hrs
    Thesis: up to 6 s/hrs
    Writing workshops: 6-15 s/hrs
    Literature courses: 6 s/hrs
    Tutorials or directed reading: up to 6 s/hrs

Other Requirements: Oral examination on thesis project; elective courses permitted outside the Department in related fields.

Degree: PhD in English (with Creative Dissertation Option, poetry, fiction, some creative nonfiction)

Type of Program: Studio/Academic

Required course of study: 54 s/hrs beyond the BA
Thesis: required
30 s/hrs of writing seminars, workshops, and literature courses beyond the MA requirements listed above.

Other Requirements: Qualifying examination for admission to doctoral program; demonstrated competence in one foreign language; preliminary examination in designated literary field; oral defense of dissertation.

Application Deadlines: It is recommended that applications for admission and financial aid be completed before January 1.

The Department of English offers a Master of Arts degree in Creative Writing (Plan C), a studio/academic program. The emphasis is on the writing of fiction or poetry or both, with supplemental courses in literature. The cornerstone of the program is a 2-semester sequence in either fiction or poetry. The first semester ("Narrative Craft and Theory" or "Poetic Craft and Theory") introduces the student to a broad range of literary techniques and models and to the practice of criticism at the graduate level. The second semester ("Seminar in Fiction Writing" or "Seminar in Poetry Writing") provides a graduate-level workshop in which student manuscripts are discussed in the context of the preceding course. Each of the four courses may be repeated, with a change in subtitle, up to three times. In addition, students are required to take at least two literature courses (6 s/hrs) from department courses providing graduate-level introductions to the study of English.

The program also provides a variety of options in creative writing and other areas. Students may take workshops in fiction, poetry, or expository writing and special workshops which cover other forms and genres (e.g., playwriting, screenwriting, genre writing, autobiography, personal journalism, etc.). Courses are also available in the teaching of writing, in business and technical writing, in article writing, in literary criticism, and formal academic research and writing. The department has a large Modern Studies program (including film theory) in which creative writing students may also take courses.

The most important feature of the program is the final project ("thesis") -- a substantial collection of fiction, poetry, or nonfiction, which grows out of the student's course work and independent study. The student's adviser will assist in the planning and development of this project, which is then submitted to a 3-person committee for evaluation. An informal colloquium ("oral examination") concludes the student's work in the program.

The Department of English also offers a limited number of students the option of a creative dissertation in the English doctoral program. Students must meet the academic standards of the program in literature (as demonstrated by previous course work, GRE scores, and a qualifying examination); they must also show exceptional promise as creative writers with the expectation of substantial publication before the completion of the doctorate. It is assumed that students applying to this program wish to enter careers as college teachers and mean to compete for academic positions with the best writers and scholars produced by American graduate schools.

Students in the doctoral program may take more creative writing as well as literature courses, including 12 s/hrs at the graduate seminar level. A major portion of the student's course work in literature should be selected in preparation for the first part of the preliminary examination -- a written exam covering a literary period, genre, or special topic which the student has designated as a supplemental teaching area. A second, oral part of the examination covers the student's plans for the creative dissertation. Students interested in teaching composition or applied writing may include work in those areas in their program of study. Each student is advised by a 3-member advisory board, which normally serves as the nucleus of the student's dissertation committee.

The creative writing faculty includes fiction writer Thomas Bontly (*The Competitor, The Adventures of a Young Outlaw, The Giant's Shadow*); fiction writer John Goulet (*Oh's Profit*); poet William Harrold (*Beyond the Dream, Trails Filled with Lighted Notions*); fiction writer Ellen Hunnicutt (*Suite for Calliope, In the Music Library* -- the Drue Heinz winner for 1987); poet Susan Firer (*My Life with the Czar, Underground Communion Rail, Lives of the Saints and Everything*); poet James Hazard (*The Thief of Kisses, The Outlaw Museum Guide, New Year's Eve in Whiting Indiana*); poet and fiction writer James Liddy (*In a Blue Smoke, A Munster Song of Love and War, A White Thought in a White Shade*); fiction writer Sheila Roberts (*He's My Brother, The Weekenders, This Time of Year*); poet and fiction writer Robert Siegel (*The Beasts and the Elders, In a Pig's Eye, The Kingdom of Wundle*); poet Marilyn Taylor (*Accident of Light, In Shadows Like These*); and nonfiction writer Carolyn Washburne (*Women in Transition, For Better, For Worse, A Multicultural Portrait of Colonial Life*).

Visiting writers and adjunct faculty have included Raymond Carver, Elizabeth Cullinan, Robert Bly, Tim O'Brien, Marvin Bell, James Dickey, Lisel Mueller, Susan Engberg, Robley Wilson, Jr., Gerald Stern, Jack Gilbert, William Heyen, Marge Piercy, Marilyn Hacker, Gordon Weaver, and Eavan Boland.

The program publishes a national literary magazine, *The Cream City Review*, which is edited by graduate students and advised by a faculty board.

From 7 to 10 teaching assistantships are available annually. TA's in the creative writing program normally teach one section of Freshman Composition and one of Introduction to Creative Writing. One project assistantship is also available through the program. The university offers University Fellowships and Advanced Opportunity Fellowships as well as out-of-state tuition remission to a number of qualified students. Applications for financial support must be received by mid-January for the following fall. Applicants not yet admitted to the program should be sure to send a writing sample (30 pages fiction, 20 pages poetry) in addition to other application materials.

For further information on the Creative Writing Program at UWM, contact Thomas Bontly, Coordinator of Creative Writing, <bontly@scd.uwm.edu>.

214

University of Wisconsin, Stevens Pt.
Stevens Point, WI 54481

(715) 346-4757
FAX (715) 346-4215
e-mail: m2willa.uwsp.edu

Degrees offered: BA, BS, MST

Degree: BA or BS in any field with a minor in Writing or Scientific and Technical Writing

Required course of study: The writing program at the University of Wisconsin–Stevens Point is broad and diverse. The minor requires 12-15 credits of writing courses selected from among poetry and fiction writing workshops, freelance writing, outdoor writing, business writing, editing and publishing, advanced expository writing, scientific and technical writing, and independent writing. Students may also choose to specialize with a scientific and technical writing minor.

The English Department offers courses in period literature, literature of the masters, and in-depth studies of poetry, drama, the English novel, and the American novel. In addition to 12-15 credits of writing, the writing minor requires 3 credits in Introduction to the Study of Literature, 3-6 credits in literature, and 3 credits in language study. At least 12 credits must be at the 300-level or higher.

Degree: MST, Master of Science in Teaching English

This is a 30 credit masters program designed for teachers of English. Teachers may select for their program of study a course that has numerous graduate offerings in writing and the teaching of writing. One of the culminating project options is the creation of a portfolio that includes professional and creative writing.

The writing faculty includes Dr. Lawrence Watson (*Montana 1948, In a Dark Time, Leaving Dakota*); Ruth Dorgan, a widely published freelance writer; Dr. Donna Decker, noted for her performance poetry and readings; Dr. William Lawlor (*The Beat Generation: A Bibliographical Teaching Guide, Let's Go Down to the Beach*); poet Dr. Richard H. Behm (*The Book of Moonlight, When the Wood Begins to Move, Simple Explanations*); Dr. Dan Dieterich and Dr. Hank Sparapani (respected writing consultants to industries and businesses across the country; Dieterich also oversees the editing and publishing of manuscripts by students in a course he teaches); Dr. John Coletta (director of the Scientific and Technical Writing Minor).

A student organization, University Writers, provides a forum for students to discuss their writing outside of the classroom. They also sponsor visits to campus by regional and national writers and publish *Barney Street*, the campus literary magazine.

The University of Wisconsin–Stevens Point has one of the oldest writing across the curriculum programs in the nation. It also hosts an annual high school writer's workshop, where the best writers from Wisconsin schools have a chance to discuss their writing and interact with faculty. UWSP is also an affiliate site of the National Writing Project, leading the way in helping teachers improve themselves as writers and teachers of writing.

The English Department at the University of Wisconsin–Stevens Point is also home to a nationally recognized journal, *Issues in Writing*, which publishes articles on writing in Education, Business and Industry, Science and Technology, Government, and the Arts and Humanities. Its goal is to publish work that cuts across the traditional boundaries separating disciplines, genres, and writing traditions.

For more information, please contact Michael Williams, Chairman, Dept. of English, at the above address.

❖University of Wisconsin, Whitewater
800 West Main Street
Whitewater, WI 53190-2121

For more information, contact the Director, Dept. of Modern Languages and Literature.

Wittenberg University
Springfield, OH 45501

(937) 327-7057
FAX (937) 327-6341
e-mail: dix@wittenberg.edu
website: http//www.wittenberg.edu or
www.wittenberg.edu/academics/engl/newpage/
index.html

Degrees offered: (Major, Minor) BA in English, with a Writing Concentration, Writing Minor

Required course of study: 128-132 s/hrs total
Writing Minor: 20 s/hrs (interdisciplinary)
English Major/Writing Concentration: 36 s/hrs; with 16 s/hrs in writing courses (poetry, fiction, playwriting, screenwriting, journalism, creative nonfiction)

Other Requirements: "Gen Ed" requirements (48-50 s/hrs or 12 courses), consistent with liberal arts education. Comprehensive exams in most majors, major theses in many departments. Honors option. Language requirement. Math requirement.

Catalog available free on request: (800) 677-7558, or e-mail: admission@wittenberg.edu.

Application Deadlines: Early Decision, December 15 (binding); Early Action: January 15.

The English major consists of 9 literature courses in a semester system (15 weeks plus exams), distributed over periods, authors, genres, and themes, and includes one methodology course and a capstone Senior Seminar in which majors write a long critical paper. The English Major with a Writing Concentration also consists of 9 courses, with similar distributions, with 3 of the 9 being writing courses (1 intro, 2 upper level), plus the Senior Seminar in which the student compiles a creative writing project in one or more genres. Four regular staff, active in their areas, teach advanced courses in fiction, poetry, playwriting, screenwriting, journalism, technical writing, and creative nonfiction (personal essay, memoir, autobiography, literary journalism, and travel narrative).

The Writing Minor consists of 5 writing courses chosen from across the curriculum, taught by faculty from History, Biology, Business, Sociology, and Theater, as well from the English Department as per above. A training course for peer writing tutors may count here.

Effective writing is seen as an essential part of the liberal arts curriculum at Wittenberg. Writing is emphasized from entrance placement exams on and is monitored by all faculty in all departments across the student's 4-year career. Students receiving a "U" (unsatisfactory writing report) in any course are required to attend the Writers' Workshop, a peer tutoring center -- a free service staffed by trained student writers, available to weak and strong writers alike. (Faculty on occasion avail themselves of Workshop editorial assistance.) Students with U's must submit essays to the University Writing Committee for evaluation and will not graduate until deemed proficient. At least 7 of every student's courses (28 s/hrs) must come from courses designated as "Writing Intensive" (WI in the catalogue, requiring a minimum of 4,000 words of graded writing and rewriting).

Training in Journalism consists of beginning and advanced courses, writing for or holding an editorial position on the weekly *Torch*, and the option of an internship on a city newspaper. Students have been placed on large metropolitan (Washington, Philadelphia) papers as well as local and state, and with area TV stations (Dayton, Columbus). The Journalism program has its own computer network with terminals for every student. Wittenberg does not offer a degree in Journalism *per se*, except as may be designed by individual students. Students may also design their own Communications Major or Minor from selected courses.

The Creative Writing program is extensive; beginning courses are taught (by 3 or more faculty) every term. These may emphasize one major genre but all three (poetry, fiction, and drama) are taught in Beginning Creative Writing. Advanced courses run every semester in these main genres as well as periodically in creative nonfiction, screenwriting, personal essay, and so on. The playwriting course includes actors working for credit; novice playwrights can work from their characters made flesh the same week they're invented. The screenwriting course involves committing a section of script to finished video, edited in continuity style. Independent studies are an option for writers wanting to go beyond the advanced courses -- with Imogene Bolls in poetry, Kent Dixon in fiction and other prose forms, Steve Reynolds in playwrighting, and with other faculty as appropriate. All are published in their fields. An honors thesis is also an option. Between 5 and 10 professional writers visit the campus per year to give readings, workshops, or serve short residencies. In the recent past: Carol Muske, Robert Pinsky, Geoffrey Woolf, Carl Bernstein, Eavan Boland, John Updike, Joyce Carol Oates, Bharati Mukherjee, Nuyorican Poets. Several student plays are selected yearly for full production. Public reading of student creative work is encouraged and is a requirement in the Senior Writing Seminar.

There are annual awards (cash and honor) in different genres, including expository writing and a hybrid Creativity Award. Faculty and students win competitions at state and national levels. Locally, students may find forums for their work (including artwork) in the school literary magazine (*The Witt Review*), the school paper, the East Asian Studies journal, History journal, and *Spectrum*, a journal of expository writing edited by the Writers' Workshop. There are various writing contests throughout the year, e.g., in the Women's Studies Program or the Literary Awards.

For more information, contact either the English Dept., (937) 327-7057, or Dr. Kent Dixon, (937) 327-7069. e-mail: <dix@wittenberg.edu>.

College of Wooster
Wooster, OH 44691
(330) 263-2402

For more information, contact Writing Program Director, Dept. of English.

Wright State University
Dayton, OH 45435
(937) 775-3136

Degrees offered: BA, MA

Degree: BA in English with an Emphasis in Creative Writing

Required course of study: 56 q/hrs in the major (above freshman level)
    Writing workshops: 24 q/hrs
    Literature courses: 32 q/hrs

The BA in English with an Emphasis in Creative Writing is designed to provide the talented undergraduate writer with both extensive workshop experience, frequent consultation with the writing faculty, and traditional study of British and American literature. Production of a publishable collection of stories or poems may be developed through "independent study" in the context of the English Honors program. A number of Creative Writing Scholarships (usually about $1,000) are awarded each year. The national award-winning undergraduate literary magazine, *Nexus*, provides additional editorial and publishing experience for program students.

Creative writing students may also be interested in obtaining an Undergraduate Certificate in Professional Writing, which will be awarded after additional course work (21-22 q/hrs) in Business Writing, Technical Writing, Research Writing, Graphics, Editing for the Media, etc. The certificate may be useful in securing work in business and industry as a technical writer or editor.

Degree: MA in English with Creative Writing Option

Type of Program: Studio/Academic

Required course of study: 48 q/hrs
    Thesis: 8 q/hrs
    Writing workshops: 8 q/hrs
    Other writing courses: 4 q/hrs
    Literature, Composition, and Rhetoric, or TESOL courses: 20 q/hrs

Other Requirements: 8 q/hrs Methods and Materials of Research and History of Literary Criticism or Rhetoric; graduate portfolio.

The MA in English with Creative Writing Option is designed for students of superior ability who wish to combine advanced work in creative writing with study for an MA in one of three concentrations: Literature, Composition and Rhetoric, or TESOL. Students take 28 q/hrs in courses and seminars taught by English Department faculty, and 20 q/hrs in related courses designed for writing students. At least 2 creative writing workshops are required, and the student must complete a creative writing thesis under the direction of a member of the writing staff. The thesis (8 q/hrs credit) should be a work of imaginative writing of substantial length and merit, usually a novel or novella, or a collection of poems and/or short stories. There is no foreign language requirement, but candidates for the degree are required to submit an academic portfolio at the end of the program.

Creative Writing students may also be interested in obtaining a Graduate Certificate in Professional Writing, which will be awarded after additional course work (21-22 q/hrs) in Business Writing, Technical Writing, Research Writing, Graphics, Editing for the Media, etc., along with an internship. This certificate can prove very useful in securing work in business and industry as a technical writer or editor.

Two types of financial aid are available. A limited number of scholarships (up to $1,200 per year) may be awarded to university graduate students on the basis of academic excellence. Graduate teaching assistantships are available: the stipend for first-year assistants is $7,100; for second-year assistants, $7,500.

Creative Writing program faculty include poet Gary Pacernick, author of the collections *Credence* and *The Jewish Poems* and a critical book, *Memory and Fire: Ten American Jewish Poets*, and editor of *Images*, a poetry journal; fiction writer James Thomas, author of *Pictures, Moving*, which was nominated for the Pulitzer Prize, editor of *Sudden Fiction, Sudden Fiction International*, and *Best of the West*, an annual anthology, recipient of 2 NEA grants, a Stegner Fellowship, and a Michener Fellowship; and fiction writer Frank Dobson, author of *The Race Is Not Given* and winner of the 1994 Zora Neal Hurston/Bessie Head Fiction Writers Award.

Students also have the opportunity to meet and hear well-known visiting writers. Visiting writers in the program have included Kenneth Koch, Richard Howard, Howard Nemerov, Marge Piercy, Max Apple, Donald Hall, Robert Bly, John Ashbery, Joy Williams, Grace Paley, Tillie Olsen, Rita Dove, Allen Tate, Margaret Atwood, and Gwendolyn Brooks.

For more information, contact Chris Hall, Director of Graduate Studies, Dept. of English.

❖University of Wyoming
Laramie, WY 82071-3353

(307) 766-6452

Degrees offered: BA, MA

Length of Residency: Two years

Application Deadlines: MA -- March 15 preferred.

The University of Wyoming enrolls 10,000 students in uncrowded classes with low student-to-faculty

ratios and opportunities to study creative writing as an individual interest or part of the BA in English and MA with an emphasis in creative writing. Undergraduate courses include 2 semesters of fiction or poetry writing at introductory to intermediate levels and upper-level workshops.

The MA in English with creative writing concentration combines literary study with substantial work in imaginative writing. Thirty s/hrs of credit are required, with 3-9 s/hrs in advanced writing courses. The remaining s/hrs include American and English literature and a course in criticism, literary theory, or applied linguistics. Before taking an oral examination, students complete creative projects -- typically groups of stories, collections of poetry, short novels, or portions of full-length novels.

The current staff consists of fiction writer, essayist, and journalist Vicki Lindner (*Outlaw Games*, co-author of *The Money Mirror: How Money Reflects Women's Dreams, Fears, and Desires*), fiction writer Alyson Hagy (*Madonna on her Back* and *Hardware River*) and poet, fiction writer, and essayist David Romtvedt (*Crossing Wyoming, How Many Horses, A Flower Whose Name I Do Not Know*). Visiting writers teach both semester- and week-long courses in the spring semester. So far they have included memoirist Hettie Jones, fiction writer Dagoberto Gilb, nonfiction writer, poet, and novelist Rosemary Daniell, Western environmental and nature writer Donald Snow, poet and nonfiction writer Carolyne Wright, dramatist Rosalyn Drexler, video-script writer Edward Robbins, magazine editor Stephanie von Hirschberg, and fiction writer Melanie Rae Thon.

The writing program is enhanced by excellent faculty throughout the Department and solid offerings in literature, criticism, and theory and practice of composition and some professional writing courses. The student-edited *Owen Wister Review* is published twice a year. Teaching assistantships are available to qualified applicants (currently $7,290 a year with full tuition remission). Applicants must submit, by March 15, GRE aptitude scores, undergraduate transcripts, 3 letters of recommendation, and a writing sample.

For further information, contact Keith Hill, Chair, Dept. of English.

❖Xavier University of Louisiana
Palmetto Street
New Orleans, LA 70125

For more information, contact the Director, Dept. of English.

York University
236 Vanier College
Toronto, Ontario, Canada, M3J 1P3

(416) 736-5910, ext. 77020

Degree offered: BA in Creative Writing

Required course of study: 7 courses in the major (42 s/hrs). This includes AS/EN 2020.06 (see below) and 3 full-year workshops in 2 of the following genres: Prose Fiction, Poetry, Playwriting, Screenwriting; and 3 full-year non-workshop courses from a selected list of English, Humanities, and Fine Arts offerings.

Other Requirements: Students are not generally accepted into the major until they are in their third year of studies; however, in the second year, they should normally have taken AS/EN 2020.06 (Introduction to Creative Writing: poetry, prose fiction). In the first 2 years, certain courses in English, Humanities, and Fine Arts are recommended as background and preliminary study. Students who are not majors can take all workshops; entrance to second- and third-year workshops (and fourth-year workshops for non-majors) is by portfolio. In addition to course requirements for the major, students must complete the 13 full-year (elective or non-elective) courses (or their equivalents) required by the University in order to complete their degree.

The Faculty of Arts and the Faculty of Fine Arts offer a program in Creative Writing under the Honours Programme of either Faculty. The primary objective of the Creative Writing Programme is to give students who have the talent and the ambition for a writing career the opportunity to develop the talent significantly and to make it the center of a program of university study. Two major assumptions inform this program: the first that the capabilities of talent can be increased through training and the second that the necessary curriculum for aspirant writers consists of their native language and the writing idioms of past and contemporary writers. The program, therefore, aims in its lower years to acquaint students with the various ways of writing which the leading writers of our time have made possible. Students begin to write in an expanding environment of literary and linguistic knowledge.

In the upper years, the program encourages specialization in one or 2 genres and aims to expose students to the history of formal experimentation and growth in particular genres.

A third objective of the program is to take into account the unpredictability and variety of the interests of writing students. This program permits students to follow idiosyncratic combinations of courses, provided that they can demonstrate to their advisor the relevance of these courses to their writing ambitions.

The program is fortunate to have had as workshop instructors some of the leading writers in Canada, including Governor General's award winners such as poet B.P. Nichol and novelist playwright M.T. Kelly. Distinguished poets such as Don Coles, Frank Davey, Lola Lemire Tostevin, Libby Scheier, and prose writers such as Susan Swan, Michael Ondaatje, Elizabeth Harvor, and Katherine Govier have taught or are at present teaching with us. In addition, the program sponsors a Creative Writing Students' Association and, through Canada Council, a yearly Reading Series in which Canada's best writers are invited to discuss their work.

For more information, contact Dan Summerhayes, Writing Program Coordinator.

❖Youngstown State University
414 Wick Avenue
Youngstown, OH 44555-3415

For more information, contact the Director, Dept. of English.

Conferences
Colonies
&
Centers

● **Indicates members of Writers' Conferences & Festivals**

http://www.gmu.edu/departments/awp/wcf

Amherst Writers & Artists
24 N. Prospect Street
Amherst, MA 01002
(413) 256-0240

Contact: Richard N. Bentley.

●Antioch Writers' Workshop
P.O. Box 494
Yellow Springs, OH 45387
(513) 866-9060

Length of Residency: One week (7 days).

When: Mid-July or late August.

Application Deadline: June 1.

Cost: Tuition $475; room & board not included in the cost of tuition.

Description: The first Antioch Writers' Workshop was held in July 1986, organized by Judson Jerome (poetry columnist for the *Writers' Digest*) and Bill Baker (professor emeritus, Wright State University). The workshop has been held every second week of July since, administered by an independent non-profit organization under a management agreement with Antioch College. Over the past eight years we have developed a national reputation for excellence and congeniality; each workshop includes approximately 110 people, faculty, participants, and volunteer "work fellows" who form a lively, intense community of writers.

We offer classes in fiction, nonfiction, poetry, scriptwriting, and other genres such as writing for children and short-short fiction. Editors and agents are on hand. Opportunities for participants to read and/or have their work read with critique are frequent.

Faculty: 1993 faculty included Joyce Carol Oates (keynote speaker), Joe David Bellamy, Mary Grimm, and Sandra Love (teaching the short story), James Thomas (teaching flash fiction), Ralph Keyes (teaching nonfiction), Stanley Plumly and Imogene Bolls (teaching poetry), George Ella Lyon (teaching Writing for Children), and more.

Financial Assistance: The Judson Jerome Scholarship, administered by *Writers' Digest*, pays tuition, room, and board for the winner of a poetry competition. The Betty Crumrine Scholarship pays tuition only for a local single parent. There are also approximately 15 work fellowships for writers who are local and/or returning.

Contact: Judy Da Polito, Director, can be reached at the above phone numbers and address. A brochure will be mailed upon request.

University of Arizona Poetry Center
Summer Residency Program
1216 North Cherry Avenue
Tucson, AZ 85719
(520) 321-7760
e-mail: poetry@u.arizona.edu
website: http://www.coh.arizona.edu/poetry/

Length of Residency: One month.

When: During months of June, July, and August. Dates chosen by resident.

Application Deadline: February 15 - March 15 postmark annually.

Cost: None.

Description: The Poetry Center provides an individual writer with a place to create in a quiet neighborhood of this southwestern desert city. The guest cottage is an historic adobe located two houses from the nationally acclaimed collections of the University of Arizona Poetry Center, and two blocks from the University campus.

Writers interested in this one month residency should submit no more than 10 pages of poetry or 20 pages of fiction or literary nonfiction. Send three copies of work and SASE for reply. Manuscripts will not be returned. Manuscripts should be typed on white letter-sized paper. Name should not appear on work. Applicant shall not, at time of submission, have published more than one full-length work. Self-published works and chapbooks excepted. Unpublished writers are encouraged to apply.

Manuscripts accompanied by cover letter stating name, address, day/evening phone numbers, and titles of submitted work should be sent to the above address.

Contact: David Penn or Alison Deming.

The Art of Nonfiction Conference
39 Trillium Way
Amherst, MA 01002
(413) 545-5924

Contact: Madeleine Blais, Director.

●Art of the Wild
SVCW/CAS
Box 2352
Olympic Valley, CA 96146
(916) 752-1658

Contact: Jack Hicks, Director.

●Ashland Writers' Conference
295 E. Main, Suite 14
Ashland, OR 97520
(541) 482-2783

Contact: The Director.

Aspen Playwrights' Festival
110 E. Hallam Street, #116
Aspen, CO 81611
(970) 925-3122
(800) 925-2526
FAX: (970) 920-5700

When: Mid-September.

Cost: $350.

Description: Workshops in playwriting for budding and experienced playwrights, craft lectures, talks with directors, producers and agents, readings, Q&A's, special events.

●Aspen Writers' Conference
Drawer 7726
Aspen, CO 81612
(970) 925-3122
(800) 925-2526
e-mail: aspenwrite@aol.com
website: http://www.aspen.com (then click on literature)

Length of Residency: One week.

When: Mid-June.

Application Deadline: No deadline, but space is limited.

Cost: $495; $795 with room and board.

Description: The Aspen Writers' Conference is in its 22nd year and offers small workshops in poetry, fiction, and nonfiction. Writers of all levels of experience are welcome. In addition to small workshops, the Conference includes daily craft lectures, talks with agents, editors, and publishers, evening readings, and special events.

Faculty: 1998 faculty included: Ron Carlson, Janice Eidus, Mary Crow, Bernard Cooper, Jan Greenberg, and Tracy Wynn. Past faculty includes: Derek Walcott, Charles Simic, Jane Smiley, Ed Hirsch, Gerald Stern, Shelby Hearon, Marcia Southwick, Madeleine Blais, and others.

Financial Assistance: Scholarship assistance is available based on available funds -- apply by sending a letter explaining financial need with application.

Contact: Jeanne McGovern, Executive Director.

Aspen Writers' Foundation
110 E. Hallam Street
Aspen, CO 81611
(970) 925-3122
(800) 925-2526

Length of Residency: June 21-26.

When: Writers' Retreat June 21-June 24, Readers and Writers Literary Festival June 24-June 26.

Application Deadline: April 30, 1999.

Cost: Retreat $250, Festival $150.

Description: A four-day writers' retreat (intensive, small workshops with notable faculty authors, plus free time to write) followed by a three-day literary festival (agents, editors, readings, industry talks, receptions, round-table discussions).

Faculty: To be announced January 1999.

Financial Assistance: Some scholarships for retreat are available.

Associated Writing Programs Annual Conference
Tallwood House, Mail Stop 1E3
George Mason University
Fairfax, VA 22030
(703) 993-4301
FAX (703) 993-4302
e-mail: awp@gmu.edu
website: http://web.gmu/.edu/departments/awp

Length of Residency: Three days (Thursday through Saturday).

When: March or April.

Cost: $115 for members of AWP; $135 for non-members; $25 for students. Attendees must pay for their own accommodations.

Description: The Associated Writing Programs (AWP) is a nonprofit organization of writers, teachers, students, and creative writing programs. Each year, in a different city of North America, AWP hosts its Annual Conference, which features: meetings and caucuses for teachers, writers, publishers, and arts administrators; a bookfair; poetry, fiction, and nonfiction readings; a keynote address by a major contemporary writer; panel discussions on a wide range of literary issues; a tribute to a major contemporary writer; and forums on the teaching of creative writing.

AWP also provides other services for writers and teachers including: *The Writer's Chronicle*, a journal of contemporary letters and the teaching of creative writing; the Award Series, a competition for the discovery and publication of excellent new works of fiction, poetry, and creative nonfiction; a *Job List* and career placement service for writers and teachers; competitions for discovering the best student writing and student literary magazines; and advocacy on behalf of freedom of expression, funding for the arts, excellence in teaching, and fair employment practices in higher education.

Contact: Roxanne French-Thornhill for more information on institutional or individual membership, the Annual Conference, or any of AWP's other services.

●Association of Personal Historians
24 North Prospect Street
Amherst, MA 01002
(413) 256-0240

Contact: The Director.

Atlantic Center for the Arts, Inc.
1414 Art Center Avenue
New Smyrna Beach, FL 32168
(904) 427-6975
FAX (904) 427-5669
e-mail: program@atlantic-centerarts.org
website: www.atlantic-centerarts.org

Length of Residency: Three weeks.

When: Five-six times per year.

Application Deadline: Varies; approximately four months prior to residency.

Cost: $800 includes 3-week residency fee and on-site housing ($300 if staying elsewhere).

Description: Atlantic Center for the Arts, an interdisciplinary artists-in-residence community, was established in 1979 for the purpose of providing midcareer artists with the opportunity to work with some of the world's most distinguished master artists. Each residency features three Master Artists from different disciplines -- literature, musical composition, visual arts, and performing arts -- who each work with eight to ten midcareer (Associate) artists. Artists spend three hours/day with their group -- talking, sharing ideas, exchanging, and critiquing -- and the rest of the time working on their art. Collaboration is encouraged but not required. Atlantic Center is situated on 67 acres of lush, tropical vegetation bordering a pristine bay, three miles from the Atlantic Ocean. On-site housing (28 rooms with private baths), discipline-specific work studios, and dining room with commercial-size kitchen are available.

Faculty: The residency program is unstructured by staff. Each residency takes on its own format by the Master and Associate Artists. Former Master Artists include Allen Ginsberg, Marilyn French, Carolyn Forché, Reynolds Price, Sonia Sanchez, John Ashbery, Francine du Plessix Gray, and W.P. Kinsella.

Financial Assistance: Limited scholarships are available. Applicants must first be accepted into the residency program (Master Artists set criteria and make selection). No application fee.

Contact: The Program Department. A mailer listing the year's upcoming residency dates and Master Artists is mailed each August, and throughout the year, as requested. E-mail at above address. Visit our website for a list of upcoming artists, residency information, and application procedures.

●Avalon Writing Center, Inc.
4340 Hideaway Lane
P.O. Box 183
Mills, WY 82644
(307) 235-6177
FAX (307) 235-6177
e-mail: fehanson@juno.com

Length of Residency: Five days, six nights.

When: Third week in July.

Application Deadline: March 1.

Cost: $1,475 including room and board, workshops; late registration $1,585.

Description: Avalon Writing Center, Inc. Writers' Retreat allows the serious writer to focus for five days and six nights entirely upon writing, photography, and renewing the five senses.

This exclusive retreat is held on the historical Mayland Ranch located in the Big Horn Mountains of Wyoming, at remote Snowshoe Lodge, located high above the valley floor. This retreat offers a beautiful setting, rich with opportunities to experience the natural and historical attractions of the region.

Guest workshop leaders yearly; staff of three offers instruction in writing, marketing, and art.

Faculty: Diana Mayland, artist; Frances Hanson, Director; Larry Brown, historian; and Earl Jensen, biology.

Financial Assistance: None.

Contact: Frances E. Hanson, Director.

Banff Centre for the Arts
Office of the Registrar
P.O. Box 1020, Station 28
Banff, AB T0L 0C0 Canada
(403) 762-6180
FAX (403) 762-6345

Length of Residencies: Writing Studio (5 weeks).
Radio Drama Workshop (2 weeks).
Dramatic Writing Workshop (2 weeks).

When: Writing Studio: May/June.
Writing Workshops: November/December.

Application Deadlines: Writing Studio: January 10.
Writing Workshops: July 31.

Cost: Writing Studio: $2,735 CF includes tuition, room, and partial board costs.
Writing Workshops: $1,094 CF includes tuition, room, and partial board costs.

Description: Located in the mountains of Canada's first national park, The Banff Centre for the Arts is a year-round continuing education facility providing a wide range of opportunities for professional artists to develop and expand their creativity.

Applicant will normally have published a body of work (book(s), stories/poems in magazines or anthologies), and will be working on a book-length manuscript or a manuscript-in-progress. They will be interested in working with an editor during their Banff residency.

Workshop residents will develop original scripts with editorial help from the program editor. Final scripts will be given a reading by professional actors.

Enrollment to the Writing Studio is limited to 20. Enrollment to the Writing Workshops is limited to 5.

Faculty: Noted Canadian faculty, by appointment.

Financial Assistance: By application. Maximum award includes tuition, room, and a portion of the board costs.

Contact: Contact the Office of the Registrar for more information and the required application form.

Beyond Baroque Literary/Arts Center
P.O. Box 2727
681 Venice Boulevard
Venice, CA 90291
(310) 822-3006
FAX (310) 827-7432
website: www.beyondbaroque.org

When: Ongoing writing workshops with local and visiting writers.

Cost: Some are free, some are paid.

Description: Beyond Baroque was founded in 1968. It is the leading literary arts center in Southern California. It presents more than 80 weekly readings per year, offers weekly free workshops and monthly open readings, houses an active small press bookstore (12,000 volumes), and small press library, publishes occasional chapbooks, anthologies, and magazines, and presents interdisciplinary programs including theatre, film, music, and gallery exhibitions. Beyond Baroque is committed to promoting the writing, presentation, publication, and distribution of a full range of literary works by contemporary living artists. It is a nationally recognized center for innovative contemporary literature and locally serves as a dynamic venue for readings, performances, books, film, and visual art. It is one of the few national sites that archives and sells chapbooks. (Donations accepted.)

Contact: Pi Ware, fiction workshop, Jessica Pompei, poetry workshop, and Allan M. Jalon, poetry workshop.

●Blooming Grove Writers' Conference
P.O. Box 515
Bloomington, IL 61702
(309) 438-2816

Length of Residency: One week.

When: Usually first week of August each year.

Application Deadline: For reduced fee, and for manuscript submission: June 30 (we encourage manuscript submission because of the nature of the program).

Cost: $25 pre-registration fee; $25 per manuscript, both non-returnable; $200 conference fee; room/board package is about $145-150 for the week (Sunday afternoon through Friday afternoon); commuters may purchase individual meals.

Description: The conference is a teaching-learning experience with morning classes in fiction, nonfiction, poetry, and writing for children/youth (including picture book writing and illustrating). Small afternoon workshops on the same areas, limited to 15 persons in each workshop, focus on participants' manuscripts. Two instructors read, critique, and hold individual evaluation sessions with each person submitting a manuscript in advance (by June 30).

The conference also includes marketing seminars with editors and agents, trade and small/literary press; open mike readings; and evening programs by instructors and special guest writers. Instructors are invited who are excellent writers and teachers.

Faculty: Past workshop/class instructors have included Phyllis Barber, Harry Mard Petrakis, Ellen Hunnicutt, Eve Shelnutt, Janet Burroway, Madeleine L'Engle, Bill Nelson, Michael Dorman, Brigit Pegeen Kelly, Ralph Burns, Grace Butcher, Fred Shafer, Kevin Stein, Lucia Getsi, James Cross Giblin, Dorothy Haas, Stephanie Lurie, Avi, Val Gregory, Bobette McCarthy, Sharon Fiffer, Sharon Solwitz, Sandy Asher, Paul Darcy Boles.

Financial Assistance: A limited number of partial scholarships are available; limited assistance for youth 14 and up. Purpose of the program is to help writers, both beginners and experienced, to writer better. Thus, we emphasize manuscript assistance, contacts with leadership, and a conference fee that entitles participants to the total program offered.

Contact: Director at address and telephone above, for information and brochures. Newsletters are also available.

Blue Mountain Center
Route 28, Box 109
Blue Mountain Lake, NY 12812
(518) 352-7391

Length of Residency: 4 weeks.

When: 4 sessions are held between approx. June 15-Oct. 31.

Application Deadline: February 1.

Cost: Voluntary contribution; $20 application fee.

Description: 14 artists and writers live and work at the Center for 4 weeks. Room and meals are provided. The Center is located in the Adirondack Mountains, in a quiet wooded setting on a lake. The Admissions Committee is especially interested in writers whose work shows social and environmental concern.

Contact: Harriet Barlow, Director.

Boise State University Writers & Readers Rendezvous
Boise State University
Office of Continuing Education
1910 University Drive
Boise, ID 83725
(208) 385-1639

Length of Residency: 3 days.

When: Held in October of each year.

Application Deadline: Contact BSU Office of Continuing Education.

Cost: $100; room is extra.

Description: The BSU Writers & Readers Rendezvous takes place annually each October in the Idaho resort community of McCall on Payette Lake. Each year writers and readers gather for readings, panels, and workshops. Optional credit is available through Boise State University Office of Continuing Education.

Faculty: Past faculty has included: Richard Shelton, William Kittredge, Annick Smith, Judith Freeman, Robert Wrigley, Clay Morgan, Pam Houston, Ridley Pearson, Marilynne Robinson, Gary Gildner, Mary Clearman Blew, and others.

Contact: Above address.

●The Bread Loaf Writers' Conference
Middlebury College
Middlebury, VT 05753
(802) 443-5286
e-mail: blwc@middlebury.edu
website: http://www.middlebury.edu/~blwc

Length of Residency: Eleven days.

When: August 11–22, 1999.

Application Deadline: April 1st for financial aid applications.

Cost: $1,690 (1998).

Description: The Conference provides an opportunity for dialogue among established and beginning writers; the program consists of lectures, workshops, classes, meetings with visiting editors and literary agents, informal conversation.

Faculty (1999): Nonfiction: Clark Blaise, Patricia Hampl. Poetry: Michael Collier, Toi Derricotte, Edward Hirsch, Carl Phillips, Alan Shapiro, Jane Shore, Ellen Bryant Voigt. Fiction: Andrea Barrett, Richard Bausch, Jennifer Egan, Percival Everett, Margot Livesey, Thomas Mallon, Bharati Mukherjee, Howard Norman, C.E. Poverman, Helena Maria Viramontes.

Financial Assistance: We offer three types of financial aid. Fellowships are awarded to writers who have published a first original book; scholarships are offered to published writers who have not published a first book. Work-study scholarships are given to unpublished but promising writers. There is no application fee.

Contact: Mrs. Carol Knauss.

Breaking Into Movies Conference
2001 NW 32nd Street
Oklahoma City, OK 73118
(405) 528-7836

Contact: Karl Grant.

Bucknell Seminar for Younger Poets
Stadler Center for Poetry, Bucknell Hall
Bucknell University
Lewisburg, PA 17837
(717) 524-1853

Length of Residency: Four weeks.

When: June and July.

Application Deadline: March 1.

Cost: Bucknell will provide tuition, room, board, and places for writing. Fellows are responsible for their own transportation.

Description: The Seminar provides an extended opportunity for undergraduates to write and to be guided by established poets. It balances private time for writing, disciplined learning, and camaraderie among the Fellows. Staff poets conduct two workshops each week, offer readings of their own verse, and are available for tutorials. Fellows also give poetry readings. Students from American colleges who have completed their sophomore, junior, or senior years may compete for eight fellowships. Applications should include academic transcript, two supporting recommendations (at least one should be from a poetry-writing instructor), and a 10-12 page portfolio. A letter of self-presentation (a brief autobiography stressing commitment to poetry writing, experience, and any publications) should accompany the application. If the applicant wishes to have the portfolio returned, a stamped, self-addressed envelope should be enclosed.

Faculty: Cynthia Hogue, director; Nicole Cooley, co-director; Deirdre O'Connor, seminar associate; Steven Styers, assistant to the director; and the visiting poet-in-residence.

Financial Assistance: See above.

Contact: Cynthia Hogue, Director.

●Bumbershoot Arts Festival
P.O. Box 9750
Seattle, WA 98109
(206) 281-7788

Contact: The Director.

California Writers' Club
2214 Derby Street
Berkeley, CA 94705
(510) 841-1217

Length of Residency: Weekend: Friday noon through Sunday lunch.

When: July of each year.

Contact: Dorothy Benson.

Cape Cod Writers' Center
c/o Cape Cod Conservatory
Route 132
West Barnstable, MA 02668
(508) 375-0516

Length of Residency: One week.

When: Late August.

Cost: Approximately $600 including housing/meals.

Financial Assistance: 4 scholarships.

Contact: Joseph A. Ryan, Executive Director.

●Catskill Poetry Workshop
Hartwick College
Oneonta, NY 13820

Length of Residency: One week.

When: July.

Cost: $750, including room and board.

Description: The Catskill Poetry Workshop offers an opportunity for talented writers to apply themselves to the craft and art of poetry in a supportive atmosphere. The seven-day program includes workshops, classes on craft, evening readings by staff and guest writers, and individual instructional conferences, assuring sustained dialogue with the faculty.

Contact: The Director.

Centrum Artist-in-Residency Program
P.O. Box 1158
Fort Worden State Park, WA 98368
(360) 385-3102

Length of Residency: One month.

When: September–May.

Application Deadline: October 1.

Cost: $10 application fee.

Description: Each year, between fifteen and twenty artists are selected for fully-subsidized one-month residencies, including housing, studio space (where applicable), a stipend of $300 and $100 toward materials for visual artists using the printmaking studio.

All residencies take place at Fort Worden State Park and Conference Center, where Centrum leases space from the State of Washington for artistic and educational programs. Fort Worden is a 440-acre park less than two miles from downtown Port Townsend on Washington's Olympic Peninsula. Resident housing is in modest, self-contained cottages, an easy walk from beaches, tennis courts, and miles of wooded hiking trails.

Following the October 1 deadline, new applications will be juried by a panel representing various disciplines.

Contact: Marlene Bennett.

●Charleston Writers' Conference
English Department
College of Charleston
Charleston, SC 29424
(803) 953-5664
e-mail: allenp@copc.edu

When: Mid-March.

Cost: $125, $50 individual manuscript critique, $20 paper critique workshop. Local hotels are $75-$89.

Description: Morning workshops and special presentations. Afternoon panels on publishing, genre, and the writing life.

Faculty: In 1998, Bret Lott, Abigail Thomas, David Todd, W.D. Wetherell, Cornelius Eady, Lola Haskins, Linda Lee Harper, Thomas Lynch, Tom Paxton, Suzanne McDermott, Judith Appelbaum, and Jennifer Robinson.

Contact: The Director.

Chattanooga Conference on Southern Literature
P.O. Box 4203
Chattanooga, TN 37405-0203
(423) 267-1218
(800) 267-4232
website: www.newschannel9.com/aec

When: Thursday, Friday, Saturday, April 15-17, 1999.

Cost: $35 per person; $25 for students and senior citizens.

Description: The Chattanooga Conference on Southern Literature invites to Chattanooga a number of critically-acclaimed writers of southern fiction, criticism and poetry. Since its inception in 1981, this biennial event has attracted over 50 writers for the purpose of discussing their works in lecture and on panels. Additionally, the Fellowship of Southern Writers convenes during the Chattanooga conference to confer awards in fiction, non-fiction, poetry, drama, and for lifetime achievement.

Contact: Arts & Education Council, Susan Robinson, Executive Director.

Clarion West Writers' Workshop
340 15th Avenue East, Suite 350
Seattle, WA 98112
(206) 322-9083

Length of Residency: Six weeks.

When: Mid–June through July.

Application Deadline: April 1.

Cost: $1,400 ($1,300 if application received by March 1). Dormitory housing is about $800, not including meals. There is a $25 application fee.

Description: The Clarion West Writers' Workshop prepares writers for professional science fiction and fantasy writing careers. It has been held annually at Seattle Central Community College since 1984. Twenty students are selected based on their fiction writing samples. Instructors for each week are established writers and editors in the field. Recent instructors include: Terry Bisson, Pat Cadigan, Ellen Datlow, Samuel R. Delany, Gardner Dozois, Geoff Ryman, Lucius Shepard, and Connie Willis. Classroom emphasis is on critiquing stories written at the workshop, supplemented by open discussions and personal conferences. Seattle offers an active literary and cultural life.

Financial Assistance: A limited number of partial scholarships are available. Optional academic credit is available through Western Washington University. Contact Clarion West for application procedure.

Colorado Mountain Writers' Workshop
Colorado Mountain College
Spring Valley Center, 3000 County Road 114
Glenwood Springs, CO 81601
(970) 945-7481

Contact: Doug Evans, Director.

The Concord Writing Center
57 Main Street
Concord, MA 01742
(508) 287-4042

Contact: The Director.

Craft of Writing Conference
University of Texas at Dallas
Greater Dallas Writer's Association
P.O. Box 830688 CN1.1
Richardson, TX 75083-0688
(214) 883-2204

Length of Residency: 2 days.

When: September.

Application Deadline: July 19 for manuscript contest or first day of conference.

Cost: $195 (includes one lunch and banquet).

Description: Writers and aspiring writers may choose from 28 workshops dealing with all aspects of writing, from query letters to characterization, from screenplays to dealing with an agent. We present information on getting published and how to produce publishable work. A manuscript contest with cash prizes is held in conjunction with the conference. Categories for submission include novel, contemporary romance, historical romance, science fiction/fantasy/horror novel, mystery/suspense, western/action/adventure, short story, children/young adult, nonfiction book, and screenplay. Manuscript critique sessions are also held where participants may bring a work in progress. Past presenters include Millard Lamell, Denise Marcil, A.W. Gray, Monica Harris, Peter Rubie, and Anne Dunn.

Financial Assistance: One conference fee with a special manuscript contest for someone taking a writing course.

Contact: Janet Harris, Director, Continuing Education, University of Texas at Dallas.

Cuesta College Writers' Conference
P.O. Box 8106
San Luis Obispo, CA 93403
(805) 546-3176

Length of Residency: 2 days.

When: Mid-September.

Application Deadline: September 16.

Cost: $70.

Description: The Writers' Conference offers 28 separate workshops on a broad range of topics, including fiction, poetry, screenwriting, nonfiction, agenting, children's literature, new technology, and legal issues. Program also includes two major keynote speakers and a closing session where participants and workshop leaders interact in small groups.

Beautiful San Luis Obispo is a quiet resort town, located exactly midway between Los Angeles and San Francisco.

Faculty: Carol Higgins Clark, Paula Huson, Leonard Tourney, Earlene Fowler, Elisabeth Spurr, Catherine Ryan Hyde, Robert F. Gish, Anne Sheldon, and Michael Vidor.

Financial Assistance: None available.

Contact: Connie Wambolt, Community Education, Cuesta College.

●Cumberland Valley Fiction Writers' Workshop
Dickinson College
P.O. Box 1773
Carlisle, PA 17013-2896
(717) 245-1291
FAX (717) 245-1942

Length of Residency: One week (6 days).

When: Third week of June.

Application Deadline: May 15 for submitting manuscripts; applications are accepted until spaces are filled on first-come basis.

Cost: $400 for tuition, $200 for a room on campus.

Description: The first Cumberland Valley Fiction Writers Workshop was held in June 1990. The Workshop provides the serious aspiring fiction writer an opportunity to work closely with an established fiction writer who is also an experienced teacher. Participants meet with the same writer throughout the week in small workshops (limited to 10 participants each) to have their manuscripts read and critiqued; in addition to workshop sessions, participants meet in individual conferences with their workshop teacher. The week's activities include evening readings by faculty, a Writers Roundtable in which faculty respond to questions submitted by participants, social get-togethers and free time to explore local attractions (hiking on the Appalachian Trail, visiting the Gettysburg battlefield, canoeing on the Juniata River, flyfishing on the LeTort and Yellow Breeches creeks).

Faculty: Faculty are chosen on the basis of the quality of their writing and teaching, their openness and accessibility. Faculty have included Lee K. Abbott, Madison Smartt Bell, Patricia Henley, Colum McCann, Jay McInerney, Debra Monroe, Lorrie Moore, Robert Olmstead, Michael Parker, Janet Peery, Melissa Pritchard, Sheila Schwartz, Darcey Steinke, and Paul Watkins.

Financial Assistance: None.

Contact: Judy Gill, Director (e-mail: <gill@dickinson.edu>). Brochure with application form will be sent upon request. Brochure and application form available online at our website, <http://www.dickinson.edu/departments/engl/cvfww.html>.

Deep South Writers Conference
English Department
University of Southwestern Louisiana
P.O. Box 44691
Lafayette, LA 70504-4691
(318) 482-6906

Length of Residency: 4 days.

When: Third weekend in September.

Application Deadline: Usually pre-registration ends September 1, but participants may register up to day of conference for added fee.

Cost: $25–$40 without workshops. Workshops are an additional $40.

Description: Writers' conference with readings, craft lectures, and workshops in poetry, fiction, nonfiction, children's literature, and drama.

Faculty: Varies from year to year, but always includes members of USL's faculty: Burton Raffel, Sheryl St. Germain, and Darrell Bourque. Past invited faculty have included Robert Hass, Brenda Hillman, Tim O'Brien, Gerald Stern, Kelly Cherry, Berthe Amoss, and James Dickey.

Financial Assistance: No financial assistance available.

Contact: Jack Ferstel.

Desert Writers Workshop at Pack Creek Ranch
Canyonlands Field Institute
P.O. Box 68
Moab, UT 84532
(801) 259-7750
(800) 860-5262
website: www.canyonland.fieldinst.org

Length of Residency: Three and a half days.

When: Early November.

Application Deadline: Early October.

Cost: $440 (includes lodging and meals).

Description: Canyonlands Field Institute is a nonprofit educational organization which promotes a better understanding and respect for the fragile and unique cultural and natural history of the Colorado Plateau. The goal of our annual Desert Writers Workshop is to address the vital connection between humans and the natural world. We offer sections in nonfiction, fiction, and poetry.

Faculty: Past instructors include William Kittredge, Richard Shelton, William Stafford, Terry Tempest Williams, Ron Carlson, Craig Lesley, Linda Hogan, Ann Zwinger, Pam Houston, and Alison Hawthorne Deming.

Dobie Paisano Fellowship Project
Dobie House, 702 E. Dean Keeton Street
Austin, TX 78705
(512) 471-8542

Length of Residency: Six months.

When: September–February, March–August.

Application Deadline: January 22.

Cost: $10 application fee; no cost to fellow for residency except long distance telephone.

Description: An annual fellowship available to writers, providing a living allowance and free residence at Frank Dobie's ranch, Paisano, outside Austin, Texas. Two six-month fellowships with $1,200 a month living allowance are awarded. Applicants must submit sample of their writing with outline of work they expect to accomplish at Paisano. Available to native Texans, persons who have lived in Texas 2 years, or persons whose published work has Texas as the subject.

Financial Assistance: $7,200 living allowance for six months.

Contact: Dr. Audrey N. Slate, Director.

Dorland Mountain Arts Colony
P.O. Box 6
Temecula, CA 92593
(909) 676-5039
FAX (909) 696-2855
e-mail: dorland@ez2.net

Length of Residency: 1–2 months.

When: All year.

Application Deadline: March 1 & September 1.

Cost: $300 per month, 1/2 is required six months prior to residency; $50 non-refundable scheduling fee.

Description: Dorland is located on a 300 acre nature preserve in foothills overlooking the Temecula Valley of Southern California. The tranquil environment provides uninterrupted time to writers, playwrights, composers, visual artists, sculptors, and other artists for serious concentrated work in their respective fields. Residents are housed in individual rustic cottages with private baths and kitchens. Propane gas is provided for cooking, refrigeration, and hot water. Lighting is by kerosene lamps and heat by wood stoves. There is no electricity.

Dorland encourages multicultural and multidiscipline applications. Applications and guidelines are available at our website or send SASE to above address.

Contact: Admissions.

DownEast Maine Writer's Workshop
P.O. Box 446
Stockton Springs, ME 04981
(207) 567-4317
FAX (207) 567-3023
e-mail: 6249304@mcimail.com

Length of Residency: 3 or 7 days.

When: May, July, October.

Description: DownEast Maine Writer's Workshops take place on 3-day holiday weekends and during the long July 4th week. They are: "Writing for the Children's Market," (3 days); "Fiction," (3 days); "Nonfiction," (3 days); "Creative Writing," (7 days); and "How to Get Your Writing Published," (3 days). These limited-sized workshops are individually geared to those who are always promising to get serious about their writing, published authors needing motivation, and aspiring writers struggling to change rejections into acceptances. If for some reason students can't attend complete 3- or 7-day programs, they can register for the specific days they believe will be the most valuable. Students may attend either Fiction, Nonfiction, or the all-inclusive "Creative Writing" workshop.

Duke Writers' Workshop
The Bishop's House
Duke University
Durham, NC 27708
(919) 684-6259

Length of Residency: Five days.

When: Late June.

Application Deadline: May 15.

Cost: $695 includes room and board.

Description: The Duke Writers' Workshop offers you a week of intensive focus on creative writing as a two-part process -- the *art* of writing (the discovery of your individual materials and voice), and the *craft* of writing (the shaping of your imaginative materials into a form which is accessible to a larger audience). Admission to the Workshop is on a first-come first-served basis, rather than by competition. We believe that if you are serious enough about your writing to make the commitment to attend, you should be so honored by our faculty's best efforts. Admission, however, is limited to a small group -- 8-12 people -- depending on the genre. Our faculty has accepted the responsibility to challenge you to grow according to your own personal objective for the week. Toward this end, criticism and instruction are balanced. A spirit of generosity and support, rather than competitiveness, is the atmosphere we seek to cultivate during the week. Small group morning meetings are devoted to lecture and round-table critique of student's works-in-progress and in-class assignments. You will also receive a private half-hour conference with your primary instructor. Large group meetings are held several evenings during the week for readings and discussion. This conference is now held in a beautiful retreat center on the North Carolina beach.

Faculty are mostly from North Carolina and are members of our creative writing staff for year-round courses.

Contact: Georgann Eubanks, <geubanks@mail.duke.edu>.

Eastern Kentucky University Creative Writing Conference
English Department
Eastern Kentucky University
Richmond, KY 40475
(606) 622-5861

Length of Residency: One week.

When: Third week in June.

Application Deadline: May 20.

Cost: $80 undergraduate and audit; $115 graduate (Kentucky students); $220 out-of-state students; Dormitory rooms rent for $39 (double) and $55 (single) per week.

Description: The Eastern Kentucky University Writing Conference was founded in 1962 by Byno Rhodes for writers to enjoy fellowship and manuscript criticism together. William Sutton took over in 1972, and directed the conference for 20 years. The emphasis is on smallness (12-15 writers) and individual attention. Mornings are given over to reading, writing, and manuscript revision. Afternoons and evenings are for lectures, workshops, and readings by outstanding writers. EKU is located in the world-famous Bluegrass Region of Kentucky.

Faculty: Past workshop teachers and visiting writers have included Donald Justice, Richard Marius, Guy Owens, Gregory Orr, David Citino, Maura Staunton, and Gordon Weaver. EKU faculty on the staff include William Sutton, Harry Brown, Dorothy Sutton, Hal Blythe, and Charlie Sweet.

Contact: Please send SASE to Harry Brown, Director, for more information and a brochure outlining registration procedures.

The Edward F. Albee Foundation
14 Harrison Street
New York, NY 10013
(212) 226-2020

Length of Residency: One month.

When: June, July, August, September.

Application Deadline: Applications accepted between January 1 and April 1.

Cost: None.

Description: The Foundation maintains the William Flanagan Memorial Creative Persons Center (better known as "The Barn") in Montauk, on Long Island in New York, as a residence for writers, painters, sculptors, and composers. The Center is presently open from June 1st to October 1st, and can accommodate comfortably five persons at a time. Residencies are for one month periods of time. The standards for admission are, simply, talent and need. Located approximately two miles from the center of Montauk and the Atlantic Ocean, "The Barn" rests in a secluded knoll which offers privacy and a peaceful atmosphere. The Foundation expects all those accepted for residence to work seriously and to conduct themselves in such a manner as to aid fellow residents in their endeavors. Writers and composers are offered a room; visual artists are offered a room and studio space. Residents are responsible for their food, travel, and other expenses. The environment is simple and communal. Residents are expected to do their share in maintaining the condition of "The Barn" as well as its peaceful environment.

Financial Assistance: The Foundation offers residencies only; no financial grants or scholarships are available.

Contact: David Briggs.

Environmental Writing Institute
Environmental Studies Program
Rankin Hall
University of Montana
Missoula, MT 59802
(406) 243-2904

Length of Residency: Five days.

When: Late May.

Application Deadline: March 31.

Cost: $550.

Description: The Environmental Writing Institute was created in 1989 to provide a forum for environmental essayists, journalists, scientists, outdoor writers, and natural historians to gather from around the country and share ideas through their writing. It is limited to 14 participants who have successfully competed for space in the Institute through the manuscripts they submit with their application. The Institute is co-sponsored by the Environmental Studies Program at the University of Montana and the Teller Wildlife Refuge in Corvallis, Montana, about 40 miles from the University. Participants in the Environmental Writing Institute meet and live in remodeled, rustic farm buildings at the edge of 1,300 acres of timbered riverbottom, croplands, and uplands. Above the Refuge rise the castellated peaks of the Bitterroot Range.

Faculty: The Environmental Writing Institute is directed by an environmental writer of national distinction. In 1996, Richard Nelson was the director.

Financial Assistance: If their manuscripts are competitive, one or two graduate students from the University of Montana are admitted with scholarships to the Institute. For the other participants, there are no scholarships available through the Institute.

Contact: Hank Harrington, Environmental Studies Program, University of Montana, Missoula, MT 59812; <e-mail: hrh@selway.umt.edu>.

Feminist Women's Writing Workshop, Inc.
P.O. Box 6583
Ithaca, NY 14851

Length of Residency: Eight days.

When: Mid-July.

Application Deadline: May 15th.

Cost: $595, tuition, room, and board.

Description: Summer Conference held annually at Hobart/William Smith Colleges in Geneva, NY. Workshops, critique sessions, solitude for writing. Women of all genres, whether novice, emerging, or published welcome. A safe, encouraging environment. Private rooms and meals provided.

Financial Assistance: Send letter with financial needs, writing sample. Some partial fee scholarships available.

Contact: Margo Gumosky and Kit Wainer, Co-directors.

●Fine Arts Work Center in Provincetown
24 Pearl Street
Provincetown, MA 02657
(508) 487-9960
e-mail: fawc@capecod.net

Length of Residency: One week.

When: June 20 to August 28, 1999.

Application Deadline: Open enrollment.

Cost: Tuition $425, housing $400.

Description: Week-long courses in creative writing and visual arts. Call for a complete catalog.

●Fine Arts Work Center in Provincetown
24 Pearl Street, Box 565
Provincetown, MA 02657
(508) 487-9960

Length of Residency: Seven months.

When: October 1 – May 1.

Application Deadline: February 1.

Description: The Fine Arts Work Center in Provincetown awards fellowships each year to 10 writers and 10 visual artists. Fellows are selected based on the quality of work submitted. Though there is no age limit, the Center aims to aid emerging talents of outstanding promise who have completed their formal training and are already working on their own.

Fellows are provided with living space at the Center and a small monthly stipend from October 1 to May 1. There are no classes or workshops. Members of the Writing Committee are available to Fellows for manuscript consultations. Throughout the season there is a series of readings by distinguished visiting writers.

The Center was created to encourage and support writers through its belief that the freedom to work without distraction in a community of peers is the best condition for creative growth.

Contact: Send SASE to Fine Arts Work Center.

●Fishtrap, Inc.
P.O. Box 38
Enterprise, OR 97828
(503) 426-3623
e-mail: fishtrapor@aol.com

When: Mid–July.

Cost: Workshop $220, Gathering $175.

Description: The Fishtrap week begins with eight workshops. Workshops are three hours/day for four days; limit 12 per workshop. Emphasis on writing here, not manuscript review. Gathering is theme oriented. 1998's theme was "Work," featuring writers who write about their own work: cops, soldiers, technocrats, and farmers.

Faculty: Recent seasons have included Dorianne Laux, Valerie Miner, Kent Anderson, Luis Alberto Urrea, and Maynard Lavadour.

Financial Assistance: Five fellowships (inquire for need based scholarships).

Contact: The Director.

The Flight of the Mind
622 S.E. 29th Avenue
Portland, OR 97214
(503) 236-9862
FAX (503) 233-0774
e-mail: soapston@teleport.com

Length of Residency: Two separate one-week workshops.

When: Last two weeks in June.

Application Deadline: April 19 (late applications accepted).

Cost: $785 for one week, includes single room and all meals ($595 for dorm room and all meals).

Description: Since 1983, the Flight of the Mind has offered two week-long workshops each summer (five classes each session with 12 to 14 participants in each). Classes meet for three hours daily. Evening programs include readings and presentations by workshop leaders and participants. Fees include all workshops, accommodations, all meals, and all evening programs.

The workshops are held at a retreat center on the scenic McKenzie River in the foothills of the Oregon Cascades. In their spare time, participants can take hikes, go river rafting, soak in hot springs, and explore nearby lakes, waterfalls, and lava beds.

The Flight of the Mind attracts women from many cultures and lifestyles, ranging in age from early twenties to over eighty. The workshop leaders bring a feminist philosophy to their work as writers and teachers, and encourage the creation of a group that is cohesive and supportive.

Past workshop teachers have included: Ursula K. LeGuin, Grace Paley, Lynne Sharon Schwartz, Rosellen Brown, Olga Broumas, Lucille Clifton, Toi Derricotte, Naomi Shihab Nye, Elizabeth Woody, and Judith Barrington.

Financial Assistance: Several scholarships are offered in varying amounts.

Contact: Judith Barrington, Director. Brochures are mailed in mid-January. To get on the mailing list, send your name and address along with a first class stamp.

●Florida Suncoast Writers' Conference
Department of English
University of South Florida
Tampa, FL 33620
(813) 974-2403

Length of Residency: Three days.

When: Early February.

Cost: $135 for three days or $50 for single day.

Description: The Florida Suncoast Writers' Conference, first held in 1972, is a how-to-do-it program on the art of writing, conducted for aspiring and published writers by professional authors, editors, publishers, agents, and other figures active in the literary world. A keynote address by a celebrated literary figure is followed by more than 50 workshops offered over the three-day period. Topics include the Novel, the Short Story, Poetry, Nonfiction Books and Articles, Memoir, Mystery and Suspense, Science Fiction, Screenwriting, Children's and Young Adult Literature, and various other subjects relating to today's markets and opportunities for writers. There are also special programs and social events, including a banquet on the second evening. Such events are planned to afford ample opportunity for exchanging ideas and making and renewing friendship. Situated on the St. Petersburg campus of the University of South Florida, the conference provides a lovely bayfront setting that is generally accompanied by the ideal weather of Florida in February. The campus is convenient to nearby hotels, as well as such places of interest as the Salvador Dali Museum and the Museum of Fine Arts. Beaches are only 15 minutes away. Approximately 400 participants attend the Conference, and over 20 literary professionals (novelists, poets, agents, screenwriters, etc.) serve as workshop leaders.

Past speakers and workshop presenters include John Updike, Marvin Bell, William Styron, P.D. James, David Guterson, Jeffrey Good, Carolyn Forché, Marge Piercy, Sonia Sanchez, and Edward Albee.

Financial Assistance: Scholarships are awarded to local full-time students.

Contact: Please contact Steve Rubin, Director, for further information.

●The Frost Place's Annual Festival of Poetry
Ridge Road
Franconia, NH 03580
(603) 823-5510

Length of Residency: Seven days.

When: Early August.

Application Deadline: Mid-July.

Cost: Approx. $425 tuition (not including room and board).

Description: Begun in 1977, the annual Festival of Poetry is held at Robert Frost's 1915 farm, eight acres of woods, fields, and lawn overlooking the White Mountains. A summer resident-poet is joined by nine nationally established poets to be faculty to 45 participants. Daily lectures, workshops, and readings.

Faculty: Recent seasons have included Amy Clampitt, Donald Hall, Sydney Lea, Molly Peacock, William Matthews, Jane Kenyon, and many others.

Financial Assistance: Budget payment of tuition.

Contact: Executive Director.

●Green Lake Christian Writers Conference
Green Lake Conference Center/American Baptist Assembly
Highway 23
Green Lake, WI 54941-9599
(414) 294-3323
(800) 558-8898

Length of Residency: One week.

When: Early July.

Application Deadline: June 15.

Cost: $85 program fee plus $438 for room and meals.

Description: Since 1948 this annual conference has served writers by providing instructors who are published authors and experienced at being both friend and coach. Instructors are happy to work with manuscripts and make marketing suggestions when required. A highlight of the week is the closing session when many of the writings are shared at a closing night "Showcase."

Workshops will be offered in Poetry, Essays, Finding and Developing the Writer in You and Devotional Writing. Other sessions will be devoted to subjects like Marketing What You Write, Writing the Nonfiction Article, Writing for Children, Biographical Writing and Revision.

Faculty: Robin Chapman-Prof. U/W Madison, Poetry; Gianfranco Pagnucci-Prof. of English U/W Platteville, Life Studies, Essays; Lenore Coberly-Teacher of Creative Writing, Madison, Developing the Writer in You; Melvin Lorentzen-Author, Carol Stream, IL, Biography, Inspiration, plus many more.

Financial Assistance: Little is usually available.

Contact: Jan DeWitt, Vice President of Program.

Green River Writers, Inc.
Novels-In-Progress Workshop
11906 Locust Road
Middletown, KY 40243
(502) 245-4902

Length of Residency: One week.

When: Third week of March, 1999.

Application Deadline: January 15, 1999.

Cost: $350 tuition, $22 per night housing (private, shared bath), $20 per night housing (shared). Meals not provided, though fridge & microwave are available, restaurants nearby.

Description: This ninth annual Novels-in-Progress Workshop is comprised of 5 to 7 small groups of participants (5-7 in group) each working with the published novelist of his/her choice, Monday through Friday. The weekend is given over to activities involving agents and editors, with an opportunity for those with finished manuscripts to have samples read and evaluated by agents & editors.

Faculty: In the past we have had such writers as Steve Womack, Betty Receveur, Jim Wayne Miller, Elaine Palencia, Bob Mayer, Gary Devon, Sara Frommer, etc.

Financial Assistance: Little financial assistance available at this point; those interested should contact Mary O'Dell, Director, as we do have a scholarship fund in place and are accepting contributions.

Contact: Mary E. O'Dell, Director, for a registration form and information.

Green River Writers, Inc.
11906 Locust Road
Middletown, KY 40243
(502) 245-4902

Length of Residency: One week.

When: Mid-July.

Application Deadline: July 12.

Cost: $75 for all week, $55 workshop weekend only, $20 retreat only (nonmembers); $22 per night private w/semiprivate bath, $20 shared room. Meals not provided, though fridge and microwave are available, restaurants nearby.

Description: This retreat begins with a workshop weekend during which professional writers hold workshops and critiquing/editing sessions. Following is a week of retreat during which participants write, read and peer-critique. Impromptu participant-led workshops are held at will.

Forty or fewer participants usually attend this event; this allows for much personal attention; no one gets lost in the crowd. Basic premise -- all work is accepted as valuable, no value judgement is placed on content, subject matter, etc. Critiquing is done with effectiveness of piece in mind.

Faculty: In the past we have employed such workshop leaders as Jim Wayne Miller, Lee Pennington, Leon Driskell, Wade Hall, Sarah Gorham, Malcolm Glass, etc.

Financial Assistance: Little financial aid is usually available, since fees are minimal; GRW Inc. is a non-profit organization.

Contact: Mary E. O'Dell, Director, for more information and a registration form.

●Guadalupe Cultural Arts Center
1300 Guadalupe Street
San Antonio, TX 78207
(210) 271-3151
FAX (210) 271-3480
e-mail: guadarts@aol.com

Length of Residency: Five days per session. Three to five sessions are held, generally in sequential order, sometimes concurrently.

When: June.

Application Deadline: April 15.

Cost: Varies, from $150 to $350 per session.

Description: Five three-hour classes of ten to twelve competitively selected student writers are conducted by well-known writers. The week of classes generally concludes with a public reading by the class at the Guadalupe Book Shop. Applicants should submit a ten-page writing sample in the discipline of their choice between January 1 and April 15. Submissions are judged blind by the instructor/writer. Notification of acceptance/rejection is made by May 5. Housing is at student expense. Several downtown B&Bs can be suggested in the $50 to $75 range.

Faculty: Sandra Cisneros is the only regularly scheduled instructor. Past instructors have included: Joy Harjo, Juan Felipe Herrera, Rolando Hinojosa, Bryce Milligan, Pat Mora, Naomi Shihab Nye, Virgil Suarez, and others.

Financial Assistance: Scholarships (reduced tuition) are given on the basis of need. Inquire by letter or phone after acceptance.

Contact: Bryce Milligan, Literature Program Director.

The Hambidge Center for Creative Arts and Sciences
P.O. Box 339
Betty's Creek Road
Rabun Gap, GA 30568
(706) 746-5718

Length of Residency: Two weeks to two months.

When: Year-round, except December, January, February.

Application Deadline: January 31 (for main season); August 31 for late season.

Cost: $400 per week; cost to artists: $125.

Description: The Hambidge Center was founded in 1934 by Mary Crovatt Hambidge as a studio and cottage-weaving industry. Her artistry as a weaver won her the Gold Medal in Textiles at the 1937 Paris World's Fair. Fabrics hand-woven at the Hambidge Center were sold in her shop in New York City to Presidents Roosevelt and Truman, Georgia O'Keefe, and other luminaries of her time.

After her death in 1973, the Hambidge Center became an art center where classes were taught and a few residencies were provided for artists. In 1988, the Board of Trustees made the decision to drop the art classes, which are offered in several nearby schools, and focus on the Artists' Residency Program. The program as it now exists began in 1989 and has grown steadily, attracting artists from across the U.S. and the world. The property and its thirteen buildings (on 600 pristine acres in the Blue Ridge Mountains) are listed on the National Register of Historic Places.

Our mission is to create, protect, sustain, and improve upon facilities and an environment in which creativity and a dynamic interchange between artists from different fields may take place; to provide periods of residency in this environment for artists of exceptional talent and diverse heritage during which they may contemplate, conceive, and ultimately create without demands or distractions. 80 or so fellowships are awarded annually.

Financial Assistance: Partial fellowships make the $125/week fee possible. Further assistance can sometimes be provided on a limited basis. There is an application fee of $20.

Contact: Judith Barber, Executive Director. Please write or call for applications (SASE).

●Hassayampa Institute for Creative Writing
Yavapai College
1100 E. Sheldon Street
Prescott, AZ 86301
(520) 776-2281
FAX (520) 776-2082

When: Late July.

Cost: $300.

Description: The Hassayampa Institute for Creative Writing is a summer gathering of writers and poets for six days of intensive writing, conversation, panels, and readings. The Institute offers writers of all levels the opportunity to work closely with a number of distinguished, nationally-known writers in historic Prescott, located in the central mountains of Arizona.

Faculty: Marge Piercy, Alberto Rios, Luci Tapahonso, Ron Carlson, Ira Wood, T.M. McNally, Peter Iverson, and Demetria Martinez.

Contact: The Director.

Hawk, I'm Your Sister
P.O. Box 9109
Santa Fe, NM 87504
(505) 984-2268

Length of Residency: Eight days.

When: October.

Application Deadline: September.

Cost: $975.

Description: This is a writing retreat/canoe trip in Boquillas Canyon, Big Bend National Park, Texas; for women.

Faculty: River Guide: Beverly Antaeus. Writing Instructor: Sharon Olds.

Contact: Beverly Antaeus.

●Haystack Writing Program
PSU Summer Programs
P.O. Box 751
Portland, OR 97207
(503) 725-3484
FAX (503) 725-4840

Length of Residency: One-week and weekend workshops.

When: July 1 through mid-August.

Application Deadline: First come, first served.

Cost: $350-$400 (tuition only).

Description: The Haystack Program began in 1969 as an artists' retreat and colony on the Oregon Coast. It is designed to support and provide writers, musicians, and artists with a space for pursuit of their creative abilities. An intensive schedule of morning and afternoon sessions with evening readings and assignments allows writers of all kinds to make rapid progress without the distractions of home. The inspiring backdrop of the Pacific Ocean and the charm of Cannon Beach itself, a small coastal community of artists, adds to the supportive environment. The atmosphere is enhanced by music classes, film projects, artists' easels, and nature hikes. Small classes (15 maximum) with well-known published writers features in-class writing assignments, lectures, discussions, critique sessions, and other writing exercises. Every summer the program hosts approximately 350 participants who come from around the world; over half of them are writers.

Faculty: Instructors have included Marilyn Chin, Ursula K. LeGuin, Craig Lesley, Sandra McPherson, Mark Medoff, Tom Spanbauer, William Stafford, Sallie Tisdale, and many other fine writers.

Contact: The Director.

Helene Wurlitzer Foundation of New Mexico
P.O. Box 545
Taos, NM 87571
(505) 758-2413
FAX (505) 758-2559

Length of Residency: 3 months.

When: April 1 through September 30.

Application Deadline: Open.

Cost: None.

Description: Rent-free and utilities-free housing in Taos, New Mexico offered to persons involved in the creative, not interpretive, fields in all media. Anyone who wishes to apply should write or fax for an application form.

Hemingway Days Writers' Workshop & Conference
P.O. Box 4045
Key West, FL 33041
(305) 294-4440

Length of Residency: Three days, held as part of a week-long festival celebrating the birthday of Nobel laureate Ernest Hemingway.

When: Third week in July.

Application Deadline: Information about registration is available in May of every year, but those interested in attending may write at any time to have their name put on the mailing list.

Cost: $120 for all sessions and social events, $105 if paid before June 10th. Discount hotel packages are available.

Description: Each year the Hemingway Days Festival, named one of the top ten summer festivals by *Vacation* magazine, celebrates the Nobel laureate's birthday with a week of storytelling, short story, Hemingway trivia, Hemingway look-alike, fishing, and arm-wrestling contests, as well as a street fair and a 5-K sunset run. The Hemingway Days Writers' Workshop & Conference is held the first four days of the festival. On Sunday the Conch Republic Prize for Literature honoree reads from his/her work. Monday is devoted to presentations, discussions and readings in fiction; Tuesday is devoted to poetry; and Wednesday is devoted to presentations and discussions of Hemingway's life and works.

Faculty: Past "faculty" have included John Updike, Alicia Ostriker, James Dickey, Peter Matthiessen, Tess Gallagher, Bob Shacochis, Joy Harjo, Cornelius Eady, Jonis Agee, James W. Hall, Li-Young Lee, William Kittredge, Martin Espada, Peter Meinke, and a number of Hemingway family members and scholars.

No financial assistance available.

Contact: Hemingway Days Festival or the director, Dr. James Plath, Dept. of English, Illinois Wesleyan University, Bloomington, IL 61702-2900, (309) 556-3352, e-mail <jplath@titan.IWU.edu>.

Highland Summer Conference
Eng. 490
Buchanan House Lower Level
Box 7014
Radford University
Radford, VA 24142
(540) 831-5366; (540) 831-6152
FAX (540) 831-5004
e-mail: jasbury@runet.edu

Length of Residency: Two weeks.

When: Last two weeks of June.

Application Deadline: June 1.

Cost: Regular tuition for 3 hour class (undergraduate or graduate) plus $25 Conference fee.

Description: The Appalachian Regional Studies Center, in collaboration with the Department of English, will conduct the 22nd annual Highland Summer Conference. The Conference, a lecture-seminar-workshop combination, is conducted by well known guest writers and offers the opportunity to study and practice creative writing within the context of regional culture. Past authors include: Jim Wayne Miller, Wilma Dykeman, David Huddle, Denise Giradina, Sharyn McCrumb, Nikki Giovanni, and others.

Contact: Dr. Grace Toney Edwards, Director, (540) 831-5366; Jo Ann Asbury, Assistant to Director, (540) 831-6152.

Highlights for Children
803 Church Street
Hondesdale, PA 18431
(717) 253-1080
FAX (717) 253-0179

Contact: Jan Keen, Director.

●Hofstra University Summer Writers' Conference
250 Hofstra University
UCCE
Hempstead, NY 11549
(516) 463-5016
FAX (516) 463-4833

Length of Residency: Two weeks, 1st week includes a Writers Conference for High School Students.

When: 2nd and 3rd weeks of July.

Application Deadline: June 15.

Cost: Non-credit: $375 for 1 workshop; $600 for 2. Undergraduate and graduate: call for tuition rates. High School Student Writers' Conference: $165 (1 week).

Description: The Summer Writers' Conference at Hofstra University seeks to nurture and encourage writing talent through the presence, stimulus, and creative authority of writers-in-residence. The conference, a cooperative venture of the Creative Writing Program, the English Department, and University College for Continuing Education, offers workshops in fiction, nonfiction, poetry, children's literature, and playwriting/scriptwriting. Participants may join any two of them, for credit (graduate or undergraduate) or on a non-credit basis. Workshops, led by master writers, include both group and individual sessions and total more than 25 contact hours between students and writers. In addition, agents, editors, and publishers make luncheon presentations during the conference, and authors and students read from published work and works in progress. Receptions, barbecues, and a conference dinner provide additional opportunities to meet informally with participants, master writers, and guest speakers. The pastoral campus of Hofstra University is enriched with thousands of mature evergreen and deciduous trees, including many rare species and varieties. Magnificent Atlantic beaches on Long Island's nearby south shore complement our campus-arboretum. Excellent train service and highways connect Hofstra to New York City, twenty-five miles west of the campus (the Manhattan skyline is visible from the library).

Past faculty and speakers have included Denise Levertov, Robert Olen Butler, Carole Maso, Oscar Hijuelos, Maurice Sendak, Cynthia Ozick, Nora Sayre, and William Hoffman.

Contact: Director, Liberal Arts Studies.

Hurston/Wright Writers Week at V.C.U.
P.O. Box 842005
Richmond, VA 23284-2005
(804) 225-4729

Length of Residency: One week (five days).

When: July 14-18, 1997.

Application Deadline: April 1, 1997.

Cost: $400 tuition only, $700 tuition, room, and board.

Description: Hurston/Wright Writers Week at Virginia Commonwealth University was first held in the summer of 1996. The week is sponsored by the Zora Neale Hurston/Richard Wright Foundation, which presents each spring an award to African-American college fiction writers. Hurston/Wright Writers Week is designed to address the shortage of summer writing workshops that target for inclusion African-American writers. The workshop is open to all, both published and unpublished writers. In its first year the week attracted writers from all over the country. Workshops in fiction, poetry, and nonfiction are offered.

Faculty: In 1996, Toi Derricotte, David Bradley, Bob Shacochis, Gloria Wade Gayles, Susan Shreve. In 1997, Maxine Clair, Jewelle Gomez, Dennis Danvers and Calvin Forbes.

Financial Assistance: A limited number of tuition remission grants of up to $300.

Contact: The Director.

●Hurston/Wright Writers' Week at Saint Mary's College of California
P.O. Box 4686
Moraga, CA 94575-4686
(510) 631-4088
e-mail: writers@stmarys-ca.edu

When: Late July.

Cost: $400 for tuition, $ for tuition, room, and board.

Description: Hurston/Wright Writers' Week invites applications from unpublished as well as published writers and anyone seeking to master the writer's craft. Entrance to the workshops is competitive and the program is designed for writers seeking an intensive critique of their work by some of the country's most talented writers as well as by workshop participants.

Faculty: Past faculty include David Haynes, Elmaz Abinader, Patti Griffith, Junot Díaz, and Nikki Finney.

Contact: The Director.

Idyllwild Arts Academy
P.O. Box 38
52500 Temecula Road
Idyllwild, CA 92459
(909) 659-2171 ext. 380

Description: Idyllwild Arts Academy is a private, nonprofit boarding high school for the arts. This creative writing program is for talented high-school students from grades 9-12 who want a specialized training in the arts as well as a solid academic curriculum. Admission is by portfolio.

Contact: Donald A. Put, Director (e-mail <daput@pe.net>).

●IMAGINATION: A Writers' Conference and Workshop
Division of Continuing Education
Cleveland State University
3100 Chester Avenue
Cleveland, OH 44114-4604
(216) 687-4522
FAX (216) 687-6943

Length of Residency: 5½ days.

When: July.

Application Deadlines: Workshops: Sample manuscripts postmarked by May 19.

Cost: Full participation with manuscript: workshops plus conference classes, readings, and colloquium (additional charge for college credit) $420. Conference, classes, readings, and colloquium $225. One-day *Colloquium on the Business of Writing* only $115.

Description: The Imagination Conference, first held in 1991, is a conference about strong imaginative writing without genre bias or boundaries. Morning workshops are small and each group works in turn with every member of the faculty. During the week each workshop student also meets in an individual conference with a second faculty member to go over his or her work. Afternoon lectures, classes, and discussion groups address the practice, the theory, and the politics of writing as well as issues of craft. There are daily readings by conference faculty, a professional performance of selected student work, and student readings.

The conference incorporates a one-day colloquium on the nuts and bolts of writing for publication, which can also be registered for separately. The colloquium features agents and editors from major publishers, small presses, journals, and magazines. Approximately 60 writers attend the workshop and 60-100 more attend the conference and colloquium. Non-credit, undergraduate, and graduate credit options are available.

Faculty: Karen Joy Fowler, Reginald Shepherd, Tananarive Due, Debra Spark, Sheila Schwartz, Elizabeth Cook-Lynn, Molly Gloss, Steve Lattimore, Ruth L. Schwartz.

Financial Assistance: Scholarships are available each year, based on need. There is a $10 manuscript reading fee.

Contact: Neal Chandler, Conference Director, for more information and application forms.

●Indiana University Writers' Conference
Ballantine Hall 464
Bloomington, IN 47405
(812) 855-1877
e-mail: stanton@indiana.edu

Length or Residency: 1 week.

When: June 27–July 2.

Application Deadline: May 14.

Cost: $350.

Description: The Indiana University Writer's Conference is the second oldest writers conference in the country, and attracts nationally prominent writers who are also excellent teachers. Both workshops and craft classes are offered in Fiction and Poetry.

Faculty: Poetry: Rodney Jones, Allison Joseph, Mary Jo Salter, Charles Webb. Fiction: Jesse Lee Kercheval, Brad Leithauser. Classes: David Wojahn, Manny Martinez, Jon Tribble.

Financial Assistance: Several small scholarships of $75–$100.

Contact: Maura Stanton, Director.

The International Film Writers Workshops
2 Central Street
P.O. Box 200
Rockport, ME 04856
(207) 236–8581
FAX (207) 236–2558
website: http://www.MEWorkshops.com

Length of Residency: One- and two-week Master Classes and 4-week Summer Screenwriters Residency.

When: Tuscany, Italy: May. Rockport, Maine: July, August, and September.

Cost: Tuition: One-week Master Classes: $695 to $795. 4-Week Screenwriters Retreat: $1,595. Application fee: $35 and $300 course deposit required. Room and board: $375/week to $665/week.

Description: The Workshops were established in 1973 as a conservatory for creative storytellers and imagemakers; filmmakers, photographers, and writers. Today, The Workshops offer more than 200 one-week workshops and Master Classes in all areas of creative storytelling: feature films, video, documentaries, public and corporate television, magazine photography and screenwriting. The Workshops provides a total immersion environment in a delightful setting on the Maine Coast, with a creative and supportive community of fellow artists, writers and a professional staff. Writers meet mornings to share and critique work, work with actors on dialogue and scene development, then spend the afternoons and evenings in writing, attending lectures, and screenings. Master Classes in feature film screenwriting, documentary project development, television writing, and a one-month writers' residency are available. The Workshops also offers a self-tailored MFA program in screenwriting each summer, as well as two-week screenwriters workshops in Tuscany, Italy in May 1996; and Oaxaca, Mexico in the winter of 1997.

Rockport is a small harbor village, halfway down the Maine Coast, 4 hours north of Boston, 8 hours from New York City. Portland Airport is 80 miles away. The Workshops have an airport van service on weekends. Cars are not necessary. Bikes can be rented. Everything is within walking distance and handicap accessible.

Faculty: The Faculty includes Academy Award–winning screenwriters: Janet Roach, Michael Miner, Christopher Keane, Stanley Ralph Ross, Grant William, Rachael Fields, and John Markus.

Financial Assistance: 25% tuition discounts are provided for enrolling in additional workshops. Half-price tuition stand-by is also available where room permits. Half-price scholarships are also available for talented writers. Refund policy: complete refund, less $35 application fee, for withdrawal prior to 60–days before course begins. $50 withdrawal fee is charged for withdrawal less than 30–days. $300 deposit is retained for withdrawal less than one–week before course begins.

Contact: Write or call for a catalogue of workshops and courses.

The International Women's Writing Guild
Remember the Magic
IWWG's Summer Conference at Skidmore College
P.O. Box 810, Gracie Station
New York, NY 10028
(212) 737-7536
FAX (212) 737-9469
e-mail: iwwg@iwwg.com
website: http://www.iwwg.com

Length of Residency: Seven days.

When: Second week in August.

Application Deadline: None.

Cost: $700 including room and board ($300 for commuters).

Description: The first summer conference of the International Women's Writing Guild was held in 1978 at Skidmore College in Saratoga Springs, New York, and has been there ever since. The conference is open to any woman regardless of portfolio and offers close to 60 writing workshops every single day, making it possibly the largest writing conference in the United States. The workshops fall into the following major headings: 1) Writing: The Nuts & Bolts of It (i.e., The Play and the Playwright, Basics of Journalism, Writing and Selling TV/Film Scripts, Finding the Travelogue, Poems of Self and Others, etc.); 2) Transformation of Self (i.e. Intensive Journal Workshop, Improving Your Writing Through Childhood Memories, Writing the Autobiography in Your Own Words, Women Writing Journals, etc.); 3) Non-linear Knowledge; 4) The Arts & The Body. Participation in the conference is entirely self-directed. Attendees may take as many or as few of the plethora of workshops offered. Evening programs consist primarily of open readings of work written by attendees. Situated in the foothills of the Adirondack Mountains, Saratoga Springs itself is a delightful Victorian town offering its own cultural diversions as well as healing mineral baths. One of the few problems that exists is finding the time to do everything that is offered, both by the conference and its beautiful surroundings. Some 450 women attend this summer conference every year from all over the world, and many have found this a catalytic life experience.

Financial Assistance: Partial scholarships are available.

Contact: Hannelore Hahn, Executive Director.

International Writers Center
Washington University
Campus Box 1071
7425 Forsyth Boulevard
St. Louis, MO 63105-2103
(314) 935-5576
FAX (314) 935-2103
e-mail: iwc@artsci.wustl.edu
website: http://www.artsci.wustl.edu/~iwc

Description: The International Writers Center was established at Washington University to build on the strengths of its resident and visiting faculty writers; to serve as a focal point for writing excellence in all disciplines and in all cultures; to be a directory for writers and writing programs at Washington University, in St. Louis, the United States, and around the world; and to present the writer to the reader. The International Writers Center publishes *The St. Louis Literary Calendar* and *Bestiary* and presents the International Writers Center Reading Series, which has featured Paul Auster, David Bradley, Anthony Butts, Mary Caponegro, Anne Carson, Cyrus Cassells, Rosemary Catacalos, Marilyn Chin, Lydia Davis, Lynn Emanuel, Francisco Goldman, Emily Grosholz, Jessica Hagedorn, Michael Hofmann, Yusef Komunyakaa, Sarah Lindsay, Ben Marcus, Steven Millhauser, Paul Muldoon, The Nuyorican Poets Café Live!, Michael Ondaatje, Ben Okri, Patricia Powell, Joanna Scott, Susan Stewart, and David Foster Wallace.

We also present international literary conferences and publish books of the proceedings. *The Writer in Politics* (1992) featured Breyten Breytenbach, Nuruddin Farah, Carolyn Forché, Mario Vargas Llosa, Antonio Skármeta, and Luis Valenzuela; *The Writer and Religion* (1994) with Eavan Boland, J.M. Coetzee, William Gaddis, Amitav Ghosh, A.G. Mojtabal, and Hanan al-Shaykh; and *The Dual Muse: The Writer As Artist, The Artist As Writer* (1997), with Jennifer Bartlett, Breyten Breytenbach, Tom Phillips, and Derek Wolcott. In 2000 the Center will present *Twenty-one on Twenty: Literature of the Twentieth Century*.

The Writer in Politics was published by Southern Illinois University Press in 1996 and *The Writer in Religion* in 1999. *The Dual Muse* exhibition catalogue and symposium volumes are available through John Benjamins Publishing Company, Amsterdam.

Faculty: The Director is William H. Gass.

Contact: Lorin Cuoco, Associate Director, or Michelle Komie, Program Coordinator.

●The Iowa Summer Writing Festival
Division of Continuing Education
116 International Center
The University of Iowa
Iowa City, IA 52242
(319) 335-2534
website: www.uiowa.edu/˜iswfest

Length of Residency: One week or weekend programs.

When: June and July.

Application Deadline: First come, first served, until spots are filled.

Cost: $375–$400 per week, $175 per weekend. Housing is additional with several options offered.

Description: The 13th annual Iowa Summer Writing Festival continues the tradition of excellence in writing for which The University of Iowa is world renowned. Workshops are labeled as appropriate for beginning, intermediate, and advanced writers of all genres including short fiction, novel, poetry, essay, screenwriting, writing for children, playwriting, and more. Participants have the morning free to write or attend special programming; afternoons are spent in workshops. We plan several evening activities, including a weekly reading by a writer of note. Approximately 1,500 writers attend the Festival each year and choose from among 140 different workshops.

Faculty: Past workshop leaders have included: Lee K. Abbott, Marvin Bell, Hope Edelman, Elizabeth McCracken, and Susan Power.

Financial Assistance: No financial aid is available from the Festival. Application fee is a $17 deposit.

Contact: Peggy Houston and Amy Margolis, coordinators, for a catalog and more information.

The Island Institute
P.O. Box 2420
Sitka, AK 99835
(907) 747-3794
e-mail: island@ptialaska.net
website: www.ptialaska.net/˜island/index.html

Length of Residency: One month.

When: January, April, November of each year.

Application Deadline: August 15 each year for November of that year and January and April of the following year.

Cost: Travel costs to Sitka (not to neighboring communities mentioned below), incidentals during residency. Housing and food stipend provided.

Description: Our Resident Fellows Program is for writers and humanities scholars whose work demonstrates an interest in the integration of the arts, humanities, and sciences. The program is two-fold, offering residents an opportunity to pursue their work, but also having them participate in a community activity once a week. Such activities vary according to the expertise of individual residents, and have included readings, workshops, exhibits, public talks and discussions, visits to school classes, and media interviews. Whenever possible, residents also travel to one of the nearby smaller communities in Southeast Alaska for a two to four day visit with similar community activities. Individuals may apply for whichever month best suits them. Native Americans or people whose work focuses on Native cultural issues are encouraged to apply for the January position which coincides with a Native Arts program at a local University.

Financial Assistance: Housing and food stipend provided. No assistance for travel at this time.

Contact: Carolyn Servid or Dorik Mechau, Co-Directors.

The Jack Kerouac School of Disembodied Poetics
The Naropa Institute
2130 Arapahoe Avenue
Boulder, CO 80302
(303) 444-0202
(800) 795-8670

Length of Residency: One to four weeks.

When: July.

Application Deadline: No deadline, early registration recommended as enrollment is limited.

Cost: Non-credit 1 week=$375, 2 wks=$630, 3 wks=$930, 4 wks=$1,260, MFA credit (permission required) 4 wks=$2,160, BA credit 2 wks=$750, 4 wks=$1,590.

Permanent Faculty: Anne Waldman, Andrew Schelling, Bobbie Louise Hawkins, Anselm Hollo, Jack Collom, Keith Abbott.

Financial Assistance: Limited assistance available for students enrolled at least half-time in degree programs, primarily loans. File applications as soon as possible, at least eight weeks before tuition due date.

Contact: Information Desk.

Jackson Hole Writers' Conference
Box 3972 U.W. Station
Laramie, WY 82071
(800) 448-7801

Contact: The Director.

Kalani Eco-Resort, Institute for Culture and Wellness
Artists-in-Residence Program
RR 2, Box 4500
Kehena Beach, HI 96778
(800) 800-6886 (USA & Canada)
(808) 965-7828 (International and Hawaii Island)
website: http://www.maui.net/~ramdm/kh.html

Length of Residency: 2 weeks to 2 months.

When: Year-round. Weather is always gentle. Greatest availability in Spring and Fall.

Application Deadline: Our application can be completed and returned at any time. Accepted year-round.

Cost: Professional artists qualify for a 50% reduction off standard lodging costs of $60-$85/day.

Description: Kalani Eco-Resort is a great any-time get-away! The only coastal lodging facility within Hawaii's largest conservation area, characterized by sunny days, cool ocean breezes and tropical forests. Kalani treats you to healthful cuisine, a relaxing pool/spa facility, thermal springs, a dolphin beach, spectacular Volcanoes National Park, and traditional culture. Because we're nonprofit we can operate in this unique area and we are your best choice for a fun and affordable vacation-education. Our international and native staff look forward to sharing with you a memorable experience of Aloha! Call for schedule of writing seminars and other events.

Faculty: Past writers and instructors in residence include: Ram Dass, Tom Spanbauer, Garret Hongo, Helen Duberstein, Dalian Moore, Walter Williams, Mark Thompson, Malcolm Boyd, Sandra Gould Ford.

Financial Assistance: No assistance is available beyond a 50% discount in lodging costs.

Contact: Richard Koob, Director.

Kenyon Review Summer Writers Workshops
The Kenyon Review
Kenyon College
Gambier, OH 43022
(614) 427-5208
FAX (614) 427-5417
e-mail: kenyonreview@kenyon.edu

Description: Workshop groups in fiction, short short-story fiction, playwriting, and poetry will focus each day's writing with intensive conversation, exercises, and detailed readings of participants' work. Just as important will be the opportunity offered for individual writing and for personal dialogue with workshop leaders. A series of distinguished poets and fiction writers will also visit for readings and for discussions with participants, individually and in small groups.

Contact: The Director.

●Key West Literary Seminars, Inc.
9 Sixth Street
Plum Island, MA 01951
(888) 293-9291
e-mail: keywest@seacoast.com

When: Mid–January.

Cost: $295.

Description: Each year the Key West Literary Seminar explores a different topic of literary interest. Seminar features panel discussions, readings, lectures, book signings, festive Key West parties, and intimate gatherings. 1999 seminar will be followed by four days of small writers' workshops.

Contact: The Director.

Key West Writers' Workshop
5901 College Road
Key West, FL 33040
(305) 296-9081 ext. 302
FAX (305) 292-5155
e-mail: weinman_i@popmail.firn.edu
website: www.firn.edu/fkcc/kwww.htm

Length of Residency: Mostly weekend workshop series; one five-day week workshop.

When: Winter and Spring, mostly January, February, April.

Application Deadline: December, or approximately one month prior to workshop.

Cost: Weekends $250, Five-day week $450 (these are tuition prices only).

Description: One of the best little workshops in America. Led by major writers, poetry and fiction. Weekend workshops limited to 10 or 12 members. Workshops completely run as writer–leader wishes. Competitive submission (except for five-day week workshop).

Faculty: Previous faculty has included: John Ashbery, Ann Beattie, Philip Caputo, James W. Hall, Alison Lurie, Les Standiford, Robert Stone, Edmund White, Richard Wilbur, and Joy Williams.

Financial Assistance: Some, only to local (county) residents.

Contact: Irving Weinman, Director.

●Latin American Writers' Workshop
International Literary Arts Programs, Inc.
2618A St. Charles Avenue
New Orleans, LA 70130
(504) 899-8212
FAX (504) 539-9530
e-mail: 102130.3200@compuserve.com
website: http://www.treebranch.com/worldwriter/LAWW
http://www.treebranch.com/worldwriter/program.htm

Contact: Trevor Top.

Legal Workshop for Writers
445 C. East Cheyenne Mountain Blvd. #328
Colorado Springs, CO 80906
(800) 580-2808

Contact: The Director.

Leighton Studios for Independent Residencies
The Banff Centre for the Arts
Box 1020, Station 22
Banff, Alberta
Canada T0L 0C0
(403) 762-6180
FAX (403) 762-6345

Length of Residency: One week to three months.

When: Year-round.

Application Deadline: Ongoing. Apply at any time, preferably 8 to 16 months ahead of desired period of attendance. Maximum residency is three months per year.

Cost: $526/week (includes room, studio, and a flex-meal plan).

Description: The Leighton Studios, which are in a quiet wooded area slightly apart from the Centre's main buildings, offer retreat space for artists working independently. The eight separate, specially designed studios provide time and space for artists to produce new work. Established writers, composers, musicians, and visual artists of all nationalities are encouraged to apply for residence. Artists working in other mediums at the conceptual stage of a project will also be considered.

Financial Assistance: Artists may be eligible for financial assistance for studio fees.

Contact: Please contact the Enquiries/Information Center Officer for application forms.

●Lifelong Learning Center Writers' Conference
Northland College
Ashland, WI 54806
(715) 682-1341
FAX (715) 682-1691

Contact: The Director.

The Loft
c/o Pratt Community Center
66 Malcolm Avenue Southeast
Minneapolis, MN 55414
(612) 379-8999
e-mail: loft@loft.org
website: www.loft.org

Length of Residency: Year round classes and workshops; periodic.

When: Awards and residency programs

Application Deadline: Varies by program.

Cost: Award program applications; $10. Tuition: $17–$300.

Description: The Loft began in 1974 when a group of writers started meeting in the loft of a Minneapolis bookstore. They were brought together by the belief that for writers to grow artistically, they needed to form a community with other writers and readers. This single idea has remained central at the Loft, as it has grown into the nation's largest and most comprehensive literary center. The main service region is Minnesota and bordering states. National programs include an annual prize in poetry and fiction (with publication in the *Michigan Quarterly Review*) and availability of our journal on craft.

Faculty: Guest writers have included Wendi Coleman, Marilyn Hacker, Rita Dove, Denise Levertov, Amiri Bakara, Ntozake Shange, John Irving, and others. Current and past instructors include Pat Francisco, Judith Guest, Kate Green, Ellen Hart, Carol Bly, Deborah Keenan, and others.

Financial Assistance: Scholarships are available.

Contact: Mary Cummings, Education Director.

Manhattanville College's Summer Writers' Workshop
2900 Purchase Street
Purchase, NY 10577
(914) 694-3425

Length of Residency: 5 days.

When: Late June.

Application Deadline: June 10.

Cost: $560.

Description: Manhattanville's Writers' Week program offers the opportunity to spend an intensive week of writing and working closely with some of the country's finest writers and teachers of writing. In small morning workshops and in private conferences, participants at all stages of development -- novice to advanced -- sign up for one of seven genres. A special workshop entitled "The Writers' Craft" has been introduced for the benefit of beginners who wish to master the elements of creative writing. Afternoons feature a methods workshop for teachers of writing. This workshop will help teachers utilize their own writings to develop curriculum for the classroom. There will be a poetry reading by Mark Doty, a tour of *Reader's Digest*, etc.

Faculty: Elizabeth Winthrop, Faye Moskowitz, Stephanie Strickland, Louise Ladd, Patricia Lee Gauch, Maxine Clair, Elizabeth Isele, Joan Silber, Sandra Tyler, C. Drew Lamm, William Valentine.

Contact: Ruth Dowd, RSCJ, Dean, Adult & Special Programs, Manhattanville College.

Maritime Writers' Workshop
Dept. of Extension & Summer Session
University of New Brunswick
P.O. Box 4400
Fredericton, NB
Canada E3B 5A3
(506) 454-9153
FAX (506) 453-3572

Length of Residency: 1 week.

When: Early July.

Application Deadline: None; applications are processed as received and writers are accepted as long as there is space.

Cost: $350 tuition. Single room and board costs approximately $275; shared double room and board, approximately $255. (All priced in Canadian dollars.)

Description: Since 1976, Maritime Writers' Workshop has offered a one-week intensive, practically-oriented summer program designed to help writers develop and refine their skills. The program encourages serious work throughout the week, with attention to the professional standards which govern manuscript preparation and editorial demands. It is open to novice as well as more established writers. Classes, limited to a maximum of ten writers each, are offered in four categories -- Fiction (two sections), Nonfiction, Poetry, and Writing for Children. Participants choose one of these four areas and submit a short manuscript of not more than 20 pages. These writing samples often form the basis of class discussions. In addition to daily workshop sessions, the schedule includes lecture/discussion sessions, a private consultation with the instructor, time for writing and conversation, readings, and various social events. The atmosphere is welcoming, supportive, and non-competitive.

Faculty: Faculty changes each year, but always consists of nationally-recognized Canadian writers. In 1998, fiction classes were led by Carol Malyon and Kent Thompson, the poetry class by Brian Bartlett, nonfiction by George Galt and writing for children by Julie Johnston.

Financial Assistance: Scholarships up to the full cost of tuition are awarded on the basis of talent and need.

Contact: Glenda Turner, Coordinator.

● **Marjorie Kinnan Rawlings Writers Workshop:**
Writing the Region
P.O. Box 12246
Gainesville, FL 32604
(352) 378-9166
(888) 917-7001
FAX (352) 373-8854
e-mail: shakes@nervm.nerdc.ufl.edu

Length of Residency: Five days.

When: July 28-August 1, 1999.

Application Deadline: None; however, workshops are closed when they reach capacity.

Description: Discover the nuances and techniques of regional writing. This five-day workshop includes fiction, nonfiction, poetry, screenwriting, writing for children, historical writing, travel writing, writing a regional guidebook, humorous writing, investigative and controversial journalism, writing from a sense of place, illustrating, an artist's life at the Creek, what publishers expect from authors, a talk about Marjorie Kinnan Rawlings's life at the Creek, selling a script, editing tips, drama, contract law, writing with an ear for dialogue, freelancing, writing for the media, performances of participants works, a trip to Cross Creek, the home of Marjorie Kinnan Rawlings, a photography expedition, and more. Workshop sizes are limited. The five-day program is a combination of small hands-on workshops, talks, and group activities; a trip to Cross Creek, continental breakfasts, luncheons, and afternoon receptions are included. Optional evening activities are planned.

Faculty: Michael Gannon, Patrick Smith, Peter Meinke, Page Edwards, Kevin McCarthy, Mike Magnuson, Shelley Fraser Mickle, John Cech, Lee Gramling, Sarah Bewley, Kate Barnes, Valerie Rivers, Idella Parker, Marilyn Maple, Walda Metcalf, Doris Bardon, Sidney Homan, Murray Laurie, Sam Gowan, Bill Maxwell, Jeff Klinkenberg, Michael McCready, Ken Scott, David and June Cussen, John Moran, and Ken Scott.

Contact: Norma H. Homan.

Mark Twain Writers Conference
921 Center Street
Hannibal, MO 63401
(800) 747-0738

Contact: Cyndi Allison, conference coordinator, for information on 1999 events.

●Marrowstone Institute: Marrowstone Conference for High School Writers
Box 92
Nordland, WA 98358
(360) 379-0268
FAX (360) 379-0268
e-mail: cbangs@olympus.net

When: Mid–June.

Cost: $275, including room and board.

Description: An intense immersion in the craft of writing, limited to 27 students (aged 16–18). Teacher/Student ratio 1/9, plus guests and discussion leaders. All events take place at a historic waterfront park and conference center near Port Townsend, WA. Several guest writers will do readings and participate in discussions.

Contact: Carol Jane Bangs, Director.

Maui Writers Conference
P.O. Box 968
Kihei, HI 96753
(808) 879-0061 (phone and voice mail)
FAX (808) 879-6233
e-mail Mauicon@aol.com
http://www.maui.com/~sbdc/writers

Length of Residency: Four days.

When: Labor Day Weekend.

Application Deadline: July 15th postmark for early sign-up discount.

Cost: $395 early sign-up, $495 after July 15 postmark.

Description: Four intense, rewarding days of inspiration and learning. Subjects covered during this conference include: Fiction for the '90s, Creative Nonfiction, The Craft of Screenwriting, The New World of Multimedia, The Business of Writing, Journalism, Poetry, Children's Books, Cookbooks and Food Writing, Self-Publishing, Technical Writing, and Regional Publishing.

Financial Assistance: The Russell Burns Scholarship Fund supports our Young Writers of Hawaii program, in which local high school students who share a keen interest in writing are offered scholarships to the Conference. No other full or partial scholarships to attend the Conference are available at this time.

Contact: Please contact the Conference Coordinator for more information.

Mendocino Coast Writers Conference
College of the Redwoods
1211 Del Mar Drive
Fort Bragg, CA 95437
(707) 961-1001

Length of Residency: Two days.

When: Early June (Friday and Saturday).

Application Deadline: Preregister by May.

Cost: $130 Pre, $150 regular.

Description: 10 workshops, 2 general addresses, 8 lectures, and 15-minute private critiquing sessions. Beach fire reading for participants, Gourmet Pizza Party Mixer, Patio Lunch Buffet.

Faculty: 22 authors, editors, publishers, and agents.

Financial Assistance: None this year.

Contact: Marlis Manley Broadhead, Director, English Dept., 205 Morrill Hall, Oklahoma State Univ., Stillwater, OK 74078. (405) 744-9474, e-mail: <marlis@vm1.ucc.okstate.edu>.

●Mid-Atlantic Creative Nonfiction Writers' Conference
Goucher College
1021 Dulaney Valley Road
Baltimore, MD 21204
(410) 337-6200
e-mail: cnf@goucher.edu
website: http://www.goucher.edu/~cnf

When: Mid-August.

Cost: $640 before July 15, $690 after July 15; $150 for manuscript evaluation, $250 for room and board.

Description: Workshops focusing on the art of creative nonfiction; defining the elements of creative nonfiction including scene, dialogue, description, and the importance of factual substance in essays or articles. Focus on storytelling. Discuss interviewing and immersion techniques and basic editing techniques. You must choose a workshop focus -- either literary journalism or essay/memoir. Workshops will be limited to 15 participants.

Faculty: Previous faculty have included Diana Hume George, Marita Golden, Dinty W. Moore, and Paul Wilkes. Guest writers have included Barry Lopez, Joyce Carol Oates, George Plimpton, and Ntozake Shange.

Contact: The Director.

●Midland Writers Conference
Grace A. Dow Memorial Library
1710 West St. Andrews
Midland, MI 48640
(517) 837-3442
e-mail: kred@ulc.lib.mi.us

When: Usually the second Saturday of June.

Cost: $40/$50 (fee changes two weeks before Conference).

Description: Offered since 1980 and sponsored by the Grace A. Dow Memorial Library this annual Saturday conference serves as a forum for about 125 writers to meet, exchange ideas, discuss problems with professionals, and learn about different areas of the writing profession. It opens with a keynote address by a distinguished author and continues with a series of concurrent sessions on various aspects of writing and publishing.

Faculty: Keynoters have included: Dave Barry, Mary Higgins Clark, Kurt Vonnegut, David Halberstam.

Contact: Please contact the Conference Coordinator for more information or brochure.

Midwest Writers' Conference
6000 Frank Avenue NW
Canton, OH 44720
(330) 499-9600

Length of Residency: Two days.

When: Early October.

Application Deadline: Early August for the manuscript contest, and mid-September for conference registration.

Cost: $65.

Description: The Midwest Writers' Conference was established in 1968 to provide an annual focal point for various activities of the Greater Canton Writers' Guild. The Conference provides an atmosphere in which aspiring writers can meet with and learn from experienced and established writers through lectures, workshops, competitive contests, personal interviews, and informal group discussions. The environment of the Conference also provides an atmosphere for networking among participants.

Faculty: Tom Wolfe, bestselling author; David Baker, Associate Professor of English at Denison University; Steven Bauer, Associate Professor and Director of Creative Writing at Miami University; Kat Snider Blackbird, instructor of creative writing at Kent State University; Arnold Cheyney, Emeritus Professor of English at The University of Miami (Florida); Jeanne Cheyney, writer and illustrator; Sandra Gurvis, author and editor; Frank Jones, author, artist, cartoonist, lecturer, and teacher; Ken Miller, reporter, photographer; Peter Miller, President of PMA Literary & Film Management, Inc.; Ed Moody, author, freelance writer and photographer; Maryann Myers, author; Kirk Polking, former Director of Writer's Digest School, former editor of *Writer's Digest Magazine*; William Pomidor, contributing editor for several medical education journals, instructor at Neoucom; Andrew Zack, agent for the Scovil Chichak Galen Literary Agency, Inc., contributing editor for Tom Doherty Assoc., Publishers of TOR and Forge Books.

Financial Assistance: There is no financial aid available.

Contact: Debbie Ruhe, Assistant Director, The Office of Corporate and Community Services.

Midwest Writers' Workshop
Department of Journalism
Ball State University
Muncie, IN 47306
(317) 285-8200

Length of Residency: One week.

When: Late July.

Application Deadline: July 15.

Cost: $185 (not including room and meals).

Description: The 23rd annual Midwest Writers Workshop features instruction in fiction, nonfiction, and poetry as well as special sessions and Writing Basics and Advanced Track units. The workshop closes with a Saturday evening banquet. Sessions are held throughout day with special lectures in the evening in addition to Talkabouts where participants share their work. A writer-in-residence and agent-in-residence meet individually with participants for critiques of articles and proposals.

Faculty: 1996 faculty: Mary Evans, agent-in-residence; Margo LaGattuta, poetry; Patrick LoBrutto, editor-in-residence; R. Karl Largent, writing basics; Holly G. Miller, advanced track; Alanna Nash, nonfiction; Susan Neville, fiction; Janette Oke, special guest.

Financial Assistance: Ten full tuition ($185) scholarships are available. Apply with letter and writing sample.

Contact: Earl L. Conn, Department of Journalism, Ball State University, Muncie, IN 47306.

The Millay Colony for the Arts
P.O. Box 3
Austerlitz, NY 12017-0003
(518) 392-3103
e-mail: application@millaycolony.org

Length of Residency: One month.

When: Year-round.

Application Deadline: February 1, May 1, September 1.

Cost: None.

Description: The Millay Colony gives residencies to writers, composers, and visual artists. Residencies are for one month and usually cover a period from the 1st to the 28th of each month. The Ellis Studio, which was opened in October, 1974, is a year round work and living space which can accommodate one visual artist, composer, or writer at a time. The Colony provides all food at no cost to the residents. Weeknight dinners are prepared. Breakfast and lunch food is available. Residents prepare their own weekend meals. There is no application fee, and no fee for a Colony residency. However, the Colony does depend on gifts for its existence, and welcomes contributions.

Contact: Gail Giles, Assistant Director.

Mississippi River Creative Writing Workshop in Poetry and Fiction
St. Cloud State University
St. Cloud, MN 56301
(612) 255-3061

Length of Residency: Two weeks.

When: Usually 2nd and 3rd week of June.

Application Deadline: Before first summer session. Register through SCSU summer session.

Description: The first week will include discussions of poetry and fiction writing techniques. Daily student writing experiments will also take place. During the second week, one published writer will visit each day to discuss his/her writing and to answer questions concerning writing techniques.

Faculty: Rotating faulty. Bill Meissner, author of 3 poetry books and one collection of short fiction, is the SCSU writer/teacher.

Contact: (612) 255-3061 for information.

Mississippi Valley Writers Conference
Augustana College
c/o Student Center
Rock Island, IL 61201

Length of Residency: Five days.

When: Early June.

Application Deadline: May 15.

Cost: Registration: $25; $50 per workshop (includes manuscript evaluation); $40 each additional; $20 per audit.

Description: Augustana College in Rock Island, Illinois, will host the annual Mississippi Valley Writers Conference. Scenically located along the rolling Mississippi River, Augustana has a long and distinguished history of providing opportunity for enrichment in the arts.

Nine one-hour workshops will be offered daily, in the areas of beginning professional writing, poetry, juveniles, nonfiction, writing romantic fiction, novel basics, short story, novel manuscript seminar, and photography. Each of these workshops will be led by a practicing and professional writer. Each workshop participant will be entitled to submit a manuscript for criticism and to have a private conference with the workshop leader. A manuscript is required for the novel manuscript seminar workshop.

In addition to the daily workshops, a variety of special evening events are on the agenda. An autograph party, fun auction, and Awards Banquet are also scheduled.

Financial Assistance: $25 awards in each workshop; additional memorial awards.

Contact: David R. Collins, MVWC Founder/Director, 3403 45th Street, Moline, IL 61265.

Mount Hermon Christian Writers Conference
P.O. Box 413
Mount Hermon, CA 95041
(831) 335-4466
FAX (831) 335-9218

Length of Residency: 5 days/4 nights.

When: Palm Sunday weekend, annually (Friday lunch through Tuesday lunch). 1999: March 26-30.

Application Deadline: Day of conference, but 14-day advance preferred.

Cost: $525 to $730, including room, board, registration, and $300 tuition, depending upon accommodations chosen (deluxe, standard, or economy).

Description: Founded in 1970, the Mount Hermon Christian Writers Conference is an intensive hands-on, how-to conference, taught by a faculty of 40-45, made up of magazine editors and publishing representatives from the major Christian publishers and magazines in the country. Mornings feature an extended track for intensive work in a continuing subject; afternoons offer multiple workshop choices. Excellent for all, from beginner to intermediate to advanced/published writer. Special Advanced Track available. Held at the beautiful 440-acre Mount Hermon Christian Conference Center in the heart of the Santa Cruz Mountain redwoods, near San Jose, California. All aspects of writing for the Christian market are included: children, youth, adult, fiction, nonfiction, magazines, books, poetry, marketing, etc.

Faculty: Have included Sally Stuart, Al Janssen, Charles Swindoll, Jerry Jenkins, Harold Ivan Smith, Bill Butterworth, Ron Allen, Jeannette Clift George, Tim Stafford, Howard Hendricks,

Calvin Miller, Roger Palms, Ted Engstrom, Earl Palmer, and Elizabeth Sherrill.

Financial Assistance: Campership grants available to 30–40% of conference costs upon application. Other scholarships available.

Contact: David R. Talbott, Director of Specialized Programs, Mount Hermon Association, Inc., P.O. Box 413, Mount Hermon, CA 95041.

Mountain Writers Series
2812 SE 22nd Avenue
Portland, OR 97202
(503) 232-4517

Contact: The Director.

●Napa Valley Writers' Conference
Napa Valley College
1088 College Avenue
St. Helena, CA 94574
(707) 967-2900, ext. 1112

Length of Residency: One week.

When: Last week of July–first week of August.

Application Deadline: Scholarship application May 15; application deadline June 1.

Cost: $475 per person, not including room and board.

Description: The Napa Valley Writers' Conference is now in its 18th year as one of the best and most prestigious summer writing programs. Since its beginnings as an informal summer gathering of writers, the conference has remained a place to convene for fellowship, serious work with a focus on craft, and a week spent beside the hills and valleys that have made the Napa Valley famous. The simple, intimate nature of the conference has in the past attracted such distinguished poets and fiction writers as Alice Adams, Russell Banks, Frank Bidart, Rosellen Brown, Fredrick Busch, Ethan Canin, Carolyn Forché, Louise Glück, Jorie Graham, Robert Hass, Brenda Hillman, Garrett Hongo, Diane Johnson, Galway Kinnell, Carolyn Kizer, Anne Lamott, Sandra McPherson, Czeslaw Milosz, Robert Pinsky, and Ellen Bryant Voigt. At a time when more attention is being paid to commercialism and marketing in the field of literature, the Napa Valley Writers' Conference has maintained its emphases on process and craft. It also has remained small and personal, fostering an unusual rapport between faculty writers and conference participants, who find the Napa experience both nurturing and challenging. Participants will register for either the poetry or the fiction workshops, but panels and craft talks will be open to all writers attending. The faculty will read from their work in literary evenings that are open to the public and often hosted by Napa Valley wineries.

Financial Assistance: There are a limited number of partial scholarships available, awarded on the basis of merit and need. Limited accommodations in local homes are available on a first-come, first-served basis for a fee of $20 for the week.

Contact: Sherri Hallgren, Managing Director.

Nature Within
26767 County Road 12
Somerset, CO 81434
(970) 929-6575

Length of Residency: 5 days.

When: Early July.

Application Deadline: June 30.

Cost: $595, including food, room and board.

Description: The schedule is arranged on a consistent daily basis to allow maximum contact with faculty and fellow participants as well as ample free time for writing, exploring, and enjoying the amenities of the ranch. The program is designed to help writers improve their writing skills, bring forth views on nature and community, and discover their "nature within."

Faculty: Jorie Graham, poetry; James Galvin, fiction; Christopher Merrill, nonfiction.

Financial Assistance: None.

Contact: Dori or John Lee, Karen Chamberlain, Directors.

New England Writers Workshop
Emerson College
100 Beacon Street
Boston, MA 02115-1523
(617) 824-8567

Length of Residency: One week.

When: June 7-11, 1999.

Application Deadline: May 25.

Cost: $550 ($175 additional for dorm room and breakfast).

Description: Five intense days of classes, conferences, visiting lecturers, and readings.

Faculty: Director C. Michael Curtis, Pamela Painter, Christopher Tilghman, and Elizabeth Cox.

Contact: C. Michael Curtis, *The Atlantic Monthly*, 77 N. Washington Street, Boston, MA 02114.

●New England Writers' Workshop at Simmons College
300 The Fenway
Boston, MA 02115
(617) 521-2220
FAX (617) 521-3199

Length of Residency: One week.

When: Early June.

Application Deadline: Mid-May.

Cost: $550 Tuition; $150 Residence.

Description: The New England Writers' Workshop at Simmons College provides a unique opportunity for participants to meet and talk with experienced and distinguished authors, editors, and agents. For five intensive days, professional and aspiring writers assess each other's work and explore the problems and rewards of writing for publication.

Boston and its literary heritage provide a stimulating environment for a workshop of writers.

Simmons College is located in the Fenway area near the Museum of Fine Arts, Symphony Hall, the Isabella Stewart Gardner Museum, Fenway Park, and many other places of educational, cultural, and social interest.

Most participants work in adult fiction: novels and short stories. The groups meet in morning classes to critique manuscripts. Each afternoon guest authors, editors, and agents speak and answer questions. Further conversation among speakers, workshop leaders, and participants is usually possible, as well as individual consultations with workshop leaders.

This is the workshop's 19th year. Guest speakers in the past have included authors Rick Moody, Ann Beattie, Elizabeth Berg, Tim O'Brien, Stephen King, John Updike, as well as editors from *The New Yorker*, Houghton Mifflin Company, *The Atlantic Monthly*, William Morrow Co., and others.

Contact: Cynthia Grady for more information.

●New Letters Weekend Writers Conference
Arts and Sciences Continuing Education
University of Missouri-Kansas City
4825 Troost Bldg., Rm. 215
5100 Rockhill Road
Kansas City, MO 64110
(816) 235-2739

Length of Residency: One weekend (Friday evening through Sunday afternoon).

When: Late June.

Application Deadline: June 1.

Cost: Non-credit $130, credit approx. $130 per credit hour (fees subject to change).

Description: New Letters Weekend Writers Conference participants work with professionals in a city setting. Topics include making and marketing fiction and poetry, creative and selling nonfiction, opportunities in broadcast media, and the art and craft of stage and movie writing.

Faculty: James McKinley is conference director. Lecturers include Conger Beasley, Jr., Mitch Brian, Carolyn Doty, Frank Higgins, Speer Morgan, Kathrin Perutz, Trish Reeves, Robert Stewart, and Gloria Vando.

Financial Assistance: New Letters gives small scholarships.

Contact: James McKinley.

New York State Summer Writers Institute
Skidmore College
Saratoga Springs, NY 12866
(518) 584-5000, ext 2264

Length of Residency: 2 or 4 weeks.

When: July.

Application Deadline: None.

Cost: Tuition for the 1993 Institute for 4 weeks was $1,130; 2 weeks was $565. Room and board are available for an additional fee. Rates subject to change.

Description: The New York State Writers Institute, established in 1984 by award-winning novelist William Kennedy at the University of Albany, offers courses for undergraduate and graduate credit and will also enroll a substantial number of non-credit students. Standard three-hour class meetings three days each week will be supplemented by a program of Tuesday and Thursday afternoon round-table sessions with visiting faculty. Monday through Friday evenings the program sponsors public readings by visiting and staff writers. An extraordinary staff of distinguished writers, among them winners of such major honors as the Pulitzer Prize and the National Book Award, will serve as Institute faculty members.

Faculty: 1993 teaching faculty included Amy Hempel, Leonard Michaels, Francine Prose, Marilynne Robinson, Richard Howard, Robert Pinsky, James Miller, and David Rieff with visiting writers Russell Banks, Ann Beattie, Frank Bidart, Mary Gordon, William Kennedy, and Joyce Carol Oates.

Financial Assistance: Limited financial aid is available.

Contact: For an application and information please contact Maria McColl, Secretary, NYS Summer Writers Institute.

Norcroft: A Writing Retreat for Women
32 East First Street #330
Duluth, MN 55802

Contact: The Director.

University of North Alabama Conference
Department of English
University of North Alabama
Florence, AL 35632-0001
(205) 760-4494
FAX (205) 760-4329

Contact: Lynne Butler, Director.

The North Carolina Writers' Network (NCWN)
3501 Hwy 54 West, Studio C
Chapel Hill, NC 27516
(919) 967-9540
FAX (919) 929-0535
e-mail: ncwn@sunsite.unc.edu
website: http://sunsite.unc.edu/ncwriters

Length of Residency: NCWN offers workshops, conferences, readings, awards, scholarships, and other literary events throughout the year.

Cost: Free to $140 (for full conference weekend); workshops typically $30-50.

Description: The North Carolina Writers' Network is a nonprofit literary organization dedicated to serving writers at all stages of development, wherever they may be located. In addition to the programs mentioned above, NCWN publishes a bimonthly newsletter, an annual North Carolina Literary Resource Guide, among other writer-related publications.

Faculty: Past conference faculty members have included William Styron, Ellen Bryant Voigt, Amos Oz, Eavan Boland, Gwendolyn Parker, John Ehle, Fred Chappell, Lee Smith, Doris Betts and more.

Financial Assistance: Student and teacher scholarships sometimes available.

Contact: The North Carolina Writer's Network staff at (919) 967-9540, or send SASE for info packet to: NCWN, P.O. Box 954, Carrboro, NC 27570, or see NCWN on the Internet.

●University of North Dakota Writers' Conference
English Dept. Box 7209
University of North Dakota
Grand Forks, ND 58202
(701) 777-2768
FAX (701) 777-3650
website: http://www.und.nodak.edu/dept/library/events/writers.htm

Contact: The Director.

Northwest Writing Institute
Lewis & Clark College
0615 Southwest Palatine Hill Road
Portland, OR 97219
(503) 768-7745
FAX (503) 768-7747

Length of Residency: Various workshops range from three day weekends to ten once–a–week meetings to week–long all day sessions (during the summer).

Cost: Relates to length of workshop.

Description: The Northwest Writing Institute of Lewis & Clark College seeks to bring together a community of writers for reflective experiences in the practice of writing. Working on campus, the Institute offers a broad range of graduate courses for teachers and adult writers, occasional programs and resources for undergraduate students on campus, selective programs for young writers, and several focused public programs which bring together the professional and public communities of the city, state, and region. The Institute often has the opportunity to respond quickly to program needs at the college and in the community.

Faculty: Teachers who use writing in their curriculum, publishing writers, and college instructors.

Financial Assistance: Occasional grant support.

Contact: Diane McDevitt or Kim Stafford.

Of Dark & Stormy Nights
Mystery Writers of America – Midwest Chapter
P.O. Box 1944
Muncie, IN 47308-1944
(765) 288-7402
e-mail: spurgeonmwa@juno.com

Length of Residency: One day.

When: Second Saturday in June.

Application Deadline: May 15.

Cost: $140 (includes continental breakfast and full luncheon).

Description: Of Dark & Stormy Nights, held in the Chicago suburb of Rolling Meadows, Ill., is a concentrated one–day workshop for mystery and true crime writers at all levels of experience.

Successful writers join experts in other fields, editors, and agents share information throughout individual presentations and panel discussions.

Faculty: Recent faculty members include Barbara D'Amato, Eleanor Taylor Bland, Jeanne M. Dams, Hugh Holton, Wendi Lee, Janet Riehecky, Marion Markham, Jeremiah Healy, Deborah Brod, Karl Largent, James D. Brewer, Philip O'Shaughnessy, Mark S. Fleisher, Alexander Obolsky, Kathryn Kennison, Shelly Rueben, Charles King, Sara Paretsky, Max Allan Collins, Marnie Schulenburg, Barbara Collins, Laura Lynn Leffers, Elizabeth Daniels Squire, Ruthe Furie, Sara Hoskinson Frommer, Michael Allen Dymmoch, Clark Davenport, Dennis E. Hensley, David Linzee, Michael S. Kahn, Fred Hunter, Allen and Alex Matthews, Mark Richard Zubro, Gary Warren Niebuhr, Sam Reaves, Helen Esper Olmstead, Michael Raleigh, David J. Walker, Terence Faherty, Susan Andrews, Penny Warner, Esmond Harmsworth, Jane Jordan Browne, Barbara Kuroff, and Linda Allen.

Contact: Wiley W. Spurgeon Jr., Director.

●The Oklahoma Fall Arts Institute
P.O. Box 18154
720 N.W. 50th
Oklahoma City, OK 73154
(405) 842-0890
website: http://www.telepath.com/okarts

Length of Residency: 4 days, Thursday through Sunday.

When: September–October.

Application Deadline: None. Classes fill quickly. Early registration is encouraged. Course catalog becomes available in late spring.

Cost: $450 includes tuition, room, and board.

Description: Six hours of workshops per day with faculty of national reputation. Workshops offered in poetry, fiction, nonfiction, and writing for children. Participants are housed at Quartz Mountain Arts and Conference Center in Southwest Oklahoma. Quartz Mountain is a beautiful, isolated location perfect for the uninterrupted study of writing. Evenings include faculty readings, musical concerts, and informal gatherings.

Faculty: TBA. Faculty have included Marvin Bell, Lucille Clifton, Donald Hall, Reginald Gibbons, Anita Skeen, Terry Tempest Williams, and others.

Financial Assistance: Limited scholarships available to College and University educators and public school teachers in Oklahoma.

Contact: Christina Newendorp, Asst. Director of Programs.

Once Upon A Time...
Santa Fe Community College
Community Services Office
P.O. Box 4187
Santa Fe, NM 87502-4187
(505) 438-1251

Length of Residency: One day.

When: Mid–July.

Application Deadline: June 28 for early registration fee.

Cost: $68 before June 28, $82 after June 28.

Description: A conference on writing and illustrating children's books, sponsored by the Community Services Division of Santa Fe Community College. Subjects covered during the conference include: the basic structure of the picture book, discover writing on the Net, creating mood and atmosphere, how to structure a novel for children, developing fictional characters, how to create manuscripts that sell, examine the market trends and learn practical steps for getting your foot in the door for publication, and what to do now that you've sold your novel.

Contact: Please contact the Conference Coordinator for more information.

●Open Road Writing Workshops
P.O. Box 386
Amherst, MA 01004
(413) 259-1865
e-mail: mpettit@alumni.princeton.edu

Contact: The Director.

Oregon Rock Eagle Writing Festival
3140 Portland Street
Eugene, OR 97405
(503) 343-9516

Contact: The Director.

Ozark Creative Writers, Inc.
6817 Gingerbread Lane
Little Rock, AR 72204
(501) 565-8889
FAX (501) 565-7220
e-mail: pvining@aristotle.net

Length of Residency: 3 days.

When: Second weekend in October.

Application Deadline: August 30 (to enter competitions).

Cost: $50 prior to September 1st, $60 afterwards.

Description: A writer's conference with excellent speakers who are prolific publishing writers. Satellite speakers fill afternoon of the two full days. Main speaker fills morning sessions. Two banquets; banquet fee is not included in registration (nor lodging).

Faculty: Seven member, nonprofit, incorporated board invites six to eight published authors.

Financial Assistance: None.

Contact: Peggy Vining, Counselor (501) 569-8771, or above address. Send SASE prior to May 1 for contest brochure and program information.

Pacifica Graduate Institute Poetry Symposium
249 Lambert Road
Carpinteria, CA 93013
(805) 969-3626 Ext. 123
FAX (805) 565-1932

Contact: Barbara McClintock, Director.

Palm Springs Writers' Conference
646 Morongo Road
Palm Springs, CA 92264
(619) 864-9760
FAX (619) 322-1833

Length of Residency: 4 days.

When: Beginning of May.

Application Deadline: Conference date.

Cost: $299-$349, including some meals, not hotel.

Description: A curriculum of all writing disciplines (except poetry) taught by working writers, editors, and agents. Manuscript evaluations are available, as well as one-on-one consultations with editors and agents. Classes from 8 a.m. to 10 p.m. during four days of intensive instruction.

Faculty: Dean R. Koontz, Ray Bradbury, Joseph Wambaugh, Sue Grafton, Harlan Ellison, Michael Spilave, Iris Rainer Dart, Olivia Goldsmith, Kelly Lange, Roderick Thorp, Gerald Petievich, Jack Adler, Otto Penzler, Arthur Lyons, Julie Smith, Raymond Strait, plus editors and agents.

Financial Assistance: Some scholarships available for needy high school and college students.

Contact: Arthur Lyons.

●Palmetto Writers' Conference
P.O. Box 587
Pendleton, SC 29670

Contact: Wayne Link.

Paris Writers' Workshop
20 Blvd. du Montparnasse
75015 Paris, France
011-331-4566-7550
FAX 011-331-4065-9653
e-mail: wice@wice-paris.org
website: www.wice-paris.org

Length of Residency: Five days.

When: Starts last Sunday in June.

Application Deadline: See website or contact WICE for details.

Cost: FF2,000 for all participants; accommodations and travel not included.

Description: This annual workshop is sponsored by WICE, a nonprofit educational and cultural institute offering innovative, high-level adult instruction in English in Montparnasse, the literary heart of Paris. First held in 1988 and limited to 40 participants, the PWW offers a positive atmosphere in which writers can watch their skills flourish. Students, who come from all over the world, pick a workshop in one of several genres: fiction, poetry, nonfiction, or creativity, for example. Following a Sunday evening reception, intensive workshops are conducted each morning (Monday-Friday). In the afternoon, participants meet with their writer-in-residence or attend lectures on topics such as memoir writing, the ethics of nonfiction, editing and marketing. There are evening readings by the writers-in-residence and special guests. The program culminates with a student reading Friday afternoon. Participants are encouraged to submit a manuscript, although this is optional. Those who do not wish to submit a manuscript may enroll as auditors.

Faculty: Past workshop teachers have included Grace Paley, Andrei Codrescu, Jayne Anne Phillips, Diane Johnson, and C.K. Williams.

Financial Assistance: Two half-tuition scholarships are offered each year. Please contact WICE or see the website for more information.

Contact: Rose Burke or Ellen Hinsey, co-directors of the Paris Writers' Workshop and the Creative Writing Program at WICE.

Peripatetic Writing Workshop & Colony
West Village Sta., Box 20093
New York, NY 10014
(212) 924-0781
FAX (914) 688-9730
e-mail: mhughesny@aol.com

Length of Residency: Ireland, one week; Woodstock, 10 days.

When: Ireland, late June; Woodstock, mid to late July.

Application Deadline: Ireland, April 1st; Woodstock, June 1st.

Cost: $1,000 Ireland; $800 Woodstock.

Description: Designed as a cross between artists' colony and writing conference, open to writers of every level and particularly valuable to writers working on full-length fiction or nonfiction manuscripts or short story collections. It offers: a quiet place to write with structured hours, weekly tutorials, 50 ms. pages per week, workshops, a professional weekend with the chance to meet and speak individually with publishing figures. Guests in 1998 included: Penguin Books Executive Editor Jane von Mehren; Algonquin Books Publisher Elisabeth Scharlatte; Charlotte Sheedy Agency, Neethi Madan, agent; Agent Mary Evans of Mary Evans, Inc.

Faculty: M.E. Hughes and Maureen Brady. Hughes teaches advanced fiction at New York University; Brady teaches in New York City at The Writer's Voice and N.Y.U. Hughes is author of *Precious In His Sight*, Viking; Brady is author of *Folly* and *The Question She Put To Herself* and *MidLife*. Also, Lisa Carey, *The Mermaids Singing*, in Ireland.

Financial Assistance: Inquire about work-study program.

Contact: M.E. Hughes & Maureen Brady. Peripatetic funded in part by New York State Council of the Arts.

●**Ploughshares International Fiction Writing Conference**
Emerson College European Programs
100 Beacon Street
Boston, MA 02116-1523
(617) 824-8567
FAX (617) 824-8618

Length of Residency: 2 weeks.

When: June, July.

Application Deadline: May 1.

Cost: $2,245 including room and board, 4 academic credits.

Description: Be an expatriate writer for two weeks. A distinguished faculty works closely with selected fiction writers in team-taught workshops and individual conferences. In the unique setting of a renaissance castle in the Dutch Country-side, the emphasis is on technique, revision, and literary values.

Faculty: Alexandra Marshall, Askold Melnychzuk, James Carroll, Alexandra Johnson, Pamela Painter, Thomas E. Kennedy. Visiting writer: John Updike.

Financial Assistance: Through Emerson College. $1,000 Robie MacAuley Fellowship awarded to best manuscript submitted with application by April 1.

Contact: Program Coordinator.

Pocono Mountains Retreat
Society of Children's Book Writers and Illustrators (SCBWI)
708 Pine Street
Moscow, PA 18444
(717) 842-2802

Length of Residency: Three days.

When: Third or fourth weekend in April.

Application Deadline: April 1.

Cost: $300 including room and board.

Description: The Pocono Mountains Retreat is sponsored by the Eastern Pennsylvania chapter of the Society of Children's Book Writers and Illustrators. Formed in 1968 by a group of Los Angeles-based writers for children, and now with over 10,000 members, the SCBWI is the only national organization for professional authors, illustrators, and publishers of children's literature. The retreat, held annually since 1993, provides serious writers a mixture of inspiration and professional opportunities in a charming country setting. Besides hearing lectures that aim high, blending the philosophical with the practical, writers share their work with other practitioners of the craft, editors and art directors from trade presses, agents, and other professionals in the field.

Faculty: Past faculty have included such award-winning authors as Nancy Willard, Patricia Lee Gauch, Richard Peck, Louis Sachar, Janet Taylor Lisle, Liz Rosenberg, and Bruce Coville, along with major illustrators, literary agents, and editors from major publishing houses such as Crown, Dial, Orchard, Viking, and Scholastic/Blue Sky.

Financial Assistance: One full scholarship and one tuition-only scholarship are available to SCBWI members who show exceptional promise and could not otherwise afford to attend the retreat.

Contact: For more information, contact Susan Campbell Bartoletti, Director.

Poetry Center
Passaic County Community College
College Boulevard
Paterson, NJ 07505-1179
(973) 684-6555

Description: The Poetry Center at PCCC sponsors the Allen Ginsberg Awards, The Paterson Poetry Prize, The Paterson Fiction Prize, the Paterson Prize for Books for Young People, *The Paterson Literary Review (PLR)*, a poetry library, and a series of readings and workshops.

Contact: Maria Mazziotti Gillian, Director.

Poets & Writers Literary Horizons
Publishing Seminars
72 Spring Street
New York, NY 10012
(212) 226-3586
FAX (212) 226-3963
e-mail: info@pw.org

Length of Residency: Single-session and multiple-session courses.

When: Classes are offered October–November and February–April.

Cost: $10–$195.

Description: The Poets & Writers Literary Horizons program is a new initiative from one of the largest nonprofit literary service organizations in the country. Literary Horizons offers professional development opportunities for writers at all stages of their careers. Our seminars, now in their third year, focus on how to publish poetry, fiction, and creative nonfiction with greater success. Writers will learn about the references and resources that will be of help to them, strategies for narrowing down the publishing market, and techniques for evaluating the editorial styles and interests of editors and agents. Guest agents and editors are part of the multiple-session courses, which also teach writers how to negotiate rights and contracts and how to build their audience. Special-topics lectures and single-session courses for women's writing and gay and lesbian writing are also available.

Faculty: Instructors for the program are Poets & Writers staff members Amy Holman, Director of Literary Horizons, and Heather Shayne Blakeslee, Associate Director of the program. Guest speakers and instructors have included C. Michael Curtis from the *Atlantic Monthly*, Carol Houck Smith from W.W. Norton, Wendy Weil of the Wendy Weil Literary Agency, Martha Stone from the *Harvard Gay & Lesbian Review*, and Jenine Gordon Bockman from *Literal Latté*.

Contact: For a free packet of information on publishing and a Literary Horizons program brochure, please contact Heather Shayne Blakeslee, Associate Director of Literary Horizons, for more information.

Pomotawh Naantam Ranch Workshop
26767 County Road 12
Somerset, CO 81434
(303) 929-6571
FAX (303) 929-6585

Contact: Jon and Dori Lee, Directors.

●Port Townsend Writers' Conference
Box 1158
Port Townsend, WA 98368
(360) 385–3102

Length of Residency: Ten days.

When: Mid–July annually.

Application Deadline: July 1.

Cost: $425 tuition; housing and food available at low cost.

Description: For over 20 years the Port Townsend Writer's Conference has set the standard for serious literary gatherings. A mixed schedule of readings, lectures, workshops, conferences, panels, and social events is complimented by free time to write and to enjoy the natural beauty of the waterfront site.

Faculty: All faculty are present for the whole conference. 1998 faculty: Ursula K. LeGuin, Olga Broumas, Terry Tempest Williams, and David Bottoms.

Financial Assistance: A limited number of partial tuition scholarships are available. Application deadline is May 1.

Contact: Sam Hamill, Director.

Ragdale Foundation
1260 N. Green Bay Road
Lake Forest, IL 60045
(847) 234–1063
FAX (847) 234–1075
e–mail: ragdale1@aol.com
website: http://nsn.nslsilus.org/ljkhome/ragdale

Length of Residency: Two weeks to eight weeks.

When: Year-round except in May and last two weeks of December.

Application Deadline: January 15 and June 1.

Cost: $20 application fee; $15 per day includes room and board.

Description: Mission: To provide a quiet place for artists and writers to work. The Ragdale Foundation houses twelve artists, writers, composers, and performers at a time for periods from two to eight weeks. Constructed in 1879 by architect Howard Van Doren Shaw in the Arts and Crafts style, the Ragdale estate is located in Lake Forest, Illinois, 30 miles north of Chicago. The foundation adjoins 55 acres of virgin prairie and is listed on the National Register of Historic Places. Daily life at Ragdale is quiet and serene, offering artists time to focus on their work. Residents have breakfast and lunch on their own. Dinner is a communal meal followed by informal readings, recitals, slide presentations, or relaxation. Residents may be requested to participate in occasional public readings or presentations.

Faculty: Former writers–in–residence include: Alex Kotlowitz, Jackie Mitchard, Jane Hamilton, Sara Paretsky, Carol Anshaw, and Maureen Seaton.

Financial Assistance: Fellowships include the Frances Shaw Fellowship for Women Over the Age of 55.

●Rappahannock Fiction Writers' Workshop
P.O. Box 633
Carlisle, PA 17013-0633
(717) 243-3205
e-mail: ficwriters@aol.com

Length of Residency: Five days.

When: August.

Application Deadline: Contact Director.

Cost: $345 tuition.

Description: A combination workshop/retreat where aspiring writers can work closely with well-established writers in a lovely environment. Each participant receives an intensive review of a pre-submitted story or novel excerpt. Emphasis: the study of craft and the creation of an energized community of writers.

Faculty: 1999: Robert Olmstead, Lee K. Abbott, Janet Peery, and Michael Parker.

Contact: The Director.

●Recursos de Santa Fe
826 Camino de Monte Rey, Suite A3
Santa Fe, NM 87505

Contact: Steven Lewis.

Richard Hugo House
1634 Eleventh Avenue
Seattle, WA 98122
(206) 322-7030
FAX (206) 320-8767
e-mail: welcome@hugohouse.org
website: www.hugohouse.org

Length of Residency: Classes, workshops, and award programs of various lengths.

Application Deadline: Varies by program.

Cost: Tuition: from $30 to $300.

Description: Located in a big, old Victorian house in Seattle's Capitol Hill neighborhood, Richard Hugo House is a place for people who love writing and reading. Hugo House is a community place where people gather to celebrate, learn about, and practice writing and reading. Through innovative programs and events, we strive to make the process of writing a meaningful and useful part of our culture and community life. Here readers and writers have a place where their talents go to work, advancing critical thought, shaping our culture, and exploring the craft of writing. Our primary areas of service are Seattle and the Pacific Northwest region.

Faculty: Current and past instructors include Rebecca Brown, Madeline DeFrees, Matthew Stadler, David Mahler, and Jan Wallace.

Financial Assistance: Scholarships are available.

Contact: Kirsten Atik, Administrative Assistant.

Robert Quackenbush's Workshops
460 East 79th Street
New York, NY 10021
(212) 744-3822

Length of Residency: Five days.

When: Annually, the 2nd week in July.

Application Deadline: June 30.

Cost: $550 covers all costs of the workshop, which does not include housing and meals.

Description: This intensive, individualized five-day children's book writing and illustrating workshop is limited to 8 persons and begins with each student planning a book which is ready for the publisher by the week's end. Daily classes begin at 9 a.m. and end at 4 p.m. with an hour break for lunch. Classes are held at the Manhattan studio of Robert Quackenbush, author/artist of over 150 books for young readers. Evenings are free to enjoy New York City's unique cultural and research facilities. Focus of the class is on picture books. Philosophy: Everyone has a unique story to tell.

Contact: Robert Quackenbush.

Rocky Mountain Writers Guild, Inc.
837 15th Street
Boulder, CO 80302
(303) 444-4100

Description: Call or write for updated information on new programs.

Contact: James Hutchinson, Executive Director.

Rogue Valley Writers' Conference
Extension Programs
SOSC
Ashland, OR 97520
(503) 552-6331

Contact: The Director.

ROM/CON
1555 Washington Avenue
San Leandro, CA 94577
(510) 357-5665
FAX (510) 357-1337

Length of Residency: 4 days.

When: August 14, 15, 16, 17 in Houston, Texas.

Application Deadline: July 15.

Cost: $175.

Description: Writers' conference: all you need to know about publishing but did not know who to ask. Our conference is the place for you. 13 years of experience.

Faculty: Quality workshops given by well-known authors, editors, publishers, and agents; plus writing teachers.

Financial Assistance: None.

Contact: Barbara Keenan, at above phone and fax number.

RopeWalk Writers' Retreat
University of Southern Indiana
8600 University Boulevard
Evansville, IN 47712
(800) 467-8600
(812) 464-1863

Length of Residency: One week.

When: Mid-June.

Application Deadline: Approx. May 10 (scholarship application approx. April 15).

Cost: $425 -- includes breakfast and lunch daily; does not include dinner or housing. Housing costs range from $100-$500 per week.

Description: The RopeWalk Writers' Retreat was founded in 1988 to take advantage of the unique atmosphere of New Harmony, Indiana. New Harmony is the site of two 19th-century utopian experiments and has a long history of intellectual exploration and experimentation. Our goal at RopeWalk is to provide participants with expert instruction and critiques from the faculty; an opportunity to share with other writers; a break from the everyday world; and a time to write in an atmosphere that is both relaxing and mentally stimulating. Workshops are limited to 12 participants each with four or five workshops offered each year.

Faculty: Faculty have included: Bob Shacochis, Pam Houston, Rust Hills, Joy Williams, Amy Hempel, Larry Levis, Ann Beattie, Ellen Bryant Voigt, William Matthews, Michael Martone, Stephen Dobyns, Mark Jarman, Roxanna Robinson, Dave Smith, Heather McHugh, John Hawkes, Phil Levine, Judith Ortiz Cofer, Barry Hannah, Andrew Hudgins, Erin McGraw, and David St. John.

Financial Assistance: Partial scholarships are available based upon merit. Occasionally, full scholarships are awarded. The amount of scholarship funding varies from year to year.

Contact: Linda Cleek, Conference Coordinator, University of Southern Indiana Extended Services, 8600 University Blvd., Evansville, IN 47712. e-mail: <lcleek.ucs@smtp.usi.edu>.

●San Jose State University
Center for Literary Arts
One Washington Square
San Jose, CA 95192-0088

Contact: The Director.

San Juan Writers Workshop
Canyonlands Field Institute
Recapture Lodge
P.O. Box 68
Moab, UT 84532
(801) 259-7750
(800) 860-5262
website: www.canyonlandsfieldinst.org

Length of Residency: Three and a half days.

When: Mid-March of each year.

Application Deadline: By February of each year.

Cost: $440 includes lodging and meals.

Credit: University semester credit available for additional filing fees.

Description: Canyonlands Field Institute is a nonprofit organization which promotes a sustainable future for the Colorado Plateau through field education programs. Established in 1997, the San Juan Writers Workshop encourages writers to explore the ways surroundings -- home and away, and especially in the natural world -- shape emotions, thoughts, and actions. Field studies of the natural and cultural history of the area will provide a model of "ecological literacy" that can be used to examine their own home places as well as the terrain of the heart. Participants study with two faculty members and a naturalist during the workshop.

Faculty: Instructors have included Ellen Meloy, Ann Weiler Walka, Robert Michael Pyle, and Scott Russell Sanders.

Santa Barbara Book Publishing Workshop
P.O. Box 4232-866
Santa Barbara, CA 93140-4232
(805) 968-7277
FAX (805) 968-1379
Fax-on-demand (805) 968-8947; Request document 167

Length of Residency: Two days.

When: 1997: Jan. 11-12, May 3-4, Aug. 2-3, Nov. 8-9.

Application Deadline: Workshops are limited to 18 participants and fill up 6-8 weeks in advance.

Cost: $495.

Description: Nonfiction book marketing, promoting, and distributing.

Faculty: Dan Poynter and Mindy Bingham.

Contact: Para Publishing, Patricia Finn.

●Santa Fe Community College Writers' Conference
6401 Richards Avenue
Santa Fe, NM 87505
(505) 428-1251
FAX (505) 428-1302
website: http://www.santa-fe.cc.nm.us

Length of Residency: 2–3 days.

When: Usually 2nd week in February.

Application Deadline: For presenters: September of the previous year; for participants: up to opening day, as available.

Cost: Generally +/– $175.

Description: The Writers' Conference at Santa Fe Community College is a week-end long event comprising several keynotes, panels with distinguished authors, editors, publishers, etc., breakout working sessions with accomplished teachers, entertainment at open mikes, luncheon readings, and participant networking.

Faculty: Past keynotes and faculty have included Natalie Goldberg, John Nichols, Denise Chavez, and Levi Romero. In 1999 our invited guests are John Nichols (*The Milagro Beanfield War*), Digby Wolfe (*Laugh-In*), and many distinguished professionals from around the State of New Mexico.

Contact: Writers' Conference at Santa Fe Community College, The Center for Continuing Education, Santa Fe Community College at above address.

Santa Fe Writers' Conference
Recursos de Santa Fe
826 Camino De Monte Rey
Santa Fe, NM 87505
(505) 988-5992
FAX (505) 989-8608
e-mail: recursos@aol.com
website: www.recursos.org

Length of Residency: 5 days.

When: July 28 – August 2, 1999.

Application Deadline: While there is no formal deadline, workshop is limited to 60 participants and selection of workshop leader is on basis of first come, first served.

Cost: $560 (non-resident, tuition, reception dinner, lunches); $850 (resident, tuition, shared room, reception dinner, breakfasts, lunches); $1,055 (as above, with single room).

Description: Workshops, under the leadership of distinguished poets and writers, limited to 12 participants each, focus on critiques of student work. Also lectures, readings, panel discussions, and individual conferences. Over five intense days, both professional and aspiring writers discuss the art and technique of writing poetry and prose. Acceptance into program based on submission of manuscript, no longer than 10 pages, double-spaced.

Faculty: The past year's workshops were conducted by Christopher Merrill, Antonya Nelson, and David St. John. Previous workshop leaders include Alice Adams, Robert Haas, Elizabeth Hardwick, E. Annie Proulx, Robert Stone, and Elizabeth Tallent.

Contact: Stephen Lewis, Conference Coordinator.

Santa Monica Writers Conference
English Department
Santa Monica College
1900 Pico Boulevard
Santa Monica, CA 90405-1628
(310) 452-9242

Description: Contact the English Department for updated information.

Contact: English Department, Santa Monica College.

Seminar in Poetry Writing
11 Chestnut Street
Melrose, MA 02176
(781) 662-7806

Length of Residency: Ten weeks, four sessions a year beginning in September, January, March, and June.

When: Tuesdays, 8:00–10:00 pm.

Cost: $175 per session.

Class Limit: 10.

Description: The Seminar in Poetry Writing, established in 1978, is an intensive, independent workshop designed for serious poets with advanced writing skills. In-depth class discussion of poems is complemented by tutorial conferences providing personal attention for individual needs. Manuscript evaluations and marketing advice are provided with an eye toward publishing.

Meetings are held in Belmont, MA, in the Greater Boston area, easily accessible by public transportation or car. A program of independent study is offered for out-of-state poets. Applications are accepted year-round. Applicants are asked to submit eight poems and a biographical sketch, including data on publications, if any.

Faculty: The Seminar is directed by Harold Bond, MFA, University of Iowa. His poems have appeared widely in anthologies and leading periodicals, including *Harper's Magazine, The New Republic, The New Yorker, Ploughshares*, and *Saturday Review*, and he is the author of three books of poetry. A past NEA fellow, he is a longtime member of the teaching staff at the Cambridge Center for Adult Education.

The Seminar is conducted with the participation of invited editors, publishers, and well-known poets. Visiting faculty have included Olga Broumas, Sam Cornish, Stephen Dobyns, Forrest Gander, Mary Karr, Thomas Lux, Elizabeth McKim, Roland Pease, Jr., Patricia Smith, Gerald Stern, and Rosanna Warren.

Contact: Harold Bond.

●Sewanee Writers' Conference
University of the South
310 St. Luke's Hall
735 University Avenue
Sewanee, TN 37375
(615) 598-1141
FAX (615) 598-1145

Length of Residency: 12 days.

When: Second half of July, beginning on a Tuesday, ending on a Sunday.

Application Deadline: Rolling admissions policy. We begin accepting applications in early February and generally continue to accept applications, as space is available, through May.

Cost: $1,205 in 1998.

Description: This annual conference, first offered in 1990, is directed by Wyatt Prunty (poet, Carlton Professor of English). It is held over 12 consecutive days beginning with the third Tuesday in July. Each year approximately 100 participants selected on the basis of manuscript submissions have the opportunity to meet and work with distinguished poets, fiction writers, and playwrights. The program features workshops (fiction, poetry, playwriting) with 15 members in each workshop, individual hour-long manuscript conferences, discussion groups focusing on model texts, and presentations by literary agents, reviewers, critics, editors of literary and commercial periodicals, and editors representing university and commercial presses. A full schedule of readings, craft lectures, panel discussions, and formal and informal talks, together with a variety of social events, allow many opportunities for exchange. Accommodations are available in single or double residency rooms, and meals are served in the dining hall. Enrollment is competitive; qualified participants are invited to apply for a limited number of fellowships and scholarships.

Faculty: During the nine years of its existence, the Sewanee Writers' Conference has had the following faculty members in attendance: Russell Banks, Pinckney Benedict, James Gordon Bennett, Kent Brown, Robert Olen Butler, John Casey, Laura Maria Censabella, Dave DeChristopher, Elizabeth Dewberry, Ellen Douglas, Stanley Elkin, Horton Foote, Carol Frost, Ernest Gaines, Marianne Gingher, Emily Grosholz, Rachel Hadas, Wendy Hammond, Anthony Hecht, Amy Hempel, John Hollander, Ann Hood, Tina Howe, Andrew Hudgins, Mark Jarman, Diane Johnson, Donald Justice, Maxine Kumin, Romulus Linney, Margot Livesey, Charles Martin, Alice McDermott, Susan Minot, Mary Morris, Kent Nelson, Howard Nemerov, Tim O'Brien, Joe Ashby Porter, Francine Prose, Mark Richard, Mary Jo Salter, Brent Spencer, Robert Stone, Mark Strand, Chase Twichell, Mona Van Duyn, Derek Walcott, and Stephen Wright. Visitors have included Georges and Anne Borchardt, Sidney Burris, C. Michael Curtis, Peter Davison, Diana Finch, Peter Franklin, Robert Giroux, David R. Godine, Henry Hart, John T. Irwin, Jon Jory, Andrew Lytle, J.D. McClatchy, Arthur Miller, Pat Mulchay, Wyatt Prunty, Alice Quinn, Robert Richman, Steve Ross, Dave Smith, Monroe K. Spears, William Styron, Peter Taylor, Jarvis Thurston, Leslie Wells, and Richard Wilbur.

Contact: Cheri Bedell Peters, Conference Administrator.

Shenandoah International Playwrights Retreat
Route 1, Box 167-F
Staunton, VA 24401
(540) 248-1868
e-mail: shenarts@cfw.com

Length of Residency: Four weeks.

When: August, September.

Application Deadline: February 1.

Cost: Fellowships cover costs.

Description: The Shenandoah Playwrights Retreat exists to provide young and established writers a stimulating, challenging environment to test and develop new work in a safe haven, free from the pressures of everyday living. Playwrights come to us from around the U.S. and the world. Each year, the Retreat brings guest playwrights from different regions of the world to join with American playwrights in this creative exploration. The writers work in close and intense collaboration with our multicultural company of dramaturgs, directors, and actors. What occurs is a simultaneous "on-the-feet/on-the-page" exploration of each play, culminating in a staged reading before an audience of invited professionals and advocates.

Faculty: Robert Graham Small is an accomplished dramaturg, director, lighting designer, and teacher with extensive national and international experience. He has worked in residence for Yale Repertory Theatre and Drama School, Pan Asian Repertory Company, and Chealsea Theatre Center. He has twice directed for Joseph Papp and the NY Shakespeare Festival. Dramaturgical and developmental work includes the Eugene O'Neill National Playwrights Conference, The New Harmony Project, and 18 years at Shenandoah.

Financial Assistance: Fellowships cover costs.

Contact: Robert Graham Small, Director, or Kathleen Tosco, Managing Director, for more information.

Shenandoah Valley Writers' Guild
c/o Professor Cogan
Lord Fairfax Community College
Middletown, VA 22645
(540) 869-1120

When: May 14.

Application Deadline: May 10.

Cost: $40, including lunch.

Description: Keynote Speaker plus morning and afternoon workshops.

Faculty: Area professional writers.

Financial Assistance: None.

Contact: Professor Cogan.

The Sitka Symposium on Human Values and the Written Word
The Island Institute
P.O. Box 2420
Sitka, AK 99835
(907) 747-3794
e-mail: island@ptialaska.net
website: www.ptialaska.net/~island/index.html

Length: One week annual symposium.

When: Each June, usually the third week.

Application Deadline: No application. Early registration by May 1 gives discount on tuition, but registrations are taken up to the beginning of the conference up to the limit of 55 participants.

Cost: Tuition: $220 by May 1, $250 after. Housing: $49/night single; $59/night for two.

Description: Sometimes thought to be a writers conference, the Sitka Symposium is rather a week–long gathering that aims to put both written and oral traditions to the service of ideas. It is for writers, readers, and anyone interested in the central questions posed by each year's specified theme. A guest faculty of five include poets, novelists, essayists, natural historians, folklorists, Native Americans, community leaders, and others whose work pertains to the year's theme. Activities include presentations by faculty, panel, and group discussions, readings, optional writing groups and individual manuscript critiques, and a summer solstice evening cruise. College credit is also available. Held concurrently with a chamber music festival and in a town with a spectacular natural setting that offers hiking, sea kayaking, wildlife viewing, and other outdoor activities.

Faculty: Past faculty have included Gary Snyder, Margaret Atwood, Barry Lopez, Robert Hass, Carolyn Forché, Ursula Hegi, Alison Deming, Robert Michael Pyle, Scott Russell Sanders, Rina Swentzell, Linda Hogan, Stephanie Mills, Wes Jackson, John Keeble, Richard Nelson, Gary Nabhan, Teresa Jordan, Pattiann Rogers, Lorna Goodison, Nora Dauenhauer, Chet Raymo,

Hugh Brody, James Nageak, John Haines, Sheila Nickerson, William Kittredge, William Stafford, and others. Different faculty serve each year.

Financial Assistance: Scholarships occasionally available, but not on a regular basis.

Contact: Carolyn Servid or Dorik Mechau, Co-Directors.

Snake River Institute
Postal Box 128
Wilson, WY 83014
(307) 733-2214
FAX (307) 739-1710

Length of Residency: One to five days.

When: June through October.

Application Deadline: None.

Cost: Call or write for details.

Description: The Snake River Institute, located in Jackson Hole, Wyoming, was founded in 1988 to present programs in the arts and humanities which celebrate the cultures and communities of the American West. Part of fulfilling this mission brings teachers of writing together with students to improve their writing skills and experience surrounding landscapes. One to five-day workshops run throughout the summer and fall. The Institute focuses mainly on writing programs which foster the individual's creative voice. The Western Landscape serves as inspiration. Workshop sizes are small (6-17) to provide an intimate and personal experience for each participant.

Past faculty: Marvin Bell, Kay Morgan, Christopher Merrill, Pamela Painter, Joan Stone, Charles Levendosky, Theresa Jordan, Patricia Limerick, Hannah Hinchman, and David Romtvedt.

Financial Assistance: Limited financial aid and work study is available for all programs. Please contact the office to receive an application.

Contact: Samantha Strawbridge, Program Coordinator for full details.

Society of Children's Book Writers
P.O. Box 20233, Park West Finance Station
New York, NY 10025-1511

Length of Residency: One day.

When: Usually first Saturday in November.

Application Deadline: Conference date.

Cost: $65 SCBW members, $70 non-members; $15 additional on day of conference.

Description: One-day conference includes keynote speaker, workshops running concurrently, editors' panel, book sales, Golden Kite Award presentation, light breakfast, and party-book signing.

Faculty: Authors, illustrators of children's books, editors, agents, and packagers change yearly.

Financial Assistance: None available for conference.

Contact: Conference Director at above address for any information, or Frieda Gates at (914) 356-7273.

●Sofer, The Jewish Writer's Workshop
Olin-Sang-Ruby Union Institute, UAHC
555 Skokie Blvd., Suite 225
Northbrook, IL 60062
(847) 509-0990
FAX (847) 509-0970
e-mail: dunnfried@aol.com

When: August.

Cost: $250-$360 (depending on chosen accommodations).

Description: The Jewish Writer's Workshop is a unique four day event for all who write whether in pursuit of profession or pleasure. Sofer will provide you with the opportunity to further hone your craft, explore new streams of interpretation, and let you share your work with others who can support your efforts. A key element of this program is the opportunity to study with prominent Jewish writers in small groups of eight to ten participants. Workshops will focus on style, revision, creativity, interpretation, and public presentation while providing response from faculty and fellow participants. Themes of the workshop emphasize a) poetry writing, b) fiction writing, c) creative nonfiction, and d) playwriting.

Faculty: Gerald Stern, Steve Stern, Roger Kamenetz, and Don Maseng.

Contact: The Director.

Southern California Society of Children's Book Writers and Illustrators Writer's Day
11943 Montana Avenue, #105
Los Angeles, CA 90049
(310) 820-5601

Length of Residency: One day.

When: Mid-April.

Application Deadline: April 8.

Cost: $60-80 (Bring lunch or purchase nearby).

Description: SOCA-SCBWI offers an annual one-day conference focusing on the craft of writing for children. The conference is held on the grounds of a private school in San Gabriel, California.

Faculty: Our annual Writers' Day features authors, editors, and others involved in the field of children's literature. This year's faculty features widely acclaimed author/illustrator Patricia Polacco, award-winning author Dian Curtis Regan, agent Virginia Knowlton from Curtis-Brown, editor Sandra Arnold, Sid Tessler, CPA, and others.

Financial Assistance: $5 early-bird discount.

Contact: Judy or Stephanie at above phone number for a flyer or information.

Southern California Writers Conference, San Diego
4555 Rhode Island
San Diego, CA 92116
(619) 291-6805

Length of Residency: Four days.

When: Mid-February (over the Presidents' Day weekend).

Application Deadline: Up to start of conference.

Cost: $350/$430 for full conference with lodging ($250 for non-residents).

Description: The SCWC began in 1986 as an outgrowth of the Writers' Bookstore and Haven in order to nurture and encourage those involved in the writing community. The conference continues to support working writers in all fields with goals toward polish and publication. Intensive workshops reach all levels, from beginners to published writers. Morning and afternoon workshops are offered in fiction, nonfiction, travel writing, poetry, the business of writing, article publication, and writing for and selling to screen. Several workshops, as well as late night read-and-critique sessions, offer writers a chance to present their ongoing work for comments and constructive feedback. Also featured is an agents' panel and evening speakers. Although busy, the long-holiday-weekend conference affords writers time to mix and mingle with peers, agents, and editors in a warm, welcoming setting.

Faculty: Past workshop leaders and visiting writers have included: Dallas & JoAnne Barnes, George Bernau, Jacqueline Briskin, Mark A. Clements, Sharleen Cooper Cohen, Michael Collins, Robert Ferrigno, D.C. Fontana, Phyllis Gebauer, Elizabeth George, C. Jerry Hannah, Ken Kuhlken, Dennis Lynds, William Murray, T. Jefferson Parker, Linda Segar, Gayle Stone, S.L. Stebel.

Contact: Michael Steven Gregory, Director, for information and application forms. Phone calls welcomed.

Southwest Florida Writers' Conference
8099 College Parkway
Fort Myers, FL 33906-6210
(813) 489-9226

Length of Residency: two days.

When: Always the fourth Friday & Saturday in February.

Application Deadline: One week in advance requested.

Cost: $79 for two days, with optional evening social.

Description: This will be the 17th Annual Writers' Conference in Ft. Myers. Each day begins with a keynote address, and includes workshop sessions on topics such as fiction, nonfiction, screen writing, children's writing, travel writing, finding an agent, and many times a presentation by a publisher/editor. The average attendance for the two days is between 150-200 participants. The goals of the conference are to provide access to successful professionals in literary and popular areas, and to allow ample opportunity for networking with peers and presenters. The keynote speakers for 1996 were George Plimpton and Stephen Humphrey Bogart.

Faculty: The conference staff includes a Director, Coordinator, support personnel, and an Advisory/Planning Board that is comprised of published writers, bookstore owners, librarians, etc., that are interested in promoting writing for beginners through seasoned professionals. Past presenters have included P.D. James, Peter Matthiesson, Carl Hiassen, Lorian Hemingway, and many others.

Financial Assistance: There are limited full scholarships available based on established financial needs. There are also student rates that are about one third the cost of the conference.

Contact: For more information please contact Joanne Hartke, Conference Director.

Southwest Writers Workshop
1338 Wyoming Blvd. NE, Suite B
Albuquerque, NM 87112
(505) 293-0303
FAX (505) 237-2665

When: September 17–19, 1999.

Contact: For information and a brochure, send a SASE to the above address.

●Split Rock Arts Program
University of Minnesota
335 Nolte Center
315 Pillsbury Drive SE
Minneapolis, MN 55455-0139
(612) 624-6800
e-mail: srap@mail.cee.umn.edu

Length of Residency: Individual workshops are one-week intensives.

When: July and August.

Application Deadline: Registration begins in late March. Registrations accepted until workshop reaches maximum enrollment.

Cost: Varies by workshop. Approx. $450/weekly workshop.

Description: The Split Rock Arts Program, which began in 1984, is a summer series of week-long residential workshops in writing and visual arts led by nationally renowned practicing artists-in-residence. Split Rock's small workshops and intensive format provide plenty of one-to-one contact with these exciting artists. There are up to 40 workshops to choose from, and everyone is treated as an artist, a learner, and most important, a participant. Split Rock is an opportunity to completely immerse yourself in an art away from the distractions of daily life as part of a community of people with similar interests and values. You may also earn University of Minnesota credit if you choose.

Home for Split Rock is the University of Minnesota's Duluth campus. UMD is set in the green hills near the city's summit, where you look out on the wide vista of Lake Superior and the small, friendly port of Duluth. 150 miles north of the Twin Cities, Duluth is also the gateway to the magnificent North Shore of Lake Superior and the beautiful natural settings are a ready source of inspiration and solitude.

Faculty: Past faculty include Paulette Bates Alden, Charles Baxter, Sandra Benítez, Carol Bly, Michael Dennis Browne, Lucille Clifton, Jane Hirshfield, Linda Hogan, Dorianne Laux, Naomi Shihab Nye, Mickey Pearlman, Faith Sullivan, Lawrence Sutin, Jane Resh Thomas, Catherine Watson, Nancy Willard, Jane Yolen, Al Young, and more.

Contact: Call or write Split Rock at the above address to receive a catalog with full information. A limited number of scholarships, based on submitted work and need, are available. Procedures for application are included in the catalogue.

●Squaw Valley Community of Writers
P.O. Box 2352
Nevada City, CA 95959
(530) 583–5200 Summer only
(530) 274–8551 Fall/Spring/Winter

Length of Residency: 1 week.

When: 1999 Poetry, July 24–31; Fiction, August 7–14; Screenwriting, August 7–14.

Application Deadline: May 10.

Cost: $580, including tuition and room.

Description: Each Workshop is one week in length with workshops in poetry, fiction, nonfiction, and screenwriting. Mornings include workshops, craft lectures, and staff readings.

Financial Assistance: Scholarships are available. Requests for financial aid must accompany submission/application, and will be granted on the perceived quality of manuscript submitted and financial need of applicant.

Contact: Brett Hall Jones, Executive Director.

❖Stadler Semester for Younger Poets
Stadler Center for Poetry
Bucknell Hall
Bucknell University
Lewisburg, PA 17837
(717) 524–1853

Length of Residency: One semester (January to May).

When: Spring semester.

Application Deadline: November 1 of preceding year.

Cost: See "Financial Assistance" below.

Description: The Stadler Semester is distinctive in allowing undergraduate poets almost four months of concentrated work centered in poetry. Guided by practicing poets, the apprentice will write and read poetry and will receive critical response. The Fellow selected will work with Bucknell's writing faculty and the visiting Poet-in-Residence. The Fellow will earn a semester of academic credit by taking four units of study: a tutorial or individual project with a mentor poet, a poetry-writing workshop, a literature course, and an elective.

Undergraduates from four-year colleges who have had at least one course in poetry writing are eligible to apply; most applicants will be second-semester juniors. Applications should include an academic transcript, two supporting recommendations (at least one from a poetry-writing instructor), and a letter from the academic dean granting permission for the student to attend Bucknell for a semester. A 10–12 page portfolio of poems and a letter of self-presentation (a brief autobiography that expresses commitment to poetry writing, cites relevant courses, and lists any publications) should also accompany the application.

Faculty: Cynthia Hogue, director; Nicole Cooley, co-director; and the visiting Poet-in-Residence.

Financial Assistance: Fellows are responsible for the tuition, room, and board costs they would pay at their own colleges. Where Bucknell's charges exceed those of the home institution and the student can demonstrate need, a scholarship will be available.

Contact: Cynthia Hogue, Director.

State of Maine Writers' Conference
P.O. Box 7146
Ocean Park, ME 04063-7146
(207) 934-9806

Length of Residency: 4 days, Tuesday through Friday noon.

When: Late August.

Application Deadline: None.

Cost: $100 registration fee which includes all conference sessions, the Wednesday buffet ticket, Conference Poetry Tournament booklet, and snack-time refreshments. Accommodations are not included.

Description: Founded in 1941, this annual 4-day conference is an eclectic program which features lectures, poetry and prose readings, and workshops, as well as social events. Extra-curricular events such as a buffet and a conference tea are open to your invited guests. Typical titles include topics like: Can Politics and Writing Mix? An Editor Looks at Writing and Editing; Capturing Your Culture -- Preserving Your Roots; and Dialogue. Several contests are held in conjunction with the Conference and modest cash prizes are awarded. There is a Contest Announcement flyer available in March each year. Send an SASE please. Some contests take place during the conference and are related to instruction received there. The emphasis is on writing to publish, including both poetry and prose subjects as well as background information and skills development.

Faculty: Varies annually with about 60% repeaters, 40% new or different. Among recent past faculty have been: John Lovelace, managing editor of *The Methodist Reporter*; Neil Rolde, author of *So You Think You Know Maine* as well as a two volume *History of Maine*; Lewis Turco, author of *Dialogue*, a Writer's Book Club selection; Betsy Sholl, Maine poet; and Christopher Keane, novelist and screenwriter.

Financial Assistance: None available.

Contact: Richard F. Burns, chairman, (207) 934-9806 (summer); (416) 596-6734 (winter); e-mail address is <rburns@wnec.edu>.

●Steamboat Springs Writers Conference
P.O. Box 774284
Steamboat Springs, CO 80477
(970) 879-9008
e-mail: freiberger@compuserve.com

When: Annual conference in July.

Application Deadline: July 1.

Cost: $35 (prior to June 1), $45 (after May 31).

Description: Sponsored by Steamboat Springs Art Council and Writers Group, this annual event offers maximum exchange between instructor and students within a minimum time frame. Format emphasizes writers' participation within a seminar format. Novices and polished professionals enjoy the pleasurable learning experience guaranteed by the old train Depot's relaxed and friendly atmosphere.

Faculty: Past faculty has included agent Carl Brandt; authors Rex Burns, Elaine Long, Ed

Bryant, Russell Martin; poets Anne Waldman, Jack Collom, Don Revell; children's writers Barbara Steiner and Mary Calhoun.

Contact: Harriet Freiberger, Director.

Stonecoast Writers' Conference
98 Falmouth Street
University of Southern Maine
Portland, ME 04103
(207) 780-4947

Length of Residency: 9 days.

When: Late July.

Application Deadline: July 1.

Cost: $395.

Description: The Stonecoast Writers' Conference is for students, teachers, and others seriously interested in writing who seek to improve their written work. The staff consists of generous, inspiring, and personable professional writers with distinguished experience in teaching and a substantial record of written achievement. Workshops include: Creative Nonfiction; Genre Writing; Fiction Writing: Developing Short Story Material; Fiction Workshop: Short Stories; Poetry Workshop; Novel Workshop.

Faculty: Past faculty have included Lucie Brock–Broido, David Bradley, Denise Gess, Walter Mosley, Connie Porter, Kenneth Rosen, Sharon Sheehe Stark, Monica Wood, Gerald Stern, Carolyn Chute, and others.

Financial Assistance: Limited scholarships available. Contact Conference Director.

Contact: Barbara Hope, Summer Session.

Summer in France Writing Workshop
HC 01, Box 102
Plainview, TX 79072
(806) 889-3533

Length of Residency: July 1–July 27th each year.

Application Deadline: June 15.

Cost: $2,700 covers course of study, shared accommodation, orientation, Paris excursions and museum entrance fees. Some single accommodations may also be available.

Description: Small classes with tutorials.

Contact: Bettye Givens, at the above address.

●Summer Seminar for Writers
Sarah Lawrence College
Bronxville, NY 10703
(914) 395-2373

Description: The Seminars provide writers, published and unpublished, with the opportunity to deepen their craft through daily work in small, intensive workshops, and in individual meetings with acclaimed poets, fiction writers, and nonfiction writers. Each morning, participants spend a minimum of 2 1/2 hours in workshop exploring the relationship among language, literary form, and personal experience. The focus of the workshops is on discovering the rich possibilities within each writer's material. Afternoon sessions are reserved for writing, and for individual meetings with faculty to read and analyze manuscripts. There will be optional panels on publishing and editing and field trips into New York City. In the evenings, several special readings are scheduled.

Contact: The Director.

Summer Writers' Workshops
Manhattanville College
2900 Purchase Street
Purchase, NY 10577
(914) 694-3425

Length of Residency: Five days.

When: Last week in June.

Application Deadline: 2nd week in June.

Cost: $560 non-credit.

Description: Manhattanville's Writers' Week program offers the opportunity to spend an intensive week of writing and working closely with some of the country's finest writers and teachers of writing. In small all-morning workshops and in private conferences, participants at all stages of development -- novice to advanced -- sign up for one of seven workshops. A special workshop entitled The Writers' Craft has been introduced for the benefit of beginners who wish to master the elements of creative writing. Afternoons feature a methods workshop for teachers of writing. Faculty readings, session with editors and agents, and a lecture by an eminent writer complete the program.

Faculty: Past workshop teachers and visiting writers have included: April Bernard, Maxine Clair, Mark Doty, Patricia Griffith, Phillip Lopate, Cynthia Ozick, Sheri Reynolds, and Elizabeth Winthrop.

Contact: Please contact Ruth Dowd, RSCJ, Dean, Adult and Special Programs for more information and the brochure.

Summer Writing Workshop in Dublin, Ireland
Eastern Washington University
English Dept. MS 25
Cheney, WA 99004-2415
(509) 359-7064

Length of Residency: Two weeks.

When: August.

Cost: Approximately $825 for tuition, bed, and breakfast.

Description: Students attend workshops in Dublin, Ireland.

Faculty: Director, James McAuley. Visiting writers -- leading Irish authors.

Financial Assistance: Two $500 tuition scholarships, competitive, mss. requested with workshop application.

Contact: The Director.

●Sun Valley Writers Conference
P.O. Box 957
Ketchum, ID 83340
(208) 726-6670

Description: A four-day event where readers and writers gather together to consider themes presented by fiction and nonfiction writers, poets, journalists, and filmmakers. Panel discussions, readings, and talks fill the day and early evening.

Contact: The Director.

Sunken Garden Poetry Conference
Miss Porter's School
60 Main Street
Farmington, CT 06032
(860) 676-4493

Contact: The Director.

Taos School of Writing
P.O. Box 20496
Albuquerque, NM 87154
(505) 294-4601
FAX (505) 294-7049
e-mail: spletzer@swcp.com

Length of Residency: 6 days.

When: July 18-24.

Application Deadline: May 15.

Cost: $1,095 (includes tuition, meals, and room -- double occupancy.

Description: The Taos School of Writing was begun in 1993 by award-winning author Norman Zollinger as an opportunity for writers to study fiction and nonfiction techniques in the solitude and natural beauty of the secluded Taos Ski Valley in New Mexico. Classes are limited to 12 students and a total enrollment of 60. A manuscript submission of 20 pages is required for acceptance. No restriction on subject matter or style; however, we currently do not accept poetry or screenplays. Each morning begins with two and a half hours of classwork led by a faculty member. Student manuscripts previously critiqued by faculty and class members are discussed as well as specific writing techniques needed to improve any problems presented in the manuscripts. Lunch is followed by two hours of unstructured time for one-on-one interviews with a faculty member, reading, writing, hiking, discussion groups, etc. Late afternoon features a speaker session followed by time for questions. After happy hour and dinner, we meet for panel discussions, student and faculty readings, etc. One evening we attend a performance by the Taos School of Music students at the St. Bernard Lodge in the ski valley.

Speakers from past years have included Tony Hillerman, Roger Zelazny, Erica Holzer, and Richard Bradford. Brochures mailed upon request. A SASE is appreciated.

Faculty: Jim Belshaw, Jean Blackmon, Jeanie Fleming, Susan Glodt-Stern, Paula Paul, Michael A. Thomas, and Richard S. Wheeler. **Speakers:** Norman Zollinger, David Morrell, Suzy McKee Charnas, Denise Chavez, and Stephen R. Donaldson.

Financial Assistance: None at present.

Contact: Suzanne Spletzer, Administrator at above address, telephone, fax, and e-mail.

To Get Ink Writer's Conference
Writers of Kern
P.O. Box 6694
Bakersfield, CA 93386-6694

Length of Residency: One day.

When: September.

Application Deadline: August 10.

Cost: Members: $75; non-members: $85.

Trenton State College Writers' Conference
Department of English
Trenton State College
Hillwood Lakes CN4700
Trenton, NJ 08650-4700
(609) 771-3254

Length of Residency: One-day conference.

When: Usually in March or April.

Application Deadline: None except for submission of manuscripts: one month before.

Cost: Registration for day: $40; $10 additional for each workshop. Lower rates are available for students. Evening feature speaker admission $5-$8.

Description: Begun in 1982, this annual one-day conference is usually attended by 800-1,000 writers at all levels of competence, as well as readers interested in meeting their favorite authors. The conference offers a day of concurrent panels, workshops, and readings by famous and successful authors, literary agents, editors, and publishers. Participants may choose from a variety of over 20 workshops in the following genres: fiction, both short story and novel; poetry; play, television, and screenwriting; literature for the young; magazine and newspaper journalism or nonfiction books. There are also workshops in breaking through writer's block. For those submitting manuscripts, there is a short story and poetry contest with $100 and $10 first and second prizes.

Faculty: Past speakers have included: Alice Walker, Kurt Vonnegut, Joyce Carol Oates, Saul Bellow, Joseph Heller, Toni Morrison, William Styron, E.L. Doctorow, John McPhee, Galway Kinnell, Ken Kesey, and many other world-famous writers.

Contact: Jean Hollander, Director, for brochure/registration forms.

●Truckee Meadows Writers Conference
4001 S. Virginia Street
Reno, NV 89502
(702) 786-7816
e-mail: mikedcroft@aol.com

Contact: The Director.

Tulsa Arts & Humanities Council
2210 South Main
Tulsa, OK 74114
(918) 584-3333

Contact: The Director.

Tyrone Guthrie Centre
Annaghmakerrig, Newbliss
Co. Monaghan, Ireland

Length of Residency: Variable.

When: All year-round.

Application Deadline: Every two months.

Cost: IR£1,200 to IR£1,600 per month.

Description: The Tyrone Guthrie Centre was founded in 1981 in the family home of the great director Sir Tyrone Guthrie. The Big House is a living museum full of books, paintings and furniture redolent of the cultured life of the Anglo-Irish Ascendancy. Each resident has a comfortable apartment and a studio if necessary. The cost covers all food, lodging, heating, etc. Roughly 200 writers, painters, sculptors, composers, and other creative people use the place every year. The 300 acre estate is a haven for wildlife and a great place for long contemplative walks.

Faculty: Other professional artists who might be in residence.

Financial Assistance: Occasionally available through special awards.

Contact: Bernard Loughlin, Director.

UCLA Extension, The Writers' Program
10995 Le Conte Avenue #313
Los Angeles, CA 90024
(800) 388-UCLA

Length of Residency: Adult continuing education -- no residency required.

When: Ongoing quarterly courses in a variety of formats, including week-long intensives for students coming from out of town, weekend workshops, etc.

Application Deadline: Open enrollment for most classes, with rolling applications for advanced classes accepted four times a year: September for Fall quarter, December for Winter quarter, March for Spring quarter, and June for Summer quarter.

Cost: Varies, usually between $205 and $325 per course, depending on length and mastery level.

Description: The Writers' Program offers courses taught by professional writers in screenwriting, fiction, poetry, playwriting, nonfiction, writing for young people, and creativity. These courses, designed for adult learners, most of whom already have undergraduate degrees, are offered in a variety of formats. Also, once a year (in summer), the Writers' Program offers a series of four-day screenwriting intensives that allow students from out of town to take such courses as *Introduction to Screenwriting*, *Animation Writing*, *Writing the Thriller*, and other courses.

Faculty: All working, professional writers in their fields. Many instructors have won major local and national awards, including O. Henry Awards, Pushcart Prizes, Academy Awards and Emmy Awards; others have been nominated for National Book Awards and Pulitzer Prizes.

Financial Assistance: None available.

Contact: Meryl Ginsberg, Program Manager.

Ucross Foundation Residency Program
2836 Highway 14-16 East
Clearmont, WY 82835
(307) 737-2291

Length of Residency: Two weeks to 8 weeks.

When: August to early December; late January to early June.

Application Deadline: October 1 (for Jan – June) and March 1 (for Aug – Dec).

Cost: None.

Description: The Ucross Foundation Residency Program provides individual workspace, living accommodations, uninterrupted time, and the experience of the historic High Plains landscape to selected artists and writers. Applications are reviewed and residents are selected by a rotating panel of professionals in the arts and humanities. The quality of an applicant's work is given primary consideration in the reviewing process. Eight positions are available in various disciplines at one time. Formal application must be made by obtaining and completing an information form which, when submitted, must include a work sample and a description of the project the applicant plans to do while at Ucross.

Financial Assistance: None.

Contact: Barbara Campbell.

Vancouver International Writers Festival
1243 Cartwright Street
Vancouver, BC V6H 4B7
Canada
(604) 681-6330
FAX (604) 681-8400
e-mail: viwf@mindlink.bc.ca

Length of Residency: 5 days.

When: October.

Cost: Events individually ticketed at $10-15. Participating writers are paid an honorarium/ travel costs/accommodation.

Description: The Festival attracts almost 9,000 people and presents approximately 40 events in three venues during five days on Granville Island, located in the heart of Vancouver, British Columbia.

The format of the Festival has traditionally been one of diversity, focusing on presenting Canadian and International writers and providing them with an often rare opportunity to interact with each other as well as with the audience. The Festival is committed to its goal of providing a diversity of events where writers and readers can celebrate the written arts.

The Vancouver International Writers Festival also presents a very successful Author Series throughout the year. Featured authors in the Series have included Michael Ondaatje, Gloria

Steinem, Margaret Atwood, Paul Theroux, John Irving, Alice Munro, and Robertson Davies. Audience response to the Series is extremely positive and the festival plans to continue presenting notable authors to a public audience.

The Vancouver International Writers Festival has established itself with local, national, and international writing communities as a respected forum for both writers and readers in an environment that is challenging, stimulating, and enjoyable!

Contact: Alma Lee, Producer.

Vancouver Summer Publishing Intensives
515 West Hastings Street
Simon Fraser University
Vancouver, BC V6B 5K3
Canada
(604) 291-5093
(604) 291-5073
FAX (604) 291-5098
e-mail: <cs_hc@sfu.ca>

Description: Select from 33 one- to five-day courses in publishing arts, business, and technologies for emerging and seasoned publishing professionals. Courses are offered in writing, photography, design and illustration, calligraphy, typography, editing, proofreading, interactive software design, Internet and E-zine publishing, desktop publishing, book and CD-ROM marketing. UBC campus accommodations are available.

Contact: Laura Gruell at (604) 291-5093, or Natalie Makortoff at (604) 291-5073.

●Vermont College Post-Graduate Summer Writers' Conference
Vermont College MFA in Writing
Montpelier, VT 05602
(802) 828-8637
e-mail: vikki@norwich.edu

When: August.

Description: The conference includes small workshops in poetry, short fiction, creative nonfiction, and the novel. Master classes include advanced seminars on crafts, theory, and aesthetics. Issues to be addressed in forums will be writing, publishing, editing, and teaching. Individual consultation with faculty is available.

Faculty: In 1998, Ellen Lesser, Bret Lott, Christopher Merrill, Sena Jeter Naslund, Deborah Diggs, Richard Jackson, Bruce Weigl, and Roger Weingarten.

Contact: The Director.

●Vermont Studio Center
P.O. Box 613
Johnson, VT 05656
(802) 635-2727
FAX (802) 635-2730
e-mail vscvt@pwshift.com
website: www.vermontstudiocenter.com

Length of Residency: 2-12 week residencies year-round.

Cost: $2,900 4-week residency.

Description: The Vermont Studio Center is a creative community offering 2- to 12-week residencies year-round to 12 writers, 24 painters, 12 sculptors, and 4 printmakers per month. Admission decisions are based on each applicant's writing sample, resume, and references, and are made without regard to finance or genre.

Each of the 12 one-month residency periods features two Visiting Writers whose work falls into one of three genres (poetry, fiction, or nonfiction). Each Visiting Writer gives a reading, a craft lecture, and is available for a one-hour conference with residents in his/her genre. 1999 Visiting Writers include A.R. Ammons, Andrei Codrescu, Mary Gaitskill, Brenda Hillman, Bob Shacochis, David Wojahn, and Robert Wrigley.

Financial Assistance: Each year, 24 Full Fellowships are awarded; the Fellowships are awarded on merit and cover all residency fees. In addition, 3/4 of each year's Residents receive VSC Grants or Work-Exchange Aid; Grants and Aids can substantially reduce the Residency fee and are awarded based on a combination of merit and documented financial need.

Contact: Write to receive a Writing Residency brochure, which includes an application, a detailed description of the residency format, and Fellowship and Financial Aid information. The application fee is $25, and all applications will be responded to in 4-6 weeks.

University of Vermont
Summer Writing Program
322 South Prospect Street
Burlington, VT 05401
(802) 656-2085

Length of Residency: 2-3 weeks.

When: July.

Application Deadline: Rolling admission.

Cost: $790 in-state, $1,549 out-of-state, $675 room and board.

Description: Now in its fourth season, the Summer Writing Program is designed to bring serious writers and writing students together with outstanding faculty in workshops that are supportive and non-competitive, yet demanding. The prime focus of the program is on writing, and constructive help from other writers.

Faculty: David Huddle, John Engels, Philip Baroth, Daniel Lusk, Stephen Dobyns, Rhea Wilson, Nancy Shulins, Jean Marzollo, Karen Hisse, Daniela Painter, Sharon Sheehe Stark, Tom Wicker, William Least Heat Moon, Bill Roorbach.

Contact: Daniel Lusk and Peter Lourie, Directors.

●Victoria School of Writing
P.O. Box 8152
Victoria, BC V8W 3R8
Canada
(250) 598-5300
FAX (250) 598-0066
e-mail: writeawy@islandnet.com
website: http://www.islandnet.com/vicwrite

Length of Residency: Five days.

When: July, third week.

Application Deadline: June 15.

Cost: $475 Can. ($435 before May 1).

Description: Craft-centred, intensive, combines a sense of retreat with easy access to downtown Victoria. A small school (about 70 participants) in a private residential school in a natural, park-like setting in Victoria's Lake Hill district. Workshops in poetry, fiction, literary nonfiction, literature of the fantastic, and editing work-in-progress, all led by experienced writers. An opening address and social gets writers ready for morning workshops that focus on participants' work. In the afternoons, for those who are not writing quietly or outside in the 22 acres of rolling land, there are open mike sessions, a lecture series which gives fascinating glimpses into the writing process of our distinguished faculty, and a one-on-one consultation with your instructor. Evenings include public readings by author-instructors in the downtown area of Victoria, near the excitement of the Inner Harbour, and on the last night a friendly gathering. Inexpensive accommodations and meals are available on-site, with flexibility for special dietary needs. All buildings used are wheelchair accessible. Applicants must submit two copies of 3-10 pages (20 pages for the work-in-progress workshop) of recent work for evaluation by the instructors.

Faculty: Past faculty have included: P.K. Page, Al Purdy, Susan Musgrave, Tom Wayman, Gail Anderson-Dargatz, Marilyn Bowering, Leon Rooke. 1999 faculty include: Daphne Marlatt, Mark Jarman, Patricia Young, Terence Young, and Tom Henry.

Financial Assistance: Some assistance with tuition and some scholarships are available. Contact the school for details.

Contact: Margaret Dyment, Registrar, for further details and application forms.

Villa Montalvo Artist Residency Program
15400 Montalvo Road
P.O. Box 158
Saratoga, CA 95071-0158
(408) 741-3421

Length of Residency: One to three months.

When: Year-round.

Application Deadline: March 1 and September 1.

Cost: None.

Description: Villa Montalvo is a 19-room Mediterranean-style villa on 176 acres which include both redwood trails and formal gardens. Villa Montalvo was built in 1912 by Senator James D. Phelan, a former mayor of San Francisco, U.S. Senator, and patron of the arts. At his death in 1930 he left Villa Montalvo as a legacy for the support and encouragement of music, art, literature, and architecture. The first Artist-in-Residence was invited to Montalvo in 1942. Montalvo now hosts up to 25 Artists-in-Residence per year for free residencies of one to three months. Artists live in separate apartments with kitchens, and provide their own meals. Artists come together once a week for a dinner. Approximately half of artist residents are writers.

Montalvo's 175 acres are open as a public arboretum and provide artists the opportunity for long walks on the 4-5 miles of hiking trails through the redwoods. In addition, Montalvo supports a very active summer arts program including regularly-scheduled concerts, theatre, and literary events, which artists in residence are invited to attend free of charge. These surroundings and activities provide an added inspiration for creative pursuits.

Anyone may apply who has completed formal training or the equivalent and is engaged in the production of art on a professional level. Montalvo's facilities best serve the needs of writers, composers and painters, although successful projects have been done in many other areas ranging from environmental sculpture to platinum print photography. Artists at an early stage of their career, as well as established artists are welcome.

Financial Assistance: Four fellowships of $400 are offered each year, one specifically to a female artist, and one specifically to a visual artist. These are awarded on the basis of merit.

Contact: Lori A. Wood, Artist Residency Program Manager, for information and application forms.

The Virginia Center for the Creative Arts
Mt. San Angelo
Sweet Briar, VA 24595
(804) 946-7236
FAX (804) 946-7239

Length of Residency: Two weeks to one month.

When: Open year-round, three admission periods.

Application Deadline: September–December: May 15 deadline; January–April: September 15 deadline; May–August: January 15 deadline.

Cost: $30/day.

Description: Separate working and living quarters, all meals provided, 24 artists at a time (visual artists, writers, and composers). Complete freedom from distraction and daily responsibilities. A "working retreat." Gallery space for exhibition during the summer months. See application.

Fellows may use the facilities of nearby Sweet Briar College. VCCA is located on a 450-acre estate at the foothills of the Blue Ridge mountains, approximately 60 miles south of Charlottesville.

Financial Assistance: Some available, based on need. We ask that everyone pay what they can. Some pay double the daily fee of $30, some pay nothing and send us money when they can.

Contact: Please contact: William Smart, Director; Craig Pleasants, Assistant Director; Sheila Gulley-Pleasants, Admissions Coordinator.

Walden Residence for Oregon Writers
Northwest Writing Institute
Campus Box 100
Lewis & Clark College
Portland, OR 97219
(503) 768-7745

Length of Residency: 6 weeks.

When: 3–6 week residencies, spring through summer of each year.

Application Deadline: November 30 of each year.

Cost: None. Room and partial board provided.

Description: Oregon writers are offered the opportunity to pursue their work at a beautiful mountain farm in Southern Oregon during 3–6 week residencies. Applicants submit a project proposal and a writing sample. This program is sponsored by a private citizen.

Contact: Diane McDevitt or Kim Stafford.

Washington Independent Writers Spring Conference
733 15th Street NW, #220
Washington, DC 20005
(202) 347-4973

Length of Residency: One evening, one full day (9 am to 6:30 pm).

When: Usually the third Saturday in May of each year.

Application Deadline: Registration may be done up until the day of the Conference.

Cost: $100 for members, $150 for non-members, $185 to join WIW and attend the Conference (subject to change).

Description: Washington Independent Writers was established in 1975 to promote the mutual interests of freelance writers and to provide its members with a variety of services. Since then, WIW has grown rapidly in both scope and stature. In addition to offering its members such resources as a newsletter, Job Bank, grievance committee, and health insurance, it conducts professional and social forums for the exchange of information and ideas, plays an active role in issues that affect the independent writing profession, and strives to correct unfair practices in the field.

Faculty: WIW's staff consists of an Executive Director, Assistant to the Director, Job Bank coordinator/Insurance coordinator, and newsletter editor. Its bylaws provide for officers and a Board of Directors who are elected by the members and who are responsible for the affairs of the association. Writers of all fields are invited to teach at each Conference. Keynote speaker in 1998 was celebrity biographer Kitty Kelley.

Financial Assistance: Partial scholarships are available to members of WIW who are financially unable to attend the Conference.

Contact: Clyde Linsley, Spring Conference Chair, (703) 354-7565; Isolde Chapin, Executive Director, (202) 347-4973.

●Wesleyan Writers' Conference
Wesleyan University
Middletown, CT 06459
(860) 685-3604
FAX (860) 685-2441
e-mail: agreene@wesleyan.edu
website: www.wesleyan.edu/writing/conferen.html

Length of Residency: An intensive one-week program for boarding and day students.

When: Annually, the last week in June.

Application Deadline: Rolling admission for regular applicants; applications for scholarships and fellowships are due April 16.

Cost: In '98, boarding student rate $775, housing and meals included. Day student rate $660, includes meals.

Description: The Wesleyan Writers Conference, now in its 43rd year, welcomes established writers, new writers, and anyone interested in writing as literary craft. The program includes seminars, readings, informal workshops, and manuscript consultations, all designed to give you new perspectives on your work and to introduce you to others who share your interests. The Conference runs for six days and offers an intensive program of day and evening events; you might try to do everything -- we encourage fiction writers to try literary journalism and nonfiction writers to try poetry -- but you are also welcome to spend your time simply writing or reading on Wesleyan's beautiful lawns.

Faculty: Our distinguished faculty (fiction writers, poets, screenwriters, literary journalists, and publishing people) have included Robert Stone, Dorothy Allison, Amy Bloom, Maureen Howard, Jane Smiley, Tom Drury, Chris Offutt, Joanna Scott, Fae Myenne Ng, Roxanne Robinson, Madison Smartt Bell, Richard Bausch, George Garrett, Henry Taylor, Dana Gioia, Robert Phillips, Molly Peacock, Elizabeth Spires, Donald Justice, Richard Howard, Luc Sante, Lis Harris, William Finnegan, James Gleick, Phyllis Rose, David Halberstam, and Katha Pollitt.

Financial Assistance: Several teaching fellowships and a range of full or partial scholarships are available to fiction writers, poets, and writers of nonfiction. The Barach Teaching Fellowship is awarded to a nonfiction writer and the specially endowed Jon Davidoff Scholarships are offered to working journalists; Jakobson Scholarships support fiction writers and poets.

Contact: For further information, please call Anne Greene, Director. If you have a brief query, you are welcome to e-mail us at <agreene@wesleyan.edu>.

●West Virginia Writers' Workshop
West Virginia University
P.O. Box 6296
Morgantown, WV 26506
(304) 293-3107 ext. 451
FAX (304) 293-5380
e-mail: jharms@wvu.edu
website: http://www.as.wvu.edu/~rgoldman/wvww/index.html

Length of Residency: Four days.

When: End of July.

Application Deadline: Mid-May.

Cost: $270 plus housing (an additional $70 to $100).

Description: The West Virginia Writers' Workshop is an intensive four-day conference featuring workshops, individual conferences, readings, panel discussions, and craft lectures. The Workshop offers the established as well as aspiring writer an opportunity to work closely with nationally renowned authors of poetry, fiction, and nonfiction. Workshops are limited to no more than 12 participants. Approximately 60 writers attend the conference each year.

The conference is held on the campus of West Virginia University, which is nestled in the rolling green highlands of the Appalachian Mountains and on the banks of the Monongahela River.

Past workshop teachers and visiting writers have included Peter Cameron, David Wojahn, Pinckney Benedict, Laura Kasischke, Maggie Anderson, David Baker, Michael McFee, Meredith Sue Willis, Ann Hood, Tom Andrews, Gerald Costanzo, Ed Ochester, Gail Galloway Adams, Irene McKinney, and others.

Financial Assistance: Full and partial scholarships are available, some on the basis of merit, others determined by need. Please indicate your interest in support when applying.

Contact: James Harms, Director of the West Virginia Writers' Workshop, for information and an application.

●White River Writers' Workshop
P.O. Box 2317
Batesville, AR 72503-2317
(501) 793-1766
e-mail: ahbudy@aol.com

Length of Residency: 1 week.

When: June.

Application Deadline: Scholarships/Fellowships – April 1, Final Deadline – May 15.

Cost: Tuition $425; lodging $325; total: $750.

Description: A selective, week-long workshop focusing on the reading and writing of poetry. Activities include workshops, individual conferences with faculty members, working on oral readings, craft lectures, panels, and participant/faculty readings. Each evening's faculty readings are free and open to the public.

Faculty: Philip Dacey, Stephen Dunn, Lawrence Raab, C.D. Wright, Andrea Hollander Budy, Lee Potts.

Financial Assistance: Deadline April 1. Up to five scholarships and five fellowships are awarded. Scholarships cover the full cost of tuition; fellowships cover the full costs of tuition, room, and board. Scholarships are open to poets who have published individual poems in literary journals, fellowships to poets who have published 1, but no more than 2, full-length collections.

Contact: Andrea Hollander Budy, Director, Lyon College, P.O. Box 2317, Batesville, AR 72503.

●Wildacres Writing for Adults
233 S. Elm Street
Greensboro, NC 27401
(919) 273-4044
(800) 635-2049
e-mail: judihill@aol.com
website: http://members.aol.com/judihill

Length of Residency: One week.

When: July.

Application Deadline: May.

Cost: $460, includes room (double), meals, and workshop.

Description: Wildacres is a residential workshop limited to approximately 90 writers. We offer small critiquing classes (limited 10 to a group) in Novel, Short Story, Poetry, and Creative Non-fiction. The rooms are lovely and the meals are delicious.

Contact: Judith Hill, Director.

●Wildacres Writing for Children
233 S. Elm Street
Greensboro, NC 27401
(919) 273-4044
(800) 635-2049
e-mail: judihill@aol.com
website: http://members.aol.com/judihill

Length of Residency: One week.

When: Mid-July.

Cost: $450, which includes room, meals, and workshop fee.

Description: Wildacres Childrens Writers is a residential workshop limited to 50 writers. We offer classes in Young Adult, Middle Grade, Picture Book and Creative Nonfiction.

Contact: Judith Hill, Director.

Wildbranch Workshop in Outdoor, Natural History, & Environmental Writing
Sterling College
Craftsbury Common, VT 05827
(802) 586-7711
(800) 648-3591
e-mail: wldbrnch@sterlingcollege.craftsborg.vt.us

Length of Residency: One week.

When: June.

Application Deadline: May 15 (some flexibility).

Cost: $650 for tuition, $200 for room and board.

Description: A week-long workshop of classes, lectures, discussion groups, and readings in the craft and techniques of fine writing about the world outdoors. For part of each day participants work with one of the residential faculty members. The rest of the day offers a range of other classes and workshops, with ample time to write, to socialize, and to enjoy the Vermont countryside.

Faculty: Ted Gup, Gale Lawrence, Joel Vance, H. Emerson Blake, Jim Schley, Edward Hoagland.

Financial Assistance: Several $200 scholarships are available to help defray tuition expenses.

Contact: David W. Brown, Director.

●The William Joiner Center for the Study of War & Social Consequences
University of Massachusetts
100 Morrissey Boulevard
Boston, MA 02125-3393
(617) 287-5850

Length of Residency: Two weeks.

When: June 21–July 2, 1999.

Application Deadline: May 15th.

Cost: $140.

Description: This workshop -- open to writers of fiction, nonfiction, poetry, and translation -- involves two weeks of working sessions and individual consultations with distinguished writers. The faculty includes Vietnam veterans and others whose lives have been altered by the experience of war, but applicants with diverse interests and backgrounds are encouraged to apply.

Visiting writers join the teaching staff in a series of readings, seminars, and panel discussions. Special events held at the University of Massachusetts-Boston and at other Boston locations will be open to both workshop students and the general public.

Faculty: Bruce Weigl, Martin Espada, Larry Heinemann, Lady Borton, Demetria Martinez, John F. Deane, Eva Bourke, Marilyn Nelson, Fred Marchant, Martha Collins, Tim O'Brien,

Doug Anderson, Robert Creeley, Carolyn Forché, Keith Wilson, Denise Chavez, Lloyd Schwartz, and James Carroll.

Financial Assistance: None.

Contact: T. Michael Sullivan.

University of Wisconsin at Madison School of the Arts at Rhinelander
Room 713, Lowell Center
610 Langdon Street
Madison, WI 53703
(608) 263-3494

Length of Residency: One week.

When: Late July.

Application Deadline: July 1.

Cost: $130-265.

Description: One week interdisciplinary educational program in the arts -- visual arts, folk arts, music, drama, writing, photography, and dance. Held in northern Wisconsin.

Financial Assistance: Tuition for Wisconsin residents only.

Contact: Kathy Berigan, Administrative Coordinator.

The Woodstock Guild's Byrdcliffe Arts Colony
34 Tinker Street
Woodstock, NY 12498
(914) 679-2079

Length of Residency: One to four one-month sessions from June through September.

When: June-September.

Application Deadline: Mid-April. Applications received after this date are considered on a space-available basis.

Cost: June and September $400; July and August $500.

Description: On the National Register of Historic Places, the Byrdcliffe Arts Colony is one and a half miles from Woodstock's center. Woodstock is located 90 miles north of New York City in the Catskill Mountains. The Colony was founded in 1902 and has offered summer residencies to writers, playwrights, and visual artists ever since. The Guild's residency program offers residents an opportunity to work up to 16 weeks in a peaceful environment.

Financial Assistance: Limited scholarships are available to applicants fulfilling requirements.

Contact: Sondra Howell, Program Director.

World Academy of Arts and Culture
(Governing board of World Congress of Poets)
3146 Buckeye Court
Placerville, CA 95667
(916) 626-4166

Length of Residency: 3–5 days.

When: August.

Application Deadline: Membership for invitation to a WCP held each year. Membership dues every January. $25 to USA office payable: WAAC/WAP.

Cost: Determined by the host nation's Min. Culture/Education.

Description: Papers on subject presented a.m. plenary session. Poetry reading in p.m. then cultural events visited by bus (p.m./evening). 3–5 day symposium on poetry of themes set by host nation.

Faculty: Dr. Tin-wen Chung, Pres./Taipei; Rosemary C. Wilkinson, Sec. Gen./USA; Dr. Chi-lung Wang, Dep. Sec. Gen./Taipei.

Contact: Rosemary C. Wilkinson.

●Writers at Work
P.O. Box 1146
Centerville, UT 84014-5146
(801) 292-9285
FAX (801) 466-1323

When: July.

Cost: $430 before April 30, $455 after.

Description: Since 1985, Writers at Work has been bringing emerging and experienced writers together with editors, publishers, and agents at its annual summer conference in the captivating mountain-resort setting of Park City, Utah. The week-long program includes intensive morning workshops in fiction, poetry, nonfiction, and screenwriting, special workshops for high-school age writers, and afternoon panel discussions, lectures, and miniworkshops. There will be two public readings daily.

Contact: The Director.

The Writer's Center
4508 Walsh Street
Bethesda, MD 20815
(301) 654-8664
website: www.writer.org

Description: The Writer's Center, a nonprofit, membership-service organization, is a resource for writers, publishers, and anyone interested in contemporary literature. Activities include writing workshops; classes in desktop publishing, HTML, and web page design; author readings; a book gallery of independent press books, books on writing, and literary magazines; special events such as conferences, lectures, and meetings; and a job bank. The Center publishes *Poet Lore*, a 108-year-old literary magazine, and *Writer's Carousel*, a bimonthly tabloid journal. Members receive *Writer's Carousel*; reduced prices on workshops, events, and books; and access to workspace, word processing equipment, and the job bank.

Contact: Allan Lefcowitz, Artistic Director.

Writers' Conferences & Festivals
Associated Writing Programs
Tallwood House, Mail Stop 1E3
George Mason University
Fairfax, VA 22030
(703) 993-4301
FAX (703) 993-4302
e-mail: awp@gmu.edu
website: www.gmu.edu/departments/awp/wcf

Description: Writers' Conferences & Festivals is a professional service organization open to anyone interested in the management of a writers' conference, literary center, festival, or any organization that offers literary programming and instructions. An annual membership fee of $150 makes you eligible for all services: an annual meeting (held at the AWP Annual Conference, the largest national gathering of writers, teachers, publishers, and literary administrators); *The Director*, a biannual newsletter; *The Writers' Chronicle*, AWP's literary journal, published six times a year; an address bank; the National Scholarship Program; group discounts on advertising rates with national literary magazines; teacher referral services; listings in this guide and on the WC&F website; technical support; and the general support, advocacy, and promotion of a large national association. If you are serious about developing and managing the best possible conference for lovers of writing and books, you should be a member of WC&F. The organization provides a network by which conference directors may meet and share information about fundraising, recruitment of faculty, scheduling, advertising, promotion, housing, liability, the application process, and more. Founded in 1990, WC&F is now a division of the Association Writing Programs, a nonprofit organization.

Contact: David Fenza, Executive Director.

●WritersCorps
1331 H Street, NW
Washington, DC 20005-4703
(202) 347-1734
e-mail: kennyc@humanities-wdc.org

Description: WritersCorps is a powerful community service program that utilizes the written word to strengthen the development and potential of some of our country's most marginalized populations. WritersCorps send accomplished writers into underserved communities to teach creative writing programs. Typically these residences last from 9 months to a year. Since 1994, more than 12,000 people of virtually all races, cultures, and ethnicities have dramatically improved their reading, writing, critical analysis, and verbal communications skills, thanks to WritersCorps' award-winning programs in the Bronx, New York, San Francisco, and Washington, DC.

Contact: For more information, contact Kenneth Carroll at the above address, phone, or e-mail.

Writers' Forum
Pasadena City College
1570 East Colorado Boulevard
Pasadena, CA 91106-2003
(626) 585-7608

Length of Residency: This a one-day writers' conference.

When: A Saturday in mid-March.

Application Deadline: Up to the day of the conference.

Cost: $100 (includes lunch).

Description: From 150–200 people attend this conference, which began in 1954 under the leadership of the late and legendary Pasadena writing teacher Helen Hinckley Jones. The day is organized into three sessions -- each with three speakers to choose from -- and we end the day with a panel discussion by literary agents, editors, or writers of a particular type.

Faculty: Each year we include guest speakers discussing poetry, writing for children, screenwriting, fiction, and nonfiction, so that everyone's area of interest is represented. Recently our speakers have included Rene Longstreet, Jill Morgan, Jim Stinson, Ken Atchity, Jack Grapes, Sandy Dykstra, and Eve Bunting. The emphasis is on good teachers, giving practical advice, so that beginners as well as those already in print are challenged and stimulated.

Contact: Nino Valmassoi, Director of Extended Learning, to receive a brochure.

Writers In The Rockies TV & Film Screenwriting Conference
1980 Glenwood Drive
Boulder, CO 80304–2329
(303) 443–4636

Length of Residency: Weekend (days only).

When: Late August.

Application Deadline: August 10.

Cost: $200.

Description: 13th Annual Conference. Held at Chautauqua Park Community House at base of Rocky Mountains. Two days of intensive interaction with high–profile Hollywood industry professionals. Enrollment limited to 50 participants to retain intimate "fireside chat" quality. Casual atmosphere. Materials and two meals provided. Lodging available, but early reservations required. Contact Chautauqua Park Association for cottage information: (303) 442–3282.

Faculty: Not determined as of this date.

Contact: Carolyn Hodges, Director.

Writers' Institute Courses
The Our Lady of the Lake University
411 SW 24th Street
San Antonio, TX 78207–4689
(210) 434–6711 Ext. 382
FAX (210) 436–0824

Contact: Peggy Kneip, Director of Continuing Education.

❖●The Writers Project, Inc.
P.O. Box 3098
Princeton, NJ 08543–3098
(609) 275–2947
FAX (609) 275–1243
e–mail: mbcd26b@prodigy.com
 or fokkertri@aol.com

Length of Residency: One to two weeks.

When: Year-round, but generally May through August.

Application Deadline: Varies. Please inquire.

Cost: Please inquire, varies from $750 to $1,750. Inclusion of room and board varies. $25 application fee.

Description: The Writers Project was founded in 1992. It seeks to foster creative writing about farming, the horse industry, and ranching to ensure that these and other historic ways of life remain vivid subjects in American literature and society. The Project offers two or more workshops per year at agriculture-linked locations, including family-owned cattle ranches, family-owned dairy farms, horse breeding farms, horseracing tracks and their support facilities, museums, and veterinary research centers and clinics. The Project's workshops are subject driven, but individual writer's portfolios may be discussed as well. The workshops are structured to immerse the writer in every aspect of a subject, to provide the writer with a working knowledge of a way of life that will, in turn, lend authenticity to the writer's work. The workshops offer unparalleled access to the animals, people, and places that continue to contribute to our history. For the writer, the experience is intense; a two-week workshop may offer only two or three free days in its schedule. But writing time is plentiful and the experience, set within a rewarding series of scenic locations and within a wholly informal working atmosphere, offers an uncensored look into endeavors that are often as foreign to the writer as they are fascinating. There is no limitation placed upon creative form within writing. Access to faculty and support personnel is exceptional. University credit can be arranged. The Project also offers year-round editing and publication-assistance service to workshop alumni. Some of the 1999 workshops being planned include the sixth renewal of the popular June workshop at historic Churchill Downs in Louisville, Kentucky, including visits to the Kentucky Derby Museum and the world-famous Thoroughbred breeding farms near Lexington; a spring semester-long workshop for high school students in Minnesota; plus the fifth renewal of the popular July workshop at Ruidoso Downs and surrounding ranches in the Capitan and Sacramento ranges of central New Mexico. Residencies for individual writers may also be available for workshop alumni at these and other locations.

Faculty: The creative writing faculty has included Lee K. Abbott, Angela Ball, Gerald Costanzo, John Dufresne, Gretel Ehrlich, Gary Gildner, Jana Harris, Jim Heynen, Greg Michalson, Jeffrey Skinner, Henry Taylor, Leslie Ullman, and Paul Zimmer, plus visiting writers. Many of the faculty return each year while others of equal distinction are added. Please inquire for specific details.

Financial Assistance: Varies. Tuition reductions are sometimes given, based on availability of funds and the quality of the writer's portfolio and publications history.

Contact: Karl Garson, President.

Writers Retreat Workshop
Write It/Sell It
P.O. Box 139
South Lancaster, MA 01561
(978) 368-0287

9314 South Evanston Place #1204
Tulsa, OK 74137
(918) 298-4866 phone/FAX
e-mail: wrwwisi@aol.com
website: www.channell.com/wisi/

Length of Residency: Ten days, nine nights.

When: May.

Application Deadline: Because this is a workshop, space is limited. Apply ASAP.

Cost: $1,620 (new students), $1,460 (returning students). Fee includes tuition, room, board, and workshop materials.

Description: The nationally acclaimed Writers Retreat Workshop was founded in 1987 by Gail Provost and her husband, the late Gary Provost. At the time of his death, Gary was arguably the nation's leading teacher of writing for publication. In the peaceful surroundings of a Kentucky retreat center, five miles from Cincinnati Airport, Gary's legacy lives on. For serious-minded writers committed to learning the craft of novel writing, a dedicated staff of proteges offer students Gary's in-depth course of study, step-by-step. Through daily classes, assignments, diagnostic sessions, continuing feedback, brainstorming with staff, talks, and consultations with visiting authors/editors/agents, writers dramatically improve their writing technique, self-editing skills, and understanding of the publishing business.

Faculty: Core staff include WRW Instructor Carol Dougherty, Editor-in-Residence Lorin Oberweger, and Mentors: Director Gail Provost, Assistant Director Lance Stockwell, and Author Dr. Keith Wilson. Guests include: Author Gregory McDonald; Executive Editor and Vice President,Warner Books, Rick Horgan; Author/Editor Elizabeth Lyon; Agent, The Literary Group, International, Jim Hornfischer.

Contact: To receive an updated brochure, phone (800) 642-2494.

Writers Workshop (Southern Baptist)
127 Ninth Avenue North
Nashville, TN 37234
(615) 251-2294

Length of Residency: Four days.

When: July 15-18.

Application Deadline: July 1.

Cost: $67 (includes cost of training, materials, and a banquet).

Description: An outside specialist will teach basic writing skills and present the challenge of writing as a form of Christian ministry. Editors will present some of the kinds of writing opportunities available through Sunday School Board publications. Participants will submit a short writing sample which will be evaluated as part of the workshop. The seminar is for anyone interested in sharpening basic writing skills or in learning more about writing opportunities for the Baptist Sunday School Board. Registration is limited to 70.

Faculty: Robert J. Hastings and editors of the Sunday School Board of the Southern Baptist Convention.

Contact: Church Program Training Center at above address for more information and application forms.

Writers Workshop in Science Fiction
Center for the Study of Science Fiction
English Department
University of Kansas
Lawrence, KS 66045
(913) 864-3380
e-mail: jgunn@falcon.cc.ukans.edu

Length of Residency: Two weeks.

When: Early June.

Application Deadline: June 1.

Cost: $400 (not including room and board).

Description: The Writers Workshop in Science Fiction offers two intensive weeks of story workshopping on the University of Kansas campus. Three stories, submitted before the start of the workshop, constitute the principal material for critiques; one story is revised over the first weekend. A variety of writers and editors are guests, including the winners of the John W. Campbell Award for the best SF novel of the year and the Theodore Sturgeon Award for the best short SF of the year, who are guests of the Campbell Conference that concludes the Workshop and focuses on a single topic in SF. An Intensive English Institute on the Teaching of Science Fiction begins with the Conference and deals with the literature genre.

Faculty: James Gunn is director and principal faculty. Frederik Pohl is a guest for the last two days, a Pocket Books editor for the second week, and other writers and editors are present for a week.

Contact: James Gunn.

Writing By The Sea Writers Conference
7 Chestnut Oak Drive
Cape May Court House, NJ 08210
(609) 463–8119 or (609) 465–6088

Length of Residency: One week.

When: First week in November.

Application Deadline: October 10.

Cost: $300 conference only.

Description: Writing By the Sea was begun in 1990 by international journalist Natalie Newton. Since that time, the conference has expanded to include workshops in fiction and nonfiction. Participants have one hour seminars on Sunday with all of the workshop instructors, followed by an intensive Monday–Thursday workshop on a selected subject. Private meetings with instructors and literary agents are available free of charge.

Faculty: Previous faculty include James Allen, literary agent; Robert Brown, editor of Princeton University Press; Page Edwards, literary novelist; Frank Grees, writing coach; Patricia Hagan, romance novelist; Peter Miller, literary agent; Natalie Newton, journalist and editor; Regula Noetzli, literary agent; David Poyer, novelist; Richard Rashke, nonfiction author; and Jurgen Wolff, screenwriter.

Contact: Natalie Newton, Director.

Writing for Publication Successfully
Villanova University
Villanova, PA 19085
(610) 510–4625

Length of Residency: Two days (Friday/Saturday).

When: Spring.

Cost: Variable: $100 non–credit; $360 graduate credit (1997 fees).

Description: A step–by–step approach to writing success from query to publication. An investigation of writing related activities: outlets, royalties, rejections, editor-author relationships, etc.

Faculty: Ray Heitzmann, Ph.D., Director. Guest lecturers vary.

Financial Assistance: None.

Contact: Ms. Lee Stack, at the above address.

Writing the Land Conference
P.O. Box 263
Eastland, Saskatchewan
Canada S0N 0T0
(306) 265-4119 FAX/phone

Contact: Terry Jordan, Director.

●Writing Women's Lives
Recursos de Santa Fe
826 Camino de Monte Rey
Santa Fe, NM 87505
(505) 988-5992
FAX (505) 989-8608
e-mail: recursos@aol.com
website: www.recursos.org

Length of Residency: Five days.

When: January

Application Deadline: While there is no formal deadline, workshop is limited to 60 participants. Selection of workshop leader is on basis of first come, first served.

Cost: $575 (non-resident, reception dinner, lunches); $835 (tuition, shared room, reception dinner, breakfasts, lunches); $1,035 (as above, with single room).

Description: Workshops, under the leadership of distinguished poets and writers, limited to 12 participants each, focus on critiques of student work. Also lectures, readings, panel discussions, and individual conferences. Over 5 intense days, both professional and aspiring writers practice the craft of writing about women and explore the art of bringing women's perspectives to the page. Discussion topics may include: class, sexuality, and ethnicity; language and dialogue; literary genre; and dominant paradigms within our culture that influence expression.

Faculty: This year's faculty includes Jo Giese, Marilyn Krysl, Melissa Pritchard, Jewell Parker Rhodes, and Susan Fox Rogers. Previous workshop leaders include Pam Houston, Pamela Painter, Toi Derricotte, Kay Leigh Hagan, Demetria Martinez. Acceptance into program based on submission of manuscript, no longer than 10 pages, double-spaced.

Contact: Dr. Robin Jones, Director or Stephen Lewis, Conference Coordinator.

●Writing Your Self
Recursos de Santa Fe
826 Camino de Monte Rey
Santa Fe, NM 87505
(505) 988-5992
FAX (505) 989-8608
e-mail: recursos@aol.com
website: www.recursos.org

Length of Residency: Five days.

When: October 8-13, 1999.

Application Deadline: While there is no formal deadline, workshop is limited to 60 participants. Selection of workshop leader is on basis of first come, first served.

Cost: $560 (non-resident, tuition, reception dinner, lunches); $850 (resident, tuition, shared room, reception dinner, breakfasts, lunches); $1,055 (as above, with single room).

Description: Workshops, under the leadership of distinguished poets and writers, limited to 12 participants each, focus on critiques of student work. Also lectures, readings and individual conferences. Over 5 intense days, both professional and aspiring writers discuss the art and technique of memoir, autobiography, and the personal essay.

Faculty: The past year's workshops were conducted by Artistic Director Phillip Lopate, Alix Kates Shulman, Sallie Bingham, and William deBuys. Previous workshop leaders include Lopate, Bingham, Lucy Grealy, Stanley Crawford, Vivian Gornick, and John Thorndike. Acceptance into program based on submission of manuscript, no longer than 10 pages, double-spaced.

Contact: Stephen Lewis, Conference Coordinator.

Yaddo
Box 395, Union Avenue
Saratoga Springs, NY 12866
(518) 584-0746

Length of Residency: Up to two months.

When: Year-round, closed two weeks in September.

Application Deadline: January 15, August 1.

Description: Residency program for professional creative artists working in one or more of the following media: choreography, film, literature, musical composition, painting, performance art, photography, printmaking, sculpture, and video. Room, board, and studio space are provided. No stipends. Approximately 200 guests have residencies each year.

Contact: Admissions Coordinator, Corporation of Yaddo.

●Yellow Bay Writers' Workshop
Center for Continuing Education
The University of Montana
Missoula, MT 59812-1900
(406) 243-4470
FAX (406) 243-2047
e-mail: hhi@selway.umt.edu

Length of Residency: Seven days.

When: Mid–August.

Application Deadline: July 1.

Cost: $840 includes all events, meals, and single-occupancy lodging; $815 includes all events, meals, and double-occupancy lodging; $495 commuter, all events, opening reception, and barbecue.

Description: The Yellow Bay Writers' Workshop provides a useful, pleasant and stimulating atmosphere in which a writer can develop and improve skills. The workshop seeks to broaden the community of writers around the country by bringing together participants and faculty in an informal, inspiring western Montana setting. During the seven days of residency, participants attend workshops, craft lectures/discussions, attend faculty and student readings, and consult with faculty. Ample time is available for writing and recreation on the lakeshore.

Faculty: Past Yellow Bay faculty includes Bill McKibbon (nonfiction), David Long (fiction), Diedre McNamer (fiction), and Pattiann Rogers (poetry).

Financial Assistance: Scholarships are available through Hellgate Writers, Inc., a Missoula-based literary organization. Scholarships include "The McGuane Family Scholarship" —— usually goes to a Montana writer, one for a Native-American writer, and a possible tuition-only scholarships depending on available funding. Submit 10 poems or a work of fiction or nonfiction (limited to 25 pages), a letter stating financial need, a cover sheet listing: choice of faculty, name, address, summer phone number, and list of submitted works. Applications are judged in a blind manuscript process. Submit Yellow Bay registration form to reserve a space. Submit scholarship application by June 10 to: YBWW Scholarship Fund, Hellgate Writers, Inc., P.O. Box 7131, Missoula, MT 59807, (406) 721-3620.

Contact: For information on YBWW contact the above address.

Zen Mountain Monastery
1 South Plank Road
P.O. Box 197
Mount Tremper, NY 12457
(914) 688-2228

Length of Residency: Conference generally runs 3 days (Friday evening to Sunday afternoon); individual retreats of 1 week to 1 month each summer and winter (with afternoons free for writing).

When: Variable; please contact Information Center for Program Catalogue (published bi-annually).

Application Deadline: None.

Cost: Weekend workshops average $165–$235; Individual retreats $575–$675/month (weekend conferences included), $175/week (weekend workshops not included).

Description: Zen Mountain Monastery is a Zen Buddhist monastic training center located on 230 acres of nature sanctuary in the foothills of the Catskill Mountains. Programs include weekend conferences organized around themes frequently of interest to writers (e.g., nature poets, haiku, journal mind); all conferences are conducted within the context of the on-going Zen monastic training. The Monastery also offers 1 week to 1 month residential retreats, which in the summer and winter offer afternoons free for writing.

Faculty: Previous faculty have included Allen Ginsberg, Anne Waldman, Natalie Goldberg, Mark Strand, and Robert Creeley; faculty are invited based on their ability to integrate their work with the teachings of Zen and Buddhism.

Financial Assistance: Work exchange scholarships available on a limited basis; please contact the Information Officer for further information.

Contact: Joy Jimon Hintz, Information Officer; call for general information, program catalog, or brochure on residential retreats.

APPENDIX:
AWP GUIDELINES
FOR CREATIVE WRITING PROGRAMS
& TEACHERS OF CREATIVE WRITING

AWP PROGRAM DIRECTORS COUNCIL POLICY
GUIDELINES FOR ADJUNCT FACULTY IN
MEMBER WRITING PROGRAMS

HALLMARKS OF A SUCCESSFUL
GRADUATE PROGRAM
IN CREATIVE WRITING

HALLMARKS OF A SUCCESSFUL
UNDERGRADUATE PROGRAM
IN CREATIVE WRITING

AWP GUIDELINES
FOR CREATIVE WRITING PROGRAMS
& TEACHERS OF CREATIVE WRITING

Introduction

The institutional membership of the Associated Writing Programs, a national, nonprofit corporation founded in 1967, includes a majority of the graduate degree programs in creative writing in the United States. AWP, which is supported, in part, by grants from the National Endowment for the Arts, is the primary source, nationally, of information on creative writing programs. *The AWP Official Guide to Writing Programs* (ninth edition, 1999) is the only comprehensive listing available.

Enrollment in writing workshops continues to grow, and new writing programs are established regularly, but the Master of Fine Arts in creative writing--the degree supported by AWP as an appropriate "terminal degree" for the practicing writer/teacher--is still misunderstood by many administrators whose responsibilities include approving new programs and hiring writing teachers. Aside from this document, we know of no other comprehensive set of guidelines regarding the hiring and tenure of writers who teach, their appropriate credentials, or academic policies affecting them.

Therefore, the Board of Directors of the Associated Writing Programs has approved a statement on writing program curricula and academic policies regarding the hiring, promotion, and tenure of writers teaching at the college level. This statement was drafted at the conclusion of a two-year study conducted by the AWP Curriculum and Academic Policy Committee, chaired by Ellen Bryant Voigt (then at Goddard College) and Marvin Bell (University of Iowa) and revised and reaffirmed in 1985 and 1991 by the AWP Board of Directors. It reflects AWP's ongoing commitment to the quality of teaching in this field, and AWP's continued support of writers in the academy.

GUIDELINES FOR TEACHERS OF WRITING

Hiring, Rank, and Tenure

It is the position of the Associated Writing Programs that decisions regarding the hiring, rank, and tenure of teachers of creative writing should be based on the quality of the individual's writing and teaching. Academic degrees should not be considered a requirement or a major criterion which would overrule the importance of the writer's achievement in the art. It is further urged that significant creative work be viewed as the equivalent of a terminal degree by administrative and academic members of the institution.

If, however, a terminal degree is required, it is recommended that the Master of Fine Arts be considered the appropriate credential for the teacher of creative writing. Holders of this degree may also be prepared to teach literature courses as well as composition and rhetoric. AWP reminds institutions that the degree itself, and programs that award the degree, vary considerably; and it is recommended that a prospective teacher's individual competencies be examined closely.

317

AWP assumes that the Master of Fine Arts in creative writing or its equivalent includes at least two years of serious study; a creative thesis (booklength collection of creative work); completion of coursework in form, theory, and literature, including contemporary writers; and a substantial amount of individualized writing study, with criticism and direction of the student's writing by experienced writers through workshop, tutorial, independent project, or thesis preparation.

AWP believes that writing program faculty, who as creative writers are best qualified to make assessments of a candidate's work, should be given the responsibility of making professional decisions about their peers, and that their evaluations of the candidate, and their recommendations, should be given the utmost weight in the review process.

Parity

It is the position of AWP that creative writers be given parity with scholars in terms of salary, including senior positions at the top of the salary range, and that the MFA degree be considered the equivalent of the PhD in literature, linguistics, or composition. While the system of part-time or visiting writing faculty is often used to increase the breadth of a program's offerings, such a system should not exclude writers from access to full-time, tenure-track positions and the possibility of renewal.

Course Load

According to the 1978 AWP survey, the majority of writing faculty members carry a course load of either two or three courses per semester or quarter in graduate creative writing programs. It should be noted that many institutions define "writing workshop" as equivalent to teaching two courses because of the additional work required in conferences, tutorials, and thesis preparation that writing students need for the development of their work. Other institutions consider a writing workshop equivalent to one literature course. AWP recommends that the course load for both undergraduate and graduate writing teachers be defined in a way that recognizes the importance of individualized attention to the student's creative work and increased amounts of conference and preparation time required. AWP also reminds institutions that a teaching writer needs large amounts of time to do his or her own creative work.

Workshop

The 1978 AWP survey indicated that most teachers of writing felt they were most effective in the workshop format, and that the majority of workshops have a class size of 11–20. AWP recommends that workshop size not exceed 15, and that 12 be viewed as desirable and most effective.

Additional Recommendations

It is the position of AWP that teaching writers must have access to a liberal policy of leave and sabbatical. As with other arts, the writing teacher will be effective as a teacher only insofar as he or she is active and engaged as a writer; and large, recurring periods of time devoted to the writer's own work are crucial to continued effective teaching.

AWP believes that writers should have the major voice in decisions concerning the hiring and retention of creative writing faculty, admission of students to the writing program, the awarding of degrees in writing, the writing program's budget, and the allocation of physical resources. AWP believes that writers in the academy are best qualified to make such judgments in regard to creative writing programs.

A DESCRIPTION OF WRITING PROGRAM CURRICULA

Although they share common goals, criteria, and characteristics, writing programs in this country are now many and diverse. AWP does not advocate one approach to the study of writing over another, but does seek, through its guide to programs, to help the student writer locate those programs which are most compatible with his or her goals and expectations. Prospective students using the guide are urged to read each program description carefully, and to pay special attention to the faculty listing, the course work distribution and other degree requirements, and the statement of the program's aims.

The AWP Official Guide to Writing Programs makes a distinction between, on the one hand, courses in writing offered by an undergraduate or graduate literature program or department, and, on the other, a coherent curriculum in literature and creative writing designed for writing students. The primary aim of writing programs, through work in writing, form and theory, contemporary writers and/or traditional literature, is to help students become better writers, although liberal arts education and/or professional training may be secondary aims. Writing programs are also characterized by the presence of active and experienced writers on their faculties, and the student's own creative work is seen as the primary evidence for decisions about admission and graduation. It should be noted that "creative writing" has traditionally encompassed poetry, playwriting and scriptwriting, translation, fiction, and other imaginative prose.

Graduate writing programs are listed in *The AWP Official Guide* in the following descriptive categories: **Studio, Studio/Academic**, and **Traditional Literary Study and Creative Writing**. Although the aims and specific curricula of programs within each category differ considerably, the following general distinctions may be fairly made:

Studio writing programs place primary emphasis on the student's writing experience within the program. In this way, they most closely parallel studio programs in music, dance, and the visual arts. Most of the degree work is done in workshops, independent writing projects or tutorials, and thesis preparation. The study of form and theory, and of contemporary writers, may be incorporated into workshops or offered through separate courses. Faculty of such programs are selected for their achievement in the creative forms and not for scholarly work. Students are admitted to such programs almost wholly on the basis of a writing sample, and in turn the significant degree criterion is the quality of the thesis manuscript.

Studio/Academic writing programs usually place equal emphasis, in their curricula, on the student's writing and literature coursework, believing that the study of literature is crucial to one's development as a writer. These programs vary considerably in the structure and amount of literature requirements, but frequently rely on the regular English department faculty, noted for scholarly achievement, for many of the literature course offerings, while writers on the program faculty offer form and theory courses, workshops, and thesis direction. Studio/Academic programs often require some kinds of comprehensive examinations, and candidates are expected to be equally well-prepared in literature and in writing. Admission is determined primarily by the quality of the original manuscript.

Programs in **Traditional Literary Study and Creative Writing** offer work in writing with experienced writers on the faculty, and allow a creative thesis, but also expect that a significant amount of the degree work will be completed in the study of literature, usually in courses taught by English department faculty. Such programs tend to align themselves firmly with the academic tradition, and emphasize training their students as literature teachers as well as writers. Often, they actively use the same criteria for admission and degree award that are applied to candidates in literature, including the comprehensive examinations and the language requirements.

ADDITIONAL RECOMMENDATIONS

It is generally felt among creative writing program faculties that a series of readings and/or brief residencies by established writers is an important dimension of a writing program, offering students an immediate connection to contemporary literature and exposure to a variety of voices and aesthetic approaches. Because such a series is seen as integral to the curriculum, writing faculty should have the largest voice in determining the participants in such a series.

--The AWP Board of Directors

AWP PROGRAM DIRECTORS COUNCIL POLICY GUIDELINES FOR ADJUNCT FACULTY IN MEMBER WRITING PROGRAMS

AWP recognizes that adjunct faculty can play a valuable and sometimes necessary role in writing programs and individual writing courses, but AWP discourages overdependence on adjunct faculty. AWP recognizes that its member institutions are diverse in their students, goals, and resources, and respects the autonomy of each member institution in assigning faculty duties, responsibilities, and privileges in its best interest. Nevertheless, AWP has a strong proprietary interest in maintaining high standards of teaching, the professional and literary development of its members, and the quality of the student experience in creative writing courses and programs. Therefore, AWP recommends that all member institutions abide by the spirit of the following guidelines for the use of adjunct faculty in creative writing programs and creative writing, professional writing, and composition courses within English, the Liberal and Fine Arts, and other curricula.

1. For teaching creative writing courses, member institutions will employ only writers fully qualified by degree (MA, MFA, PhD) and/or active engagement with their craft, including but not limited to publication.

2. Adjunct faculty will be treated as fully professional colleagues and given the same resources, commensurate with their duties, as regular faculty members, including office space, library and audio-visual support, and secretarial and administrative support. They will be invited to contribute to faculty meetings and other forums in a manner in keeping with their institutional policies. Where possible, they will also be given a fair share of department funds for travel and professional development.

3. Adjunct faculty will be compensated according to a good-faith standard that recognizes their value to the mission of the program. Compensation includes but is not limited to salary, and will vary by institution and region, but AWP urges each member institution to develop a compensation scale that rewards the professional accomplishments of adjuncts and that reflects honorably upon the institution.

4. Adjuncts will share in the ancillary privileges accorded regular faculty, e.g. parking, use of gymnasium facilities, Internet access, free courses for professional development, etc.

5. Adjuncts paid on a per-course basis will not be expected to assume other institutional duties, such as committee work, advising, and administration, unless compensated in a fair manner. AWP recognizes the enthusiasm and expertise of adjunct faculty members, who may voluntarily undertake such duties, but such volunteerism must be accepted in good faith and never abused. There must never be any sense of coercion, either overt or implied.

6. Class size limits for courses taught by adjuncts will be the same as for similar courses taught by regular faculty.

7. Adjuncts will be given access to the institutional health insurance program at a reasonable and fair rate. At public institutions, state laws and procedures may make this difficult, but AWP recommends very strongly that a good-faith effort be made to provide for the physical well-being of adjuncts -- both for their own welfare and for the morale and effectiveness of the program.

8. There are a number of humane models for designing adjunct faculty contracts that ensure both a term of job stability for adjuncts and their most useful contribution to the program, especially those who may teach several years in the same program: three years nonrenewable, yearly with increases

based on length of service, etc. AWP recognizes that different programs require different models and therefore endorses no specific plan. But AWP does strongly urge all programs to develop a model that minimizes stress, dislocation, and discontinuity, and maximizes creativity, institutional loyalty, and a strong commitment to students. AWP stands ready to advise any program on various models and to help any member program develop the best model for its needs.

9. In any matter not specifically addressed in these guidelines, programs should act with good faith and treat adjuncts with professionalism and fairness.

HALLMARKS OF A SUCCESSFUL GRADUATE PROGRAM IN CREATIVE WRITING

Graduate programs in creative writing have evolved over the past 30 years to offer a range of artistic experiences, approaches, and courses of study. Because there are many paths by which one may become a writer, the curricula vary from program to program. AWP encourages this variety and innovation while it also sets general guidelines to help ensure a high quality of artistic literary training within these programs. Although the courses of study vary, AWP has noted the following shared characteristics among successful programs that nurture a culture of creativity, vitality, intellectual and artistic rigor, and fruitful cooperation. These definitive hallmarks also form the basis for *The AWP Guidelines for Creative Writing Programs*.

As stated in *The AWP Guidelines*, AWP maintains that the MFA is the appropriate terminal degree for professors of creative writing and literature. AWP acknowledges, however, that other graduate degrees may require courses of study similar to that of the MFA. Although some graduate programs confer degrees other than the MFA, these programs may also facilitate a writer's development as an artist and as a teacher. AWP has developed these hallmarks for departments and programs that accept a creative work of writing for the thesis requirement. These hallmarks enumerate the components of an education that best prepares a student to complete a successful creative thesis and to become a professional writer and teacher of writing and literature.

A successful creative writing program has accomplished writers as faculty members, a rigorous curriculum, talented students, and strong administrative support, all of which are complemented by the assets that distinguish a generally excellent academic institution. The AWP board of directors recommends that a creative writing program undergo annual self-evaluation and periodic independent assessment in its effort to offer the best education for writers and to make the best possible contributions to contemporary letters. Independent assessments are especially valuable to programs that have been operating for fewer than ten years.

To facilitate, structure, and focus a program's self-evaluation or independent assessment, the AWP board of directors has established 26 hallmarks within 5 general categories as follows:

Accomplished Faculty

1. A strong, stable core faculty of distinguished publishing writers in full-time, tenured or tenure-track positions, so that students may study with a different writer each semester during a two- or three-year program of study. Core faculty have distinguished themselves as artists who have published significant work in one or more of the following genres: fiction, poetry, creative nonfiction, dramas, or screenplays. Core faculty members share equally in teaching, mentoring, and thesis direction duties.

2. Faculty who are both working writers and committed teachers, who routinely make themselves available to students outside of class. Such faculty are professionally active, not only publishing creative work, but also providing leadership in the profession through national, regional, and local service. They are promoted and tenured based on publication of creative work, demonstrated ability as teachers, and contribution to the university and greater literary

community. The program should have clear criteria based on these qualities to designate, hire, and promote creative writing faculty.

3. Distinguished visiting or adjunct faculty to supplement the work of the regular faculty.

4. A diverse combination of faculty members who provide expertise in various genres of writing as well as a variety of approaches to their craft, based on aesthetic differences related to their literary, ethnic, cultural, and other backgrounds.

Rigorous and Extensive Curriculum

1. An integrated, rigorous curriculum consistent with the mission of the program as studio or studio/academic, two types of programs established by *AWP Guidelines for Creative Writing Programs*. This curriculum provides graduate-level creative writing workshops and seminars taught by core creative writing faculty on craft, theory, and contemporary literature. The program should provide an enabling progression of both practice and study in the literary arts in order to prepare the student for a life of letters and to equip the student with the skills needed for writing a publishable book-length creative work for the thesis.

2. A good faculty-to-student ratio as established by AWP's guidelines, allowing for class size of 11–20 students.

3. Courses in the catalog curriculum offered regularly and with consistent quality in the actual course schedule every semester or quarter.

4. A good series of lectures, readings, and workshops by visiting writers to extend the regular faculty's ability to provide a variety of approaches to the art and craft of writing.

5. Student access to other classes in literature, journalism, publishing, composition, or communications taught by distinguished faculty.

6. An affiliation with a journal or other literary publishing opportunities that can provide editorial experience.

Excellent Students and Support for Students

1. A high ratio of applicants to admissions; generally high and selective admissions standards.

2. Financial support available to a large percentage of MFA students in the form of fellowships, scholarships, teaching or research assistantships, travel grants, etc.

3. If teaching assistantships are available, a regular program of TA training and mentoring to ensure that TAs develop good pedagogical methods and benefit from the experience of a skilled teacher.

4. Graduate student representation in decisions of policy and practice: the program is responsive to graduate needs and has a mechanism for evaluating its effectiveness annually while it periodically conducts larger, more comprehensive reviews of how to best serve the needs of students.

5. A high percentage of matriculated students who graduate from the program (and a low number of students who drop out or transfer out of the program).

6. A high number of students who go on to publish significant work.

Strong Administrative Support

1. Strong leadership by the MFA director in planning, staffing, devising curriculum, and advocating program needs to the university administration.

2. High morale and a sense of cooperation and collegiality among students and faculty; an atmosphere of open discussion and mutual support, as well as respect for cultural and ethnic differences.

3. A strong commitment of support from the dean and higher administration, including but not limited to financial resources, salary support, paid release time for faculty to pursue creative work, and clerical/administrative support for the program director.

4. A healthy relationship with the department in which the program is housed.

5. A strong, positive presence in the local community established through deliberate outreach.

6. Membership in AWP and other appropriate local, regional, and national associations to assure its faculty and students access to timely information about contemporary letters and the teaching of creative writing.

Other Complementary Institutional Assets and Infrastructure

1. A special focus, initiative, resource, or other opportunity for students that distinguishes the program from other comparable programs.

2. Faculty and student access to a good library with extensive holdings in contemporary literature and an adequate budget for adding new titles to those holdings, including new periodicals.

3. Classrooms, offices, and other spaces adequate to conduct workshops, conferences, readings, etc., which promote an atmosphere conducive to concentration, listening, and focused work.

4. Internet access and computer labs for research and training in computer skills, including those required for desktop publishing.

AWP HALLMARKS OF A SUCCESSFUL UNDERGRADUATE PROGRAM IN CREATIVE WRITING

For their undergraduate students, many colleges and universities offer minors or concentrations in creative writing, and a few schools offer majors, or BFA programs, in creative writing. The Associated Writing Programs (AWP) recognizes that colleges and universities have different strengths and missions, and AWP encourages innovation and variety in the pedagogy of creative writing. Among its member programs, however, AWP has recognized common elements of successful undergraduate programs in creative writing.

These hallmarks represent a superior undergraduate program that offers a minor or a concentration in creative writing. Many of the hallmarks resemble those of a strong graduate program, but the undergraduate hallmarks differ from the graduate hallmarks especially in regard to curriculum. For undergraduate writers, a good four-year curriculum requires more general studies of literature, the arts and sciences, and the fine arts; it also provides extracurricular experiences in writing, publishing, and literature. Whereas a Master of Fine Arts program in creative writing places equal emphasis on the practice of craft and on the study of literature, an undergraduate program places a stronger emphasis on the study of literature.

Because a writer must first become a voracious and expert reader before he or she can master a difficult art, a strong undergraduate program emphasizes a wide range of study in literature and other disciplines to provide students with the foundation they need to become resourceful writers -- resourceful in techniques, styles, models, ideas, and subject matter. The goal of an undergraduate program is to teach students how to read critically as writers and to give students the practice of writing frequently so that, by creating their own works, they may apply what they have learned about the elements of literature. An undergraduate course of study in creative writing gives students an overview of the precedents established by writers of many eras, continents, and sensibilities; it gives students the ability to analyze, appreciate, and create the components that comprise works of literature. A successful undergraduate program accomplishes all this through various means: through instruction from publishing writers who are gifted teachers, through a rigorous and diverse curriculum, through excellent support for students, through the administration's effective management, and through the institution's extracurricular activities, general assets, and infrastructure.

To help institutions structure and focus their self-evaluations, long-range plans, or independent assessments of their programs, the AWP Board of Directors has established the following hallmarks.

Accomplished Faculty

1. Full-time, tenure-track or tenured faculty members teach a significant majority of creative writing courses. The core faculty is composed of writers whose work has been published by nationally known, professional journals and presses respected by other writers, editors, and publishers. Writers will have published significant work and at least one book in each of the genres they teach (for playwrights, significant stage or film production may replace traditional publication). The program has core faculty members who are expert and accomplished in three or more of the following genres: fiction, poetry, creative nonfiction, drama, or screenplays.

2. Faculty members are publishing writers and committed teachers who routinely make themselves available to students outside of class. Faculty members are professionally active, not only publishing creative work, but also participating in national, regional, and local organizations and activities related to teaching, literature, and the arts. Most faculty are experienced teachers of composition, literature, and other courses; however, the criteria for promotion, assignment of classes, and tenure of creative writing faculty focus on publication of creative work, demonstrated ability as teachers of creative writing, and contributions to the university and greater literary community.

3. Distinguished visiting full-time or adjunct faculty include writers whose credentials equal or surpass the members of the program's core faculty. Visiting or adjunct faculty teach primarily, if not exclusively, courses in creative writing; they are not used inappropriately to supplement other departmental staffing needs.

4. In universities, a graduate creative writing student's training may include teaching introductory or intermediate undergraduate courses in creative writing; however, the program's faculty members prepare and supervise the graduate teaching associates.

5. A program's faculty provides depth and expertise in at least three genres and in various aesthetics and philosophies of the craft of writing. A diverse faculty provides a range of aesthetic points of view related to literary, ethnic, cultural, or other influences. For each genre offered in the program's curriculum (poetry, fiction, nonfiction, etc.), the core faculty includes one or more individual members per genre, who each have publications primarily in that genre. A program's faculty resources are supplemented, not replaced, by visiting full-time faculty, adjunct instructors, or graduate teaching associates.

6. Since undergraduates with a minor or a concentration in creative writing must also study a wide range of literature, the program, or the department in which the program operates, also has an excellent full-time faculty of scholars who teach a wide range of courses that cover many authors, eras, and continents of literary history.

Rigorous and Diverse Curriculum

1. Students takes courses that provide a broad background in literature, the arts and sciences, and the fine arts; and they enjoy other extracurricular experiences essential to an undergraduate education. Although students in a creative writing program are not necessarily English majors, it is important that an institution offers courses in literary studies that are historically, intellectually, geographically, and culturally wide-ranging and varied. For the minor, or for the concentration, students take a balance of courses in literary studies and creative writing with less than 50% of the courses in creative writing. Students should take courses that explore a wide variety of literature, both past and present, as well as courses that apply various forms of literary criticism. Students should be proficient in a second modern or classical language.

2. A tiered curriculum provides introductory, intermediate, advanced courses, and an independent study, a senior thesis, or capstone course in creative writing. Programs provide a practicum, such as an internship, and advising on job opportunities and graduate schools. A system of prerequisites, which tracks courses taken and grades achieved, assures that students take courses in an appropriate order. Because too much specialization too soon is generally not in a young writer's best interest, students in undergraduate writing programs typically are required to take writing workshops and seminars in more than one genre. The best undergraduate creative writing program offers advanced courses in at least three or more separate genres (fiction, poetry,

creative nonfiction, drama, screen writing). A senior thesis, project, or capstone course completes the program, requiring both a longer creative manuscript and a critical paper. In the junior or senior year, a student completes an appropriate internship.

3. Introductory creative writing courses have class size restrictions equal to or less than an institution's restriction for composition classes (but no greater than 22 students). Intermediate and advanced courses have class size restrictions of 12-18 students, with a maximum of 15 students in advanced workshop classes (optimum workshop class size: 12 students).

4. Courses are listed in the school's catalog and offered regularly so that students may complete the program in a timely manner consistent with other programs at the school.

5. Creative writing courses, including workshops, include craft texts and literary texts (anthologies, books by individual authors, literary periodicals) that offer appropriate models for student writing. Workshops also include anthologies or other primary works and critical texts. Undergraduate workshops are generally more structured than graduate workshops, since it is not assumed that students know the elements of prosody or storytelling. Undergraduate workshops, especially at the introductory level, require students to work in various forms, styles, modes, and genres.

6. Lectures, readings, and workshops by visiting writers (especially those from outside an institution's state or region) extend the regular faculty's ability to present a variety of approaches to the art and craft of writing.

Excellent Support for Students

1. Undergraduate students participate in all facets of the program, both curricular and extracurricular, and are not marginalized by graduate students or faculty. Students serve on committees relevant to the undergraduate creative writing program.

2. Students edit their own literary magazine (50% or more is devoted to literary works) with a faculty advisor who guides but does not censor their editorial process. The majority of published works are by undergraduate students. The editorial staff is not represented excessively among the magazine's contributors.

3. Students have regular opportunities to participate in public readings of their works, including solo readings for students completing a senior thesis or project.

4. Students participate in programs that promote and celebrate literature, writing, and reading in their communities.

5. Internship opportunities are available for creative writing students in a variety of writing, editing, and publishing professions. A formal affiliation with a professional literary journal or press is especially desirable.

6. Creative writing students are as academically competitive and qualified as students in other undergraduate departments. Financial aid for creative writing students is comparable to the support for students in other departments. Both the institution and the program work in consort to enroll qualified students of different backgrounds, social classes, and races. A significant number of students continue their studies in graduate programs and go on to publish their work.

Administrative Support

1. A program director (tenured or on tenure-track) provides strong leadership in planning, budgeting, staffing, and advocating the needs of the program to the administration. The director maintains a productive relationship not only with the department in particular that sponsors the program, but also with the institution and local community in general.

2. A high sense of collegiality exists among students and faculty. An open atmosphere invites discussion, collaboration, and diverse cultural and ethnic contributions.

3. The dean and higher administration demonstrate a strong commitment to the program, including but not limited to support for financial resources, salaries, release time for faculty to pursue creative projects, and clerical/administrative assistance to the director. A special focus, initiative, resource, or other opportunity for students distinguishes the creative writing program from other comparable programs.

4. The program maintains membership in AWP and other appropriate local, regional, and national associations to assure that its faculty and students have access to timely information relevant to contemporary letters and opportunities in creative writing.

Other Complementary Assets and Infrastructure

1. The program sponsors a visiting writers program that includes public readings but also offers students private opportunities for workshops and discussions with visiting writers. Visiting writers represent a wide variety of styles, genres, and backgrounds.

2. The program sponsors a festival, workshop, or conference that attracts an audience from outside the school with whom students can interact intellectually and creatively.

3. Faculty and student access to a good library with extensive holdings in contemporary literature and an adequate budget for adding new titles to those holdings, including new periodicals.

4. Classrooms, offices, and other spaces adequate to conduct workshops, conferences, readings, etc., which promote an atmosphere conducive to concentration, listening, and focused work.

5. Internet access and computer labs for research and training in computer skills, desktop publishing, and web page design.

6. The program encourages students to travel to readings, workshops, festivals, conferences, and other special events. As much as possible, the program provides support for student travel and participation in such events; this support is especially important for students of colleges and universities in remote areas.

7. Affiliation with a professional literary journal allows students to observe and, for advanced students, to assist in the process of editing and managing the journal.

8. Students participate in literary competitions, including the national Intro Awards competition and the AWP Program.

Indices

GRADUATE & UNDERGRADUATE PROGRAMS
LISTED BY STATE

ALABAMA

ALASKA

ARIZONA

ARKANSAS

CALIFORNIA

COLORADO

CONNECTICUT

DISTRICT OF COLUMBIA

FLORIDA

GEORGIA

HAWAII

IDAHO

ILLINOIS

LOUISIANA

MAINE

MARYLAND

MASSACHUSETTS

MICHIGAN

NEW HAMPSHIRE

NEW JERSEY

NEW MEXICO

NEW YORK

NORTH CAROLINA

NORTH DAKOTA

OHIO

OKLAHOMA

OREGON

PENNSYLVANIA

RHODE ISLAND

SOUTH CAROLINA

SOUTH DAKOTA

TENNESSEE

TEXAS

UTAH

VERMONT

VIRGINIA

WASHINGTON

WEST VIRGINIA

WISCONSIN

WYOMING

CANADA

UNITED KINGDOM

WALES

GRADUATE & UNDERGRADUATE PROGRAMS
LISTED BY DEGREES OFFERED

ASSOCIATE OF ARTS (AA)

UNDERGRADUATE DEGREE WITH MINOR, OPTION, EMPHASIS, OR CONCENTRATION IN WRITING (BA)

UNDERGRADUATE MAJOR (BA, BFA) IN WRITING

BACHELOR OF SCIENCE (BS)

BACHELOR OF SCIENCE IN EDUCATION (BSE)

MASTER OF ARTS (MA)

MASTER OF ARTS IN LIBERAL STUDIES (MALS)

MASTER OF FINE ARTS (MFA)

MASTER OF FINE ARTS (MFA) IN NONFICTION

CENTERS, COLONIES & CONFERENCES LISTED BY STATE

ALABAMA

ALASKA

ARIZONA

ARKANSAS

CALIFORNIA

NEW YORK

NORTH CAROLINA

NORTH DAKOTA

OHIO

OKLAHOMA

OREGON

WASHINGTON

WEST VIRGINIA

WISCONSIN

WYOMING

CANADA

FRANCE

IRELAND

Tools & Services

As a writer, you know how solitary the literary life can be. And if you teach writing, you also know how important it is to keep up with all the latest ideas, debates, and controversies in contemporary literature and education. Since 1967, the Associated Writing Programs has provided the tools and the company of fellow spirits to make work easier for writers and teachers.

Listed below are some of AWP's services. They are divided into three categories: (1) Membership services, whose benefits include the *The Writer's Chronicle, AWP Job List, &* discounts for participation in AWP events. (2) Placement Services. *You must be a member to use Placement Services.* (3) Publications.

Membership Services

• **The Writer's Chronicle.** $20 for six issues, ($25 in Canada) or $32 for twelve issues ($40 in Canada). News, debates, interviews, information, & essays for writers & teachers. Every issue includes listings of grants, awards, & publishing opportunities.

• **Individual Membership.** $57 per year ($67 in Canada). Includes subscription to *The Writer's Chronicle,* plus *AWP Job List & Job List Online,* a listing of employment opportunities for writers in higher education, editing, & publishing. Members shape the services of AWP, as members elect directors to the AWP Board.

• **Graduate Student Membership.** $37 ($42 in Canada). A non-voting membership, it includes subscriptions to *The Writer's Chronicle & AWP Job List.* You must send a photocopy of a valid student ID.

Clip out this form and mail to:
Associated Writing Programs,
Tallwood House, Mail Stop 1E3,
George Mason University,
Fairfax, VA 22030
or fax it to (703) 993-4302.
If you have any questions, please call
(703) 993-4301, or email awp@gmu.edu

For Writers

Placement Services
(only for members)

• **Placement Service.** $62 per year. Maintenance, photocopying, & 10 mailings of your dossier to prospective employers by your request. $30 for 10 additional mailings, or $5 per mailing.

• **Limited Placement Service.** $32 per year. For members who plan to send their dossier only a few times each year. Maintenance of your file, photocopying, & 5 mailings— $5 for each additional mailing.

Membership Services
☐ **The Writer's Chronicle**
☐ **Individual Membership**
☐ **Grad. Student Membership**

AWP Official Guide to Writing Programs

AWP Official Guide to Writing Programs. $25.95, postage included. ($27.95 in Canada) Describes over 300 creative writing programs in the U.S. & Canada. The most comprehensive listing available. Published with Dustbooks.

Placement & Guide
○ Placement Service
○ Limited Placement
☐ Guide to Writing Programs

Total enclosed $_____

_____
Your name (please print)

_____
Mastercard or Visa Number

_____
Expiration Date   Phone

_____
Signature

_____
Address

_____
City   State   Zip

_____
E-mail address

I would like to contribute this amount to AWP: $_____

Check or money order to AWP. Payment must be in U.S. funds, drawn on U.S. bank, or use your Visa or Mastercard. Contact the AWP office for overseas rates.

small school, small program

(small cost)

Rhode Island College in Providence offers small classes, plenty of teacher/student contact and low tuition. Programs lead to the B.A. and M.A. in English/Creative Writing.

Faculty: Cathleen Calbert, Mark Anderson,
   poetry. Thomas Cobb, fiction.
Recent visitors include Robert Pinsky, James Tate,
   Charles Simic, Ann Hood, Rosellen Brown,
   Ann Harleman, Thomas Lux, Richard Price,
   Marilyn Nelson, Wally Lamb.

Contact: Director of Creative Writing, Department of English, Rhode Island College, Providence, RI 02908

RHODE ISLAND COLLEGE

MA Creative Writing Emphasis

University of Nebraska at Kearney

Degrees Offered: BA, MA
Degree: MA in English with Creative Writing Emphasis
Required course of study: M.A. 30 total hours
Creative Writing Courses: 12 hours for emphasis
Literary Studies: 9 hours
Electives: 3 hours
Creative Thesis: 6 hours

Admission requirements will be the same as for the current M.A. program with one modification. The writing sample of a prospective student should include the following: one academic essay (5-10 pages) and a 15-page creative writing sample from one of the following genres: Fiction, Poetry, Creative Nonfiction, or Drama Writing (for stage or screen).

Program Contents

The emphasis in Creative Writing will be a studio/academic degree of 30 hours, with 12 hours required in creative writing courses. Students can choose from courses such as Creative Nonfiction, Fiction Writing, Poetry Writing, Creative Writing for Teachers, Prosody, Drama Writing, and the Ft. Kearny Summer Writers' Conference. Of these courses, Creative Nonfiction, Fiction Writing, Poetry Writing, and Drama Writing may be repeated for up to six hours each. The limit on P courses for the Creative Emphasis students will be 12 hours.

Students must also take 9 hours of coursework in literary studies. This should include 3 hours of course work in American literature and 3 hours of course work in English literature. The additional 3 hours of credit in literary studies are to be selected by the student in criticism or theory, either English 806 or English 807. The 12 hours of Creative Writing courses and 9 hours of Literary Studies comprise 21 of the total 30 hours required for the English M.A. degree with an emphasis in Creative Writing. An additional 3 hours of credit are to be taken either in a course which would prepare the student to teach writing as a Graduate Assistant at UNK or an elective course if the student chooses not to be a GA. The final six hours of credit toward the degree will be for the development of a Creative Thesis in poetry, fiction, creative nonfiction, or drama writing.

The English Department faculty will be able to support the curriculum for the emphasis. The program will be enriched by the Reynolds Reading Series and by the annual Ft. Kearny Summer Writers' Conference. Moreover, graduate students in the program will have opportunities to do editorial work for in-house journals.

Graduate Creative Writing Courses

We offer Poetry Writing, Fiction Writing, Drama Writing, Creative Nonfiction, Seminar in Prosody and Creative Writing for Public School Teachers.

Information:
Write or call Steve Schneider, Director of Graduate Studies in English, University of Nebraska at Kearney, Department of English, Kearney, Nebraska 68849-1320 at (308) 865-8297or schneiders@unk.edu

Creative Writing Faculty

Charles Fort, Reynolds Chair in Poetry
M.F.A. Bowling Green State University
Graduate Faculty Member

Author of *The Town Clock Burning* and *Darvil* . A MacDowell Fellow, Fort has received major literary awards from the Poetry Society of America, Writer's Voice, and the Randall Jarrell Poetry Prize. He has published his work in eleven anthologies of poetry.

Barbara Emrys, Associate Professor
Ph.D. Florida State University
Graduate Faculty Member

Her fiction has appeared in *Prairie Schooner*, *Short Story*, *Sacred Ground*: *Writing about Home* (Milkweed Editions) as well as *Portland*, *Paragraph*, *Sun Dog*, and many national journals. She received the Mary Roberts Rinehart award in nonfiction, and is an experienced editor and journalist.

Steven P. Schneider, Associate Professor
M.F.A., Ph.D. University of Iowa
Graduate Faculty Member

Author of *A.R. Ammons and the Poetics of Widening Scope* (Fairleigh Dickinson University Press) and editor of *Complexities of Motion: Essays on the Long Poems of A.R. Ammons*. His poetry has appeared in *Prairie Schooner*, *The Literary Review*, *The Beloit Poetry Journal*, and many other national literary journals. Professor Schneider is a winner of a Merit Award in Poetry from the Nebraska Arts Council. He is also the co-author of two non-fiction books.

Susanne George, Professor
Ph.D., University of Nebraska at Lincoln
Graduate Faculty Member

Author of the *Adventure of The Woman Homesteader: The Life and Letters of Elinor Pruitt Stewart* and *Kate Cleary: A Literary Biography with Selected Works*; ed. *Wellsprings: Poems by Six Nebraska Poets* and *The Platte River: An Atlas of the Big Bend Region*; poems and nonfiction in such works as *Leaning to the Wind*, *By Grit and Grace*, *A Hold Row to Hoe* and *The Sandhills and Other Geographies*.

Recent visiting writers have included: Frank Conroy, Novelist; David Lee, Poet Laureate of Utah; William Kloefkorn, Poet Laureate of Nebraska; Lucy Wang, Playwright and Screenwriter; Tillie Olsen, Writer; Josip Novakovich, Poet and Essayist; and Charles Simic, Poet and Pulitzer Prize Winner.

Additional faculty in the English Department with creative writing, teaching, or publishing experience will offer support.

The Department publishes *The Platte Valley Review* and the *Carillon*, both of which accept student work. Internships on publishing projects and grant support are available. Graduate assistantships are also awarded.

Ft. Kearny Writers' Workshop 1-3 hours
A summer week-long workshop in creative writing for those who would like to improve their abilities in writing poetry, fiction, and drama.

Fort Kearny Summer Writers Conference

MASTER THE ART OF ENGLISH

Join the ongoing conversation about literature and writing with dedicated scholars in the Master of Arts in English program at the University of St. Thomas. Diversify your reading, challenge your thinking and sharpen your writing. Enjoy small, evening classes in a variety of topics. Financial aid and fellowships are available for degree-seeking students.

Fall 1999 application deadline: April 1, 1999

If you would like more information, please call (651) 962-5628, or (800) 328-6819, Ext. 2-5628, or send e-mail to: jebukowski@stthomas.edu.

UNIVERSITY OF
ST. THOMAS
ST. PAUL, MINN.

PROGRAM FACULTY & AREAS OF ACADEMIC SPECIALTY:

Young-Ok An (Ph.D., University of Southern California), *Romanticism, 18th- and 19th-century British literature, literary theory, postcolonialism and cultural critique*

Michael Bellamy (Ph.D., Wisconsin-Madison), *American literature, writing theory, Joyce, utopian studies*

Susan J. Callaway (Ph.D., Wisconsin-Madison), *Director, UST Writing Center; composition theory and pedagogy, writing center theory and administration, writing across the curriculum*

Kanishka Chowdhury (Ph.D., Purdue), *Postcolonial literature and theory, British and American multicultural literature, cultural theory*

Catherine Craft-Fairchild (Ph.D., Rochester), *Restoration and 18th-century British literature, feminist theory, psychoanalysis and film theory, history of the novel*

Heid Erdrich (M.A./M.A., Johns Hopkins), *Poetry and fiction writing, Native American literature, multicultural and bicultural literature*

Robert C. Foy (Ph.D., Minnesota), *Shakespeare, English Renaissance literature, drama, literature and the Bible, Far Eastern literature*

Michael C. Jordan (Ph.D., North Carolina-Chapel Hill), *Comparative literature, literary theory, classical Greek literature, philosophical anthropology, history and theory of liberal education*

Kelli Larson (Ph.D., Michigan State), *18th- and 19th-century American literature, modern American literature*

Ray MacKenzie (Ph.D., Kansas), *17th-and 18th-century British literature, French classicism, Byron, technical writing*

Claudia May (Ph.D., California-Berkeley), *Ethnic studies; African-American and Chicano/Chicana literature, Caribbean literature and theory*

Michael A. Mikolajczak (Ph.D., Wisconsin-Milwaukee), *16th-and 17th-century British literature, Milton, religion and literature, rhetoric; editor of Logos: A Journal of Catholic Thought and Culture*

Leslie Adrienne Miller (Ph.D., Houston), *Creative writing, contemporary American poetry, rhetorical theory and criticism, British romanticism, medieval literature*

Robert K. Miller (Ph.D., Columbia), *Rhetorical theory, writing pedagogy, literary nonfiction, American literature since 1865*

Mary Rose O'Reilley (Ph.D., Wisconsin-Milwaukee), *20th Century poetry, poetry-as-genre, early 20th-century British fiction, literary nonfiction*

Lon Otto (Ph.D., Indiana), *Creative writing, the novel since World War II, modern poetry, Faulkner*

Joan Piorkowski (Ph.D., Temple), *18th-century British literature, prose fiction, Gothic literature, composition, basic writing*

Brenda J. Powell (Ph.D., North Carolina-Chapel Hill), *Director, Luann Dummer Center for Women; literature by women, mythology and classical literature, multicultural literature*

Thomas Dillon Redshaw (Ph.D., New York University; senior fellow, Institute of Irish Studies, The Queen's University, Belfast), *modern and contemporary Irish literature, British literature between the wars, 17th Century British literature; editor, New Hibernia Review: A Quarterly Record of Irish Studies*

Mary R. Reichardt (Ph.D., Wisconsin-Madison), *American literature through 1914, early American women's literature, autobiography, Midwest and regional literature*

Donald Ringnalda (Ph.D., Ohio University), *Comparative literature, Third World and Native American literature, contemporary American drama, Vietnam War literature*

Erika C. Scheurer (Ph.D., Massachusetts-Amherst), *Composition theory and pedagogy, Emily Dickinson*

Andrew J. Scheiber (Ph.D., Michigan State), *19th-and 20th-century literature, literary criticism, literature and linguistics, women's studies, history of the novel*

Rev. Martin Warren (Ph.D., Minnesota), *Medieval and early modern literature, Chaucer, the Lollards, English Mystics, religion and literature, computer technology in education*

Rev. Robert Wellisch (Ph.D., Minnesota), *Victorian literature, 18th-and 19th-century novel, European literature*

The University of St. Thomas admits students of any race, color, creed and national or ethnic origin.

UNIVERSITY

master of english

OF SOUTH

in creative writing

ALABAMA

LOCATION: Mobile, Alabama, birthplace of Mardi Gras. Close to warm water beaches, Biloxi casinos and New Orleans. Comfortable port city living, thriving historical downtown, affordable for a student.

FACULTY: Novelists: **James White**, Program Director (*Birdsong*, Methuen; *California Exit*, Methuen; *Where Joy Resides: A Christopher Isherwood Reader*, Farrar Straus and Giroux, Guggenheim and Fulbright Fellowships) and **Tom Franklin** (*Poachers: Stories*, William Morrow; *Hell at the Breech*, forthcoming from William Morrow; Arkansas Arts Council Grant; Writers at Work Literary Non-fiction Award).

Poet **Sue Walker** (*Traveling My Shadow*, Negative Capability Press; *Shorings*, South Coast Press; *The Appearance of Green*, Nightshade Press; *Marge Piercy: Critical Views*, forthcoming from Greenwood Publishers; editor of *Negative Capability*, several awards for poetry and non-fiction).

Adjunct faculty include non-fiction writer **Robert Bahr** (*The Hibernation Response*, William Morrow; *The Virility Factor*, Putnam's; *Least of all Saints*, Prentice Hall) and screenwriter Brian Overstreet (MFA, New York University).

DEGREE REQUIREMENTS: 12 hours of writing seminars, 6 hours thesis, 18 hours literature. Reading knowledge of one foreign language, oral thesis defense.

ABOUT THE PROGRAM: Financial assistance available. Limited enrollment, small workshops, annual host of Gulf Coast Association of Creative Writing Teachers and of The Fairhope Conference, where students are encouraged to meet professionals who can mentor them in their careers. Recent visiting writers include Marge Piercy, Margaret Atwood, James Schevill and Diane Wakoski.

For Information, write:
Creative Writing Program/Humanities 240
USA
Mobile, Alabama 36688

MY DEAR, I DON'T CARE WHAT THEY DO SO LONG AS THEY DON'T DO IT IN THE STREET AND FRIGHTEN THE HORSES.

Mrs. Patrick Campbell
(Beatrice Stella Tanner Campbell)

MFA in CREATIVE WRITING
boise state university

For more information:
Robert Olmstead, Director
Boise State University
Department of English
1910 University Drive
Boise, Idaho 83725

http://english.idbsu.edu/mfa

PROFESSIONAL WRITING PROGRAM

University of Missouri-Kansas City

An Interdisciplinary Master of Arts

This interdisciplinary curriculum allows each student to design and pursue a personal program of study using the resources of a campus and community support system unequaled in this part of the country. The list of opportunities available to writing students is rich and varied: internal and external internships, experience with the international literary magazine *New Letters* and its companion audio-literature program *New Letters on the Air,* or with the small literary press BkMk Press, seminars, master-classes with visiting writers, writing conferences, and tutorials, in addition to the traditional classes. Graduates of this 33-hour program are awarded a Master of Arts with a professional-writing emphasis in one of the three areas of concentration.

Three Areas of Concentration
◊ Fiction and Poetry
◊ Stage- and Screenwriting
◊ Print and Electronic Journalism

The Resident Faculty:

Ralph Berets - Screenwriting
Gregory D. Black - Communications, Film
Michelle Boisseau - Poetry, Fiction
G.S. Sharat Chandra - Fiction, Poetry
Angela Elam - Broadcast Journalism

Charles Hammer - Fiction, Journalism
Felicia Londre - Playwriting
James McKinley - Fiction, Journalism
Robert Stewart - Poetry, Journalism
Robert Unger - Print Journalism

Recent Visiting Writers and Writers-in-Residence

Martin Amis, Mary Catherine Bateson, Gwendolyn Brooks, Christopher Buckley, Janet Burroway, Gerald Early, Richard Ford, Paul Fussell, Tess Gallagher, Adam Gopnik, Molly Ivins, Mark Jarman, Alison Joseph, William Henry Lewis, Barry Lopez, Hilary Masters, David McCullough, Walter McDonald, Lynn McMahon, Terrence McNally, Grace Paley, Kathrin Perutz, Robert Pinsky, Chaim Potok, Richard Rhodes, William Jay Smith, John Updike, Miller Williams and Al Young.

for more information contact:
James McKinley
Director, Professional Writing Program
UMKC, 5101 Rockhill Road, Kansas City, MO 64110-2499
Phone: (816) 235-1120   Fax: (816) 235-2611
e-mail: mckinleyj@umkc.edu

UMKC

or visit us at the www.umkc.edu *website*

—financial aid available—